Intelligent Systems for Business:
Expert Systems with Neural Networks

TheWadsworth Series in Management Information Systems
Peter G. W. Keen, Consulting Editor

Intelligent Systems for Business: Expert Systems with Neural Networks, Fatemeh Zahedi

Database Systems: Design, Implementation, and Management, Peter Rob and Carlos Coronel

Forthcoming Titles:

Networks in Action: Business Decisions and Technical Choices, Peter G. W. Keen

Information Technology in Action, Peter G. W. Keen

Software Engineering for the 1990s, Sue Conger

Microcomputers for Managers, Bay Arinze

Business Systems Analysis and Design, William Davis

Intelligent Systems for Business: Expert Systems with Neural Networks

Fatemeh Zahedi

University of Massachusetts, Boston

The Wadsworth Series in
Management Information Systems

Wadsworth Publishing Company
Belmont, California
A Division of Wadsworth, Inc.

Publisher: Frank Ruggirello
Editorial Assistant: Rhonda Gray
Production Editor: Karen Garrison
Managing Designer: Andrew Ogus
Print Buyer: Randy Hurst
Art Editor: Nancy Spellman
Compositor: Electronic Technical Publishing
Cover: Andrew Ogus
Signing Representative: John Moroney
Printer: R. R. Donnelly & Sons, Crawfordsville
Cover Illustration: Nick Backes

Printed in the United States of America

1 2 3 4 5 6 7 8 9 10—97 96 95 94 93

Library of Congress Cataloging-in-Publication Data
Zahedi, Fatemeh
    Intelligent systems for business : expert sytems with neural networks / Fatemeh Zahedi.
        p. cm.
    Includes bibliographical references and index.
    ISBN 0-534-18888-5
    1. Industrial management—Data processing. 2. Industrial management—Decision making. 3. Expert systems (Computer science) 4. Neural networks (Computer science) I. Title.
HD30.2.Z34 1993
658.4'03'0285633—dc20   92-25249

To two Ls that can't be simulated, imitated, or copied:
Love and my daughter Lara.

Preface

Systems with intelligence have become increasingly more valuable in business information systems and in the decision-making process. This type of system boosts productivity, creates consistency, helps novices, and works nonstop. This book shows how to create intelligent systems, reviews the theories that provide legitimacy for these systems, and illustrates areas in which they are used.

There are two distinct fields with the goal of creating intelligent systems: expert systems and neural networks. Expert systems have a relatively longer history of development and deployment in business. That is why the book dedicates ten chapters (3–12) to a discussion of expert system topics. Expert systems have two basic approaches: logic-based and object-oriented. There is also the hybrid system, which combines the two approaches in order to utilize the advantages of both. The neural network application in business is a recent phenomenon, and is expected to grow rapidly. The last two chapters of the book are dedicated to the introduction of neural networks and their applications.

This book has a number of unique features:

- An introduction to expert systems and neural networks in a unifying framework of intelligent systems.

- An accessible review of the theoretical foundation of expert systems.

- A presentation of the object-oriented approach in a nontechnical, yet detailed fashion.

- A review of hybrid expert systems in which rule-based and object-oriented approaches are combined.

- An in-depth discussion of three expert-system software products: a deductive-based expert system (LEVEL5), an inductive-based expert system (1st-CLASS), and two hybrid tools (LEVEL5 OBJECT and KAPPA-PC). A chapter on each product offers the reader an opportunity to get hands-on experience in creating prototype expert systems.

- The coverage of introductory and essential topics as well as advanced subjects in expert systems. The advanced topics are identified as optional in each chapter.

- The presentation of more than 50 cases of real applications of expert systems and neural networks in domestic and international industries and governments, as well as in areas in which expert systems and neural networks are being integrated.

- An appendix that reviews the ID3 method—a well-known inductive method in expert systems.

- Two appendices that list sources for expert systems and neural networks.

- An appendix on one of the popular and powerful neural-net tools, NeuralWorks Professional II/Plus.

- Tutorial diskettes for LEVEL5 and 1st-CLASS and demo diskettes for KAPPA-PC, LEVEL5 OBJECT, and NeuralWorks Professional II/Plus are available for this book through your local Wadsworth representative or by contacting David Garrison, Marketing Manager, Wadsworth Publishing Company, 10 Davis Drive, Belmont, California, 94002.

Structure of the Book

The book contains 14 chapters, most of which are self-contained. Figure P.1 shows that Chapters 1, 3, 6, 7, 8, and 13 are self-contained, and therefore could be covered out of sequence. Sections with "optional" in their headings are not prerequisites for the nonoptional sections of the chapters that follow. In other words, for introductory courses and nontechnical general reading, skipping "optional" sections will not cause any problem.

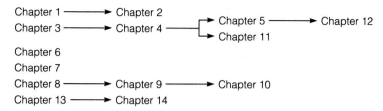

Figure P.1 The Dependency of Chapters

Chapters are grouped into six parts, as discussed below:

Part I

The first part consists of Chapters 1 and 2. It introduces the field of intelligent systems and their role in business decision making. This part offers simple and general discussions of expert systems and neural networks, and puts these two areas in the perspective of business decision making and productivity tools. Chapters 1 and 2 are recommended to all readers.

Part II

The second part consists of Chapters 3 and 4. It covers the theoretical foundation of logic-based expert systems. There are two basic approaches in expert systems: logic-based and object-oriented (including semantic nets and frames). Chapter 3 discusses the components of expert systems and then reviews those topics of mathematical logic on which expert systems are built. This review identifies the foundation of rule-based and predicate-based methods (two major methods used in the logic-based approach). Chapter 4 extends Chapter 3 to multiple inference and demonstrates the foundation on which inference engines are built.

The coverage in the second part is solid but accessible. Whenever the discussion goes further than a simple introduction, the word "optional" appears in the title of the section.

For undergraduates, some practically oriented graduate courses, and general readers, the optional sections could be skipped. Theoretically oriented graduate courses and general readers with a good grounding in abstract concepts may find the optional sections of interest.

Part III

The third part consists of Chapters 5 through 7. It gives the reader hands-on experience in using a deductive tool (LEVEL5 in Chapter 5) and an inductive tool (1st-CLASS in Chapter 6). Chapter 7 discusses the practical issues in developing expert systems.

Chapter 5 depends on the introductory parts of Chapters 3 and 4. Chapters 6 and 7 do not have a strong dependency on other chapters. I recommend reading Chapter 7 after some hands-on experience in creating a small expert system in Chapter 5, Chapter 6, or both.

Part IV

The fourth part consists of Chapters 8 through 10. It discusses the object-oriented approach and the hybrid method for combining rule-based and object-oriented approaches. Chapter 8 is an introduction to the object-oriented approach and its use in expert systems. It covers the topic in some depth, without being too technical. The advanced concepts are identified as "optional." This chapter is required for all readers.

Chapter 9 covers the hybrid approach. For undergraduate courses and general readers, a brief review of the chapter will suffice. Some of the graduate courses may dwell on this chapter and even conduct additional research on its topics. Chapter 10 is intended to show how a hybrid tool works. For undergraduate courses and general readers, a demo session will suffice. For a more advanced course, in-depth coverage and hands-on experience with the demo diskette will equip the student with a good understanding of the software.

Part V

The fifth part consists of Chapters 11 and 12. It contains advanced topics in expert systems: uncertainty, software evaluation, and liability issues. For undergraduate courses and general readers, a brief review of nonoptional sections will be adequate. Advanced courses should cover these topics in some depth, especially Chapter 11, because these are areas of active research and future advancement in expert systems.

Part VI

The sixth part consists of Chapters 13 and 14. This part introduces neural networks, compares them with expert systems, and shows samples of their applications. The nonoptional sections of Chapters 13 and 14 are good readings for all. Advanced courses and theoretically oriented readers will be interested in the optional sections of these chapters.

Appendices

There are four appendices in this book. Appendix A gives a brief review of the ID3 method. Appendices B and C report sources (companies and software products) for expert systems and neural networks. Appendix D briefly reviews NeuralWorks Professional II/Plus neural network tool.

Instructional Materials

The book is accompanied by the following instructional materials:

- Instructor manual
- Student version of LEVEL5
- Student version of 1st-CLASS
- Demo diskette for KAPPA-PC
- Demo diskette for LEVEL5 OBJECT
- Demo diskette for NeuralWorks Professional II/Plus

Acknowledgments

The publication of this book would not have been possible without the efficiency and foresight of my publishing editor, Frank Ruggirello, and the keen expertise of Peter Keen. I am grateful for their support in this project. The book has been reviewed by a number of reviewers at different stages of its development and publishing life. Various pieces of this book were reviewed by some who have remained anonymous to me. I would like to thank them for their comments and encouragements. I extend my special thanks to all reviewers including: Professor Lotfi Zadeh, University of California, Berkeley; Dr. Mark Musen, Stanford University School of Medicine; Professor Judea Pearl, University of California, Los Angeles; Professor Ali Emdad, Morgan State University; Professor Carl Clavadetscher, California State Polytechnic University; Professor André Everett, University of Otago, New Zealand; and Professor Jay Liebowitz, George Washington University.

The book was tested in my expert systems courses and Professor Oscar Gutierrez's course at the University of Massachusetts/Boston. I would like to express my thanks to Professor Gutierrez and all students, especially Robert Brockman, who read the chapters with care and offered feedback.

My special thanks go to Linda Kincaid, my editor, whose vigilance for clarity and simplicity of presentation has kept me on my toes and my feet on the ground. The book was written when my life went through a drastic change. I would like to thank Professor Kamran M. Dadkhah for his encouragement in the early stages of this book, and my mother Rafat, who with her unconditional love and unequivocal faith has given me the courage to dream.

Fatemeh (Mariam) Zahedi
January 1992

I plant my hands in the garden.
I will bloom, I know, I know, I know,
and sparrows will nest
in the hollows of my ink-stained fingers.

Persian Poet Forough Faroukhzad, "Another Birth"

Foreword

The aim of the Wadsworth MIS Series is to help you build an effective career. Career building goes beyond getting a job. In the field of information systems, jobs change radically because the technology itself moves so quickly and so radically. Many new job descriptions have already been created in the 1990s: programmer in multimedia applications, specialist in business process reengineering, Microsoft Windows application developer, and wide area network expert on frame-relay, to name just a few.

Someone else will own your job, but you own your career. Building a career in the MIS field requires a solid grounding in the skills and knowledge that underlie the many ongoing surface changes in technology and applications. Yet you must also keep up-to-date in key areas. That is what this book offers. It will help you be a builder of effective tools that can greatly enhance decision-making in public- and private-sector organizations.

Those tools—expert systems and neural networks—have evolved over a forty-year period, with some major successes, frequent overhyping among software vendors, false starts, breakthroughs in theory, and continuing improvements in development aids. There is now a body of proven theory and practice that provides the foundation for a comprehensive grounding in the design and delivery of expert systems. While the surface details of the technology will surely change, this core knowledge will be as valid in the year 2015 as it is today and will help you adjust to the shifts between now and 2045.

These are not arbitrary dates. For students graduating in 1995, 2015 is twenty years into their career, the time when they will get key promotions or jobs as the outcome of their effort, grounding, and ability to adapt to rapid change as the norm. The year 2045 is when they can expect to retire at the end of a successful career.

We can be sure that in the twenty-first century there will be a career for builders of expert systems because the potential payoff is so huge and the challenges just as large. Expert systems augment human capacity. They do not replace human thought anymore than the motor car replaces human feet. At its best, the field of expert systems has been an adventure in the experiment of applying computer hardware, software, analytic methods, plus lessons from cognitive psychology, linguistics, philosophy, and mathematics to decisions that really matter.

In this book, you will find examples of such decisions, ranging from Merced County, California, transforming speed of response to welfare applicants from five to six weeks to a maximum of three days, to financial service organizations dramatically improving the risk management that is the core of their business (and a key element in what they charge, who files for Chapter 11, and whether or not you get your loan or mortgage), to Anderson Memorial Hospital saving millions of dollars and improving patient care through neural networks, to Mitsubishi's cutting office building energy costs by 24 percent through an expert system based on "fuzzy logic." These decisions matter in the sense that they affect quality of life, social policy, or economic survival. The more than fifty examples of expert systems and neural networks provided in this book highlight not just the progress of the field but why it has, and should have, ambitious aims.

None of the examples are "gee whiz" applications nor is there any magic formula for getting value from expert systems technology. Indeed, the field has been more one of disappointment and overpromises than of successes. Many technical specialists mistook the technology for the tools. Tools are for real people. To build tools, the tool maker has to understand the people, the context, and practical limits. He or she—you—have to bring a solid theoretical, technical, and empirical background to the task in order to build the right tools and ensure they will be used and provide results.

Many books on expert systems offer the theoretical, the technical, or the empirical. Fatemeh Zahedi's book is a fusion of all three. It is reliable;

there is no aspect of the foundations of expert systems field that it neglects or takes a biased position on. It is comprehensive, covering every major topic that a skilled tool maker needs. It is realistic, focusing on practice while doing justice to theory and history. It is timely; her coverage of neural network architectures, object-oriented design, fuzzy logic, and individual development languages are often more up-to-date than many practitioners' knowledge.

Up to now, expert systems have been a niche within the wider field of information system development, and neural networks have been entirely outside the mainstream. One disturbing implication of Professor Zahedi's book is that within the next five years, every developer of decision support systems, executive information systems, financial models, manufacturing planning systems, and even transaction processing systems will need to be familiar with what she describes. This is subversive in that expert systems are moving beyond being a job where your résumé shows you have four years' experience in C^{++}, to being a core element in the design and implementation of any type of decision-making tool. In 1982, the term "user-friendly" did not exist. Imagine saying in a job interview, "I'm sorry, I don't know anything about user-friendly graphical interfaces." We are not yet in a comparable situation with expert systems, but they show every sign of becoming as essential a part of the grounding for the career programmer, analyst, designer, developer, and consultant in every area of MIS.

Thus, this book is not only for the "specialist" but for anyone in MIS. It is also a beautiful book, by someone who knows how to teach.

Peter Keen

Table of Contents

PART II   THE THEORETICAL FOUNDATION OF EXPERT SYSTEMS

CHAPTER 3   Knowledge Representation Based on Logic   63

CHAPTER 4   Inference and Knowledge Processing   105

PART III   PRACTICAL ASPECTS IN APPLYING EXPERT SYSTEMS

CHAPTER 5   Deductive Reasoning Tools and LEVEL5   149

CHAPTER 6   Inductive Reasoning with 1st-Class   187

PART IV   OBJECT-ORIENTED REPRESENTATION AND HYBRID METHODS

CHAPTER 8   Object-Oriented Representation and Design   277

PART V   ADVANCED TOPICS IN EXPERT SYSTEMS

CHAPTER 11   Uncertainty in Expert Systems   415

PART I

INTRODUCTION

The objective of Part I is to introduce the reader to the field of intelligent systems and their applications in business. This part consists of Chapters 1 and 2.

Chapter 1 shows that expert systems and neural networks provide managers and decision makers with qualitative methods that complement the existing quantitative methods for decision making. It also presents a brief history of the development of expert systems and neural networks.

Chapter 2 shows why expert systems and neural networks are useful tools for managerial decision making in business and economics.

Introduction

Thus grew the tale of Wonderland:
Thus slowly, one by one,
Its quaint events were hammered out–

Alice's Adventures in Wonderland

Chapter Objectives

The objectives of this chapter are:

- To introduce the important features of expert systems and neural networks that make them desirable tools for decision making

- To present a brief history of the development of artificial intelligence and neural networks

---

KEY WORDS: Quantitative method, algorithms, qualitative methods, intelligent system, machine intelligence, macro models of intelligence, micro models of intelligence

---

Introduction

This first chapter provides an overview of what has been learned over the past two decades about the use of quantitative tools for decision making. Those quantitative tools that have been most successful and their reasons for success are highlighted. The chapter then looks at their main limitations and points out the distinctive qualitative nature of expert systems (ES) and neural networks (NN). A key point to note is the extent to which complex decision making that involves judgment does not easily fit into the quantitative approach. ES and NN open up new opportunities, several of which we illustrate from real-world corporate experience; American Express's Authorizer Assistant is an outstanding example.

The chapter then reviews the history of machine intelligence, artificial intelligence (AI), and neural networks, focusing on the development of practical tools and on the specific problem areas that theorists and developers have encountered.

The aim of this first chapter is to provide a sense of the foundations of ES and NN. We do not cover any technical material; the main question we address is, what do ES and NN have to offer the decision maker and how much practical progress have we made in developing effective tools?

1.1 Expert Systems and Neural Networks as Qualitative Tools

Decision making in business requires processing quantitative information and qualitative knowledge. Expert systems and neural networks provide the needed methodologies for dealing with qualitative aspects of decision making.

At the beginning of the enlightened history of man, numerical terms had a qualitative origin, distinguishing "one" from "more than one," as one can still detect in certain languages, such as Greek. Commerce and crafts stimulated the development of numerical and quantitative techniques to the point where every aspect of business and economics, and modern human life in general, is measured by some quantitative yardstick, such as time, weight, length, profit, wealth, and income. In the last two centuries, as the advances in mathematics quickened, so did applications of quantitative techniques for increasing our understanding of business and economic systems, leading to better predictions and improved decisions.

Case: American Express Credit Authorization

Credit cards are a fact of life. Although they may ultimately cause the downfall of Western civilization as we know it, they have firmly entrenched themselves in society.

Credit cards provide certain benefits and disadvantages to both card holders and the issuing financial institution. For instance, one of the most unnerving things that can happen to you as a credit card holder involves using the card when you know you're close to your limit.

There are a tense few seconds while the cashier runs that precarious plastic through the little magnetic code reader hooked up to a phone line, then waits for the authorization number on your credit slip, and you are home free.

Unfortunately, if you're a compulsive or power shopper with an acute case of "drastic plastic," you might have to suffer humiliation: the cashier tells you, "This card is over the limit. You'll have to either pay cash, or give me another card, or put this thing back. And, geez, now I have to write up another receipt." As you try to find enough cash to cover your purchase, the 12 people behind you start mumbling things about you that even your mother never knew.

But there is a reason for all this anguish. Credit card fraud amounts to a multibillion-dollar annual loss for the credit card industry. Hardest hit each year are the most popular cards: Master Card, Visa, and American Express.

These companies have started taking steps to stop fraud; for example, using holograms affixed to the card to prevent duplication. You've seen these wonderful little creations on the lower right-hand corner of newer cards: the multicolor dove you can rotate as it takes flight and the corporate logo superimposed over a wire-frame model of the world, to name two.

Holograms have created an obstacle to counterfeits, but they don't have any effect on cards used fraudulently by the rightful owners or cards that have been stolen and not yet reported. American Express has turned to expert systems to help with this particular aspect of the problem and has created a system called the Authorizer's Assistant.

American Express and some of its subsidiaries, most notably its Shearson Lehman brokerage, have been active in expert system development since the early 1980s. One of the first publicized expert systems was Shearson's K:Base, a program that performs interest rate swaps in the financial market. K:Base was developed by Shearson with Gold Hill Computers Inc. and Symbolics Inc., and for the first time a major financial institution was willing to discuss its activity in AI.

American Express prides itself on offering a wide range of financial, business, and entertainment services through its various affiliations, including travel service, insurance coverage, and card division.

But the company is best known for its prestigious pieces of green, gold, and platinum plastic. This prestige is the result of American Express's card authorization system and credit registry (for tracking a cardholder's complete set of cards, not just the American Express card). It is the authorization system American Express set out to improve using expert system technology.

Let's start with the basics. American Express provides each of its retailers (stores, hotels, restaurants, bars) with one of its automated validation—or authorization—systems. These gizmos allow the merchant to check the status of the card at the time of purchase.

Now, think of all the different things people might use the card for at any given moment: checking into a hotel, picking up the bar tab after a stag party, towing a car after an accident, or buying a fur coat. Each of these scenarios and thousands more are telecommunicated into a central American Express authorization office every minute, every hour, 24 hours a day, every day.

The logistics of such an operation are mind boggling. Needless to say, authorizations are not handled by anybody's PC. For years, American Express has employed IBM mainframes for the basic authorization procedures involved in each card check. American Express is what is known in computing circles as a "big blue shop." This means it is a heavy-duty customer of IBM, requiring lots of equipment, support, and software.

American Express uses an IBM 3090 series mainframe for authorization. The 3090 is then accessed by users over the 3270 network, which includes 3278, 3279, and 3178 series terminals. The network itself actually extends to more than 100 users at individual terminals.

Think of 100 queries on the same topic with different variables bombarding the mainframe simultaneously in a relatively constant stream. Think about the fact that the mainframe is designed to handle relatively common queries. Then think about how many calls have to be turned over to human experts for actual verification or decision making.

Finally, think about doing this until, say, the end of the world. Now you have an idea of the American Express dilemma.

The company's history of involvement with expert systems led it to consider creating an automated authorization system: not just a prototype of a semi-useful, occasionally employed expert system, but one that would work in real time and could be connected to the installed mainframe for access to the existing database.

The criteria for the system, in addition to the technical requirements just mentioned, were fairly straightforward:

1. Minimize fraud and credit losses from improper or incorrect authorizations.
2. Assist in making more accurate authorization, more quickly and frequently.
3. Reduce training time and associated costs for authorizers.
4. Stabilize authorization staffing levels by transferring certain responsibilities to the computer system.

The system also had to be able to show its chain of reasoning at given points in the operation—a fairly common capability in most current expert system tools and shells. It also had to be fairly easy to maintain, with the ability to incorporate new company policies in a minimal amount of time; obviously, that eliminated compiler-based systems.

American Express looked for the appropriate product and vendor and eventually settled on Inference Corp. to help with its large-scale development plan. This Los Angeles, Calif.-based company is the vendor of the Automated Reasoning Tool, a Lisp development tool usually referred to by its acronym, ART. ART is considered by many users to be the most comprehensive of the larger tools (those that cost more than $30,000 and run on something bigger than a PC AT) and the most complex.

Inference had built a pretty good reputation through its work with aerospace and aeronautics companies, notably the National Aeronautics and Space Administration and Lockheed Missiles and Space Co. NASA and Inference developed NAVEX, one of the most famous early commercial expert systems, used for navigational tracking of space flights.

Inference agreed to develop the Authorizer's Assistant to conform to all American Express's criteria. Therefore, Inference couldn't just hand American Express the most recent version of ART and say "have at it." Eventually the system had to be fully deployable to American Express for internal use. Two important points about ART are worth mentioning. First, the program allows for incremental rule compilation during development, which means new rules can be inserted without having to go through entire recompilation of an application. This was appealing because of American Express's need for revisions based on corporate policy changes.

Second, ART is capable of synchronous processing. Although this may be met with remarks like "So what?," it was important to American Express to be able to exchange data with IBM 3090 to utilize shared information between the two environments.

Started in early 1986, the system began with prototypes, as all good expert systems do. The companies used Symbolics 3645 Lisp machine for development purposes since ART on a 3645 is supposed to be one of the fastest-performing cohesive systems.

But what kind of information was important to use in the knowledge base? After all, if you're over your limit, you don't get to use the card, right? What's the big deal?

Hah! Not so fast. First of all, American Express is different from other credit companies in that it has no predefined credit limit. The company imposes spending ceilings for individual cardholders based on their ability to pay their monthly statements, which are always due in full. So oftentimes, users of the card may not know how much they are allowed to spend in a given time period until the company determines that maybe the cardholder is in over his or her head.

Thus a dilemma arises if an individual who customarily runs up a maximum of $200 per month suddenly makes a purchase of $15,000. This would require human authorization because of the mitigating factors involved.

Primary concerns are: "Is the card being used by someone other than the original cardholder? Could it be stolen or a fake? Could the cardholder have gone berserk and embarked upon a murderous shopping spree?" Although the last question is not an official American Express designation, I'm sure it gives you an idea of the possibilities.

Other factors also come into play. If Monday's authorization for a card came in from Sacramento, Calif., Tuesday's authorization for the same card came from Manila, Philippines, Wednesday's from Stockholm, Sweden, Thursday's from the Bahamas, and Friday's from Anchorage, Alaska, something fishy is probably going on.

The system has to be able to track strange travel patterns given the location of previous authorization sites. Not that any of these are strange places to use the card; it's just strange if the user appears to only have stopped in each place for the sole purpose of using the credit card.

As if this weren't enough, the system also has to address the problem of discrepancies. When discrepancies do occur, how will the customer be queried? The Authorizer's Assistant couldn't just give the instruction to have the card holder arrested by the local federales.

It was decided that the program would help by supplying a set of courteous questions to the merchant on the other end in case a problem arose.

Back to the mechanics. The first prototype took almost six months to complete and consisted of 520 rules configured for forward chaining. Currently, Authorizer's Assistant has about 1,000 rules, and both companies expect it to have about 1,500 by the time it is fully deployed this summer [1987].

By Harvey P. Newquist III, "In Practice: American Express and AI: Don't Leave Home Without Them," *AI Expert*, April 1987, pp. 63–65, reprinted with permission from *AI Expert*.

In business and economics, systems are identified by their components. For example, a manufacturing plant has employees, profit, sales, machinery, and capital. Many of these components are measurable in a quantitative metric, such as number of employees or dollar amounts of sales. If we can measure all components of a system in a quantifiable fashion and can formalize the relationships among them by mathematical functions, then we can use quantitative methods to analyze the system, solve problems, and recommend decisions.

1.1.1   *Quantitative Methods as Tools for Analysis and Decision*

Since the Second World War, *quantitative methods* have become the most important tools for formalizing, analyzing, and, at times, solving business and economic problems. Among these methods are optimization models by which one can optimize (maximize or minimize) one (or more) objective function(s), while taking into account constraints in financial, technical, physical, legal, and policy aspects of the system.

The combination of the objective function and constraints functions is called the formulation of the problem or system. In other words, we formalize those aspects of the system we are interested in by a set of quantitative variables and functions. Using this formalization, we can follow a well-defined computational procedure to find the best answer for the formulated problem.

The most successful optimization method is linear programming, which has been used in numerous areas. More complex optimization methods, such as nonlinear programming and dynamic programming, are used for solving more complex business and economics problems.

Another popular quantitative category of tools is statistics and econometrics. Using observed data, these methods estimate functional relationships among various system variables. In this category of tools, the functions are always mathematical, and the variables are mostly quantitative, although categorical variables are allowed in some methods. Estimated functions represent a formalization or a model of the system. We use these functions to analyze business or economic systems, forecast future values of system components, or measure impacts of various policies or decisions on the system.

Another set of tools are decision analysis methods, used in decision problems that involve selecting an alternative from a set of alternatives. In such problems, alternatives have many attributes or features. In this set of tools, too, one can estimate utility functions of decision makers based on their quantitative responses to questions. Here, the system (the preference structure of the decision maker) is formalized with a function.

These are quantitative approaches that do not require formalizing all aspects of a system by mathematical functions. In such cases, the system is represented by an *algorithm*. An algorithm is a step-wise set of rules, which can be used to produce the desired solution or response. For example, in the simulation method, the system is represented by a set of steps that, if followed, will simulate the working of the system. In the simulation of a waiting line system, such as a grocery check out line, the customers arrive in the system according to a probability distribution, wait in the queue for their turn, receive service, and leave the system. Computerizing this process by quantitative representation of the system, such as using probability functions to simulate the arrival and service time of a customer, keeping record of those in the queue and those being served, and advancing time, one can represent the working of the system on the computer. Another example is the nonutility methods of decision analysis, where following an algorithm for rating various attributes of alternatives under consideration yields ratings for alternatives, which the decision maker could use in making his or her decision.

1.1.2   Can Quantitative Methods Address All Problems?

While these and other quantitative methods have been quite successful in addressing system problems with quantitative components, they falter when a problem has a strongly qualitative nature. A recurring complaint of managers, decision makers, and policy makers has been that these methods ignore those important aspects and components of business and economic systems that are not easily quantifiable.

For example, the optimization formulation of a problem may recommend a solution requiring the CEO of the company to make changes considered radical. The CEO believes that radical changes may have a negative impact on the morale of employees, and hence labels the solution as undesirable. The question is how can one formalize this aspect of the problem? Functional relationships and quantitative methods cannot easily formalize "radical change" or its impact on the "morale" of the employees. Business and economic problems may have dimensions that do not lend themselves to quantitative measures and functional formulation of relationships.

Questions have also been raised regarding cases where patterns of quantitative data are so complex that no mathematical function can meaningfully represent them. For example, although one can measure all features of a face, such measures cannot be translated into mathematical functions for comparison with other faces. Similarly, movements of the stock market index are so complex that the best we can do is to characterize it as a random walk. We cannot formulate a mathematical function to represent its movements in a time interval, and compare it with the corresponding functional forms in other time intervals.

We can rarely find purely quantitative systems. Many aspects of business and economic systems do not lend themselves to quantifiable measurements, and many business and economic structures do not fit into mathematical functions. Expert systems and neural networks offer *qualitative methods*, or tools for the formal analysis of systems' qualitative aspects.

Case: Oil-Drilling Expert

Texaco, the oil-industry giant, uses a PC-based expert system to help drilling engineers diagnose and manage drilling-fluid problems. The system, which is written in Exsys Corp.'s (Albuquerque, N. M.) Exsys and Exsys Professional expert system environments, captures and exploits the expertise of Texaco's chemical engineers.

In drilling a well, a series of viscous fluids are pumped down the shaft to flush out cuttings, stabilize the rock to prevent blowouts, and perform other crucial operations that can precipitate as much as a quarter of the well's cost. Because of the task's sensitive nature and the "heavy chemistry" involved, drilling engineers must often rely on company chemists, whose time is limited and who can't be everywhere at once.

Kenneth Skillern, a senior research scientist with Texaco, developed the system several years ago after attending a seminar on expert system technology. Management expressed interest in Skillern's proposal to build a question-driven expert system that could help engineers detect fluid problems and make proper recommendations. According to Skillern, the system now "handles all phases of the drilling of the well. If problems occur, it knows what to do."

During a typical session, the user will have the choice of two screens: question-driven and word or numeric input. After a 10–15 minute question-and-answer session, the system will reach its conclusions, print a report, and offer recommendations (which may include the immediate notification of company chemists). The result is that engineers can approach their drilling problems more confidently and, even if they can't, Skillern says that "they'll have a lot of questions answered before they call the company chemists." The system has been invaluable as a training tool.

In addition to the tangible benefits of the system's deployment, Skillern claims that the expert system development process itself helped company chemists "take knowledge 'snapshots' and compare notes to uncover the gaps and weaknesses in our knowledge. The whole process really stimulated a cooperative effort among experts and helped us pool our thoughts."

Texaco is pleased with the system and plans to deploy similar Exsys-based tutorial programs.

By Justin Kestelyn, "Application Watch," *AI Expert*, May 1991, p. 71, reprinted with permission from *AI Expert*.

1.1.3   Qualitative Nature of Expert Systems and Neural Networks

One definition of expert systems is a set of computer programs that are based on artificial intelligence methods and are designed to serve as tools for making decisions. This definition equally applies to neural networks, with the exception that the computer program structure of neural networks is based on the structure of biological neural systems. A system created based on either the expert system or neural network approach is called an *intelligent system*.

Artificial intelligence and one of its most successful areas—expert systems—use symbolic manipulation, and are qualitative by nature. One of the most common methods of knowledge representation in expert systems is in the form of the IF-THEN rule, such as:

```
IF a decision requires radical changes
THEN it may have a negative impact on employee morale
```

The research in artificial intelligence has underlined what cognitive psychologists have known for some time—the human reasoning process is mainly qualitative.

The research in neural networks indicated that one can learn, remember, and compare complex patterns via a network of interconnected neurons. This representation is qualitative in the sense that no mathematical function is needed to store and recall patterns and relationships. Hence, neural networks too, have opened a new way to deal with qualitative structures that could not easily be formalized with the traditional quantitative techniques.

Thus, artificial intelligence and neural networks together present alternative methods of representing, storing, and processing information that are closer to human cognition and, at the same time, do not use the traditional quantitative methods. Researchers of *machine intelligence*—intelligence simulated on computers—probed into human information processing in their quest for understanding and simulating intelligence. In the process, they came up with alternative methodologies that address some of the old perplexing questions of practitioners about how to represent, formalize, and process the type of information and knowledge that does not fit the mold of quantitative methods.

1.1.4   Machine Intelligence

Although the dream of objects with human intelligence is as old as recorded history, the interest in simulating human intelligence on the computer started in the 1940s, when computers exhibited potential well beyond what had been remotely feasible before. It was at this time that the topic of human information-processing methods became an urgent issue. The question of whether a computer could be given human intelligence depended on our understanding of how humans process their thoughts and information.

To make intelligent machines required an understanding of intelligence itself. This led to an investigation of how humans process, learn, remember, and forget information. In the early attempts to understand human information processing for the purpose of simulating it on computers, researchers had access to two distinct bodies of knowledge: theories on *macro* aspects of human intelligence, and theories on *micro* aspects of intelligence. The macro aspects form the foundation of artificial intelligence, and the micro aspects are the foundation of neural networks.

Macro and Micro Models of Intelligence

The macro theories look at the human brain as a black box. They are not interested in how the human brain functions chemically or physiologically. They are interested in the logical process by which humans translate input information into knowledge, and in the thought process that arrives at new conclusions based on acquired knowledge and new facts. Philosophers, logicians, cognitive scientists, behavior psychologists, linguists, decision analysts, and information scientists are among those who are interested in macro theories.

It was, therefore, natural for a group of researchers interested in machine intelligence to choose the macro approach to investigate human intelligence for the purpose of transferring it to computers. They created the field of artificial intelligence.

The list of professionals who have interests in artificial intelligence from one perspective or another is lengthy, and includes computer scientists—for the hardware and software aspects of artificial intelligence—and engineers, who make intelligent components and intelligent machines such as industrial robots or control components. Linguists are interested in artificial intelligence as a tool to investigate language. Mathematicians are interested in artificial intelligence for using it to prove theorems and study logic. Business managers and policy makers are interested in artificial intelligence for its potential as a business decision tool. It is quite evident that in both development and applications, artificial intelligence is a multi-disciplinary field.

The micro approach to human intelligence treats the brain as a white or clear box. Researchers in this approach investigate the brain to discover how it operates, how it transfers information from external stimuli to internal signals, where and how it stores information, how it categorizes knowledge, how it remembers relevant information, how it forgets, and more importantly, how it learns. Various areas in the medical profession have claims on brain research, including neurologists, biologists, neuroscientists, neurobiologists, psychologists, and cognitive scientists.

To investigate the possibility of simulating human intelligence, another group of researchers interested in machine intelligence chose to fashion their models of human intelligence after the way the brain functions. They developed the field of neural networks. Their unit of analysis became neurons or groups of similar neurons. As in the brain itself, neural networks have layers of interconnected neurons that fire up signals. These signals are transmitted through a network to other neurons. When a signal arrives at a neuron, it may excite or inhibit the activity within a neuron. Once a neuron is sufficiently excited, it fires signals to others. Information is stored as the strength of interconnection among neurons. Thus, knowledge is represented in the form of a series of interconnected neurons, the structure of their interconnections, and the strength of their interconnections.

The list of professionals interested in neural networks is similar to those interested in artificial intelligence. Although the method differs, the outcome of artificial intelligence and neural networks should be the same—simulation of some intelligence on computers.

Historical Foundations for Modeling Intelligence at Macro Level

In various forms, the human thought process at the macro level has been a topic of interest to philosophers, logicians, and mathematicians long before the advent of the computer. About 24 centuries ago, Aristotle used logic to explain his thought process: If we posit that "all men are mortal" and "Socrates is a man," then "Socrates is mortal." This was a *deductive rea-*

soning approach, starting from the knowledge that "all men are mortal," using the fact that Socrates is a man, and deriving the conclusion about the mortality of Socrates.

In the seventeenth century, Descartes declared that "thought" was the essence of being, and believed "reason" was the basis for developing his unification method. He used his method to integrate geometry and algebra. George Boole in *The Laws of Thought* published in 1854 showed how logic dating back to Aristotle could have a calculus of its own. Gottlob Frege developed a mathematical language for logic in 1884.

In the early twentieth century, Bertrand Russell and Alfred North Whitehead developed a purely formal and mechanical approach to mathematical reasoning. Later in the 1930s, Kurt Gödel and Jacques Herbrand developed the concept of computability. Before the advent of computers, Alan Turing connected their ideas to computability on a theoretically envisioned digital machine. These developments facilitated the transfer of logical reasoning to computers in the form of *automatic theorem-proving*—being able to prove mathematical theorems from a given set of assumptions, similar to what mathematicians do. This is the foundation on which the field of artificial intelligence has been built.

Historical Foundations for Modeling Intelligence at Micro Level

Micro models of intelligence use the brain as the foundation for simulating intelligence. The brain has been one of the most fascinating and puzzling parts of human anatomy. However, by the 1940s a wealth of knowledge had already been developed about the functioning of animal and human brains at the micro level. As Shepherd [1988] describes in his historical account of developments in neurobiology, by the 1940s Galvani [1798] had already discovered the electrical activity of neurons, Cajal [1891] had shown that the brain is made up of independent neurons that are interconnected, Sherrington [1897] had proposed that nerve cells communicate with each other via synapses, and Langley, Loewi, and Dale [1920s] had discovered that neurons communicate through neurotransmitters (chemical substances) that transmit nerve cell signals.

Putting the discoveries together, it was known that the brain consists of small processing units called neurons. The neurons are massively connected and communicate through electrical and chemical signals. In 1952, the Nobel Prize winners Hodgkin and Huxley developed a mathematical model for the measurement of the neurons' electrical signals. An understanding of the general structure of brain functions had already emerged by the time the interest in machine intelligence became a practical topic for researchers. This is the foundation on which the neural networks field has been built.

1.2 A Brief History of Artificial Intelligence

In the early 1950s, the artificial intelligence pioneer and Nobel Prize winner Herbert Simon and his colleague Allen Newell at Carnegie Institute of Technology (now Carnegie-Mellon University) developed Logic Theorist, which proved theorems using logic (or more accurately, one of the formalized branches of logic, called propositional calculus). They were euphoric about it. Simon and Newell, the pioneers in the field, declared in their work published in 1958 that "... there are now in the world machines that think, that learn and that create. Moreover, their ability to do these things is going to increase rapidly until—in a visible future—the range of problems they can handle will be coexistensive with the range to which the human mind had been applied."

In 1956, Dartmouth College held the Dartmouth conference, the first artificial intelligence gathering attended by artificial intelligence pioneers: Marvin Minsky, John McCarthy (Dartmouth College), Nathaniel Rochester (IBM), and Claude Shannon (Bell Lab). They called the area of their common endeavor "artificial intelligence." John McCarthy proposed the lofty goal of artificial intelligence on the basis that "every aspect of learning or any other feature of intelligence can in principle be so precisely described that a machine can be made to simulate it." This conference witnessed the announcement of Logic Theorist as the first artificial intelligence computer program.

The early years of artificial intelligence were dedicated to developing general methods and software for computer processing. During these years, Newell, Simon, and Shaw (who joined them from RAND in 1956) developed General Problem Solver (GPS) [1957], and McCarthy developed Lisp (LISt Processing) at MIT as the artificial intelligence general programming language in 1958.

The next important milestone came in 1965—the year Robinson developed the resolution method for automatic theorem proving, and Zadeh developed fuzzy logic. In 1968, Quillian developed the semantic net approach for knowledge representation.

The second half of the 1960s witnessed the emergence of the practical side of artificial intelligence—expert systems. Starting in 1965, Feigenbaum and Buchanan developed DENDRAL, for determining the chemical structures of molecules. In 1969, Martin and Moses developed MACSYMA, a math expert system. Pioneering work in expert system development continued in the early 1970s with HEARSAY I and HEARSAY II for speech recognition, MYCIN for medical diagnosis, and PROSPECTOR for mineral explorations.

In the early 1970s, a new wave of software development took place, this time designed specifically for expert systems. In 1970, Roussell and Colmerauer developed Prolog; Van Melle, Shortliffe, and Buchanan developed the EMYCIN shell from MYCIN in 1973; and Forgy created OPS for programming expert systems in 1977.

On the conceptual side, Minsky developed frames for knowledge representation in 1976, and one year later, Dempster and Shafer developed their theory of evidence. In 1978, Buchanan developed the concepts of meta-rule and rule induction.

In 1978, McDermott started developing R1 (later XCON), a commercially successful expert system for aiding in computer configuration at Digital Equipment Corporation. In 1980, Symbolics started the development of Lisp machines and artificial intelligence emerged from labs and entered the commercial world. (See Giarratano and Riley [1989] for a chronicle of artificial intelligence developments.)

Thus, in a period of less than three decades since the inception of artificial intelligence, expert systems—its most successful application—entered the mainstream of computerized decision-making tools as intelligent systems. However, expert systems did not remain the sole intelligent tool in the market for long, neural networks followed soon after.

1.3 A Brief History of Neural Networks

Neural networks began with the pioneering work of McCulloch and Pitts, published in 1943. This early development of neural networks was concerned with showing that one could use neural networks for coding logical relations such as "x AND y" or "x OR y." This emphasis of neural networks quickly changed to using them to model brain structure. McCulloch and Pitts realized that their approach could be used for modeling the brain's process of pattern recognition and classification.

In 1949, Donald O. Hebb suggested that the strength of connections among neurons in the brain changes dynamically. When two neurons are activated by the same stimulus, the strength of their relation increases, such that when one is activated, the other one becomes activated, too. An external evidence of this is observed in animal conditioning. For example, in the Pavlov experiment, a dog was fed when a bell rang. Then, whenever the bell rang, the dog salivated.

In 1958, Frank Rosenblatt developed *perceptrons*—the first neural network architecture—which were based on the McCulloch and Pitts model. His major contribution was to suggest dynamic modification of the weights that represent the strength of interconnections among neurons. When combined with Hebb's proposition, the modifiability of weights among neurons was interpreted as the learning process of neural networks. The same year, John Von Neumann's last writing, *The Computer and the Brain*, crystallized the connection of the nervous system and machine intelligence. The pioneers of neural networks were as euphoric as their artificial intelligence counterparts. Rosenblatt declared in 1958 that he had developed a machine that could form original ideas.

This was a major turning point in neural networks. From this point onward, developing and improving methods of learning in neural networks became the topic of intense investigation. In 1960, Widrow and Hoff developed ADALINE (adaptive linear neuron), in which they used the difference between the activity of neurons and their desired outputs for changing interconnection weights among the neurons, thus training a network to learn to produce the desired output from a given input. During the 1960s, artificial intelligence and neural networks became competitive approaches for simulating intelligence on computers.

Another turning point in neural networks occurred in 1969 when Minsky and Papert (two famous artificial intelligence researchers) published the book *Perceptrons*, in which they showed that one-layer neural networks could not represent some simple systems such as [(x AND NOT y) OR (y AND NOT x)]. Once one-layer neural networks were shown to be inadequate, they conjectured that multi-level neural networks would not perform any better.

Before this conjecture was proved wrong, it created a ten-year hiatus in neural networks research because it dried up financial support for neural networks research projects and diverted researchers from the field. Still a handful of dedicated researchers continued the work during these dark days. One of the prominent and productive among them was Stephen Grossberg, who continued his work in modeling neural networks based on the neurobiological evidence of brain functions. When the interest in neural networks was renewed again, Grossberg had already laid substantial groundwork for the field.

In 1982, John Hopfield, a well-known physicist, observed the similarity of a neural network system with a recently discovered material called a "spin-glass." The similarity between spins of atomic patterns and neurons was first noted in 1954 by the neuroanatomist Brian Cragg and the physicist Nervill Temperley. However, it was Hopfield's observation of the similarity of neural networks and spin-glass in 1982 that renewed substantial research interest in neural networks and established them once more as a legitimate area of inquiry.

Thus, in the mid-1980s, research interest in neural networks intensified again. In 1987, Robert Hecht-Nielsen mathematically disproved Minsky and Papert's conjecture about multi-layer neural networks not being able to perform better than one-layer neural networks. Research and application in neural networks increased during the second half of the 1980s. Numerous commercial software products simulating various neural network methods entered the market. Under Stephen Grossberg's leadership, the International Neural Network Society (INNS) was founded. This society held its first meeting in Boston in 1988. In 1987, IEEE (the Institute of Electrical and Electronics Engineers) held its first international conference on neural networks.

Case: Medical Neural Networks

Any good physician should be interested in the "personality" of his or her practice—how long patients remain hospitalized, the average severity of illness, the rate of success or patient mortality. If you were such a physician, you'd probably also want to know how your practice stacks up against those of your colleagues. With that kind of information, it would be easy to discover which approaches work best for your patient, and when.

This information is now available on both an individual and a hospital-wide level thanks to a neural-network-based system developed by Steven Epstein, director of system development and data research at South Carolina's Anderson Memorial Hospital. Featuring networks trained in BrainMaker (California Scientific Software, Grass Valley, Calif.), CRTS/QURI is designed, according to Epstein, "to provide a profile of the 'average physician' so doctors can see how they practice medicine as compared to their peers." The system is in use at three large hospitals (500+ beds each) and one hospital system (1,500+ beds).

At the heart of Epstein's system is the goal of equating length of hospital stay with severity of illness; the result is the ability to predict length of stay and type of hospital discharge (including death) based on given diagnosis. Epstein attempted to meet that goal initially with statistical regression analysis, but the data was too divergent. After reading about BrainMaker in a magazine, he decided to take a new approach and ultimately trained his network to predict diagnosis severity with a 95% success rate. Said Epstein, "BrainMaker's numbers were so good I couldn't believe them."

Epstein used seven types of variables—diagnosis; complications; relevant body systems (respiratory, cardiovascular, neural, and so on); surgical and nonsurgical procedures; and admission category—to train the network. Training data was drawn from a pool of 80,000 cases and 473 diagnoses; each diagnosis comprised 400–1,000 examples. After the data files were dumped from a mainframe onto the PC-based CRTS/QURI database, NetMaker, BrainMaker's preprocessing component, converted them into neural-net files for training.

But Epstein didn't stop there. Once the network was trained to predict severity, he built two more networks for each diagnosis: one to predict resource allocation and one to predict type of hospital discharge. Each diagnosis network uses 26 input and one output variable and was trained in about four hours on a 386-based PC.

The sum of these networks, CRTS/QURI, is used to provide physicians with profiles of their individual practice, an "average" practice, and of the entire hospital. For a typical evaluation, Epstein will analyze a given hospital's records to identify problem diagnoses called DRGs. He then asks the resident physicians to select a single DRG and determines which physician group—internist, surgeon, resident, and so on—primarily encounters the DRG.

Here's where the networks come into play. Epstein uses the system to target the specialty groups and provides each physician with a one-page summary, which is generated with the help of Paperback Software's VP-Expert. This summary provides a hospital the comparative evaluation of length of stay as related to diagnosis severity and five pages of supporting graphs. Epstein then has personal consultations with each physician to present the results and answer any questions.

The results have been dramatic. Hospitals are able to make financial decisions based on their resources and the comparative resource requirements of each diagnosis; Epstein claims that in the second year alone of deployment at Anderson Memorial the hospital saved millions of dollars. And on the personal physician level, doctors are finding the weak spots in their practices. According to Epstein, "simply by increasing awareness, we're shortening the length of hospital stays and reducing mortality." He also claims that, interestingly enough, "I've had doctors tell me 'the fact that you're using neural networks in this system made me take a second look.'"

By Justin Kestelyn, "Application Watch," *AI Expert*, February 1991, pp. 71–72, reprinted with permission from *AI Expert*.

In the joint conference of IEEE and INNS in 1989, the "Business/Economics Special Interest Group" within INNS was formed. The 1989 conference contained numerous reports on the research on applications of neural networks, and featured a number of software products and hardware boards for neural networks.

Neural network potential will increase as we expand our knowledge of how the brain functions and as computers with many processors, each representing a set of neurons, become commercialized and affordable. Thus, neural network research will continue in labs in the foreseeable future. This however does not prevent the commercial use of developed methods in neural networks, a process that one may claim started in 1989.

Conclusion

While quantitative methods have been successfully developed and used in the analysis of business and economic systems and decision making, the qualitative aspects of such problems have not been fully formalized. Thus, expert systems and neural networks fill the gap by including the qualitative aspects of decision making into computerized systems. To accomplish this task, the two fields have aspired to simulate human intelligence and the brain on computers, creating machine intelligence.

References

Anderson, James A. and Rosenfeld, E. (Eds.) 1988. *Neurocomputing: Foundations of Research*, MIT Press, Cambridge, MA.

Carpenter, Gale A. 1989. "Neural Network Models for Pattern Recognition and Associative Memory," *Neural Networks*, Vol. 2, No. 4, pp. 243–257.

Charniak, E. and McDermott, D. 1985. *Introduction to Artificial Intelligence*, Addison-Wesley, Reading, MA.

Davis, R. and Buchanan, B. G. 1984. "Meta-level Knowledge," Chapter 28 in *Rule-Based Expert Systems*, B. G. Buchanan and E. H. Shortliffe (Eds.), Addison-Wesley, Reading, MA, pp. 507–530.

Dreyfus, Hubert L. and Dreyfus, Stuart E. 1988. "Making a Mind versus Modeling the Brain: Artificial Intelligence Back at a Branchpoint," *The Artificial Intelligence Debate—False Starts and Real Foundations*, S. Graubard (Ed.), MIT Press, Cambridge, MA, pp. 15–43.

Duda, R. O. and Shortliffe, E. H. 1983. "Expert Systems Research," *Science*, Vol. 220, No. 4594, April, pp. 261–268.

Giarratano, Joseph and Riley, Gary. 1989. *Expert Systems: Principles and Programming*, PWS-KENT, Boston, MA.

Grossberg, S. 1969. "Some Networks that Can Learn, Remember, and Reproduce any Number of Complicated Space-time Patterns, I," *Journal of Mathematics and Mechanics*, Vol. 19, pp. 53–91.

Hecht-Nielsen, R. 1987. "Kolmogorov's Mapping Neural Network Existence Theorem," in *The Proceedings of the First IEEE International Conference on Neural Networks*, M. Caudill and C. Butler (Eds.), Piscataway, NJ, IEEE Service Center, pp. 11–14.

Hopfield, J. J. 1982. "Neural Networks and Physical Systems with Emergent Collective Computational Abilities," *Proceedings of the National Academy of Sciences*, Vol. 79, pp. 2554–2558.

McCorduck, Pamela. 1988. "Artificial Intelligence: An Aperçu," *The Artificial Intelligence Debate—False Starts and Real Foundations*, S. Graubard (Ed.), MIT Press, Cambridge, MA, pp. 65–83.

McCulloch, W. S. and Pitts, W. 1943. "A Logical Calculus of the Ideas Immanent in Nervous Activity," *Bulletin of Mathematical Biophysics*, Vol. 9, pp. 127–147.

Minsky, M. and Papert, S. 1969. *Perceptrons*, MIT Press, Cambridge, MA.

Newell, Allen and Simon, Herbert. 1981. "Computer Science as Empirical Inquiry: Symbols and Search," *Mind Design*, John Haugeland (Ed.), MIT Press, Cambridge, MA.

Rosenblatt, Frank. 1958a. "The Perceptrons: A Probabilistic Model for Information Storage and Organization in the Brain," *Psychological Review*, Vol. 56, pp. 386–408.

Rosenblatt, Frank. 1958b. "Mechanism of Thought Processes," *Proceedings of a Symposium at the National Physical Laboratory*, Her Majesty's Stationary Office, London, Vol. 1, p. 449.

Rumelhart, David E.; McClelland, James L.; and the PDP Research Group (Eds.). 1986. *Parallel Distributed Processing*, Volumes I and II, MIT Press, Cambridge, MA.

Shepherd, G. M. 1988. *Neurobiology*, second edition, Oxford University Press, New York, NY.

Simon, Herbert A. and Newell, Allen. 1958. "Heuristic Problem Solving: The Next Advance in Operations Research," *Operations Research*, Vol. 6, January–February, pp. 1–10.

Struik, D. J. 1948. *A Concise History of Mathematics*, Dover Publications, Inc., New York, NY.

Von Neumann, John. 1958. *The Computer and the Brain*, Yale University Press, New Haven, CT.

Widrow, B. and Hoff, M. E. 1960. "Adaptive Switching Circuits," *Institute of Radio Engineers WESCON Convention Record*, part 4, August, pp. 96–104.

Widrow, B. and Winter, R. 1988. "Neural Nets for Adaptive Filtering and Adaptive Pattern Recognition," *Computer*, Vol. 21, pp. 25–39.

Zahedi, F. 1987. "Qualitative Programming for Selection Decisions," *Computers and Operations Research*, Vol. 14, No. 5, pp. 395–407.

Zahedi, Fatemeh. 1987. "Economics of Expert Systems and the Contribution of OR/MS," *Interfaces*, Vol. 17, No. 5, pp. 72–81.

Questions

1.1   What is the significance of qualitative and quantitative methods in business problem solving?

1.2   What are the categories of quantitative methods for business analysis?

1.3   How can we use expert systems and neural networks in solving business problems?

1.4   What are the historical similarities of artificial intelligence and neural networks?

1.5   What is the difference between artificial intelligence and expert systems?

1.6   What is the difference between the macro and micro models of intelligence? To which category do expert systems belong? To which category do neural networks belong?

Case Questions

1. Refer to the American Express Credit Authorization case. Discuss other areas of credit authorization that can benefit from the application of expert systems.

2. How could expert systems be used in a credit company that has credit ceilings for its cardholders?

3. Discuss the human authorizers' possible positive and negative reactions to the use of expert systems.

4. What would be your recommendations for encountering the negative reactions of employees towards the implementation of an expert system?

5. Compare the expert system application in the American Express Credit Authorization case with that in the Oil-Drilling Expert case. What are their similarities? What are their differences?

6. Compare the application of expert systems in the Oil-Drilling case with the application of neural networks in the Medical Neural Networks case. What are their similarities? What are their differences? What is the type of input required for each case?

CHAPTER 2

Why Are Expert Systems and Neural Networks Needed?

2.5.2. Algorithmics in Quantitative Methods vs. Heuristics in Qualitative Methods

2.5.3. The Debate over Machine Intelligence

We used to think that if we knew one, we knew two, because one and one are two. We are finding that we must learn a great deal about "and."

Sir Arthur Eddington

Chapter Objectives

The objectives of this chapter are:

- To discuss the applications of expert systems and neural networks

- To review the economic forces that necessitate the use of such systems

- To review some of the unresolved issues in artificial intelligence and neural networks

KEY WORDS: Synergy, intelligent database systems, productivity tools, integrated approach, heuristics

Introduction

This chapter focuses on the economic and technical reasons for applying expert systems (ES) and neural networks (NN). The first section reviews some of the early successful applications of expert systems and discusses some of the recent use of intelligent systems. We see that companies in the United States as well as in Europe and Japan are engaged in creating expert systems for various functions within their organizations. The neural networks have a shorter history of real-world application; the first section reports some of the major applications of NN.

The second section of this chapter discusses the economic factors that make ES and NN essential decision-making tools, and traces the desire for increased productivity from the nineteenth century to the present. We show that we have arrived at a stage of development in which further increases in labor productivity require investment in intelligent tools of the type expert systems and neural networks offer.

The use of ES and NN is not limited to the stand-alone systems; there are numerous efforts to integrate ES and NN with other information-system tools in order to formalize the qualitative aspects of these systems and give them "intelligence." Thus, we observe the *synergy*, or combination, of ES with database systems creating what is called *intelligent database systems.* Similarly, we observe the synergy of ES and NN with statistics and decision support systems. Attempts have been made to combine ES and NN, and to create intelligent systems that benefit from the strengths of both. The process of cross-fertilization and integration is ongoing.

Although ES and NN offer novel methods that address the need for formalizing the qualitative aspects of human knowledge, they are far from complete. There is a healthy skepticism about what these systems can accomplish. Research in this area has raised questions like, What is intelligence? How can we transfer or measure intelligence? How can we tell if an intelligent system is working correctly? The development of intelligent systems has stirred interesting philosophical debates across a multiple of disciplines involved in the field. The last section of this chapter reviews some controversial issues that are relevant to the applications of the technology.

The cases in this chapter give you a glimpse of the diversity of areas in which intelligent systems are applied.

2.1 Applications of Expert Systems and Neural Networks

Although one may apply expert and neural network systems for interpretation, prediction, diagnosis, planning, monitoring, debugging, repair, instruction, and control, the most successful applications of expert systems and neural networks are in *categorization* and *pattern recognition.* Such a system classifies the object under investigation (an illness, a pattern, a picture, a chemical compound, a drilling prospect, a word, the financial profile of a customer, a maintenance job) as one of numerous possible categories that, in turn, may trigger the recommendation of an action (such as a treatment plan or a financial plan).

Since expert systems have been one decade ahead of neural networks in entering the commercial market, they have a far greater list of reported successful applications. An expert system requires extensive effort in the collection of knowledge and expertise in the area in which it is applied. A neural network requires careful system design and choice of learning method.

2.1.1   Applications of Expert Systems

The early successful applications of expert systems were in mathematics, speech, and medicine. They were developed mainly for the purpose of demonstrating the feasibility and usefulness of expert systems. MACSYMA was one of the early expert systems developed at MIT. It has a knowledge base for solving algebra, trigonometry, differential, and integral problems in math. HEARSAY was an early attempt in using expert systems for speech recognition. MYCIN was developed for making diagnoses and recommending treatment for blood infection. Later, other systems (INTERNIST, CADUCEUS, CASNET, and PUFF) were developed for diagnosis and treatment of internal ailments, glaucoma, and lung diseases. Applications of expert systems to other areas such as chemistry (DENDRAL), geology (PROSPECTOR), and engineering (SACON) proved the universality of the approach.

The first major commercial application of expert systems was in the configuration of computers based on a customer's specifications and needs by Digital Equipment Corporation (R1, later renamed XCON). Today, numerous companies are engaged in the development of expert systems. Schorr and Rappaport [1989] report on some 27 interesting real-world applications of expert systems in areas such as aerospace, the military, banking and finance, manufacturing, retail, personnel management, biotechnology, emergency services, law, manufacturing assembly, manufacturing design, media, and music.

For example, when NASA launched the space shuttle *Discovery* in 1988, it used expert systems in its Mission Control Center to make flight management decisions [Muratore et al. 1989]. Huston [1989] reports on an advising system for the risk analysis of 12,000 domestic General Motors dealerships. Another GM expert system (Charley) is designed to help novice technicians decide when to schedule equipment for preventive maintenance.

Another interesting application of expert systems in financial economics and financial management is in the area of foreign currency. The job of foreign currency traders is quite complex. They have to process a large amount of data, take into account historical trends, determine the importance of any new event, and make buy or sell decisions a number of times during the course of a day. Manufacturers Hanover Trust has developed an expert system called TARA (Technical Analyst and Reasoning Assistant) to assist the foreign currency traders [Byrnes et al. 1989]. The profitability and acceptability of TARA have proven it to be a successful system.

Thompson and Bailey [1990] report a number of expert systems used in the public sector, other than the military. For example, the Environmental Protection Agency uses an expert system to determine the cost and payment schedules for those responsible for polluting the environment. The Nuclear Regulatory Commission uses an expert system to monitor the performance of power plants. A varied mix of public agencies are now developing or using expert systems, including the Immigration and Naturalization Service, United States Postal Service, Department of Transportation, Internal Revenue Service, Department of Energy, and some state agencies.

Feigenbaum, McCorduck, and Nii in their book [1988] have reviewed a number of well-known, big companies that use artificial intelligence to achieve higher productivity and profits. The following is a sample of the reported applications of expert systems.

Northrop has developed an expert system for the planning process in manufacturing jet fighters. A typical jet fighter requires 20,000 plans, each taking up hours of human planning and frequent revisions. The application of expert systems has reduced this planning time by a factor of 12 to 18.

IBM has had about 50 major expert systems in use and 120 more in development as of 1988. One of these applications is the Logistic Management System, which helps the managers and operators control the manufacturing process of microelectronics chips. The Diagnostic Expert for Final Test is another expert system at IBM used to help test technicians diagnose the cause of failure of assembled products. In addition to providing consultation help, this system has reduced the training time of test technicians from 14–16 months to 3–5 months. Yet a third system at IBM (CASES) helps engineers and managers follow business procedures and prepare bureaucratic paperwork.

American Express has developed the expert system called Authorizer's Assistant to aid the authorizers in deciding whether to approve or reject a credit card charge. A computerized system automatically makes a decision for 80 percent of the charges by checking the statistical pattern of the cardholder's spending habit. The authorizers decide the remaining 20 percent that fall outside the regular spending patterns of the cardholder. Since American Express credit cards do not have a preset spending limit and the authorization decision must be made in less than 70 seconds, decision errors could be costly, leading to either uncollectable charges or customer dissatisfaction. The use of the expert system increases the consistency, quality, and speed of the authorization decision.

At Du Pont, 200 expert systems have been in use and 600 more have been under development as of 1988. Feigenbaum, McCorduck, and Nii report that these systems have been designed for solving diagnostic, selection, and planning problems.

Texas Instruments has chosen expert systems and artificial intelligence as a major strategic approach both for internal use and the external market. Texas Instruments uses expert systems in many facets of its manufacturing and planning. It also sells expert system products and custom-designed systems to customers.

In Japan, Nippon-Kokan Steel has captured the rare and disappearing expertise of its troubleshooting giant blast furnace operators, before these experts retire and their expertise is lost forever. The expert system is used in-house, and will be marketed for export. As Japan exports its traditional steel industry to developing nations, troubleshooting expert systems of this kind will be part of the package deal.

Expert system applications have flourished in Europe, especially in Britain, where artificial intelligence research has been strong and active. An example is the expert system developed by the British National Health Service. With 11,200 rules, it qualifies as one of the largest expert systems in the world. This system is used to help health service professionals evaluate the performance of national medical-care providers in Britain.

2.1.2   Applications of Neural Networks

Neural networks have been applied in solving a wide variety of problems, ranging from traveling salesman optimization to vision problems. Neural networks, like expert systems, are best at solving classification problems. They have the added advantage of performing successfully where other methods readily fail—recognizing and matching complicated, vague, or incomplete patterns.

Research projects for the applications of neural networks cover a surprising number of diverse fields. One of the first and best-known applications of neural networks is in the newly installed bomb detectors in some U.S. airports. This device is called SNOOPE and uses neural networks to determine the presence of certain compounds from the chemical configurations of their components.

Another area of intense research for the application of neural networks is in character recognition and handwriting recognition. This line of research has immediate use in banking, credit card processing, and other financial services, where reading and correctly recognizing handwriting on documents is of crucial significance.

The pattern recognition capability of neural networks has been used to read handwriting. In processing checks, the amount of the check must normally be entered into the system by a human. A system that could automate this task would expedite check processing and reduce errors. The human part in this system would be in the examination of those checks that the machine rejects. One such system has been developed by HNC (Hecht-Nielsen Co.) for BancTec.

Neural networks also have been used in financial risk assessment. Nestor (a neural network consulting firm) has used neural networks technology to develop a system for mortgage insurance decisions [Reilly et al. 1990]. Using the data from cases decided by underwriters, the system learns to emulate the decision-making process of the mortgage underwriters and to categorize the risk of loans as good or bad.

Another application of neural networks is in large diagnostic systems, as reported by Casselman and Acres [1990]. DASA/LARS is one such system, developed by GTE under a defense contract to discover spectrum anomalies in satellite communications. This system is already operational at the Defense Satellite Communication System.

Sejnowski and Rosenberg in 1987 have applied neural networks to convert text to speech. NETtalk (which uses DECtalk for synthesizing voice) is one of the systems developed for this purpose. This system can learn to read aloud.

Neural networks have been used for natural language processing. One such case is the use of neural networks for deriving language rules. Yet another area of neural network applications is in image compression. Since the storage and transmission of images require too much memory, neural networks were applied for compressing images, making image processing manageable. Image processing and pattern recognition form an important area of neural network applications because of its importance in vision, one of the most actively researched areas of neural networks.

A 700-page publication on research in neural network applications contains summaries of numerous papers of neural networks in a variety of areas. This document, produced from IJCNN-90 [International Joint Conference on Neural Networks 1990], contains reports on using neural networks in areas ranging from robotics, speech, signal processing, vision, and character recognition to musical composition, detection of heart malfunction and epilepsy, fish detection and classification, optimization, and scheduling. Most of the reported neural network applications are still in the research stage. That means that we will witness a wide range of neural network applications entering the market in the near future.

2.2 Economics of Expert Systems and Neural Network Systems

Strong economic incentives exist for developing expert systems and neural networks as *productivity tools* to increase the monetary productivity of labor. Here we examine the underlying economic motives for developing expert systems and neural networks, and specify the features that make such systems commercially successful. We review the historical background on the economic consequences of technological progress in the United States, and identify the type of technical advances that are likely to produce swift market responses. Given the above perspective, we identify the areas of artificial intelligence, expert systems, and neural networks that are more promising in meeting the immediate market demand for technical innovations in production tools.*

2.2.1 Technology as Impetus for Progress

"The division of labour, . . . , so far as it can be introduced, occasions, in every art, a proportionate increase of the productive powers of labour" [Adam Smith 1937, p. 5]; ". . . the invention of all those machines by which labour is so much facilitated and abridged, seems to have been originally owing to the division of labour" [Adam Smith, p. 9].

Adam Smith's two golden rules, the *division of labor* and the *division of labor between man and machine*, summarize the production maxims that fueled U.S. industry's unprecedented advances, from the inventions of farm machinery between 1783 and 1860 to the electrical era of 1860 to 1900, and on to the development of the automobile, the assembly line, and mass production technology between 1900 and 1930. Despite the extensive and rising reliance on machinery, the technological advances of the last four decades **(1)** have not changed the monetary productivity of workers, **(2)** have changed

---

*Parts of this section are based on the paper "Economics of Expert Systems and the Contribution of OR/MS," by Fatemeh Zahedi, *Interfaces*, Vol. 17, No. 5, 1987, pp. 72–81, with permission from the Operations Society of America and the Institute of Management Sciences.

the mix of the labor force, and (3) consequently, have led to the need for productivity tools that expert systems and neural networks could satisfy. These three aspects are the economic forces behind the applications of expert systems and neural networks.

Workers' Share in Production

With our increasing reliance on machinery, one might conjecture that labor's share in the total value of production would decline. Yet historical data do not always support this argument, especially for the period from World War II to the present. Lebergott [1984] reports that from 1870 to 1920, worker earnings grew as much as the increase in the net productivity of labor.

As Figure 2.1 shows, from 1929 to 1945, the share of the nation's private sector employee compensation in the gross domestic product (GDP) declined. However, since 1946, employee compensation has held stable at about 50 percent of the GDP. In other words, in the last four decades, employees have received a fixed share of the value of the gross domestic product.

Furthermore, Figure 2.2 breaks down the employee compensation into two major sectors: manufacturing and service, and shows that the share of wages in these two sectors has remained fixed. Service wages held a steady share of about 43 percent of the GDP since 1945, while manufacturing wages held at about 60 percent of GDP until 1983, when they dropped slightly.

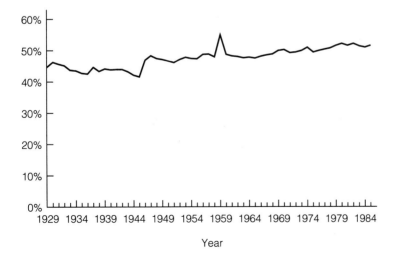

Figure 2.1 Percentage of Employee Compensation in GDP

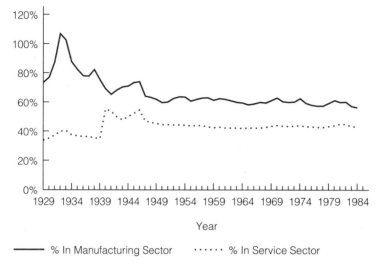

Figure 2.2 Percentage of Wages in GDP in Manufacturing and Service Sectors

We conclude that the share of labor in the monetary value of production has not declined in the last four decades. Thus, introducing more advanced machineries has not reduced the share of employee compensation in the total value of the production. We will see that this factor gives an important push to the application of productivity tools.

Case: Scheduling Freight Trains

Delays caused by scheduling conflicts for freight trains loaded with perishable foods or goods that have to be delivered on time are costly. Burlington Northern Railroad of Ft. Worth, Texas, has cut back on its delays and costs by employing an expert system running on SPARC-based UNIX workstations from Sun Microsystems—the Service Maintenance Planner (SMP).

Burlington Northern's primary problem was the lack of communication between its train schedulers and its maintenance crews. With 900 trains running daily on 11 corridors (routes) comprising approximately 25,000 miles of track in 26 states, the increasing delays were threatening business. By early 1987, the problem had escalated until something had to be done.

According to Glenn Galen, Artificial Intelligence Systems manager for Burlington Northern's information-systems department, hand-drawn charts were too time-consuming. Burlington Northern's chief of maintenance suggested using a knowledge-based expert system to detect scheduling conflicts and resolve them before they became problems, but no commercial software was available to do the job.

Carnegie Group Inc. was called upon to write a highly specialized program running on Sun workstations that generated charts in as little as 20 seconds. In addition, any changes to the charts can be made in less than two minutes. Schedulers can detect conflicts at a glance by looking at the graphic display provided by the workstation. They can call up any corridor on the screen and check its 24-hour activity, including train and maintenance schedules.

Galen states, "The SMP applies human expertise and experience to coordinate train and maintenance timing and to resolve conflicts. That's where the AI comes in. To develop the SMP, we used the existing schedule database and added expert knowledge of our schedulers, combining the two sources into our knowledge-based system."

The pairing of Knowledge Craft AI software and Sun's UNIX-based SPARC stations gives Burlington Northern clear graphics and greater speed, two key factors in the success of its smooth ride.

By Patty Enrado, "Application Watch," *AI Expert*, July 1991, p. 78, reprinted with permission from *AI Expert*.

Change in the Mix of the Labor Force

Given technological advances, the professional division of labor, and the increasing division of labor between man and machine, one might wonder why labor's monetary share in the value of production has not declined. Alfred Marshall, during his tour of the United States in 1875, observed that "in all matters of this kind the leadership of the world lies with America, and it is a not uncommon saying there, that he is the best business man who contrives to pay the highest wages" [Marshall 1920, p. 550]. The U.S. companies were first to recognize that they could generate more profit by using expensive machines with fewer, but higher paid, employees.

The higher paid worker, however, is not the *same* worker who was there before the introduction of a new technology. In a free market, there is no economic reason to pay more for the same work. More advanced machinery requires a higher level of training, and hence higher pay. In other words, the advance of production technology has increased the skill required of labor, leading to higher wages.

While wages have increased continually since the 1870s, the last four decades have marked a rather unique feature in the production mix of labor and capital. In the period from 1945 to 1985, workers' proficiency has increased in the same proportion as technological progress, thus keeping labor's monetary share in production value almost constant. In other words, as employers have used relatively more advanced machinery and less labor in production of a unit of output, the share of private sector labor compensation in the gross domestic product has remained constant because workers have become more skilled and better paid.

In sum, the technological advances of the last four decades have not increased the productivity of the same worker, they have raised the productivity of another, more skilled worker. Thus, modern production technology has been in the service of increasing total profit, regardless of the share of labor in the value of output. This has prompted a change in the mix of the labor force and has made it more proficient and skilled.

A counterargument to the above conclusion is that the technological advances might have reduced the cost of capital goods, or have increased the production power of capital without changing the labor force. For example, if $100 of capital goods and one worker are used to produce $200 worth of output, then doubling the production power of the same $100 capital would require two workers with the same pay and an output of $400. Hence, the share of wages in the output would remain the same. This explanation, however, requires that the ratio of total wages to total capital stock be on the rise in the last four decades. But the evidence shows the opposite—in fact, the ratio of private sector employee compensation to capital stock has steadily and slowly declined during this period, from 83 percent in 1946 to 57 percent in 1982, as shown in Figure 2.3.

We can therefore conclude that the technological progress of the last four decades required significant changes in the type of workers, leading to a large, professionally trained work force.

Need for Productivity Tools

From the previous section, we see that in order to increase productivity, one must continue to increase the proficiency of the employees. Physical limitations—such as the number of skilled workers, the time lag in training such workers, and ultimately, the limited span of human life—make the continuation of the present trend of increasing workers' skill in production rather costly, if not impossible. Hence, production technology will be forced to advance in directions in which the skill of labor does not have to rise so rapidly.

Figure 2.3   Percentage of Employee Compensation in Capital Stock

Case: Grinder Troubleshooting

Ford Motor Co.'s Rawsonville plant in Ypsilanti, Mich., manufactures fuel-injection needles. The pride of the plant is a series of computer-guided, high-precision grinders, which grind the needles to precise specifications. Because of sensitive computer controls and frequent subtle adjustments, these needles often become flawed and cannot be recognized as such until testing, when the manufacturing process is over. To compound these difficulties, the grinders were designed in Europe, and troubleshooting expertise is not readily available.

In late 1988, Ford deployed the Fuel Injector Diagnostic System, which was built in Carnegie Group's TestBench. This system diagnoses grinder problems by guiding operators through a question-and-answer session, suggesting appropriate troubleshooting tests and advice. When the results of these tests have guided the system to diagnoses, it generates repair procedures. The system has been valuable because it reduces factory downtime and performs as an excellent troubleshooting tutor for plant personnel.

By Justin Kestelyn, "Application Watch," *AI Expert*, March 1991, p. 72, reprinted with permission from *AI Expert*.

In the present era of professional workers, technology could improve their productivity in two ways:

- First, since productivity (the quality and quantity of output) increases with work experience, one must find ways to transfer experience to the inexperienced worker without the common time lag, that is, using tools that help a novice perform at the level of an experienced worker.

- The second way is to look for new machinery or tools that could increase the productivity of the *same* worker without additional training.

Such tools would have to help professional workers increase the quantity and quality of their output. The division of labor between man and machine can increase productivity only when the machinery helps workers in areas where they are the weakest. Both the ancient abacus and the modern computer are examples of such machines.

Computer use by the professional labor force is still fairly limited, encompassing mechanical tasks such as word processing, and limited computations and presentations, such as spreadsheets, graphics, data communications, and database packages. Real productivity gains will be realized when the computer can help the professional in specialized production tasks. This requires the study of professional tasks and of how computer software can help to increase the productivity of people performing those particular tasks. This is a job in the domain of expert systems and neural networks.

2.2.2   *Expert Systems and Neural Networks as Productivity Tools*

In light of these requirements, let us review the developments in expert systems and neural networks for their potential as business and economic productivity tools.

Researchers have already discovered that the aspects of human intelligence that are most difficult to simulate are what man does without any apparent effort, such as vision, language (including speech recognition), common sense, and creating new research in vision and language are in the field of robotics; robots, by nature, are machines that replace workers and, at the same time, require a higher degree of proficiency in the workers that work with or manage them. The immediate business and economic applications of expert systems and neural networks are in the kind of tools that improve the productivity of the same professional worker.

Business expert systems and neural network systems can assist professional workers and decision makers by making expertise more widely and consistently available. If well developed, such systems are:

- *Untiring.* They are available 24 hours a day.

- *Immortal and permanent.* If maintained regularly, they do not retire, die, or resign.

- *Consistent.* Such systems make the same recommendation. They are not, by nature, emotional or biased, unless they are programmed to be so!

- *Duplicable and distributable.* One can produce multiple copies of such a system and use it in many locations.

Case: Hispanic Math Project

The Technology Based Learning and Research Dept. at Arizona State University in Tempe, Ariz., has implemented the Hispanic Math Project, a three-part interactive, multimedia expert system for teaching and evaluating math skills of kindergarten through twelfth-grade students.

The user-interface aspect, developed using IBM's Info Windows and M-Motion Video platforms, allows control of laserdiscs and touch-screen technologies. The expert system interprets student progress to Arizona State University's host computer using text processing, spreadsheets, database management, graphics, and modem communications. The expert system interprets, predicts, diagnoses, plans, monitors, instructs, and controls a student's work through its computer-aided learning station. It analyzes why a student missed a question or segment. The adaptive testing, based on 20 specific questions, determines the placement level of a student in a specific training unit. Students may choose an English audio translation of instructions on the screen, but for non-English-speaking students, a Spanish audio track is available.

The Hispanic Math Project, funded by the National Science Foundation and equipped with IBM hardware, is run by Gary Bitter and Marvin Tanner.

By Patty Enrado, "Application Watch," *AI Expert*, July 1991, p. 78, reprinted with permission from *AI Expert*.

Thus, it is possible for the professional to have an untiring, immortal, unemotional, permanent, consistent aid to consult with. The skill of the system could increase as its knowledge is expanded, hence aging may make the system more reliable. Such a system can increase the productivity of professionals.

2.2.3   Features of Expert Systems and Neural Networks as Productivity Tools

For expert systems and neural networks to be the answer to the quest for professional productivity, they must have certain features:

- Intelligent systems cannot remain custom-made, except when they are the early models for future mass-market production. Some companies with adequate resources, specialized functions, and extensive internal use have developed custom-made expert systems for strategic decision making. However, the real economic impact of expert systems and neural network systems as productivity boosters will be from standardized systems developed for various business and production functions and mass marketed.

- The systems must be flexible, capable of being modified or expanded according to the special circumstances of the organization.

- The systems must be extremely user-friendly and natural language-oriented so that they require no special training or additional knowledge from professional users.

- The systems must (a) increase the skill of the novice professional to the level of the experienced one, (b) increase the professional's quality and quantity of output, or (c) reduce the skill required to do a particular task.

- The mass use of systems will require that performance standards or proven track records be established. They must also be workable on microcomputers, have cheap hardware of their own, or be on mainframes with timesharing capability.

2.2.4   Combination of Quantitative and Qualitative Tools

We have seen in the definition of expert systems and neural networks (Chapter 1) that the goal of intelligent systems is to serve as a consultant to decision makers. This goal is shared by decision support systems, or any of the business and economics quantitative methods.

Both qualitative and quantitative methods are designed to help the decision maker. But while qualitative methods incorporate qualitative knowledge and relations, quantitative methods have long championed the value of quantitative knowledge. Thus the two fields have developed different solution techniques, adapted to the type of knowledge they each favor—one exact and numerical and the other inexact and inferential.

Professionals in the labor force use both exact and inexact knowledge in their work. Productivity tools designed to aid these professionals must encompass both types of knowledge and use both approaches to solve a problem.

2.3 The Synergy of Conventional and Intelligent Systems

Existing information technology and quantitative methods have proved highly useful tools in business and economic analysis. Expert systems and neural networks can successfully complement these techniques by formalizing the qualitative aspects of the system. There is evidence that the process of this synergy has already started in various types of systems and across a number of methods.

2.3.1 Synergy of Expert Systems and Database Systems

Databases are the most successful and widely used systems in management information systems. Their ability to organize, maintain, and retrieve a large volume of data has proven the immediate value of information systems in any business or government organization. One may argue that database systems have had a major role in launching the information revolution and in creating the label of *information age* for the postindustrial era.

In their conventional form, database systems are *passive*. That is, the ultimate added value of a database system depends on how its users use it and how its users interpret the information obtained from it. In other words, the value of the database depends on the intelligence, expertise, and creativity of its users.

One can increase the value of a database system by rendering it intelligent—by making it able to discover patterns and errors that, in a conventional database system, would be the task of its users. By adding intelligence to databases, one can make them *active*. Such an intelligent database can discover new patterns and knowledge from data, can check the quality of its own data, and help the user in finding the needed data, even if the user provides incomplete, vague, or erroneous answers to the questions asked by the system.

2.3.2   *Synergy of Expert Systems and Statistics*

There are numerous statistical and econometric techniques for data analysis and forecasting. Statistical packages such as SPSS, SAS, BMDP, MINITAB, SHAZAM, LIMDEP, and RATS contain numerous methods for statistical model specification and estimation techniques. These packages, too, are passive, in that they assume the user has the complete knowledge of all techniques and remembers what is the best and most efficient method to use in each case. However, even if the user knows which method to use, deciphering the manual to find the correct command is not an easy task. The explanation of the computational methods and statistical results in these packages could be greatly improved by adding an intelligent interface to them.

Intelligent statistical packages have a more active role. They can *help* the user in choosing the most appropriate approach, and in finding the correct software command. John Chambers was first in 1981 to note that using expert systems in statistical packages would make them intelligent and more useful. There are now a few relatively intelligent statistical packages in the market.

One of the early attempts in developing such a package was REX (Regression EXpert), developed in 1982 [Gale and Pregibon 1982]. This software contains enough knowledge to help the user safely apply a simple linear regression. REX can be used in conjunction with the S statistical package.

Another intelligent statistical package is SAM (for Statistical Analysis Mentor) [Athey 1989]. The methods in this package are relatively elementary, at the first or second level of statistics courses in business and economics. Its purpose is to help the novice user.

Although the existing intelligent statistical packages are mostly at the elementary level, they clearly are the indicators of the potential for a synergy between expert systems and statistics at the software level.

The synergy of expert systems and statistics is not limited to intelligent software. Research projects are underway to connect these two areas more closely. For example, Zahedi has shown that one can use statistical techniques to estimate relationships when the system generates its data in a qualitative fashion, as in expert systems. As expert systems become more popular, we will see more attempts to create a synergy between the two areas.

2.3.3   *Synergy of Neural Networks and Statistics*

Statistical techniques and neural networks are both *inductive* methods. That is, in both fields, the relationship between input and output is constructed from a data set. This makes the comparison and synergy between the two almost unavoidable.

One such synergy is reported in financial risk management by Marose [1990]. ADAM is a system that is designed for classifying the risk category of corporate loan applicants by Chase Manhattan Bank for $300 million in annual corporate loans. This system is a hybrid of statistical techniques and neural networks. From the historical data, it identifies the patterns for classifying the riskiness of loan applicants. For each case, it matches the applicant's financial profile with the patterns obtained from the historical data, and forecasts the corporation's riskiness for the next three years.

Because of their underlying statistical foundation, and due to their ability to recognize complex patterns, neural networks have attracted the attention of statisticians and econometricians. Already, Halbert White, a well-known econometrician, has made a number of detailed theoretical analyses, comparing some learning methods in neural networks with estimation techniques in econometrics. We almost surely will see more systems combining the two.

2.3.4   *Synergy of Decision Support Systems Tools with Expert Systems and Neural Networks*

Decision support systems (DSS) are "computer-based support systems for management decision makers who deal with semi-structured problems" [Keen and Scott-Morton 1978]. This is a broad definition that encompasses all systems that can aid managers. Expert system and neural network applications designed for managerial decision making fit this definition well. That is why some consider expert systems a type of decision support system.

Popular among the software tools used in developing DSS are spreadsheets (such as Lotus 1-2-3) and worksheets (such as IFPS). The worksheets are also called DSS generators and are expected to have more capability for modeling than spreadsheets.

The focus of DSS is on semi-structured and unstructured decision problems, and many such problems have significant qualitative components. Therefore, it is desirable to have intelligent DSS tools, the software products that have the function of the expert system or neural network software as well as an intelligent user-interface.

Some spreadsheet products have add-on units for developing expert systems within the software. On the other hand, some expert system products in the market (such as Guru) have a spreadsheet integrated within the software, such that one can access spreadsheet data as part of the expert system's knowledge base.

Fordyce [1987] reports the development of ALB (Automated Ledger Book) at IBM, in which the worksheet and expert systems software are integrated into one. He argues that the use of expert systems in DSS tools enhances the *cognitive* support of the software. Such support could be in the added knowledge about the variables and functions within the DSS, and in helping to change the relations from words to equations, in manipulating and working with equations, and in increasing the user-friendliness of the interface.

Once we accept the desirability of intelligent DSS tools, it is natural to expand it to combine DSS tools with neural networks. This concept has been applied in developing Mathematica, developed by Wolfram Research Inc. In this software package, one can create notes, graphs, animation, texts, equations, and neural networks. These functionalities make the software an appropriate tool for creating intelligent decision support systems.

2.4 An Integrated Approach to Expert Systems and Neural Networks

Real-world problems have qualitative and quantitative dimensions. Real-world users of decision tools can benefit from more qualitative capabilities and increasing user friendliness. The history of new and successful systems indicates that they must eventually be integrated with the systems that now exist within organizations.

To enter the mainstream of business computing, a system has to communicate and be integrated with other business systems. Expert systems and neural networks are no exception. One may argue whether the "intelligence" of expert systems and neural networks is "true" or "humanlike." But there is no doubt that they offer useful approaches that can enhance and complement the existing methodologies for problem solving and decision making. Therefore, it is essential that expert systems and neural networks become integrated with the existing tools and systems available to decision makers and problem solvers.

The need for an *integrated approach* to expert systems and neural networks is already acknowledged. For example, Bigus and Goolsbey [1990] have demonstrated that for solving a truck dispatching problem, they have integrated database functions, an expert system software tool, and a neural network software tool. The integration allows for the removal of artificial barriers among the quantitative and qualitative methods, and among the existing and new systems.

One can approach integration in two ways: independent software products that have plugs to other systems, and integrated products that contain all important functionalities needed within an organization. The first achieves integration through *compatibility* and the second group attains integration through *self-sufficiency*.

One can find examples of both approaches in various software products in the market. For example, six functionalities have emerged as the most commonly needed computerized tasks for organizational and personal purposes: spreadsheet analysis, word processing, database management, data communications, graphics production, and statistical analysis. To integrate these functionalities, some software vendors have chosen to produce products that perform some or all of these tasks with different degrees of completeness. Symphony and Framework are examples of self-sufficient packages containing these functions (at different levels of sophistication).

There are many other packages that are designed for one or two of these functions but have the capability to import from and export to other packages. For example, many spreadsheet packages can import data from Lotus 1-2-3 and dBase files. The degree and extent of compatibility varies among such packages. Many self-sufficient packages provide some degree of compatibility, as well. To provide compatibility for packages that are not compatible, there are facilitator software products in the market.

Discussion of the synergy of expert systems and neural networks shows that the integration process of expert systems and neural networks with the other business systems has already started. Expert system products are ahead in this aspect, because most expert system software products have hooks to the outside and accept database files and programs written in general languages such as C or Pascal.

However, expert systems and neural networks have a long way to go before achieving conceptual and software integration with the existing information technology. This is the challenge of expert systems and neural networks in the future as they join the battery of tools and systems used in tackling decision problems in a world of increasing sophistication and complexity.

2.5 Issues in Artificial Intelligence and Neural Networks

Artificial intelligence, expert systems, and neural networks are methods with a history far shorter than other established methodologies. They have not achieved their full development potentials, and the acid of time has not sufficiently tested their metals yet. There is healthy skepticism about the ultimate capabilities of these methods. Do we really know what *intelligence* is? Can we transfer intelligence? Is it possible to represent intelligence in software or hardware? Do these methods have any valid computational basis?

It will be a long time—if ever—before one can safely say that such questions have been addressed fully. Here we review issues of correctness of answer and computational methods that are of great importance in the applications of these technologies.

2.5.1 The Criteria for Measuring Machine Intelligence

One of the important issues in the application of any method is the criteria by which one may judge the correctness of the answers the method produces. In other words, how do we establish whether an answer is correct?

In quantitative methods, the criterion for the correctness of a result is established theoretically within the method itself, or is accepted within the field as a sensible rule or a generally accepted assumption (or axiom). For example, in optimization, the criterion for the correctness of an answer is whether it has the highest or the lowest possible value for the objective function. One may formulate a problem to maximize profit. The correctness of its computation is whether the recommended solution yields the highest possible profit.

In statistics, too, when we use regression to estimate the functional relations among a set of variables, the criteria for the correctness is whether the observed points have the minimum square distance from the estimated regression line or curve. Or, when we have an identity or definition, the correctness of the computation is given within the definition. We test it by checking whether the identity holds. For example, the correctness of the computation of the gross national product (GNP) is whether it is the sum of consumption, saving, and tax. Similarly, the correctness of adding two numbers is whether the agreed upon arithmetic rules of addition are followed.

The question is how one can say when an expert system or a neural network system has produced a *correct* answer. Or, when can we claim that a machine has acquired intelligence? One answer is that since we model human intelligence, the method must produce answers compatible with answers given by humans. The experience with the application of expert systems shows that while this proposition seems simple, it may be problematic in practice.

For example, one application of expert systems is in bank lending, where the system must, based on the applicant's financial profile, decide whether or not a loan should be approved. The question is which loan officer should be the one whose knowledge is stored in the system, and whose answer is what the system produces in each case?

This is one of the decisions that must be made at the time of system development. An expert system may contain the common knowledge of all bank officers. In this case, the system is called a *knowledge-base* system. Or, the bank may choose one or more of its best bank officers as the provider of knowledge and correct answers. In this case, the system would contain the special expertise of the chosen loan officers, and may be called an *expert system*. One may go even further, and attempt to collect the knowledge of a select group of bank officers from across the nation, and their answers would be the criteria of correctness. In this case, one may call the system a *super expert system*. In our discussion, we will use *expert systems* as a generic title encompassing all three system types.

A similar question exists in neural networks. No matter which model of neural networks is used, the criterion for its legitimacy is whether or not its output is similar to the way a human responds. Again, the question is who should be the model for such a system. The answer is similar to the one for expert systems: It is a decision to be made at the development stage.

Using the Turing test is an alternative answer to the question of how one can establish the existence of machine intelligence. This test requires a person to act as a judge and ask a series of questions without knowing whether it is the machine or a human answering the questions. If this person cannot tell which one (the machine or the human) has responded, then the machine has intelligence.

Although the Turing test is theoretically valid, at present it is rarely used in its original form for judging the intelligence of real-world applications of systems based on expert systems and neural networks. One reason is that such systems, which require a deep and vast knowledge of the world, have not been built, and may not be feasible in the near future. (There have been some promising efforts made in this direction, though, such as those by Douglas Lenat and his colleagues in creating CYC [Lenat et al. 1986 and Lenat and Guha 1990].)

Another reason may be that real-world applications are less concerned with the existence of an all-encompassing intelligence in a machine. The main interest in such systems at present is in their ability to capture, formalize, and process qualitative knowledge and information within a given domain in order to help professionals in their jobs.

2.5.2 Algorithmics in Quantitative Methods vs. Heuristics in Qualitative Methods

Since the correct answer is almost always well-defined in quantitative methods, computations in these methods are *algorithmic*. This means that there are step-wise rules one should follow to arrive at the correct answer. The simple example is the rule for adding two positive integer numbers. Step one is to write the second number below the first by lining up the digits from the right; step two is to add the two digits in the first right-hand column; step three is to write down the right digit of the answer; step four is to carry the remaining digits to the second column, and repeat steps two to four for all remaining columns. One can show that every time this procedure is followed, the correct answer is obtained.

This is not the case for artificial intelligence, expert systems, and neural networks. Since the correct answer lies within the human model, the methods of artificial intelligence and neural networks are *heuristic* in nature. That means that one may use several strategies and rules to improve the outcome. They mimic what humans do in their problem solving. Take the game of chess. There are no fixed and certain steps that one can follow to win a game. A chess player encounters a number of options in each turn, and chooses the one that *looks* more promising. The player would have developed some rules of thumb from previous games, and would use them in selecting the next move.

Similarly, when a musician tries to memorize a piece of music, there is no fixed step-wise, algorithmic method that he can use to ensure perfect recall of the score. The musician must rely on his experience and rules of thumb to learn the score in a given time interval. The accuracy of recall depends on the skill of the musician, and a perfect recall is never guaranteed.

Since human intelligence and cognition in addressing complex tasks and problems use a heuristic approach, so do artificial intelligence, expert systems, and neural networks.

2.5.3   *The Debate over Machine Intelligence*

Both artificial intelligence and neural networks have come under criticism for not delivering on their lofty claims, and for failures in accomplishing what probably were not their main mission to begin with. There are two main criticisms:

- One of the most common criticisms of machine intelligence is that AI and neural networks cannot capture some aspects of human intelligence— such as common sense. In some other aspects such as language and vision, the breakthroughs have been slow and small, although neural networks have shown a greater potential in these areas. Yet in other areas, such as modeling the intelligence to control physical movements in humans, the efforts are just beginning. It is true that artificial intelligence and neural networks are far from their intended goals, but no progress is linear, and the goal is far too great to expect its accomplishment in such a short time. In less than four decades, useful and practical accomplishments have been substantial.

- Another set of criticisms of artificial intelligence and neural networks is that we have learned little about human intelligence from these systems. Philosophers who consider artificial intelligence as part of their field because it concerns itself with the definition of intelligence, mind, reasoning, and rationality, are disappointed that artificial intelligence has not brought new insight to a philosophical understanding of these concepts. Some claim that we have not yet achieved *any* intelligence on the computer because we cannot reproduce the behavior of even a six-year-old child on the machine [see, for example, Dennett 1988; Putnam 1988; Penrose 1989; and Searle 1990].

Although such concerns may be legitimate, and certainly will provide the impetus for pushing forward the frontiers of machine intelligence, the discussions in this book are concerned with what has been accomplished so far, and how one may put these accomplishments to use as productivity tools.

Conclusion

This chapter discussed the applications of expert systems and neural networks, and reviewed the economic forces which necessitate the use of such systems.

Systems developed using the principles of expert systems and neural networks are called intelligent systems. We have begun to see the development of intelligent systems in which the conventional information systems are combined with expert or neural network systems. In other words, there is a trend in combining the existing information-system technology with that of expert systems, and more recently, neural network systems, thus creating intelligent information systems. Examples of these hybrid systems are intelligent databases, intelligent spreadsheets, and intelligent statistical packages. The process of combining technologies has been extended further to include the attempts to combine expert systems and neural networks into one technology.

While the researchers and business system developers are energetically discovering innovative applications of intelligent systems, the field is still struggling with some unsettled fundamental issues, among which are the concept of *intelligence* and the problem of measuring the intelligence of systems.

References

Athey, Susan. 1989. "SAM: Statistical Analysis Mentor," PC AI, Vol. 3, No. 6, November–December, pp. 56–60.

Bigus, Joseph P. and Goolsbey, Keith. 1990. "Integrating Neural Networks and Knowledge-Based Systems in a Commercial Environment," *Proceedings of the International Joint Conference on Neural Networks*, in Washington, DC, Volume II, January, Lawrence Erlbaum Associates, Hillsdale, NJ, pp. 463–466.

Byrnes, Elizabeth; Campfield, Thomas; and Connor, Bruce. 1989. "TARA: An Intelligent Assistant for Foreign Traders," in *Innovative Applications of Artificial Intelligence*, H. Schorr and A. Rappaport (Eds.), AAAI Press, Menlo Park, CA, pp. 71–77.

Casselman, F. and Acres, J. D. 1990. "A Large Diagnostic System Using Neural Networks," *Proceedings of the International Joint Conference on Neural Networks*, in Washington, DC, January, Volume II, Lawrence Erlbaum Associates, Hillsdale, NJ, pp. 539–542.

Caudill, Maureen and Butler, Charles. 1990. *Naturally Intelligent Systems*, MIT Press, Cambridge, MA.

Dennett, Daniel C. 1988. "When Philosophers Encounter Artificial Intelligence," in *The Artificial Intelligence Debate: False Starts, Real Foundations*, Stephen R. Graubard (Ed.), MIT Press, Cambridge, MA, pp. 283–295.

Doukidis, G. I. and Paul, R. J. 1985. "Research into Expert Systems to Aid Simulation Model Formulation," *Journal of the Operational Research Society*, Vol. 36, No. 4, pp. 319–325.

Feigenbaum, E.; McCorduck, P.; and Nii, H. P. 1988. *The Rise of the Expert Company: How Visionary Companies Are Using Artificial Intelligence to Achieve Higher Productivity and Profits*, Random House, New York, NY.

Fordyce, Kenneth J. 1987. "Looking at Worksheet Modeling Through Expert Systems," in *Expert Systems for Business,* Barry G. Silverman (Ed.), Addison-Wesley, Reading, MA, pp. 246–286.

Gale, W. A. and Pregibon, D. 1982. "An Expert System for Regression Analysis," in *Computer Science and Statistics: Proceedings of the 14th Symposium on the Interface*, K. W. Heiner, R. S. Sacher, and J. W. Wilkinson (Eds.), Springer-Verlag, NY, held July 1982 at Rensselaer Polytechnic Institute, Troy, NY, pp. 110–117.

Gale, William A. 1986. "REX Review," in *Artificial Intelligence and Statistics*, W. A. Gale (Ed.), Addison-Wesley, Reading, MA, pp. 173–227.

Graubard, Stephen R. (Ed.) 1988. *The Artificial Intelligence Debate: False Starts, Real Foundations*, MIT Press, Cambridge, MA.

Grant, T. J. 1986. "Lessons for O.R. from A.I.: A Scheduling Case Study," *Journal of the Operational Research Society*, Vol. 37, No. 1, pp. 41–57.

Hayes-Roth, F.; Waterman, D.; and Lenat, D. B. (Eds.) 1983. *Building Expert Systems*, Addison-Wesley, Reading, MA.

Holroyd, P.; Mallory, G.; Price, D. H. R.; and Sharp, J. A. 1985. "Developing Expert Systems for Management Applications," *Omega*, Vol. 13, No. 1, pp. 1–11.

Huston, Michael A. 1989. "Analyst: An Advisor for Financial Analysis of Automobile Dealerships," in *Innovative Applications of Artificial Intelligence*, H. Schorr and A. Rappaport (Eds.), AAAI Press, Menlo Park, CA, pp. 28–42.

International Joint Conference on Neural Networks. 1990. *Proceedings of the International Joint Conference on Neural Networks*, in Washington, DC, Volume II, January, Lawrence Erlbaum Associates, Hillsdale, NJ.

Keen, P. G. W. and Scott-Morton, M. S. 1978. *Decision Support Systems: An Organizational Perspective*, Addison-Wesley, Reading, MA.

Lebergott, S. 1984. *The Americans: An Economic Record*, W. W. Norton, New York, NY.

Lenat, Douglas B.; Prakash, Mayank; and Shepherd, Mary. 1986. "CYC: Using Common Sense Knowledge to Overcome Brittleness and Knowledge Acquisition Bottlenecks," *AI Magazine*, Vol. 6, No. 4, Winter, pp. 65–85.

Lenat, Douglas B. and Guha, R. V. 1990. *Building Large Knowledge-Based Systems*, Addison-Wesley, Reading, MA.

Marose, Robert A. 1990. "A Financial Neural Network Application," *AI Expert*, Vol. 5, No. 5, May, pp. 50–53.

Marshall, Alfred. 1920. *Principles of Economics*, eighth edition, MacMillan and Co. Limited, London.

Muratore, John F.; Heindel, Troy A.; Murphy, Terri B.; Rasmussen, Arthur N.; and McFarland, Robert Z. 1989. "Space Shuttle Telemetry Monitoring by Expert Systems in Mission Control," in *Innovative Applications of Artificial Intelligence*, H. Schorr and A. Rappaport (Eds.), AAAI Press, Menlo Park, CA, pp. 3–14.

Musgrave, J. C. 1983. "Fixed Reproducible Tangible Wealth in the United States 1979–82," *Survey of Current Business*, August, pp. 62–65.

O'Keefe, R. M. 1985. "Expert Systems and Operational Research—Mutual Benefits," *Journal of the Operational Research Society*, Vol. 36, No. 2, pp. 125–129.

O'Keefe, R. M.; Belton, V.; and Ball, T. 1986. "Experiences with Using Expert Systems in O.R.," *Journal of the Operational Research Society*, Vol. 37, No. 7, pp. 657–668.

Parsaye, Kamran; Chignell, Mark; Khoshafian, Setrang; and Wong, Harry. 1989. *Intelligent Databases: Object-Oriented, Deductive Hypermedia Technologies*, John Wiley and Sons, New York, NY.

Penrose, Roger. 1989. *The Emperor's New Mind*, Oxford University Press, Oxford, England.

Phelps, R. I. 1986. "Artificial Intelligence—An Overview of Similarities with O.R.," *Journal of the Operational Research Society*, Vol. 37, No. 1, pp. 13–20.

Putnam, Hilary. 1988. "Much Ado About Not Very Much," in *The Artificial Intelligence Debate: False Starts, Real Foundations*, Stephen R. Graubard (Ed.), MIT Press, Cambridge, MA, pp. 269–281.

Reilly, D. L.; Collins, E.; Scofield, C.; and Ghosh, S. 1990. "Risk Assessment of Mortgage Applications with a Neural Network System: An Update as the Test Portfolio Ages," *Proceedings of the International Joint Conference on Neural Networks*, in Washington, DC, Volume II, January, Lawrence Erlbaum Associates, Hillsdale, NJ, pp. 479–482.

Schorr, H. and Rappaport, A. (Eds.) 1989. *Innovative Applications of Artificial Intelligence*, AAAI Press, Menlo Park, CA.

Searle, John R. 1990. "Is the Brain's Mind a Computer Program?" *Scientific American*, Vol. 262, No. 1, January, pp. 26–31.

Sejnowski, T. I. and Rosenberg, C. R. 1987. "Parallel Networks that Learn to Pronounce English Text," *Complex Systems*, Vol. 1, pp. 145–168.

Smith, Adam. 1937. *An Inquiry into the Nature and Causes of the Wealth of Nations*, based on the fifth edition 1789, The Modern Library, New York, NY.

Thompson, Donna M. and Bailey, David L. 1990. "Financial Expert Systems," *PC AI*, Vol. 4, No. 2, March–April, pp. 20–23, 55–56.

U. S. Department of Commerce. 1982. *Fixed Reproducible Tangible Wealth in the United States, 1925–79*, GPO, Washington, DC.

U. S. Government. 1986. *Economic Report of the President*, GPO, Washington, DC.

White, Halbert. 1989. "Neural Network Learning and Statistics," *AI Expert*, Vol. 4, No. 12, December, pp. 48–52.

Zahedi, Fatemeh. 1984. "A Survey of the MS/OR Field," *Interfaces*, Vol. 14, No. 2, March–April, pp. 57–68.

Zahedi, Fatemeh. 1987. "Economics of Expert Systems and the Contribution of OR/MS," *Interfaces*, Vol. 17, No. 5, September–October, pp. 72–81.

Zahedi, Fatemeh. 1991. "An Introduction to Neural Networks and a Comparison with Artificial Intelligence and Expert Systems," *Interfaces*, Vol. 21, No. 2, March–April, pp. 25–38.

Zahedi, Fatemeh and Dadkhah, Kamran. 1990. "The Application of Statistics to AI Models—Using Logit for Inductive Reasoning," working paper, University of Massachusetts, Boston, MA.

Questions

2.1 What are the economic factors that necessitate the application of expert systems and neural networks?

2.2 Using more machines in the workplace implies a smaller share of employee wages in the total cost of production. Is this statement correct? Why?

2.3 Why do we need productivity tools?

2.4 What are the characteristics of expert systems and neural networks that make them good productivity tools?

2.5 Why do we need to combine qualitative and quantitative methods in business decision tools?

2.6 Discuss areas in which you think expert systems and neural networks could contribute to the productivity and profitability of an organization.

2.7 Discuss the synergy of expert systems and neural networks with the conventional technologies in information systems.

2.8 What are the issues being debated in the fields of artificial intelligence and neural networks?

Case: Expert System Applications in Advertising

Despite recent advances in the application of decision support systems to the media and budgeting areas, current advertising decision support tools are of little assistance in helping managers deal with the qualitative aspects of advertising decision making. This is significant because both budgeting and media selection have many qualitative aspects. In addition, creative strategy has largely been ignored in the decision support system revolution because of its qualitative nature.

Advertising decisions such as competitive response strategy, audience response strategy, audience segmentation, budget allocation, positioning strategy, advertising copy and layout, advertisement production, copy testing, media selection, media scheduling, and campaign control all have significant qualitative aspects which influence both performance and costs. Since these strategic decision areas have qualitative aspects, human judgment is required in order to make effective decisions. These decisions have three characteristics in common; they are: (1) complex—involving numerous interacting behavioral variables; (2) situational—variables involved and their relative importance are time and environment dependent; and (3) unstructured—incomplete and potentially inaccurate information must be used in decision-making.

The current decision support tools typically utilize rigid procedural programming and quantitative modeling to process large numerical databases, which limits their usefulness in advertising decision-making. However, the use of expert system tools that process both qualitative and quantitative information show significant promise for improving advertising decision making.

A number of expert systems have already been developed for use as management decision tools. The leading areas of application have been: (1) logistics, with applications focusing on inventory management and transportation, and (2) finance, with applications involving credit, tax, and financial planning areas. Other managerial areas experiencing considerable expert system activity are customer service and sales. However, there have been relatively few applications of expert system technology to advertising. Here, we describe four systems: two systems developed for newspapers that tangentially interact with advertising, one system for direct mail and one for sales promotion.

The first of the newspaper publishing expert systems is the Expert Publishing System developed by Crosfield CSI, a supplier of transaction systems for the publishing industry. This system aids daily newspaper publication through the use of three expert systems: (1) an expert space reservation system provided on-line, front-end advertising order-processing and newspaper space management; (2) an expert paper layout system for plotting the size and shape of editions, for configuring presses, and for dummying editions with ad and editorial structures; and (3) an expert production control system for deadline analysis and materials management.

The Press Lineup Advisor designed by Rockwell International Corporation aids newspaper publishers in determining printing plate positioning on presses. The expert system takes into consideration the number and sizes of newspaper editions, the number and types of color pages, and the press configuration available. Advertising personnel also use the system to configure ad layouts.

The first expert system related directly to advertising has been developed for direct marketers. MORE, an expert system developed by Persoft, Inc. provides direct-mail decision support. MORE provides the manager with an automated ability to screen and control a mailing list on a name-by-name basis. The system analyzes each individual on the mailing list considering (1) direct-mail purchase date; (2) frequency of response to previous mailings; and (3) how the individual might typically purchase as a result of a direct-mail contact.

Entemann and Cannon have developed an expert system designed to assist the sales promotion manager. Using the ESIE (Expert System Inference Engine), the developers have used existing published empirical research to develop a set of rules. This body of knowledge has been organized to provide guidance on sales promotion decisions.

Condensed from "Applications of Expert Systems in Advertising," by Robert Lorin Cook and John M. Schleede, *Journal of Advertising Research*, June–July 1988, pp. 47–55, reprinted with the permission from *Journal of Advertising Research*.

Case Questions

1. Discuss reasons for the relatively slow pace of expert system applications in advertising.

2. Identify the qualitative aspects of inventory management, transportation, and finance which make them good candidates for the use of expert systems in their decision-making process.

3. Find the original article on which this case is based in your library. Identify and discuss the expert system applications in inventory management, transportation, and finance for which the original article provides references.

4. Identify and discuss other areas of management decision making that can benefit from applications of expert systems.

Case: Neural Network Application in Risk Assessment of Mortgage Applications

Nestor's multiple neural network technology has been applied to many problems; among them, applications in signal processing for character recognition, in medicine, in vision, industrial inspection, diagnostics, speech and recognition. One particular problem domain that has been under investigation is that of automated decision-making and risk assessment for mortgage insurance underwriting.

Mortgage risk assessment begins with mortgage origination. A mortgage originator filters the general population of potential property owners according to a set of simple guidelines on acceptable ranges for such risk measures as the proposed loan-to-value ratio, the ratio of proposed obligations to income, etc. Fannie Mae and others in the secondary mortgage market publish guidelines that serve to qualify and segregate the home loan applicant pool into risk categories. Some of the higher risk loans are referred for private mortgage insurance. The process of determining whether or not a loan applicant should be accepted for mortgage insurance involves in effect a second underwriting. If the applicant exhibits an acceptable level of risk, he will be sold insurance. Mortgage insurance applicants are by nature a higher risk group than the general population of mortgage applicants. These applicants have already been underwritten by the mortgage originator and assessed as less secure cases. Thus, this second order underwriting performed by the mortgage insurer is bound to be more difficult, and prone to greater uncertainty.

The mortgage insurance problem can be divided in two parts. The first problem is that of automating the decision-making process of the underwriters. This can be served by constructing a system that can learn to emulate the decisions that underwriters make on mortgage applications. The strategy of applying a neural network approach to this phase of the problem is to capture data that represents loan application information together with the corresponding judgments that an underwriter has made on each application. The pool of data represents judgments from a number of underwriters. The neural net system trains to emulate the decision-making of this collection of experts on the problem.

A different aspect of the problem arises not from the use of the network in automating the human decision-making, but rather from the use of the network to improve upon the quality of the decisions through its ability to learn to estimate some measure of the risk of a loan applicant's defaulting on his mortgage payments. Underwriters for loan originators and private mortgage insurance companies do not perform this task flawlessly. Although these insurance underwriters typically decline approximately 20% of the applicants they review, of the remaining accepted group, some 20% will go delinquent during the course of the loan. Approximately 6% will eventually lead to losses as a result of claims. The peak in claims rates occurs some three to five years after the loan is granted. Because any feedback from an incorrect decision occurs some number of years after the decision is made, and because of the high turnover in underwriter staffing, there is little opportunity to improve on the underwriters' judgments from observations of historical outcomes.

Although the economic payoff of improving the quality of the underwriting decisions can be substantially greater than that of simply automating and replicating their current decision-making trends and practices, the acceptance of the former can require a higher level of commitment and reliance upon the technology. It is relatively easy to immediately verify whether or not the system is deciding as the underwriter would decide. From the simple perspective of "trusting the machine," it requires more commitment to accept that the machine, when disagreeing with the underwriter, is actually making the *better* decision about something that may happen in three to five years from now.

The neural network that was used for this application is a derivative of an RCE network. The RCE network is a three-layer network that is developed and patented by Cooper, Elbaum and Reilly. Essentially, the network trains by committing cells on its single internal layer that represents prototypical "exemplars" of the pattern classes that it sees in the training set. It automatically selects from the training set the exemplars that are to be stored in memory, storing in its weights the values that define the prototype features. Associated with each prototype cell is a cell threshold, a number that captures the extent to which this prototype's exemplar will participate in the classification of incoming new patterns. This cell threshold represents a region of influence around the prototype in the pattern space.

Data used for the risk assessment study was taken from a collection of some 111,080 home mortgage loans from the period of July 1984 to December 1986. The status of the loans was noted as of December 1987, and this served as the classification of "good" and "bad" loans. For the initial study, "bad" was designed as any loan which had gone delinquent at least once in the period from origination through the end of 1987. A total of 758 good applications and 844 bad applications was used for the risk assessment study.

The results of the initial study are that for a certain percentage of the applications (10%), it is possible to predict with 95% accuracy the loan which, if granted, would go delinquent in payment. (Delinquency is not the same as default, but it is a necessary precursor.) If the system's decisions are accepted at this throughput (10% of applications), then some number of good applications will also be called "bad." Rejecting such loan applicants would amount to turning away good business. Since the cost of replacing this lost business is far less than the cost associated with underwriting loans that go to claim, this 10% throughput represents an operating point with a viable economic benefit.

Condensed from "Risk Assessment of Mortgage Applications with Neural Network System: An Update as the Test Portfolio Ages," Douglas L. Reilly, Edward Collins, Christopher Scofield, and Sushmito Ghosh, *The Proceedings of the International Joint Conference on Neural Networks*, Washington, DC, January 1990, Volume II, pp. II.479–II.482, reprinted with permission from Lawrence Erlbaum Associates, Inc., Hillsdale, NJ.

Case Questions

1. Discuss risk management in other areas in which a similar neural network system may prove to be a good decision-making tool.

2. What were the information requirements for developing the neural network system in this case?

3. Could the developers have used statistical techniques in solving this risk-assessment decision problem? Why?

4. What are the advantages (if any) of developing a neural network system over the application of statistical techniques?

5. Do you see a potential for using both neural networks and statistical methods in developing a risk-assessment decision tool? How?

6. What was the role of database in developing the neural network for this case? Discuss the synergy of database systems and neural networks within the context of this case.

II

THE THEORETICAL FOUNDATION OF EXPERT SYSTEMS

The objective of Part II is to introduce the reader to the structure of expert systems and the theoretical foundation of the logic-based reasoning method. This part consists of Chapters 3 and 4.

Chapter 3 discusses the structure of expert systems and briefly reviews mathematical logic, which forms the foundation of single inference reasoning in expert systems.

Chapter 4 covers reasoning methods in expert systems including deductive, inductive, single, and multiple reasoning.

Undergraduate business students with minimal quantitative background and professionals with little interest in the theoretical foundation of expert systems can skip the sections identified as "optional." Scanning these sections without regard to the details of the mathematical logic will give the reader some idea of the soundness of the reasoning performed in expert systems. The optional sections are intended for graduate students with quantitative skills and professionals who are interested in the detailed examination of the reasoning process in expert systems.

CHAPTER 3

Knowledge Representation Based on Logic

The same persons who cry down Logic will generally warn you against Political Economy. It is unfeeling, they will tell you. It recognizes unpleasant facts. For my part, the most unfeeling thing I know of is the law of gravitation: it breaks the neck of the best and most amiable person without scruple, if he forgets for a single moment to give heed to it.

John Stuart Mill

The principles of logic and metaphysics are true simply because we never allow them to be anything else.

A. J. Ayer

Chapter Objectives

The objectives of this chapter are:

- To discuss the structure of expert systems and their major components

- To present the theoretical foundation of logic-based knowledge representation

- To discuss the rule-based method

- To review the predicate method

KEY WORDS: Domain knowledge, knowledge base, knowledge representation, inference engine, knowledge management, outside hooks, meta knowledge, rule-based representation, modus ponens, hypothetical syllogism, propositional logic, propositional calculus, predicate logic, predicate calculus

---

Introduction

This chapter begins with an introduction to the structure of expert systems, and discusses the major system components, or the building blocks, that one can find in every expert system.

One of the vital components of an expert system is its knowledge base. One can represent knowledge in a knowledge base more than one way. We can categorize the knowledge representation methods into two groups: *logic-based methods* and *object-oriented methods*. In this chapter, we discuss the logic-based methods of representing knowledge (they consist of the rule-based method and the predicate calculus method). The object-oriented methods of knowledge representation are discussed in Part IV.

The theoretical foundation of logic-based methods of *knowledge representation* is mathematical logic. Here we discuss basic fundamentals of mathematical logic, and show how rule-based knowledge representation and the predicate method of knowledge representation are directly derived from propositional logic and predicate calculus (two subcategories of mathematical logic). Most of the discussions regarding predicate logic have "optional" in their title. These are the topics that need not be covered in depth in most of the undergraduate and some MBA courses. However, a cursory reading of the optional sections shows predicate logic and predicate calculus lead to logic-based languages such as Prolog.

The chapter ends with the mortgage loan expert system case. Since this case will be the running example throughout the book, it is a good idea to read it carefully. Using the theoretical discussions in this chapter, the last section codes the knowledge base for the mortgage loan case both in the rule-based method and in the predicate method. This is a good point for emphasizing that logic-based knowledge representation has a strong theoretical foundation, and one does not need the syntax of a language or software product for coding knowledge in this method.

Although coding the mortgage loan case in the predicate method is optional, it is a good introduction to the Prolog language, because this language is designed for coding the predicate calculus method of knowledge representation. A comparison of the coded knowledge base in the rule-based method and the predicate method demonstrates the simplicity of the first method as opposed to the power of the second.

3.1 Structure of an Expert System

In any expert system, one can distinguish four major factors: domain knowledge, knowledge base, human component, and expert system software, as shown in Figure 3.1.

3.1.1 Domain Knowledge

Humans have knowledge in a variety of domains. For example, an individual may have knowledge in many areas, such as sports, food preparation, personal care, and driving. This person also may be an expert in one or more professional fields. An expert system normally is given knowledge within a particular area for which it is designed to solve problems or make recommendations. This area is called *domain knowledge*. For example, in a mortgage loan expert system, the domain knowledge includes all criteria, principles, and information pertaining to the decision on granting or denying a mortgage loan.

In the development of any expert system, the first step is to determine what the domain is. Although it sounds simple, determining what part of the domain knowledge should be included in an expert system can be a major hurdle in expert system development.

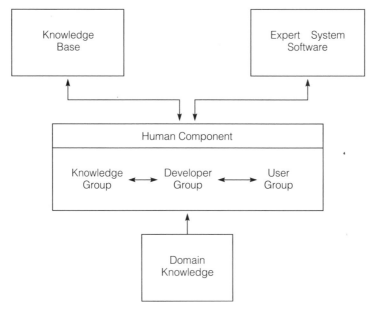

Figure 3.1 Factors in an Expert System

3.1.2   Knowledge Base

The *knowledge base* is the part of the domain knowledge that the expert system must contain. For example, the knowledge base of a medical expert system contains a portion of the medical knowledge pertinent to the purpose of the expert system. Similarly, the knowledge base of a mortgage loan expert system represents the rules, procedures, criteria, and formalized expertise used by a particular financial institution for approving or denying mortgage loans.

As a larger portion of the domain knowledge is incorporated into an expert system, its knowledge base grows in size. However, an overly large knowledge base could reduce the efficiency of the expert system and increase the possibility of inconsistency in the knowledge base, caused by conflicting rules or procedures. Chapter 7 discusses the systems analysis and design issues in developing large expert systems.

3.1.3   Human Component

As in any other system, people play a major role in expert systems. One can group the human players in expert systems into three general categories:

- Knowledge group

- Developer group

- User group

Knowledge Group

This group consists of individuals who create the content of the knowledge base. They determine, through many iterations of trial and error, what constitutes expertise within the domain knowledge, and formalize its structure. This group consists of the *domain expert* and the *knowledge engineer*. The domain expert is the person or group whose knowledge of the domain must be emulated by the expert system. For example, in a medical expert system for lung disease, the human expert could be the best-known lung specialist. Similarly, for a mortgage loan expert system, the human expert could be one or a group of the bank's best loan officers.

The domain expert knows a great deal about the domain knowledge. However, such an expert usually does not know how to formalize the knowledge such that it can be transferred to computers. The knowledge engineer works with the human expert to formalize the domain expertise in such a way that it can be transferred to the machine.

Developer Group

The developer group either programs the system from scratch or works with an existing expert system software product. This is the group that builds the expert system in close cooperation with the knowledge group and the user group.

User Group

This group consists of individuals who will use the expert system. Depending on the purpose of the expert system, the user could be a regular user, such as a novice bank officer who consults the expert system for additional expertise before deciding on a particular bank loan application. The user could be an irregular user, such as a bank loan applicant who is using the system to see whether he will be granted the loan. The needs of the system users have an important role in the design of the expert system.

The roles of human participants in an expert system are not clearly delineated. For example, with adequate training, a human expert could also play the role of knowledge engineer. The knowledge engineer is closely associated with the developer group. One person may serve more than one of the above functions in an expert system.

3.1.4 Expert System Software

In the early development of computer programs for expert systems, it became clear that a number of programming tasks were repeated in every program, while the coding of the knowledge specific to the problem area changed from one program to another. This led to the development of expert system *shells*. In expert system shells, the components common to all expert systems are separated from the knowledge base.

EMYCIN (Empty MYCIN) was the first expert system shell and was evolved from MYCIN (the first major medical diagnosis expert system). In this shell, the knowledge domain (medical knowledge) was removed from the software, and the remaining shell became a general tool for developing expert systems in other domains. Separating domain knowledge from the rest of the system was an important step that paved the way for the introduction of general expert system software products to the market.

Today, expert system software is far more sophisticated than EMYCIN, and its components have grown in power and in the diversity of tasks it can perform. Such software products are programmed to address the needs of the typical user group. In creating an expert system, one can simply enter the coded knowledge into the system and run it. However, most expert system software products have facilities for accommodating the special needs of a particular application, such as importing and processing data from an external source.

As shown in Figure 3.2, the typical expert system software has the following components:

- Coded knowledge base

- Knowledge representation

- Inference engine

- Knowledge management

- Outside hooks

- Meta knowledge

Coded Knowledge Base

The coded knowledge base is the knowledge base coded for the expert system software. There are several methods for coding knowledge. Even when two expert system products use the same method, their syntax of encoding knowledge may vary, depending on the design of the software. Once the knowledge is coded according to the software syntax, then the other components of the software can access and process it.

When an expert system is consulted about a particular problem, the expert system must get the relevant facts about that problem. The system combines these facts with the coded knowledge base to derive new conclusions and make recommendations. After the consultation session is over, most expert systems purge problem-specific facts from the system. However, some systems allow the user to modify the knowledge base on the basis of new conclusions. Some expert systems keep a library of facts regarding various problems within the knowledge domain. This library could be used for a variety of purposes, such as validation of expert systems, reasoning by analogy, and inductive reasoning. These topics are discussed in Chapters 4 and 7.

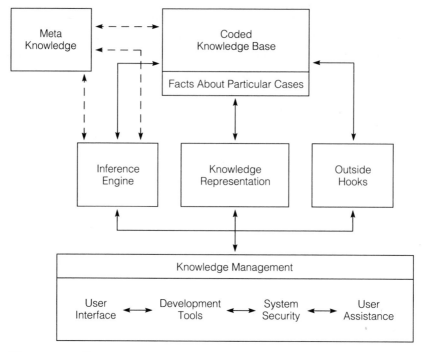

Figure 3.2 Components of Expert System Software

Knowledge Representation

The knowledge representation component of the expert system software provides the syntax for encoding knowledge. The knowledge representation could take the form of:

- Rules

- Predicates

- Semantic nets

- Frames

- Objects

In this chapter, we will discuss rule-based and predicate methods for knowledge representation and will observe that both have logic as their theoretical foundation. One can categorize semantic nets, frames, and objects as object-based methods, which are discussed in Chapters 8 and 9.

The knowledge representation component of expert system software normally allows for uncertainty, lack of clarity, or lack of confidence in the knowledge included in the knowledge base, or in the facts regarding a particular problem. Chapter 11 covers the treatment of uncertainty in expert systems.

Inference Engine

The *inference engine* processes and combines facts related to a particular problem, a case, or a question with the knowledge from the knowledge base in order to come up with a result, a conclusion, or an answer. Depending on the form of knowledge representation, an inference engine may apply one or more strategies for processing knowledge. In all cases, the approach of the inference engine is a heuristic one. That is, the inference engine uses rules of thumb that in most cases would result in *good enough* or *humanlike* answers. This is in contrast to quantitative methods, which mostly use algorithmic methods to arrive at the *correct* answers, where correct is defined according to prespecified criteria.

An inference engine has to search the knowledge base for pieces of knowledge that are relevant to the problem at hand. It may apply different search strategies. Furthermore, to link one piece of relevant knowledge to another in order to derive a conclusion, the inference engine may adopt backward chaining or forward chaining. These topics are discussed in detail in Chapter 4.

Knowledge Management

The *knowledge management* component of expert system software consists of the following facilities:

- User interface
- Development tools
- System security
- User assistance

The *user-interface* facility allows the user to interact relatively easily with the expert system. The user can enter the facts pertinent to the problem at hand by answering questions asked by the system. He or she can interrogate the system for the reasons behind a question the system poses or the system's conclusion. These are called the *why* and *how* capabilities.

For example, in a bank loan expert system, the system may ask for the length of time the applicant has been at his present address. The user can ask the reason for this question by entering the *why* mode. Furthermore, once the system concludes that the loan should be approved, the user may ask *how* the system has arrived at this conclusion. The user-interface facility has many more capabilities, which will be discussed in more detail in Chapter 7.

The *development tools* are the facilities for entering encoded knowledge to the system, checking for errors and inconsistencies within the system, and programming special features into the expert system.

The *system security* allows the developers to protect parts of the knowledge base from unauthorized access. Expert systems containing crucial and confidential knowledge could have layers of authorized access to various or all parts of the knowledge base.

The *user-assistance* facility of the expert system consists of help features provided by the software manufacturer, as well as assistance features programmed by the developer group for the special needs of the system's user group.

Outside Hooks

The *outside hooks* component of the expert system software gives the system a channel of communication to other systems. At present, most expert systems are designed to work as stand-alone systems. However, as the role of expert systems grows within organizations, the need to exchange data, information, and knowledge with other systems will increase. Thus, expert system software products that can interact with other expert system software products as well as with other types of software (such as popular database management, spreadsheet, and graphics products) will have a better chance of survival in the market.

Meta Knowledge

The *meta knowledge* component is not a common component in expert system software. Meta knowledge means knowledge about knowledge. When the expert system is large and complicated, the presence of a meta knowledge base and the ability of the inference engine to use it could contribute greatly to the system's efficiency and versatility.

For example, in the bank loan expert system, there could be knowledge about what particular pieces of the knowledge base become inoperative when the state economy experiences a period of severe decline, or the bank has shown declining profits for a number of quarters. When the applicant is in a special group, such as those with inadequate credit records, then the sequence of processing certain parts of the knowledge base should change, and special procedures must be activated. The meta knowledge base also could include information about the expert system's limitations in order to tell the user whether it has enough expertise for making a recommendation.

Case: Expert System for Paint Job

A retail firm in Holland, HEMA, has about 200 department stores, which sell various products, including paint. This company has created an expert system called Paint Advisor that helps the customers with their paint needs. The system advises the customer on how to do a proper paint job, makes recommendations for tools and products, and gives the customer a cost estimate. If a customer selects a given product for a specific job, the system performs an evaluation of the product for him or her. It also displays all the relevant information about the products discussed during the consultation and prints out a complete set of recommendations for the customer.

The system is implemented on the Knowledge Engineering System expert system software (by Software A&E) and runs on special in-store terminals that have only 12 keys for user interface. The Paint Advisor system has 280 rules and it costs between $150,000 and $200,000 to complete. The company expects to get a return on its investment through an increase in paint and tools sales.

Adapted from "In Practice," by Harvey P. Newquist III, *AI Expert*, October 1990, p. 65, reprinted with permission from *AI Expert*.

3.2 Logic-based Knowledge Representation

As discussions in the previous section indicate, formalizing knowledge plays a crucial role in the development of artificial intelligence and expert systems. One can separate knowledge representation into two broad categories: logic-based and object-based. We will discuss the logic-based approach in this chapter, and defer the discussion of object-based methods to Chapter 8.

3.2.1 Rule-based Representation

Rule-based representation is one of the most popular methods of knowledge representation in expert systems. The idea of rule-based representation started with Post in 1943 and was extensively used in systems developed by

Simon and Newell, two pioneers in artificial intelligence and expert systems. They called this method of representation *production rules*.

Originally, production rules had the form:

$$IF \quad <conditions> \quad THEN \quad <action>$$

which is also the model of the human method of generalizing and learning. Later, production rules took a more general nature, and became one of the most common modes of knowledge representation in expert systems—rule-based systems. Rules in their more general meaning can have the following interpretations:

$$IF \quad <conditions> \quad THEN \quad <conclusion>$$

or

$$IF \quad <antecedent> \quad THEN \quad <consequent>$$

or

$$IF \quad <evidence> \quad THEN \quad <hypothesis>.$$

Thus, a rule has two parts: The *IF* part indicates conditions, an antecedent or evidence; and the *THEN* represents the conclusion, consequent, or a hypothesis that one can generate from the evidence. Examples of production rules are:

```
IF  the applicant has had the same job for more than two years
THEN  the applicant has a steady job.
```

In this example, the statements the applicant has had the same job for more than two years and the applicant has a steady job are examples of a proposition or statement.

A rule can have more than one proposition in its antecedent or conditions. The following is an example of such a rule:

```
IF   the applicant has a steady job
 AND  the applicant has adequate income
 AND  the applicant has good credit ratings
 AND  the property is in an acceptable location
THEN approve the loan.
```

There are shorthand, but less obvious, ways to write rules. For instance, instead of

$$IF \ X \ THEN \ Y$$

where X and Y are two propositions, one can write

$$X \rightarrow Y$$

with the same meaning. For example,

```
IF   the applicant is 18 or older
THEN the applicant can apply for a loan.
```

has the same meaning as

the applicant is 18 or older $\rightarrow$

the applicant can apply for a loan.

Although the methods for reasoning and inference are discussed in more detail in the next chapter, it would be instructive to demonstrate here how one can reason with rules. Reasoning with rules is based on two rules of inference:

- Modus ponens

- Hypothetical syllogism

Modus Ponens

Modus ponens means that when you have a rule, and you establish that the antecedent or the condition of the rule is true, you can conclude that the consequent or the conclusion of the rule is also true. In other words,

IF X THEN Y
X is true

---

conclude : *Y is true.*

For example, assume that in the knowledge base we have the rule

```
IF   the applicant is 18 or older
THEN the applicant can apply for a mortgage loan.
```

Consider the case of applicant Smith. We know for a fact the applicant is 18 or older, so we can conclude that the applicant (Smith) can apply for a mortgage loan.

Hypothetical Syllogism

Hypothetical syllogism means that when the conclusion of one rule is the antecedent of a second rule, then you can establish a third rule whose antecedent is that of the first rule and whose consequent belongs to the second rule. In other words,

$$IF \quad X \quad THEN \quad Y$$
$$IF \quad Y \quad THEN \quad Z$$

$$conclude : IF \quad X \quad THEN \quad Z.$$

For example, from the following two rules

```
IF   the applicant is married
THEN the property is jointly owned
and
IF   the property is jointly owned
THEN the mortgage loan may have a cosigner
```

we can conclude that

```
IF   the applicant is married
THEN the mortgage loan may have a cosigner.
```

As we will see in the next section, modus ponens and hypothetical syllogism are two inference rules in logic.

3.2.2 Logic as the Foundation for Knowledge Representation

One can define logic as methods for formalized reasoning. Logic emphasizes form rather than content. That is, we may reason about two entirely different topics, but the reasoning may have the same form. For example, we may reason that:

- An increase in the money supply causes inflation; inflation causes an increase in the trade deficit; consequently, an increase in the money supply causes an increase in the trade deficit.

- Approving a mortgage loan requires adequate income; John does not have an adequate income; consequently, John's loan application is not approved.

- A person exposed to radiation has a high risk of developing cancer; John has been exposed to radiation; consequently, John has a high risk of developing cancer.

In all of these cases, the reasoning is similar, but the subject matter is different. Formal logic allows us to use similar reasoning processes in unrelated fields.

The foundation of logic dates back to Aristotle (384–322 B.C.), who used limited symbolic representation in his reasoning. However, formalized logic was greatly enhanced when the German mathematician and logician Leibniz (1646–1716) and later the British mathematician Boole (1815–1864) applied the symbolic abstraction of mathematics to logic, and laid the ground for mathematical logic.

Mathematical logic can be divided into four areas:

- Propositional logic

- Propositional calculus

- Predicate logic

- Predicate calculus

Although the distinction between propositional logic and propositional calculus is not always made clear in many texts, we will use the terms here in their precise meaning. This distinction will prove useful in the understanding of knowledge representation methods.

Case: Expert System Application in Corporate Accounting

The use of computer systems is growing rapidly in the areas of auditing, taxation, personal financial planning, and corporate planning, implementation, and control. Artificial intelligence now is being used in computer systems to provide access to the judgment of the best experts in a given field.

Although artificial intelligence and expert systems have been a part of accounting for a number of years, the use of expert systems is growing phenomenally. Expert systems are being developed for use in auditing, income taxes, personal financial planning, and corporate accounting. Expert systems are available to assist management accountants in all phases of corporate accounting including implementation and control as well as internal auditing.

IBM's FAME and Texas Instruments' Capital Investment System are examples of corporate financial planning discussed in Chapter 4. Here we discuss the expert system application in corporate accounting.

Expert systems are being developed and implemented to handle high-volume transactions requiring decision making by an accountant before the transaction can be entered in the accounting records. Some of the areas that are adaptable to the use of expert systems are revenue recognition, transfer pricing, cost flow and cost accumulation, evaluation of credit worthiness, and revenue and expense allocation in conglomerates with both domestic and foreign subsidiaries. EXXON's material transfer pricing system is an example of such systems.

EXXON acquired an Atlantic Richfield Co. accounting system, Integrated Capital and Operations Reporting (ICOR), that Anderson Consulting is customizing and enhancing to meet EXXON's needs. ICOR is a large mainframe-based system with more than 1,000 modules. For the Materials Subsystem, one of 11 subsystems of ICOR, EXXON is developing a global database to manage and account for inventories and fixed assets in numerous fields and warehouse locations.

This expert system has three knowledge bases that are used to determine the appropriate transfer prices for inventory and equipment moved from one location to another with or without change of ownership; to determine the sales and taxes related to these transactions; and to prepare the journal entries to record the transactions. The expert system will interface the operational events with the financial information and accounting systems of ICOR.

1. *Transfer Pricing Knowledge Base.* EXXON has a number of joint operating agreements that specify the type of transfer price to be used between EXXON and other participants. EXXON also transfers inventory and equipment between company-owned projects and divisions. As a result, EXXON must determine the types of transfer prices needed to maintain the accounting records at the various locations, such as book value, average warehouse cost, current market value, and agreed-upon contractual price.

2. *Sales and Use Tax Knowledge Base.* The determination of sales and use taxes can be quite complex. Inventory and equipment used domestically are taxed at different rates and by different taxing jurisdictions than materials used offshore or for transshipment to other states. The tax due and the taxing authority also can change depending on the use of, and/or the type of, inventory. Some materials are tax exempt in some jurisdictions. In addition, if the inventory or equipment is used for a different purpose than anticipated when purchased, the applicable tax rates and taxing jurisdictions can change.

3. *Journal Entry Knowledge Base.* A knowledge base also has been created to record the transfers of inventory and equipment. A single physical transfer of inventory can require as many as 30 separate journal entries. This knowledge base uses the transfer prices and sales and use taxes from two other knowledge bases to prepare the journal entries and to bill joint operation participants when a transfer between entities has occurred. The journal entries generated by the knowledge base feed directly into the validation and posting process of the general ledger. The knowledge base is designed to accommodate changes in accounting policies and accounting structures without requiring major changes to the structure of the knowledge base.

EXXON's expert system records 1,500 transactions a night using compiled mainframe version for faster performance. The expert system enables EXXON to account for transactions in a day or two that previously required more than a month to record. Thus, the timeliness and throughput from use of the expert system are exceptional. EXXON anticipates that the use of this expert system will eliminate the processing bottleneck caused by these transfers because 90% of the transactions can be handled without human intervention. If the system does not have all the information needed to record the transaction, then an accountant is called in to help.

The expert system will allow EXXON to move toward user maintenance in the long run. The initial coding is being done by Anderson Consulting to the specifications of EXXON's experts, but EXXON will do the long-run maintenance.

EXXON anticipates that the expert system will provide benefits in three areas: manpower savings, improved cash flow, and better decisions. First, EXXON expects the computer processing of the transfers of inventory and materials to reduce staffing needs because the expert system has replaced human processors. Second, the company expects savings from quicker processing of transfers that will enable to bill joint operation participants sooner, thus speeding up cash receipts. Third, the more timely recording of the financial effects of transfers will lead to better decisions regarding inventory and equipment.

Excerpts from "Expert Systems for Management Accountants," by Carol Brown and Mary Ellen Phillips, *Management Accounting*, January 1990, pp. 18–23, reprinted with permission from *Management Accounting*.

3.3 Propositional Logic

Propositional logic is the most elementary and fundamental part of mathematical logic, and it constitutes the theoretical foundation of knowledge representation with rules. It consists of *elementary propositions*, such as the applicant is married, or the budget deficit has increased this year.

One cannot break down the elementary propositions to simpler propositions. We use *connectives* to create *compound propositions*. For example, the budget deficit has increased this year and the stock market is unstable, is an example of a compound proposition in which the connective *and* connects two elementary propositions.

We represent elementary propositions or statements with *statement letters* $A, B, \ldots$. The *connectives* or *propositional operations* are:

Common Name	Formal Name	Symbol
not	negation	¬
and	conjunction	∧
or	disjunction	∨
if ... then	conditional	→
if and only if	biconditional	↔

3.3.1   Use of Connectives

Connectives are used to combine propositions. The formal name of such propositions is *statement form* or *statement formula*. Statement forms are compound propositions whose components themselves could be compound propositions. We will use $A, B, \ldots$ to represent both elementary and compound propositions.

In propositional logic, we want to establish the truth (T) or falsity (F) of the statements. T and F are called the *truth values* of the statement.

3.3.2   Truth Tables for Connectives

To establish the truth or falsity of a statement, one needs to know the truth tables of connectives used in the statement. Below we discuss the truth tables for various connectives: negation, conjunction, disjunction, conditional, and biconditional.

Negation

If we have a statement represented by the statement letter A, then $\neg A$ has the opposite truth value. The nature of the negation could be shown in a *truth table* as

A	$\neg A$
T	F
F	T

Note that $\neg\neg A = A$.

Example. Assume we have the proposition or statement

the applicant is married

which has a truth value of T. It is obvious that

¬the applicant is married

meaning that the applicant is not married has a truth value F. Moreover,

¬the applicant is not married

is the negation of the negation of a true statement, so its truth value is T. Note that a proposition is not always stated in positive form. For example, the following could be true

> *the applicant is not married.*

In this case, its negation

> $\neg$*the applicant is not married*

would be false, or has F as the truth value.

Conjunction

The conjunction connective *and* is shown as $\wedge$. The conjunction connects two statement forms (or formulas) such as

$$A \wedge B \qquad (\neg A) \wedge B.$$

Example. The following example gives content to the statement forms above:

> *the applicant is married* $\wedge$
>
> *the applicant has applied for a mortgage loan*

and

> $\neg$*(the applicant is married)* $\wedge$
>
> *the applicant has applied for a mortgage loan.*

The conjunctive connective has the following truth table:

A	B	$A \wedge B$
T	T	T
F	T	F
T	F	F
F	F	F

That is, a statement form with a conjunction is true only when both its parts are true. For example, the following statement form

> $\neg$*(the applicant is married)* $\wedge$
>
> *the applicant has applied for a mortgage loan*

is true only when the applicant is not married and the applicant has applied for a mortgage loan.

Disjunction

The disjunction connective *or* is represented as ∨; it connects two statement forms as well, and has the following truth table:

A	B	$A \lor B$
T	T	T
F	T	T
T	F	T
F	F	F

Example. The disjunction connective can be used in statements like:

$$A \lor B.$$

The following could be the context of the above statement form:

> *the applicant has adequate income to get a mortgage loan* ∨
>
> *the applicant has adequate assets to get a mortgage loan.*

This statement form has T as its truth value when either parts or both parts of the statement form are true.

Example. A more complex form of using disjunction is when we combine it with other connectives, such as either the applicant is married or the applicant is not married and has adequate income for a mortgage loan, which can be formalized as

$$A \lor (\neg A \land B).$$

Conditional

The conditional connective, *if-then*, represented as →, connects two statement forms: if A then B or $A \rightarrow B$. A is the *antecedent* of the conditional and B is its *consequent*. The conditional is false only when the antecedent is true and the consequent is false. That is, the truth table for this connective is

A	B	$A \rightarrow B$
T	T	T
F	T	T
T	F	F
F	F	T

Example. The following is a conditional:

```
IF   the applicant has adequate income
THEN the applicant can apply for a mortgage loan
```

which can be represented as

$$A \rightarrow B$$

where A represents the applicant has adequate income, and B represents the applicant can apply for a mortgage loan. This conditional is true when both A and B are true. It is also true when A is false and B is true. In other words, the applicant may not have adequate income, but could still qualify for a mortgage loan for other reasons, such as adequate assets. The statement form is true when both A and B are false. That is, it is possible that the applicant does not have adequate income and does not qualify for a mortgage loan. The statement form is false only when A is true and B is false. That is, when the applicant has adequate income, the applicant must qualify for a mortgage loan. Otherwise, the statement form would have F as its truth value.

Note that in the previous truth table for the conditional when the antecedent is false, the statement form is true regardless of the truth value of the consequent. This may, at times, look unusual. For example, the following two statement forms are true because the antecedent of both is false.

```
IF  the capital of France is New York  THEN  2 x 2 = 5
IF  the capital of France is New York  THEN  2 x 2 = 4.
```

In other words, the truth value of a conditional depends solely on the truth value of its antecedent. More formally, one can prove that $A \rightarrow B$ is equivalent to $\neg A \lor B$. That is, when A is not true, the conditional is true regardless of the truth value of B. When A is true, then the truth value of the conditional is determined by the truth value of B.

Note that in the previous example we did not discuss the content; the emphasis was purely on the *formal* truth value of these statement forms. However, to have meaningful results, one should ensure that the antecedent and consequent of the conditional operator are related, which was not the case in the above example. In other words, we can only check the *syntax*, or the form of statements, by propositional logic. The *semantic* or meaning of propositions depends on the knowledge domain to which the propositional logic is applied. It is the knowledge engineer's responsibility to ensure that propositions make sense.

Biconditional

If we have $A \rightarrow B$ and $B \rightarrow A$, this is the case of B *if and only if* A and is shown as $A \leftrightarrow B$. The connective $\leftrightarrow$ is called biconditional. A biconditional

$A \leftrightarrow B$ is true when both A and B are true. Hence, the truth table of this operator is

A	B	$A \leftrightarrow B$
T	T	T
F	T	F
T	F	F
F	F	T

Example. We want to formalize the following: the applicant can apply for a mortgage loan only if the applicant has good credit ratings. This could be formalized as

the applicant can apply for a mortgage loan $\leftrightarrow$

the applicant has good credit ratings

or

$$A \leftrightarrow B.$$

3.3.3 Establishing the Truth Value of a Statement Form

Since the statement forms (or formulas) are recursively constructed from statement letters (elementary propositions) and other statement forms, we may use numerous connectives in a statement form. Therefore, the use of parentheses clarifies the statement form to which a connective applies. To avoid extensive use of parentheses, the following priorities for the connectives are established:

Priority	Connective
1	( )
2	$\neg$
3	$\wedge$
4	$\vee$
5	$\rightarrow$
6	$\leftrightarrow$

The statement forms inside the parenthesis follow the same order of connective priorities.

Example. The following are examples of statement forms:

$$B$$

$$A \wedge \neg C$$

$$\neg(B \wedge C \vee A)$$

$$((A \vee B) \wedge (C \vee \neg D)) \rightarrow E.$$

Note that in the second statement form in this example, $\neg$ applies to C before the conjunction $\wedge$.

It is obvious that we can express all compound propositions by statement forms. This allows us to establish the truth value of a compound proposition.

Example. Formalize the following statement and show that it is always true: if the applicant has adequate income for a loan and the applicant gets a loan, then either the applicant does not have adequate income for a loan or the applicant gets the loan. This statement looks contradictory. But let us first formalize it in the following form:

$$(A \wedge B) \to (\neg A \vee B),$$

where A represents the applicant has adequate income for a loan, and B represents the applicant gets a loan.

To establish the truth table of this compound proposition or statement form, we should establish the truth value of its components and then combine the components according to the truth table of their connectives.

A	B	$\neg A$	$A \wedge B$	$\neg A \vee B$	$(A \wedge B) \to (\neg A \vee B)$
T	T	F	T	T	T
F	T	T	F	T	T
T	F	F	F	F	T
F	F	T	F	T	T

Since the truth value of $(A \wedge B) \to (\neg A \vee B)$ is T for all truth values of A and B, the original statement is always true.

3.3.4   Tautology and Contradiction

When the truth value of a statement form is always T no matter what the truth values of its components are, that statement form is a *tautology*. On the other hand, when the truth value of a statement form (or formula) is always F no matter what the truth value of its components are, that statement form is a *contradiction*. Note that a statement form could be neither a tautology nor a contradiction, because a statement could be true only some of the times.

We can use the truth table to establish whether a statement form is a tautology. This is similar to proving the universality of a statement form in all cases. This gives propositional logic a strong tool for the analysis of statement forms.

3.3.5   Truth Functions (Optional)

In establishing the truth value of statement forms, values T and F are not the only binary symbols to use. One can choose to use 1 and 0, instead. The statement forms could be regarded as *Boolean functions, binary functions*, or *truth functions*. A truth function is a type of function that returns only two values, T and F or 1 and 0.

We can form a truth function $f(X,Y)$ from statement forms in which only the connectives $\neg$, $\wedge$, $\vee$ are used. For example, consider the following table for a truth function:

X	Y	$f(X,Y)$
T	T	F
F	T	F
T	F	T
F	F	T

Then, this function could be characterized by the following statement form:

$$(X \wedge Y) \vee (\neg X \wedge Y) \vee (X \wedge \neg Y) \vee (\neg X \wedge \neg Y).$$

In other words, for the function to have a truth value, one of the above statement forms in the parentheses should hold. However, the first two statement forms in the parentheses result in F for the truth value of the function. In a disjunction, when parts that have F as truth values are of no consequence, the statement form representing the truth value of the function as T or as 1 is

$$(X \wedge \neg Y) \vee (\neg X \wedge \neg Y).$$

Example. Data from a bank loan officer indicates the following:

Income Level	Credit Ratings	Loan Approved
high	good	yes
high	bad	yes
low	good	yes
low	bad	no

The truth function of this set of data is

X	Y	$f(X,Y)$
T	T	T
T	F	T
F	T	T
F	F	F

where X represents income level, taking T for high and F for low value. Similarly, Y represents the credit ratings, with truth values of T for good ratings and F for bad ratings. The truth value of the function is T according to the following:

$$(X \wedge Y) \vee (X \wedge \neg Y) \vee (\neg X \wedge Y).$$

3.4 Propositional Calculus

Propositional calculus is the abstract and axiomatic formulation of propositional logic. A calculus—a formal theory or formal system—has the following components:

- Countable set of symbols or alphabets.

- Statement forms (or formulas) consisting of the combination of symbols and elementary statement forms (formulas).

- A set of axioms that are the initial formulas.

- The rules for deriving formulas from axioms or other formulas. This is called the "rule of inference." Modus ponens is one such inference rule.

- A set of formulas called *derived* or *well-formed formulas (wff's)* that are determined or derived from axioms or other formulas by using the rule of inference in a well-defined and effective manner.

In a formal theory or in calculus, a *proof* is the direct consequence of the rule of inference applied to axioms or well-formed formulas (wff's). Wff's are the statements or formulas already determined or proven. Therefore, in propositional calculus, one can start from axioms and apply the rule of inference to them to produce wff's, to which the rule of inference is applied again. This process allows proving theorems and new wff's in the propositional calculus.

From the previous discussions, one can observe that a rule-based system is a simplified form of propositional calculus. The propositions within the knowledge base form the symbols or alphabets of the system. These propositions are connected by connectives, usually negation (NOT), conjunction (AND), disjunction (OR), or conditional (IF ... THEN). Thus the compound propositions or rules in the knowledge base are the set of initial axioms or formulas of the system. Its rules of inference are modus ponens and hypothetical syllogism. Applying the rules of inference to the axioms and wff's derived from these axioms, one can attempt to establish the truth of wff's of interest.

In other words, the recommendation of an expert system is a wff of interest derived by applying the rules of inference to the contents of the knowledge base (axioms) and the intermediate conclusions (other wff's) already derived from the axioms.

As we will see in Chapter 11, rule-based systems do not always adhere closely to the formal process of propositional calculus. However, propositional calculus provides the theoretical foundation for this approach.

3.5 Predicate Logic (Optional)

Propositional logic provides us with tools to formulate and manipulate propositions and reduce them to simplified forms. It does not, however, have the power to break down the proposition and work within the internal structure of propositions. Consider the following example.

```
every worker can apply for a loan
smith is a worker
consequently:  smith can apply for a loan.
```

Propositional logic cannot accommodate the above, because it does not break down the structure of the proposition. Hence, it does not recognize that a worker is an instance of every worker.

In *predicate logic*, the proposition is broken down into a predicate and the subject of the predicate. A *predicate*, $P()$, is a logical function, hence its possible values (or range) are T and F. For example, the proposition Smith is a worker would be written as

$$is - a(smith, worker),$$

where is-a is the name of the predicate, and the predicate has two arguments: smith and worker. We could have defined this predicate differently, as

$$is - a - worker(smith).$$

In this case, the predicate has one argument. Note that in both cases, the range of the predicate (or the logical function) is T or F, while the domain of its arguments (or the values the arguments can take) depends on the context.

Arguments of a predicate could take both qualitative and quantitative values. For example, the proposition 10 is greater than 2 could be written as the predicate

$$> (10, 2) \quad or \quad greater(10, 2),$$

where the name of the predicate in this case is either $>$ or $greater$, and it takes two numerical arguments. The general form of this predicate is $> (X, Y)$ where variables X and Y are the arguments of the predicate. The domain of this predicate is the set of all real number pairs.

3.5.1   *Predicates (Optional)*

Predicates that cannot be divided into other predicates are called *elementary predicates*. Using the connectives, these predicates could be combined to form *compound predicates*.

For example, let $P_1(X, Y)$ and $P_2(X)$ be two predicates. Then we can write

$$P_1(X, Y) \wedge P_2(X)$$

$$P_1(X, Y) \rightarrow P_2(X)$$

$$P_1(X, Y) \vee P_2(X).$$

Example. We use the following predicate to show that X is Y's boss:

$$boss(X, Y).$$

Furthermore, to show that X is a Y in profession, we have

$$is - a(X, Y).$$

Now we can code the following statement. Smith is a worker and Jones is Smith's boss, which implies that Smith is a systems analyst.

$$is - a - worker(smith) \ \wedge \ boss(jones, smith)$$

$$\rightarrow \ is - a(smith, systems \ analyst)$$

Note that X or Y could take the form of a function.

Example. The predicate *greater* could have a function as one of its arguments:

$$greater(X, f(Y, a)),$$

which means that X is greater than function f, where a is a constant and f has a function form, such as

$$f(Y, a) = a * Y.$$

3.5.2   Quantifiers (Optional)

There are two types of quantifiers in predicate logic:

- Universal quantifier

- Existential quantifier

Universal Quantifier

A predicate, such as $P(X)$, has the variable X as its argument. To show that the predicate is true for all values of X, we use the universal quantifier $(\forall X)$, and have the predicate as $(\forall X)P(X)$.

   Example. All workers earn wages could be written as

$$(\forall X)earn - wages(X),$$

where the domain of X is the set of all workers.

Existential Quantifier

To express that the predicate is true only for some values of X, we have the existential quantifier as $(\exists X)P(X)$.

   Example. Some bank loans are approved can be coded as

$$(\exists X)approved(X),$$

where the domain of X is bank loans.

   Combining the predicates and the quantifiers remedies the shortcomings of propositional logic, in that it allows us to break down the structure of the proposition. Going back to the example at the start of this section, we had every worker can apply for a loan; Smith is a worker; consequently, Smith can apply for a loan. The following formalizes it as

$$(\forall X)(is - a - worker(X) \rightarrow apply(X)),$$

combined with

$$is - a - worker(smith),$$

results in

$$apply(smith).$$

Chapter 4 discusses how this conclusion is reached.

   Note that the parentheses in the conditional $(is - a - worker(X) \rightarrow apply(X))$ delineate the *scope* of the universal quantifier. If we had

$$(\forall X)is - a - worker(X) \rightarrow apply(X),$$

then the quantifier would apply only to the antecedent and not to the consequent. In other words, X is a dummy name and is local to the predicate where it is used, and the similarity of the argument name in $is-a-worker(X)$ and $apply(X)$ is of no consequence. Their similarity becomes important when both fall within the scope of the same quantifier.

3.5.3   Bound and Free Variables and Quantification (Optional)

In both universal and existential quantifiers, a variable that appears both in the quantifier and in the predicate is called a *bound* variable. In

$$(\forall X)earn-wages(X),$$

the variable X is a bound variable because it appears in both the quantifier and the predicate. When applied to a particular application, the interpretation of a bound variable is that it takes on the values within a given domain. In this example, X takes on the names of all wage earners.

Now take the following example. One can always find a better job. This can be represented as

$$(\exists Y)better-job(X,Y),$$

where the domain of X and Y is jobs in the market. In this example, X is a *free* variable because it does not appear in the quantifier.

The addition of a quantifier such as $(\forall X)$ or $(\exists Y)$ is called the *quantification* of a variable.

3.5.4   Relation of Quantifiers and Connectives (Optional)

One may consider the universal quantifier as a generalization of conjunction. That is, rather than writing

$$P(a_1) \wedge P(a_2) \wedge \cdots \wedge P(a_i),$$

where $\{a_1, a_2, \cdots, a_i\}$ is the domain of X, we write it as $(\forall X)P(X)$. This generalization is even more interesting when X has continuous or infinite elements in its domain. Hence, in one sense, the universal quantifier is the continuous counterpart of the conjunction.

Similarly, one may consider the existential quantifier as the general form of disjunction. That is, instead of writing

$$P(a_1) \vee P(a_2) \vee \cdots \vee P(a_i),$$

we may simplify it as $(\exists X)P(X)$. Again, since X, in this form, may take continuous values, the existential quantifiers generalize disjunction to include the continuous case as well. Thus, in the case where the predicate argument has a finite domain n, we have

$$(\forall X)P(X) \quad equiv. \quad P(a_1) \wedge P(a_2) \wedge \cdots \wedge P(a_n)$$

$$(\exists X)P(X) \quad equiv. \quad P(a_1) \vee P(a_2) \vee \cdots \vee P(a_n).$$

Example. In a firm, all employees have health insurance. One can formalize this fact by using conjunction and listing every employee:

$$P(adam) \wedge P(jones) \wedge P(lee) \wedge \ldots \wedge P(wang),$$

where P is the predicate representing has health insurance. Or, one can summarize this by

$$(\forall X)P(X),$$

where the domain of X is employees within the firm.

3.5.5   Multiple Quantifiers (Optional)

It is also possible to have more than one quantifier for one predicate. For example, every nation has some commodities to export could be written as

$$(\forall X)(\exists Y)P(X, Y),$$

where having commodities to export is the predicate P, and the domain of X is the world's nations and the domain of Y is the world's commodities.

Using the relations of the conjunction and disjunction,

$$(A \wedge B) \quad equiv. \quad \neg(\neg A \vee \neg B),$$

we have

$$(\forall X)P(X) \quad equiv. \quad \neg((\exists X)\neg P(X))$$

$$(\exists X)P(X) \quad equiv. \quad \neg((\forall X)\neg P(X)).$$

This allows the manipulation of quantifiers and their transformation from one to another type. We will see in Chapter 4 that such manipulation gives predicate logic a powerful tool for automatic reasoning.

3.6 Predicate Calculus

Predicate calculus is based in the concepts of predicate logic. Additionally, it has axioms and rules of inference. Applying rules of inference to the axioms of predicate calculus, one can find well-formed formulas (wff's), which in turn can be used to find other wff's. This is the process of theorem proving.

The simplest predicate calculus is *first order predicate calculus*, in which the quantifiers apply only to the arguments within the predicates, not to the predicates themselves. Predicate calculus is used in languages of artificial intelligence, especially in Prolog.

In summary, logic-based knowledge representation consists of the rule-based and predicate methods. The rule-based method has propositional calculus as its theoretical foundation. The predicate method is based on predicate calculus. In Chapter 4, we will see how one can reason using logic-based methods.

3.7 Knowledge Representation for a Mortgage Loan Expert System

In this section, we will discuss the content of the knowledge base for a simplified mortgage loan expert system and then encode it, using both the rule-based method and the predicate method of knowledge representation.

3.7.1 Mortgage Loan Case

The knowledge base of a mortgage loan expert system contains the following information. To get a mortgage loan, the applicant must have a steady job, acceptable income, and good credit ratings; and the property should be acceptable. If an applicant does not have a steady job, then he must have adequate assets. The amount of the loan cannot be more than 80 percent of the property value, and the applicant must have 20 percent of the property value in cash.

The definition of a steady job is that the applicant should have been at the present job for more than two years. The definition of adequate assets is that the applicant's properties must be valued at ten times the amount of the loan, or the applicant must have liquid assets valued at five times the amount of the loan.

An acceptable property is one that either is located in the bank's lending zone with no legal constraints, or is on the bank's exception list. The credit ratings check is done manually.

The definition of adequate income is as follows. If the applicant is single, then the mortgage payment must be less than 70 percent of his net income.

If the applicant is married, then the mortgage payment must be less than 60 percent of the family net income.

In the next section, this knowledge base is coded in the rule-based representation method.

3.7.2 Knowledge Base Represented in Rule-based Method

The content of the knowledge base could be coded using the rule-based method in the following manner. To simplify the presentation, we will use IF-THEN, NOT, AND, and OR to represent the connectives.

1. IF the applicant has a steady job
    AND the applicant has adequate income
    AND the property is acceptable
    AND the applicant has good credit ratings
    AND the amount of loan is less than 80% of the property value
    AND the applicant has 20% of the property value in cash
   THEN approve the loan
2. IF the applicant has adequate assets
    AND the applicant has adequate income
    AND the property is acceptable
    AND the applicant has good credit ratings
    AND the amount of loan is less than 80% of the property value
    AND the applicant has 20% of the property value in cash
   THEN approve the loan
3. IF the applicant has a job
    AND the applicant has been more than 2 years at the present job
   THEN the applicant has a steady job
4. IF the property is in the bank's lending zone
    OR the property is on exception list
   THEN the property is acceptable
5. IF the family income is adequate
    OR the single income is adequate
   THEN the applicant has adequate income
6. IF the applicant is married
    AND the mortgage payment is less than 60% of the family

```
              net income
    THEN the family income is adequate
  7.IF NOT the applicant is married
      AND the mortgage payment is less than 70% of the
        applicant's net income
    THEN the single income is adequate
  8.IF the applicant has properties with a value greater than
        10 times the loan
      OR the applicant has liquid assets greater than 5 times
        the loan
    THEN the applicant has adequate assets.
```

Note that in this encoded knowledge base, we have represented every piece of knowledge as a proposition. In Chapters 5, 6, and 10, we will see that it is possible to have quantitative values and attributes within the rules.

3.7.3   Knowledge Base Represented in Predicate Method (Optional)

In this section, we represent the same mortgage loan knowledge base using the predicate method. To reduce the number of parentheses, assume that a quantifier has the entire conditional as its scope. Furthermore, we follow the common convention that variables are specified by capital letters at the end of the alphabet, and the constants are specified with lowercase letters. For example, in the following wff's, *steady, good, adequate,* and 0.80 are constants, while X, Y, Z, V, and U are variables.

(1)
$$(\forall X)(\forall Y)(\forall Z)(\forall V)(\forall U)job(X, steady) \land property(Y, acceptable)\land$$
$$loan(Z) \land propertyvalue(V) \land credit(X, good)\land$$
$$income(X, adequate) \land less(Z, f(V, 0.80))\land$$
$$hascash(X, U) \land greater(U, f(V, 0.20)) \rightarrow approve(X, Y, Z).$$

Note that in (1), the domain of X consists of all applicants, the domain of Y is mortgage properties, the domain of Z is loan amounts, the domain of V is property values, and the domain of U is cash assets. Furthermore, the second argument of predicate *job* could be *steady* or *notsteady*. Similarly, the second argument in the predicate *credit* could take *good* and *bad* as values, and that in *income* takes values *adequate* and *notadequate*. In the predicate *less*, the notation f denotes a function that determines 80 percent of the property value V. Similarly, the predicate *greater* has f as the second argument for computing 20 percent of the property value. The function f in these two predicates has the following specifications:

$$f(V, 0.80) = V * 0.80$$

$$f(V, 0.20) = V * 0.20.$$

The representation in (1) here corresponds with rule (1) in the previous section. Note that (1) here accomplishes more than its corresponding rule in the previous section because it checks to see if the amount of the loan is less than 80 percent of the property value. The proposition in the rule-based representation assumes that this would be done manually. As was mentioned in the previous section, it is possible to make the computations automatic in the rule-based method. An example of this is presented in Chapter 5.

(2)
$$(\forall X)(\forall Y)(\forall Z)(\forall V)(\forall U) assets(X, adequate) \wedge property(Y, acceptable) \wedge$$

$$loan(Z) \wedge propertyvalue(V) \wedge credit(X, good) \wedge$$

$$income(X, adequate) \wedge less(Z, f(V, 0.80)) \wedge hascash(X, U) \wedge$$

$$greater(U, f(V, 0.20)) \rightarrow approve(X, Y, Z),$$

where domains of variables are the same as those in (1). This conditional is equivalent to rule (2) in the rule-based representation.

(3) $(\forall X)(\forall Y) hasjob(X) \wedge yearsatjob(Y) \wedge greater(Y, 2) \rightarrow job(X, steady).$

Here, Y's domain is the number of years the applicant has been at the present job. Note that we have used Y as number of years in (3) and as the mortgage property in (1) and (2). This is perfectly acceptable because, as was mentioned before, the variables are local within each predicate; and it does not matter which variable names are used as arguments in other predicates. This becomes more clear in Chapter 4.

(4)
$$(\forall Y) member(Y, zonelist) \vee member(Y, exceptlist) \rightarrow property(Y, acceptable).$$

In (4), the predicate *match* signifies whether the property is on the *zonelist* or the *exceptlist*.

(5) $(\forall X) familyincome(X, adequate) \vee singleincome(X, adequate)$
$\rightarrow income(X, adequate).$

Here, the predicates *familyincome* and *singleincome* have *adequate* and *notadequate* as the values of their second argument.

$$(\forall X)(\forall M)(\forall N)(\forall Z)married(X)\wedge$$

(6) $\quad netincome(X,N)\wedge mortpay(X,Z,M)\wedge$

$$less(M,f(N,0.60))\to familyincome(X,adequate),$$

where the domain of N is X's net family income, and the domain of M is the mortgage payment. The function f is defined as before.

$$(\forall X)(\forall M)(\forall N)(\forall Z)\neg married(X)\wedge$$

(7) $\quad netincome(X,N)\wedge mortpay(X,Z,M)\wedge$

$$less(M,f(N,0.70))\to singleincome(X,adequate),$$

where the domains of N and M are defined in (6).

$$(\forall X)(\forall V)(\forall Z)(\forall U)loan(Z)\wedge$$

$$(hasproperty(X,V)\wedge greater(V,f(Z,10)))\vee$$

(8)

$$(hasliquid(X,U)\wedge greater(U,f(Z,5)))$$

$$\to assets(X,adequate),$$

where the domain of V is the value of property assets, the domain of U is the value of liquid assets, and the domain of Z is loan amounts. The function f has the same definition as before.

The next chapter shows how an inference engine processes this encoded knowledge base to arrive at useful conclusions.

Conclusion

Factors of an expert system include domain knowledge, the knowledge base, the human component, and the expert system software. Domain knowledge is the major building block of expert systems. The knowledge relevant to the problem at hand is represented in the knowledge base. Since all expert system software products require encoding knowledge into their knowledge bases, the problem of formalizing knowledge is of great importance even in ready-to-use expert system software.

In order to formalize the relevant knowledge, one must first acquire and understand the knowledge that goes into the expert system. The process of collecting and organizing the relevant knowledge is called knowledge acquisition. The content of the knowledge base is determined at this step. The second step is to encode the content of the knowledge base into the expert system.

The issue of knowledge acquisition is addressed in Chapter 7. Here we will assume that we have already determined the content of the knowledge base, and focus on methods to represent or encode knowledge into the knowledge base. A basic understanding of knowledge representation methods facilitates an accurate encoding of relevant knowledge into the expert system.

One can separate knowledge representation methods into two general categories: logic-based and object-based. This chapter discussed logic-based knowledge representation, and Chapter 8 contains a discussion of object-based methods.

There are two methods of knowledge representation that have logic as their theoretical foundation: the rule-based method and the predicate method. Rule-based representation is based on propositional logic and calculus, while the predicate method is based on predicate logic and calculus. Although neither of the two representations adhere 100 percent to their fundamental mathematical theories, understanding these theories helps us to decide when we are on firm ground, and when we must be on the lookout for the possibility of unfounded conclusions.

This chapter reviewed the fundamental components of propositional logic, including connectives and their truth tables, how to establish the truth value of a statement, tautology and contradiction, and truth functions. Propositional calculus has the same foundation as the propositional logic plus the axioms of the domain in which it is applied.

Predicate logic has predicates, quantifiers, bound and free variables, connectives, and multiple quantifiers as its main components. Predicate calculus consists of the same components as predicate logic plus the axioms of the knowledge domain.

To demonstrate the difference between logic-based and predicate-based methods of knowledge representation, the last section of this chapter presented a small knowledge base for a mortgage loan expert system. The content of this knowledge base is encoded both in rule-based and predicate-based methods.

References

Gallier, Jean H. 1986. *Logic for Computer Science: Foundations of Automatic Theorem Proving*, Harper and Row, Publishers, New York, NY.

Hogger, Christopher John. 1984. *Introduction to Logic Programming*, Academic Press, Inc., London, England.

Jackson, Peter; Reichgelt, Han; and van Harmelen, Frank. (Eds.) 1989. *Logic Based Knowledge Representation*, MIT Press, Cambridge, MA.

Luger, G. F. and Stubblefield, W. A. 1989. *Artificial Intelligence and the Design of Expert Systems*, The Benjamin/Cummings Publishing Co., Redwood City, CA.

Mandelson, Elliott. 1987. *Introduction to Mathematical Logic*, third edition, Wadsworth & Brooks/Cole Advanced Books & Software, Monterey, CA.

Questions

3.1 Why is domain knowledge important in expert systems?

3.2 What is a knowledge base and what does it contain?

3.3 What are the roles of people in expert systems?

3.4 What is the difference between a knowledge base and a coded knowledge base?

3.5 Discuss the major components of expert system software.

3.6 What is the outside hook in expert system software?

3.7 Why should an expert system have an outside hook to other systems in an organization?

3.8 What is the meaning of *formal* in formal logic?

3.9 What are the four areas of mathematical logic?

3.10 What are the connectives in propositional logic?

3.11 What is the difference between statement form and statement formula?

3.12 Compare the truth tables of conjunction and biconditional. What is the difference between them?

3.13 What is the difference between propositional logic and propositional calculus?

3.14 What is a calculus?

3.15 What is the relation between propositional calculus and rule-based knowledge representation?

3.16 What is a predicate? What values does a predicate take?

3.17 Why are quantifiers important? What knowledge representation problems do quantifiers resolve?

3.18 What is the difference between the universal and existential quantifiers?

3.19 What is quantification?

3.20 What is the relation between the universal quantifier and the conjunction connective?

3.21 What is the relation between the existential quantifier and the disjunction connective?

3.22 What is the difference between predicate logic and predicate calculus?

3.23 What is the significance of mathematical logic in expert systems?

3.24 What is the use of predicate logic and predicate calculus in expert systems?

3.25 Does any area of mathematical logic incorporate uncertainty about the state of knowledge or a fact?

Problems

3.1   Give two examples of meta knowledge for a bank loan expert system.

3.2   Assume you are designing an expert system for screening job applicants. Give an example of meta knowledge for this expert system.

3.3   Give an example of a rule for a job applicant screening expert system.

3.4   Form two compound propositions by using connectives.

3.5   Give two examples of elementary propositions.

3.6   Write the formal negation for the proposition the loan is not approved.

3.7   Give three examples of rules for a mortgage loan expert system.

3.8   Code the following statement by breaking it down into elementary propositions and using the appropriate connectives: Every job applicant must have a college diploma and more than four years of experience. If a job applicant has not finished college or has a two-year certificate, then more than eight years of experience is required.

3.9   Use symbols to represent the elementary propositions in the previous question in order to produce a symbolic representation of the problem.

3.10 Determine if the following statement form is a tautology

$$A \vee T \leftrightarrow T$$

where T stands for true.

3.11 Show that in the following two statements, one is true if and only if the other is true:
(1) Smith is a worker and either Smith has enough assets or Smith has adequate income

to get a loan. (2) Either Smith is a worker and has enough assets or Smith is a worker and has adequate income to get a loan. (Hint: Use propositional logic and establish that the statement form connecting the two parts with a biconditional is a tautology.)

3.12 Give two examples for each type of quantifiers. Use them with a two-argument predicate.

3.13 Formalize the following statements: (1) For every man there is a woman. (2) All loan applications are checked for completeness. If an application is not complete, then action on the application is stopped and the applicant is notified.

3.14 Represent the statements in the previous question in the form of predicates.

3.15 Add rules to the mortgage loan example to accommodate the possibility that the applicant could have a partner (not a spouse) who would share in the payment of the mortgage.

3.16 Code the following in the rule-based representation method: If the job applicant is educated in accounting, marketing, or MIS, then he/she has the right education for the job. The applicant is considered to have the required experience if he/she has 2 or more years in accounting, marketing, or MIS. If the applicant does not have experience in accounting, marketing, or MIS, then he/she must have 4 or more years of experience. To qualify for the job, the applicant should have both the right education and the required experience. If an applicant does not have the right education, to qualify for the job, he/she must have at least 10 years of experience in accounting, marketing, or MIS.

3.17 Code the statements in the previous question in the predicate representation method.

Case: Lawn Advisor

Many homeowners spend a great deal of time and money to take care of their lawn. The minimum care for a lawn is to mow it on a regular basis in the growth season, to fertilize it a number of times per year, and to water it on the dry days. But, the minimum care does not guarantee a lush and beautiful lawn. Lawns are attacked by pests or fungal diseases, and may be burned by too much fertilizer or too little moisture. A diseased lawn changes color to pale green, gray, pink, yellow, or brown, it may have regular or irregular patches, it may have mold, or it may stop growing. The diseases appear at different times of the year.

Check out lawn care books from your local library, and consult with your local horticulturist to develop rules for diagnosing the lawn diseases based on the physical symptoms of the lawn.

Case: Expert Systems for Risk Management

There is nothing mystical about managing risk. It is a matter of establishing and enforcing lending guidelines, gathering and analyzing information, and monitoring situations. Risk management is an information problem: What you don't know can indeed hurt you.

Automated information systems help banks manage risk by helping them better capture, analyze and monitor information about loans. The systems also assist the bank in consistently enforcing lending policy.

The systems do not replace the loan officer or credit analyst, say Marc Brammer, senior marketing manager at Crowe Chizek & Co. Rather, the systems allow the loan officer to structure deals more easily, generate a more thorough analysis, and conform to the bank's lending policy. Ideally, using automated tools, any lending officer will make the same decision regarding a loan—the same decision that the review committee would make.

At one time, expert systems were thought to be the answer. The technology promised to let the bank capture the wisdom of its best lenders. The system would analyze the request, measuring it against bank policies and the collective lending wisdom of its knowledge data base.

However, Martin Sleath, vice president of Fair Isaac & Co., San Rafael, Calif., a leader in quantitative credit-risk analysis, argues that cloning the experience of superior bankers offers no advantage and possibly some disadvantages compared to empirically analyzing and quantifying the lending experience. For instance, "You have a problem with rejects, people you have no experience with," he says.

Clearly something happened on the way to full-blown expert systems. The systems were slow in coming, difficult to develop and very costly when they arrived. Very few actually made it to market. Of those, Syntelligence's Lending Advisor became the best known, although it never penetrated more than a handful of banks.

Syntelligence filed for bankruptcy in December 1990. In April, however, a consortium of Crowe Chizek & Co., South Bend, Ind.; Sun Alliance Insurance Group, London; and the Continuum Co., Austin, Texas, purchased the assets, including Lending Advisor and Lending Examiner. Crowe Chizek, the marketer of Financial Analyst's Management and Authoring Systems (FAMAS), a credit analysis spreadsheet, took on the marketing of Syntelligence products in the banking industry.

Lending Advisor is a commercial banking system based on artificial intelligence (AI) and expert system technology. For each borrower, the system analyzes industry risk, financial performance, management competence and projected financial performance. Lending Examiner helps credit and loan administrators evaluate existing loans.

At Security Pacific Bank, Seattle, Wash., Lending Advisor speeded up the loan decision process by helping the loan officer do more complete initial research and evaluation. "Lending Advisor raises all the critical questions and issues," says Dennis Long, senior vice president.

One benefit of the system, he says, comes from pointing out inconsistencies. For instance, a loan officer might give management a strong rating on an application, but Lending Advisor's analysis of the borrower's financial performance might show that it fell below the industry average. The lending officer then would have to provide additional information to back up his strong management rating or explain the discrepancies in the financial analysis.

As a result, some loans that would have been approved without Lending Advisor are rejected, while others that would have been rejected may be approved. For example, a $1.6 million loan approved before the bank instituted Lending Advisor turned bad, Long recalls. But, "If we put all the information we had at the time into Lending Advisor, we wouldn't have done the deal," he says.

The system is being used by about 20 lenders at the bank. "Our most expert people like it because it endorses their own thinking and really boosts their confidence. A few people feel threatened by it, but it is not optional." A bank-wide rollout of Lending Advisor was delayed due to the bankruptcy of Syntelligence.

Cogensys, San Diego, makes an AI-based credit judgment system for consumer lending and residential mortgage decisions. This spring [1991], Cybertek acquired the company. Other vendors also are preparing AI-based systems. Data Select Systems, Woodland Hills, Calif., plans to introduce Expert Planning System, an expert system addressing real estate lending. The PC-based program tracks construction and commercial mortgage loans from structuring through underwriting, say Sean McCracken, vice president/marketing. Expert Planning System is being beta tested at Pittsburgh National Bank, First American Bank and Dominion Bank.

ITT Commercial Finance, St. Louis, also hopes to introduce an AI-based lending system for banks similar to the system its in-house analysts use for floor-planning and receivables-based lending. The system prompts the lender through data gathering and then compares the information against the expert knowledge base to produce a decision.

In the retail credit arena, American Management Systems (AMS) has been applying expert technology in its Automated Credit Application Processing System (ACAPS), which performs prescreening, credit-bureau information retrieval, and decision making, although AMS does not represent ACAPS as an AI-based system. ACAPS supports revolving credit, installment loans, mortgage and retail charge cards.

There are three important aspects to determining retail credit risk, says Peter DiGiammarino, AMS vice president/finance industry—the quantitative scoring model, the integration of the score with the other information in the system, and the decision process itself.

The greatest risk occurs in the gray area just above and below the credit scoring cutoff line. "This is where the strictly quantitative approach fails," DiGiammarino says. At this point, AMS invokes expert-system technology to take the analysis beyond basic credit scoring. The system applies rules from a knowledge base against case-specific data.

Fair Isaac's solution combines credit bureau and customized credit scoring. To expand lending, prospective borrowers who fall just below the acceptable customized credit score can be approved if the credit bureau score is acceptable. To tighten credit, applicants whose custom scores fall just above the cutoff line wouldn't be approved unless they also scored above the cutoff for the credit bureau score.

The Bank of Boston uses ACAPS for all customer credit except mortgages and credit cards, says Paul Mangelsdorf, director of portfolio management. The bank installed the system last August in its Massachusetts operations and is rolling it out to bank operations in other states.

At the moment, however, the bank uses ACAPS primarily to automate data gathering. The system edits and verifies the accuracy of data and checks for duplicates and fraudulent applications, a key risk management step in itself. It automatically draws the report from the credit bureau and performs credit scoring. At that point, the application is passed along to a credit analyst, who still must analyze the information.

The big payback now is speed and consistency. Bank of Boston does much consumer loan business, for instance, through auto dealers. "The dealer wants consistency. He needs to be sure that if he gives the bank a credit application that meets certain requirements, the bank will approve it quickly," Mangelsdorf says. With a system such as ACAPS, the bank can promise quick, consistent credit decisions, while managing its risk.

Condensed from "Cloning Loan Experts in the Struggle to Limit Risk," by Alan Radding, *Bank Management*, July 1991, pp. 48–50, reprinted with permission from Bank Administration Institute.

Case Questions

1. Discuss the differences between a custom-made expert system designed for internal use in an organization, and a ready-to-use expert system that is developed to be used by many firms.

2. Why are ready-to-use expert systems, such as the ones discussed in this case, far slower in development and commercial success than the custom-made expert systems?

3. As ready-to-use expert systems enter the market, the question of buying a ready-to-use expert system application or developing it from scratch becomes an issue. If you were to decide between "buying a ready-to-use expert system" and "developing it from scratch," what factors would you take into account in making the choice?

4. What are the benefits of using expert systems in banking?

5. Discuss the drawbacks of relying too heavily on expert systems for banking decisions. Do you think that an expert system could replace a loan officer? Why?

CHAPTER 4

Inference and Knowledge Processing

Reason itself is a matter of faith. It is an act of faith to assert that our thoughts have any relation to reality at all.

G. K. Chesterton

RUSSELL: But then I have led a very sheltered life. I had no contact with my own body until the spring of 1887, when I suddenly found my feet. I deduced the rest logically.

Alan Bennett

Chapter Objectives

The objectives of this chapter are:

- To discuss the deductive reasoning methods

- To show the multiple inference process in expert systems

- To discuss the inductive reasoning method in expert systems

- To review the ID3 method for inductive reasoning

- To review the case-based approach

KEY WORDS: Deductive reasoning, modus tolens, pattern matching, inductive reasoning, single inference, multiple inference, backward chaining, forward chaining, search methods, ID3, case-based reasoning, reasoning by analogy

---

Introduction

This chapter follows the theoretical discussions of Chapter 3, and explains the reasoning process used by expert systems. We are interested in reasoning methods because they allow us to combine various pieces in the knowledge base and arrive at a conclusion or recommendation.

Reasoning methods are divided into two categories: *inductive* and *deductive* methods. Deductive reasoning is the method used in propositional and predicate calculus. By using deductive reasoning, the inference engine of an expert system combines the rules (or predicates) to arrive at the final answer.

Combining two rules (or two predicates) has a strong theoretical basis in proposition calculus (and predicate calculus). This is the topic of the single inference section in this chapter. However, the knowledge base has numerous rules or predicates. This poses a number of problems, such as the order in which the rules (or predicates) should be combined and how the knowledge base should be searched. These topics are addressed in the multiple inference section of this chapter. Multiple inference is based on heuristic approaches and does not have the same theoretical foundation as the single inference process of deductive reasoning.

In the last section of this chapter, we discuss the inductive method of reasoning. This method does not require rules or predicates. Instead, it derives its conclusion from a set of observed cases. This method of reasoning, therefore, is based on observations from experience, rather than on predetermined rules or predicates. One of the well-known inductive methods is ID3, which is discussed in the last section of this chapter. One can also use this method to derive rules for the knowledge base. In Chapter 6, we use a software product (called 1st-CLASS) that uses this method for reasoning.

The box on the applications of expert systems reports 21 expert systems built and deployed by large domestic and international organizations. This list provides further evidence that expert systems have found their place in the organizational decision-making tool bag.

4.1 Reasoning Methods

Knowledge representation methods allow us to encode or formalize qualitative facts and knowledge. This formalization is of little use without the ability to reason with the encoded knowledge base. In numerical computations, we measure and represent aspects of a problem by numbers. But it is the power of arithmetic computation and algebra, which puts the numbers into use, generating new and useful numbers. In an expert system, too, it is through reasoning and inference that we can generate new and useful knowledge, conclusions, and recommendations. Therefore, it is through the power of processing knowledge that one can create new knowledge and draw valuable conclusions.

Inference methods fall into two general categories:

- Deductive reasoning

- Inductive reasoning

The *deductive reasoning* process starts with a set of axioms, or commonly accepted premises, that one cannot derive from a system itself. Using these axioms and well-formed formulas (wff's), which have already been proven or accepted, one can use deductive reasoning to *deduce* new conclusions or wff's. In other words, in deductive reasoning one starts with premises that are already proven or accepted. Based on these premises and using the inference rules, one can derive new facts or conclusions. Deductive reasoning is the inference approach in formal logic, and we have already seen examples of deductive reasoning in the rule-based systems of Chapter 3.

The *inductive reasoning* process does not start with any given premise. It starts with observed data and observed cases, and then generalizes from them to build new rules. Statistics is one of the fields that is based on inductive reasoning. In constructing an expert system, the creation of a knowledge base is the central issue and the major problem. Inductive methods have been used to aid the knowledge engineers in the creation of a knowledge base.

Although deductive and inductive reasoning are two theoretically sound approaches to reasoning, they do not solve all the reasoning problems faced by expert systems. To increase the power and efficiency of an expert system, other methods with less theoretical underpinnings have been employed. These are heuristics of various types, such as reasoning with meta knowledge, and abduction as the inference method. We review some of these methods in this chapter.

4.2 Deductive Reasoning in Expert Systems

Let's look at the process of deductive reasoning in artificial intelligence and expert systems for logic-based systems. The reasoning method in logic is deductive. This means that the system starts with a given set of accepted axioms, statements and facts, which comprise the knowledge base and facts related to a given problem. "Reasoning" means applying rules of inference to the problem facts and the content of the coded knowledge base in order to arrive at new conclusions and recommend solutions.

The inference process consists of two parts:

- Single inference

- Multiple inference

Case: Expert Systems for Corporate Financial Planning

Many corporate expert systems are developed for internal use by a single company while others may be used by any company. These systems emphasize long-range planning and include the income tax effects of the decisions. Two expert systems providing advice for companies considering major acquisitions include IBM's FAME and Texas Instruments' Capital Investment System. FAME is used by IBM sales personnel to provide investment information to customers, while Capital Investment System is used for internal investment decisions at Texas Instruments.

IBM's FAME is a large, interactive system used to assist customers to make decisions about the purchase, conditional purchase, or lease of mainframe computers. FAME also provides sensitivity, competitive, and financial analysis together with justification for the recommended plans. The system considers the operating costs, the tax savings from depreciation, the software costs, and the cost of maintenance contracts. The system helps the purchaser determine the correct accounting treatment to use in recording the asset cost.

Texas Instruments' Capital Investment System is used worldwide by more than 190 department managers at Texas Instruments for preparing reports used to make capital investment decisions regarding acquisitions of equipment. The system is menu and question driven, permits customization by allowing parameters to be set, describes the conditions necessary for installation of the equipment, describes legal requirements including environmental impact statements, and is easy for the employee to use. The system provides a full investment presentation package of 17 forms that includes payback and cash flow analysis, and provides an option of whether the investment decision is worthwhile. The system has built-in controls that do not permit data to be illogical.

The system was designed so that the most experienced people at Texas Instruments provide the knowledge for the preparation of the investment decision reports. The system has reduced report preparation time. Before the system was developed, the reports frequently were prepared by new employees because most of the company's engineers considered this task unpleasant.

Texas Instruments' annual acquisitions exceed $600 million, and, thus, some of the most important capital investment decisions were based on data provided by the least experienced employees. Texas Instruments believes the system prevents expenditures for unneeded equipment. The system now is self-sustaining and requires only an hour a month to maintain.

Single inference refers to the process of applying inference rules to combine two pieces of knowledge to derive a new premise. This new premise is not necessarily the solution to the problem, or the system's final recommendation. Rather, it could be an intermediate step in a long process of numerous inferences that eventually lead to a final recommendation.

Multiple inference refers to the sequence or the order of applying the single inference process to the entire knowledge base in order to derive final conclusions. The single inference and multiple inference together form the knowledge-processing capability of an intelligent system. Therefore, it is essential to have a basic understanding of these two types of inference in expert systems.

4.3 Single Inference in Deductive Reasoning

In Chapter 3, we observed that propositional calculus is the foundation of rule-based knowledge representation. Therefore, it is essential to understand the inference process used in propositional logic and calculus. We also noted that predicate calculus is the underlying theory for predicate knowledge representation. Therefore, it is important to understand the inference process in predicate logic and predicate calculus. The following two sections provide a simple overview of the inference process for these two types of knowledge representations.

4.3.1 Inference in Propositional Logic and Calculus

There are a number of rules of inference in propositional logic that allow us to derive new statements from combining two previously accepted ones. Most important among them are:

- Modus ponens

- Hypothetical syllogism

- Modus tollens

Modus Ponens

One of the most widely used rules of inference is modus ponens, which was discussed briefly in Chapter 3. The modus ponens rule of inference has the following form:

$$A \rightarrow B$$
$$A$$

$$conclude: \ B$$

Here we say that since A is true, $A \rightarrow B$ has *fired*, and resulted in the conclusion that B is true. Another way of summarizing modus ponens is in the form:

$$((A \rightarrow B) \wedge A) \rightarrow B,$$

that is, when it is true that A implies B and we know that A is true, then we can conclude B. Note that modus ponens allows the manipulation of qualitative knowledge in the same spirit that addition allows the manipulation of numbers.

Modus ponens or any other rule of inference has to be a tautology for it to be applicable to all statement forms. For modus ponens to be a tautology, the statement form $((A \rightarrow B) \wedge A) \rightarrow B$ must be true no matter what the truth values of A and B are. The following truth table shows that modus ponens is indeed a tautology.

A	B	$A \rightarrow B$	$(A \rightarrow B) \wedge A$	$(A \rightarrow B) \wedge A) \rightarrow B$
T	T	T	T	T
T	F	F	F	T
F	T	T	F	T
F	F	T	F	T

Modus ponens makes it possible to combine a rule $(A \rightarrow B)$ with a fact A and make a new conclusion B.

Most rules have more than one proposition in their conditions or antecedents. For example,

the applicant has a job
∧the applicant has been at the job for more than 2 years
→ the applicant has a steady job
the applicant has a job
∧the applicant has been at the job for more than 2 years

———————————

conclude : the applicant has a steady job

Here, to use modus ponens, both conditions of the antecedent must be true.

Hypothetical Syllogism

Hypothetical syllogism is another important rule of inference. It has the following form:

$$A \rightarrow B$$
$$B \rightarrow C$$

———————————

$$conclude :\ A \rightarrow C$$

This rule of inference makes it possible to combine two rules and derive a new rule. In other words, one can *chain* rules together. This becomes an important process in the multiple inference part of expert systems.

Another way to present the hypothetical syllogism is

$$(A \rightarrow B) \wedge (B \rightarrow C) \rightarrow (A \rightarrow C)$$

We leave it to the reader, as an optional exercise, to derive the truth table of hypothetical syllogism and show that it, too, is a tautology.

We have already seen examples of hypothetical syllogism in Chapter 3. Below is another example.

the applicant is qualified → application forms must be completed

application forms must be completed → mail application forms

Applying the hypothetical syllogism results in

the applicant is qualified → mail application forms

Modus Tollens

Modus tollens is the rule of inference used when the negation of a fact is established. It has the following form:

$$A \to B$$
$$\neg B$$
_____

$$conclude: \ \neg A$$

In other words, once we know that the consequent of a rule is not true, we can conclude that the antecedent of the rule is not true. Using a construct similar to the case of modus ponens, one can show that modus tollens is a tautology.

Example. We can apply modus tollens to the following:

the applicant is qualified $\to$ *the loan is approved*
$\neg$the loan is approved
_____

$conclude: \ \neg the \ applicant \ is \ qualified$

In other words, we know that the loan will be approved when an applicant is qualified. Since the loan is not approved, we conclude that the applicant did not qualify for the loan.

The above example shows that compared to modus ponens, modus tollens is a less useful rule of inference because its emphasis is on the negation of facts, while most expert systems focus on establishing facts in the positive form. However, modus tollens may be used to cut short inference paths that do not lead to any useful conclusion.

There are many more tautologies in propositional logic. However, for our purpose the above discussion on the rules of inference should provide adequate background for understanding the single inference process in rule-based expert systems.

As we have seen in Chapter 3, the determination of rules of inference is a major component of propositional calculus. Rule-based systems are the application of propositional calculus and use modus ponens and hypothetical syllogism as in their inference process.

Pattern Matching in Inference

The rules of inference discussed above imply a *pattern matching* that is important in encoding knowledge for the knowledge base. The examples of propositions show that the semantics of a proposition involve phrases consisting of many words. When we apply a rule of inference, say, modus ponens, and assume that A and $A \to B$ are true, it is important that the semantic content of A matches that in $A \to B$ perfectly. This is because the system does not break down the components of a proposition.

For example, an expert system's inference engine does not have any means to ascertain that *the applicant is a worker* has the same meaning as *the applicant works*. Therefore, it considers these two propositions as distinct and different, and will not be able to draw any conclusion from:

the applicant is a worker → *the applicant qualifies for loan*

the applicant works

because the condition of the rule does not match exactly with the fact that *the applicant works*. This is an important point to remember when encoding knowledge in the form of rules into the expert system.

Mortgage Loan Case Revisited

Take the following three rules from the mortgage loan case introduced in Chapter 3:

```
1. IF the family income is adequate
      OR the single income is adequate
   THEN the applicant has adequate income

2. IF the applicant is married
      AND the mortgage payment is less than 60% of the
          family net income
   THEN the family income is adequate

3. IF NOT the applicant is married
      AND the mortgage payment is less than 70% of the
          the applicant's net income
   THEN the single income is adequate.
```

For Smith's particular case, we have the following facts:

```
4. the applicant is married

5. the mortgage payment is less than 60% of the family
   net income.
```

Matching (4) and (5) with the conditions in (2) *fires* (2). That is, applying modus ponens results in the conclusion that:

```
6. The family income is adequate.
```

Matching (6) with one of the two conditions in (1) makes the antecedent of (1) true, because the truth table of OR (discussed in Chapter 3) has shown us that when one of the two parts is true, the statement form is true. Using modus ponens again, we conclude that

```
7. The applicant has adequate income.
```

(7) is the conclusion reached by applying rules of inference to the facts (4), (5), and (6) of Smith's case and the content of the coded knowledge base represented by (1), (2), and (3).

4.3.2   Inference in Predicate Calculus (Optional)

Predicate knowledge representation is most closely tied to predicate calculus. Understanding the inference process in such systems requires a basic review of inference in first order predicate calculus.

Predicate calculus uses rules of inference in propositional calculus. In other words, modus ponens and hypothetical syllogism are also used in predicate calculus. However, remember that predicate calculus has predicates and quantifiers (existential and universal) that do not exist in propositional calculus.

Quantifiers provide more power for the system because one can break down the content of propositions into predicates. At the same time, they require additional arsenals for inference; pattern matching for predicates is more involved, and one has to deal with the quantifiers that come before predicates. This is accomplished by *unification*, which is discussed in the next section.

In predicate calculus, one can manipulate wff's (well-formed formulas), and simplify them by successive substitutions. This capability has led to the development of another inference approach called *resolution*, discussed in a later section. Resolution is the inference method used in systems with theorem proving and automatic reasoning capability that can prove theorems from their axioms.

4.3.3   Unification (Optional)

Let us go back to the example of Chapter 3, and assume we have the following conditional and fact:

$$(\forall X)(is - a - worker(X) \rightarrow apply(X))$$

$$is - a - worker(smith)$$

We follow the convention that variables are specified by capital letters at the end of the alphabet, and constants are specified with any lowercase letters, even when they are proper names. The parentheses around the conditional show that the scope of the universal quantifier is the entire conditional.

The question is how the inference engine matches $is - a - worker(smith)$ and the conditional. First, one has to deal with the universal quantifier. Since this quantifier applies to both parts of the conditional, one can drop it from the conditional. This is allowed because it is one of the two rules of inference in first order predicate calculus. First order predicate calculus starts with these two rules of inference and derives the other rules of inference as wff's.

$$is - a - worker(X) \rightarrow apply(X)$$

$$is - a - worker(smith)$$

Now, we can match the predicate $is - a - worker$ in the conditional with that in the fact, and replace X with $smith$ in the condition part of the conditional. But this replacement carries through for every X in the conditional. That is, it also applies to $apply(X)$. This yields $apply(smith)$. The process of matching the predicates and replacing the arguments of the matched predicates is called *unification*. Replacing X with $smith$ is called *binding*.

The predicate may involve existential quantifiers, such as in the following example: "Every applicant has a social security number." We can encode this piece of knowledge as

$$(\forall X)(\exists Y)(has - socsecno(X, Y))$$

where X has the domain of applicants, and Y has the domain of social security numbers. As we have seen, when the universal quantifier is at the start of the wff, we can simply remove it. Since Y depends on who X is, it is replaced by a function name and then the existential quantifier is also removed. Thus, we have

$$has - socsecno(X, f(X))$$

If Y does not depend on X, then it is replaced by a constant in the domain of Y, and then the existential quantifier is removed. The process of removing the existential quantifier is called *Skolemization*.

When the quantifiers are not at the start of the wff, there are a number of substitution rules that one can use to manipulate the wff, in order to put the quantifiers at the start of the wff. Furthermore, binding of arguments should be in such a way as to preserve the most general form of the statement. In other words, if there is more than one choice for binding an argument of a predicate, the first priority goes to the one which preserves the generality of the wff. We do not go into the technical details of these substitution rules. References at the end of this chapter contain a number of books that discuss this topic in detail.

Mortgage Loan Case Revisited

Take the following wff's from the mortgage loan case. The universal quantifiers are removed, as just discussed.

(1)
$$familyincome(X, adequate) \lor singleincome(X, adequate)$$
$$\rightarrow income(X, adequate)$$

(2)
$$married(X) \land netincome(N) \land mortpay(M)$$
$$\land less(M, f(N, 0.60)) \rightarrow familyincome(X, adequate)$$

(3)
$$\neg married(X) \land netincome(N) \land mortpay(M)$$
$$\land less(M, f(N, 0.70)) \rightarrow singleincome(X, adequate)$$

We have the following facts about Smith's case:

(4)
$$married(smith)$$

(5)
$$netincome(2000)$$

(6)
$$mortpay(1100)$$

The unification process would be as follows. The predicates (4), (5), and (6) match with those in (2) to produce:

(7)
$$married(smith) \land netincome(2000) \land mortpay(1100)$$
$$\land less(1100, 1200) \rightarrow familyincome(smith, adequate)$$

where the function f has produced

$$f(2000, 0.60) = 0.60 * 2000 = 1200$$

used in the predicate *less*. Since all conditions of (7) are true, using modus ponens, we have

(8) $familyincome(smith, adequate)$

as true. Then the predicate in (8) matches one of the conditions in (1). Since this antecedent has $\vee$ or OR as the connective in its antecedent, then its antecedent becomes true when one of the conditions is satisfied. So we have

(9)
$familyincome(smith, adequate) \vee$

$singleincome(smith, adequate) \rightarrow income(smith, adequate)$

Since the first condition is true, then the consequent should also be true:

(10) $income(smith, adequate)$

which is the conclusion reached from using the specific case for Smith and applying the knowledge base represented in three wff's (1), (2), and (3).

4.3.4   Resolution (Optional)

There is another inference process for automatic reasoning based on predicate calculus. This method, called *resolution*, makes it possible to prove theorems and derive useful conclusions from a set of facts and a knowledge base. Resolution has a sound theoretical foundation in first order predicate calculus. Although the process of resolution looks tedious, it is based on simple ideas, shown in the following steps:

- Step 1. Assume what you want to prove is false.

- Step 2. Repeatedly apply substitutions to combine and simplify wff's.

- Step 3. If you get a false or contradictory result, then what you set out to prove is true.

The idea of the first step is straightforward. For example, if you want to know whether $income(smith, adequate)$ is true, Step 1 starts by assuming $\neg income(smith, adequate)$ as one of the facts of the case.

Step 2 is more involved because there are numerous ways to substitute one wff with another using already proven wff's. This step is like using proven mathematical formulas or mathematical identities in order to simplify a complicated formula. This step by itself involves a number of additional steps:

- 2.1. To reduce the complexity of handling repeated substitutions, the conditional connective is removed by using its equivalent formula. $A \rightarrow B$ is the same as $\neg A \vee B$ because both have the same truth tables and one can show that

$$(A \rightarrow B) \leftrightarrow (\neg A \vee B)$$

  is a tautology.

- 2.2. Put the wff in standard form by changing the name of variable arguments such that each variable name would be used only for one quantifier. For example,

$$(\forall X)P_1(X) \vee (\forall X)P_2(X)$$

  should be changed to

$$(\forall X)P_1(X) \vee (\forall Y)P_2(Y)$$

  to make clear which variable is within the scope of each quantifier. In other words, the variable for each quantifier should have a unique name.

- 2.3. Move the quantifiers to the start of the wff, using the substitution formulas. This is already discussed in the previous section on unification. Once all quantifiers are moved to the start of the wff, it is said to be in *prenex* form.

- 2.4. Once the wff is in prenex form, remove the universal quantifiers from the prenex form of wff, and use Skolemization to remove the existential quantifiers.

- 2.5. Apply substitution formulas repeatedly until you get a false or contradictory conclusion.

In Step 3, arriving at a contradiction proves that the negation of what we want to show is false, so it must be true. This is called proving by *contradiction*.

We do not intend to go into detail about resolution here. However, the following example is intended to give a flavor of how the process of resolution works.

Example. Take a simplified part of the knowledge base of the mortgage loan example. We want to know if Smith has adequate income for the loan.

(1) $(\forall X) familyincome(X, adequate) \rightarrow income(X, adequate)$

(2) $(\forall X)(\forall N)(\forall M) married(X) \wedge netincome(N) \wedge mortpay(M)$
           $\wedge\, less(M, f(N, 0.60)) \rightarrow familyincome(X, adequate)$

(3) $married(smith)$

(4) $netincome(2000)$

(5) $mortpay(1100)$

Step 1 requires that we add the negation of what we are interested in proving:

(6) $\neg income(smith, adequate)$

Step 2.1 requires that we get rid of conditionals in (1) and (2) by using the equivalence between $A \rightarrow B$ and $\neg A \vee B$. Watch for the use of parentheses for the correct grouping:

(7) $\neg((\forall X) familyincome(X, adequate)) \vee income(X, adequate)$

(8) $\neg((\forall X)(\forall N)(\forall M) married(X) \wedge netincome(N) \wedge mortpay(M)$
           $\wedge\, less(M, f(N, 0.60))) \vee familyincome(X, adequate)$

Step 2.2 is not needed here because variables are clearly named such that in each wff, the variable within the scope of each quantifier has a unique name.

Step 2.3 requires that we move quantifiers to the beginning of the wff. Using one of the formulas in Appendix A, we know that when negation is applied to $\forall$ as in $\neg(\forall X)\ldots$, it becomes $(\exists X)\neg\ldots$. Using this in (7) and (8), we get

(9) $(\exists X)\neg familyincome(X, adequate) \vee income(X, adequate)$

(10) $(\exists X)(\exists N)(\exists M)\neg(married(X) \wedge netincome(N) \wedge mortpay(M)$
           $\wedge\, less(M, f(N, 0.60))) \vee familyincome(X, adequate)$

Now these wff's are in prenex form.

Again, look for the use of parentheses for the correct specification of the scope of the quantifiers. Step 2.4 requires removing quantifiers. Here, since we have only existential quantifiers, we should Skolemize it. There are no universal quantifiers, so we can put an acceptable constant in place of X,

N and M in order to put the wff's in the Skolem form. The only acceptable constants in this example are *smith*, 2000, and 1100. So we have

(11) $\neg familyincome(smith, adequate) \lor income(smith, adequate)$

and

(12) $\neg(married(smith) \land netincome(2000) \land mortpay(1100)$
        $\land\ less(1100, f(2000, 0.60))) \lor familyincome(smith, adequate)$

Step 2.5 requires repeated substitutions and simplification. We move the negation ($\neg$) inside the parentheses in (12). This changes the connective ($\land$) to connective ($\lor$) and vice versa:

(13) $\neg married(smith) \lor \neg netincome(2000) \lor \neg mortpay(1100)$
        $\lor\ \neg less(1100, f(2000, 0.60)) \lor familyincome(smith, adequate)$

From (3), (4), and (5), we know that the first three parts of (13) are false, so conclude that the fourth part must be true for (13) to be a true wff in our knowledge base. That is

(14) $familyincome(smith, adequate)$

must be true. Using (14) in (11), we note that the first part of (11) is false. So the second part must be true for (11) to remain a true statement in our knowledge base. So we conclude that

(15) $income(smith, adequate)$

must be true. (15) is a contradiction of (6). Thus Step 3 is completed and we conclude that the question we started with: *income(smith, adequate)?* has "yes" as the answer.

Resolution is the method used for proving theorems and for answering questions from a knowledge base. It is a powerful tool for automatic reasoning. Although the process of resolution is tedious when done manually, the computer can perform its steps indefatigably. Resolution is the inference method used in Prolog, one of the artificial intelligence programming languages.

Case: Applications of Expert Systems

In the ninth annual Association for American Artificial Intelligence (AAAI) conference in Anaheim, Calif. in 1991, companies presented twenty one applications that they had built and deployed. The following is a short report of these applications.

- Northwest Airlines has developed an expert system with Anderson Consulting and using ART on Sun-4s that helps it audit passenger airline tickets—something it used to do manually for 60,000 tickets a day.
- American Airlines has an expert system in ART-IM for managing its frequent flier program. With all the restrictions and perks that go with frequent flier deals, as well as trying to keep up with the competitions, AA had AI handle the task of monitoring one of its most popular flier incentives. The program runs in an IBM environment including PS/2s and a 3090 mainframe.
- American also has its Maintenance Operation Center Advisor (MOCA), which maintains the more than 350 planes that AA flies. It was developed in ART and runs on a microExplorer.
- SYLLABUS, a system used to develop curricula for students in the United Kingdom, runs on a Macintosh and was developed in Lisp. The program helps save costs by producing schedules, which must include all courses and teacher availability information.
- Lubrizol has an expert system for developing federally required documentation on the more than 10,000 chemical products it manufactures. The application is integrated with DB2 on a 3090 mainframe using Aion's ADS tool.
- Cognitive Systems unveiled its Automatic Letter Composition system, which generates correspondence to customers at a credit card company.
- Hewlett-Packard has developed AGATHA, an expert system that tests and diagnoses failures on complex personal computer boards. Written from scratch in Prolog, the program has been deployed at three of the company's manufacturing and field test facilities.
- The Thallium Diagnostic Workstation, developed for the U.S. Air Force School of Aerospace Medicine, uses a rule structure to assist physicians in making consistent diagnoses about heart workups on Air Force fliers. The product combines machine vision with machine learning using a USAF developed algorithm called METARULE.
- General Dynamics' Electric Boat group has developed a case-based system to handle the problems of manufacturing nonconformance in the building of ships and submarines. The company has deployed the system using its own case-based methodology, after building prototypes in rule-based systems KEE and GoldWorks.
- Draper Labs has an application developed internally that assists in the design of complex assembly systems that can share data between disparate groups working on different parts of an assembly system.
- The Lamb Group has created a Computer-Aided Mechanical Expert Systems (CAMES), which designs material handling equipment in the pulp and paper industries. The Lisp-based system has already designed almost 1,000 machines for the company.
- Nippon Steel has designed the Quality Design Expert System (QDES) for ensuring quality production of customized steel products. The 3,000-rule system runs on Sun machines and was developed using ART.
- DEC has the Crash Analysis Troubleshooting Assistant (CANASTA). It assists computer-support engineers in analyzing the whys and wherefores of operating system

crashed. It was built with a rule-based shell that DEC uses internally called Foxglove.

• NYNEX's MAX is a maintenance advisor system which is used by the telephone company to help diagnose problems via a customer-support phone line. The application runs in 42 maintenance centers in the Northeast. It is built in ART with some additional Lisp coding, and runs on Sun SPARC stations.

• Sun America has an expert appointment system, which helps it with regulations requiring all agents and brokers be appointed to the State Board of Insurance in each state for each product line of insurance sold. This paperwork nightmare was alleviated by creating a system in ART that is integrated into the company's entire computer network.

• AL2X (pronounced alex) is developed by AL2X Corporation to assess the financial stability of commercial banks. The product was written in Borland's Turbo BASIC.

• Dun & Bradstreet has its Credit Clearing House expert system that assists the financial services giant in assigning credit ratings and dollar-specific credit limitations to companies in the clothing industry. The 800-rule system resides on a series of DEC VAX stations and is written in ART.

• The Swiss Bank has produced CUBUS, a system which—like D&B system—assigns credit to commercial customers based on a valuation involving holdings and estimated financial solvency. The company runs the system under ART-IM for PS/2s (after abandoning T1 Explorer) and expects to save $1.5 million each year using the system. For acronym fans, CUBUS stands for Computerunterstutztes Bnitotsuntersuchungssystem.

• The U.S. Army has TIME, an application for generating documents based on headquarters decision-makers, who often do not have the time to write documentation themselves. TIME stands for TRADOC Issue Management System, and TRADOC is short for Training and Doctrine Command. The UNIX-based system was built in COPE, a generic knowledge-acquisition environment built by the Army.

• The State of California has developed the Travel Expense Claim System (CALTREC), which helps in the approval of expense claims made by approximately 70,000 state employees who travel on state business annually. Originally developed in IBM's ESE and then ported to AICorp's KBM, the system has been deployed on IBM mainframes.

• SAIC has created a knowledge-based system to support nuclear test ban treaty verification, which analyzes seismic data to determine if unauthorized nuclear testing is occurring somewhere in the world. The ART-based system is used daily at the Center for Seismic Studies in Washington, D.C., and contains 250 rules.

Excerpts from "In Practice: The Magic Kingdom of AAAI," by Harvey P. Newquist III, *AI Expert*, October 1991, pp. 59–61, reprinted with permission from *AI Expert*.

4.4 Multiple Inference in Deductive Reasoning

So far we have been concerned with how one can combine a couple of rules or well-formed formulas (wff's) by the proper inference method. A real-world knowledge base contains numerous rules or wff's. The question is in what order these rules should fire or predicates should unify. Here is where the heuristic nature of artificial intelligence and expert systems comes into play because there is no set order or *algorithm* that would guarantee an answer in a reasonable time. For example, when we use artificial intelligence in the game of chess, the number of possible moves is so great that examining every one of them would go beyond the lifetime of human players and many generations of their descendants. Although there are few knowledge bases as large as the number of moves in chess, generating a system response in a reasonable amount of time is crucial to any real-world expert system.

In other words, while the single inference in artificial intelligence has a solid theoretical foundation, applying rules of inference to the entire knowledge base requires tools for analysis and *heuristics*—useful rules of thumb—that could improve the speed of the system response. Here we discuss some of the tools used to analyze the knowledge base, and common approaches for *multiple inference*.

4.4.1 Graphs, Trees, and the And/Or Graph

Graph

One of the most effective tools for analyzing the logic structure of the knowledge base is *graph theory*. Graph theory is a powerful field in mathematics, with the added advantage that graphs are an easily understandable method of presentation. In graph theory, a graph consists of nodes connected by arcs (Figure 4.1a). In a *directed graph*, the direction an arc takes when connecting two nodes is important (Figure 4.1b). A *path* in a graph is the sequence of nodes and arcs connecting the beginning node of the path to the end node of the path. A *cycle* is a path where the ending node of the path is the same as the beginning node (Figure 4.1c).

Tree

A tree is a directed graph with no cycles, which starts with a beginning node (called the *root*) and ends with ending nodes (called *leaves*). Paths

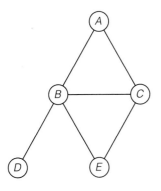

a. Graph

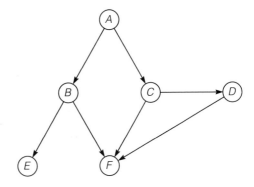

b. Directed graph, with paths $A - B - E$, $A - C - F$, $A - C - D - F$, and $A - B - F$

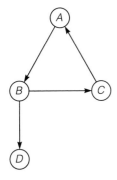

c. Graph with a cycle, $A - B - C$

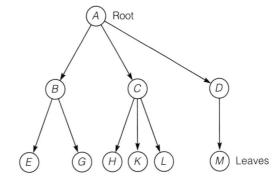

d. Tree with branches such as $A - B - E$, $A - B - G$, and $A - C - H$

Figure 4.1   Types of Graphs

start from the root and end with leaves in a tree, and there is only one path from the root to each leaf (Figure 4.1d). Graphs and trees are used extensively in artificial intelligence and expert systems, such as the and/or graph and decision tree. We will discuss the and/or graph here and present the decision tree in the discussion of inductive reasoning.

And/Or Graph

Since a knowledge base contains many pieces of information, methods summarizing the solution process or the *state space* of the problem are of great value. One such method is the and/or graph. In such a graph, one can show rules or predicates with nodes and arcs. For example, we can present

$A \vee B \rightarrow C$ as Figure 4.2a. This constitutes the OR part of the graph. On the other hand, $A \wedge B \rightarrow C$ is shown as Figure 4.2b. Note that the two arcs in Figure 4.2.b are connected by an arc, signifying that both A and B must be true in order to reach the conclusion C from this rule.

One can use the and/or graph to have a state space representation or solution process in a knowledge base. Figure 4.3 shows the and/or graph for the mortgage loan example.

As this figure demonstrates, one can observe the structure of the solution process or state space in one glance. We will see in the chapter on knowledge acquisition that the and/or graph is helpful in identifying the completeness of rules in the knowledge base and in checking for possible inconsistencies within the knowledge base.

4.4.2 Backward and Forward Chaining

Multiple inference involves testing rules or predicates to find the one which must fire next. In multiple inference, the sequence of testing is also important. Two well-known and commonly used methods of multiple inference in expert systems are backward and forward chaining. In backward and forward chaining, rules or predicates are tested in the order they appear in the knowledge base. They differ in the selection of the rule for testing.

Backward Chaining

In *backward chaining*, the multiple inference starts with a question or goal. For instance, in the mortgage loan example, the reasoning process starts with the goal or question about the approval of the mortgage loan of an applicant. Note that the goal or answer to the question is the consequent or the THEN part of a conditional. In this method, the inference engine

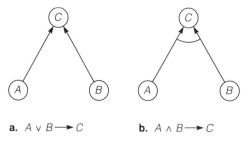

a. $A \vee B \longrightarrow C$ **b.** $A \wedge B \longrightarrow C$

Figure 4.2 And/Or Graph

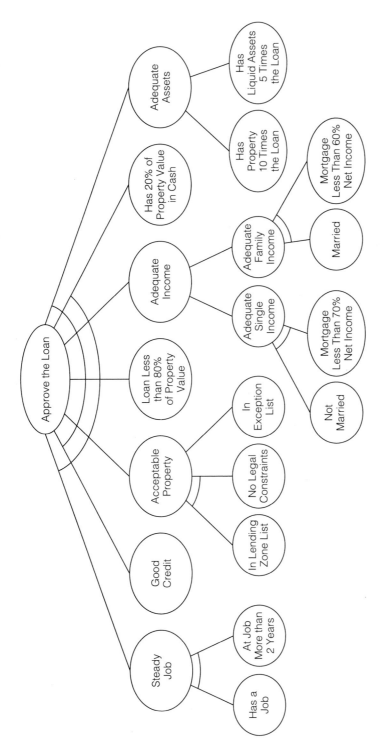

Figure 4.3 And/Or Graph for the Mortgage Loan Example

starts from the consequent of a rule, and goes *backward* to the antecedent or IF part of the rule. Let us demonstrate backward chaining with a simple abstract example first, then we will see how backward chaining works in the case of the mortgage loan expert system.

Example. Assume that the knowledge base consists of the following rules:

$$A \rightarrow C$$
$$D \rightarrow E$$
$$B \wedge C \rightarrow F$$
$$E \vee F \rightarrow G$$

Figure 4.4 shows the and/or graph for this example. The goal is to establish whether G is true. The inference engine within the expert system checks to see which rule has G as its consequent. It is the last rule. To conclude from this knowledge base that G is true, one must show that either E or F is true. Therefore, E becomes the current goal of the system. The inference engine checks to see which rule has E as its consequent. The second rule fires and now the current goal of the system becomes D. The inference engine checks to see which rule has D for its consequent. It finds no rule.

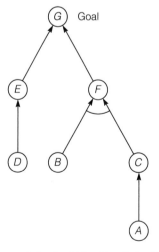

Figure 4.4   And/Or Graph for Backward Chaining

Therefore, it asks the user to provide the information about D. If the user says that D is true, the inference engine concludes that E is true (from the second rule), and then concludes that G is true (from the last rule).

Now assume that the user answers that D is false. The system fails to establish the truth of E. Note that we do not say E is false. The reason is in the truth table of the conditional in Chapter 3. When the antecedent of a conditional is false, the consequent could either be true or false.

Since the inference engine did not get anywhere by pursuing E, it *backtracks* and picks up F to get at the goal G. F is in the consequent of the third rule with both B and C as required conditions; thus B and C become the current goal. Since B is not in the consequent of any rule, the system asks the user if B is true. If the user answers no, then no matter what C is, the conditional part of the third rule will be false. In this case, the inference engine has failed to establish that G is true.

If the user answers that B is true, then the inference engine will pursue C. Since C is in the consequent of the first rule, A becomes the current goal. No rule has A as its consequent, therefore, the system asks the user about the truth value of A. If the answer is that A is true, the first rule leads to the truth of C, and the third rule (with the true answer for B) leads to the truth value for F, which in turn establishes that G is true.

Now let us consider the mortgage loan example in Chapter 3 with its and/or graph in Figure 4.3. The goal is to see whether the loan should be approved. This is the consequent of rules (1) and (2) in section 3.7.2 of Chapter 3. Since the inference engine goes sequentially from the beginning of the knowledge base, it tests (1) and the propositions of this rule become the current rule. The first proposition test is whether the applicant has a steady job. This is in the consequent of rule (3). It asks the user if the applicant has a job. Assume the answer is no. The inference engine does not go any further in (3). Since it could not show that the applicant has a steady job, it does not go any further with rule (1) either, because to conclude the goal using rule (1), all its conditions should hold.

Failing to achieve a true answer for the goal from (1), the inference engine searches the knowledge base again, and uses (2) to establish the goal. The first proposition in this rule is whether the applicant has adequate assets. This becomes the current goal. It searches the knowledge base from the beginning to see which rule has this proposition as its consequent. It finds rule (8). So the first proposition of this rule becomes the current goal. The inference engine scans the entire knowledge base to see if any rule has the applicant's properties as the consequent. It does not find any. So it asks the user whether the applicant has properties with a value greater than ten times the loan. If the answer is yes, the inference engine concludes that the applicant has adequate assets and attempts to check the truth value of other conditions in rule (2). If the user answers no, then the system asks whether the applicant has liquid assets greater than five times the loan. If the user says no, the inference engine does not go any further because it has failed to establish the truth of the goal. If the user's answer is positive, then the inference engine attempts to check the truth value of the second proposition in rule (2). The rest of the multiple inference based on backward chaining for this example is left as an exercise for the reader.

Backward chaining is also called *goal driven* for the obvious reason that it starts with the objective of satisfying a goal. It is used in many expert systems and in Prolog. Note that the inference engine asks the questions for which it needs an answer; the user does not need to enter all the facts at the start of the inquiry.

Forward Chaining

In *forward chaining*, the system requires the user to provide facts pertaining to the problem. The inference engine tries to match each fact with the antecedent or the IF part of a rule. If the match succeeds, the rule fires and the truth of the consequent of that rule is established and is added to the known facts of the case. This process continues until the inference engine has drawn all possible conclusions by matching facts to antecedents of rules in the knowledge base. Among these conclusions could be the goal(s) of the system.

Example. Consider the abstract example discussed in the section on backward chaining. In this example, if we start with the known facts that A and B are true, then the inference engine uses A and the first rule to conclude that C is true. Then it uses B and C and the third rule to conclude that F is true. It uses the truth of F and the last rule to establish that G is true.

Note that forward chaining is *data driven* because it starts with the data about the case and moves forward from the antecedents of rules to conclude their consequents. As an exercise, apply forward chaining to the mortgage loan example.

Backward chaining is useful when the number of goals is small, and the and/or graph of the knowledge base does not have numerous levels. In some systems, to avoid searching for many goals, the user has the choice of telling the inference engine which goal it must pursue. This is called *goal selection by the user.*

Forward chaining performs well when the number of goals is large, the user has a given set of facts at the start of the inquiry, and wants to find the implications of these facts. It is possible to combine backward and forward chaining. Some expert system products allow for combining the two methods of multiple inference.

4.4.3   Search Methods: Depth-first and Breadth-first

The discussion of the and/or graph and backward and forward chaining demonstrates that the sequence of applying rules of inference to the knowledge base is an important issue in processing knowledge. More specifically, the inference engine must know how to *search* the state space or the structure of the knowledge base. Thus, *search methods* are of importance to multiple inference in artificial intelligence and expert systems. There are two well-known search methods: depth-first and breadth-first.

Depth-first Search Method

In the backward chaining example in the previous section, we saw that the inference engine goes down one path of the and/or graph, then backtracks up to its closest parent with an untested path, and goes down the new path to its end. Figure 4.5a shows this process. This is searching through the and/or graph with the depth-first search method.

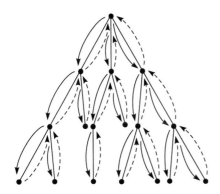

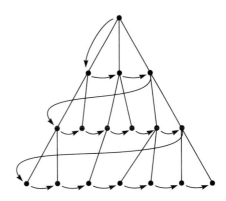

a. Depth-first
   Search Method

b. Breadth-first
   Search Method

Figure 4.5   Search Methods

Breadth-first Search Method

The other method of searching the and/or graph is the breadth-first method. In this approach, all nodes on the same level are tried first before going to the next level. Figure 4.5b demonstrates the search sequence in this approach.

These two methods have their own advantages and disadvantages. The depth-first method is commonly used with backward chaining. However, when the and/or graph is very deep (that is, when the graph has many levels), this search may become very inefficient. It also fails to find the shortest path (or the smallest number of nodes) for satisfying the goal. The depth-first method performs well when there are numerous nodes at each level, and the and/or graph is not very deep.

The breadth-first method, on the other hand, does not perform well when there are numerous nodes at each level because the inference engine has to keep track of all the children of each active node that could lead to a conclusion for the goal. An active node is a node that is the start of a path that may lead to establishing the truth of a goal. When each node in the and/or graph has many children, the number of active nodes becomes combinatorially explosive. That is, the system has to keep track of many paths at the same time. This makes the processing prohibitively slow. The advantage of the breadth-first search method is that it finds the shortest path for satisfying the goal. Hence, this method performs well when nodes are not numerous at each level, and finding the shortest path for satisfying the goal is of importance for solving the decision problem.

The preceding discussion of search methods demonstrates that there is no single search method for all problem types. That is why there are a number of heuristics for search methods, such as *depth-first iterative deepening* and *best-first* methods. These heuristics were developed to improve the efficiency of the search. For the discussion of these and other heuristics see the references for this chapter, such as Luger and Stubblefield [1989].

In evaluating an expert system software product for developing an expert system in a given knowledge domain, especially a system with a large knowledge base, one must be aware of the product's search method, and its fit with the structure of the problem or the state space.

4.4.4   Other Heuristics in Expert Systems

Since multiple inference in expert systems lacks a universal methodology that applies to all types of knowledge bases, a number of heuristics exist that could be of use for some problem types. None have a solid theoretical basis, but can have practical value in some applications. Among these heuristics are:

- Reasoning by abduction

- Reasoning by generation and test

- Reasoning using meta knowledge

Reasoning by Abduction

The abduction rule of inference has the form that if we have the rule that $A \rightarrow B$, and B is true, we conclude that A is true. This is not a tautology, and does not have the theoretical support of the propositional logic. However at times, it could be useful in reducing the scope of the search when the state space is very large.

Reasoning by Generation and Test

In reasoning by generation and test, the system generates hypotheses and tests them to see if any are true. Again, when the state space is very large, this search strategy may be helpful in identifying useful conclusions and reducing the requirement of searching the entire state space.

Reasoning Using Meta Knowledge

We have already seen in Chapter 3 that meta knowledge is knowledge about the knowledge base. For large knowledge bases, one can have meta knowledge controlling the choice of rules in the search process. The rules of meta knowledge may exclude a certain part of the knowledge base under given circumstances. This way the inference engine will have a smaller state space to search.

Furthermore, the meta knowledge may change the order of rules under given circumstances. The change in the order of rules changes the order of the search, which, in turn, reduces the state space for the search. Therefore, the meta knowledge reasoning changes the search process performed by the inference engine.

Ideally, the meta knowledge should be able to tell the inference engine which search mechanism, or even what reasoning process, it should follow. This could increase the versatility and power of expert systems. On the other hand, developing domain-specific meta knowledge is not an easy task. This could be one reason why the concept of meta knowledge and its role as the controller of the knowledge base and inference engine are not commonplace in expert system software products.

4.4.5   Shallow and Deep Reasoning

Some have criticized rule-based knowledge representation for being a *shallow* method, in that rules do not specify a causal reason for going from antecedents to consequents. This could be partly due to the nature of the knowledge domain. For example, in the mortgage loan example, there is no causal reason to believe that staying at a current job for more than two years would make the job a steady one. This is only an indication used by the expert or the procedure developed by the bank from past experience.

On the other hand, when there is a causal relationship, it can be added to the knowledge base as a rule. In the mortgage loan example, for instance, assume that it is scientifically shown that when a person stays at a job for more than two years, the employer and the employee create a psychological bond that causes the job to become a steady one. In this case, one can develop two rules: (1) staying at a job for more than two years creates a psychological bond between employer and employee, (2) a psychological bond between employer and employee leads the job to become a steady one.

Even when one does not know the causal relationship for the reasoning, one can always add an explanation to the rule describing why the antecedent leads to the consequent of the rule. Many expert system software products allow an explanation to be added to a rule as part of the syntax of the rule. This, however, is not part of the formal theory of logic. Rather, it is developed as a practical necessity.

Other methods of knowledge representation, especially the object-based methods discussed in Chapter 8, are said to be deep reasoning methods because they provide more structure for showing the causal relations. This, however, is more a function of how the knowledge is coded into the knowledge base than of the representation method itself.

4.5 Inductive Reasoning in Expert Systems

Most inference rules in artificial intelligence and expert systems have their theoretical basis in deductive reasoning. But the fact remains that most of our learning is through experience, which is an inductive process. That is, after we are exposed to a number of similar circumstances that lead to a certain consequence, we generalize and develop rules for dealing with that group of circumstances. For example, after the bank experiences a relatively high number of delinquent cases with borrowers who have had new jobs, the bank develops the rule that the applicant should have a steady job to be qualified for a loan. This process of going from specific cases to general rules is called *inductive reasoning.*

Some methods are inductive by nature. For example, in quantitative methods, the field of statistics is inductive in nature because it uses observed data in order to develop generalized functional relationships among system variables. In qualitative methods, we will see in later chapters that the neural networks approach is an inductive method, where the system uses data in order to develop a structure that is generally applicable to similar problems.

Although artificial intelligence and expert systems are deductive, they use inductive reasoning as well. The inductive approach in artificial intelligence and expert systems is necessitated for two reasons:

- As we will see in Chapter 7, developing rules for the knowledge base is not an easy task, and at times could be impossible. Inductive reasoning is used to help the expert and knowledge engineer in developing rules for the knowledge base.

- The knowledge domain does not lend itself to rule-based or predicate representation, and domain experts do not reason using rules or predicates.

In such cases, using inductive reasoning could be a useful approach in expert systems. Methods for inductive reasoning in expert systems include:

- Decision trees
- ID3
- Case-based approach: reasoning by analogy

4.5.1 Decision Trees

In the inductive reasoning approach, we must have a set of representative cases for which we already know what the goal or the decision value is.

Decision Tree for the Mortgage Loan Case

Assume that we have the following data for the possible cases in the mortgage loan system:

steady job	*adequate assets*	*adequate income*	*approve loan*
yes	yes	yes	yes
yes	no	yes	yes
no	yes	yes	yes
no	no	yes	no
yes	yes	no	no
yes	no	no	no
no	yes	no	no
no	no	no	no

Figure 4.6 shows the decision tree for this example.

Following the paths or branches, one can develop rules. For example, the first top branch indicates that if the applicant has a steady job, adequate assets, and adequate income, then the loan should be approved. Note that in this case, one does not even need the rule. Setting up the decision tree itself could be a method of knowledge representation. To make an inference based on this decision tree, it would be enough to match the facts with one of the branches of the decision tree.

Let us note a number of features in this example. First, the data is a complete representation of all possible cases. It does not have the nature of sample data in statistics. Rather, it is a set of all possible values of attributes of the decision and the outcome of the decision.

Second, no error is allowed in the data set. Third, the decision tree, as presented in Figure 4.6, is quite inefficient. For example, once it is established that the applicant does not have a steady job and adequate assets, the loan is denied. In other words, we could have dropped the last node (adequate income) in the last branch of the tree in Figure 4.6, because the adequacy of income is an irrelevant attribute in this case.

The decision tree in its raw form is inefficient. The question is whether we can find a tree with a minimum number of nodes that could represent the data in full. In fact, we can, using a method called ID3, which is discussed in the next section.

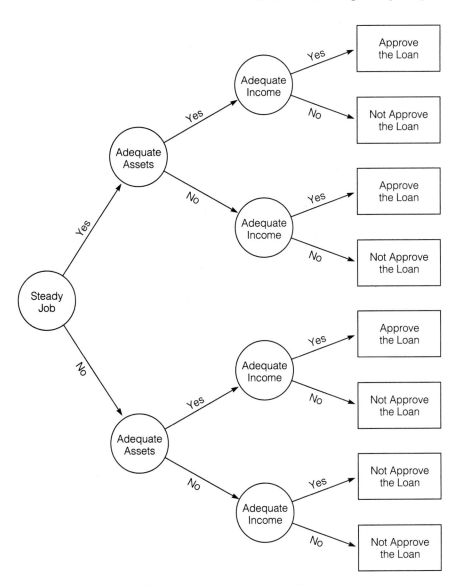

Figure 4.6 Decision Tree for the Mortgage Loan Case

4.5.2 ID3

ID3 was developed by Quinlan [1983]. This method finds the decision tree with the minimum number of nodes that could represent the data. It chooses as the first node the attribute that has the most discriminating power. For example, in the previous data set, the most discriminating attribute is "adequate income," because if the applicant does not have an adequate income, the loan application will not be approved. This point is not obvious by visual inspection. One needs a computation procedure to determine which attribute has the most discriminating power. Appendix A explains the computational details of ID3 as applied to this data set. Figure 4.7 shows one of the two decision trees which ID3 recommends for it.

If we compare Figure 4.6 with Figure 4.7, we notice that the number of branches in Figure 4.7 is considerably less. This translates to a more efficient search. Furthermore, when the possible values of attributes are not binary, such as high, medium, and low, ID3 finds the most effective way of branching from the node that has multiple values or even continuous numerical values. This reduces the combinatorial explosion of the decision tree and makes it possible to use the decision tree as an inductive method of knowledge representation and reasoning in expert systems. ID3 is used in the 1st-CLASS expert system software, which is discussed in Chapter 6.

Note that once the appropriate decision tree is found, one can use it directly to match its branches with the facts of a given problem, and reach a conclusion. Alternatively, one can encode the branches of the decision tree using rule-based or predicate knowledge representation. For example, the decision tree in Figure 4.7 for the goal of approving the loan could be

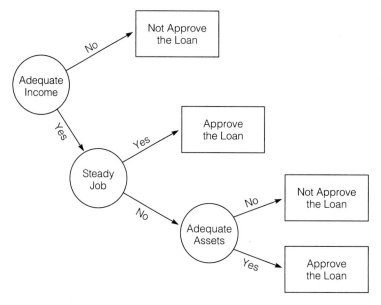

Figure 4.7 Decision Tree for the Mortgage Loan Case as Recommended by ID3

represented as:

```
IF  the applicant has adequate income
   AND  the applicant has a steady job
THEN  approve the loan

IF  the applicant has adequate income
   AND NOT the applicant has a steady job
   AND  the applicant has adequate assets
THEN approve the loan.
```

Similarly, the predicate presentation is:

$$income(X, adequate) \land job(X, steady) \rightarrow approve(X)$$

$$income(X, adequate) \land \neg job(X, steady) \land$$

$$assets(X, adequate) \rightarrow approve(X).$$

4.5.3 Case-based Reasoning and Reasoning by Analogy

Case-based reasoning and its related approach, *reasoning by analogy*, constitute alternative methods of reasoning and inference in expert systems. Some knowledge bases do not lend themselves to rule-based or predicate encoding. A notable example of such knowledge bases is legal knowledge bases. Most of the reasoning in such systems is based on previous rulings or cases. In such knowledge bases, rulings that are the basis for legal reasoning must be coded into the database of cases. For a new case, one can match the facts or attributes of the case against those in the database. Once a match is found, then one can use the precedent case to reason about the new case. As new cases with differing attributes come into existence, they too are added to the database of cases.

We learn from past cases, and rely on our previous experiences to quickly recognize and categorize a new situation or solve a new problem. We first establish that the new situation is adequately similar to one we have seen before, or the new problem matches with a problem we have solved before. Even when the match is not perfect, the previous solution may give us a partial answer to the new problem, and guide us in solving the new problem while avoiding past mistakes and pitfalls.

Case-based reasoning (CBR) is modeled after this aspect of human intelligence. CBR can be divided into two categories: classification and problem solving. In *classification* CBR, the system establishes whether or not a new case should be treated like an existing case. In this category of CBR, the system should come up with the pros and cons of why a new case should (or should not) be treated like an existing case.

In the *problem-solving CBR*, the system attempts to solve the new problem by establishing its similarity to a problem for which the system has a solution. The solution may be complete or partial. If the match is not complete, the existing solution may provide only a partial answer, and more reasoning would be needed to arrive at a complete answer. Some applications of CBR use both classification and problem-solving approaches in their reasoning process.

The critical issues in CBR are: How should we organize existing cases so that the computer can search the database of cases with adequate efficiency? What are the criteria for choosing a relevant case or a reasonable match? How can we adapt the solution of a matched case to fit the novel aspects of the new problem? These are among major issues under active investigation in CBR.

The CBR approach is also used as a heuristic to modify an existing knowledge base and learn new cases. Case-based learning is one method of what is called *machine learning* in artificial intelligence. Other learning heuristics in artificial intelligence may be found with books with "machine learning" as part of their titles.

Conclusion

There are two logic-based knowledge representation methods: rules and predicates. One can use inference methods in logic to derive new conclusions from combining the knowledge base and facts for a given problem. Knowledge representation and inference methods go hand in hand; together they make it possible to process knowledge. With knowledge representation methods one can model the qualitative aspects of a system. This is similar to formulating a problem in quantitative methods. For a model to be of any use, it should provide answers to decision questions, or *solve* decision problems. This is the task performed by rules of inference in expert systems.

To apply domain knowledge to a given problem, humans reason and arrive at a conclusion. Thus, an expert system that attempts to mimic human problem solving must use reasoning as its problem-solving method. There are two types of reasoning: deductive and inductive. Deductive reasoning starts with a set of axioms or the knowledge base, while inductive reasoning starts with observed data and cases.

The logic-based knowledge representation methods—rules and predicates—are based on logic, which is deductive in reasoning. Since rules are based on propositional logic, rule processing is based on inference methods in propositional logic. Similarly, for processing predicates, we must look into the inference methods in predicate calculus. That is why we discussed the reasoning methods of propositional and predicate calculi in the single inference section of this chapter.

Logic provides us with a single inference: how one can combine two pieces of knowledge or fact to arrive at a new conclusion. We know that a knowledge base contains numerous pieces of knowledge. The question then becomes in what order various pieces of knowledge must be processed, which is the process of multiple inference. Backward and forward chaining are among the common approaches in multiple inference. Various search methods constitute heuristics applied in multiple inference processing.

Although logic is the theoretical foundation of rule-based and predicate methods, many expert systems do not adhere to the principles of logic at all times, and apply other reasoning methods as well. Among such methods is inductive reasoning, which is the process of going from specific cases to general rules. ID3 is one of the best-known inductive reasoning methods. Other inductive approaches include case-based reasoning and reasoning by analogy.

References

Carbonell, Jaime. (Ed.) 1990. *Machine Learning: Paradigms and Methods*, MIT Press, Cambridge, MA.

Charniak, Eugene and McDermott, Drew. 1985. *Introduction to Artificial Intelligence*, Addison-Wesley, Reading, MA.

Defense Advanced Research Project Agency (DARPA). 1989. *Proceedings of Case-Based Reasoning Workshop*, in Pensacola, Florida, May, Distributed by Morgan Kaufmann Publishers, Inc., San Mateo, CA.

Hogger, Christopher John. 1984. *Introduction to Logic Programming*, Academic Press, Inc., London, England.

Jackson, Peter; Reichgelt, Hans; and van Harmelen, Frank. (Eds.) 1989. *Logic-Based Knowledge Representation*, MIT Press, Cambridge, MA.

Luger, George. F. and Stubblefield, William. A. 1989. *Artificial Intelligence and the Design of Expert Systems*, The Benjamin/Cummings Publishing Co., Redwood City, CA.

Mandelson, Elliott. 1987. *Introduction to Mathematical Logic*, third edition, Wadsworth & Brooks/Cole Advanced Books & Software, Monterey, CA.

Quinlan, J. Ross. 1983. "Learning Efficient Classification Procedures and Their Application to Chess End Games," in *Machine Learning, An Artificial Intelligence Approach*, R. S. Michalski, J. F. Carbonell, and T. M. Mitchell (Eds.), Tioga Publishing Co., Palo Alto, CA, pp. 463–482.

Questions

4.1   Compare the inductive and deductive reasoning methods. Give one example for each.

4.2   What is the difference between single and multiple inference? Why is the distinction between the two important in expert systems?

4.3   What are the major rules of inference in propositional logic and calculus?

4.4   Why are rules of inference important in expert systems?

4.5   Show the truth table for hypothetical syllogism, and prove that it is a tautology.

4.6   What is the difference between modus ponens and modus tollens? Which one is more useful in expert systems and why?

4.7   Why is pattern matching important in expert systems?

4.8   How does pattern matching take place in predicate calculus?

4.9   What is Skolemization? What is its role in unification?

4.10 What is the difference between unification and resolution in reasoning with predicate calculus?

4.11 What is the difference between a graph and a tree?

4.12 Why is the and/or graph a useful tool for the analysis of the knowledge base?

4.13 What is the difference between forward and backward chaining?

4.14 What are search methods? What is their role in expert systems?

4.15 What is shallow reasoning? In an expert system, what can we do to decrease the shallowness of reasoning?

4.16 What are some of the methods in inductive reasoning?

4.17 What does ID3 do to make the decision tree a more useful method of knowledge representation?

4.18 What are other heuristics in expert systems? Do they have theoretical foundations?

4.19 What is meta knowledge reasoning? In what type of expert system could meta knowledge reasoning be of great use?

Problems

4.1 Give two examples of inference using modus ponens, hypothetical syllogism, and modus tollens.

4.2 Give two examples of Skolemization.

4.3 Draw the and/or graph for the following knowledge base, assuming that G is the goal:

$$A \rightarrow H$$

$$B \rightarrow C$$

$$(A \wedge D) \vee (C \wedge E) \rightarrow F$$

$$F \vee H \rightarrow G$$

4.4 Use the knowledge base in the previous question to show how backward chaining works.

4.5 Draw the and/or graph for the following knowledge base:

$$E \vee F \rightarrow A$$

$$H \rightarrow B$$

$$I \vee (J \wedge K) \rightarrow C$$

$$(A \wedge B \wedge C) \vee (A \wedge C \wedge D) \rightarrow G$$

where the above statement letters have the following meaning:

```
A = the applicant has a steady job
B = the applicant has adequate income
```

```
C = the applicant has good credit rating

D = the applicant has adequate assets

E = the applicant has been at the present job for the past 3
    years

F = the applicant has received a raise in the last year

H = the applicant's net income is 1.5 times the monthly
    mortgage

I = the applicant has paid all monthly payments on time

J = the applicant has a line of credit more than 2 times the
    loan

K = the applicant has cash more than 50% of the loan

G = approve the loan.
```

4.6   Draw the and/or graph for the mortgage loan case.

4.7   Set up the decision tree for the following data:

adequate education	adequate experience	good interview	approve hiring
yes	yes	yes	yes
yes	no	yes	yes
no	yes	yes	yes
no	no	yes	no
yes	yes	no	yes
yes	no	no	no
no	yes	no	no
no	no	no	no

4.8   Give an example of a knowledge domain where case-based reasoning would be a more appropriate method.

Case: Financial Advisor

In dealing with increased global competition, large commercial banks now offer a full range of financial services, which include not only the traditional checking/saving accounts and loans, but also insurance products and brokerage services. In providing the brokerage services to bank customers, the bank employee is required to answer customers' questions regarding the various types of financial products, such as their risk level, minimum investment, tax advantage, and recent perfomance. In answering customers' questions and making recommendations, the bank broker must consider the customer's attributes, such as his or her tax bracket, age, level of income, and types and amounts of assets and loans.

Interview your finance instructor(s) as the expert(s) to develop rules for an expert system that provides advice for financial investment. Discuss the type of databases you wish to hook up to such an expert system.

Case: Expert System Applications in Corporate Income Tax

Expert systems that examine income tax issues are now in use at many major accounting firms, the IRS, and a variety of businesses for international taxation, corporate tax planning, special issues in corporate tax, personal income taxes, personal and corporate financial planning. The tax planning expert systems of the major accounting firms also are used in auditing deferred income tax accruals.

Coopers & Lybrand, Deloitte & Touche, and Price Waterhouse use expert systems to optimize the international tax position of their corporate clients with constraints set by users. Coopers & Lybrand and KPMG Peat Marwick use expert systems for income tax planning and auditing deferred income tax accruals.

Many industries have special taxation rules, so industry-specific expert systems complement a general tax-planning expert system or are independent self-contained systems. Coopers & Lybrand added two modules to its general corporate tax-planning system, one for the insurance industry and another for the oil and gas industry. Price Waterhouse developed a system for regulated investment companies.

Excerpts from "Expert Systems for Management Accountants," *Management Accounting*, by Carol Brown and Mary Ellen Phillips, January 1990, pp. 18–23, reprinted with permission from *Management Accounting*.

Case Questions

1. Discuss the desirable features of an expert system used for the preparation of personal income tax.

2. Give two examples of the rules for personal income tax.

3. Write the examples in Question 2 in the predicate method.

4. Interview your accounting professor or a tax accountant to develop rules for deciding whether to itemize expenses in the preparation of a personal-income tax return.

5. Draw a decision tree for the rules in Question 4.

6. Convert the rules in Question 4 into predicate statements.

III

PRACTICAL ASPECTS IN APPLYING EXPERT SYSTEMS

The objective of Part III is to introduce the reader to the practical aspects of developing expert systems in business. This part consists of Chapters 5, 6, and 7.

Chapter 5 contains a brief introduction to two major languages used in artificial intelligence (Lisp and Prolog). However, the bulk of this chapter is a hands-on introduction to LEVEL5, an expert system software tool. There is a student version of LEVEL5 attached to the book that can be used for practice. LEVEL5 is an example of a deductive reasoning tool for expert systems.

Chapter 6 contains a hands-on discussion of 1st-CLASS. This tool is an example of an inductive approach in expert systems. A student version of this software is also available for this book.

In an application-oriented course, the use of both Chapters 5 and 6 is recommended. However, if the course has a more conceptual orientation, covering either Chapter 5 or 6 will suffice. The discussion of Lisp and Prolog in Chapter 5 is expository in nature, and can be skipped in business courses with a greater emphasis on conceptual topics. The sections with "optional" in their titles contain details about the software and can be skipped without diminishing the students' understanding of the software tool.

Chapter 7 covers systems development and knowledge acquisition topics in expert systems. It discusses the organizational and communication issues in developing and evaluating expert systems. Chapter 7 is essential for any reader who is interested in the unique issues in developing expert system applications. It is essential for all business expert systems courses.

CHAPTER 5

Deductive Reasoning Tools and LEVEL5

Every tool carries with it the spirit by which it has been created.

Werner Karl Heisenberg

Chapter Objectives

The objectives of this chapter are:

- To discuss the working of an expert system software through a hands-on experience with LEVEL5

- To briefly review the languages designed for programming expert systems: Lisp and Prolog

---

KEY WORDS: LEVEL5, editing, compiling, running, user interface, interface development, outside hooks, certainty factor, Lisp, Prolog, expert system programming languages

---

This chapter could be used with the demonstration diskettes attached to this book for hands-on experiments with the LEVEL5 software tool. Those who prefer to have a general understanding of the tool without practicing with the diskettes can read the chapter and refer to the tables, which demonstrate the working of the software.

Introduction

This chapter is the first to show how the theoretical concepts discussed in Chapters 3 and 4 are operationalized into expert system software products and languages for deductive reasoning. This chapter continues to use the mortgage loan case, and guides the student to create a prototype mortgage-loan expert system using LEVEL5, the software covered in this chapter.

The focus of this chapter is to give the reader hands-on experience in creating prototype expert systems. The software used for this purpose is LEVEL5. The syntax of this software is discussed here, while helping the reader create the mortgage loan system. You do not need a separate software manual for LEVEL5 to create prototype expert systems because the coverage of LEVEL5 is detailed enough for the purpose of this chapter.

The last section of this chapter introduces two major languages used in artificial intelligence and expert systems: Lisp and Prolog. You will not become a Lisp or Prolog programmer with the two short, optional sections on these languages. Rather, the purpose is to show how the mathematical-logic foundation discussed in the previous two chapters is operationalized into these languages and to give you a flavor for how these languages work. If you are in a position to decide to "make" or "buy" the software for an expert system, you may need a rudimentary familiarity with these languages. The last two sections of this chapter give you this familiarity.

The case boxes in this chapter continue to emphasize the diversity of expert system applications and to provide you with ideas for your expert system projects.

5.1 LEVEL5

Most of the expert system applications require a number of common features. Programming all these features from scratch could take time and involve bugs that may be difficult to discover. There are numerous software products on the market that have built-in facilities addressing the common needs of most applications, and many offer capabilities that allow the application developer to custom-design additional features into the system.

Here we discuss the working of one such tool, called *LEVEL5*. The discussion of LEVEL5 in this chapter is intended to be used in conjunction with the student version of LEVEL5, an option available for this book. Those who are not interested in gaining a working knowledge of the software can read the chapter without practicing with the software. This would give them a general overview of what could be accomplished with an expert system software product.

Some of the advanced features of LEVEL5 are not included in the student version of the software. These advanced features are discussed only briefly in this chapter. Using a feature not included in the student version will cause an error message informing you that the keyword is not supported in this version.

5.1.1 *General Features of LEVEL5*

LEVEL5 has an embedded inference engine, editor, and a language called PRL (Production Rule Language) for coding the knowledge base into the system. The software allows the developer to customize the user interface by adding additional information and explanation. One of the advantages of LEVEL5 is its simplicity, which makes the learning period short.

The inference engine in LEVEL5 is primarily designed for backward chaining inference. (Backward chaining is described in Chapter 4.) It also can perform forward chaining if the knowledge base is coded for forward chaining.

In backward chaining, the goals that the inference engine must attempt to establish are entered in the goal section of the software. The body of the knowledge base is in the form of IF-THEN rules. In LEVEL5, the uncertainty is modeled by way of confidence factors, using a combination of fuzzy set and probability approaches (discussed in Chapter 11). Most of the user interface features of LEVEL5 are already designed into the software, which makes the software easy to use. All custom-designed user-interface enhancement must be included as a part of the knowledge base. LEVEL5 has the capability to interact with dBASEII and III files. (The mainframe version of LEVEL5 can interact with a variety of file types.) The developer can divide the knowledge into multiple knowledge bases, and chain them together in the inference process.

Thus, what the developer enters into the system consists of:

- Coded knowledge in the form of rules and goals

- Additional texts and statements for the user-interface enhancement

- Statements for turning on some of the optional features of the software

All are entered into one file (or more when there are multiple knowledge bases), which automatically takes the extension ".PRL".

LEVEL5 has a simple and easy-to-use editor, by which the developer can create the ".PRL" file. Once the content of the knowledge base is entered into the editor and saved, it must be compiled. The compilation of the ".PRL" file translates the human-oriented coded knowledge base into a machine-oriented code, which would be more efficient when the system executes the program. The file containing the compiled version of the knowledge base automatically receives the extension ".KNB".

The content of the knowledge base file could be divided into a number of distinct sections:

- TITLE statement

- Control section

- Goal section

- Rule section

- User-interface section

- END statement

In what follows, we discuss these sections in more detail.

5.1.2   *Essential Sections in the Knowledge Base*

A knowledge base must have a minimum of the TITLE and END statements, as well as the goal and rule sections. The knowledge base must start with the key word TITLE followed by a line of text identifying the expert system, and must end with the key word END on the last line of the knowledge base.

Propositions in LEVEL5

Propositions in LEVEL5 are called *facts*. There are four types of facts in LEVEL5: simple, numerical, string, and attribute-value facts. One can use these facts to form rules in the knowledge base.

The *simple fact* is the logical proposition discussed in Chapter 3; it takes true and false values. The *numerical fact* takes numerical values. The *string fact* is similar to the numerical fact, with the difference that it takes string values. A string value should be enclosed in double quotes. The *attribute-value* fact consists of two parts: attribute and value. The *attribute* part is similar to a proposition, with the exception that this proposition takes categorical values. For example, the credit rating is an attribute, which takes values good, fair, and bad.

LEVEL5 supports both *compound* and *multi-compound* data types. In the compound data type, only one item of a list could be true. For example, the attribute credit rating could only take one value of the list good, fair, bad. In the *multi-compound* data type, several items of a list may be true. For example, the attribute college degree may take several values in the list: BA, BS, MA, MS, MBA, PhD, DBA, MD. (We will see in a later section that one can declare a multi-compound data type in the control statement MULTI.)

Rules in LEVEL5

Facts are used in rules. In PRL, a rule starts with the key word RULE followed by a name or title for the rule. Key words in LEVEL5 are in capital letters. The next line starts with the key word IF followed by a proposition. The antecedent of the rule could have connectives: AND and OR. If the antecedent of the rule has more than one proposition, the second proposition starts on the next line, beginning with the connective. The consequent of the rule starts on a new line with the key word THEN. One can use the AND connective in the consequent, but OR is not allowed in the consequent. In other words, LEVEL5 rules are not in the form of the Horn clause, as is the case in Prolog.

Case: Scheduling Advisor

Stone & Webster Engineering, an advanced-technology consulting firm based in Boston, has developed a modular production-scheduling system called the Production Scheduling Advisor that features an embedded expert system written in New York City–based Information Builders' LEVEL5. The Advisor helps plan daily production for a forecast period of as long as one year and can accommodate facilities with multiple units, storage, and recycle streams that produce intermediate raw materials as well as finished products.

The heart of the system is a proprietary implementation of an interactive Gantt chart that lets users manipulate their production schedules in conformity with given constraints. The chart permits access to inventories, production constraints, and production cycles, which may be shortened, lengthened, or rescheduled. Users model their production processes with a spreadsheet module that accepts specifications by week, month, order, or in combination. The Advisor's optimization module satisfies production constraints, minimizes inventory violations, and prioritizes tasks as efficiently as possible.

The LEVEL5 module facilitates the Advisor's scheduling operations. It contains 225 generic product rules that are applied when the system determines production capacity and demand, the order in which products are manufactured, and the consequences of typical production constraints (such as common transfer lines). The expert system also diagnoses production-cycle problems for the user by analyzing inventory-violation patterns. Following the diagnosis, more specific rules may be added to help the scheduler to meet its goals. In some cases, this diagnosis supersedes the optimization module's proposed production cycle.

Gavin Finn of Stone & Webster points out that for Union Carbide, one of the Advisor customers, "The scheduling task has been fundamentally changed. Scheduling time has been shortened and many more alternatives are possible.... Using the system, if you want to change a rolling schedule at the last minute, you can do so without modifying your basic plan. You become much more responsive to the marketplace."

By Justin Kestelyn, "Application Watch," *AI Expert*, May 1991, p. 72, reprinted with permission from *AI Expert*.

In the mortgage loan case, one of the rules for approving a loan may be:

```
RULE 1 for approving the loan
IF credit rating IS good
AND net income to mortgage ratio > 1.5
AND net income to mortgage ratio <= 2
AND there are some assets
THEN the decision IS approve
AND the points := 2
```

The first line in this example contains a description of the rule. The body of the rule starts on the second line. The proposition in the first condition of the antecedent is an attribute-value type. The key word **IS** compares the attribute **credit rating** with the categorical value **good**. In the second condition, the fact is numerical and is compared with the numerical value 1.5. The third condition is a simple fact, which takes a true or false value. For the simple facts, one does not need to specify values. The fourth condition requires that the simple proposition **there are some assets** be true. Later, we will see the difference in processing simple facts as opposed to attribute-value facts.

In the previous rule, the consequent assigns the value **approve** to the attribute **the decision**. LEVEL5 uses uppercase for reserved words, such as **IS** and **ARE**. The reserved word **IS** is used for both comparison (in the antecedent of a rule) and value assignment (in the consequent) for the attribute-value facts. Symbols **ARE** and \ are equivalent to **IS** in attribute-value facts. Thus, **the decision is approve** is considered a simple fact, while **the decision IS approve** is an attribute-value fact.

The second proposition in the consequent assigns the value 2 to the numerical fact **the points**. In LEVEL5, ":=" assigns numerical values, while "=" represents a relational comparison. The first proposition of **THEN** must be either a simple or an attribute-value fact. The subsequent propositions in the consequent could be of any type, and are considered the *side effect* of the rule. In the above example, the assignment of 2 to **the points** is a side effect of the rule.

Goals in LEVEL5

In backward chaining, the inference engine needs to know the propositions for which the backward search should take place. These propositions are specified in the goal section. Goals consist of numbered propositions, where the numbers indicate the order by which the inference engine must search the knowledge base.

For example, the loan mortgage system may have the following goals:

```
1. the decision IS approve
2. the decision IS reject
```

The inference engine performs backward chaining to search for the first goal. If it achieves the first goal, it stops, and outputs the result. Otherwise, it continues searching for the second goal. If it fails to reach any of the listed goals, it stops and declares that no goal is achieved.

A goal may have one or more subgoals. For example,

```
1. the decision IS approve
     1.1 the decision on loan details is made
2. the decision IS  reject
     2.1 the anti-discrimination checks are made
```

When the first goal is attained (the loan is approved), the system should attempt to achieve the goal of deciding on the details of the loan, such as the interest rate, amount, duration, and monthly mortgage payment. When a loan is rejected, the system must make sure that the rejection is not discriminatory. The inference engine searches for a subgoal only when its parent goal is achieved. There may be more than one subgoal. However, when the inference engine achieves one subgoal at the lowest level of the goal hierarchy, it stops the search and does not attempt to achieve other subgoals on the same level.

5.1.3   Editing, Compiling, and Running an Application

LEVEL5 opens into an initial main menu with three options:

```
==> Run a knowledge base
    Edit a knowledge base
    Compile a knowledge base
```

The arrow ==> shows the current selection; pressing the return key performs the option. The ↑ and ↓ keys move ==> for changing the current option. The Edit option opens the editor for the developer to enter the knowledge base into the system. The Compile option compiles the knowledge base, and Run runs the system to perform user consultation.

The last line on the screen shows the active function keys; the numbers correspond to the F1 through F10 function keys on the keyboard. Pressing F10 exits the system, and F9 activates help on this screen. F5 allows us to change the default directory.

- Install and start your LEVEL5 student version, and test the active function keys on the main menu.

- Change the directory to where a new knowledge base is to be stored. This could be a disk drive or a subdirectory on the hard disk.

LEVEL5 Editor

Choosing the Edit option allows you either to edit an existing knowledge base or to create a new one.

- Choose the Edit option and use the function key F2, labeled New, for starting a new knowledge base.

- Enter the knowledge base as shown below:

```
TITLE a prototype for the mortgage loan case

! You can use comment lines like this to make notes
!    which are helpful in documenting the system

! This is the goal section of the knowledge base

1. the decision IS approve
2. the decision IS reject

! This is the rule section of the knowledge base
```

```
RULE 1 for approving the loan
IF credit rating IS good
AND net income to mortgage ratio > 1.5
AND net income to mortgage ratio <= 2
AND there are some assets
THEN the decision IS approve

RULE 2 for approving the loan
IF credit rating IS good
AND net income to mortgage ratio > 2
THEN the decision IS approve

RULE 3 for approving the loan
IF credit rating IS fair
AND net income to mortgage ratio > 2
AND there are some assets
THEN the decision IS approve

RULE 1 for rejecting the loan
IF credit rating IS bad
THEN the decision IS reject

RULE 2 for rejecting the loan
IF NOT there are some assets
AND NOT credit rating IS good
THEN the decision IS reject

RULE 3 for rejecting the loan
IF NOT there are some assets
AND net income to mortgage ratio < 2
THEN the decision IS reject

! The knowledge base ends with an end statement.

END
```

- After entering the knowledge base, save it with the save option on F3, and call it mortloan. This creates the file MORTLOAN.PRL, which is the ASCII file containing what you have entered. You can change the contents of this file using the Edit option or any word processor that can generate an ASCII file output.

- You can compile it with F4, or return to the main menu by F10 (labeled Menu), choose the Compile option, and choose mortloan.

- After successful compilation, the system creates the file mortloan.KNB, which contains the machine code of the knowledge base. If the compilation produces error messages, use the editor to make the corrections.

- Once the knowledge base is compiled, you can run it with F3 (Run), or enter F8 to return to the main menu, and choose the Run option and the name of the knowledge base you just compiled.

Running a Knowledge Base

In running a knowledge base, the inference engine chooses the first goal, and tries to establish its truth. In doing so, it needs to establish the truth of the propositions in the antecedent of the rules containing the goal in their consequent. The inference engine stores all the facts obtained from the user or established through the inference process in what is called the *working memory* or the *session context*.

To establish the truth of these propositions, the inference engine first checks to see if the working memory contains the truth of the proposition. If not, it checks to see if the proposition is in the consequent of another rule. If so, the antecedent of that rule becomes the new intermediate goal. This step constitutes the backward chaining process (discussed in detail in Chapter 4). If the proposition is not in any rule's consequent, the inference engine prompts the user to provide the information. Thus, the system automatically prompts the user for the facts it needs, and displays the goal it reaches.

5.1.4   User Interface in LEVEL5

In running the system, you will notice that a great deal of the user interface is already programmed into LEVEL5. This makes it possible for the developer of the expert system to rapidly create a prototype of the expert system.

In running the example in the previous section, you notice that when LEVEL5 needs to ask the user for the value of a proposition, it uses the wording of the fact within the rule. Furthermore, it uses the text of the attained goal to inform the user of the conclusion it has reached. Thus, the developer does not need to worry about designing the user interface in order to run the system.

The user interface in expert systems is not limited to the input and output communications between the system and the user. One of the distinguishing features of expert systems is the ability to show the user the line of reasoning leading to a conclusion, and informing the user why a particular fact is needed. This is called the *explanation capability* of the expert system.

In LEVEL5, the function key marked **WHY** gives the user the option of accessing a number of menus:

- FACT

- RULE

- REPT

- OPTN

The **FACT** menu gives the user access to the facts entered by the user so far, and the facts within the knowledge base, categorized into fact types. It also gives the user the option of trying new answers within the same session.

The **RULE** menu allows the user to access the current rule that led to the current query, the rules with the same consequent as the current rule, and the list of all rules within the knowledge base. This menu also allows the user to look at the previous or forthcoming rule used by the inference engine.

The **REPT** (short for report) menu shows the user the line of reasoning used by the inference engine to arrive at its present state. Furthermore, the user can look at the knowledge tree of the entire knowledge base.

The **OPTN** (short for option) menu provides the user with the option of saving the session, calling back a saved session, or starting the session all over again and trying new answers.

Thus, in running the system, the user, at any point, has the option of asking the system for the reasoning behind a question, as well as for detailed information on the content of the knowledge base and the session's facts and line of reasoning.

These menus are not included in the student version of LEVEL5. The function key **WHY** in the student version shows only the line of reasoning and the current rule the inference engine is pursuing.

5.1.5 User-Interface Development

The default user interface in LEVEL5 is helpful in the rapid development of a system prototype. However, the development of an operational expert system invariably requires the developer to enhance and customize the user interface to the special needs of the system's user group.

The user interface in LEVEL5 could be customized using the following PRL statements:

- DISPLAY

- TEXT

- EXPAND (not available in the student version)

DISPLAY

One can use this statement in the TITLE in order make the opening screen of the system more informative. For example, in the mortgage loan system, we can have:

```
TITLE A prototype for the mortgage loan case DISPLAY
=======================================================

    MORTGAGE LOAN CONSULTATION SYSTEM

      FOR SINGLE FAMILY LOANS

   Please have all the application information ready
   before starting the system. Answer the questions
   as the system prompts you. If any question is not
   clear, use the function key with EXPL label.
            H A V E   A   N I C E   D A Y
=======================================================
1. the decision IS approve
2. the decision IS reject
. . . . . . . . . .
```

The content of the display is what is on the line after the DISPLAY statement, and before any other key word or system-defined sections. In this example, the display content starts with the second line and ends at the goal definition section. When the user runs the system, the content of the display will appear on the screen first. If the display requires more than one page of the screen, the system automatically displays one page and has labeled keys for moving pages up and down.

- Add this display to the mortgage loan case, and run the knowledge base.

DISPLAY can also be used in conjunction with rules. For example, the THEN part of a rule may include a display with a name, such as **DISPLAY** approve-info. The content of the display is coded following all the rules in the knowledge base. When the antecedent of the rule becomes true, the display is shown to the user as a side effect of the consequent. For example,

```
RULE 1 for approving the loan
IF credit rating IS good
AND net income to mortgage ratio > 1.5
AND net income to mortgage ratio <= 2
AND there are some assets
THEN the decision IS approve
AND  DISPLAY approve_info
.......
all the remaining rules
.......
DISPLAY approve_info
Subsequent to the approval of the loan, you should make
sure that the interest rate is determined, and
the loan applicant is immediately notified.
END
```

The content of the display starts from the line after the **DISPLAY** key word and name, and continues up to the next PRL statement or key word.

- Add additional displays to the knowledge base you have already created in order to make the final recommendations more meaningful to the user.

TEXT

A fact can have up to 60 characters on one line. This limits the length of a proposition. Since the inference engine matches facts character by character (including blank spaces), lengthy propositions increase the probability of typographical errors, preventing the inference engine from matching identical propositions. This creates a logical error in the knowledge base that may not be easily discovered.

On the other hand, since the propositions are used by LEVEL5 to form the inquiries to the user, a short proposition may not clearly communicate to the user the meaning of a question. Defining a TEXT for a proposition at the end of the knowledge base allows the system to replace the content of the TEXT for the proposition when prompting the user to enter a value for a fact, or when it is declared as the system's final conclusion.

For example, in the mortgage loan case, we can add the following texts to replace the simple fact there are some assets, the attributes net income to mortgage ratio and the decision, and the values approve and reject. These texts must be added after all the rules are entered and before the END statement.

```
TITLE ...
the goals section
the rules section

TEXT there are some assets
The applicant has documented that he/she owns properties
and liquid assets, with a total market value of 20% or
more of the amount of the loan.

TEXT net income to mortgage ratio
The applicant's net income (income minus all
expenses) divided by the estimated amount of monthly
mortgage to be paid by the applicant if the loan is approved.

TEXT the decision
The system recommends that

TEXT approve
this loan application should be approved.

TEXT reject
this loan application should be rejected.
END
```

When the user runs the system, these texts will be displayed to replace the shorter version of the facts used in rules.

- Add these texts to the mortgage loan case and run the system to see the effect of adding **TEXT** in the user interface.

EXPAND

In some cases, the system may have more than one user type, such as experienced and novice users. The developer of the system may wish to add additional explanation for a novice user, without bothering the experienced user with unnecessary explanations.

The developer may use the **EXPAND** option in order to add further explanation to the system regarding a particular fact. If a fact has been **EXPAND**ed, whenever the user is prompted for that fact, a function key marked **EXPL** appears on the screen. By pressing this function key, the user can see the additional explanation for the fact.

For example, the developer may want to explain why the system is asking about the assets of the applicant with an **EXPAND** statement similar to the following:

```
TITLE ...
the goals section
the rules section
TEXT and DISPLAY contents
. . . . . . .
EXPAND there are some assets
The reason for asking whether the applicant has
some assets is that either his/her credit rating
is not good, or the net income of the applicant
does not adequately cover the monthly mortgage payment.
. . . . . . .
END
```

- Identify the facts in the mortgage loan case that should be expanded. Add the needed statements to the system.

The **TEXT**, **DISPLAY**, and **EXPAND** statements come at the end of the knowledge base, and their order is of no consequence.

5.1.6   Treatment of Uncertainty in LEVEL5

LEVEL5 allows for the incorporation of uncertainty in facts and rules by attaching a *certainty factor* to every type of fact. The certainty factor ranges from 0 to 100, while the certainty factor of -1 represents a fact that is undetermined (not yet known), and -2 represents a fact whose value is declared as unknown by the user. The default value of the certainty factor is 100. (Chapter 10 discusses how PRL combines certainty factors of rules and facts.)

Getting the Confidence Factor from the User

If the facts in the knowledge base have certainty factors below 100, the developer can prompt the user for the certainty values of the facts by turning on the confidence prompting:

```
TITLE ....
CONFIDENCE ON
goal section
.........
```

Alternatively, if only a select number of facts have certainty factors below 100, they could be listed as:

```
TITLE ....
CONFIDENCE there are some assets
AND  credit rating
AND net income to mortgage ratio
AND the decision
```

As this example shows, all types of facts—simple, numeric, attribute, and string—could be declared in the CONFIDENCE statement.

- Add these statements to the mortgage loan case, and run the knowledge base to see the effect of turning the confidence on.

The system has a threshold of 50. When the certainty factor of a fact falls below this level, the inference engine ceases to use the fact in its inference process. The developer could change the threshold by:

```
TITLE ....
THRESHOLD = 60 (not available in the student version)
.........
goal section
```

Confidence Factors in the Knowledge Base

The developer can assign confidence factors to the consequents of a rule, reflecting the expert's confidence in the rule. This is done by using CONFIDENCE or its abbreviation CF as shown in the following example:

```
RULE 2 for approving the loan
IF credit rating IS good
AND net income to mortgage ratio > 2
THEN the decision IS approve    CF 95
```

If the consequent has more than one proposition, each one may have its own CF value.

One can also access the value of the confidence factor of a fact by the function CONF. For example:

```
TITLE ....
THRESHOLD = 60
CONFIDENCE ON
1. the decision IS approve
   1.1 issue warning about decision reliability
2. the decision IS reject
..........
RULE 1 warning for low confidence
IF CONF(the decision IS approve) < 80
THEN issue warning about decision reliability
AND DISPLAY warning
..........
DISPLAY warning
The confidence factor for approving this loan
is [CONF(the decision IS approve)(4,0)].
This value is below 80, which means
that this decision is not reliable, and
requires further investigation.
```

- Add this statement to the mortgage loan knowledge base, and run the knowledge base.

In the previous example, when the confidence factor of the decision to approve the loan falls below 80, the user is given the warning about the low reliability of the decision. The [name] in DISPLAY shows the value of *name*, in this case the confidence factor of the decision IS approve. When *name* is numeric, [name(x,d)] shows the number of spaces (x) and decimal places (d) used to print the numerical value. In the above example, four spaces are used for printing the confidence factor, without any decimals.

Alternatively, one can use the BAR function to display the confidence factor of a fact, as in the following example:

```
RULE 1 for approving the loan
IF credit rating IS good
AND net income to mortgage ratio > 1.5
AND net income to mortgage ratio <= 2
AND there are some assets
THEN the decision IS approve
AND BAR the decision IS approve
```

- Experiment with using the BAR function in the knowledge base you have already created.

5.1.7 System Control Statements

LEVEL5 has a number of control statements that allow the developer to change the features of the knowledge base. Here is the list of a selected number of such statements in the order they should appear after the TITLE statement and before the goal section.

```
! shared among chained knowledge bases
SHARED SIMPLEFACT
SHARED ATTRIBUTE

! database declaration
OPEN...AS...FOR...CALLED
```

```
! type declaration
SIMPLEFACT list of facts
ATTRIBUTE  list of facts
NUMERIC    list of facts
STRING     list of facts

CONFIDENCE ON  (not available in the student version)
GOAL SELECT ON (not available in the student version)
MULTI   list of attribute facts
THRESHOLD = a number (not available in the student version)
EXHAUSTIVE list of facts
FILE
```

Since the student version does not have these features, we will not go into the details of all these control statements. The following brief review is to demonstrate the capability of the full version of the software.

In LEVEL5, it is possible to divide the knowledge base into a number of independent knowledge bases, and then chain them together. The facts that are shared among these knowledge bases are declared as **SHARED**. One can use the **CHAIN** statement in a rule in the form of: **CHAIN the name of knowledge base**. This will connect the knowledge base to the chained knowledge base, sharing the facts declared as **SHARED** between them.

The developer does not need to declare the type of facts in the knowledge base. The inference engine infers the type of the fact from the content of the rules. For example, when a fact is compared with a number, then the inference engine assumes that the fact has a numeric type.

However, in large knowledge bases, it is dangerous to leave the type identification to the rule contents, because an error in a rule may corrupt the whole knowledge base. Therefore, it is safer for the developer to declare the types of various facts. When a rule contains a comparison that violates the type declaration, the system produces an error message. The following is an example of the fact declaration in the mortgage loan case:

```
SIMPLEFACT there are some assets
ATTRIBUTE credit rating
AND the decision
NUMERIC net income to mortgage ratio
```

As with all control statements, when there is more than one fact in a control statement, each new fact should be on a new line, starting with the key word **AND**.

The control statement **GOAL SELECT ON** allows the user to choose the goal that the inference engine must follow. The use of this control statement is tricky. To use this option, the goal hierarchy must have only one goal at the lowest level of each category.

The **MULTI** control statement allows the user to enter multiple values for an attribute. For example, an applicant could have more than one type of assets. In this case, the system, in one query, asks the user to identify all asset types.

In the **EXHAUSTIVE** control statement, the developer orders the inference engine not to stop when one rule establishes the truth (or other value types) for a fact. Instead, the inference engine must examine exhaustively all the rules in which the fact is used. In such a case, the inference engine chooses the proposition that has the highest certainty factor.

The **FILE** and database declaration are parts of outside hook in LEVEL5.

5.1.8   Outside Hooks in LEVEL5

LEVEL5 communicates with other software products in a number of ways:

- With an ASCII file

- With a program written in a programming language

- With dBASEII and dBASEIII data files

- With graphical files

The **FILE** control statement opens an ASCII file, and reads from and writes into the file with the commands: FILE, PRINT, READ, and WRITE.

The communication with an outside program is by the **ACTIVATE** command, which executes an executable file that is a .BAT, .COM, or .EXE file. The commands **SEND** and **RETURN** send the value of facts to the program, and receive input from the executed program.

Communication with a dBASEII or dBASEIII file is through the control statement:

```
OPEN pathname\filename AS DBIII FOR WRITE :
CALLED a reference name
```

The filename is the name of the database file, the key words DBII and DBIII identify the database type, the key word READ (read-only access), or WRITE (both read and write access) identifies the type of access. The symbol (:) is used for the continuation of the statement on the next line. The reference name is used to refer to the database file in rules. The fields of the database file are accessible within the knowledge base. Within the rules, they can be used as facts (numerical, string, simple facts). Within the rules, the developer may change the value of the field. The database commands, such as ADVANCE, APPEND, DELETE, EOF, LOCATE, RECNO, and POSITION, allow the developer to traverse through the records of the database file, query it for a particular value of a field, and change the content of the database file. This is an example of an active communication between an expert system and a database software.

The communication with a graphical image is by the statement PAINT. This statement is similar to DISPLAY with the exception that it displays the content of an image file.

5.1.9 Other Features in LEVEL5

PRL has a number of other features. The following is a sample of such features. In a rule, one can store the confidence factor of a fact in a numerical fact as b := CONF(fact name). The fact b could be used in other rules.

If the knowledge base is expected to have a number of facts regardless of the goals, the developer can force the inference engine to ask for the value of the fact by the statement ASK fact name. The ASK statement could be the antecedent of a rule with the bogus top level goal, such as get info as its consequent.

The connective NOT negates a fact. The difference between NOT there are some assets and there are no assets is that, in the first case, once the inference engine establishes that there are some assets is false, the NOT there are some assets fact becomes true. In the second case, even when the falsity of the existence of some assets is established, the inference engine prompts the user for the truth value of the statement there are no assets. Thus, using negation saves the user from answering duplicate questions.

The connective OR has priority over AND. Combining AND and OR in one rule could be tricky. Consider the following example:

```
RULE 1
IF A
AND B
OR C
THEN D
```

The priority is A AND (B OR C). The rule succeeds if A and B or A and C are true.

One can save the content of a consultation session by including CONTENT SAVE filename in a rule. To access a stored session, the command RESTORE filename should be included in a rule. One can also make the inference engine to restart the session while keeping the facts obtained from the previous session by the command LOOP.

5.2 Programming Languages for Expert Systems

One can use conventional programming languages (such as C and Pascal) to program expert systems and AI applications. Furthermore, some of the present expert system products are coded in C or Pascal, and Prolog was first coded in FORTRAN. However, the qualitative nature of knowledge processing requires languages that are designed for handling the symbolic and logical nature of expert systems. *Lisp* and *Prolog* are the two most important languages for programming AI applications and expert systems.

Lisp is a procedural language that is designed for processing and handling symbolic expressions, mostly qualitative in nature. Prolog, developed long after Lisp, is a declarative language, designed for the presentation and processing of knowledge represented in predicate calculus. It has a close tie to the topics discussed in Chapters 3 and 4.

This section provides a brief introduction to Lisp and Prolog. This introduction is not intended as a comprehensive coverage of these languages, but it will give the reader the flavor of each language. This minimum familiarity is needed when the tool for an expert system application is chosen.

5.2.1 *A Brief Review of Prolog (Optional)*

Prolog (for Programmation et Logique) was first developed in the early 1970s by Colmerauer and his group at the University of Marseille-Aix, and was intended for programming theorem proving in mathematical logic. Early computational inefficiency of the language was rectified in the late 1970s when David Warren and his colleagues developed an efficient implementation of Prolog.

At present, Prolog is one of the two most important AI languages, and has numerous implementations and dialects with different capabilities. In what follows, we discuss some of the fundamentals of this radically different programming language for AI and expert systems, using a subset of DEC-10 and Arity/Prolog [Marcus 1986].

Prolog is a declarative (as opposed to procedural) language, in that it codes the state of the knowledge, rather than listing a computational sequence of statements. Prolog is designed directly for coding predicate calculus, using the *Horn clause*. A Horn clause could be described as an IF-THEN construct in which the connectives AND and OR are not allowed in the consequent.

Prolog uses predicates (discussed in Chapters 3 and 4), similar to those we have seen in Chapter 3. For example, credit(X) is a predicate that takes one parameter X (or has an *arity* of 1).

Prolog uses the comma (,) to represent AND, semicolon (;) for OR, and "not" for NOT connectives. The conditionals in Prolog are in the form of Horn clauses, and start with THEN. The symbol (:-) represents the conditional connective. Thus, an IF-THEN in Prolog has the following form:

```
decision(X,approve) :- credit(X,good), >(ratio,1.5),
    assets(X,some), job(X,steady).
```

In this example, if the credit is good, the ratio of the property value to the loan is greater than 1.5, there are some assets, and the applicant's job is steady, then approve the loan. The symbolic fixed values, such as "good" and "some" are specified in lowercase in Prolog. Variables start with an uppercase letter in Prolog.

Simple facts are coded in the form of predicates, such as

```
job(smith,steady).
assets(smith,some).
decision(smith,Y).
```

One can run Prolog in the interpreter mode, where the system shows a prompt like "?-" to indicate that it is ready to take questions from the user. Assume that we have already entered the above three facts. Now, if we enter assets(smith,X) as a question, Prolog returns some. The session has the following form:

```
?- assets(smith,X).
X = some -> ;
no
```

Processing in Prolog is in the form of *pattern matching* and *unification.* When Prolog sees the predicate assets(smith,X), it attempts to match the predicate name with what it has in its knowledge base (or database). Once it finds a match, it attempts to unify the parameters of the matched predicates according to the following rules: variables always unify with other variables and fixed values. Fixed values match only with their identical fixed values. For example, smith matches only with itself in other predicates. (More complex structures and matching are possible, but they are not discussed in this introductory review.)

In the preceding example, once X is *instantiated*—matched with a fixed value—Prolog returns its value to the user. The symbol -¿ asks the user if Prolog should search for other values of X. When the user enters (;), Prolog discards the instantiated value of X, and tries to find other possible values for X. When it fails to do so, it returns no.

In addition to pattern matching and unification, Prolog uses backward chaining to make inferences with the conditionals and rules. To see how this works, let us code a simple version of the mortgage loan case in Chapter 3:

```
decision(X,approve) :- credit(X,good), >(ratio,1.5),
    assets(X,some), job(X,steady).
decision(X,approve) :- credit(X,good), >(ratio,2).
decision(X,approve) :- credit(X,fair), >(ratio,2),
    assets(X,some), job(X,steady).
credit(X,Y) :- bank_report(X,Y), card_report(X,Y).
job(X,steady) :- has_job(X), years_at_job(X,Y), >(Y,2).
assets(X,Y) :- liquid(X,Y); property(X,Y).
```

Now, assume that we have the following facts for Smith's application:

```
>(ratio,1.5).
liquid(smith,some).
```

```
bank_report(smith,good).
card_report(smith,good).
has_job(smith).
years_at_job(smith,3).
```

Now, the user runs the Prolog interpreter and asks whether the loan should be approved:

```
?- decision(smith,approve).
yes
```

When Prolog sees the user's question, it matches the predicate decision with the consequent part of the first well-formed formula (or rule, using less precise but simpler language). The fixed value smith binds with variable X in the first rule, and all Xs in the first rule are instantiated to smith.

Prolog then attempts to establish the truth of the conditions of the first rule. First, it has to establish that credit(smith,good) is true. Prolog accomplishes this by matching the third and fourth facts with the conditions of the fourth rule, and instantiating Y to good.

If Prolog fails to establish the truth of the first condition, it stops its search in this rule, because no matter what the truth value of other conditions are, the rule will fail. Thus, a rule with conjunction connectives fails as soon as the Prolog inference engine fails to establish the truth of one condition. On the other hand, the rule succeeds as soon as the first condition of a disjunctive (OR) connective succeeds.

Continuing with the example, once the first condition proves true, Prolog moves to test the truth of the second condition. The second condition is directly matched with the first fact. The condition assets(smith,some) becomes true from the second fact liquid(some), matching with the first condition of the last rule, instantiating Y to some. To establish the last condition of the first rule, the inference mechanism of Prolog attempts to verify the truth of job(smith,steady), in which it succeeds by using the last two facts in the fifth rule. Note that ">" is one of many built-in predicates in Prolog.

Prolog uses a backward-chaining process to identify the predicates whose truth values are needed for attaining the goal identified by the user. If Prolog could not infer the truth of the decision predicate, it would erase all the unification it has made for the first rule. This is called *backtracking*. It then starts the same process by examining the conditions in the second rule. If it succeeds, it reports to the user. Otherwise, it backtracks and attempts to arrive at the value of the decision predicate from the third rule. If this, too, fails, it backtracks and returns "no" as the answer to the user.

Case: Expert System for Credit Decisions

AT ITT Commercial Finance Corp., based in St. Louis, MO., every credit decision maker, regardless of how long the person has been with the company, can use the experience and knowledge of its senior credit experts with the help of the Expert Credit System (ECS). Installed throughout ITT's 23 offices in the United States, Canada, and the United Kingdom, ECS boasts 250 users.

ECS analyzes credit information, identifies credit-proposal strengths and weaknesses, and offers credit recommendations to ITT managers. Because ECS is user-friendly, managers can easily go through the whole process of gathering and inputting information and receive consistent credit recommendations on a daily basis.

ECS was developed by Harvey Gers, Kurt Ruhlin, and Emery Saladin of ITT, and Arthur D. Little consultant Karl Mate. ECS runs on DOS, which is used throughout the company. The ITT system developers wrote the program in Prolog because the language made writing the knowledge base and definitions easy. The choice to use Arity rested on the company's established track record and its product's quick execution and code compilation. Additionally, Borland's Paradox database allows portability to mainframes, a switch ITT may choose to do in the future.

Careful planning of ECS has paid great dividends, according to project manager Ruhlin. ECS was awarded ITT's 1990 Corporate Quality Award. Over the past two years and a half since its installation, ECS has saved approximately $500,000 in hard cash. Although difficult to quantify, the million-dollar savings in bad loan write-offs has been attributed to ECS. In ITT's book, ECS gets the highest credit rating.

By Patty Enrado, "Application Watch," *AI Expert*, September 1991, p. 64, reprinted with permission from *AI Expert*.

The following is the code for the mortgage loan case of Chapter 3. Comparing the code with the predicate statements of Chapter 3 shows that Prolog rules have a one-to-one correspondence with well-formed formulas in predicate calculus.

```
approve(X,Y,Z) :- job(X,steady), property(Y,acceptable),
                  loan(Z), property_value(V),
                  credit(X,good), income(X,adequate),
                  <(Z, V * 0.80),
```

```
                        has_cash(X,U),
                        >(U, V * 0.20).
        approve(X,Y,Z) :- assets(X,adequate), property(Y,acceptable),
                        loan(Z), property_value(V),
                        credit(X,good), income(X,adequate),
                        <(Z, V * 0.80),
                        has_cash(X,U),
                        >(U, V * 0.20).
        job(X,steady) :- has_job(X), years_at_job(Y), >(Y, 2).
        property(Y,acceptable)) :- member(Y,zone_list);
                                   member(Y,except_list).
        income(X,adequate) :- family_income(X,adequate) ;
                           single_income(X,adequate).
        family_income(X,adequate) :- married(X), net_income(X,N),
                               mort_pay(X,Z,M), <(M, N * 0.60).
        single_income(X,adequate) :- not married(X), net_income(X,N),
                               mort_pay(X,Z,M), <(M, N * 0.70).
        assets(X,adequate) :- has_property(X,V), loan(Z),
                           >(V, Z * 10).
        assets(X,adequate) :- has_liquid(X,U), loan(Z),
                           >(U, Z * 5).
        zone_list(.(element1,.(element2,.(element3.....)))).
        except_list(.(item1,.(item2,.(item3....)))).
```

Assuming the following facts of Smith's application, the process of pattern matching and unification leads to approval of the loan. Perform the matching and unification to see how Prolog reaches this decision.

```
loan(100000).
married(smith).
net_income(smith,2300).
mort_pay(smith,100000,1200).
property(lot_no_5555, X).
property_value(150000).
has_cash(70000).
credit(smith,good).
has_job(smith).
years_at_job(4).
```

Prolog has more capabilities than we can begin to cover in this brief introduction, such as recursion, the use of cut (!) to stop it, and the ability to handle complex data structures including lists. However, this brief introduction shows that Prolog is not procedural—that is, it does not process the coded statements sequentially, as the procedural languages do. It is declarative in that the state of knowledge is declared in Prolog. The built-in inference mechanism in Prolog uses the declared knowledge to arrive at a conclusion.

As we will see, Lisp does not have such a built-in inference mechanism; the inference mechanism and search method must be explicitly coded by the developer in Lisp. This demands more programming time, and, at the same time, gives the developer more flexibility and control over the processing of the system.

5.2.2   *A Brief Review of Lisp (Optional)*

Lisp (LISt Programming or Processing) is another AI language. It is one of the oldest procedural languages, first developed by McCarthy in 1958, and it was the only official language of AI before Prolog. Lisp has grown to address the programming needs of the AI community, and has many implementations and dialects. This brief introduction is based on Common Lisp [Winston and Horn 1989].

Lisp is a procedural language like C, BASIC, and Pascal. However, Lisp is designed for symbolic processing. For this reason, its syntax is drastically different from that of other procedural languages.

The foundation of Lisp is symbolic expression, or *s-expression*. It consists of wordlike objects called *atoms* or a list consisting of atoms or other lists. For example, credit is an atom, (credit smith good) is a list, and so is (property lot-no-5555 X).

The focus of Lisp is functions. The major syntax components of Lisp are in the form of functions. For example, if we enter (+ 2.5 3.4) in the Lisp interpreter, it returns 5.9. In this list, (+) is a built-in function in Lisp, and 2.5 and 3.4 are the parameters of the function.

Lisp has a number of built-in functions. One group of such functions is for arithmetic operations, such as $+, -, *, /$. Another group of functions is for processing lists. Among this group are the car, cdr, and append functions. For example, assume that we have the list (decision approve smith). Then, the Lisp interpreter returns the following:

```
your inquiry: (car '(decision approve smith))
Lisp response:    decision

(cdr '(decision approve smith))
   (approve smith)

(append '(decision approve smith) (50000))
   (decision approve smith 50000)
```

In this example, car picks up the first item in the list, and cdr returns all the list elements except the first one. The append function appends two lists together.

In Lisp, all s-expressions are evaluated, in that Lisp tries to match the list against what already exists in the knowledge base, except for numerical values that are evaluated to themselves. To stop the evaluation process, and to tell Lisp that it should take an s-expression as is, one must use either the function name quote or enter the symbol (') before the opening parenthesis. In the earlier examples, the facts have the (') symbol.

The items in the list could themselves be lists of lists, thus allowing the programmer to create a tree or hierarchy of elements within a list, creating structures with varying degrees of complexity. One can access the inner structure of a complex list by nesting car and cdr. For example,

```
(car '((decision approve) smith 50000))
   (decision approve)

(cadr '((decision approve) smith 50000))
   approve
```

In this example, the cadr first applies car to the list to get (decision approve), it then applies cdr to the result to get approve. One can use as many a and d as needed in c...r to access the hierarchy of lists within lists of an s-expression. There are many more Lisp functions to manipulate lists in Lisp.

Among other important built-in functions in Lisp are setq, and, or, cond, and defun. To see how these functions work, consider the following example:

```
'(credit good)
'(> ratio 1.5)
'(assets some)
'(job steady)

(defun decision (X)
   (cond   (and (credit good)
                (> ratio 1.5)
                (assets some)
                (job steady))    t
          t                (setq X approve)
          t                '(the decision is))))
```

In this example, the **defun** function defines a function with the name decision and the parameter list (X). The body of the function follows the parameter list. In the body of this function, **cond** specifies the set of conditions to be satisfied in the form of

```
(cond <condition 1>  <test 1>
      <condition 2>  <test 2>
      . . . . . .    . . . . . .
      <condition n>  <test n>)
```

The **cond** checks the first condition with the test value; if it succeeds, it goes to the next condition, otherwise it returns the test value of the last test value.

Case: Gate Scheduler

If you think you've got a complicated scheduling problem, try coordinating all the gates with their respective flights at a major airport. As if the coordination weren't difficult enough, a single delayed or canceled flight can have repercussions for the entire airport and its gate schedule. Strangely enough, this facet of airport management is one of the most underautomated processes in the friendly skies.

Texas Air has a better way to solve the problem. Its GateKeeper system, which is written in Common Lisp and runs on VAXs and 386-based PCs, helps personnel design and maintain gate schedules in real time. GateKeeper's database has access to flight arrival/departure, passenger, maintenance, and routing data, and features a knowledge base that captures information about gate layout, airplane prep, and other constraints. It formulates a gate-schedule scheme, typically for a single airport day.

GateKeeper's most valuable feature, however, is its ability to modify schedules in real time. The system has a parser that processes messages from airport networks, which it stores in its database. GateKeeper can also verify the accuracy of entered data and will detect contradictory or erroneous information.

By Justin Kestelyn, "Application Watch," *AI Expert*, June 1991, p. 64, reprinted with permission from *AI Expert*.

The cond function can have complex conditions. In the preceding example, the first condition itself consists of a number of s-expressions within an and function, which behaves as an "and" connective—it fails and returns nil if one of its conditions does not hold. Otherwise, it returns the value of its last condition. The function or succeeds once one of its conditions becomes true, and returns the value of that term.

In Lisp, t is the key word for true, and nil stands for false. Furthermore, anything that is not nil is considered a true value. Thus, the fact that Lisp or and and return values that are neither true nor false does not create obstacles in programming of knowledge represented in predicate calculus. However, this has been a source of continuing controversy about the language.

Going back to the above example, once the and function succeeds, the setq function puts the parameter of the function equal to approve, and creates the list '(the decision is), which is the last term in the cond function. The function returns the value of its parameter as approve. Note that the use of t forces the second and third terms of the cond function to always be true.

Lisp has numerous built-in functions, and complex and recursive capabilities. This brief review is intended to highlight the fact that programming an expert system in Lisp is similar to programming in any other language, with the exception that Lisp has the symbolic processing nature that is appropriate for handling the qualitative nature of expert systems.

Lisp and Prolog are languages that are commonly used in programming expert systems. However, non-AI languages, such as C and Pascal, have also been used in programming expert systems. The common feature of all such programming is that the developer must design and program the expert system from scratch.

Conclusion

Although the theory of mathematical logic has provided expert systems with theoretical validity, it is the software that has made expert systems a practical decision making tool.

The expert system developer has the choice of programming the system from scratch using a programming language, or relying on one of many expert system software products, which have built-in facilities common in such applications. In Chapter 7, the aspects of "make" or "buy" decisions in developing an expert system are discussed. The common features of expert system products are listed in detail in Chapter 12.

In this chapter, we introduced the typical options available to a developer in the form of software products and languages. More specifically, this chapter introduced an expert system software product (LEVEL5) and the two major languages developed for programming an expert system from scratch: Prolog and Lisp.

The reasoning mechanism and user interface of expert systems have many features in common. Hence, it is quite natural to have expert system products in which these common features are already built-in, and the developer does not have to reinvent the wheel by programming them from scratch. This chapter reviewed these features in LEVEL5. First, the general and essential features of the software were discussed, and then a hands-on review showed how to edit, compile, and run the system. LEVEL5 has a default user interface and additional facilities for enhancing the default user interface. The chapter also reviewed control statements, outside hooks, and other features of LEVEL5. In Chapter 10, we show the enhancement of this product, called LEVEL5 OBJECT, which combines the logical and object-oriented knowledge representation methods.

Prolog and Lisp were briefly reviewed here. These languages are used to program the knowledge base, inference engine, and user interface, although Prolog has a built-in inference mechanism.

References

Information Builders Inc. 1990. *LEVEL5 User Manual, PC Version 1.3,* Information Builders Inc., New York, NY.

Marcus, Claudia. 1986. *Prolog Programming: Applications for Database Systems, Expert Systems and Natural Language Systems*, Addison-Wesley, Reading, MA.

Winston, Patrick Henry and Horn, Berthold Klaus Paul. 1989. *Lisp*, third edition, Addison-Wesley, Reading, MA.

Questions

5.1 Describe the general features of LEVEL5.

5.2 What is the difference between the user interface and the user-interface development? Discuss it using the features of LEVEL5.

5.3 Discuss additional user development tools that you, as a developer, may wish to see added to LEVEL5.

5.4 Why is it a good idea to declare the type of facts in LEVEL5?

5.5 What are the outside hooks in LEVEL5? What is the significance of outside hooks in the business applications of expert systems?

5.6 Discuss the significance of interaction between expert systems and database systems in the business applications of expert systems.

5.7 How does LEVEL5 treat uncertainty in the knowledge base?

5.8 What is the function of **THRESHOLD** in LEVEL5? What happens if we increase it? What happens if we decrease it?

5.9 How can a developer inform the user of the level of confidence of a fact or conclusion in LEVEL5?

5.10 Discuss the advantages and disadvantages of using an expert system product like LEVEL5 as opposed to programming the application in Prolog or Lisp.

5.11 What features, if any, in Prolog and Lisp make them superior to the conventional languages in programming expert systems?

5.12 Compare and contrast Prolog and Lisp. Discuss the applications in which one language has an advantage over the other.

5.13 What is the significance of pattern matching and unification in Prolog?

5.14 What is a Horn clause? What is its relevance in Prolog?

5.15 Lisp is said to be a functional language and Prolog a declarative language. Identify the major features in the two languages that would justify such labels.

5.16 Why is the symbol ' (or the function quote) needed in Lisp?

5.17 Describe defun and cond functions in Lisp.

5.18 Do the and and or functions in Lisp behave differently from the conjunctive and disjunctive connectives in mathematical logic?

Problems

5.1 In the example in this chapter, write the rules for the subgoal 2.1 in LEVEL5.

```
2. the decision IS reject

2.1 the anti-discrimination checks are made
```

5.2 Develop a prototype for the job applicant expert system in LEVEL5.

5.3 Assume we have the following Prolog statements in the knowledge base. Discuss what Prolog's answer will be if you enter decision(smith,reject) at the Prolog interpreter's prompt.

```
job(X, unsteady) :- has_job(X, no), assets(X,none).

job(X, unsteady) :- has_job(X, yes), years_at_job(Y),

                    <(Y,2).

decision(X, reject) :- job(X,unsteady).

the facts for Smith are:

has_job(smith, yes).

years_at_job(1).
```

5.4 What is the difference between credit rating is good and credit rating IS good? How does LEVEL5 prompt for the value of these two facts?

5.5 Write the Prolog statements for the realistic determination of an applicant's credit rating in the mortgage loan case in this chapter.

5.6   Assume you are given the following in Lisp. What does Lisp return in each case?

```
(car '((decision approve) (loan 100000)))

(cdr '((decision approve) (loan 100000)))

(cadr '((decision approve) (loan 100000)))
```

5.7   Identify a decision problem for which an expert system is an appropriate tool, and develop a prototype for the system in LEVEL5.

5.8   Code the following statements in LEVEL5 for an expert system that checks the qualification of job applicants. The goal of the system is to establish whether or nor the applicant qualifies for a job in the company. "If the job applicant is educated in accounting, marketing, or MIS, then he/she has the right education for the job. The applicant is considered to have the required experience if he/she has 2 or more years in accounting, marketing, or MIS. If the applicant does not have experience in accounting, marketing, or MIS, then he/she must have 4 or more years of experience. To qualify for the job, the applicant should have both the right education and the required experience. If an applicant does not have the right education to qualify for the job, he/she must have at least 10 years of experience in accounting, marketing, or MIS."

Case: Expert System for University Admission Office

The admission of undergraduate and graduate students at the university requires a number of criteria, and a series of rules to handle exceptional cases. Furthermore, the decision for the eligibility of the applicant for financial aid and loans is another aspect of the admission process.

The intended goal of the system is to identify the university applicants who either meet the minimum requirements for the university admission or fall into one of the exceptional categories. Such applicants are called "potentially acceptable." If an applicant is potentially acceptable, and has applied for financial assistance or loan, the system must determine the eligibility of the applicant for financial aid.

Imagine that you are the admission officer of your university. Develop rules for identifying the potentially acceptable applicants, code the rules in LEVEL5, and create a system that implements your rules.

Case: Expert System Application in Human Services

In California, the Merced County Agency of Human Services was losing ground to a bureaucratic paper chase: social workers were spending more time transcribing as many as 1,500 pieces of information, figuring out which of the more than 1,000 kinds of forms needed to be completed for each case, and rechecking calculations against a stockpile of regulation manuals, than interviewing and helping their clients. Morale was low, and staff turnovers reached 35 percent a year. The cost of constantly training replacements became an additional burden to the county. The welfare-eligibility system was simply not working.

Merced County turned to Chicago-based Anderson Consulting to develop an expert system that would quickly and efficiently determine client eligibility and keep a continuing file on each case. The end result became the Merced Automated Global Information Control (MAGIC) system.

Working with a knowledge base of a social worker's reasoning, MAGIC develops individual interviews for applicants and chooses appropriate questions for social workers to ask. Working from the answers, the system decides what additional information is needed. MAGIC relieves social workers of having to transcribe the information and calculate eligibility. According to Rita Kidd, Merced County's project director for MAGIC, "The flow of information is more uniform and complete. MAGIC is truly a self-guiding system."

Bob Carlson, senior manager at Anderson Consulting, states, "We had three visions for Merced County: increase service delivery, manage the quality of delivery more effectively, and present clients with more equitable decisions." MAGIC determines eligibility immediately after the interview and generates payments the next day. It solved the logistical problem of sharing client information among several workers in each eligibility area (aid to dependent children, food stamps, medical care, foster care, and emergency and refugee assistance) by letting one person access necessary information across all areas for a single household. Clients find the results fair because a computer has reached an arbitrary conclusion.

Anderson Consulting employed the ADS knowledge-system shell by Aion because it was appropriate for this rule-intensive application and would best handle the implementation of the rule-based processing. Part of the program was written in C. MAGIC runs on the HP UNIX and PCs, but can integrate with mainframes. MAGIC was built to be scalable; instead of investing on a mainframe, the county can add more servers or workstations to handle larger workloads. Since its initial installation in August 1990, MAGIC has gone through several revisions. Once operating on 2,500 rules, MAGIC now handles 5,500 rules.

Based on an independent assessment by Ernst and Young, Merced County is projected to save $4–6 million for 1991 at the county, state, and federal levels. The savings include operational costs, errors in benefit payments, management, recruitment and training supervision, and staff reduction. Social workers who once labored over 168 cases for 90 households can ably manage 300–500 cases for 240 households.

Because of the reduction in job-related stress, staff turnovers have decreased to 16 percent annually. Even training replacements have been cost-effective because MAGIC is user friendly.

MAGIC is turning out to be a success story for Merced County and a model system for other social-service agencies to emulate. Indeed, 57 counties in California are looking into MAGIC, which handles 1 percent of the state's welfare-eligibility caseload. As Carlson notes, "You need a vision to build a smart system."

Condensed from "Application Watch: Helping People Help People," by Patty Enrado, *AI Expert*, October 1991, p. 64, reprinted with permission from *AI Expert*.

Case Questions

1. Imagine that you live in a society with an ideal welfare system (your ideal). Develop rules that determine the eligibility of applicants for the areas mentioned in the case.

2. Create a prototype for your ideal welfare expert system using LEVEL5.

3. Interview a welfare officer in your area and come up with the eligibility rule for food stamps.

4. Implement your answer to Question 3 in LEVEL5.

5. Discuss the type of user interface needed for an expert system in the area of human services.

6. Discuss other areas in human and community services where the application of an expert system could be helpful in improving the quality and efficiency of services.

7. Discuss possible positive and negative reactions welfare employees may have toward the deployment of expert systems on their jobs.

8. What are possible organizational impediments in deploying an expert system in a welfare office?

CHAPTER 6

Inductive Reasoning
with 1st-CLASS

"Data! Data! Data!" he cried impatiently. "I can't make bricks without clay."

Sherlock Holmes in *The Adventure of Copper Beeches*,

by Sir Arthur Conan Doyle

No data yet.... It is a capital mistake to theorize before you have all the evidence. It biases the judgement.

Sherlock Holmes in *A Study in Scarlet*, by Sir Arthur Conan Doyle

Chapter Objectives

The objectives of this chapter are:

- To demonstrate the working of an inductive method in expert systems via the use of 1st-CLASS

- To show how one can obtain production rules from the decision tree, created by 1st-CLASS

KEY WORDS: 1st-CLASS, 1st-CLASS screens, 1st-CLASS methods, modular processing, development tools

---

This chapter could be used with the demonstration diskettes attached to this book for hands-on experiments with the 1st-CLASS software tool. Those who prefer to have a general understanding of the tool without practicing with the diskettes can read the chapter and refer to the figures, which demonstrate the working of the software.

Introduction

Chapter 6 continues the hands-on experience in creating prototype expert systems, this time with a software product that is based on ID3, an inductive reasoning method. The software in which ID3 is embedded is called 1st-CLASS. We continue to use the mortgage loan case here, and guide the reader to create a prototype mortgage loan system using 1st-CLASS. There is enough coverage of 1st-CLASS to make the use of a software manual unnecessary for the purpose of this chapter.

Since 1st-CLASS is an inductive method, the input to the system is the data from the observed cases. The output of the system is a decision tree that can be used for making inferences about new cases. Furthermore, we can use the decision tree to find out the rules on which the inference is based. For this reason, one can use 1st-CLASS to help develop rules for a rule-based expert system.

The case boxes in this chapter report expert system applications that have a heavier emphasis on data. They provide you with a sample of areas in which you can use the inductive method for creating an expert system.

6.1 General Features of 1st-CLASS

1st-CLASS was developed by Hapgood (at Programs in Motion, later named 1st-CLASS) and subsequently acquired by AICorp (Waltham, MA). It uses an inductive reasoning approach, and is based on the ID3 method, discussed in Chapter 4 and Appendix A. This product is user-friendly and easy to learn. With all its ease of use and simplicity, this product offers a valuable tool for knowledge acquisition and inductive learning.

6.1.1　Input Requirements for 1st-CLASS

As with any inductive-based method, 1st-CLASS does not require the developer to have formulated rules for the knowledge base. Instead, it requires data for the representative cases within the knowledge domain. This is its major difference from the deductive-based software discussed in Chapter 5, where the rules must be developed before the software can be used. In 1st-CLASS, the input consists of raw data on representative cases.

In its data requirements, 1st-CLASS may resemble statistical software, which uses data as input. However, the data requirement in 1st-CLASS differs from that of statistical methods in an important way. In statistics, the data is a random sample of the population under study. In 1st-CLASS, there is nothing random in the selection of case data.

The input data to 1st-CLASS should represent all possible outcomes, and the developer should be confident about the reliability and exhaustiveness of data. Although 1st-CLASS does take into account the possibility of less than certain data, the method used in the product, ID3, considers data as certain. Thus, the inclusion of the uncertainty in 1st-CLASS is ad hoc, as it is in most existing expert system products.

The developer, with the assistance of the expert, must select representative cases and identify the important factors contributing to the decision. Consider the mortgage loan case, for example. The developer must collect representative cases that cover all possible circumstances leading to the rejection or approval of a mortgage loan. Furthermore, the developer and the expert must determine all possible factors that might have influenced the decision. The input data consists of the raw data on these factors in each selected case.

In sum, the input requirements for 1st-CLASS are the decision-related data and outcomes for the cases that represent the knowledge domain.

6.1.2   Processing in 1st-CLASS

1st-CLASS requires that the developer enter the factor names and data types, as well as the interface texts. It then prompts the developer to enter the data. The software builds the decision tree, as described in Appendix A. Once the developer and the expert feel the decision tree satisfactorily models the knowledge domain, the system could be used for reasoning and making decisions in solving new cases.

The product allows for uncertainty in data. The developer or the expert could attach a certainty weight (between 0 and 1) to the data for each case. Furthermore, the system permits conflicting data. For example, two cases with identical values for factors may have two different decision outcomes. The system chooses the case that has the highest certainty weight.

An interesting feature of 1st-CLASS is the possibility of designing modular knowledge bases. This feature allows the developer to start with a simple prototype that can be expanded later by chaining each factor to a knowledge base of its own.

Once the decision tree is created, the system is ready for making inference. Entering the reasoning process is simple and straightforward. 1st-CLASS matches the data of a new case with the branches of the decision tree. Once it finds a match, it uses the decision of that branch as the recommended decision.

Case: Insurance Underwriting

The Travelers developed and deployed a Medical Underwriting Advisor, built in 1st-CLASS FUSION for the IBM PC, to assist in individually screening the 125,000 group-policy applications the company receives each year.

Lay underwriters with little medical experience previously screened applicants according to guidelines for more than 80 medical conditions, each involving a variety of restrictions factored into the underwriting decision. Particularly complex cases were routed to professional underwriters with medical backgrounds. The Travelers decided to develop an expert system that would assist in training, reduce referrals to professional underwriters, and improve turnaround and underwriting quality.

The Medical Underwriting Advisor was developed in 1st-CLASS FUSION by one knowledge engineer; total development time was about nine months. The user examines one of 80 medical conditions and the Advisor returns the condition's underwriting implications. Alternatively, a case study can be set up and the system will ask basic medical questions. The user may then examine a particular condition, and the Advisor will ask concluding questions and produce advice. The system comprises 145 knowledge bases and more than 800 rules.

The Travelers estimates the Medical Underwriting Advisor will improve underwriting by at least $1 million per year.

By Justin Kestelyn, "Application Watch," *AI Expert*, March 1990, p. 72, reprinted with permission from *AI Expert*.

6.2 Working with 1st-CLASS

To show how 1st-CLASS works, we use the mortgage loan case introduced in the previous chapters. Assume that we have collected data for 14 representative loan cases. We have chosen a small number of cases so that we can input them using the tutorial diskette available for this book. Assume that the expert has identified four major decision factors: JOB, CREDIT, ASSETS, and INCOME. Now we are ready to enter this prototype into the system.

We start the system by entering the name of the file with the extension ".exe" (the name varies depending on whether we are using the tutorial diskette or the full version of the product). The system has six basic screens, and one can travel back and forth between these six screens by using function keys F9 to move to the previous screen, and F10 to move to the next screen. We will go through the screens for the mortgage loan case introduced in the previous chapters.

6.2.1 First Screen: Files

When the system starts, the first screen appears, as shown in Figure 6.1 This screen offers a number of options, which are identified on the first line of the

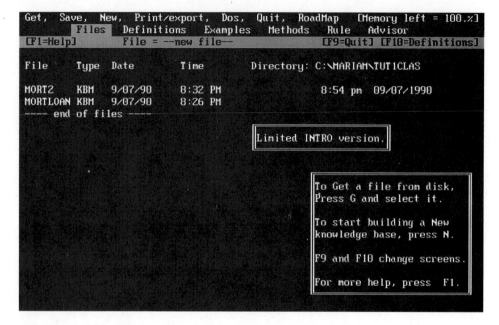

Figure 6.1   The First Screen in 1st-CLASS

screen. You can get, save, or start new files (the first three options) from this screen. You also can exit the system by choosing **Q**, the sixth option on this screen.

- Choose **New**.

- This creates a new file that will contain the knowledge base; call it mortloan.

When you save this file, it will appear as mortloan.kbm in the directory where you have saved the file. F1 is the help key in this screen.

6.2.2   Second Screen: Definitions

Using F10 moves you to the second screen, as shown in Figure 6.2. In this screen, the factors and their value types are defined for the system. The system always requires a result factor, which corresponds to the outcome or decision for each case. The options for this screen are shown on the first line of the screen. Factors and their allowable values are entered by selecting **F** (for Factor) and **V** (for Value).

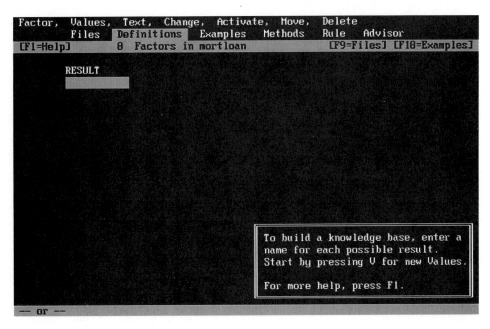

Figure 6.2   The Second Screen in 1st-CLASS

- Move the highlight to RESULT with up arrow key (↑).

- Enter C for the Change option. The system asks you for a new name to replace the default name RESULT.

- Enter DECISION. You have now changed the factor name.

- Enter approve and then reject in response to the system's prompt for possible values of the DECISION factor. Since you are done with this factor, just hit the return key to return to the Definitions screen. Your screen should now look like the one shown in Figure 6.3.

- Enter the factors and their allowable values, as shown in Figure 6.4.

Notice that the allowable values of factors in this example are all non-numeric. It is possible to have numeric values: you would not enter any value for the factor when the software prompts you for a value. By simply

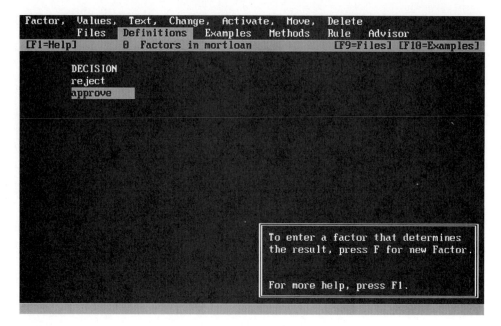

Figure 6.3   Changing the Name of the RESULT Factor

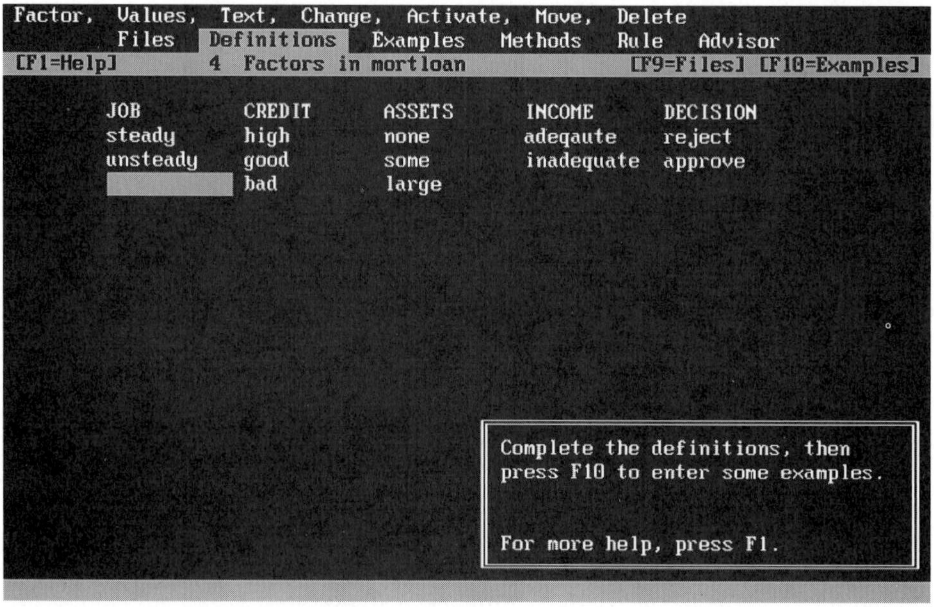

Figure 6.4   The Factors for the Mortgage Loan Case

hitting the return key, the data type of the factor would be designated as numerical.

You can change and delete a factor or an allowable value by highlighting it with one of the arrow keys, and entering the letter C or D to Change or Delete what is highlighted.

Another interesting option of this screen is Text. It is used to enter a descriptive text that the user sees when the system requests information for the factor or its value.

- Highlight the ASSETS factor, and enter T for Text. An editor appears. Enter the message shown in Figure 6.5.

- Save the content by pressing F10.

This editor has limited text-editing capabilities. One can also create links to hypertext using this editor.

The full version of 1st-CLASS has a default factor called Memo. The developer can enter text for this factor, which the user would see as a preface to starting the system.

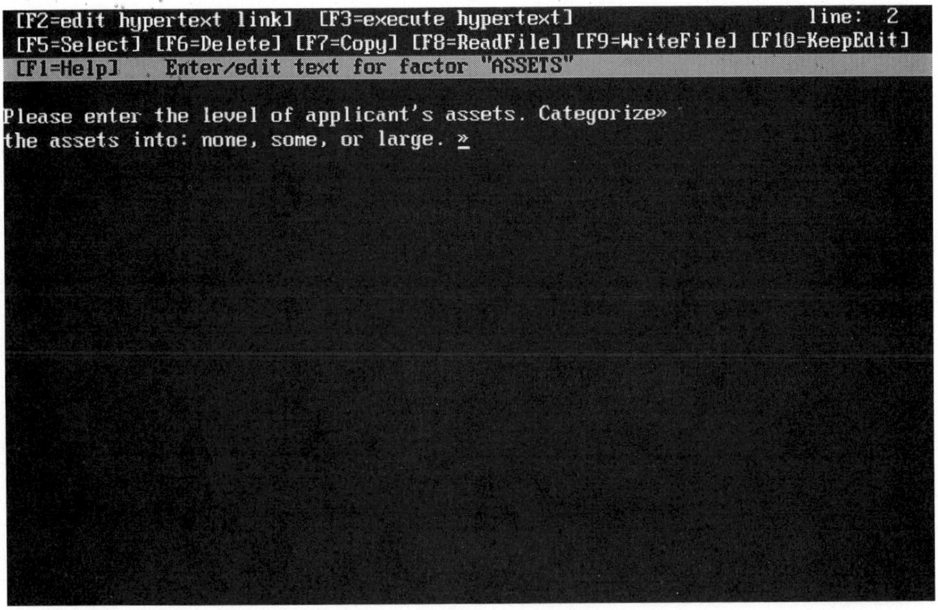

Figure 6.5 The Editor for Creating Interface Messages

6.2.3   Third Screen: Examples

Moving to the next screen with F10, we get an empty table, with the factor names as headings for its columns, as shown in Figure 6.6. This screen is designed to get the data for representative cases from the developer.

This screen contains one column called **Weight**, which is not one of the factors from the previous screen. This column represents the confidence weight for each row of data, which represents a given case. The allowable values for this column are between 0 and 1, and the default value is 1. If the expert or developer of the system is uncertain about the validity of a case, a value lower than 1 should be assigned to the weight of that case. The **Weight** column is part of the treatment of uncertainty in 1st-CLASS, which is discussed in a later section in this chapter.

- Enter **E** (for **Example**) to enter a row of data.

- The system prompts you to enter the allowable values for each factor. Highlight the correct value with the arrow key and hit the return key. Use the data in Figure 6.7 to enter the data for the mortgage loan case.

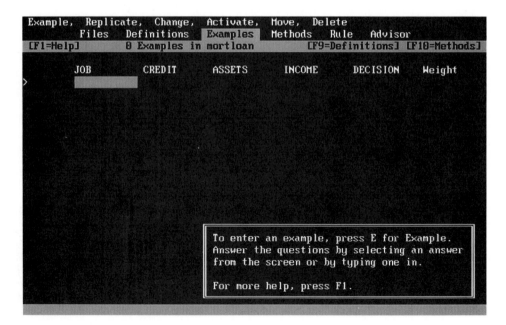

Figure 6.6   The Examples Screen Prior to Data Entry

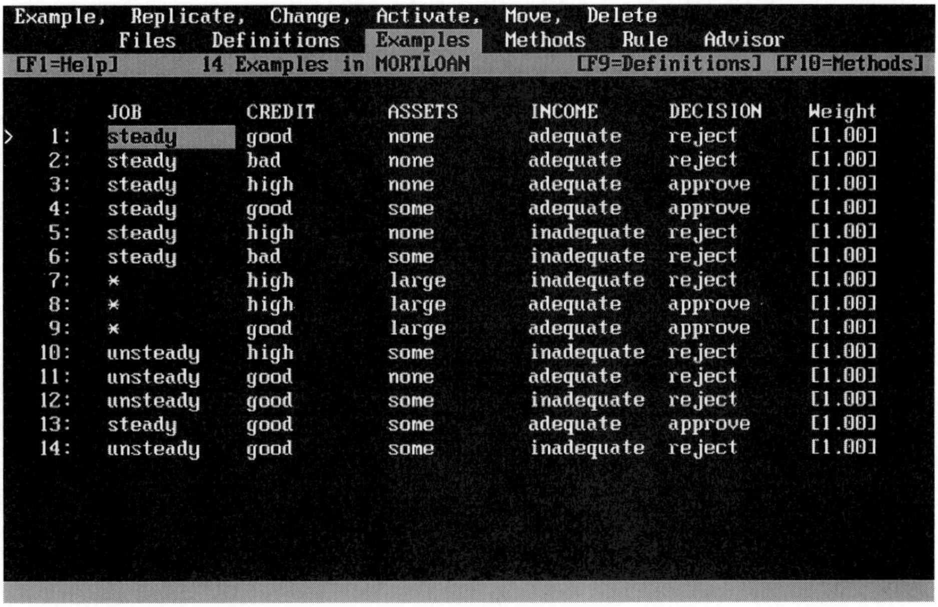

Example, Replicate, Change, Activate, Move, Delete
        Files   Definitions   Examples   Methods   Rule   Advisor
[F1=Help]   14 Examples in MORTLOAN   [F9=Definitions] [F10=Methods]

		JOB	CREDIT	ASSETS	INCOME	DECISION	Weight
>	1:	steady	good	none	adequate	reject	[1.00]
	2:	steady	bad	none	adequate	reject	[1.00]
	3:	steady	high	none	adequate	approve	[1.00]
	4:	steady	good	some	adequate	approve	[1.00]
	5:	steady	high	none	inadequate	reject	[1.00]
	6:	steady	bad	some	inadequate	reject	[1.00]
	7:	*	high	large	inadequate	reject	[1.00]
	8:	*	high	large	adequate	approve	[1.00]
	9:	*	good	large	adequate	approve	[1.00]
	10:	unsteady	high	some	inadequate	reject	[1.00]
	11:	unsteady	good	none	adequate	reject	[1.00]
	12:	unsteady	good	some	inadequate	reject	[1.00]
	13:	steady	good	some	adequate	approve	[1.00]
	14:	unsteady	good	some	inadequate	reject	[1.00]

Figure 6.7   The Data for the Mortgage Loan Case

One can change any data item by highlighting it with the arrow keys and entering C (for Change). The system prompts you to select from one of the allowable values. You can also delete the entire row by highlighting one of the elements, and entering D (for Delete).

When the value of a factor is irrelevant for a particular case, one can enter the * symbol. In the example in Figure 6.7, the (*) in rows 7, 8, and 9 indicates that JOB factor is irrelevant for the case of an applicant who has a high or good rating for CREDIT and has a large amount of ASSETS. Note that the system allows you to have identical examples, such as examples 4 and 13 in Figure 6.7.

6.2.4   Fourth Screen: Methods

Pressing F10 takes us forward to the next screen. In this screen, the system developer selects the method for producing the decision tree. The ID3 method is option O (for Optimize) in this screen. Other methods are discussed in a later section in this chapter.

- Select O, and save what you have entered when the system prompts you to do so. Your screen should now look like the one shown in Figure 6.8.

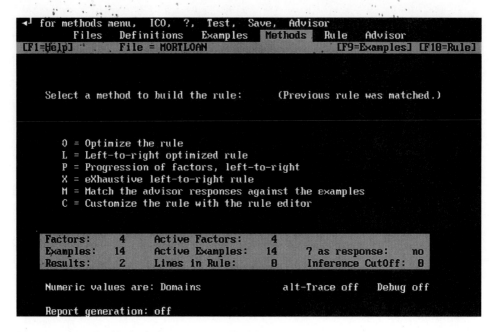

Figure 6.8   The Methods Screen in 1st-CLASS

This screen contains a summary of the knowledge base. It reports the number of factors, the number of examples, and the number of possible decisions. In some cases, one may make some examples or factors Inactive by choosing the Activate option in the Definitions and Examples screens. This option toggles between activation and deactivation. In such cases, the number of Active Factors or Active Examples would be less than what the developer has entered in the previous screen. This option allows the system developer to test the sensitivity of results with respect to a factor or a row of examples.

Furthermore, 1st-CLASS allows for "I don't know" as a valid response. This is shown as the ? symbol in this screen. By entering a (?), such an answer becomes acceptable to the system. This option is turned on and off by entering (?). However, using this option has an impact on the method of producing the decision tree, which is discussed later.

6.2.5   Fifth Screen: Rule

This screen shows the decision tree that results from the application of the selected method in the previous screen. For the mortgage loan case, Figure 6.9 shows the computed decision tree.

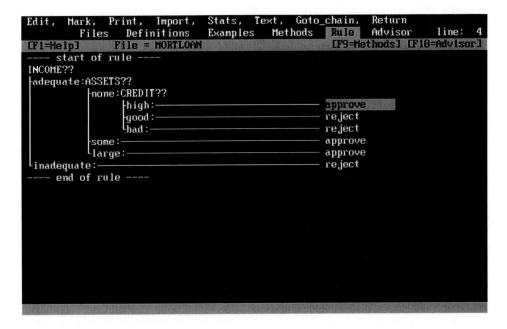

Figure 6.9   The Decision Tree for the Mortgage Loan Case

An examination of the decision tree in Figure 6.9 reveals that the JOB factor has no role in the decision process. The CREDIT factor is important only when the applicant has no assets.

The decision tree results directly from the application of ID3 to the factors and examples used in building the system. This is where the completeness of factors and examples makes a significant impact. In this example, when the applicant has adequate income and some assets, the loan is approved without considering the credit rating of the applicant. One may conclude that although the expert claims the credit rating is important, he/she does not use it in all cases. That is, the data does not support the expert's claim. Another interpretation could be that the example set does not contain sufficiently diverse cases. An examination of Figure 6.7 reveals that there is only one case in which the applicant has some assets and the credit rating is bad. This lack of adequate examples could have caused the exclusion of CREDIT as a decision factor when the applicant has some assets.

The preceding discussion indicates that the system developer must closely examine the structure of the decision tree, and test its sensitivity with respect to adding or deleting new factors and examples. As discussed in Chapter 7, the expert must play an active role in identifying factors and examples, as well as in the analysis of the decision tree produced by the software. One can perform sensitivity analysis by using the **Activate** option of the **Definitions** and **Examples** screens.

The **Rule** screen has a number of options, as shown on the first line in Figure 6.9. The developer can edit the decision tree or print it. The **Stat** option gives additional information about the decision tree.

- In the **Rule** screen, move the highlight bar to the first leaf of the decision tree, and enter **S** (for **Stat** option) to get the screen shown in Figure 6.10.

The following discussion is the interpretation of the statistics given in Figure 6.10. Some of the statistics pertain to the highlighted leaf on the decision tree, and some are true for the whole of the decision tree. The names of the system variables needed to access these statistics start with "$$" followed by single digits 1–9.

- Active examples: 14 means that all 14 examples are used in generating the decision tree. If one deactivates any of the examples, this number would be reduced. The variable name for the number of active examples is $$1.

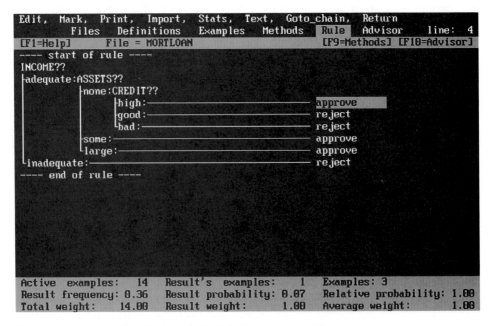

Figure 6.10   The Stat Option of the Rule Screen in 1st-CLASS

- **Result's examples:** 1 means that there is one row in the example set which contains the factors that lead to the highlighted leaf, i.e., **adequate** income, **none** for assets, and **high** for credit rating. The system variable name for this statistic is $$2.

- **Examples:** 3 indicates that the row number (3) is the basis of the branch with the highlighted leaf. The system variable name for this statistic is $$3.

- **Result frequency:** 0.36 means that of 14 examples, 5 (36%) have **approve** as the decision. More accurately, the result frequency is the sum of the weights of the examples with **approve** as decision divided by the sum of all weights. The system variable name for this statistic is $$4.

- **Result probability** shows the relative weight of the branch leading to the highlighted leaf with respect to the sum of all weights in the example set, here 1/14. The system variable name for this statistic is $$5.

- **Relative probability** is a number other than 1, used when there are conflicting decisions for the same values of factors in the example set. In this case, the decision tree shows the conflicting decisions (one with a solid line and the rest with broken lines). The relative probability of each is the ratio of the weights of those examples that produce the branch with respect to the total weights of all examples, relevant to the branch under consideration. The system variable name for this statistic is $$6.

- **Total weight:** 14 shows the sum of the numbers in the **Weight** column of the **Examples** screen. The system variable name for this statistic is $$7.

- **Result weight** shows the total weights of the examples used to arrive at the highlighted leaf. Here, there is only one example with weight 1. However, if there were 4 examples for this leaf, each with a weight of 1, the result's weight would be 4. The system variable name for this statistic is $$8.

- **Average weight** is the result's weight (discussed above) divided by the number of examples used for the highlighted leaf. The system variable name for this statistic is $$9.

The developer can access and inform the user of the values of any of these nine statistics by incorporating their variable names within the text attached to a factor or its values. In this manner, the developer can design the interface such that the user is informed of some or all of these nine statistics.

- To see how one can inform the user of the statistics of the results, attach the following text to the **DECISION** factor: "The decision has an average certainty weight of $$9. A total number of $$1 examples was used to produce this result. The relative weight of examples with a similar decision outcome is $$4."

To see how these statistics would change when the weights are less than one, we experiment by changing some of the weights in the example set in a later section of this chapter.

6.2.6   Sixth Screen: Advisor

Using F10 moves us forward to the next screen, the **Advisor** screen. This screen runs the system based on the decision tree that was derived in the previous screen, and prompts the user for answers. In doing so, the screen displays the text attached to the factors or values that were created in the Definitions screen. For example, in Figure 6.5, we created the text attached to the factor **ASSETS**. If we run the system from the **Advisor** screen, we can see that when the system asks for the value of the factor **ASSETS**, it uses the text to prompt the user, as shown in Figure 6.11, while giving the user

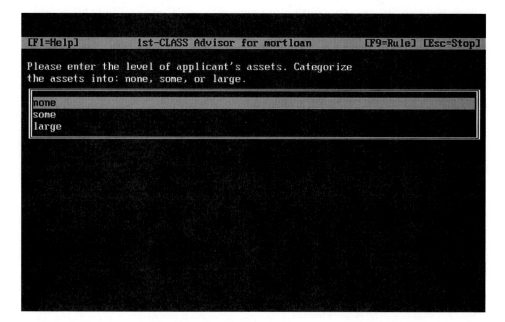

Figure 6.11   The Advisor Screen Using the Text Attached to the Factor ASSETS

the choice of one of the three allowable values for this factor. Attaching a text to a value changes the prompt for that particular allowable value.

- As an exercise, attach texts to the allowable values of ASSETS so that they become more meaningful for the user, and run the Advisor to see the outcome.

The full version of the software has the capability of running the Advisor while getting the input from a file, rather than in an interactive mode. Furthermore, one can output the outcome into a file by activating the Report generation option in the Methods screen. These options are useful when the system is being verified and validated, as discussed in Chapter 7.

6.3 Treatment of Uncertainty in 1st-CLASS (Optional)

We see from the preceding discussion that the treatment of uncertainty in 1st-CLASS is via a weight assignment to each example. To see this, we change the weights of some examples and observe the results of these changes.

- Use F9 to go back to the Examples screen. Highlight and use C (for Change) to change the first three values in the Weights column, as shown in Figure 6.12.

- Go to the Methods screen and optimize (which applies the ID3 method to the example set).

- Go to the Rule screen. Enter S to get the statistics screen as shown in Figure 6.13.

In Figure 6.13, the result frequency ($$4) has changed to 0.35 because the total weight is now 13.40 and the sum of the examples with approve as the decision is 4.70. Thus, we have

$$\frac{4.70}{13.40} = 0.35.$$

Similarly, the result probability is now 0.05, which is the ratio of 0.70 to the total weight 13.4. Observe that $$7, $$8, and $$9 have also changed.

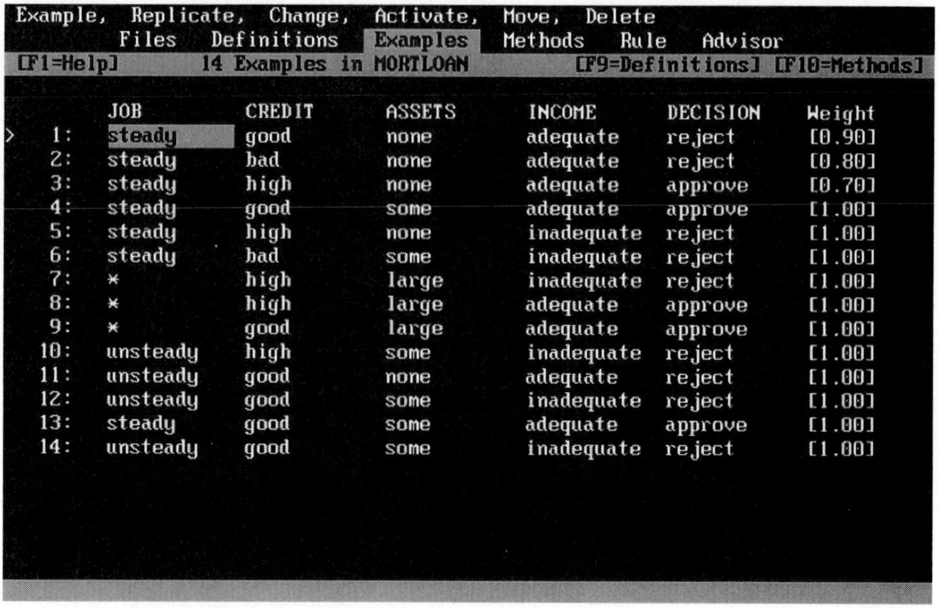

```
Example, Replicate, Change, Activate, Move, Delete
        Files   Definitions  Examples   Methods   Rule   Advisor
[F1=Help]          14 Examples in MORTLOAN          [F9=Definitions] [F10=Methods]

            JOB         CREDIT      ASSETS      INCOME        DECISION    Weight
>    1:   steady       good        none        adequate      reject      [0.90]
     2:   steady       bad         none        adequate      reject      [0.80]
     3:   steady       high        none        adequate      approve     [0.70]
     4:   steady       good        some        adequate      approve     [1.00]
     5:   steady       high        none        inadequate    reject      [1.00]
     6:   steady       bad         some        inadequate    reject      [1.00]
     7:   *            high        large       inadequate    reject      [1.00]
     8:   *            high        large       adequate      approve     [1.00]
     9:   *            good        large       adequate      approve     [1.00]
    10:   unsteady     high        some        inadequate    reject      [1.00]
    11:   unsteady     good        none        adequate      reject      [1.00]
    12:   unsteady     good        some        inadequate    reject      [1.00]
    13:   steady       good        some        adequate      approve     [1.00]
    14:   unsteady     good        some        inadequate    reject      [1.00]
```

Figure 6.12   Changing the Weights in the Loan Case

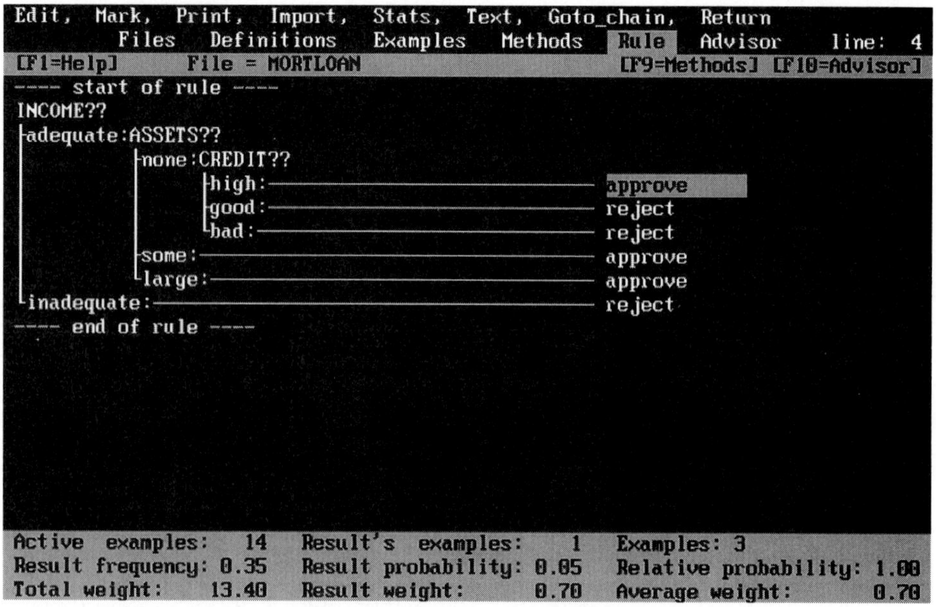

```
Edit,  Mark,  Print,  Import,  Stats,  Text,  Goto_chain,  Return
        Files   Definitions  Examples   Methods   Rule   Advisor    line:  4
[F1=Help]       File = MORTLOAN                      [F9=Methods] [F10=Advisor]
----- start of rule -----
INCOME??
|-adequate:ASSETS??
|           |-none:CREDIT??
|           |      |-high:----------------------------- approve
|           |      |-good:----------------------------- reject
|           |      |-bad:------------------------------ reject
|           |-some:------------------------------------ approve
|           |-large:----------------------------------- approve
|-inadequate:----------------------------------------- reject
----- end of rule -----

Active  examples:   14   Result's  examples:   1   Examples: 3
Result frequency: 0.35   Result probability: 0.05   Relative probability: 1.00
Total weight:    13.40   Result weight:      0.70   Average weight:       0.70
```

Figure 6.13   The Decision Tree for Uncertain Examples

1st-CLASS basically assigns a weight as a certainty factor to each example, and reports the simple sum or average of the weights. Most of the existing products on the market lack a solid treatment of uncertainty, or ignore the topic completely. Given this state of affairs, what 1st-CLASS offers is not below par in the market. However, even this ad hoc treatment of uncertainty could be improved in a number of directions.

The expert should be able to express the extent of uncertainty with respect to one factor of an example. Therefore, the uncertainty of an example's factors should be separated from the uncertainty of the decision in that example. Furthermore, the user should be able to express uncertainty for the facts. When the examples have errors, and conflicting decisions are made for the same set of factor values, there must be a better way of informing the user that errors exist within the example set. More importantly, the ID3 method needs an extension for dealing with errors in data. Because the system has a decision tree structure, it has a natural ability to incorporate any one of the uncertainty methods that use the belief net, as discussed in Chapter 11. We expect to see more development in this area in the future.

6.4 Modular Processing in 1st-CLASS

One of the interesting features of 1st-CLASS is its *modular-processing* feature. This feature allows the developer to divide the knowledge domain into independent modules, create and test these modules separately, and then link them together to create the desired system.

In 1st-CLASS, one can create an expert system prototype by treating a factor as given. Later, one can expand the system by adding more realistic details. Moreover, the decision also could be expanded to include more processing or actions. In 1st-CLASS, connecting the modules together is called backward and forward chaining. Thus, 1st-CLASS has backward and forward chaining in a special form. Let us demonstrate this with the mortgage loan case.

In Figure 6.4, we have INCOME as one of the factors with the allowable values adequate and inadequate. However, the bank officer must observe a number of other factors to establish whether or not the income is adequate. By creating another module, we can include the additional factors that establish the adequacy of the applicant's income. This module will be activated whenever the value of the INCOME factor is needed by the system. This is called backward chaining in 1st-CLASS.

The factor that is chained to another starts with the special character #.

- Go back (F9) to the **Definitions** screen, and change the name of the INCOME factor to #INCOME as shown in Figure 6.14.

Now, we must create the module that produces **adequate** or **inadequate** as its result.

- Save the **mortloan** file on the first screen and open a new knowledge base file called **income**. The name of the file should be the same as the factor for which the backward chaining is designed.

- Create the factor and example screens using the information shown in Figure 6.15.

- Save the **income** file and get the **mortloan** file from the first screen.

- Move forward to the **Advisor** screen and run the system. You will notice that when the system needs a value for the INCOME factor, it prompts you for the factors of the decision tree in the **income** knowledge base.

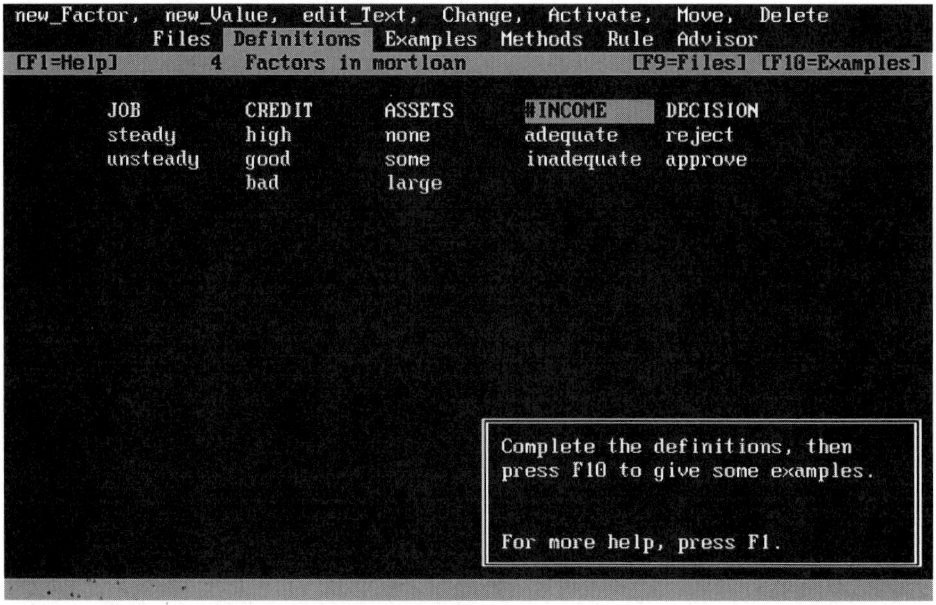

```
new_Factor,  new_Value,  edit_Text,  Change,  Activate,  Move,  Delete
         Files  Definitions  Examples  Methods  Rule  Advisor
[F1=Help]        4  Factors in mortloan              [F9=Files] [F10=Examples]

      JOB          CREDIT       ASSETS      #INCOME      DECISION
      steady       high         none        adequate     reject
      unsteady     good         some        inadequate   approve
                   bad          large


                                      ┌─────────────────────────────────┐
                                      │ Complete the definitions, then   │
                                      │ press F10 to give some examples. │
                                      │                                  │
                                      │ For more help, press F1.         │
                                      └─────────────────────────────────┘
```

Figure 6.14 Backward Chaining for INCOME

```
new_Example,  Replicate,  Change,  Activate,  Move,  Delete
            Files  Definitions  Examples  Methods  Rule  Advisor
[F1=Help]        17 Examples in income          [F9=Definitions] [F10=Methods]

          other loans  loan      net       RESULT      Weight
>   1:    yes          20000.0   1000.0    inadequate  [1.00]
    2:    yes          20000.0   2000.0    adequate    [1.00]
    3:    yes          30000.0   1500.0    inadequate  [1.00]
    4:    yes          30000.0   1200.0    inadequate  [1.00]
    5:    no           30000.0   1500.0    adequate    [1.00]
    6:    no           30000.0   1200.0    adequate    [1.00]
    7:    no           20000.0   1000.0    adequate    [1.00]
    8:    yes          40000.0   1000.0    inadequate  [1.00]
    9:    yes          40000.0   2000.0    adequate    [1.00]
   10:    no           40000.0   1800.0    adequate    [1.00]
   11:    no           40000.0   1200.0    inadequate  [1.00]
   12:    yes          40000.0   1700.0    inadequate  [1.00]
   13:    yes          40000.0   1800.0    inadequate  [1.00]
   14:    yes          30000.0   2000.0    adequate    [1.00]
   15:    yes          50000.0   2000.0    inadequate  [1.00]
   16:    yes          50000.0   2400.0    adequate    [1.00]
   17:    no           50000.0   2000.0    adequate    [1.00]
```

Figure 6.15   The Knowledge Base of INCOME Factor

The process of modularized linking of knowledge bases makes it possible to design the system in modular form. It increases the efficiency of the system because the additional knowledge base and its example set are used only when the system needs a value for a chained factor. It also provides a systematic approach for the progressive expansion of the prototype.

One can also create forward chaining in 1st-CLASS. In this case, the column representing the decision or its allowable values should get # as the starting character. Then, the system developer must create a knowledge base with the same name as the factor or the value.

If the decision column is forward chained, whenever a decision is reached, the system chains forward to the knowledge base and continues from that knowledge base. When a decision value is chained, the forward chain takes place whenever that particular decision is reached.

- To see how forward chaining operates, in the Definitions screen, change the allowable value approve to #approve, and save. Then create a knowledge base that determines the rate of interest for the approved loan, by including the factors such as the amount, type, and duration of the loan.

The RoadMap option (not available in the student version) of the first screen in 1st-CLASS shows a graphical presentation of the chained (forward and backward) modules to the existing knowledge base. Furthermore, the Goto-chain option of the Rule screen allows the developer to go to the chained knowledge base and return with the Return option. Therefore, although the knowledge bases are stored in independent modules, the system developer can have an overall picture of the structure of the modules, and travel through the independent modules without ever exiting the initial knowledge base.

6.5 Other Features in 1st-CLASS

In this section, we briefly review some of the additional features in 1st-CLASS. One feature is a number of methods (other than ID3) that are available to the system developer. The software has additional capabilities for outside hooks and user-interface development.

6.5.1 Methods in 1st-CLASS (Optional)

The Methods screen of 1st-CLASS contains a number of options for methods, other than ID3. The Left-Right method is a modified version of ID3, in which the factors are selected from left to right for the optimization of the ID3. The Exhaustive method uses all factors at every node. That is, every node uses all factors within the system. The Progressive method creates a decision tree with the nodes that consist of a sequence of factors, with no branching. This method is useful for the sequential chaining of a number of knowledge bases. The Customize method allows the developer to create a decision tree (using the Edit option of the Rule screen), regardless of the examples. The Match method does not create any decision tree. It asks for the value of factors. The factors are ordered from left to right on the Definitions or Examples screen. The system matches the user's answers to one of the examples within the example set, and produces the result or decision value for that example. The Match method acts like a database system, because it matches the input data with the record of an example within the system.

The ICO option in the Methods screen allows the system to produce more than one answer when the method is Match. As the system asks questions from the user, it shrinks the set of examples that apply to the case in hand. Normally, the system continues asking questions about factors in order to reduce the applicable example to 1 or 0. If we set the ICO value to, say, 3, the matching process stops when the set of examples relevant to the present case has three examples in it. This is useful when the example data contain errors. Furthermore, when the option of "I don't know" is on (by toggling ? option), and the user answers "I don't know," the system switches to the Match method, and starts matching the user's answers with the examples within the example set. If the value of ICO is 3, it stops when there are only three examples that match the user's answers.

6.5.2   Outside Hooks (Optional)

We have mentioned that 1st-CLASS can store its output into a file. It also can produce output-only as well as output-input hooks to external programs, written in languages such as C, Pascal, FORTRAN, and BASIC.

In the output-only hook, 1st-CLASS calls an external program to produce an output to the screen. In the output-input hook, the external program could also provide the needed value for a factor when the Advisor is working; this becomes an input to 1st-CLASS.

Accessing an outside program is possible with

$$\{CALL \ \ filename \ \ parameters\}$$

and is included within the Text option of a factor (including the result) or value. The curly braces are required to distinguish it from the regular text.

When the external program is expected to input the value of a factor, the developer should identify a memory location on which the external program writes its answer. 1st-CLASS reads the content of the memory by

$$\{READ \ \ \# \ \ FactorName\}$$

which is incorporated in the text. The # symbol denotes the return buffer in memory address. This structure enables 1st-CLASS to communicate with any executable code. It is, however, cumbersome because the developer must know the memory address where the output of the external program is written. Thus, it is easier to have the external program write its output into a file, and then read the value of the factor from the file as:

$$\{READ \ \ FileName \ \ FactorName\}.$$

The curly braces in the Text option of factors and values could be used to open dBASE III and IV files, and to search through them by commands such as SEEK, SEEKP, and GET. The file could be updated with the commands

PUT and APPEND. One can open up to four data files at any time, and can close them with the CLOSE command.

1st-CLASS has the capability to import images. The image should first be imported by the CAPTURE utility. The captured image could be displayed by the CALL command. The command, as with all other outside hooks, is incorporated in curly braces with the Text option of factors or values.

Another outside hook in 1st-CLASS is its ability to export the knowledge base by translating it into source codes written in Pascal, C, or production rules. The conversion is partial in that it only contains the decision tree, and the developer should check the variable names and functions.

6.5.3   Development Tools (Optional)

Development tools are facilities that allow the developer to design custom-made user interfaces, as well as facilities to help the developer in finding errors in the system.

In the user-interface design, we have already seen that the developer can import and display images, and use the Text option to provide information to the user. Within the Text option, the developer can set up hypertext links that allow the user to freely access additional information. The system developer has the option of creating help screens for the user by calling the HELPW utility.

For debugging purposes, we have already seen that the developer can test the sensitivity of the system by using the Activation option. The Memo default factor attached to examples allows the developer to document the system, because this factor contains development notes that have no role in the inference process. (The Memo default factor in the Definitions screen is used to create a title page for the knowledge base.)

Case: Expert System for Sailing Races

Few sporting events have been as profoundly affected by technology as yacht racing. An America's Cup challenge is usually synonymous with publicity for advanced space-age hulls, computer-designed spinnakers, and other cutting-edge innovations. The French entry for the 1992 America's Cup race will feature yet another high-tech yachting application: an on-board, work-station-based expert system. Nemo-America, which was developed by S_2O Developpement of Paris and runs on a Sun SparcStation 1, captures the sailing expertise of yachtsmen.

Yacht racing is a subtle and intricate chess game of tactical moves, countermoves, and parries. Each boat battles for position, trying to steal the adversary's wind and force it to change course and speed. Formulating and countering these tactics can be a baffling task, especially if the navigator is unsure of his or her own boat's exact position (which is a common problem). Furthermore, the crew may be unfamiliar with the waters and prevailing winds.

Nemo-America, which comprises two modules, is designed to work closely with the skipper, navigator, and tactician. The system's Positioning Expert module is crucial in determining the boat's position; it monitors radio waves from the shore and verifies position to within three meters. The system then feeds the radio-wave data into the Tactic Expert module, which contains Nemo-America's knowledge base. The Tactic Expert provides tactical analysis and recommendations on a geographical, diagrammed screen.

As an additional benefit, the system captures knowledge about the America's Cup racing rules and notifies users of rule infractions. Furthermore, the system's memory serves as an audit trail for any potential investigations.

In one demonstration, tactician Marc Bouet and a colleague simulated a race in the waters outlying San Diego harbor. The system instantly loaded the wind, current, and tidal features of the course. (It keeps such data on many well-known courses in its memory.) As the simulated race progressed with Bouet's boat in the lead, the system analyzed the situation, and made recommendations in about three seconds.

By Justin Kestelyn, "Application Watch," *AI Expert*, June 1991, p. 64, reprinted with permission from *AI Expert*.

The developer can use the **Debug** option to record the sequence of events in a file during a session. The **Trace** option allows the developer to see (within a window) what information is being recorded in the debugging file.

The developer has the option to produce a runtime version of the expert system. This version contains the decision tree and the **Advisor**, and lacks the tools for developing a knowledge base. Therefore, it requires less memory and disk space than the development version.

6.6 Using 1st-CLASS

1st-CLASS is based on inductive reasoning. It forms a decision tree from the data, and utilizes the tree for reasoning. Furthermore, 1st-CLASS can be used as a knowledge engineering tool.

6.6.1   *Inductive Reasoning with 1st-CLASS*

Reasoning with 1st-CLASS is straightforward. The system starts with the root of the decision tree, and asks about the value of the factor at the root. Depending on the user's answer, the system chooses one of the branches of the tree, and prompts the user to enter the value of that factor.

For example, consider Figure 6.9. From the decision tree, we know that the first question is about the value of the INCOME factor (assuming that it is not chained yet). If the user responds that the income is inadequate, the last branch of the decision tree is followed with the conclusion that the loan should be rejected. However, if the user selects adequate as the response, then the system prompts for the value of the ASSETS factor. If the user answers none, then the system prompts for the value of CREDIT and arrives at a decision depending on the user's answer.

Although 1st-CLASS does not use the formalism of the IF-THEN rule, it is obvious that the decision tree can be easily converted to rules. For example, the first two branches of the decision tree in Figure 6.9 could be converted into the following two rules:

```
IF   the income is adequate
   AND   there are no assets
   AND   the credit is high
THEN   approve the loan

IF   the income is adequate
   AND   there are no assets
   AND   the credit is good
THEN   reject the loan.
```

Thus, the knowledge representation in 1st-CLASS effectively follows the same rules as the logic-based representation.

6.6.2   *Combining 1st-CLASS with Other Methods*

As we have seen in Chapter 4, the decision tree obtained from ID3 can be used to generate rules as well as predicate methods of knowledge representation. In this sense, 1st-CLASS is not only an inductive-based expert system, but it could also be considered a knowledge acquisition tool. That is, even when the final knowledge base is not stored in 1st-CLASS, it can be used to help the expert discover rules and predicates within the knowledge domain. As we will see in Chapter 7, the inductive method is one of the important methods of modeling and acquiring knowledge, and 1st-CLASS is an effective and simple tool for this purpose.

Inductive methods such as ID3 are considered as important ways that an expert system may learn automatically. Therefore, this is another area in which 1st-CLASS could be augmented with other tools for providing an automatic learning capability for the system.

Conclusion

This chapter discussed the expert system software product 1st-CLASS in detail. 1st-CLASS is an example of an inductive-based software tool. Using this software provides the reader with not only a working knowledge of the product, but also an understanding of one of the important learning methods in expert systems.

This chapter reviewed the general features of the software. 1st-CLASS has six screens: Files, Definitions, Examples, Methods, Rules, and Advisor. Together, these six screens provide the developer an easy way of creating an inductive-based expert system. The chapter discussed the treatment of uncertainty in 1st-CLASS and gave a brief presentation of other features of the software, including its methods, outside hooks, and development tools.

It was shown that one can directly use the decision tree for reasoning. One can also translate the decision tree into rules. The last section of this chapter discussed using 1st-CLASS in conjunction with other methods in expert systems.

References

Thomas, Wes and Hapgood, Will. 1987. *1st-CLASS Instruction Manual,* 1st-CLASS Expert Systems Inc., Wayland, MA.

Questions

6.1   The sensitivity of the decision tree to the examples and the factors included in the system is a major issue in the application of inductive methods. Why is this issue important?

6.2   Discuss the way uncertainty is handled in 1st-CLASS.

6.3 Describe possible circumstances under which you would prefer to use a method other than ID3 to generate the decision tree.

6.4 Why is modularity important in the design of expert systems?

Problems

6.1 In Figure 6.7, drop the first two examples, and find the decision tree. Has the decision tree changed? Why?

6.2 Use the examples in Figure 6.7, and test various methods available on the Methods screen. Are the resulting decision trees different for each method? Why?

6.3 Analyze the decision trees produced in Question 2. Do they all look reasonable to you? Why?

6.4 Using the examples in Figure 6.7, turn on (?) on the Methods screen. What would be the consequence of this action? Under what circumstances would you use this option?

6.5 Use the examples in Figure 6.7, and change the values on the Weight column to represent your uncertainty. Analyze the changes you observe in the Stat option of the Rule screen.

6.6 Use the examples in Figure 6.7, and develop a knowledge base for deciding the value of the CREDIT factor. Chain it to the original knowledge base, and test the outcome. Use RoadMap and Goto-Chain options to explore the connection between the original system and the new knowledge base.

6.7 Use the examples in Figure 6.7, and design an interface screen where the user would get all nine statistics with a good description for each, whenever the system reaches a decision. (Hint: Use the text option with the DECISION factor.)

6.8 Assume that you wish to develop an expert system for job applicants. Assume that some of the factors used for hiring MIS applicants are degree, years of experience, and area of interest. Develop a set of examples for these factors, and use 1st-CLASS to find the decision tree.

6.9 Use 1st-CLASS to prototype a real-world expert system, and write the rules based on the decision tree.

6.10 Expand your system in Question 9 by adding modules in the form of forward and backward chains.

Case: Induction Method Applied to Expert System for University Admission Office

The admission of undergraduate and graduate students at the university requires a number of criteria, and a series of rules to handle exceptional cases. Furthermore, the decision for the eligibility of the application for financial aid and a student loan is another aspect of the admission process.

The intended goal of the system is to identify the university applicants who either meet the minimum requirements for the university admission or fall into one of the exceptional categories. Such applicants are called "potentially acceptable." If an applicant is potentially acceptable, and has applied for financial assistance or a loan, the system must determine the eligibility of the applicant for the financial aid.

Contact the admission office and financial aid office at your university. Collect data for the student applicants who have been accepted or rejected by the university admission office. Using the induction method and 1st-CLASS, come up with the decision tree and rules that should be used in this expert system.

Case: Expert System Application in Monitoring Gymnastic Training

Training elite international-level athletes is very time consuming, expensive, and difficult. The coach and athlete must walk a narrow path toward success. The path is bounded on one side with failure due to undertraining or inadequate work. In this case the athlete is defeated because the opponent trained harder and developed farther by virtue of his/her more demanding training. The path is bounded on the other side by failure due to overtraining. This side of the path results in defeat due to chronic fatigue, injury, burnout or some other maladaptive response on the part of the athlete.

The boundaries define a "training window"—an optimization or "Goldilocks" problem for coaches and athletes. The goal of the modern coach and athlete is to maintain the athlete within the narrow path of optimal adaptation to imposed training demands; not too much, not too little—just right. This article describes an expert system that helps coaches achieve this goal.

In 1987, the U.S. Gymnastics Federation funded a pilot study for the development of a monitoring system. The system would monitor the training of the women's national team before the 1988 Olympic Games.

After considerable research, a machine-scannable data sheet was developed specifically for capturing pertinent dosage (what the athlete does in training) and response (how the athlete adapts to the training) information. Each athlete was responsible for entering her own data every day. At the end of each week, the athletes' coaches mailed the data sheets to Dr. Sands at the University of Utah.

More than a dozen Turbo Pascal programs number-crunched, graphed, and displayed the data. The graphs and statistics were then analyzed by visual inspection for trends indicating overtraining, undertraining, or training in the athlete's window of adaptability. The written report was sent to each athlete's coach to help develop future training plans.

For a complete and consistent monitoring system, however, there was a need for adding intelligence to the programs. Dr. Sands needed a knowledge-based program to take the statistical information, analyze the trends, and make a diagnosis for each athlete.

He divided the knowledge domain into dosage, response, and injury variables. Rules were developed to deal with each of these variables and their combinations, within the context of the training plan or cycle. The training period for dosage was broken down into the last six trainings, the second to last six trainings, and the baseline back to the start of the training programs. The training period for response and injury variables was divided into the last ten trainings and the remaining baseline values. These divisions were based on 13 years experience in determining the sufficient amount of data to indicate a trend.

The completed knowledge base contains nearly 200 rules that analyze several facets of training. The program has allowed Dr. Sands to turn the data around in a much more timely fashion.

The rule-based system currently monitors the training members of the women's U.S. National Gymnastics Team, the men's U.S. National Gymnastics Team, and the University of Utah's Women's Gymnastics Team (1990 NCAA Champions). The system has correctly identified and warned many maladaptive patterns in physiological and psychological variables. This has helped detect

- illness before overt symptoms were displayed

- illness problems that led to a diagnosis of anemia

- trends in injuries

- identification of overtraining

- poor administration of the dose/response relationship by the coach

- growth spurts among adolescent athletes

- physiological and psychological reactions to paternal divorce

and many other trends.

The system monitors dose-response relationships quite well. It is simple in that it merely alerts a coach that a potential problem may exist. Little more could be hoped for in a mail-based system that provides no direct contact with athletes. Moreover, coaches are quite protective of their athletes and come to resent any major intrusions. The system has struck a happy medium in alerting coaches to a potential problem, but leaves the solution up to them. The development of this rule-based diagnostic system has given the U.S. National Gymnastics Team another very useful tool in the battle to remain on the narrow path to success.

Condensed from "AI and Athletics: Monitoring Gymnastic Training," by William A. Sands, *PC AI*, January/February 1992, pp. 52–54, reprinted with permission from *PC AI*.

Case Questions

1. Identify the features of this case that make it appropriate for using the inductive method in discovering the knowledge-base rules.

2. Suggest other areas of sport in which an expert system could prove helpful to athletes and their coaches.

3. If the system in this case was to be used by coaches, what should be the characteristics of the system user interface?

4. Interview a coach (in a sport of your choice) to identify factors that are important in training an athlete.

5. Collect data for the factors in Question 5: (i) by direct observation, (ii) by presenting hypothetical cases (doses of training for various groups) and asking a coach to give you the response for each case, or (iii) by using sports literature. Use the data in 1st-CLASS to develop a prototype expert system for sports training.

6. Use the decision tree from 1st-CLASS to derive rules for a rule-based knowledge base.

7. Show the rules in Question 6 to a coach to see if he or she agrees with the rules. Ask the coach to critique the rules and give you his or her corrections.

8. Create a rule-based expert system from your answers to Questions 6 and 7. Invite the coach to use your system and test its knowledge base.

9. Discuss the organizational impediments in deploying expert systems in sports.

CHAPTER 7

System Development and Knowledge Acquisition

It is a great nuisance that knowledge can only be acquired by hard work. It would be fine if we could swallow the powder of profitable information made palatable by the jam of fiction.

W. Somerset Maugham, *10 Novels and Their Authors*

His had been an intellectual decision founded on his conviction that if a little knowledge was a dangerous thing, a lot was lethal.

Tom Sharpe, *Porterhouse Blue*

You can't invent a design. You recognize it, in the fourth dimension. That is, with your blood and your bones, as well as with your eyes.

D. H. Lawrence

Chapter Objectives

The objectives of this chapter are:

- To discuss the developmental stages of expert systems

- To review the systems analysis features in expert systems

- To review the nature, methods, modes, tools, and issues of knowledge acquisition in expert systems

- To discuss the testing methods in expert systems

- To review the reliability issues in expert systems

KEY WORDS: Systems analysis, systems design, prototyping, system life cycle, knowledge acquisition, knowledge engineer, object-oriented methods, logical design, physical design, coding, testing, reliability

Introduction

In Chapter 7, we discuss the systems analysis and design aspects of creating an expert systems. This is an important chapter for creating any type of expert system for real use.

Since an expert system is a component of business information systems and organizational decision tools, all concepts of systems analysis and design for information systems apply here as well. However, expert systems have unique features that create issues in analyzing and designing such systems. The first two sections of this chapter focus on systems-analysis issues in expert systems.

In expert systems, like other information systems, we begin with logical design before starting to code and physically create the system. One of the most important special features of expert systems at the logical-design phase is the collection of rules (or predicates) for the knowledge base from experts and other sources. This is called *knowledge acquisition,* and is considered one of the stumbling blocks in creating expert systems. Section 7.3 of this chapter discusses various methods and issues regarding knowledge acquisition for expert systems.

At the physical design phase of expert system development, we must decide about the software, the hardware, and the method for coding the system. Examples of decisions at this phase are: "buy" or "make" the software, buy new hardware or use the existing one, selecting the method of knowledge representation, and designing the user interface. These issues are discussed in Section 7.4 of this chapter.

Once the expert system is created, we should test its reliability. The questions we ask at this stage are: Is the system coded correctly? Does the system represent the logic of the expert? Does the system work as we intended? Does the system give "correct" or "expert" help? These questions are related to the reliability of an expert system, which is discussed in Section 7.5 of this chapter.

The last section discusses the implementation issues. The success of a system is in its use. That is why user acceptance plays a major role in the success of an expert system. Furthermore, an expert system, like other "live" systems, must be maintained and updated as the domain knowledge changes. Hence, the life cycle of expert system development continues, as it does in other information systems.

The case boxes in this chapter are intended to highlight some of the issues and trends in the development of expert systems. One interesting phenomenon is the fact that some companies have started to sell the expert systems that they have originally developed and successfully deployed for internal purposes.

7.1 Stages in Developing Expert Systems

Systems analysis and design have proved to be of great importance in developing successful business information systems. They have an equally important role in expert system development. A business expert system is a computerized decision tool. When the size and strategic significance of an expert system are great, its analysis and design play crucial roles in its successful development.

Business information systems and business expert systems share common features. Both have the ultimate goal of improving the quality of the decision and control process within the business. Their applications alter the business environment, and change the day-to-day operation. In turn, they are greatly affected by the business culture and the business environment for which they are designed. Their development requires a commitment of resources and time by top managers and users. The similarities between business information systems and expert systems indicate that the development of business expert systems could greatly benefit from the use of systems analysis and design techniques. In practice, this indeed has proven to be the case.

In analyzing and designing expert systems, one must be aware of the major differences between expert systems and information systems. Differences that impact the choice of methods in analyzing expert systems are:

- Expert systems are new and less established than information systems. The top managers, experts, and users need more extensive communication and discussions to define the objectives of the expert system and grasp its capabilities and limitations. This demands an extra degree of interaction among those involved in the development of an expert system, as discussed in a later section in this chapter.

- While information systems computerize mostly the structured aspects of business processes, expert systems are designed for solving unstructured and semistructured decision problems. The developer of expert systems must impose a structure for solving such problems. This requires development approaches that allow for many iterations and trial and error, before the final product is produced. One such method is prototyping, which is discussed in the next section.

- Expert systems contain domain knowledge, which must be attained through the arduous process of knowledge acquisition and knowledge modeling. Information systems need data, whose methods of collection and storage are well established. The underlying data models in information systems are easier to attain.

- Expert systems normally come up with an *answer*, such as categorizing an object (for example, a loan application), diagnosing a problem (for example, the reason for a machine failure), or taking an action (for example, opening a valve). Information systems give input to the user, normally without producing a definite recommendation. This means that an expert system requires the added steps of validation and verification for establishing the correctness or, at least, the acceptability of its answers.

Case: Expert System for Criminal Investigation

DIANA is an expert system which is developed by Bolt Beranek & Newman for the Home Office, the criminal investigation bureau in the United Kingdom. This system is created for the intelligence analysis and interpretation of police intelligence data. It was created in collaboration with the scientific research and development branch of the Home Office in London.

DIANA uses a pattern-matching approach to analyze the gathered data. Normally, data pertaining to specific cases or police work is accumulated and then pored over by human intelligence analysts, who make reports based on their study of the material. The expert system streamlines this process by maintaining a static base while creating a dynamic knowledge base with each session. Objects created within the dynamic database can be represented graphically for visual inspection by the user, who can further manipulate them during the course of analysis. The final results can be printed out in hard copy.

BBN developed DIANA using Procyon Common Lisp, one of the most popular European Lisps, on a Macintosh IIx. The Macintosh was chosen as both a development and delivery vehicle to put users more at ease with the initial analysis sessions.

The FBI has more than twenty expert system projects. The Behavioral Science Unit of the FBI has constructed an expert system that creates personality profiles of violent criminals based on reports taken from crime scenes, media accounts, violent crime research findings, the mode of activity, and pattern analysis. In effect, the expert system examines all the information about the crime and the victim and then develops its own hypothesis about the type of person who committed the crime. This system is part of the computerization of the National Center for the Analysis of Violent Crime.

The FBI is also working on the Arson Information Management System, called AIMS. This system analyzes arson to help determine possible future locations and times that might be ripe for certain arsonists to strike. At the local level, in 1987, the Jefferson Institute for Justice Study was awarded a grant to adapt the British crime-analysis program developed by the Devon & Cornwall Constabulary in Exeter and the Savant Research Center in Coventry. The initial prototype was developed in April 1988.

At this point, burglary detectives got their first look at the system that would help them analyze information taken from burglary sites and help narrow down initial lists of suspects. Information from 300 closed burglary cases and 3,000 records about unsolved cases and known burglars were loaded into the system. Eighteen detectives were interviewed for insights into residential burglaries, who came up with 397 statements relevant to that particular type of crime, including categorical information such as the characteristics of the residence, its environment, the type of entry used by the burglar, behavior at the scene, types of materials taken and not taken, and possible mode of transportation to and from the scene.

The residential burglary system now runs on a Compaq 386 with 10MBs of hard disk memory and the software is the Gold Hill's GoldWorks expert system shell. This system was one of the first AI applications at the local level. Baltimore County Police Department was the test site of the system. Tucson, Charlotte, and Rochester are among the cities where this system is used in their police departments.

Condensed from an article by Harvey P. Newquist III, "In Practice: Bloodhounds and Expert Systems," *AI Expert*, March 1990, pp. 67–69, with permission from *AI Expert*.

7.1.1 System Development Life Cycle

In organizing the development of a relatively large expert system, one must use the system development stages common to those in information systems:

- Systems analysis

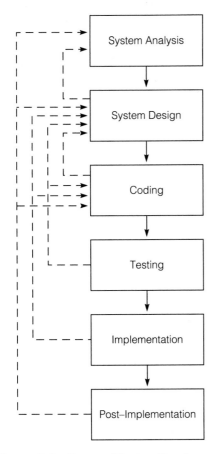

Figure 7.1 Stages of System Development in Expert Systems

- Systems design
- Coding
- Testing
- Implementation
- Post-implementation

These stages are shown in Figure 7.1, where the arrows indicate the iterative nature of the development stages.

Each stage, however, has features unique to expert systems, as shown in Figure 7.2. In the following sections of this chapter, each one of these stages is discussed in more detail.

System Analysis

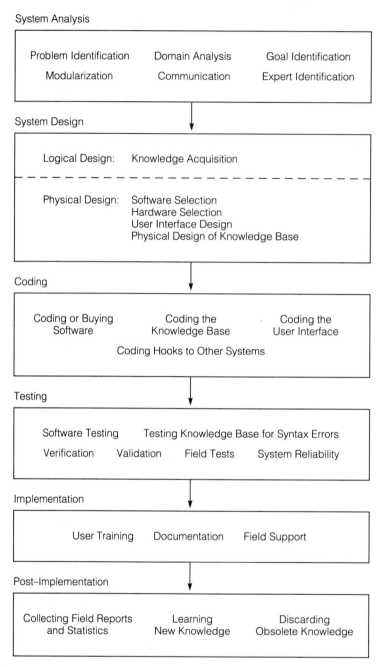

System Design

Coding

Testing

Implementation

Post–Implementation

Figure 7.2 Features of System Development in Expert Systems

The *system life cycle* approach requires a formal process in which the system developer goes through the developmental stages before arriving at the implementation phase, in which the finished product is produced. The advantage of this approach is that it provides an orderly framework for the development of an expert system, which reduces the probability of major errors and pitfalls. The disadvantage of this approach is that it takes a long time before any product with a visible outcome is produced. This makes top managers reluctant to commit financial resources to the development of the system.

7.1.2 Prototyping

Prototyping is another approach to system development. In this method, the system developer produces a system prototype in a short time. The prototype is a rough version of the system on a small scale. The developer uses the prototype to demonstrate and discuss the capabilities of the system to top management and system users. Developing the prototype helps the developer understand the problem and its domain, identify the scope of the system, and choose its future expansions. By nature, prototyping involves a number of iterations, through which the prototype is gradually altered and expanded to meet organizational needs.

Prototyping is a common approach in expert systems because of the novelty and unstructured nature of problems that these systems solve. The development of a prototype is far cheaper than the full version, and the gradual expansion of the prototype gives the managers who pay for the system more control over the cost and extent of the system.

Producing a prototype of an expert system, however, does not mean the six stages of system development are discarded. Rather, in prototyping an expert system, the developer goes through these stages in a quick and incomplete fashion, enhancing each stage in the next iteration of the prototype (Figure 7.3).

For example, in developing a prototype for a mortgage loan system, the developer would complete the systems analysis stage by identifying the problem, its domain, and its goals. But the developer may identify only, for example, 20 percent of the problem. The domain may first be limited only to loans to individuals, and the goal of the system may be limited to helping novice loan officers check their decisions with the system. The identified experts may be limited only to those loan officers in charge of approving loans for single-family houses. In the design phase, the developer may use inexpensive software, with limited capabilities, on a slow machine.

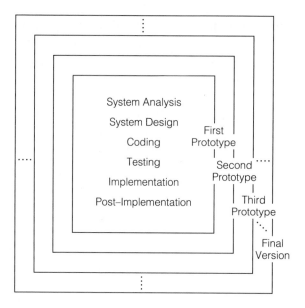

Figure 7.3 Prototyping in Expert Systems

The knowledge acquisition may involve deriving about 20 rules, and the user interface may be limited to defaults on the software. This means a very limited amount of coding. Establishing the correctness of the system does not take long, either. Hence, the prototype may be ready for demonstration in less than two weeks.

As the developer presents the system to the top managers, users, and experts, the limitations of the system become evident. This leads to the identification of future expansions of the system. Meanwhile, those involved get a taste of the capabilities and limitations of the system. Thus the prototype is used as a focal point for educating the developer in the needs of the organization, and the users and decision makers in what the system might accomplish. Furthermore, the top managers see the intermediate outcome and are able to allocate resources incrementally, which is a preferred mode of financing novel projects.

It is worthwhile to emphasize that prototyping has the same development stages as the life-cycle approach, but the completion of prototyping takes place iteratively, as shown in Figure 7.3. Therefore, no matter which of the two approaches—system life cycle or prototyping—are used, the expert system goes through the development stages. In the remaining sections of this chapter, we discuss these stages in detail.

7.2 Systems Analysis in Expert Systems

At the systems analysis stage, the developer should determine the desirability and feasibility of the system. In the case of expert systems, the developer must determine the problem for which the expert system is designed, the goals of the system, and the scope of the system. Because expert systems are dependent on knowledge, the developer must identify the sources of knowledge for various parts of the system. Finally, in expert systems, communication plays an important role in the process. Thus, establishing communication channels with those involved in the system is another aspect of systems analysis in expert systems.

7.2.1 *Problem Definition and Goal Identification*

In developing expert systems, one must first determine the problem for which the expert system is to provide a solution or advice. In other words, the major purpose of developing the system must be clear from the start, because it is the guiding light for subsequent decisions on domain and expert selections.

The purpose of an expert system could be:

- Helping novice workers

- Training workers for a job

- Supplementing workers' skill for performing more demanding tasks

- Improving customer service

- Capturing valuable knowledge

- Increasing the quality and uniformity of an existing task

For example, in a mortgage loan system, the problem could be the novice officers' lack of adequate access to expert loan officers. Then, an expert system is needed to fill the gap. Alternatively, the bank may wish to have a system for applicants to check their eligibility for a loan. Or, the bank has a single brilliant loan officer who is close to retirement, and would like to capture his or her expertise into an expert system. These are different problem types and organizational needs for developing a mortgage loan system.

The problem type impacts the subsequent development decisions. For example, an expert system intended to capture the expertise of a single loan officer has the purpose of emulating the decisions of that officer. In this case, the domain is limited to the knowledge of the officer, and the expert is already identified. The system goals are the outcomes similar to what the loan officer decides.

On the other hand, when the problem is to develop a system for the applicants to check their eligibility for a loan, one must determine the system goals. For example, the system may provide a yes or no answer to the applicant, or tell the applicant about other possibilities, such as the increased likelihood of acceptance of a smaller loan request, the availability of other types of loans, and actions the applicant could take to improve his or her chance of obtaining the desired loan.

The problem should be identified in consultation with the top managers who provide resources for the project, and potential experts and users (including those who would manage and maintain the system). Based on the type of problem, the same group should determine the system goals. The degree of the specificity of system goals increases as the project progresses. For example, in developing the mortgage loan system for applicants, the goal may be specified that the system must provide an answer: "acceptable or unacceptable," as well as give the applicant advice on alternatives relevant to the applicant's needs. Specifying the exact nature of the latter type of advice may be delayed to a later stage of the system development.

7.2.2 *Domain Analysis, Modularization, and Expert Identification*

Expert system analysis involves the determination of the domain and its major concepts. Since the developer is not necessarily knowledgeable in the domain, he or she relies on a *generalist expert* who has an overall understanding of the domain. With the help of this expert, the developer determines the major concepts within the domain. This is called *conceptualization.*

For example, in the mortgage loan expert system, the expert helps the developer to identify the major loan categories as single-family, multiple-family, and commercial. The expert helps the developer to identify the individuals and institutions involved in the process, such as the applicant, the cosigner, the applicant's lawyer, the bank's lawyer, the firm providing the credit information, and the property appraiser. The expert identifies the type and nature of decisions made regarding an application, and the *specialist experts* who may cooperate in the details of each decision type.

In some cases, the generalist expert may not be available or accessible. The developer may have to use written materials, group discussions, or existing standards as possible sources for conceptualization.

Conceptualization is the beginning of knowledge acquisition. It provides a general familiarity with the domain and allows the developer to break down the domain into modules, and to identify the experts and sources of knowledge for each module. For example, after the conceptualization, the developer of the mortgage loan may decide that the system has two modules: personal loans and commercial loans. The developer then attempts to find knowledge sources and experts within and outside the bank to help in the design and knowledge acquisition phase of the system development.

As conceptualization progresses, the developer becomes able to modify the scope and goals of the system, and make them more specific. For example, the developer may clarify with the bank's top managers that the system will not involve commercial loans at the start. However, the system must have a design general enough to accommodate commercial loans as an add-on module at a later time.

Thus, systems analysis in expert systems has the feature of iterative discovery of the concepts within the domain, which helps in clarifying and modifying the scope and goals of the system.

7.2.3   Communication Process

In this book, we refer to those involved in the development of expert systems by the generic term *developer*. The developer is not necessarily a single person. The development of large expert systems requires a development team, consisting of a number of internal employees and external consultants. The management of the team demands the same organizational skills as any large technical project. The unique feature of the expert system development team is its extensive amount of interpersonal communications with:

- Top managers and CEOs

- Experts

- Users

- Managers of the system

- Managers of the systems with which the expert system will be integrated

- Members of the development team

Top Managers and CEOs

Like any technical innovation, the application of expert systems starts with an individual playing the role of the agent of change, who introduces the concept into the organization and becomes a force behind its progress. However, the top managers and CEOs of the organization should be convinced of the viability of the approach, and its limitations. The development team must educate the managers on the subject, and keep them involved with the major decisions of the project.

Experts

The experts require the most extensive amount of interpersonal communication. Some experts may be apprehensive about the objective of the system—they may fear that the system will replace them, that they will lose control over their decisions, or that their knowledge and expertise could undergo scrutiny and criticism. It is essential to have a clear and continuous communication with the experts regarding system objectives and the tasks the system will be used for.

At the knowledge acquisition stage, interaction with the experts becomes more intense. Communication with the experts continues into the testing, validation, verification, and subsequent revision stages of the project. An early and solid rapport with the experts would go a long way toward ensuring the success of the project.

Users

Users of the expert system must be involved at the start of the analysis and participate actively throughout system development. They provide information about the needs the system must satisfy, and the user-interface design. The development team should design communication strategies with the users to keep them interested and involved.

Managers of the System

Many applications of expert systems have remained at the prototype stage, partly because no internal unit is responsible for providing technical support, and for maintaining and updating its knowledge base. The development team should identify the organizational unit most appropriate to manage the expert system. An early and steady involvement of this unit is essential for the internalization of the system.

Managers of Other Systems

Most of the major business expert systems should eventually be integrated with the other systems in the organization. (Some integration options are discussed in Chapter 9.) For example, a mortgage loan expert system may require a connection to the database on the historical data of loans granted and denied, or the database of property zones in which the bank operates. The system must be designed with the proper hook to these systems. Identifying persons in charge of such systems and establishing an early and steady communication channel with them is crucial to the system integration.

Members of the Development Team

The development group consists of heterogeneous members, ranging from the knowledge engineer, with possible degrees in cognitive psychology or liberal arts, to a computer programmer who codes the system, and systems analysts and AI specialists. After the initial stage of conceptualization, the tasks are divided among the team members. Keeping communication channels open among those with diverse tasks, such as the knowledge engineer and programmers, reduces the chance of major errors.

7.3 Knowledge Acquisition as the Logical Design

Knowledge acquisition is one of the most important, yet least formalized steps of expert system development. This is why knowledge acquisition is considered an art, a major bottleneck in the development of expert systems.

The person who collects knowledge for the knowledge base has the title of *knowledge engineer*. Acquiring knowledge requires skills not directly related to the computer system:

- Communication and interviewing skills

- Ability to organize and manage group sessions

- Willingness to learn about new knowledge domains

- Ability to handle and process a high volume of unfamiliar and technical information

Knowledge engineering requires people skills for interviewing, communicating, and managing the acquisition process from experts. It also requires an ability to absorb and summarize a great deal of information, and sort out the important and crucial pieces from nonessential parts.

7.3.1 Logical Design vs. Physical Design of the Knowledge Base

Knowledge elicitation and acquisition is a process by which the developer *models* knowledge, in that he or she transforms knowledge into a computational form. The process of modeling knowledge constitutes the *logical design* of the expert system. This process should be independent of the software or language of the expert system. The software independency of the logical design provides flexibility and freedom in modeling knowledge without the constraints a language or software product may impose. Furthermore, software selection should be guided by the nature and requirements of the domain knowledge, not the other way around. Thus, it is good knowledge modeling style to use an English-like pseudo code to document the elicited knowledge, even when developing a prototype of the system. This document is called the *logical design* of the knowledge base. The generic nature of the logical design facilitates its translation to any language or software product, and keeps track of the acquired knowledge, uncluttered by the added complexity of the syntax of a language or software product.

After the completion of the logical design, the *physical design* begins. In this phase, the developer makes the software and hardware decisions, and translates the logical design of the knowledge base into a design that accommodates the software requirements and its representation method.

Here, we discuss the knowledge acquisition as the logical design of expert systems. In a later section, we review the issues involved in the physical design of expert systems. One of the first steps in the logical design is the selection of domain expert.

7.3.2 Expert Selection

Expert system development has a unique design feature—the developer must select expert(s) who will cooperate with the knowledge engineers in creating the knowledge base. The developer should interview the experts identified in the system analysis phase of the project. The major criteria for including an expert in the development team are [McGraw and Harbison-Briggs 1989, Chapter 3; Prerau 1990, Chapters 8 and 9]:

- The recognized expertise and experience of the expert

- The availability of the expert

- The commitment of the expert to the system

- The interpersonal communication skills of the expert

The fact that an expert has the expertise is not the only qualifying condition. The expert must have time to participate in the process of knowledge acquisition, and the subsequent testing of the system. Communicating how one reaches a decision is not an easy task. In many cases, the expert is not conscious of the real method he or she actually applies in arriving at a decision. The knowledge engineer and the expert together should unravel the actual decision process. The expert's good communication skills aid the process and contributes to the quality of the knowledge base.

The expert selection involves a number of choices:

- Internal expert(s) or external expert(s)

- Single expert or multiple experts

- Individual sessions or group sessions

An internal expert works within the organization for which the expert system is being developed, while the external expert is independent from the organization. The choice between internal or external experts depends on the type and objectives of the system. One major criterion is how *smart* the expert system should be. If the system must contain the "best" available know-how, it is only natural that the developer must choose the best experts, regardless of their affiliation. This normally means including external experts in the pool. On the other hand, when the purpose of the system is to capture the rare expertise of an expert in the organization, the expert is naturally of internal type.

The number of experts also depends on the objective of the system. Except in the case where the expert system is designed to capture the expertise of a single "star" of the organization, a multi-expert knowledge base contains more reliable knowledge than a uni-expert one, especially when the domain knowledge is large and complex.

On the other hand, increasing the number of experts beyond a small group is detrimental to the quality and may hinder the progress of system development. Acquiring knowledge from a large group of experts and resolving their conflicting views makes the project lengthy, costly, and unmanageable. The developer can choose a select core of experts (between two and seven, depending on the module and its complexity) for knowledge acquisition, and use the rest for the verification and validation of the system. The topics of verification and validation are discussed in a later section of this chapter.

The decision to hold sessions with experts individually or in groups depends on the availability of experts and the methods of knowledge acquisition used.

7.3.3   Sources of Knowledge

The knowledge engineer acquires knowledge from a number of sources:

- Written sources, such as books, manuals, standard procedures

- Experts

- Observations of the actual process

Written materials are an important source of knowledge at the start, when the knowledge engineer learns the vocabularies and general topics of the domain. If the type of expertise has a procedural nature, in which a sequence of tasks are performed, direct observation of the operation also can provide input to the knowledge base. For the mortgage loan case, the knowledge engineer may observe that the bank officer always requests a report from the applicant's banks. This becomes a part of the knowledge base.

In most cases, however, experts make decisions based on an abstract and intellectual process that even experts themselves have difficulty understanding and verbalizing. The knowledge engineer should elicit knowledge from the expert by helping the expert to discover and communicate this process, using a host of knowledge acquisition methods.

7.3.4   Knowledge Acquisition Methods

A knowledge engineer uses various methods to create an abstract model of the domain knowledge. The knowledge base could be considered as the model of the domain knowledge, and the knowledge acquisition as the process of *modeling knowledge*. As such, knowledge acquisition methods constitute tools for solving this modeling problem.

There is no single formula or set method by which the knowledge engineer can successfully elicit knowledge and model the knowledge domain. In eliciting knowledge, the knowledge engineer can use a host of methods developed in psychology, cognitive science, and decision analysis under various names and procedures. These methods were developed through time for different purposes. Some have different names but a similar approach. This section categorizes and gives a generic description of the methods available to the knowledge engineer. (For an overview of many of the techniques developed in psychology and cognitive science with references to the original works, see McGraw and Harbison-Briggs 1989, Chapter 5.)

There are two basic strategies in knowledge engineering: one may start from general and overall concepts, gradually leading the expert to elicit details of a topic. Or, alternatively, one may start from the details of specific cases and help the expert establish and derive general concepts from the specific examples. Therefore, the methods of eliciting knowledge can be categorized into two broad groups:

- Top-down (or deductive) methods

- Bottom-up (or inductive) methods

Top-Down Methods

In top-down methods, the knowledge engineer organizes the acquisition sessions for discovering general concepts, rules, and objects, and then gradually goes into the details of each concept, rule, or object. We can group the top-down methods into four categories, as shown in the right branch of Figure 7.4:

- Questioning methods

- Object-oriented methods

- Quantitative methods

- Inventive methods

Questioning methods. In the *questioning methods*, the knowledge engineer interviews the expert in a series of meetings, or asks the expert to fill out a questionnaire. The knowledge engineer could use three strategies in questioning the expert:

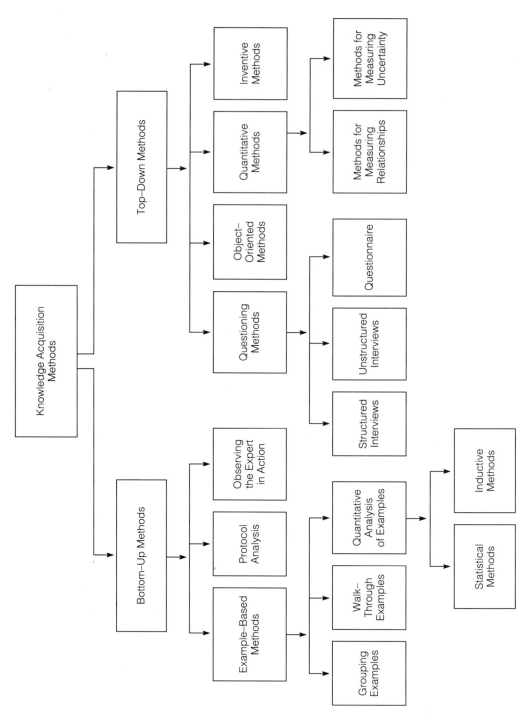

Figure 7.4 Categories of Knowledge Acquisition Methods

- Structured interviews

- Unstructured interviews

- Questionnaires

In the *structured interviews*, the knowledge engineer determines the objective of the interview. For example, for one interview session, the knowledge engineer may have the objective of determining the rules for deciding the credit worthiness of a mortgage loan applicant. The knowledge engineer prepares a number of questions in advance, and focuses the discussion on the topic. If the expert diverts from the objective of the session, the knowledge engineer refocuses the discussion back to the session's objective. This method is appropriate for the advanced stages of the knowledge acquisition, when the knowledge engineer has enough knowledge to prepare session objectives and questions.

In the *unstructured interviews*, the interview has a free format. The knowledge engineer prepares some opening questions, and asks the subsequent questions based on the expert's answers. The method is appropriate for the beginning stages of the knowledge acquisition process, when the knowledge engineer has started to explore the domain.

In cases where access to the expert is limited, the knowledge engineer may prepare a *questionnaire* for the expert to answer in writing. This method is useful for clarifying already developed topics in the advanced stages of knowledge engineering.

Object-oriented methods.   A number of knowledge elicitation methods are object-oriented. Although we discuss objected-oriented analysis and design in Chapter 8, this section briefly describes those features that are commonly used even when the system does not use an object-oriented knowledge-representation method.

In the *object-oriented methods*, the knowledge engineer focuses the interview sessions on discovering the objects within the domain. In doing so, the knowledge engineer asks the expert to group the actual objects in the field in order to form a class of objects that has a common set of attributes. Then, the knowledge engineer asks the expert to identify subclasses of objects that have distinguishing attributes.

For example, one can observe from various loan applications that one of the major objects in the mortgage loan is the applicant. So, the expert forms the class of **applicants** objects and identifies the relevant attributes of this class, such as name and address. Then, from this class, the knowledge elicitation leads to the subclasses of individual applicants and commercial applicants. The individual applicants subclass has attributes such as age, job, education, and marital status, which are unique to this subclass. The commercial applicants subclass has, say, business type, legal status, financial manager, and home state as its attributes.

As an aid to discovering the classes of objects, and their attributes and subclasses, some of the object-oriented methods use network graphs. In a network graph, each node represents an object with the attached attributes. Arcs of the network show the types of relationships among the objects, as shown in Figure 7.5a.

Another way to depict the structure of objects is the hierarchy of classes of objects. The top of the hierarchy shows the most general class of objects. The lower levels of the hierarchy contain increasingly more specific subclasses of objects, which may inherit some or all attributes of their immediate parent object. In a hierarchy, a lower node could have more than one parent node. An example of the hierarchy of objects is shown in Figure 7.5b. (Chapter 8 contains a more detailed discussion on the graphical models of objects.)

One point to keep in mind in using such graphing techniques is the principle of KISS: "keep it simple. . . ." One may easily create a complex and unreadable diagram in an attempt to show all objects and their relations within the domain. The ultimate goal of these methods is elicitation and clarification. One can use separate diagrams to show the details of objects or attributes in lower layers, or one may document the details in the form of semi-English texts or pseudo codes, attached to the diagram.

Another variation of the object-oriented method is to identify concepts instead of objects. Concepts are more abstract than objects. For example, a loan is an object, it has a real-world counterpart. "Educating applicants about their rights" is a concept, and has a more abstract nature. One can use the network or the hierarchy graphs to establish the interconnections of the concepts.

Quantitative methods.   The knowledge engineer can use quantitative methods to measure and determine:

- The extent of relationships among objects (or concepts)

- The degree of uncertainty about the domain knowledge

a. Network

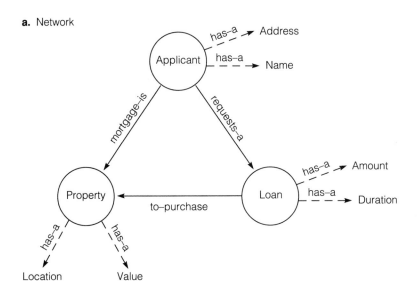

b. Hierarchy

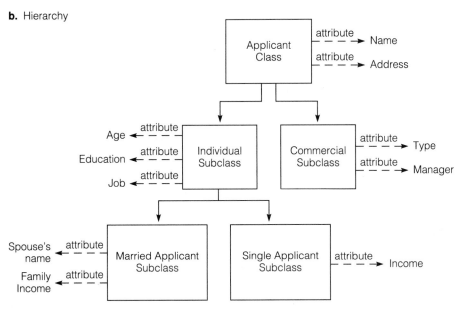

Figure 7.5   Examples of Object-Oriented Knowledge Acquisition Methods

In some cases, the expert is unable to provide a clear description of the extent of relationships among various objects (or concepts). In such cases, the knowledge engineer can use quantitative methods for helping the expert elicit the relations among the objects. These methods are developed in cognitive science and decision analysis for eliciting the degree of a decision maker's preferences and utilities, and in grouping various objects and attributes. Among these techniques are:

- Analytic hierarchy process [Saaty 1977; Zahedi 1986]

- Multidimensional scaling [Kruskal 1977]

- Hierarchical cluster analysis [Johnson 1967]

In these quantitative methods, the expert is asked to compare and express the extent of the objects' relationships in a numerical scale. Then, a mathematical algorithm is used to compute and rank the degree of relationships among the objects.

Quantitative methods have a potential application in measuring the expert's uncertainty with respect to various pieces of knowledge. The elicitation of uncertainty is one of the areas of expert systems that has not been fully developed yet. The elicitation of uncertainty depends on the selected method of uncertainty representation. Chapter 11 discusses the methods for representing uncertainty in expert systems.

Inventive methods.   The top-down methods discussed so far give the knowledge engineer the responsibility for the eliciting and modeling of knowledge. In the inventive methods, the expert is allowed a more active part in the process in one of the following roles:

- Expert as a teacher

- Expert as a partner in systematic innovation

- Expert as the knowledge engineer

The expert as a teacher would be responsible for teaching and transferring expertise to the knowledge engineer. In this case, the expert is given the responsibility for the preparation and organization of the elicitation sessions. This method is efficient at the early stages of knowledge acquisition.

Lirov [1990] suggests the idea of systematic invention in knowledge engineering. This is an abstract concept, which requires the expert and the knowledge engineer to identify pieces of knowledge that are in contradiction, and to discover solution methods for removing the contradiction. For example, the applicant's request for a loan and a less than favorable credit rating form a contradiction. The expert must provide a solution for this contradiction, which leads to the elicitation of new pieces of knowledge. In this approach, the expert and knowledge engineer form a partnership in discovering contradictions and creating solutions; this taps the expert's deep understanding of the domain.

In some cases, the expert may have both technical interest in the system and the needed training in knowledge engineering. In this case, the expert can also play the role of a knowledge engineer.

Bottom-Up Methods

In the bottom-up methods, the knowledge engineer focuses the expert's attention on specific cases, in order to help the expert abstract the decision for resolving a specific case to a more generalized rule or concept. The methods that can be grouped in this approach are (refer back to Figure 7.4):

- Example-based methods

- Protocol analysis

- Observation of the expert's decision-making process

Example-based methods.   The example-based approach constitutes the foundation of case-based learning and learning by analogy. In example-based methods, the knowledge engineer and the expert work on a number of representative cases or examples in one of the following ways (Figure 7.4):

- Grouping examples

- Walk-through examples

- Quantitative analysis of examples

In *grouping examples*, the expert groups the examples based on their similarities and differences. The knowledge engineer then asks the expert to identify the common and differentiating attributes of the examples. This process helps to determine categories of examples and the development of general rules for each category.

In the *walk-through method*, the knowledge engineer selects a number of cases previously decided by the expert, and asks the expert to walk through the decision process, which has led to the decision for each case. In doing so, the knowledge engineer and the expert recognize the contributing factors and attributes, and their role in the decision.

Methods for the *quantitative analysis of examples* could be categorized into two groups:

- Statistical methods

- Inductive methods

In the *statistical methods*, the examples must be a random sample of the cases decided by the expert(s). The data on the examples are fed into a statistical technique, such as regression analysis, in order to discover the expert's decision criteria.

In the *inductive methods*, the example set contains a representative set of all possible cases the expert has encountered. The examples are fed into the inductive method, which produces a decision tree or a set of decision rules. ID3, discussed in Chapters 4 and 6, and Appendix A, is one such method.

The quantitative techniques are tools for helping the expert discover the relations among various attributes of the decision cases. The outcomes should not be used without consultation with the expert, because the whole purpose of expert systems is to include the qualitative and non-quantifiable aspects of decision problems in the system. The quantitative methods may not be able to discover all of the qualitative aspects of the decision process.

Protocol analysis. In this method, the expert is asked to think aloud and verbalize his or her thought process while solving a set of actual (or simulated) problems and making decisions. The knowledge engineer records the process, and later analyzes the large volume of information produced from this method to discover the general rules the expert uses in solving problems. This method is useful for the nonprocedural type of problem solving, where the expert applies a great deal of mental, creative, and intellectual effort to arrive at a decision in each case.

Observation. Another bottom-up method is the observation of the expert while solving a problem. When the solution of the problem is procedural and takes place in a sequence of steps through time, observing the expert in action produces useful insight. The absence of the biases and intrusions inherent in the knowledge engineer's questions makes this approach useful.

In this method, the knowledge engineer must make sure that the expert is making decisions in the most realistic environment, including seemingly trivial matters such as sitting in the location where the expert commonly makes actual decisions. Experience shows that the realism of the expert decision is greatly influenced by the expert's mental state, on which the habitual physical environment has a significant impact.

Testimony to the impact of the physical environment on our mental process is the fact that many of us have to be in certain locations to write or study effectively. Some of us must have a pencil in our hand to think about solving a mathematical problem, or must have our fingers on the keyboard of a computer for writing on professional topics. The knowledge engineer has to be aware of the expert's particular decision environment to achieve the realism necessary for observing the expert in action.

7.3.5 Knowledge Acquisition Modes

At the start of the application of expert systems, all the knowledge engineering tasks were performed manually. However, as the field took hold, computer-assisted systems entered into the market to facilitate the process. At present, the knowledge elicitation modes could be divided into three categories:

- Manual mode

- Automated mode

- Combined manual and automated mode

Manual Mode

Manual elicitation requires a direct interaction between the knowledge engineer and the expert. The advantage of manual methods is that the knowledge engineer organizes the acquisition process, and helps the expert elicit his or her knowledge. This may reduce the possibility of major errors, or the omission of major factors from the system. The disadvantages of the manual system are that:

- The process could become lengthy, inefficient, and expensive

- The expert may feel intimidated and threatened by the possibility that the knowledge engineer may pass judgment on his or her expertise

- The development team may lack sufficient expertise in knowledge engineering

Some of the knowledge acquisition methods are inherently manual. For example, the interview methods, especially unstructured interviews, lend themselves more naturally to a manual approach. The inventive methods, such as teaching and systematic innovation, are manual systems.

Automated Mode

There are now a number of software products in the market that are designed for automatic elicitation of knowledge. The automated mode may be divided into two categories:

- Automated mode with the expert

- Automated mode without the expert

In the *automated mode with the expert*, the expert interacts with the computer. The software is designed to help the expert elicit knowledge without the assistance of a knowledge engineer.

The advantage of this type of automated method is that the expert has control over the knowledge acquisition session, and is not disturbed by the presence of the knowledge engineer. The process may move faster and more efficiently. The shortcoming of this method is that the knowledge base may have major errors and omissions. That is why a knowledge engineer must oversee the process.

In the *automated mode without the expert*, the system is fed examples to produce rules or decision trees. The example-based quantitative methods discussed in the previous subsection are the acquisition methods used in the automated mode without the expert. Such methods reduce the dependency on the expert, and are faster and more efficient. On the other hand, the knowledge engineer must check the results with an expert to make sure that they constitute an accurate, thorough, and meaningful representation of the domain knowledge.

Combined Manual and Automated Mode

The manual and automated modes have enough advantages and shortcomings to make their combination the most desirable mode of knowledge elicitation. At the start of the process, the knowledge engineer could use manual-based methods for conceptualization, modularization, and gaining insights into the knowledge domain. In some of the modules for which enough examples are available and the accessibility to the expert is limited, the knowledge engineer can use the automated mode to accelerate the elicitation of the knowledge. Later, the expert should review the results, and may make suggestions to modify the automatically developed rules. In other modules, the expert may work directly with the computer to elicit knowledge. The knowledge engineer then examines the elicited rules and may check their integrity and reliability with another expert.

7.3.6   Issues in Multi-expert Knowledge Acquisition

The knowledge engineer may use more than one expert in building the knowledge base. As long as the experts participate in different modules of the system, the process of knowledge acquisition remains unaltered for each module. In this case, the knowledge engineer must make sure that modules could be integrated without a problem. On the other hand, in most super expert systems and smart expert systems, the knowledge engineer uses more than one expert for the same module. The issues of multi-expert knowledge elicitation may be grouped into the following topics:

- Organizational issues

- Conflict resolution issues

The organizational issues of multi-expert knowledge acquisition involve questions on how to organize the experts, and how to keep the knowledge engineering process across multiple experts consistent in quality, timing, and procedure.

The first organizational question in multi-expert knowledge acquisition is whether to elicit expert knowledge individually or in a group. In some cases, physical constraints such as scheduling and geographical distance may decide the matter quickly in favor of individual elicitation. However, when the experts are in close proximity, and their schedules make group participation possible, the method could shift to group participation. It is also possible to have some modules in group form and others in individual form.

When multi-expert knowledge elicitation is performed on an individual basis, the developer may need a number of knowledge engineers to carry out the task. In this case, the developer should assign a knowledge acquisition coordinator to the responsibility of creating a uniform knowledge acquisition strategy, as well as common procedures for communication with the expert, and for the documentation of the elicited knowledge. All knowledge engineers must be equally competent. In other words, the knowledge engineer coordinator must take every precaution to eliminate variability in the quality of the elicited knowledge due to the difference in knowledge acquisition among the experts.

When the multi-expert knowledge is elicited in a group, managing the group dynamics becomes critical. The fear of being judged or disapproved of by peers could reduce some experts' contributions, while others may have a disproportionate share in input by the force of their personality rather than their expertise. The methods used in group decision making, especially the tools used in group decision support systems (GDSS), help the knowledge engineer in managing the process. Among these methods are:

- Group interaction via computers to make the views anonymous

- Long-distance group session via a local or long distance network of computers or computer terminals

- Computerized system for data collection on views, voting procedures, and consensus generation

An added advantage of computerized group sessions is that the raw input of the generated knowledge is already stored in the computer. In the case of geographically scattered experts, the long-distance group session is one possible solution.

Regardless of the form of knowledge generation in the multi-expert case, the knowledge engineer will encounter conflicting views and opinions about various pieces of knowledge. Therefore, the knowledge engineer should decide how to resolve conflicting opinions. Some of the approaches for conflict resolution are:

- The *Delphi technique*, where the conflicting opinions are collected anonymously and organized. The experts individually review and rank them. The resulting ranking is then distributed among the experts again. The process is repeated a number of times with the hope that a winning view gradually emerges.

- Voting. The experts vote to select the most agreed-on opinion or solution.

- The knowledge engineer incorporates the conflicting views in different modules. In this case, the expert system recommends more than one solution.

- The knowledge engineer asks the experts to discuss the subject until they reach a consensus.

- The knowledge engineer chooses an expert to be the arbiter of conflicts.

The choice of the conflict resolution method depends on the severity of conflicts, their impact on the quality of the knowledge base, and the degree of experts' cooperation and participation.

Case: Expert System Applications in Internal Auditing

Expert systems can be used to develop and maintain internal audit systems, to plan an internal audit, to schedule audit personnel, to assist in conducting an audit, and to assist in auditing a specific line item and its related accounts. Some examples of the use of expert systems in the internal audit function are Coopers & Lybrand's AShell program for developing and maintaining audit expert systems and KPMG Peat Marwick's system for estimating loan loss reserves.

1. *Coopers & Lybrand's AShell.* Coopers & Lybrand has developed a special computer program, AShell, to develop and maintain auditing expert systems. AShell's personal computer-based system is a comprehensive system covering the entire audit process including planning, execution, and automatic generation of work papers and audit reports. The system uses an intelligent questionnaire that leads an auditor though the entire audit process. The system contains modules that permit different parts of an audit to be executed and reported on separately. The expert system includes status tracking of the various audit functions and the ability to integrate and test mainframe transaction data in the AShell audit environment. Additional specific information about transactions is requested automatically if indicated by results of initial tests.

AShell includes the Knowledge Acquisition and Maintenance System (KAMS) that is used by internal auditors to maintain and add to the client-specific knowledge of the AShell knowledge base. KAMS is menu driven so that the knowledge base can be maintained by the audit staff. The actual auditing expert systems applications are built by compiling the output of the KAMS.

AShell has been used successfully to develop two modules of a branch compliance audit system for a major securities broker and investment banking firm. It also is used to develop a proof-of-concept demonstration system for a major commercial bank.

2. *KPMG Peat Marwick's Loan Probe.* KPMG Peat Marwick's Loan Probe is an 8,000-rule-based expert system that analyzes bank loans and determines the level of loan reserves needed. The knowledge base uses the expertise of KPMG senior managers and partners who are the firm's top banking professionals. The system's knowledge base also contains statistics and projections that are updated annually for more than 150 industries. The accountant supplies information about the financial institution, the loan and its security and guarantees, the bank's access to liquid collateral and the risk associated with the collateral's valuation, and the borrower.

Loan Probe is designed to arrive at a recommendation about the adequacy of the loan loss reserve for each loan being analyzed in the shortest possible time using the minimum of relevant information. The expert system will suggest that no reserve is necessary, that a reserve is necessary within a specific range, or that no determination can be made because of insufficient information. Loan Probe explains the logic used in reaching the loan loss reserve recommendation so the auditor can critique the explanation, and if necessary, develop a different solution. Thus, the system recognizes that an auditor might encounter a lending situation that is not considered by the system's expertise.

Loan Probe was created to assist KPMG auditors in assessing loan loss reserves for their clients. Now it is being sold to financial institutions for use by their internal audit staff.

Excerpts from "Expert Systems for Management Accountants," by Carol Brown and Mary Ellen Phillips, *Management Accounting*, January 1990, pp. 18–23, reprinted with permission from *Management Accounting*.

7.3.7 Knowledge Collection Tools

To collect and record the information in the knowledge engineering sessions, the knowledge engineer has the option of using a number of *manual* and *automated* tools.

Some of the manual tools are:

- Notetaking

- Audio taping

- Video taping

- Observing and subsequent reporting

- Written answers by the expert

The choice of knowledge collection tools greatly depends on the method of knowledge engineering. For example, protocol analysis requires audio or video taping to capture the expert's train of thought without interruption. Notetaking may be more appropriate for interviewing methods. When the knowledge engineer uses the questionnaire method, the expert's written answer is the natural tool for collecting knowledge.

The automated tools could be categorized into [Musen 1989a]:

- Symbol-oriented
- Method-oriented
- Domain-specific
- Meta tools

The *symbol-oriented* automated tools have facilities, such as rule editors, frame editors, dependency diagram editors, networks, and hypertext, and provide the user with the needed facilities for modeling knowledge. TEIRE-SIAS [Davis 1979] is an example of such tools. Almost all expert system software products have many of these tools built-in.

A *method-oriented* tool is committed to a particular method of representing knowledge. For example, Protos [Bareiss 1989] uses case-based learning as its knowledge acquisition method. Auto-Intelligence (by Intelligence Ware, Los Angeles, Calif.) automates the interview process (which is based on a model of classification based on personal construct psychology, developed by Kelley in 1955).

A tool of this type may be attached to an expert system software product, operating within the structure and syntax of the software. NEXTRA (by Neuron Data, Palo Alto, Calif.) is a method-oriented tool, which can be used in conjunction with NEXPERT and NEXPERT OBJECT, expert system products by the same company.

A *domain-specific* tool is designed for a given type of domain knowledge and a particular task within that domain. An example of this type is OPAL [Musen et al. 1987], which is a tool specifically designed for cancer chemotherapy knowledge acquisition.

The idea of *meta tools* is a new concept. It is a knowledge acquisition tool that the developer can use to generate domain-specific knowledge acquisition tools. PROTÉGÉ is the first of this kind, and has a method-oriented approach. It was used to generate a special version OPAL [Musen 1989b].

7.3.8   *Organizational Aspects of Knowledge Acquisition*

The majority of the knowledge engineering time is spent in preparing for the knowledge elicitation, and the subsequent organization and documentation of the results. The actual elicitation of knowledge normally takes less than one-third or one-fourth of the knowledge engineering time in an expert system with a large knowledge base.

Knowledge engineering requires the skills common to the management of any complex task. The following concerns add further demands on the knowledge engineer's time:

- Selecting methods and tools of knowledge engineering requires careful analysis of the expert and knowledge module by the knowledge engineer.

- When there are numerous sessions for knowledge acquisition or more than one expert and knowledge engineer, setting up procedures for knowledge acquisition is of great importance. Following a uniform procedure for knowledge engineering reduces the variability of the quality of knowledge within the knowledge base.

- Communicating with experts prior, during, and after the knowledge acquisition session facilitates the elicitation process. McGraw and Harbison-Briggs [1989] emphasize the necessity of training the expert on the mission of the expert system, and the methods of knowledge elicitation and knowledge collection to enhance the expert's enthusiasm for the system. They require that the expert should receive all the session materials in advance and be aware of the session's objective and method. After the session, the expert should receive a summary of the session's results and should have the opportunity to correct or comment on them.

- Paperwork and documentation is another time-consuming aspect of knowledge engineering. The knowledge engineer must document the elicitation process, but avoid the impulse to produce paper rather than usable knowledge. Observations, video taping, and audio taping require reporting and transcription, which has the potential to generate piles of paper. The knowledge engineer must decide on how much reporting and transcription is needed in such cases, while making sure that the source and content of the elicited knowledge is accurately documented.

- A database of experts, concepts, and vocabularies is needed when the size of the project is large and more than one knowledge engineer and expert participate in it. The organization and regular updating of this database help the knowledge engineers access the appropriate experts for different modules, without duplicating the already elicited knowledge or concepts.

- The knowledge base must be documented prior to coding. The knowledge base is not the same as the coded knowledge base. The knowledge engineer must establish an English-like pseudo code for documenting the logical design of the acquired knowledge, prior to the physical design and coding the knowledge into the expert system.

- The evaluation of the elicitation process is another required aspect of large expert systems. Feedback and reactions of the participants in the knowledge elicitation process at the early stages of the knowledge acquisition helps the knowledge engineer to improve the quality of the elicitation process. Measuring and evaluating the amount of usable knowledge obtained from every session is another way of controlling the effectiveness of elicitation sessions.

7.4 The Physical Design of Expert Systems

The logical design of the knowledge base forms the basis of the system's physical design. The physical design involves:

- Software decisions

- Hardware decisions

- User-interface design

- Physical design of the knowledge base

7.4.1 Software Decisions

The first question regarding the software is whether to program the system from scratch (*make*) or *buy* one of the numerous expert system products in the market. Usually the first prototype uses a relatively cheap software product. In a later stage, when the organization and the developer have gained enough insight about the system, and if the existing products in the market are deemed inadequate, the developer may decide to program the system from scratch.

If the *make* decision is made, then the developer must decide on the representation method and programming language, and organize a programming team to design the software. The decisions on the method of representation, language, programmers, and software design go through a number of iterations and modifications before being finalized, as shown in Figure 7.6.

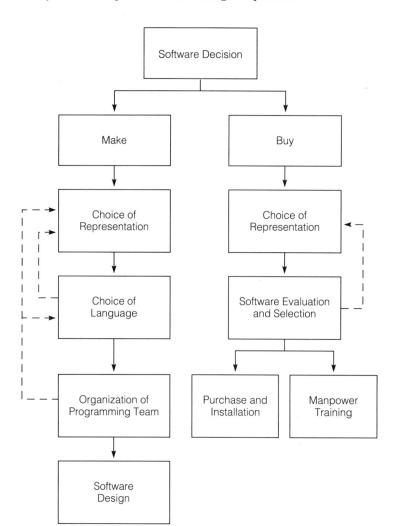

Figure 7.6 Software Decisions for Expert System Development

The *buy* decision is more common because of the availability of a wide range of expert system software products. In this option, too, the developer must decide on the method of representation and evaluate software products in the market. Evaluating the expert system software products is not a simple task. (Chapter 12 discusses the methods of software evaluation for expert systems.) Once the purchase is made, the software installation and training follow (Figure 7.6).

One important consideration in buying expert system software is the availability of the *run-time* or *field delivery* version of the software, as opposed to its *development* version. For example, in the case of the mortgage loan expert system, the programmer develops the system on the full or development version of an expert system software product. Once the system is complete and compiled, the use of the expert system does not require all the development facilities of the software. That is, the system could be used with the run-time version of the software on less powerful microcomputers.

On the other hand, the bank may wish to send, say, 1,000 copies of the system to its loan officers in various branches. When buying the software, the bank must consider the availability of the run-time version of the software, and negotiate the number of allowable copies of software that could be used in the field. If a software company has the run-time version of its software that runs on the bank's branch computers, it would receive a more favorable review because the bank would not need to buy new hardware in order to use the expert system in its branch offices.

If the expert system is complex and has to be hooked to other systems, as in the case of real-time manufacturing or control systems, the software must have strong outside hooks, specialized modules, or a programming language to allow the developer to deal with the complexity of the system.

The software decisions are closely tied to the other components of design, especially the choice of hardware and the results of knowledge acquisition.

7.4.2   Hardware Decisions

Since AI languages and expert system software products have become available for a wide range of hardware products, the speed and cost of hardware play an increasingly important role in the choice of hardware. Many software products run on micro- and minicomputers and workstations. However, the choice of minicomputers does not necessarily guarantee more speed and efficiency. Many expert system products may run more efficiently on powerful microcomputers than on minicomputers, because of the heavy overhead load in some minicomputers.

If the developer decides to *make* the software, then the choice of hardware partly depends on the availability of good and efficient compilers for the chosen AI language, as well as on the special hardware features that the expert system requires, such as graphics, voice synthesizer, and networking capabilities.

The organization's existing hardware for the development and field use of the expert system is a major consideration, especially in the early rounds of prototyping. As the nature and contributions of the expert system become more clear, the cost/benefit analysis of the system may show that a hardware investment may have a high return.

7.4.3 User-Interface Decisions

Most expert system software products have a default user interface, which prompts the user for inputs and answers to *why* and *how* questions regarding a particular input or the final advice. It provides on-line help on how to run the system, and allows the developer to add texts to questions, answers, and the introductory page. While such an interface may be adequate for early prototypes, a more sophisticated user interface may be needed when the system is implemented in the field.

User-Interface Technology

The user interface enjoys a number of technological advances for inputs to and outputs from the system:

- Menus

- Forms

- Graphics

- Symbols and icons

- Voice

- Hypertext

- Natural language

While menus, forms, and graphics for input and output are relatively commonplace, the use of symbols and icons for depicting an object and its attributes is of great value for an expert system that involves objects with which the user is most familiar. In other cases, the voice input and output is of value to users who do not have adequate time for keyboard entry (such as professionals), whose hands and eyes are occupied (such as drivers), or lack the skill for keyboard entry (such as some nonprofessional workers). In such cases, the system needs speech recognition and voice synthesizer units to understand the input and produce verbal outputs. This technology is already in use in many non-AI systems in business.

Hypertext is another technology for the user-interface design, which allows the user to move freely within a text, and select a keyword to access the related concepts or objects at other levels of the text. The hypertext as user interface, especially in expert systems, is in its infancy. However, there are already products in the market, such as Knowledge Pro (by Knowledge Garden, Nassau, N.Y.) and LEVEL5 OBJECT (by Information Builders, Inc., New York, N.Y.), which use the hypertext technology. Using hypertext creates a flexibility in movement within the system that is not available in many other products.

Natural language processing is a field of AI application in its own right. A number of non-AI software products have used this technology to allow the user to develop his or her own vocabulary, and communicate with the system in an English-like fashion. Products like Clout (by Microrim) and Intellect (by Artificial Intelligence Corp.) are add-on software used in conjunction with database management systems. These products accept questions in the user's vocabulary and translate them into system commands.

Expert systems normally do not provide answers to the user's query. Instead, the system asks the user questions regarding the data for a particular case. However, as expert systems are integrated with other business systems, particularly database management systems, one may design an expert system that provides answers to the user's queries. An example of such queries is the set of questions regarding past cases, with attributes similar to those of the case under consideration. The users of legal expert systems have queries of this type. In such systems, the use of natural language processors as the front end of the expert system increases the system's user-friendliness.

User-Interface Design

An important, and often neglected, aspect of a successful expert system is the identification of the user needs and the design of the user interface for accommodating them.

In designing the user interface, one must consider the type of the system users:

- Regular users vs. one-time users

- Computer-literate users vs. computer-illiterate users

- Internal users vs. external users

- Professional users vs. nonprofessional users

- Domain-experienced users vs. novice users

Features of the interface depend on the type of user. For example, after using the system for a while, a regular user of the system may prefer to access the system quickly, without waiting for the explanatory screens. A novice user may need far simpler screens, with a great deal of help in starting and working with the system. The internal users may have far greater opportunity to be trained on how to use the system, as opposed to external users, who may solely rely on the on-line help and off-line documents for using the system. A professional user may not be a domain expert, but has training in the domain, while a nonprofessional user may not be familiar with even the common vocabularies of the domain. The latter type of user requires a user interface with simple wordings and screens that explain the domain jargon. The developer should get to know the typical users of the system, before starting the user-interface design.

As Figure 7.7 shows, the user-interface design must address user needs within the software, hardware, resource, and manpower constraints.

For example, in the mortgage loan expert system designed to answer applicants' queries about their eligibility, the bank may need a system that

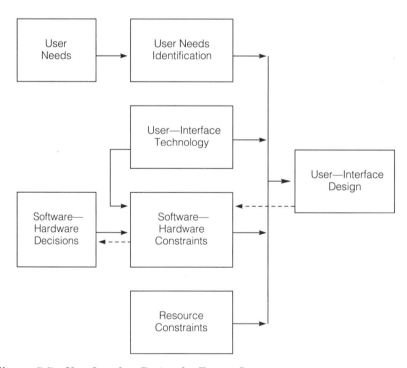

Figure 7.7   User-Interface Design for Expert Systems

could answer applicants by phone. Since the speech recognition technology at present requires repeated training inputs of the speaker's speech pattern to recognize the voice input, the system may be designed to take short entries by asking the customer to push telephone buttons. Alternatively, the bank may require that the customer come to a branch and fill out a computerized form for the expert system, or answer questions asked by the system. The choice of technology and the design of the user interface depends on the target customers (users) and the resources allocated to the project. Obviously, the choice also depends on whether it is possible to buy or make the expert system software that takes telephone signals as input and outputs verbal answers, and whether such software (with the accompanying hardware) is feasible within the financial and manpower resources available to the project.

Once the users' needs are identified and the decisions regarding user-interface technology are made, the user-interface design begins. When the users of the expert system have little technical knowledge and are apprehensive about using the system, the user interface must compensate for the users' lack of technical know-how and relieve their apprehension. Creating such a user interface is not a simple task, and its design may require more time and effort than the other components of the system.

7.4.4   The Physical Design of the Knowledge Base

When the software and hardware are in place, the pseudo-coded logical design of the knowledge base should be translated to a design compatible with the requirements of the software. The logical design is geared toward the domain knowledge; it is an abstract model of the domain knowledge. The physical design, on the other hand, accommodates the constraints and requirements imposed by the software product or the programming language; it is the implementation of the abstract model.

The physical design phase also contains:

- The design of outside hooks to the other business systems

- The modularization of the knowledge base for increasing system efficiency

- The design of hooks between the user interface and the knowledge base

- The security design for protecting the knowledge base from unauthorized access and accidental damage

- The design of warning and error messages

- The updating and maintenance procedures

In sum, the physical design is a document, based on which the system is coded and programmed. It provides a unified framework for coding and testing decisions and evaluations.

7.5 Coding, Testing, and Reliability of Expert Systems

Once the physical design of the expert system is completed, the system is ready for *coding* and *testing*. Ideally it is desirable to have a measure of reliability for the expert system. As we will see, methods for measuring the reliability of expert systems are yet to be developed.

7.5.1 Managing the Coding Process

Expert systems have a number of pieces that must be coded:

- Coding or installing the software

- Coding the knowledge base

- Coding the user-interface design

- Coding the connection of the expert system to other systems

The complexity of the coding stage depends on the "make" or "buy" decision of the software, as well as on the complexity of the user interface and the connection of the expert system to other systems. When the software decision is to program the system from scratch, or the user interface has a complex design, the developer needs software engineering procedures and techniques for ensuring the quality and integrity of the software. All available techniques and related issues in software engineering are applicable in coding expert system applications.

When the software is purchased, coding the knowledge base is the most important step of coding. Here the efforts of the knowledge engineer in documenting the elicited knowledge would pay off. A well-documented knowledge base greatly facilitates the coding of the knowledge base.

7.5.2 *Testing*

Testing the expert system takes place in various stages:

- Software testing

- Testing the coded knowledge base for syntax errors

- Verification and validation of the expert system

- Field tests

The last two categories are discussed in the next subsection.

The expert system must be tested even if the software is purchased. The producers of the software products provide users with sample examples. Using these samples and samples from other sources for testing the software help the developer discover special features and limitations of the software, before embarking on a massive effort of encoding the knowledge base.

The coded knowledge base is tested for syntax errors. (Semantic errors are normally discovered at the verification stage.) Not all expert system software products provide good error-checking facilities. Therefore, the developer must devise procedures for reducing the probability of syntax errors and increasing the possibility of discovering such errors. Modularization of the expert system helps in this respect, because the difficulty of discovering errors increases with the size of the knowledge base. Modularization allows the programmers to code the knowledge base in small and manageable modules, which makes it easier to test the knowledge base for syntax errors. If modules are entered manually, another strategy is to have two independent coders enter each module twice. A discrepancy between the results of running the two versions of a module indicates the existence of syntax errors in at least one of the two versions.

As discussed previously, there are mathematical techniques for measuring software reliability. When the system is of critical importance to the firm, the developer may use software reliability techniques to measure the reliability of the software.

Verification, Validation, and Field Tests

Verification and validation require that:

- The system must perform according to its intended design

- The system must be a good model of the real-world decisions made by the expert

Verification and validation have a relatively long history in other areas; Fishman and Kiviat [1968] were the first to use these terms in connection with testing system simulation. Since expert systems have the goal of simulating the human reasoning process, we follow the definitions used for simulation.

Verification in general means proving mathematically that a computer program behaves in a certain manner. Applied to expert systems, the verification process determines whether the expert system follows the logic provided in the knowledge base. In other words, the coded knowledge base should reflect the intended structure of the logical and physical designs. *Validation* asks whether the expert system simulates the decision process of the expert(s) to an acceptable degree by producing the *right* or an *acceptable* answer in each case.

At the verification stage, the system is still under development. Therefore, the verification tests have an internal focus. The developer looks for errors in the logical design, physical design, or programming and software codes. The expert who helps in the verification stage is in most cases the one who has been involved in the knowledge acquisition process. The data sets used for verification are mostly the ones used for developing the knowledge base. The developer may divide each data set into two parts: one part for knowledge acquisition and one part for the subsequent verification. The system also may be verified using both parts of the data set.

Validation has an external focus. The performance of the system is judged as a completed product, which has already passed the verification tests. The experts used in validating the system are usually independent from those involved in the system development. The data sets used for validation are not used in the development of the system, and could be obtained from sources outside the acquisition process.

Field testing is another element of system validation. In such tests, the developer selects a number of test sites, and puts the system into actual use. The advantage of field testing is that all aspects of the system, rather than just the knowledge base, could be examined. When the system has a complex user interface or a series of complex hooks to other systems, such field tests are crucial for successful implementation of the system.

Methods of verification and validation could be divided into four categories:

- Machine tests

- Data tests

- Human tests

- Turing-like tests

Machine Tests

Machine tests are useful for verification. In such tests, the expert system software product has facilities for identifying errors. For example, the software may find inconsistent and conflicting rules or knowledge pieces. The software may provide the capability of tracing the sequence of steps used in arriving at the final answer. It may allow the developer to compile the knowledge base one portion at a time, or compile it incrementally. The software that has a better testing and error finding capability enhances the verification stage of the system.

Data Tests

Data tests are used in both verification and validation of the system. In a data test, the data on the existing cases are fed to the system, and the output of the system is analyzed. The data set is generated from actual human decisions, which could be inconsistent over time due to fatigue or just plain limitations of human cognitive ability. Therefore, in the case of occasional differences between the data and the system, an expert should judge the quality of the expert recommendations versus the historical data.

Human Tests

Human tests are used for both verification and validation. The expert or the user are asked to use the system and judge its performance. At the verification stage, the expert and the user are internal, and at the validation stage, they are external to the design process.

In a more formal test, the system is tested against the expert. Hypothetical or actual cases are presented to both the system and the expert. The developer may ask for the expert's reasoning and match it with the system's line of reasoning. In doing so, the developer makes sure that the system and the expert have reached the same conclusion for the same reason. Furthermore, in the case of a conflict, the developer has some clue about the sources of conflict. In the verification stage, the expert is the one whose knowledge is incorporated in the knowledge base. In the validation stage, either the expert is external, or an independent expert may review the quality of the outcome of the machine versus the expert.

Another formal test for validation is to have the users in the field use the system for a given period of time. Favorable results in the field tests add to the face validity of the system. On the other hand, serious problems encountered in field tests indicate the need for further improvement of the design.

Turing-like Tests

Turing-like tests are based on the Turing test concept, discussed in Chapter 2. The focus in such tests is to see whether the answers of an expert system could pass as those of a human expert. The judges could be users, or a panel of human experts. The judges are provided with answers to a series of problems, some given by human experts and some by the expert system. If the judges are unable to identify the answer sets produced by the machine, then the system is considered to have passed this test. This type of test is appropriate for the validation stage.

7.5.3 *Reliability of Expert Systems*

As the previous discussion shows, for an expert system to provide the correct answer, its components must be designed properly and work accurately. That is, the system as a whole must be reliable.

Therefore, the *reliability* of an expert system is a concept that entails various aspects of systems evaluation and performance. Expert system reliability measures the dependability of the system in satisfactorily performing the tasks it is designed for. Expert system reliability has four major sources, as shown in Figure 7.8:

- Software reliability

- Knowledge-base reliability

- User-interface reliability

- Uncertainty structure reliability

Ideally, a measure of expert system reliability brings together the test results of these four components of the system.

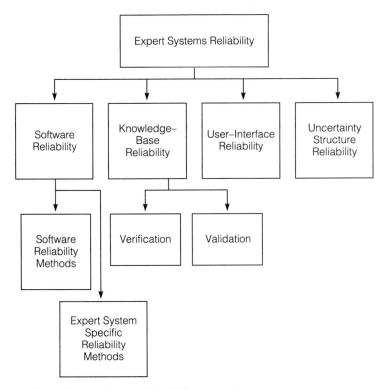

Figure 7.8 Expert System Reliability

One can model the software reliability in expert systems using the general purpose models designed for measuring software reliability. Numerous models have been developed for this purpose (see, for example, Musa et al. 1987).

The reliability of the knowledge base could be tested through the verification and validation processes, described in the previous sections. This is the area with the most methods. However, the quantitative method for bringing the results of the verification and validation together into one measure of knowledge-base reliability is yet to be developed.

The user-interface reliability tests ensure that the user interface elicits the correct answer from the user. Although field tests collect the users' reaction to the system's user interface, a systematic method for measuring the reliability of the user interface is lacking at present.

The reliability of modeling uncertainty in the system is one of the most problematic areas of expert system reliability. As we discuss in Chapter 11, modeling uncertainty in expert systems has an ad hoc nature in some cases.

Using the uncertainty model that correctly reflects the errors and the lack of precision in the domain and in the expert's knowledge is one of the most challenging tasks in expert system development. Equally challenging is the elicitation of the uncertainty data from the expert. The uncertainty model has a significant impact on the outcome of the system. At present, there are few methods for measuring the reliability of uncertainty models and the elicited data on uncertainty.

7.6 Implementation and Post-implementation of Expert Systems

The ultimate goal of any expert system is its implementation in the real world. Like any other computerized system, the implementation and post-implementation phases of expert systems require careful planning.

7.6.1 Implementation Considerations

Many expert systems do not go beyond the prototyping and testing stages. Part of this is attributable to:

- The initial unrealistic expectations of the managers

- The failure of the developer to correctly identify the problem, its domain, and domain experts

- The limited nature of the system

- The reluctance of users to use the system

- The lack of a supporting structure for maintaining and updating the system

These problems indicate that the developer has rushed into the systems design without spending adequate time in the system analysis stage.

An expert system could rarely reach the implementation phase without an active participation of users' representatives. If the system is designed for internal users, training and involvement of the users should start from the initial phases of the system. In all cases, user training is a function of the implementation phase. The system documentation as well as on-line and human technical support for the access and use of the system are essential.

In other words, users are the key to the successful implementation of expert systems.

7.6.2 Post-implementation Considerations

The development of an expert system does not end with its implementation. The system's knowledge-base manager should collect statistics on its use and gather reports of its problems to identify areas of future enhancement for the system. The special feature of the post-implementation stage of an expert system is its requirement for learning new knowledge and forgetting obsolete knowledge.

Learning is the most dynamic aspect of human intelligence. A human life consists of a continuous process of learning new information, and discarding obsolete knowledge. Expert systems do not have the ability to learn automatically. Updating the system's knowledge base is vital to its continuous use. It needs a *knowledge-base manager* within an organizational unit with the capability to update the knowledge base. A logical location could be either the user unit, or within the MIS department.

When the knowledge within the domain has a great deal of dynamism and changes regularly, it would be desirable to incorporate the automatic learning tools of neural networks within the expert system. The topic of neural networks is discussed in Chapters 13 and 14.

Conclusion

This chapter introduced the stages of development in expert systems, including system development life cycle and prototyping. It showed that expert systems, like information systems, require systems analysis and design. Systems analysis in expert systems requires problem definition and goal identification, domain analysis, domain modulation, and expert identification. One of the most important issues in systems analysis is the communication process among many players involved in developing and managing expert systems.

The design of expert systems consists of the logical design and physical design phases. Knowledge acquisition constitutes the major feature in the logical design of expert systems. It begins with the selection of experts and identification of knowledge sources. Once the knowledge acquisition process commences, the knowledge engineer should choose the appropriate methods and tools of knowledge acquisition. This chapter reviewed methods and tools available to the knowledge engineer. Using multiple experts in knowledge acquisition has many advantages. However, it creates added complexities and issues in the process. The organizational aspects of knowledge acquisition are among the crucial factors in the success of the knowledge acquisition process.

The physical design of expert systems involves software and hardware selection, user interface design, and the physical design of the knowledge base. These topics were reviewed in this chapter.

Testing the expert systems is also another major step in the development of expert systems. In this step, we make a distinction between the verification and validation of the system. The concept of expert system reliability brings together various evaluation aspects of expert systems. Expert system reliability, and the implementation and post-implementation issues of expert systems are critical development areas that have not received adequate attention in the applications of expert systems. These are the areas of future elaboration, as expert systems leave the experimental phase and mature into an everyday business tool.

References

Bareiss, E. R. 1989. *Exemplar-based Knowledge Acquisition: A Unified Approach to Concept Representation, Classification, and Learning*, Academic Press, Boston, MA.

Davis, Randall. 1979. "Interactive Transfer of Expertise: Acquisition of New Inference Rules," *Artificial Intelligence*, Vol. 12, No. 2, pp. 121–157.

Fishman, G. S. and Kiviat, P. J. 1968. "The Statistics of Discrete Event Simulation," *Simulation*, Vol. 10, pp. 185–195.

Johnson, S. 1967. "Hierarchical Clustering Schemes," *Psychometrika*, Vol. 32, pp. 241–254.

Kruskal, J. 1977. "Multidimensional Scaling and Other Methods for Discovering Structure," in *Statistical Methods for Digital Computers*, Enslein, Ralston, and Wilf (Eds.), John Wiley and Sons, New York, NY.

Lenat, Douglas B. and Guha, R. V. 1990. *Building Large Knowledge-Based Systems*, Addison-Wesley Publishing Co., Reading, MA.

Lirov, Yuval. 1990. "Systematic Innovation for Knowledge Engineering," *AI Expert*, Vol. 5, July, pp. 28–33.

McGraw, Karen L. and Harbison-Briggs, Karan. 1989. *Knowledge Acquisition: Principles and Guidelines*, Prentice Hall, Englewood Cliffs, NJ.

Musa, J.; Iannino, D.; and Okumoto, K. 1987. *Software Reliability: Measurement, Prediction, Applications*, McGraw-Hill, New York, NY.

Musen, Mark A. 1989a. "Conceptual Models of Interactive Knowledge Acquisition Tools," *Knowledge Acquisition*, Vol. 1, No. 1, pp. 73–88.

Musen, Mark A. 1989b. *Automated Generation of Model-Based Knowledge Acquisition Tools*, Pitman, London, England.

Musen, Mark A.; Fagan, Lawrence M.; Combs, David M.; and Shortliffe, Edward H. 1987. "Use of a Domain Model to Drive an Interactive Knowledge Editing Tool," *International Journal of Man-Machine Studies*, Vol. 26, No. 1, pp. 105–121.

Prerau, David S. 1990. *Developing and Managing Expert Systems: Proven Techniques for Business and Industry*, Addison-Wesley Publishing Co., Reading, MA.

Saaty, Thomas L. 1977. "A Scaling Method for Priorities in Hierarchical Structures," *Journal of Mathematical Psychology*, Vol. 15, pp. 234–281.

Zahedi, Fatemeh. 1986. "The Analytic Hierarchy Process—A Survey of the Method and its Applications," *Interfaces*, Vol. 16, pp. 96–108.

Questions

7.1 What are the special features of an expert system that make expert system development different from that of the information systems?

7.2 What is the difference between the life-cycle and prototyping approaches in developing expert systems?

7.3 What are the unique features of systems analysis in expert systems?

7.4 What are the major issues in designing an expert system?

7.5 What is the difference between logical design and physical design in expert system development?

7.6 Discuss various types of knowledge acquisition methods.

7.7 Discuss the circumstances where the deductive method of knowledge acquisition is a preferred method. Repeat the discussion for the inductive approach.

7.8   Discuss the advantages and disadvantages of a multi-expert knowledge base.

7.9   What is the significance of documentation? What are the areas of the expert system where documentation is of critical importance?

7.10 What is the difference between validation and verification in expert system development?

7.11 Discuss the significance of a reliability measure for expert systems.

7.12 What is the significance of automatic learning for the post-implementation of expert systems?

Problems

7.1   Specify the possible goals of a job application expert system, which evaluates job applicants for various positions.

7.2   What are the possible knowledge base modules for a job application expert system?

7.3   Specify the knowledge sources for the knowledge acquisition for a job application system.

7.4   What are possible user types in a job application expert system?

7.5   Identify various phases of knowledge acquisition for a job application expert system, and justify using an appropriate acquisition method for each phase.

7.6   Discuss the organizational aspects of knowledge acquisition for a job application expert system. If you choose to have a multi-expert knowledge base for this system, what methods of conflict resolution would you adopt?

7.7   Describe how you would verify and validate a job application expert system.

7.8   Refer to the case box on the application of expert systems to internal auditing. Discuss the type of AShell expert system. Identify similar systems discussed in this chapter.

7.9   What is the difference between the Loan Probe (discussed in case box on the application of expert systems to internal auditing) and the Mortgage Loan case discussed throughout the previous chapters?

7.10 What are other possible expert systems that may be developed for bank services?

7.11 Identify a problem and its domain for developing an expert system, and perform the system development functions for this system.

Case: Expert System for University Admission Office

As we saw in the case at the end of Chapter 5, the admission of undergraduate and graduate students at the university requires a number of criteria, and a series of rules to handle exceptional cases. Furthermore, the decision for the eligibility of the application for financial aid and a loan is another aspect of the admission process.

The intended goal of the system is to identify the university applicants who either meet the minimum requirements for the university admission or fall into one of the exceptional categories. Such applicants are called "potentially acceptable" applicants. If an applicant is potentially acceptable, and has applied for financial assistance or a loan, the system must determine the eligibility of the applicant for the financial aid.

Contact the admission office and financial aid office at your university. Collect their manuals and standard procedures. Identify an expert in each office. Through the process of knowledge engineering discussed in this chapter, identify the rules that are applied for identifying the potentially acceptable applicant and his or her eligibility for financial assistance.

Case: Expert System Software Spinoff

Based in Park City, Utah, The Fields Software Group is a division of cookie queen Mrs. Fields Inc. that sells retail management software based on expert systems technology. Although Mrs. Fields may seem an unlikely source for artificial intelligence software, the company's success with its homegrown expert systems encouraged executives to offer the modules for other retailers through its own software sales company. In this way, Mrs. Fields has not only capitalized on its own expertise in house but now makes money selling that expertise to others.

The Fields Software Group's packages are sold in modules for PC-based systems. Each module, or Retail Operations Intelligence System (ROI) is designed to deliver expert advice on specific areas of interest to retailers, including daily sales, labor scheduling and personnel management.

While some companies are reluctant to disclose their development in AI because of the strategic advantage that expert systems deliver, Mrs. Fields has no such qualms with its ROIs. Although the ROI prepackages much of the information required to create a custom expert system, each module still has to be tailored to a specific buyer's needs. As a result, an ROI-based system for the cookie business can wind up looking quite different than one applied for an auto parts store. The modules can be purchased for approximately $500 to $1,000 a piece, with the entire ROI system retailing for $8,000.

From the article by Harvey P. Newquist III, "Mrs. Fields Software Spinoff," *Datamation*, April 1, 1990, p. 54, reprinted with permission from *Datamation*.

Case Questions

1. Discuss the advantages and disadvantages of marketing an internally used expert system.

2. What are the issues to be considered in the systems analysis and design of an expert system that will eventually be offered in the market as opposed to those of an expert system developed solely for internal use?

Case: Expert Systems for Environmental Decision Makers

Environmental decision makers typically use well-established database and spreadsheet software. Knowledge-base systems, however, have not achieved similar acceptance. This is due to a general lack of understanding. The community of environmental specialists is not aware that knowledge-base systems can i) reliably augment decision support process, ii) operationally model decision processes, iii) interpret or supplement data from spreadsheets, databases, and other software, and iv) be configured as extensions of conventional systems.

To compound the problem, powerful, affordable development shells have been available for only a short time. Also, some expert systems have not met users' expectations. Despite these difficulties, a number of knowledge-base tools have been developed to assist with environmental decision processes, and others are under development.

In 1986, the Environmental Protection Agency (EPA) initiated efforts to evaluate the utility of knowledge-base systems. A few ad hoc evaluations were conducted through the Agency. These efforts were usually undertaken by individuals with interests both in knowledge-base programming and in a technical domain. Small prototype systems covering specific topics of interest were subsequently developed. This context influenced the initial criteria for evaluating knowledge programming technology in general. In effect, knowledge programming technology was evaluated in terms of the functional characteristics of early projects, rather than in an organized manner. Flawed or inappropriate applications adversely affected the overall view of knowledge system's usefulness. Follow-up analyses were usually not conducted. Criteria considered important by current standards, such as qualitative improvements of decisions, were not usually considered.

EPA's Risk Reduction Engineering Laboratory (RREL), was one of the early participants in knowledge system development and evaluation within EPA. The first knowledge-base system project initiated by RREL, now called the Flexible Membrane Liner System (FLEX), typifies early EPA projects. The goal was to produce systems to assist in evaluation of test data for a particular type of flexible membrane liner (FML) material. FMLs are commonly used as a barrier element in landfill construction. This project was initiated largely because FMLs were of particular interest to the funding organization. Since the first version (written in BASIC) was released in 1984, FLEX has been rewritten and revised several times. Recent versions (written in C) have expanded reporting and analysis capabilities.

Based on FLEX and a few other narrowly defined projects, EPA decided to expand development efforts. From 1985 to 1987, funding was increased and new system work was begun to assist in reviewing sections of permit applications for closing hazardous waste sites. This domain was selected as a result of an informal survey of targeted users and others acquainted with the Resource Conservation Recovery Act. The closure analysis project was assigned to a contractor, CDM Federal Programs Corporation (FPC), through a three-year support contract.

FPC's Expert System Group designed and developed the Closure Evaluation System (CES). CES produced as analysis of the quality of a site closure design based on engineering design parameters and other data characterizing a waste site and closure plan. The analytical capabilities of this system have been expanded and enhanced. CES is currently delivered as three interrelated modules. Each module can be used independently or with either or both of the others to analyze and review closure engineering parameters and concepts.

Near the end of FPC's three-year contract, FPC was commissioned to conduct a formal survey of EPA's needs for knowledge-base decision systems. This was the first attempt to evaluate potential knowledge system applications on an Agency-wide basis. Based on the results of this survey, eleven topic areas were selected as targets for application projects. The formal survey process represented a major shift in program management policy. Rather than initiating projects on the basis of development interests, application topic selection would now be based on the interests of potential user community.

Knowledge-base system development has entered a new era at RREL. RREL's current development work is directed towards providing applications that satisfy formally identified needs. Some of these needs are more broadly defined than the domains of earlier systems. The development staff includes four EPA employees and four on-site contractor specialists from Computer Science Corporation. All of the development staff have 386-class machines with state-of-the-art software products (object-oriented development shells with graphics user interface capabilities). A complement to this on-site organization is provided through a five year expert systems development support contract with CDM FPC, awarded at the end of fiscal 1990.

The major effort of RREL is currently directed toward developing a knowledge-base system that will aid in screening federal and state regulations that affect clean-up activities at Superfund sites. These regulations are referred to as ARARS (Applicable or Relevant and Appropriate Regulations). The Potential ARARS Selection Tool (PAST) will address one of the highest priority needs identified by the user survey.

Full development of this system is anticipated to be a multi-year effort. Although development activities are centered at RREL, FPC is also providing technical support and knowledge engineering for this project.

The knowledge-base system development program within RREL now has both the capabilities and funding to develop systems which can meaningfully assist the work of environmental decision makers. For the RREL program to be successful in this work, however, it is helpful to further explore the criteria used for application selection within the Agency and to also identify and evaluate factors that may impede the acceptance of future systems.

Condensed from "AI and The Environment: Knowledge-Based Tools For Environmental Decision Makers," by Daniel Greathouse and James Decker, *PC AI*, November/December 1991, pp. 29–31, reprinted with permission from *PC AI*.

Case Questions

1. User acceptance plays a major role in the success of any information system, especially in expert systems. Discuss the actions you would recommend in increasing the user acceptance in the EPA's expert systems.

2. Considering the fact that environmental issues are gaining significance in our society, discuss the type of expert systems that will be needed at EPA in coming years.

3. Cost is always an issue in developing new applications of expert systems. Discuss cost-saving technological trends that will help EPA in developing new applications.

4. Discuss trends in environmental problems and types of government employment that will necessitate an increased reliance on expert systems.

5. It is observed that in some parts of EPA (such as the Superfund Program) the personnel turnover is high. Discuss the role of expert systems in helping the agency cope with high turnover.

6. Identify areas in which EPA can use expert systems as a management control tool.

7. The authors of the article conclude that "within the next ten years at EPA, the knowledge-based systems will become (at least nearly) as prevalent as database and spreadsheet technologies." Discuss the factors that support this conclusion. What are the possible organizational roadblocks to the future massive use of expert systems at EPA?

OBJECT-ORIENTED REPRESENTATION AND HYBRID METHODS

The objective of Part IV is to introduce the reader to the object-oriented representation approach in expert systems, and to review the use of this approach in hybrid expert system tools that contain both logic-based and object-oriented methods of knowledge representation. This part consists of Chapters 8, 9, and 10.

Chapter 8 introduces object-oriented representation and design. It discusses the unique features of the object-oriented approach, and covers topics related to systems analysis and design issues in developing object-oriented systems.

Chapter 9 discusses the methods and some software tools that combine the logic-based and object-oriented knowledge representation in expert systems. This chapter introduces KAPPA, a hybrid expert system software tool, in some detail.

Chapter 10 covers LEVEL5 OBJECT, a hybrid tool, using a hands-on approach. Available for this book is a demo diskette of LEVEL5 OBJECT, which can be used to examine and demonstrate the unique features of this tool.

In undergraduate courses, the sections of Chapter 8 identified as "optional" can be skipped. In courses with a greater emphasis on the conceptual topics, and for those readers who wish to have only a general understanding of the working of hybrid tools, a brief review of either KAPPA in Chapter 9, or LEVEL5 OBJECT in Chapter 10, will be sufficient. Courses with a greater emphasis on application can benefit from a detailed examination of both KAPPA and LEVEL5 OBJECT.

CHAPTER 8

Object-Oriented Representation and Design

Knowledge is the conformity of the object and the intellect.

Averroës, *Destructio Destructionum*

In natural science, I have understood, there is nothing petty to the mind that has a large vision of relations, and to which every single object suggests a vast sum of conditions. It is surely the same with the observation of human life.

George Eliot, *The Mill on the Floss*

Chapter Objectives

The objectives of this chapter are:

- To briefly review the semantic nets, scripts, and frames modeling methods

- To cover the object-oriented programming (OOP) method for modeling knowledge

- To discuss the object-oriented analysis in expert systems

- To discuss the object-oriented design in expert systems

- To review the logical design in the object-oriented approach

- To review the physical design in the object-oriented approach

- To compare object-oriented programming languages

- To discuss the advantages and disadvantages of the object-oriented approach

---

KEY WORDS: Semantic nets, scripts, frames, object-oriented programming, inheritance, class abstraction, class hierarchy, modularity, encapsulation, object-oriented analysis, object-oriented design, polymorphisms

---

Introduction

This chapter is the first of three chapters that cover the object-oriented knowledge representation in expert systems. Section 8.1 lays the foundation for the object-oriented approach and traces its use in the early development of three well-known methods in artificial intelligence: semantic nets, scripts, and frames. These methods were developed exclusively for AI before the object-oriented approach became a hot topic in information systems.

Section 8.2 introduces you to object-oriented programming (OOP) and its major concepts, such as class abstraction, hierarchy, inheritance, instances, methods, and polymorphism. These concepts are important when using OOP, be it in expert systems or other areas of information systems.

Section 8.3 introduces object-oriented analysis (OOA) and object-oriented design (OOD) as applied to expert systems. Section 8.4 takes you further by discussing the logical design of an expert system when the knowledge is represented in the object-oriented method. In other words, this section shows you how to design classes and their relations and methods.

Chapter 7 explained that the physical design follows the logical design. The same issues and discussions concerning physical design apply equally to the object-oriented approach. However, in this approach, there is the additional issue of choice of the OOP language. There are numerous OOP languages with different structures and capabilities. We discuss and categorize these languages in Section 8.5 and then compare them with conventional programming languages in the last section of this chapter. The case boxes demonstrate real applications in which an object-oriented approach is an appropriate method of knowledge representation.

8.1 The Evolution of Object-Oriented Methods

The logic-based representation methods have been criticized for their inability to show "causal relationships" and associations among the objects. For example, in the loan application case, one may wish to know the salient attributes of an applicant, and be able to answer questions about the applicant's associations with the bank, the loan officer, his or her employer, and other banks and credit organizations. In a broad domain, such as modeling natural language processing, this problem is even more acute because the scope of possible questions and associations is much wider than a limited system such as a loan application system. The semantic nets method was developed for modeling associations among concepts or objects.

8.1.1 Semantic Nets

The *semantic nets* method has a simple and graphic structure in the form of a network. The nodes of the network represent objects or concepts, while the arcs of the network show the relations or associations among the nodes. For example, in Figure 8.1, the objects or concepts are the loan applicants, individual applicants, commercial applicants, loans, home equity loans, and commercial loans. The associations among these nodes are identified on the arcs of the network. Two association types are more frequent: *is-a* and *has-a*. The *is-a* association shows the specialization. For example, the human applicant is a special type of applicant. The *has-a* association indicates the attributes of the object. For example, the individual applicants node has income and social-security attributes.

One of the most important contributions of semantic nets to the object-oriented approach is the concept of *inheritance*. In the *is-a* association, the specialized node inherits the attributes of its parent node. For example, in Figure 8.1, the loan applicants node has two attributes: name and address. The *children* of this node are the specialized form of the general category loan applicants, and they inherit these attributes. Therefore, we do not need to repeat them for the individual applicants and commercial applicants. We see in the discussion of object-oriented programming that inheritance is one of its important features.

The development of semantic nets took place in the 1960s. The major applications of semantic nets were in the context of modeling natural language processing in AI. In 1961, Masterman used semantic nets to develop the 100 basic concepts in modeling a 15,000-word dictionary. A number of AI researchers built systems of a similar nature in the 1960s and early 1970s.

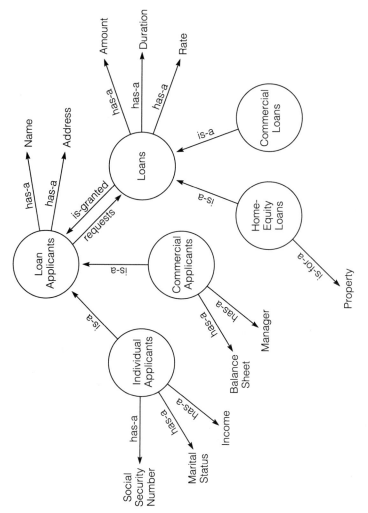

Figure 8.1 An Example of Semantic Nets

In 1969, Collins and Quillian demonstrated the theoretical application of semantic nets. They built a hierarchical network for structuring animals, birds, and special types of birds. In asking questions from the human subjects, Collins and Quillian noticed that when the question required moving up the hierarchy, the subject took longer to answer. They concluded that semantic nets are a good model of human information processing.

The semantic nets method was used to model the structure of the English language and the linguistic associations of words within sentences. The problem with using semantic nets was that the associations were too general and too diverse for any meaningful modeling. In 1974, Schank and Rieger developed a standard for modeling natural language processing and called it *conceptual dependency theory*. They identified four types of primitive concepts: actions, picture producers (such as objects), action aiders, and picture aiders. They then identified basic types of each concept. For example, they categorized basic components of actions into these twelve types: move, speak, attend, grasp, ingest, propel, expel, transfer control, transfer by physical force, transfer information, create information, and think. These basic concepts were used to model the English language.

Although semantic nets have been useful for conceptualizing complex systems, such as language structure, they have a number of shortcomings, most notably:

- The semantic nets method does not distinguish between the class of an object and a particular object, as in the individual **applicants** as a class and **smith** as an instance of the category. Later, this distinction was created by using *is-a* to identify an instance of an object and by defining another type of association: *is-a-kind-of* for identifying the subclass of a class of objects.

- The semantic nets method does not have the appropriate structure for accommodating the complex associations of the attributes of an object with other objects. For example, in Figure 8.1, the attribute **property** could itself be a node with attributes of its own.

- The presentation and structure of semantic nets for complex systems could become unmanageable.

These and other criticisms led to the continuous modification and extensions of semantic nets, which resulted in two other methods: scripts and frames.

8.1.2 *Scripts*

In their information processing, humans rely a great deal on their experience and common sense. One criticism of knowledge representation methods is that they do not embody the background experience and context.

Case: Smart Factory Outlet

FMC's Ground Systems Division in San Jose, Calif., uses a system called Layout Advisor, developed and running on Symbolics workstations, to configure the shop floor intelligently for maximum efficiency.

The plant manufactures military-transport vehicles, a multistep process that involves welding, drilling, painting, and every other manufacturing application imaginable. The factory floor is a tangle of fork lifts, trucks, and mechanized carts, all swarming like worker ants. The manufactured parts have to get from one treatment to another, and that's where intrafactory transport comes in—the products have to be delivered from one end of the factory to the other. When you consider that the shop floor comprises 120,000 square feet, the task can be intractable.

Logically enough, management had grouped machines on the floor according to their functions: drill presses in one corner, lathes in another. But this approach caused as many problems as it solved, because although the overall confusion was decreased, the time a particular product stayed on the floor was too long. When a part had graduated from one process, it had to be transported to another. And because each part is introduced to a different sequence of processes, there is no way to ensure optimal efficiency by function grouping alone.

Project engineer Larry Martin decided to investigate software that could model the flow of products through the factory, ultimately to build an "interactive floor plan." After experimenting with conventional programs on PCs, he found them inflexible and lacking in graphics capabilities, so he turned to the Symbolics workstations at FMC's Corporate Technology Center. The workstations are used by FMC primarily for scheduling and diagnostics applications.

FMC programmers downloaded the factory's CAD and process-planning applications to a workstation and put symbolics' object-oriented Genera development environment to work. They used the environment to construct graphical models of the factory machines, the shop floor itself, and the way products flow through the factory. In addition, they determined how factory-floor configuration affected manufacturing efficiency.

Within six months they had created the Layout Advisor, which can configure as many as 10,000 routings among 500 machines. The system's knowledge base captures information about processes, machine capacity, and material flow and can recommend the appropriate product routings for various manufacturing processes. In addition, users may relocate machinery on the workstation screen and the Advisor will generate the impact of the relocation on material flow.

Layout Advisor has decreased the annual distance traveled by intrafactory transport by 40,000 miles, a 51% improvement. The system has also improved budgeting, forecasts, worker communication, and factory flexibility. FMC plans to build similar systems for department planning, cell-level design, and other internal applications.

By Justin Kestelyn, "Application Watch," *AI Expert*, January 1991, p. 72, reprinted with permission from *AI Expert*.

Schank's research on conceptual dependency led to the development of the *scripts* method to model the contextual and background for knowledge.

In the scripts method, the *typical* situation or context is modeled into the script or text of a story. For example, in the case of the mortgage loan application, the script may be that the applicant contacts the loan officer. The loan officer asks a set of questions, then asks the applicant to fill out the appropriate loan application forms and to provide the necessary documents, and the script continues.

A script has a number of components. To be useful, it should have a *starting condition*. For example, the bank must offer home mortgage loans, and the applicant must need a loan. The *outcomes* of the script are that the loan is approved, the bank's cash is reduced by the amount of the loan, and the applicant receives the money for purchasing the property. The *scenes* are the possible intermediary situations that take place in time. The *actors* of the script play their *roles*, as the applicant, the loan officer, the appraiser, and others play their roles. There are items, objects, and concepts that are the actor's *props* within the script, such as cash, forms, credit rating, property, loan, bank accounts, and assets. The script variables have a list of possible values, and one can develop possible *scenarios* by using these values within the script.

The scripts approach models the contextual component of knowledge. Although it was developed for understanding and processing natural language, it can be used for formalizing dynamic aspects of a system. Most of the knowledge representation methods have a static nature. That is, the sequence of events or the dynamic aspects of the system are not explicitly modeled into the system. Instead, it is the sequence of the rules or nodes that indirectly determines the expected sequence of events or scenes. In the scripts method, this sequence is explicitly formalized into the system. When the dynamic aspect of the system is of importance, the scripts approach has the capability of modeling it into the knowledge base. The difficulty in applying the scripts method is the lack of tools for operationalizing this approach.

Although the scripts method is not a popular approach in expert system applications, it has great potential for formalizing example-based and case-based inference methods. Furthermore, we note in the discussion of the tools for analyzing and designing object-oriented knowledge representation that it lacks methods for depicting the dynamics of the system. One can apply the scripts concept as a design approach in this area.

8.1.3 *Frames*

Knowledge representation by the *frames* method was developed to address some of the inadequacies of the semantic nets. It combines some of the features of semantic nets and scripts. Minsky (1975) describes the frame theory as "data structures for representing stereotyped situations," which could be changed to fit new realities. One can think about a frame as a node of semantic nets with a complex data structure like a script. Thus, a frame represents a complex object, whose attributes are stored in *slots* of the frame.

For example, the mortgage loan system could have a frame **individual applicants**. This frame represents the class of human applicants, and belongs to the superclass of **loan applicants**. It has slots that contain the attributes of a stereotypical human applicant, such as the purpose of the application, the information an applicant provides, the responsibility of an applicant, the property, and so forth.

As Figure 8.2 shows, the concept of inheritance of semantic nets is present in the network of frames, and the relations of each frame with the others are clearly identified. For example, the **individual applicants** frame has the **applicants** frame as its superclass, and inherits its attributes. More importantly, the frames have a complex data structure in that this frame has attributes that themselves are frames. For example, the individual applies for a mortgage loan, which itself is a frame with its own attributes.

Frames also have *procedural attachment*. For example, the value in the mortgage payment slot of the **mortgage loan** frame could be the result of applying a formula in which the amount, rate, and duration slots are used. The frames can also have *demons*. A demon is the side effect of a change within the knowledge base, and gets activated when the change takes place. For example, when the value in the **amount** slot in the **mortgage loan** frame goes above, say, $1,000,000, the system invokes procedures (subroutines, or a small program) that require a more stringent check on the applicant's

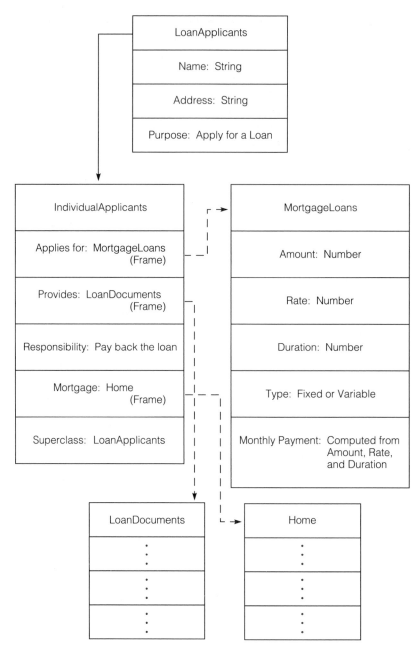

Figure 8.2 An Example of Frames

creditworthiness, or alerts a high-ranking loan officer for the supervision of the process.

The emphasis of frames is the static representation of knowledge; it lacks the dynamic formalism of scripts. More importantly, the frames method does not have a language of its own, and that makes its application costly and time-consuming. However, the frames' complex data structure in the form of slots was the precursor of the data structure of object-oriented programming languages.

8.2 Object-Oriented Programming (OOP)

Object-oriented programming (OOP for short) brings together the advances in:

- AI's object-based knowledge representation, especially semantic nets and frames

- Software engineering and systems analysis

- Conventional programming

- Systems simulation modeling techniques

- Computer graphics

At the same time, it addresses some of the concerns in the first three areas.

The development of semantic nets and frames gave OOP the concepts of inheritance and object representation. Advances in conventional programming provided the possibility of complex and user-defined data structures. In languages such as Pascal and C, the programmer is not limited to language-defined data types such as integer, real, and string. The programmer can define complex data structures. In these languages, one can define, say, an **address** data type that has components for the number, street, city, state, and zip code. Each of these components, in turn, is declared as integer, string, real, or any user-defined data type.

Software engineering and systems analysis contributed the concept of modular design and structured programming, in that the complex systems are divided into simple functional components.

The systems simulation approach and languages were the foundation for the first and most influential object-oriented programming language, which defined the field and its philosophy. Moreover, the advances in computer graphics made it possible to present and manipulate objects on the screen and to have multiple windows on one screen.

The existing needs of AI, software engineering, and conventional programming greatly contributed to OOP's sudden popularity as a paradigm, and to the marketing hype portraying OOP as a cure-all approach.

8.2.1   The Need for OOP

In AI and expert systems, the frame theory provided the fundamental concepts, but the programmer did not have a standard tool for applying them. OOP is the right tool for this approach.

In software engineering and systems analysis, the desirability of *reusable* code has been discussed for some time. In every computer project, the main cost of development, testing, and especially maintenance is in programming. It is therefore natural to think of writing the computer code in such a way that one can use part of it in other projects. The OOP approach has the promise of reusable code.

The fields of software engineering and systems analysis have championed the concept of modular design and programming, but no language had an inherent structure to force modularity. Moreover, the management of large and complex systems required a more stringent structure than simple modularity as well as an approach closer to the physical system. The OOP design and languages enforce modularity at the lowest unit of the system.

In conventional programming, there was a need for user-defined data types (or data abstraction) that would allow for a complex data structure for representing the real systems. The OOP approach has the most abstract and complex data structure.

More importantly, the maintenance cost of computer programs is a serious problem. Making changes in a complex program in response to changes in the environment sometimes costs, in the life of the program, more than its original development cost. Any method that could reduce the maintenance cost contributes greatly to the cost-effectiveness of computer systems. The OOP approach has the promise of lowering the maintenance and modification cost.

8.2.2   Class Abstraction

In modeling knowledge or programming systems, OOP *abstracts* from reality by choosing the components (objects) of the real world that matter to the problem at hand, and disregards the irrelevant aspects. In this process, OOP comes close to the way we see the world, as interacting objects.

The process of abstraction in object-oriented programming (OOP) is through the selection of relevant objects, and the identification of their relevant features, *attributes*, or *variables*. Objects with similar attributes are classified into a *class* of objects.

Classifying relevant objects starts with observing the real objects within the system, and categorizing them into classes based on their common attributes that matter to the problem. For example, in the mortgage loan system, smith, alpert, and jones are real objects. They may look and act differently, but they have common attributes that are of interest to the bank. They need mortgage loans, they have contacted the bank for the loan, and they have names for identification. Therefore, they could be classified as the individual applicants class in the system.

The attributes we have listed so far for individual applicants do not make this class of objects uniquely identifiable, because a commercial applicant, too, has the same attributes. Does this mean that a business company that applies for a loan could be considered in the class individual applicants? The answer is no. The problem is that the class of objects should contain the relevant attributes that uniquely identify the objects of a class, and exclude those that do not belong to the class. Therefore, we must include additional relevant attributes to the individual applicants class, such as social security number, marital status, job title, and so forth, in order to exclude the commercial applicants from the class.

Thus, objects are the unit of modeling in OOP, grouped into classes based on their relevant attributes. This is called *class abstraction* in OOP. The class abstraction depends on the purpose of the system and the knowledge domain. For example, in the mortgage loan system, the height, weight, race, national origin, and health status of the applicants are irrelevant, or even illegal, attributes to include in the system. However, in a medical system, these attributes must be included in the system. Thus, class abstraction is a knowledge engineering and knowledge modeling problem, as discussed in the object-oriented analysis later in this chapter.

8.2.3   Hierarchy of Classes

The classes of OOP are organized into a *class hierarchy*. Classes with some common attributes are classified into a higher level of abstraction. Moving up in the hierarchy, the classes are *generalized,* and moving down in the hierarchy, the classes are *specialized.* For example, the individual applicants and commercial applicants classes could be generalized into a more abstract class: the loan applicants. This class is called the *superclass* or the parent class of the individual applicants and commercial applicants classes, and these, in turn, are called the *subclasses*, or children of the parent class within the hierarchy.

As the system expands, the classes of loan applicants, credit card applicants, and commercial credit applicants could be generalized into the class of bank applicants, as shown in Figure 8.3. Thus, a class such as loan applicants could be both a superclass for its children and a subclass of its own parent.

In general, it is possible for a class to have more than one superclass. For example, since the bank's commercial customers normally ask for a commercial credit line, the class commercial credit applicants could have two superclasses: bank applicants and commercial customers (Figure 8.3). Later we will see that a class with more than one superclass creates the problem of multiple inheritance.

Setting up the hierarchy of classes depends on the nature of the knowledge domain, and requires a careful object-oriented analysis and design.

8.2.4 Inheritance

Setting up the hierarchy of classes with common attributes implies *inheritance* from superclass (parent) to subclasses (children). Inheritance works in

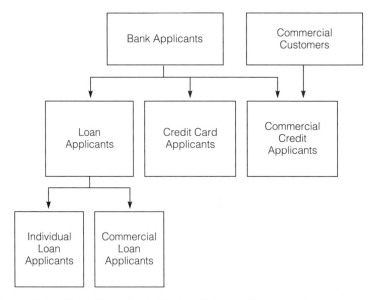

Figure 8.3 Class Hierarchy in Object-Oriented Programming

the following way. The superclass has the attributes that are common among its children. The children inherit these common attributes from their parent. Additionally, each child has its own unique set of attributes. In other words, the superclass has the general attributes; the subclass inherits the general attributes and adds its own special attributes. This is similar to what we have seen in the frames method.

Furthermore, a class could have attributes that are of the type of another class. For example, the individual applicants class has an attribute name, which itself is a member of another class called people names. This class, in turn, has the attributes first name, middle name, last name, trailing title (for Jr., Sr., MD, etc.), and titles (for Dr., HH., etc.), as shown in Figure 8.4.

A subclass could have more than one superclass and inherit from more than one. This type of inheritance is called *multiple inheritance.* Multiple inheritance is one of several unresolved topics of OOP, because it raises a number of issues that will be discussed in the object-oriented design section of this chapter.

8.2.5   Object as an Instance of a Class

A class is the model of a set of similar objects. However, in the use of the knowledge base or the execution of the program, a specific object is created that is an *instance* of the class. For example, we have the class individual applicants with given sets of attributes, some inherited and some unique to the class. When the knowledge base is used, one can create smith as an instance of this class by a statement like

```
smith := (new  IndividualApplicants)
```

This object has values for its attributes, which come from the user or a database. Thus, the object smith is an instance of the class individual applicants.

It is important to pay attention to the difference between the objects as instances, and classes as the models or abstract forms of a group of similar objects. In using the knowledge base or running the program, it is the interaction among the instance objects that produces outcome. This is the main strength of OOP, and will be explained in more detail in the following sections.

8.2.6   Methods

Each class has attached functions it can perform. These functions are called *methods.* If we imagine the attribute values of classes as their data, the

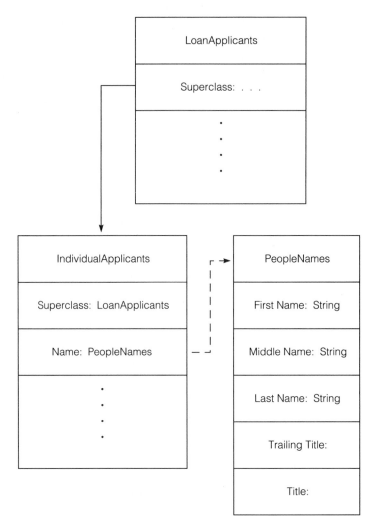

Figure 8.4   An Example of Inheritance and Class Membership in OOP

methods are the procedures or functions that use the data to produce outcomes. When an instance object of a class is created, the object is a bundle of data and computational procedures. For example, when the object smith is created as an instance of the class individual applicants, it not only has all the attributes that uniquely identify this object as an individual loan applicant, it also has all the necessary functions to perform the tasks of an applicant. Thus, smith not only looks like an applicant (because of its attributes), it also acts like an applicant (because of its methods). Thus, we are able to transfer all of the characteristics of an applicant into one object unit, bringing the model close to reality as we see it.

Let us consider the type of methods in a class. The method could be a function or procedure. It could be a mathematical computation using data, a print statement producing output, an input statement to get data from the user, or it could perform a more complex task such as creating objects (including objects in its own class), and communicating with them. A method could also contain IF-THEN rules. It is here that one can combine the logic-based representation with the object-oriented representation of knowledge.

For example, when the object smith is created, its method could trigger the creation of another object that is an instance of the mortgage loan class with specific attribute values for it, such as $40,000 for amount, 10 percent for interest rate, 30 years for duration, and fixed for loan type. Its method computes the monthly payment from the loan attribute values, as shown in Figure 8.5.

Note that a method can create an instance of any other classes or send messages to their instances. The only way a class can communicate with other classes is to send messages to their instances. Sending a message to an object is calling on one of its methods to perform its function.

A child inherits the methods of its parent. In other words, if a class can perform a task, so can its subclasses. Once a method is defined for a parent class, all its children inherit the method, and one does not need to repeat the method in the specification of the children classes.

8.2.7   *Modularity and Encapsulation*

Structured programming, decomposition, and *modularity* are the successful concepts that brought some organization to the design and implementation of software projects, and constitute one of the most important approaches in designing and creating complex computer systems. No language, however, has enforced modularity as much as OOP has. The object is a modular unit that contains its data and its functions in a capsule. No other objects can open this capsule and tell it which attributes it can use or how it should perform its functions. The only way to an object's method is to call on it to perform its function(s), and produce the outcome. This is called *message passing*. You send a message to an object, and you get back an answer or an action, which is produced from the method of that object. Passing a message is achieved by creating an instance of the object or sending a message to an already-created object.

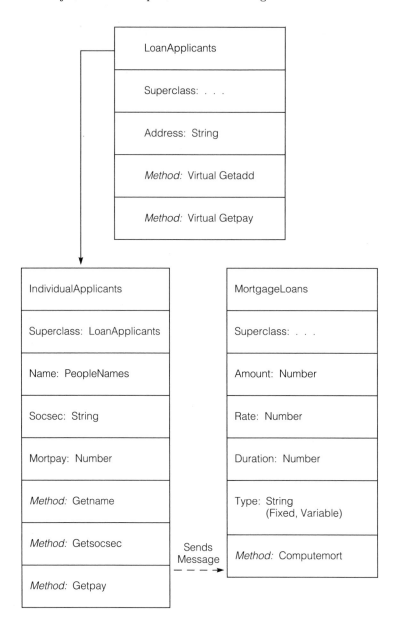

Figure 8.5   An Example of Methods in Classes of OOP

The method an object uses in order to perform its tasks is completely hidden from the other classes and their objects. The other objects that pass messages to an object do not know how the message is processed, they only get back an answer. This is *encapsulation* or *information hiding*. For example, the object smith does not know how the instance of mortgage loan computes the monthly payment (Figure 8.5). It only knows that it can use the name of the method in the mortgage loan class to compute and return the monthly mortgage payment. Therefore, parts of an object are visible to the others, and hidden parts of the object are visible only to itself and its children.

8.2.8   *External and Internal Views*

The structure of a class has two parts: *specification* and *implementation*.
   The specification of a class consists of:

- The class name

- The list and type of class attributes, including attributes that could be the members of other classes

- The superclasses from which it inherits

- The interface, which consists of the name and type of the methods in the class, what they need from the calling objects when they send a message, and what they will return as their outcome

Since the OOP languages have numerously different structures and syntaxes, we use the simplified version of Demeter^{TM} [Lieberherr and Riel 1988; Lieberherr and Holland 1988] in this chapter to show the generic form of OOP without the entanglement with various syntaxes of OOP languages. Demeter^{TM} is an English-like pseudo code for designing language-independent OOP systems.

Consider the objects in Figure 8.5. A generic code for defining the class individual applicants looks like the following:

```
class  IndividualApplicants has attributes
  name: PeopleNames    /* it is a member of PeopleNames class */
  socsec: String       /* another attribute */
  . . . . . . . . . .
  . . . . . . . . . .  /* other  attributes */
  . . . . . . . . . .
  optional attributes
    mortpay: Number    /* an optional attribute */
  end optional
```

```
    inherits from          /* listing its superclasses */
      LoanApplicants
    end inherits
    implements interface
      getname() returns PeopleNames;
      getsocsec() returns String;
      getpay() returns Number;
      ...........
      ...........          /* other methods */
      ...........
    end interface
  end class IndividualApplicants
```

where statements in /* ... */ are comments. For the sake of consistency, we have replaced the word *part* used in Demeter^{TM} with *attribute*. Furthermore, we disregard more subtle aspects of coding, such as the needed statements for constructing or destroying the object called *constructors* and *destructors*. For example, the constructor of this class is a method within the class that creates a copy of the class and gets the values of name, socsec, and others from the user of the expert system. The destructor specifies how the instance is removed from the system.

In the specification of the class, one can have optional attributes, meaning that not all instances of the class may have a value for them. If the object smith's application is denied, its attribute mortpay will not have a value. Thus, not all objects of this class have a value for mortpay.

The interface is what the outside objects can see. In this example, it contains the name of three functions that the other objects (including itself) can ask this object to perform. What the functions need from outside objects are identified in () after the name of the function. In this example, no outside data is needed, so there is no data name in the parentheses. After the parentheses is the *type* of data that the method returns to the calling object after the task is completed. For example, getpay returns an answer that is a number. Note that the interface does not contain any information about how the methods carry out their tasks, or what data they use internally. This is the principle of encapsulation.

The implementation part of the class consists of the exact codes for the class methods or functions. For example, the implementation component of the class individual applicants has the following generic look:

```
Implementation of the class IndividualApplicants
  IndividualApplicants :: getname() returns PeopleNames
    {
      /* A call to this method returns
         the content of name to the caller.
         The value of name was initialized by calling
         on a method in the PeopleNames class and storing
         what it returned in name. */
    }
  IndividualApplicants :: getsocsec() returns String
    {
      /* returns the applicant's social security */
    }
  IndividualApplicants :: getpay() returns Number
    {
      /* 1- call the method of MortgageLoan class to
            compute the mortgage payment
         2- this call brings back a number that is the amount
            of monthly mortgage payment,
              stores it in mortpay
            and returns this value to the caller. */
    }
  . . . . . . . . . .
  . . . . . . . . . .          /* details of other methods */
  . . . . . . . . . .
end class IndividualApplicants implementation
```

Here the methods are described rather than coded to keep the presentation simple. The syntax for coding a method is similar to writing a procedure, function, or subroutine in one of the conventional programming languages.

Other classes and objects see and have access to the interface part of the specification, because the interface tells others what the class can do. Other classes send messages according to what they see the object can perform. Other classes do not see the implementation part of the class. That is the hidden information that enforces the modularity at the micro level.

How much, if any, of the attribute values are visible to other classes is an open question, and will be discussed on the logical design section. This division of views of the structure of a class makes the maintenance and changes of systems much less costly, because any change in data or computational procedure is local to a class, and does not impact those that use it, as long as the interface information does not change.

We have to be careful about who is an outsider and who is an insider when we talk about the external and internal views. The class itself is obviously the insider and has all the information about its own structure. Furthermore, a subclass must know the structure of its superclasses in order to become a specialized version of them. When a class has attributes that are members of other classes, it may need to know all the specification parts of these classes. Furthermore, instances of a class may need to access the attribute values of their siblings. Section 8.4 will explore access to attribute values in the logical design of the system.

8.3 Modeling Knowledge in Object-based Representation Methods

The OOP approach brings together the modeling tradition in a number of disciplines:

- From cognitive psychology, the idea of semantic hierarchy and inheritance

- From AI, the practical applications of semantic nets and frames

- From management science and operations research, modeling the system by using the classes of objects as the unit of the program simulating the real objects that could be created and destroyed, or made active or passive

While these disciplines have tried to model the behavior of complex systems from different perspectives, they all have used objects with complex attributes and with hierarchical relations. Furthermore, the theoretical paradigms of these fields reinforce the practical wisdom of systems analysts and software engineers that modeling a complex system requires structured modularity, with the emphasis on a complete independence of modules from one another.

Thus, OOP is not just another programming method. It is a paradigm for modeling knowledge and designing systems. In this section, we review the systems analysis and design features of OOP, which help and expand the system development concepts in expert systems.

8.3.1 Object-Oriented Analysis (OOA)

One of the advantages of the OOP paradigm is that it contains the systems analysis in a set of relatively crisp steps. One does not need to impose or develop an approach for analyzing the systems in OOP; it embodies its own systems analysis approach. The *object-oriented analysis* (or OOA for short) requires:

- Determining the system goals and purposes
- Identifying the classes of objects and their relations

which can be broken down into the following steps:

- Goal analysis
- Object analysis
- Attribute and behavior analysis
- Class analysis
- Incremental analysis

The fact that the steps are well-defined does not imply, by any means, that they are easy to accomplish. Management scientists and AI researchers have grappled with them for many years.

Goal Analysis

Goal analysis is a careful feasibility study for identifying what exactly the system is expected to accomplish. It determines the framework of the analysis. All subsequent steps use this framework to decide what issues are relevant to the modeling process, and what should be set aside at present.

This step is the same as the goal analysis discussed in Chapter 7, with a difference in focus. The logic-based systems analysis focuses on *what the recommendations or actions are.* In the object-oriented systems analysis, the focus shifts to *what objects are and what they do.* In other words, in both cases, the goal analysis defines the function or action boundaries of the system to be modeled. In the logic-based analysis, the existence of objects and components are implied by their functions and actions. OOA has the additional requirement of explicitly defining the object or component boundaries of the system. Thus, OOA explicitly deals with the objects within the knowledge domain. This provides a clearer view for analyzing the domain and designing the knowledge base.

For example, in the mortgage loan case, one of the possible goals of the system in Chapter 7 was the decision to grant or deny the loan. In an OOA of the same system, one may define as a goal that the loan officer decides to grant a given amount of loan to the applicant, or to deny the applicant any loan. Here, both the object (loan officer) and the action (loan decision) are clearly defined in the system. This makes the goal specification more precise.

Object Analysis

The object analysis is an in-depth observation and analysis of the system for locating the physical and conceptual objects that have a role in achieving the system goals. The object analysis is related to the *domain analysis* components of the systems analysis discussed in Chapter 7. However, in OOA, the analysis focuses on identifying objects in the domain.

For example, in the mortgage loan system, the analyst may observe that in the decision for a loan, a number of system entities or objects have been involved, such as the applicant smith, the loan officer jones, the $40,000 loan, smith's application forms, the house at 21 Main St. for which the loan is requested, and smith's banks and credit card companies. The typical questions asked at this phase are: What are the objects in the system? Are all these objects involved in every loan decision? Can one identify the set of typical objects in every type of decision?

Attribute and Behavior Analysis

Attribute and behavior analysis is a study of the object attributes and actions to determine which ones are relevant to the system being modeled.

For example, smith is a system entity or object. The question is what attributes and behaviors of smith are relevant to the domain knowledge. As a person, smith has many attributes and acts differently in different circumstances. The question is which of them the knowledge base should contain. Here, too, the goal analysis guides the attribute and behavior analysis. Since the goal is the loan officer's decision on the loan, those attributes and actions of the applicant should be included in the system to help the loan officer to make a decision. Examples of such attributes are smith's credit history, liquid assets, properties, other loans, income, monthly expenses, and job. The possible relevant behaviors are that smith applies for a loan by filling out the application forms, asking about the rate and monthly payments for the loan, supplying the bank with the property documents, signing the loan documents, paying for the application and other costs, and so forth. The questions at this phase are: What attributes are common to all applicants? Do all behave the same? What are the differences and exceptions? These questions are part of the knowledge engineering process in the OOP approach.

Class Analysis

The object classification step groups the objects with similar attributes and behaviors into classes. For example, observation and data collection show that in every individual loan decision there is a person who applies for a loan, and the relevant attributes and behaviors of such individuals are similar. Therefore, one can group them into the individual applicants class.

In OOA, the classification of objects is relatively coarse in that it defines classes in general categories and in broad terms. At this stage, the purpose is not the detailed technical definition of objects and classes; this is done at the design stage. Here, the definition of classes draws a rough sketch of the system model, to help the owners of the system decide how far the system must go, and where the boundaries of the knowledge base should be drawn.

Note that class analysis is part of the *conceptualization* step of expert systems analysis, discussed in Chapter 7, except that the tasks here are well-defined by the nature of the OOP paradigm.

Incremental Analysis

Incremental analysis is another systems analysis concept extended to OOA. No complex system could be analyzed in one trial. In OOA, too, the analyst arrives at the final specification through trial and error and iterative refinements. OOA has the advantage that the increments have a clearer structure. Each increment either adds new classes to the system, or makes the structure of some of the existing classes more precise.

In the mortgage loan case, a simple attribute of the class, such as name with string type, may take a more complex structure after further analysis, and become a member of a more complex data structure, as shown in Figure 8.4. Another example is that the analyst may decide to concentrate on the classes of applicants who apply for a home mortgage loan, and later add other types of applicants to the system, such as commercial loan applicants, or credit card applicants.

Thus, the incremental analysis permits the system analyst to start with a rough sketch of a narrow aspect of the system, and systematically make the sketch more representative, and expand the model to include other entities of the system. Although, as discussed in Chapter 7, this is the premise of prototyping in systems analysis, the advantage of OOA is that it has a clear road map on how to proceed to increase the scope and accuracy of the prototype.

Through the iterative refinement of incremental analysis, the developer gains a deeper understanding of the domain knowledge and the system goals. The incremental analysis continues to the design stage. That is, the developer must iteratively go back and forth between analysis and design stages and make refinements at each iteration before the design becomes final.

8.3.2 Object-Oriented Design (OOD)

The development of the object-oriented knowledge base involves the system development phases, including the design stage. The variety of the OOP languages and software products and their numerous variety of syntaxes and cultures forces two stages for *object-oriented design* (OOD): logical design and physical design.

The *logical design* in OOD is concerned with that part of the design that could be accomplished independent of the language, software, or hardware used in the implementation stage. The logical design is part of the *knowledge acquisition* and *knowledge modeling* process of expert system design.

The *physical design* of OOD, on the other hand, translates the logical design to the requirements of a particular OOP software product or language. It is, therefore, obvious that immediately after the OOA, the logical design must commence. After a few iterations of the OOA and logical design, the decisions on physical design in conjunction with the selection of the software and hardware must follow.

8.4 Logical Design of the Object-Oriented Representation

In object-oriented knowledge representation, the logical design is part of the knowledge modeling or knowledge acquisition of the system, which is software-independent.

The logical design has components related to the objects, classes, class relations, and methods. Again, the relatively well-defined categories stem from the structure of the paradigm, which embodies its logical design concepts. One can break down the logical design into the following components:

- Designing classes and their relations

- Designing methods

- Designing the dynamics of the system

- Documentation of the design

- Tools for analysis and design

Case: Space Shuttle Prep

Lockheed Space Operations has used a Lisp-based expert system to help engineers prepare space-shuttle vehicles for flight.

The amount of planning and preparation that goes into a single space-shuttle mission is almost unimaginable. This planning includes not only "high level" analysis of weather conditions, trajectory paths, and computer systems; it also entails the rather mundane but essential task of checking the more than 7,000 connectors and quarter-million connector pins in each vehicle. As you would expect, this task is as time-consuming as it is expensive.

Lockheed engineers decided to take the edge out of this job with the Shuttle Connector Analysis Network (SCAN), which is coded in Lucid Inc.'s Domain/Common Lisp, and implemented on an Apollo workstation. SCAN is essentially a frame-based knowledge base that captures the connector knowledge of human analysts and mimics their thought processes. The system features real-time graphics of shuttle connector configuration and functions as an on-line diagnostic expert system.

SCAN's connector knowledge, which accounts for about 90 percent of its knowledge base, is formulated automatically from shuttle design data stored in a local database. Consequently, current data on all three shuttle vehicles can be accessed from any SCAN workstation, and the system can perform "what-if" analysis and troubleshoot electrical problems. As repairs or modifications are made, these changes in circuitry configuration are reflected in SCAN instantly.

SCAN, which took three years to develop from concept to production, is expected to pay itself off within two to three years.

By Justin Kestelyn, "Application Watch," *AI Expert*, March 1991, p. 72, reprinted with permission from *AI Expert*.

8.4.1 Designing Classes and Their Relations

The object-oriented analysis of the system creates a rough draft of classes within the system. The relations and structures of classes become more precise at the design stage. One important design element is the class hierarchy. The system designer must decide which superclasses and subclasses will be in the hierarchy, what attributes and methods should be in a superclass, and which ones are delegated to its subclasses. The decision on the hierarchy of classes again depends on the generalization of the superclasses and specialization of the subclasses.

There are issues in class design that are relatively common in modeling the knowledge. The most important topics in the class design are:

- Class hierarchy design

- Inheritance design

- Complex class design

- Class relations

- Attribute design

Class Hierarchy Design

In the class hierarchy, the subclass has access to the methods and attributes of its parents, and an object created from a subclass is considered an instance of its parents as well. Thus, the class hierarchy reveals information, while the modularity principle of OOP encapsulates and hides the information within each class of objects. If a hierarchy is extensive, with many children at each level and many levels within the hierarchy, the principle of encapsulation would be compromised. On the other hand, avoiding hierarchy takes away the inheritance capability of OOP, which is one of its strong technical and conceptual features.

In sum, a class hierarchy with numerous layers does not represent a good design. In designing the class hierarchy, the developer must strike a balance between satisfying the modularity principle that requires class independence and meeting the need for hierarchical associations among classes that weakens the extent of modularity.

Inheritance Design

Another important issue in the class design is whether the system designer should allow multiple inheritance. This is an unresolved issue in the OOP field. Multiple inheritance increases the complexity of the design and system, and creates a number of potential problems against which the system designer must guard.

One problem is that if a subclass has two parents, which themselves have a common parent, the two parents will have a set of identical attributes and methods inherited from their common superclass. When the subclass inherits from its two parents, it ends up with two sets of identical attributes and methods.

Another problem with multiple inheritance is that the parents may have attributes and methods with the same name, but with conflicting types or content. When the subclass inherits from its two superclass parents, the conflict may create logical errors, which may not be easily tractable.

Some OOP languages do not allow multiple inheritance. Of those that have this feature, Booch (1991) reports different approaches for resolving such problems.

- The software may tag the name of each inherited attribute with the name of its superclass, and allow the subclass to inherit from all its superclasses. For example, the attribute address in class loan applicants would be inherited as loan applicants: address.

- The software may specify the priority for inheritance from superclasses. In case of a conflict or repetition, the subclass inherits from the superclass with the higher priority.

- The software declares any conflict or repetition illegal, and produces error messages.

A common-sense approach to multiple inheritance is to avoid it if possible. Otherwise, one must guard against the problems it may cause by a careful design, and a meticulous screening of software.

Complex Class Design

Some class types have a more complex structure for accommodating the complexity of the system. One type of these classes could be used to avoid multiple inheritance. Demeter^{TM} accomplishes this with the *alternation* class. An alternation class is a collection of classes, and contains the common attributes and behaviors of the classes it contains.

The following example shows the use of this class type to avoid multiple inheritance. As Figure 8.6 shows, an individual applicant could be not only the subclass of the **loan applicants** class, but also the subclass of **bank customers**. This is a case of multiple inheritance. To avoid it, one can define an alternation class, called **customer applicants**, and its attributes would be those common in both classes. The two classes **loan applicants** and **bank customers** are the subclasses of the alternation class. Thus the class **individual applicants** inherits the attributes it needs from the class **customer applicants** (via its parent, the **loan applicants** class).

Multiple Inheritance:

Alternation Class:

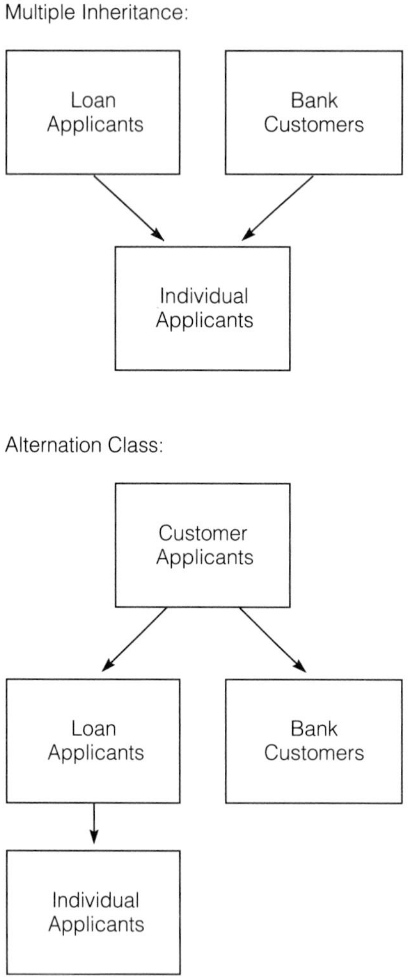

Figure 8.6   Multiple Inheritance and the Alternation Class

In the pseudo-code language of Demeter^{TM}, one can declare the following:

```
class CustomerApplicants is either
   LoanApplicants or BankCustomers
common attributes

. . . . . . . . . . .
. . . . . . . . . .          /* the list of common attributes */
. . . . . . . . . .
  optional attributes
    accountno: Number

    . . . . . . . . . .
    . . . . . . . . . .      /* list of other optional attributes */
    . . . . . . . . . .
  end optional
end common
```

A class that is created to facilitate the design, and that does not have an instance object, is called an *abstract class*. Normally in such classes, attributes are partially defined and the subclasses are expected to complete the list of attributes. This type of class may have methods that are *virtual* (defined below) and are overridden by its subclasses, or have no method at all. The customer applicants class just described is an example of an abstract class.

A *virtual* (or *void*) method resembles an empty shell and does not have any content. It is intended to be overridden by the methods in the children classes. Later, we will see that the virtual method is a powerful aspect of OOP.

Another class type is the *repetition class*, which consists of the list of objects belonging to another class. For example, we may wish to have a class that represents the pool of applicants, called applicants pool. This class is defined as a list of objects belonging to the class loan applicants. The use of complex class designs is not common in object-oriented expert systems.

Class Relations

Two classes, say, A and B, are related in the following way:

- *A* could be the subclass or superclass of *B*

- *A* could use *B* for defining the type of its attribute, or send messages via its methods to instances of *B*

(Later we will see that class A could be an instance of B, if B is A's meta class.)

Although the first type of class relation is normally documented clearly in the class hierarchy, the second type usually remains obscure in the design document. The developer must document both types of class relations. The design of classes and their relations constitutes an important step in the OOP approach, because the complexity of the system is reflected in the design of its classes.

Attribute Design

In attribute design, the analyst must decide which attributes belong to the superclass and are shared by all its subclasses down the hierarchy. A subclass has the additional attributes that specialize it as a unique child of its parents. Thus, the principle of OOP requires a subclass to have the attributes of all its parents, plus its own attributes. In the specification of a subclass, one does not need to list all the attributes the class inherits from its parent, or grandparent, upward in the inheritance hierarchy. As long as the immediate superclasses of the class are specified, the class inherits their attributes. In other words, the subclass has complete access to the attributes of the superclass, which itself has access to the attributes of its parent, and the process is repeated upward.

The opposite, however, is not true. A parent class does not have the attributes of its subclasses. Thus the inheritance has a downward direction, while access has an upward direction in the hierarchy. Yet, one must remember that any object instance of a subclass within the hierarchy is considered as an instance of all of its parents found upward in the hierarchy. Thus, an instance of the class individual applicants is also an instance of loan applicants and its superclasses higher up in the hierarchy. This has an important implication in polymorphism, discussed in the next section.

An important question in the design of the attributes is determining who is allowed to see the values of the attributes of an instance object. To deal with this issue, the attributes of a class could be divided into three categories: private, protected, and public.

The *private* attributes (*private variables*) are those whose values are not visible to other instances of the same class, or the instances of classes. For example, the name attribute of a loan applicant instance called smith should not be accessible by other loan applicants or other classes. Another name of the private attributes is *instance variables*.

The *protected* attributes (or *class variables*) are those whose values are visible to other instances of the same class. For example, the loan applicant class may have an attribute called count, which counts the number of loan applicants at any one time. This value could be accessible to all instances of this class. Therefore, the protected attributes normally contain the information across the objects of a class. Aggregate and statistical attributes fall into this category.

The *public* attributes (or *public variables*) are those whose values are visible to all classes that sent messages to the instances of this class. For example, in the class mortgage loan, the designer may wish to make the interest rate value accessible to all classes that send messages to the instances of the class.

One can declare the type of an attribute in the design by prefacing its name by private, protected, or public.

8.4.2   Designing Methods (Optional)

In modeling system processes and functions, one has to decide whether the physical process should be a method within an object, or an object itself. For example, in the mortgage loan system, we have the process of establishing the applicant's credit rating. This process could be a method in the loan officer class, with the reasoning that it is one of the tasks this object should perform. Or, one can say that it is a method in the loan applicants class because the credit rating belongs to the loan applicant. Alternatively, one can set up a class for establishing the credit rating of the applicant, and have the loan officer send a message to it asking for the rating. The decision in such cases depends on the complexity of the task, the reusability of the class, and the importance of the process to the system.

There could be functions common to all objects within the system. One can define this method in the uppermost class within the hierarchy, the class that is the parent of all classes. In this case, all classes will have access to this method. For example, if many classes of the mortgage loan application need to get credit ratings, then this method should belong to a class that is at the top of the hierarchy.

In designing the methods in OOP, the designer can utilize the powerful concept of polymorphism, which accommodates systems with complex structure.

Assume that we have one class A, which has BB, CC, and DD as its subclasses. We can define a virtual method in A (called M). Each subclass overrides M, and has its own version of M that performs a different task.

Now, if we send the message **perform M** to an instance of A, it performs its version, while BB, and CC answer to the same message, each in a different fashion. This is called *polymorphism*.

Polymorphism has a more interesting application. Assume that we have created an object instance of BB called BBO. Now, we send the message M to A. A has no instance of its own, but BBO is considered its instance, and it answers to the message, performing its own version of the M method. Next time around, an instance of CC (called CCO) is alive when the same message is sent to A. This time, CCO performs its version of M, and responds to the message. Thus, the same message to the same class could produce a different answer, depending which instance of A or its children is active at that time. One may have both BBO and CCO alive. In this case, both will respond to the message, each in its own way.

To see this with the mortgage loan case, consider the classes **loan applicants, individual applicants,** and **commercial applicants,** as shown in Figure 8.7. The following generic code, based on a simplified form of Demeter^{TM}, demonstrates the design. We have already seen the last part of this code. The **LoanApplicants** class is coded as:

```
class LoanApplicants has attributes
  address: String
  . . . . . . . . . . .
  . . . . . . . . . .          /* other attributes */
  . . . . . . . . . .
  implements interface
        /* the interface components of the class */
  virtual getadd() returns String;
      /*  the interface of a method,
          virtual means that the subclass could
          override the method */
  virtual getpay() returns void;
      /* void means that it returns nothing */
  . . . . . . . . . .
  . . . . . . . . . .          /* other methods */
  . . . . . . . . . .
  end interface
end class LoanApplicants
```

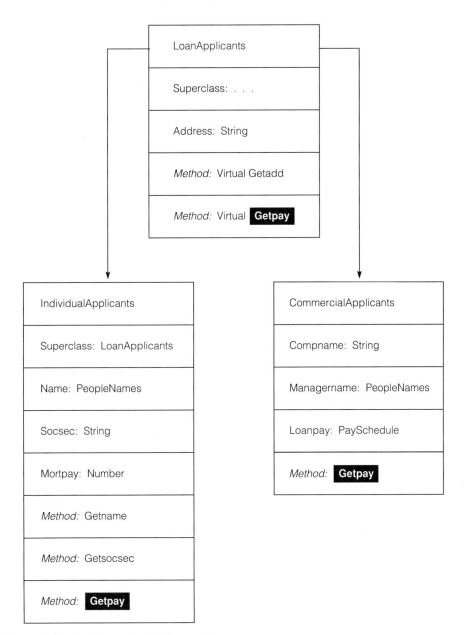

Figure 8.7   An Example of Polymorphism

The methods in the LoanApplicants class are coded as:

```
Implementation of the class LoanApplicants
  LoanApplicants :: getadd() returns String
  {
    /* returns the content of address to the caller */
  }
  virtual LoanApplicants :: getpay() returns void
  {
    /* keep the content of this method empty because it
       will be overridden by the  subclasses */
  }
  ...........
  ...........                 /* other methods */
  ...........
end class LoanApplicants implementation
```

The IndividualApplicants class is coded as:

```
class IndividualApplicants has attributes
    name: PeopleNames
    socsec: String
    ...........
    ...........            /* other   attributes */
    ...........
  optional attributes
    mortpay: Number
  end optional
 inherits from
   LoanApplicants
 end inherits
 implements interface
    getname() returns PeopleNames;
    getsocsec() returns String;
    getpay() returns Number;
    ...........
    ...........            /* other methods */
    ...........
  end interface
end class IndividualApplicants
```

The methods of this class are coded as:

```
Implementation of the class IndividualApplicants
  IndividualApplicants :: getname() returns PeopleNames
    {
        /*  A call to this method returns
            the content of name to the caller */
    }
  IndividualApplicants :: getsocsec() returns String
    {
        /* returns the applicant's social security  */
    }
  IndividualApplicants :: getpay() returns Number
    {
        /*  1- call the method of MortgageLoan class to
            compute the mortgage payment
            2- this call brings back a number that
            is the amount of monthly mortgage payment,
            stores it in mortpay, and returns this
            value to the caller.  */
    }
  ..........
  ..........            /* details of other methods */
  ..........
end class IndividualApplicants implementation
```

The CommercialApplicants class has the following code:

```
class CommercialApplicants has attributes
    compname: String
    managername: PeopleNames
    ..........
    ..........                /* other  attributes */
    ..........
  optional attribute
    loanpay: PaySchedule  /* PaySchedule is a class */
  end optional
 inherits from
   LoanApplicants
 end inherits
```

```
implements interface
   getpay() returns PaySchedule;
   . . . . . . . . . . .
   . . . . . . . . . . .              /* other methods */
   . . . . . . . . . . .
 end interface
end class CommercialApplicants
```

The methods in this class are coded as:

```
Implementation of the class CommercialApplicants
   CommercialApplicants :: getpay() returns PaySchedule
   {
      /* 1- call the method of CommercialLoan class to
            compute the payment schedule
         2- this call brings back a payment schedule for
            this applicant, stores it in loanpay, and
            returns the schedule to the caller, as well. */
   }
   . . . . . . . . . .
   . . . . . . . . . .              /* details of other methods */
   . . . . . . . . . .
end class CommercialApplicants implementation
```

The method getpay is virtual in loan applicants and is overridden by its two subclasses, each with a different content. Now, if we send a message getpay to the class loan applicant, we get a different answer, depending on which of its two subclasses individual applicants or commercial applicants has an instance. If they both have instances, both will respond to this message. This is polymorphism. The polymorphism in methods lets the objects within a hierarchy answer the message sent to their parents or ancestors. This gives OOP a great amount of power, because the user does not have to know which objects of this class are alive. By sending the message to the parent, all existing children of the parent (who have the method of the same name) would respond to the message and perform their own version of the method.

This is similar to human behavior in a group setting. If there are a number of us in a group, and we all receive a message, those to whom the message applies will respond. Thus, OOP simulates and models the system the way humans perceive it.

In a particular application, another issue in designing the methods is designing the flow or the sequence of messages passed among various objects.

This task consists of one or more classes with methods that start the process. Thus, objects represent various components of a system, and the control of the system operation is also in the hands of an object. This is also a human view of how a system works.

8.4.3 Designing the Dynamics of the System

One can control the sequence of executing and responding to messages within a class by categorizing methods into: *primary, after,* and *before.* The primary method is the response to the message. The "before" method should be executed before the primary method; the "after" method should be performed after the primary method. For example, assume that applying for a loan is the primary method. The "before" method could be that the applicant must first visit or call the loan officer to get the application forms and other information. The "after" method could be getting a lawyer to represent the applicant in processing the loan.

Although the sequence of executing messages is of importance in a system, the message management does not yet have the well-established structure of other features in the OOP paradigm. This is one area where a scripts-like method could help in the design of the class messages.

8.4.4 Documentation of the Design

To keep track of the design in a complex system, the analyst should create a dictionary for classes, their attributes, relations, and methods. At this stage, the structure of classes is coded in a semi-English pseudo code, such as Demeter^{TM}, with a clear standard for names, class attribute types, class interfaces, and class implementations. Documenting design creates a history—or paper trail—of changes, which helps in the management and organization of the process.

Some of the OOP languages, especially those based on the Smalltalk approach (discussed in a later section), provide facilities such as browsers and graphic browsers, which enable the user to document and see the class, attribute, and method definitions and relations. However, since the design takes place before coding and implementation, one must document the logical design with language-independent, standard tools.

8.4.5 Tools for Object-Oriented Analysis and Design

OOA and OOD need tools for analysis and design that can help the system developer:

- To identify classes, attributes, and methods, and their types

- To depict the hierarchy and inheritance relations among classes

- To show the connection of classes that communicate via messages

- To document the interface and implementation structure of each class

- To show the dynamic structure of methods

- To provide an overall picture of the flow of messages through time

Due to the relative recency of the OOP approach, OOA and OOD tools are sparse. The language-independent pseudo codes such as Demeter^{TM} are necessary design tools, but are not sufficient. The *dependency diagram* showing the hierarchy among classes is a method for class presentation. The figures in this chapter are incomplete examples of the dependency diagram. In such diagrams, the types of relations are more clearly identified on the arcs of the network.

One interesting concept specifically designed for OOA is Abbott's proposal (1983) to write the acquired knowledge in English text. The nouns in the text are candidates for objects and the verbs are candidates for methods. This, however, is the first approximation in the analysis, and is too dependent on the sentence structure of the text to be a reliable method.

A tool for depicting the sequence of events or the dynamics of the system is the *state transition diagram*, borrowed from the fields of operations research and engineering. This diagram is a network whose nodes are labeled according to the state of the system, and show the system's states through time. For example, in the mortgage loan system, one node may show the applicant at the start of the application process, another node would show the applicant after the completion of forms, and the arc would represent the action of filling out the forms. Although such diagrams are helpful to depict some aspects of analysis and design, the OOP-specific tools are yet to be developed for OOA and OOD.

8.5 Physical Design of the Object-Oriented Representation

The logical design of object-oriented knowledge representation takes place independent of the software and hardware on which the design will be implemented. The physical design involves translating the logical design to a design that is appropriate for a specific OOP language. Thus, the first step in the physical design is the evaluation and selection of an OOP language or software that best accommodates the logical design.

In this section, we discuss the OOP languages and their special features. The next chapter contains a review of some expert systems products that have object-oriented representation capability.

8.5.1 Object-Oriented Programming Languages

Saunders (1989) reported on more than 80 languages for OOP, and Booch (1991) lists more than 110 such languages, not counting various versions developed for different machines by various vendors. Considering that the first OOP language was publicly released in 1979, the sheer growth of the number of OOP languages within a decade indicates the extent of interest in this approach.

The first language developed for OOP was Smalltalk. In 1972, the first version of Smalltalk was developed at the Xerox Palo Alto Research Center as part of a research project for creating the smallest computer, called Dynabook, with unprecedented power and ease of use. The software for this computer was called Smalltalk. Every two years, a new version of Smalltalk was generated. In 1979, Xerox made Smalltalk80 (the current version of the software) available to outsiders, and set up a separate company, ParcPlace Systems, to market the software.

Although Smalltalk is the first OOP language to be labeled accordingly, its concepts come from the simulation language SIMULA. Although it had the power of a general language, SIMULA67, in turn, was a superset of another simulation language called ALGOL60. SIMULA was developed and became popular in Europe, but went unnoticed in the United States. SIMULA67 contained the idea of semantic nets and classes. Using SIMULA67, an object of a class would be created by the word **new** and the name of the class. An object could be in one of four states: active, passive, suspended, and terminated. An object created by **new** could continue to exist, as long as the access to the object was preserved, even after the program was temporarily or permanently terminated. This feature is called *persistence* of an object; a persistent object continues to exist long after its creator program is gone.

It is interesting to note that in system simulation, one models the real objects and their interactions within the system and through time. Having the ancestry of a simulation approach, the OOP's programming philosophy is modeling the real world. That is why the OOP languages are not just another set of computer programming languages. They define computer programming as a modeling paradigm.

8.5.2 Conventional vs. Object-Oriented Programming

Conventional and object-oriented programming are two distinct approaches used to represent a system. One can list the differences between them as:

- Function orientation vs. object orientation

- Data separation vs. data integration

- Passive functions vs. active objects

- Inherently sequential vs. inherently concurrent

- Static binding vs. dynamic binding

- Monomorphism vs. polymorphism

Function Orientation vs. Object Orientation

In all of the first three generations of computer programming languages, starting from machine-oriented languages, to mnemonic languages (such as assembly languages), to high-level human-oriented languages (such as FORTRAN, BASIC, Pascal, C), the focus of the conventional languages has been on modeling the procedural and computational aspects of systems. For example, in the mortgage loan application system, the functional units of the program would be reading the input data, computing the monthly mortgage payment, and printing the result of computation. In OOP, as we have seen, the unit of programming is a class of objects. One approach models what the system does, and the other what the system consists of and the interactions of its components.

The OOP languages move computer programming closer to the way humans perceive a system, because these languages *simulate* the components of the systems into classes of objects. Objects interact in these languages, the same way that real physical or conceptual objects interact.

Data Separation vs. Data Integration

A real object such as an applicant or a loan has both its functions and its data contained in one entity. Therefore, in OOP, data is not kept in a separate file, rather it is bundled together with the functions into one unit.

On the other hand, in conventional programming, data and functions are kept separate. The functions are in the programs, and they have the choice of accessing any data in the data files.

In OOP, data and functions are in object units. An object is allowed to see only its own data, and none of the others. This enforces modularity at all levels of the program. This way, any changes in a piece of data affect only the class of objects that use it. Conversely, any change in a class may affect the piece of data related to that class.

Passive Functions vs. Active Objects

In conventional programming, the functions are passive, in that they should be called on by other parts of the program. Once they produce their output, they go back into a passive mode again. In OOP, an object, once created, could remain active and perform its function continuously while other objects are performing their functions. This allows for concurrency, as discussed below.

Inherently Sequential vs. Inherently Concurrent

Conventional programming calls on one function at a time. Thus, the processing is inherently sequential. In OOP, objects could remain active. That is, once created, an instance of an class may continue to exist in the computer memory and its data and structure remain available to other objects in the program. An object may remain active while the program is running (or conceivably after its termination, as long as access to the object is possible), and periodically send messages to other objects. An example for the mortgage loan system is an object that periodically checks the cash reserve in the bank, and when the reserve falls below a critical level, it halts processing of loan applications, and notifies bank officials. This is called *concurrency* in OOP.

Thus, OOP has the potential of having more than one unit working at any moment, and thus the capability of running on more than one processor. Concurrent processing is an aspect that will appear again in the discussion of neural networks (Chapters 13 and 14) of this book.

Static Binding vs. Dynamic Binding

In the conventional languages, computer memory is allocated to variables when the code is compiled, that is, translated to the machine language. This is called *static binding*. In the OOP languages, the allocation of the memory could happen when the program is running. That is, the computer memory used for a method is not decided till an object is created. This is called *dynamic* or *delayed binding*. Although this seems like an innocent-looking technical difference, it allows for polymorphism, which impacts the system design to a great extent.

Monomorphism vs. Polymorphism

The conventional programming languages have static binding and monomorphism. That is, once the code is compiled, the type and name of data are determined. The dynamic binding in OOP makes it possible to use the same name to represent different methods.

As we have seen before, polymorphism gives the OOP language a powerful facility. On the other hand, polymorphism uses more memory resources than monomorphism. Some OOP languages allow the developer to identify which method has polymorphism, normally by using the word *virtual* for the type of the method, thus decreasing the memory requirement.

8.5.3   Categories of OOP Languages

The sheer number of OOP languages makes any meaningful discussions of their syntax impossible. However, we can categorize them according to different criteria, and into various cultures:

- Pure vs. hybrid

- Base-language culture

- Developer-friendliness vs. efficiency

- Type of inheritance

- Technical facilities

- The host operating system

Pure vs. Hybrid

The languages that are designed specifically for OOP are called *pure* OOP languages. Obviously, Smalltalk is a pure OOP language. After the initial success of Smalltalk, the object-oriented features were added to the popular conventional languages, producing *hybrid* OOP languages. Among hybrid languages are: C^{++}, which is an expanded version of C programming language; CLOS (short for Common Lisp Object Systems), which is an expanded version of Common Lisp; and Object Pascal, an expanded version of Pascal. The hybrid languages have to accommodate the features of the original conventional language, and this, in some cases, limits and/or alters the OOP facilities in the language.

One way to produce a hybrid OOP language is to create a front-end object-oriented facility to the conventional language, and have a pre-processor to translate the front-end to the original conventional programming language. Examples of OOP languages with such a preprocessor are Guideline C++ (by Guideline Software, Orinda, Calif.), and Advantage C++ (by Lifeboat Associates, Tarrytown, N.Y.). A more complete integration is when a new compiler is developed for the hybrid language, which is the case in C++ and its PC version Zortech C++ (by Zortech, Arlington, Mass.).

Another interesting hybrid is the incorporation of PROLOG within Smalltalk/V (by Digitalk, Los Angeles, Calif.). In this case, the OOP language is the host, and the addition is the AI language.

Base-language Culture

The second way to categorize the OOP languages is by their base-language culture. The word culture here means the common definitions and vocabularies, the way the language implements the OOP components, the general structure of the language syntax, and the technical and interface facilities within the language. Because of their different origins, the OOP languages do not share a common culture or even common vocabularies.

The following are some examples of labeling conventions. Some languages call everything "object," and others use "class" to refer to the model or the abstraction of objects, and use "object" to refer to an instance of a class. Furthermore, what we have used as "attributes" in this chapter are also called *variables, instance variables, slots, data members, fields, member objects,* and *parts* in the OOP languages. The methods are also called *operations* and *member functions* in OOP languages.

Another example of the cultural difference is attribute types. The private attributes and methods in Smalltalk culture are called *instance attributes* and *instance methods,* and the protected attributes and methods are called *class attributes* and *class methods.* The difference does not end at the naming convention. In Smalltalk and CLOS, the protected attributes are initialized in the *meta class* of each class. A meta class in these languages is the class of a class—it is a construct to initialize the protected attributes. C++ declares the attribute types directly as private, protected, and public, and does not need a meta class to initialize them.

The variation of naming conventions is a good indicator of how much the type, names, and functionality of the OOP facilities vary within the OOP languages. That is why the culture of the language is of importance in OOP.

One can identify Smalltalk, Lisp, C, Pascal, Flavors, Actor, Eiffel, and Ada cultures. Flavors is one the predecessors of CLOS. Ada is not a complete OOP languages, but contains some OOP concepts. Actor and Eiffel are two independent, pure OOP languages. Actor is culturally close to Smalltalk. Eiffel is relatively new, and is developed for both design and programming object-oriented representations.

Developer-friendliness vs. Efficiency

Another criterion for grouping the OOP languages is their developer-friendliness versus their efficiency. Smalltalk is the archetypal developer-friendly OOP language, which provides a development environment, including multiple windows, graphics, and a browser for reviewing classes, their methods, and attributes. It makes a higher demand on computer resources. The challenge of Smalltalk-like languages is to reduce system overheads and increase efficiency.

Smalltalk does not have a stand-alone application capability. That is, all classes created in Smalltalk remain in it, and add to the system overhead. Thus, one concern with the Smalltalk-like OOP languages is the possibility of stripping the software from classes that are not used in an application. An example of a language that provides such a capability is Smalltalk/V (by Digitalk).

The other end of the spectrum is C^{++}, which has high computational efficiency, but inadequate developmental environment and friendliness in interface. The challenge for the C^{++}-like languages is providing a friendlier development environment. Objective-C (by Stepstone, Sandy Hook, Conn.) combines the C efficiency with a number of Smalltalk development interface features.

Type of Inheritance

Another criterion for classification is the type of inheritance within the system. Smalltalk and most of the OOP languages based on it (including Actor) have single inheritance, while C and Lisp cultures (such as C^{++}, CLOS) and

Flavors have multiple inheritance. Eiffel, too, supports multiple inheritance. Ada does not have inheritance capability.

Technical Facilities

Other technical facilities representative of the power of an OOP language are: concurrency, polymorphism, and attribute and method types. Booch [1991] provides an in-depth review and case applications of Smalltalk, Object Pascal, C++, CLOS, and Ada for the OOP facilities (and a comprehensive reference to the OOP literature). Some of the technical features of these languages are summarized below:

	Origin	Inheritance	Polymorphism	Concurrency	Types*
Smalltalk	Pure	Single	Yes	Yes	Yes
Object Pascal	Hybrid	Single	Yes	No	No
C++	Hybrid	Multiple	Yes	Yes	Yes
CLOS	Hybrid	Multiple	Yes	Yes	Yes
Ada	OB**	None	No	Yes	No

(*) Private and protected types.
(**)Object-based, has some OOP features.
(Adopted from Booch [1991])

The overall picture emerging from the table is that Smalltalk, C++, and CLOS are at the top of the list in their OOP capabilities.

The Host Operating System

Another way to categorize OOP languages is by the hardware they run on, or more accurately, the host operating system. Of the languages discussed in this chapter, Ada and CLOS are ANSI standards published in 1983 and 1988, respectively, and do not have a primary host. The Ada compilers are mostly for the larger computer. CLOS is a new standard, and its compiler is expected to become available on all types of operating systems.

C++ was developed in AT&T Bell Laboratories by Bjarne Stroustrup. Originally, it was available on the Unix system. Now, it is available on almost all major operating systems. Smalltalk was originally designed by Alan Kay, and redesigned and programmed by Dan Ignalls (both at Xerox PARC). It was developed to run on its own computer. After its public release in 1979, Smalltalk became available on most of the micros and workstations. Object Pascal was developed in the Macintosh environment. Actor was developed on the MSDOS system, and was later introduced in a Macintosh version as well. Eiffel was developed on the Unix system.

There are a number of OOP languages available for IBM and Macintosh. Among those available for IBM PCs and compatibles are: Smalltalk–80, Smalltalk/V, Guidelines C++, Advantage C++, Zortech C++, C-Talk, Objective-C, and XLisp. For Macintosh, the available OOP languages include Smalltalk–80, Allegro Common Lisp, XLisp, XperCommon Lisp, Flavors, and MPW Pascal. The Lisp family of OOP languages is expected to be replaced by CLOS products, as the standard is implemented by various software companies. Objective-C (by Stepstone, Sandy Hook, Conn.) was selected as the development environment for the NeXT computer. The prices of the micro-based languages range from $100 to $10,000. David Betz, the developer of XLisp, has made it available for free.

8.5.4 Special Issues in the Physical Design

The selection of the OOP language has the same decision process as other types of software selection, as discussed in Chapter 12. However, one of the special features of OOP languages is their standardization of real-world classes. This means that the classes created for one application may be reusable in other applications and knowledge bases as well. This has given a new theoretical and practical dimension to the OOP paradigm.

At the theoretical level, we have the concept of *frameworks* for developing a general model for each type of domain or system. According to Johnson and Foote [1988], a framework is a set of abstract classes that represent the general knowledge of a domain.

For example, one can develop a framework for a typical mortgage loan system by designing its classes. This framework could be used by many banks. Each bank would write the subclasses to custom-design the framework to its own particular needs. In other words, in designing a knowledge base, one need not reinvent the wheel each time. Instead, one can build the system over others' experiences. This is a powerful concept that, if implemented, could dramatically reduce the development time and cost of expert systems.

On the practical side, many OOP languages provide the developer with many pre-coded classes in the form of class libraries. These are pieces of reusable code, and the developer can add to the library as new classes are created for various applications. The problem with these types of classes is that the required specification of the class should match what is available in the library, and the developer must be aware of the structure of each class within the library. In comparison, the strength of the framework approach is that the classes are clustered based on the knowledge domain. Furthermore, the classes in a framework are written as abstract classes that the developer can use as superclasses of custom-designed subclasses.

Another interesting development in the OOP paradigm is that independent companies offer the code for some standard classes. An example of such products is PluggableGauges (by Knowledge Systems, Cary, N.C.), which are pre-coded classes of graphical gauges for Smalltalk. Thus, the knowledge acquisition, physical design and software selection in OOP involve the decision to identify and use some existing designs and codes in the domain knowledge.

8.6 Advantages and Disadvantages of the Object-Oriented Approach

OOP as a knowledge representation paradigm and a software tool has a number of advantages and disadvantages, which are briefly reviewed here.

8.6.1 Advantages

One can list the advantages of OOP as:

- Human orientation

- Enforced modularity

- Reusability, extendibility, and modifiability

- Ability to deal with complex systems

Human Orientation

The most important advantage of the OOP paradigm is its ability to simulate the human view of the world. While logic-based knowledge representation has a claim on modeling the human method of reasoning, the OOP's claim is on representing the world as we see it in our everyday experience. It is a dimension that, when added to the logic-based method, increases the representational power of the knowledge base. The danger of such a mix is that it puts the combined representation method on a shaky theoretical ground.

Enforced Modularity

The OOP approach requires the analysis and design within the object classes. This requirement forces the developer to think modular, to design modular, and to program modular. As discussed in Chapter 7, a number of methods in the knowledge acquisition process attempt to create a modularity environment that is natural to the OOP paradigm. That is why OOP could be a tool for knowledge modeling even if the eventual product does not have an OOP component.

Reusability, Extendibility, and Modifiability

One of the potential benefits of the OOP approach is in creating designs and codes that can be used again. The concepts of frameworks and the availability of class libraries show this potential. It means that one can develop a general expert system for each domain, and customize it later based on the needs of each organization. This can reduce development time considerably.

Furthermore, the modularity of OOP enables the developer to start with a small prototype and expand it in an organized fashion by adding new classes to the system, and modifying some of the existing ones. This gives order and structure to the management of the system growth.

Similarly, as the domain knowledge changes, the system should be modified to incorporate the change. In OOP, one can keep the history of the change within the system. Instead of changing the structure of a class, one can create a subclass that contains only the changed attributes and methods. Thus, the hierarchy would contain a chronology of the evolution of knowledge. No other paradigm has such an archival facility.

This, however, is not always the best method for modification, because a long hierarchy could reduce the efficiency of the system. In such cases, one would change the class and restructure the hierarchy to reflect the changes with little impact on other modules of the system.

Ability to Deal with Complex Systems

All the advantages discussed above make OOP a good candidate for modeling complex systems. As we have seen before, OOP has facilities to deal with complexities such as concurrent processing and polymorphism. The experience in the application of OOP to model complex systems is that its modeling capability far surpasses the conventional programming tools.

8.6.2 Disadvantages

The disadvantages of OOP could be summarized in the following categories:

- Start-up cost and time

- System inefficiency

- Representing uncertainty

Start-up Cost and Time

The greatest disadvantage of OOP is its recency. Like any new paradigm, it suffers from the unavailability of a sufficient number of system developers and programmers proficient in the field. Thus, for any major undertaking using OOP, a learning period is needed for those involved to adopt an object-oriented perspective. It is observed that the more proficient is the person in conventional programming methods, the longer the transition period. Thus, there is a start-up cost and time involved in applying the OOP approach.

However, for the application in expert systems, this start-up could be nonexistent or minimal, because the object-oriented representation has a solid root in AI representations and in simulation methods.

System Inefficiency

Another disadvantage of the OOP languages is the computer resources that they require. This was true for the earlier versions of most of the OOP languages, but may not be true for more efficient languages, such as C^{++}. With the increase in the hardware power, this concern is losing its significance. With the availability of parallel processors, the OOP languages may prove to be even more efficient than the conventional languages. At present, the system efficiency remains a concern in the large application of OOP.

Representing Uncertainty

As a knowledge representation paradigm, OOP lacks the uncertainty management methodologies available for the logic-based approach. However, for dealing with uncertainty within the domain knowledge, the structure of OOP, with its network nature, is compatible with some of the uncertainty constructs, such as belief nets (discussed in Chapter 11). As OOP is integrated with expert system software, methods will evolve for dealing with uncertain objects and uncertainty within and across objects.

Conclusion

In Chapters 3 and 4, we discussed the knowledge representation methods in expert systems that have mathematical logic as their theoretical foundation. This chapter covered the knowledge representation methods that are based on modeling objects.

We discussed the precursors of the object-oriented approach, semantic nets, frames, and scripts. We also reviewed the basic components of object-oriented programming, which together constitute the paradigm. Semantic nets, frames, and scripts are the precursors of the more general object-oriented approach, each attempting to capture the complexity of real-world objects and their relationships.

Object-oriented approaches are rooted in the research on the human method of language processing in psychology and cognitive science. The AI modeling of natural language developed the method of semantic networks, or *semantic nets* for short. The shortcomings of the semantic net led to the extensions of this approach to *frames* and *scripts*. Both were mostly developed in the context of the AI modeling of natural language processing, although the frames approach was widely applied in many AI applications, and was incorporated in expert system software products.

Object-oriented programming emerged as a method that combined the successes of AI's object-based methods with the concerns of conventional programming for data abstraction, and the need of system designers to design systems in modular form with reusable components. The outcome was not only a programming language with a radically different approach, but a school of thought for designing systems and modeling knowledge.

Modeling and representing knowledge with the object-oriented approach requires object-oriented analysis and design. We reviewed the object-oriented analysis (referred to as OOA), and presented the design concepts in two categories: logical design and physical design. The logical design is independent of the language in which the design will be coded, while the physical design takes into account the software and hardware requirements. Object-oriented languages were reviewed in the section on the physical design. Finally, the last section discussed the advantages and disadvantages of object-oriented knowledge representation.

It did not take long for the expert system software manufacturers to realize that the power of object-oriented knowledge representation can be combined with the logic-based methods. Some languages and expert system software products on the market combine the two knowledge representation methods, as discussed in the next chapter. The power and capability of such products indicate that the combination of the two modes of knowledge representation is one of the directions of future development.

References

Abbott, R. 1983. "Program Design by Informal English Descriptions," *Communications of the ACM*, Vol. 26, No. 11.

Booch, G. 1991. *Object Oriented Design with Applications*, The Benjamin/Cummings Publishing Co., Redwood City, CA.

Coad, P. and Yourdon, E. 1990. *Object-Oriented Analysis*, Yourdon Press, Prentice Hall, Englewood Cliffs, NJ.

Collins, A. and Quillian, M. R. 1969. "Retrieval Time from Semantic Memory," *Journal of Verbal Learning and Verbal Behavior*, Vol. 8, pp. 240–247.

Dahl, Ole-Johan and Nygaard, Kristen. 1966. "SIMULA—An ALGOL-Based Simulation Language," *Communications of the ACM*, Vol. 19, Sept., pp. 671–678.

Dahl, O. J.; Myhrhaug, B.; and Nygaard, K. 1968. *SIMULA67 Common Base Language*, Publication No. S-2, Norwegian Computing Center, Oslo.

Johnson, Ralph E. and Foote, Brian. 1988. "Designing Reusable Classes," *Journal of Object-Oriented Programming*, June–July, Vol. 1, No. 2, pp. 22–35.

Lieberherr, Karl. J. and Holland, Ian M. 1988. "Formulation of the Law of Demeter," Technical Report Demeter-2, Northeastern University, June.

Lieberherr, Karl. J. and Riel, A. J. 1988. "Demeter: A CASE Software Growth Through Parametrized Classes," *Journal of Object-Oriented Programming*, August-September, pp. 8–22.

Masterman, M. 1961. "Semantic Message Detection for Machine Translation, Using Interlingua," *Proceedings of the 1961 International Conference on Machine Translation*.

Minsky, M. 1975. "A Framework for Representing Knowledge," in *The Psychology of Computer Vision*, Winston, P. H. (Ed.), McGraw Hill, NY, pp. 211–277.

Rettig, M.; Morgan, T.; Jacobs, J.; and Wimberly, D. 1989. "Object-Oriented Programming in AI—New Choices," *AI Expert*, January, Vol. 4, No. 1, pp. 53–70.

Saunders, J. 1989. "A Survey of Object-Oriented Programming Languages," *Journal of Object-Oriented Programming*, March–April, pp. 5–11.

Schank, Roger C. and Ableson, R. P. 1977. *Scripts, Plans, Goals, and Understanding: An Inquiry into Human Knowledge Structures*, Erlbaum, Hillsdale, NJ.

Schank, R. and Rieger, C. J. 1974. "Inference and the Computer Understanding of Natural Language," *Artificial Intelligence*, Vol. 5, pp. 373–412.

Snyder, Alan. 1986. "Encapsulation and Inheritance in Object-Oriented Languages," *Proceedings of Object-Oriented Programming Systems, Languages, and Applications: OOPSLA '86*, September, pp. 38–45.

Tello, Ernest R. 1989. *Object-Oriented Programming for Artificial Intelligence: A Guide to Tools and System Design*, Addison-Wesley Publishing Co., Reading, MA.

Questions

8.1 Discuss the differences and similarities among semantic nets, scripts, and frames.

8.2 What is the origin of OOP?

8.3 What does OOP offer to the fields from which it has derived its concepts?

8.4 Why is inheritance important in expert system knowledge representation?

8.5 What is the difference between the micro and macro modularity in OOP?

8.6 What are the major components of OOP?

8.7 In a knowledge base, are modularity and encapsulation useful concepts? Why?

8.8 What is the difference between OOA and OOD?

8.9 Compare and contrast the systems analysis in Chapter 7 with OOA.

8.10 What is the difference between the logical and physical designs in OOP?

8.11 What are the steps of logical design?

8.12 What issues of software selection are unique to OOP?

8.13 Should reusability and modifiability be of concern to the developer of an expert system? Why?

8.14 Discuss the advantages and disadvantages of OOP in relation to the development of an expert system.

8.15 What issues and opportunities do you see in combining the logic-based and object-oriented methods of knowledge representation?

Problems

8.1 In the job application expert system, identify the system goals, using an object-oriented knowledge representation.

8.2 What are the OOA components in the above problem?

8.3 Discuss the types of classes in OOP. Give an example for each.

8.4 What are the attribute types? Give an example for each type.

8.5 What are the class relations? Give an example for each type.

8.6 Draw a diagram of class hierarchy for the job application expert system.

8.7 Add attributes and methods to the class in the previous problem, and identify the inheritance within the hierarchy.

8.8 What is polymorphism? Give two detailed examples of it.

8.9 Describe the use of polymorphism in the design of the job application system.

8.10 Refer to the example of the mortgage loan system coded in Demeter^{TM}. Expand the example by adding attributes and methods to it.

8.11 Expand the system in the previous question to include more classes of objects.

8.12 Give a list of the tools you would like to see for analysis and design in OOP. Be as detailed as possible.

8.13 As a system developer, which categorization of the OOP languages would be useful to you?

Case: Expert System for Car Rental

Alamo Rent-A-Car, based in Ft. Lauderdale, Fla., is using an expert system developed in IBM's TIRS (The Integrated Reasoning Shell) to set car-rental prices nationwide. According to Alamo, the system has helped make it possible for Alamo to keep its prices as much as 20 percent below its competitors' while continuing to make a profit.

Before the TIRS-based system came along, managers at the company's 90 different locations had set their own prices individually and haphazardly. Because these managers weren't always in a position to make the right decision or were slow to make one at all, Alamo decided to build an expert system that would set prices for every car, in every city, every day—that's 2.8 million pricing alternatives. Furthermore, the system would have to ensure that these prices would be as low as possible while still returning profit.

The system resides on an IBM PS/2 Model 70 and is connected to Alamo's IBM S/3090 mainframe, which contains all relevant pricing information, and to a Token Ring network of other PC's. Competitor pricing information, airline reservation system data, and other information is put in the mainframe and analyzed by the TIRS system. After comparing the mainframe data to current Alamo prices, it returns a number of pricing options to the marketing staff who then modify Alamo rates as necessary.

Excerpts from "Application Watch: Price-setting with TIRS," by Justin Kestelyn, *AI Expert*, April 1991, p. 72, reprinted with permission from *AI Expert*.

Case Questions

1. Discuss the type and degree of integration needed to connect this expert system with the company's information system.

2. How did this integration requirement affect the choice of hardware and software for developing the expert system?

3. What are the features of this application that make the object-oriented approach a useful method for knowledge representation?

4. Assume this expert system is to be developed with the object-oriented approach. Identify the objects in this system.

5. Group the objects in Question 4 into classes.

6. Identify class attributes that are of importance in this system.

7. Draw the hierarchy of classes and their attributes for this expert system application. Suggest possible methods that are needed in this system.

8. Discuss the role of this expert system in managing the car rental company. What are the possible future expansions of the system?

CHAPTER 9

Hybrid Methods, Systems, and Tools for Expert Systems

I felt once more the strange equivocal power of the city—its flat alluvial landscape and exhausted airs ... Alexandria; which is neither Greek, Syrian nor Egyptian, but a hybrid: a joint.

Lawrence George Durrell, *Justine*

Chapter Objectives

The objectives of this chapter are:

- To review the hybrid methods for modeling knowledge in expert systems

- To discuss the nature of hybrid systems, such as intelligent database management systems and object-oriented database management systems

- To review some of the hybrid software products for expert systems

- To review the hybrid tool called KAPPA

KEY WORDS: Opportunistic reasoning, production systems, blackboard systems, intelligent database management systems, object-oriented database management systems, hybrid tools, knowledge-based integrated information systems

---

This chapter could be used with the demonstration diskette of KAPPA-PC available with this book for hands-on experiments with the tool.

Introduction

So far, we have seen two methods of knowledge representation: logic-based (discussed in Chapters 3 and 4) and object-oriented (Chapter 8). The question we address in this chapter is whether we can mix methods in order to increase the power of the system in representing more complex systems. To this end, we discuss hybrid methods, systems, and tools.

Hybrid methods are presented in Section 9.1. Among the well-known hybrid methods are: opportunistic reasoning, production systems, and blackboard systems. We discuss each one only briefly, to give a taste for these methods. The intention is to raise your awareness of the existence of these alternative approaches.

In Section 9.2, we observe the existing trend of creating hybrid systems to increase the power and capabilities of the system. Most notable among the hybrid systems are intelligent databases, in which the database and expert system technologies are combined, and object-oriented databases, in which the database and object-oriented technologies are integrated. Again, this section illustrates that in solving business problems and creating useful information systems, one does not have to adhere to just one approach. Instead, there is an increasing number of instances where one can combine various technologies to enhance the system's ability to provide answers to complex problems.

Section 9.3 discusses existing and exciting new tools and software products that combine various methods of knowledge representation and utilize the latest software advances. We review one of these tools (KAPPA) in relatively more depth. Chapter 10 is exclusively dedicated to the discussion of LEVEL5 OBJECT, another new hybrid tool.

Section 9.4 gives you a flavor of what the future has in store regarding the direction of creating the hybrid systems and tools. The case boxes in this chapter display a sample of real applications of the hybrid approach.

9.1 Hybrid Methods

Logic-based knowledge representation methods have the theoretical support of mathematical logic, although the incorporation of uncertainty in these methods somewhat reduces this support. Object-oriented methods, by contrast, do not have a firm mathematical foundation, but they have the support of modeling experiences in different fields for modeling large and complex systems, and have the intuitive appeal of resembling the way humans perceive the physical world. In this section, we discuss methods that have a hybrid approach, applying both logic-based and object-oriented representation. These methods focus on the problem, and use any approach that helps the system solve the problem.

Among the hybrid methods are opportunistic reasoning and the blackboard method. We briefly review them here.

9.1.1 Opportunistic Reasoning

In Chapter 4, we discussed backward chaining and forward chaining as two popular multiple inference methods. There is no set criterion for using one or the other. However, data-driven systems usually use forward chaining, and goal-driven systems use backward chaining. In a data-driven system, a typical user gives the system a set of data and looks for all the possible conclusions one can draw from the input data. In the goal-driven system, on the other hand, the user focuses on given goals or final actions.

This distinction is vague. A data-driven system has goals, and a goal-driven system uses data. Furthermore, choosing one chaining method for reasoning could be restrictive. An opportunistic system uses both backward and forward chaining, depending on the nature of the data and the degree of goal-orientation of the user. In *opportunistic reasoning*, the backward and forward mechanisms, as well as the search mechanism, are included as a part of the knowledge base, and the developer selects the circumstances suitable for applying each mechanism. One can take the idea of opportunistic choice of chaining and search one step further by including the use of any solution method within a structured frame. One successful implementation of this approach is the blackboard system.

9.1.2   Production Systems vs. Blackboard Systems

Blackboard systems and frameworks are relatively new concepts, which have their roots in production systems.

Production Systems

Newell and Simon developed production systems, which are the origin of production rules and the present structure of expert systems. A *production system* has three major components, as shown in Figure 9.1:

- The production rules
- The working memory
- The conflict resolution mechanism

A production system represents knowledge in rules. It was the production systems concept that made the rule-based systems popular.

The *working memory* has the information about all the successful results of firing rules. When the conditions of a rule match the content of the working memory, the rule fires. When the firing of a rule is successful and generates an outcome, the result is added to the content of the working memory. The working memory acts like a pad or a blackboard on which the current state of reasoning is stored.

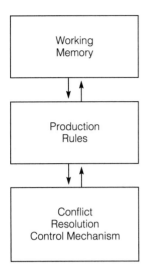

Figure 9.1   A Simplified View of Production Systems

The *conflict resolution mechanism* is needed when more than one rule becomes eligible for firing next. In this case, a criterion or a rule of thumb guides the selection of the next rule to fire. The conflict resolution mechanism resolves conflict by applying the criterion in selecting which rule should fire next. The popular conflict resolution strategies are:

- Specificity
- Simplicity
- Recency
- Antecedent-ordered
- Consequent-ordered
- Top-down
- Refractoriness

The *specificity* strategy directs the inference engine to choose the rule with the highest number of conditions in its antecedent. The *simplicity* strategy, on the other hand, directs the inference engine to choose the rule with the least number of conditions in its antecedent. The *recency* strategy means selecting the rule that uses the most recent data within the working memory of the system.

Antecedent-ordered means that the developer has attached priorities to the antecedents of rules in the knowledge base. Therefore, the rule with the highest priority should fire first. *Consequent-ordered* is similar to antecedent-ordered, with the exception that the consequents of the rules are prioritized. The *top-down* strategy gives priority to the rule that comes first in the knowledge base. The *refractoriness* strategy means that in each cycle, a rule should fire only once, thus excluding those rules that have already fired.

In a production system, one can interpret each rule as an independent unit. A unit looks at the working memory, recognizes that it can make a contribution to the working memory because its pattern has matched with some parts of the working memory, and then decides to fire. However, before firing, the control mechanism of the conflict resolution should give the rule permission to fire. Once the rule fires, it passes the firing result to the working memory. The cycle restarts when all rules again look at the working memory to see if they can contribute to it.

Blackboard Systems

Blackboard systems take the structure of production systems and expand it considerably to model complex systems. Although blackboard systems embody a variety of approaches, one can identify the following basic features, as shown in Figure 9.2 [Nii 1986]:

- Multiple independent knowledge sources

- A hierarchy of problem-solving components

- A blackboard containing the problem hierarchy

- A control mechanism

A *knowledge source* in a blackboard system is an independent portion of a knowledge base. The division of the knowledge base into *independent* knowledge sources has the same modularity feature as the object-oriented paradigm. However, knowledge representation across the knowledge sources is not limited to one method. Each knowledge source could have its own particular representation and reasoning process. The knowledge sources do not communicate with one another. They can see only the blackboard, and change only the content of the blackboard. Their activation is controlled by a control mechanism.

One of the strong features of blackboard systems is that the problem domain is divided into a hierarchy unique to that domain. The design of the

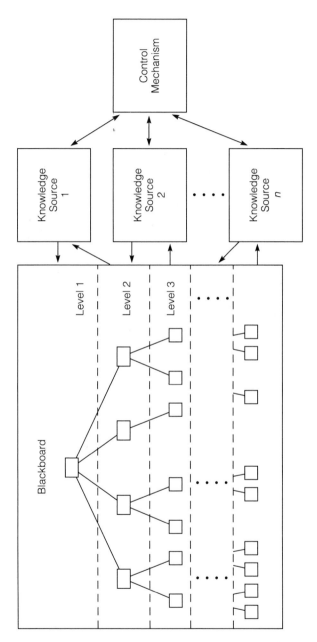

Figure 9.2 A Simplified View of Blackboard Systems

hierarchy is one of the important tasks of system design. The hierarchy could be a structure, starting from the most general deductive elements within the domain, going down to the inductive and example-based constructs of the domain. Alternatively, the hierarchy could represent the division of the system goals into smaller subgoals at the lower levels of the hierarchy. For example, in the case of the mortgage loan system, a part of the hierarchy could start from the goal of the loan approval decision, going down to the subgoals of establishing the applicant's credit worthiness, property value, adequacy of income, and so forth, as shown in Figure 9.3.

The contents of the blackboard are called the *blackboard objects*. These objects have a hierarchical structure, and have features of classes of objects in the object-oriented paradigm. That is, the blackboard objects have attribute slots, which could take complex values.

A *blackboard* is an extended version of the working memory of production systems. All knowledge sources communicate only with the blackboard, and can see the entire contents of the blackboard. Each knowledge source decides whether it can contribute to the blackboard. Once a knowledge source gets the activation permission from the control unit, it takes the information from the blackboard, performs its own reasoning process, and returns the result to the blackboard by altering the content of the blackboard.

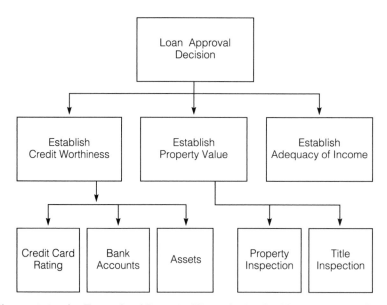

Figure 9.3   An Example of Domain Hierarchy in the Mortgage Loan System

The blackboard contains different levels or regions, representing the hierarchy of the knowledge domain. Each knowledge base can read information from one level and change the content of another level. For example, one knowledge source in the mortgage loan example may get the information from the third level of the hierarchy (Figure 9.3) about the applicant's credit card rating, bank accounts, and assets, and conclude that the applicant's credit worthiness is good, writing the result to the second level of the hierarchy.

For complex systems, the blackboard could contain multiple hierarchies. For example, if the mortgage loan is part of a larger system, its hierarchy would be one of a number of hierarchies in the system. Within this larger system, the other hierarchies could include granting commercial loans or credit cards.

The control mechanism controls the activation of the knowledge source. This task is similar to the control mechanism in production systems, with the exception that, in blackboard systems, the control is over the activation of each chunk of knowledge (stored in knowledge sources), rather than on each production rule. This increases the modularity of the system, similar to what we have seen in the object-oriented paradigm discussed in Chapter 8.

The control mechanism may have another task in the blackboard. Since the domain knowledge is divided into a hierarchy of objects, the control mechanism may be given the control over the choice of the object that should be the focus of problem solving at any moment. For example, if objects are in the form of goals, as in Figure 9.3, the control mechanism may decide which subgoal the system must pursue at any moment.

Thus, the control mechanism must decide on what is called the *focus of attention*, which consists of one of the following decisions [Nii 1986; Engelmore, Morgan, and Nii 1988]:

- Which object (or group of objects) in the blackboard gets the problem-solving priority

- Which knowledge source gets the permission to act

- A combination of the two

The systems work in the following manner:

- The knowledge sources look at the content of the blackboard, and announce whether they can make any contribution to it.

- The control selects a blackboard object, the knowledge source that can act on it, or both, as the focus of attention.

- This activates a knowledge source, which then writes its results on the blackboard.

- The process repeats again.

The blackboard paradigm provides a structure for combining various knowledge representation methods. Each knowledge source could theoretically contain its own reasoning process. The independence of the knowledge sources isolates them from the influence of others.

The blackboard approach provides a modular structure that facilitates the incremental development of the system. Thus, a system design based on blackboard systems has the effectiveness of the object-oriented paradigm, and uses strengths of logic-based knowledge representation and inference.

Modularity has computational efficiency as well. The efficiency results from the fact that the knowledge base is divided into smaller units, which makes their invocation less costly computationally.

The blackboard approach shares the concurrency feature of the object-oriented method, in that each knowledge source could theoretically be located on a different processor, while the control mechanism guides the process centrally.

9.1.3   Blackboard Shells

The idea of blackboard systems started when DARPA (Defense Advanced Research Projects Agency) initiated a research plan for speech recognition. One of the outcomes was Hearsay-II (developed at Carnegie Mellon University), where the blackboard concept was developed and implemented. Subsequently a number of systems used this concept in dealing with various complex systems. The first generalization of the approach into a shell, similar to an expert system shell, was the development of AGE (Attempt to GEneralize). A number of other blackboard shells have been developed, almost all as research projects. They include Hearsay-III (which is a shell), MXA, and BLOBS. The book by Engelmore and Morgan [1988] contains the details of these blackboard systems. The first commercial blackboard shell is ESHELL, by Fujitsu, Japan.

The blackboard paradigm has been used for tackling difficult problems in expert systems, such as continuous time representation, and manufacturing processes and sensors where the input data are continuous. Already reports of successful applications of the method in factory processes have reached publication [Larner 1990].

Four trends in expert systems encourage more extensive use of the blackboard paradigm in developing expert systems:

- The increase in the variety and complexity of the application domains of expert systems, which require, among many things, the incorporation of the passage of time and continuous inputs

- The demonstrated strength of the hierarchical, modular design, and the critical role of software in enforcing modularity

- The outlook of affordable machines with parallel processing capability

- The necessity for combining different representation and reasoning capabilities within one system, and the opportunistic and flexible applications of each, when needed

9.2 Hybrid Systems

The success of expert systems in formalizing the qualitative aspects of business problems raises the questions of whether expert system methods could be combined together, and whether they can serve to highlight the qualitative aspects of existing systems, thus creating hybrid information and decision systems. Notable hybrid systems include the combination of database management systems, the object-oriented approach, and logic-based knowledge representation in one of the following forms:

- Intelligent database management systems

- Object-oriented database management systems

- Object-oriented knowledge-base systems

- Distributed object management

These topics are discussed in the following subsections.

9.2.1   Intelligent Database Management Systems

Database management systems (DBMS) products are software designed to manage the storage, retrieval, and modification of data within an organization. The first such product was IMS, which was developed for handling data in the Apollo moon program by a joint effort of IBM and Rockwell International in the 1960s, and was later commercialized by IBM. The next two decades witnessed the rapid proliferation of DBMS products and their now universal applications in business information systems.

DBMS products have contributed greatly to the organization of business information systems. However, they can improve in a number of areas.

- The function of DBMS products is mostly passive. These products rely on the user-written applications programs to make sense out of the data.

- Most DBMS products have checks for the integrity of data, in that the database developer can specify the acceptable values and types of data in each field. However, the default integrity checks are mostly limited to the field value itself, and do not compare values across fields. Thus, a typical DBMS product may not discover that a person under 16 could not have a driver's license number.

- DBMS products do not check the nature of relations among data in order to discover unusual patterns that could indicate errors or problems. For example, it would be unusual for a credit card holder to make more than 10 purchases within a day. Such an abnormal case merits checking for the possibility of a data entry error or a stolen card.

- The user interface of DBMS products is either command-driven or menu-driven. That is, the user should either know the query commands (such as SQL) in order to interrogate the system, or rely on programmed menus for assistance in accessing data. In both cases, the query should match perfectly the content of the database. The systems do not tolerate any inaccuracy or fuzziness in the question.

The application of expert systems to a DBMS product creates the possibility of expanding the capability of the system in the above areas. *Intelligent database management systems* (or expert database systems) consist of the conventional DBMS, plus intelligence in the form of an added expert system functionality. In their book, Parsaye, Chignell, Khoshafian, and Wong [1989] describe in detail how the intelligence in DBMS could be in one of the following three areas:

- Intelligent user interface

- Intelligent integrity checks and error corrections

- Intelligent discovery

Intelligent User Interface

The user interface of DBMS products could be enhanced by adding intelligence to the system in a number of ways. One method is to add a natural language processing component of AI in the interface, such that the user could enter queries in English, rather than by command or menu. (Some of the fourth-generation languages and products also have this feature.) There are a number of add-on software products in the market that could work as the front-end to the DBMS.

A more interesting type of intelligence for the user interface is the ability of the system to respond to inaccurate or fuzzy questions. Chapter 11 describes the concepts of fuzzy sets and fuzzy logic. In an intelligent user interface, the user may enter a query such as: give me the list of all high income applicants. The system has quantitative values in the field income. The system uses a fuzzy set approach to identify and print the name of those who have high income.

Another useful type of user intelligence is the ability to recognize an inaccurate question, such as give me all information about smeth. Here the name is misspelled. The system must recognize that the user means smith. Yet other types of intelligence in the user interface are: the ability of the system to recognize queries from graphical representation and icons, and the system's capability to answer the user's question such as Why is smith not qualified for a loan?

Intelligent interfacing is now a field of active research in expert systems and could contribute greatly to the enhancement of the DBMS's user interface. Research topics include:

- Multimedia explanation facility, such as combining text and graphics to provide explanations for the user

- Explanation dialogue in which the user can ask follow-up questions to clarify the system's answers to the previous questions

Intelligent Integrity Checks and Error Corrections

The integrity checks in DBMS are intended to prevent errors from creeping into the database. While the DBMS products check the range and types of data, checking more complex errors requires additional programming. One way to increase the reliability of a database is by adding the expert system capability to the system for complex error checking. For example, in a database on the loan applicants in a bank, one of the error checking rules could be:

```
IF  the applicant has no assets
  AND  the applicant has no job
THEN  the applicant could not be in the medium or high
        income category
```

Here, again, medium or high income are fuzzy data types, and the rule uses more than one field to discover the error. The integrity check, therefore, has a knowledge base of its own.

The integrity check knowledge base could also contain information on the organization's rules and regulations. For example, the bank may require that each loan application should have one assigned loan officer. In the database of loan applicants, if the data record of an applicant does not have an assigned loan officer, then there is the possibility of a data entry error in this record.

Intelligent Discovery

Intelligent discovery is intended to reveal relationships and patterns among the data fields that could be of interest, or indicate possible errors. Part of this discovery could be through the application of statistical techniques, such as regression and time series analyses. The inductive learning and reasoning methods of the expert systems could also be applied to uncover hidden patterns in data, which could help in error detections. For example, from the database on the monthly mortgage payments, one may discover that self-employed mortgage holders have a higher tendency to miss a payment. This information is potentially important in the loan decision when the case for an application is marginal, or the pool of applicants is much larger than the available fund.

The potential contributions of expert system methods to the quality of data and user interfaces in databases are the indicators of future trends in DBMS development. The synergy of DBMS and expert systems is not limited to logic-based representation and inference. The object-oriented paradigm, too, has entered the database domain.

Case: Wire-Transfer Sentinel

WJM Technologies of Petaluma, Calif., is assisting Wells Fargo Bank in the deployment of a wire-transfer, fraud-detection expert system. The system, which will capture the expertise of wire supervisors and regulators, is designed to scan wire transfers for potentially fraudulent transactions.

The Wells Fargo system, which is only in its first phase of testing, is not your typical computer-security program. Instead of preoccupying itself with encrypted codes and passwords, the system will automatically apply the same common-sense techniques as human regulators, concentrating on unusual patterns and other giveaways. It will pass suspicious transactions, along with an explanation of its reasoning, to human supervisors for confirmation.

WJM Technologies has determined that as many as 50% of wire-transfer transactions can be successfully reviewed by the system.

By Justin Kestelyn, "Application Watch," *AI Expert*, March 1991, p. 72, reprinted with permission from *AI Expert*.

9.2.2   *Object-Oriented Database Management Systems*

Another limitation of the existing DBMS products is their inability to deal with complex data structures such as graphics, computer aided designs (CAD), images, and so forth. *Object-oriented database management systems* (OODBMS) deal with this problem.

Database management has gone through a number of phases:

- At the start, the files were in a chaotic state. Each computer program had its own file; the files were numerous, contained redundant data, and were not updated at the same time. Later, the idea of managing the files by creating master files was introduced to reduce the chaos.

- The introduction of IMS by IBM initiated the field of database management systems. IMS has a hierarchical data model. In the hierarchy model, each child record has only one physical parent record.

- The inadequacy of the hierarchical data model in dealing with complex relations among data led to the network data model (and the subsequent CODASYL standard for network data model), where a child record could have more than one parent.

- Then came the relational data model, where the records (called relations) were flat, and each file looked like a two-dimensional table. The relational data model has the mathematical foundation of set theory. The design of relational data is guided by the principles of the first, second, third, ... normal forms. The relational data model for the DBMS became popular with the introduction of the PC-based DBMS, which utilize the model in their structure. With the introduction of relational DBMS for mainframes, such as DB2, and the SQL as the de facto industry standard for relational query language, the relational data model has become the most common data model in DBMS products.

- Now, the object oriented data model is the new kid on the block, challenging the relational data model, and sparking hot debates on the advantages of OODBMS over relational DBMS.

In the relational data model, the unit representing a physical object is represented by one or more flat data records. In the object-oriented data model, an object represents the unit of database. As Loomis [1990] notes, the advantage of the object-oriented data model is that:

- It can represent complex data structures, which is not possible in relational DBMS

- It is closer to the way humans see the objects

- Its user interface is object-oriented, hence easier to use, and allows easier graphical retrieval

- In the three phases of design (human), implementation (OODBMS), and use (humans as end-users and programmers), it has a closer fit with the design and use

The advantage of the relational data model is its set theory foundation, its well-established status within the industry, and the availability of numerous reliable products in the market.

OODBMS is a structure that has object-oriented programming (OOP) features, as discussed in Chapter 8. However, it has the following additional features over what is normally available in any OOP tool [Loomis 1990]:

- The data should be persistent, in that the object, once created, is stored within OODBMS

- OODBMS should be able to store and retrieve small and large numbers of objects in an efficient manner

- OODBMS must allow the users to access the database concurrently, without any damage to the integrity of data

- OODBMS should have the capability to recover objects in the case of a system crash

- OODBMS should allow the user to ask questions about various objects

There are already some OODBMS products in the market, such as ObjectStore (by Object Design, Burlington, Mass.), G-Base/GTX (by Object Databases, Cambridge, Mass.), ITASCA (by ITASCA Systems, Inc., Minneapolis, Minn.), ONTOS (by Ontologic, Burlington, Mass.), GemStone (by Servio Corp., Alameda, Calif.), and Versant (by Versant Object Technology, Menlo Park, Calif.). Adding an object component to the existing relational databases is another avenue being pursued by DBMS vendors. Objectivity Inc. (with Objectivity/DB product) and Digital Equipment Corporation have teamed up to create object-oriented databases.

The comparison of the relational and object-oriented data models will continue for some time to come, and will, with high probability, end when a hybrid of the two models proves to be stronger than each.

9.3 Hybrid Tools

The success of the object-oriented paradigm in modeling complex systems has prompted the introduction of a number of software tools into the market. In Chapter 8, we mentioned CLOS (Common Lisp Object Systems), which is a combination of the AI language: Lisp and OOP components. Smalltalk/V has a PROLOG capability that creates a hybrid of the two knowledge presentation methods: logic-based and object-oriented.

However, the most pervasive effort in combining the two methods of knowledge representation is in the hybrid expert system software products, which also make extensive use of windows and graphics in their development and user interfaces.

9.3.1   Hybrid Software Products

The recent wave of expert system software products combines the logic-based and object-oriented knowledge representation methods. They mostly apply rules for logic-based representation. However, the propositions within rules involve testing and changing the slot values of objects. Thus, the knowledge is represented in the hierarchically structured classes of objects. The rules contain reasoning about the objects.

One of the roadblocks in combining the two knowledge representation approaches is programming the methods within objects. Products deal with this problem in different ways. Some have developed a language within the system for encoding methods, and some rely on conventional languages for this purpose.

The hybrid products take full advantage of the advances in graphics and image processing, thus adding to the resource requirements of the software. A number of products take advantage of Microsoft Windows, which provides a uniform graphical and windowing structure for all these products.

One major omission in most of the hybrid systems is the treatment of uncertainty. Many of them simply do not have any capability for dealing with uncertainty.

Among those products that have some capability for incorporating uncertainty are KAPPA and LEVEL5 OBJECT. In KAPPA, the developer can write programs in order to accommodate uncertainty. LEVEL5 OBJECT has a simple confidence factor to represent uncertain rules or facts. A review of KAPPA and a brief discussion of other products on the market provides a better understanding of hybrid tools. Appendix B presents a more comprehensive list of expert system tools on the market.

9.3.2 KAPPA

KAPPA (by IntelliCorp, Inc., Mountain View, Calif.) is a recent hybrid expert system software product that combines the logic-based and object-oriented knowledge representation methods, and uses Microsoft Windows for graphics and window management. It also has a procedural language of its own, called KAL. KAPPA itself uses KAL for knowledge representation and inference, and allows the developer to program in KAL.

KAPPA Features

The general features of KAPPA are:

- Object-oriented representation

- Rule-based representation

- Inference

- User interfaces

- Outside hooks

KAPPA has the environment and foundation of an object-oriented tool. For this reason, its strongest aspect is its object-oriented representation. KAPPA models the knowledge domain into classes of objects, with single inheritance (which can be made into multiple inheritance with the abstract classes, as discussed in Chapter 8). Classes have slots, methods, and instances. KAPPA supports polymorphism (defined in Chapter 8.) In KAPPA, slots could have other class types and could create instances of other classes.

The logic-based component of KAPPA is rule-based. However, the propositions in the rules are mostly about the object within the system. The conditions of the antecedent of a rule (the IF part) test the slot values of instances of objects, and the consequent (the THEN part) of the rule changes the slot values, sends messages to methods, and takes other actions, such as getting data from a database, updating data in a database, or executing other programs.

Goals are defined separately in different sets. Each set can be used for a different reasoning process. One can group rules into sets of rules. Each set of rules itself is an object, whose slots have rules as their values. Grouping rules into sets yields the capability of blackboard systems by treating each set as a knowledge source. However, KAPPA does not enforce independence of the rule sets; one rule could be in more than one set.

KAPPA has forward and backward inference mechanisms, and gives the developer control over selecting the inference type. It is possible to combine both inference methods in one inference process, and apply forward chaining in one set of rules and backward chaining in another set. Hence, it offers the capability of opportunistic reasoning, discussed earlier in this chapter. The developer has the option of assigning a priority to each rule. Thus, when there is a conflict, the developer can control the order of resolving the conflict. The developer also can choose the search mechanism by choosing one of the following methods: depth-first, breadth-first, best-first, or selective (as defined in Chapter 4).

The programming language KAL allows the user to define functions and procedures, as in conventional programming. The developer needs to know KAL because the methods in classes of objects must be programmed in KAL. However, KAPPA has about 240 predefined functions with relatively simple syntax, for tasks from knowledge representation to image processing and mathematical computations. There are also help facilities for using the KAL expressions. These functions handle most of the developer's needs. The developer has the option of defining user-defined functions, and adding them

to the product. KAPPA has a strong tie to the C language, and can import
C functions.

KAPPA has a strong graphical interface, especially for the object-oriented
aspect of the system. Since it runs over Microsoft Windows, it contains all
the power and facilities of Windows, as well. This becomes more clear in the
following discussion of the inner working of KAPPA.

Object-Oriented Representation in KAPPA (Optional)

KAPPA must be accessed from Microsoft Windows, because it utilizes the
windowing and graphics capabilities of Windows. KAPPA starts with three
windows, as shown in Figure 9.4. The top window has the icons for the groups
of tools within KAPPA, two of which are shown the top window, the **Object
Browser** (on the lower left) and the **Knowledge Tools** (on the lower right).

The **Object Browser** is the backbone of the system. It is where the hierarchy of classes is defined. A new knowledge base starts with the classes **Root**,
Image, and **Global**. The **Root** class is the parent of all classes. The **Global**
class contains sets of rules as its instances. (The developer can store other
data in the Global class.)

Thus, the knowledge sources or rule sets are considered objects within
the system. The developer can import and hold images in the **Image** class,
and use them as needed.

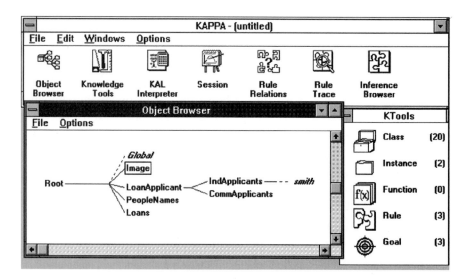

Figure 9.4   Three Starting Windows of KAPPA

To demonstrate KAPPA's features we continue the example of the mortgage loan system. In Chapter 8, we developed a number of classes for the mortgage loan system. The names of classes are shortened to fit them in the Object Browser window in Figure 9.4. The class LoanApplicant has two subclasses IndApplicants and ComApplicants. PeopleNames and Loans are subclasses of the Root class, as well.

One can easily create and edit classes, their contents, and instances by clicking the mouse on the class. This brings up a menu from which one can choose class operations, such as create subclasses, instances, edit, delete, and so forth, as shown in Figure 9.5.

Choosing the Edit option when clicking on the class LoanApplicant opens the class editor, as shown in Figure 9.6. In this editor, one can define and edit slots and methods for the class. It also shows the parent class from which this class inherits. Since the LoanApplicant class has Root as the parent, it has no inherited slot or method in this example.

One can add and modify slots with the pull-down menu Slots. For example, to add Address as a slot for this class, one chooses the New option in the Slots menu to get a window to add the name of the slot, and another window to add the value of the slot, if any. In the latter window, one can choose the Option window to define the data type for the slot. This window for the slot Address is shown in Figure 9.7.

As Figure 9.7 shows, the slots have methods. In Figure 9.7, If Needed Method means that when the slot needs to have a value, this method is activated. Before Change Method means that the function should be executed

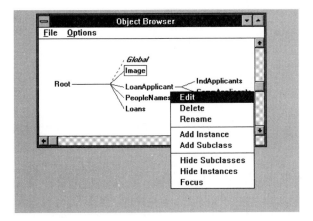

Figure 9.5   The Pull-Down Menu for Class Operation in KAPPA

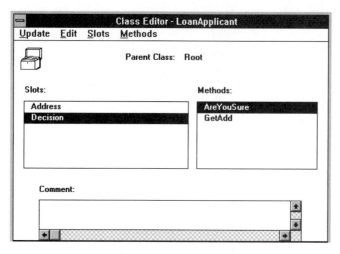

Figure 9.6   The Class Editor for the LoanApplicant Class

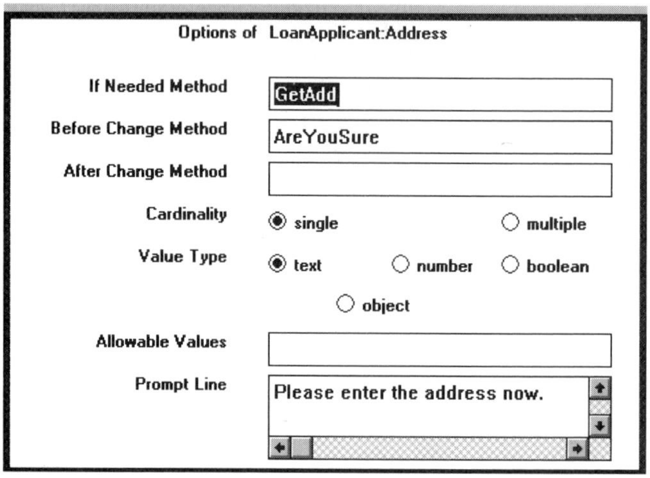

Figure 9.7   The Window for the Type Definition of the Address Slot

before the slot value is changed; and **After Change Method** means that the method is executed after the value of the slot is altered. These methods act as demons—side effects of the change in the knowledge base—and get activated when the data for the slot is changed.

These methods form a strong feature of the system, which allow for sophisticated processing of objects. In the case of the **Address** slot, it uses the method **GetAdd** when it needs value. Before any change in address, it uses the method AreYouSure to make sure that the user really intends to change the address.

Figure 9.7 shows other parts of the data structure of a slot. The slot could have single or multiple value, it could take text, number, Boolean, and object as its type. One can specify the allowable values for the slot, and in the Prompt Line enter the text that the user should see when asked for the value of this slot. In the case of no entry for the prompt line, the system uses its own default prompt. Using this editor twice, we have defined Address and Decision slots for this class. The Decision slot can take values approve and reject. Thus, the LoanApplicant class has two slots as shown in Figure 9.6.

The choice of Methods option in the class editor (Figure 9.6) results in the system asking for the name of the method, and opening the Method Editor as shown in Figure 9.8.

Arguments, an optional part of the method, defines the list of names it uses as arguments. The Body of the method consists of functions (user-defined or system-defined) in KAL that perform the purpose of the method. In Figure 9.8, the KAL function AskValue has two arguments—the class and the slot—for which the function asks the user to enter a single value. The word Self represents the class or instance to which the method belongs. One could also use TheParent, referring to the parent of the method's class. One can use any class name for this function call. The delimiter of the KAL functions is ";", and if there is more than one function in the method, they are grouped into {...} with a ";" after the closing bracket.

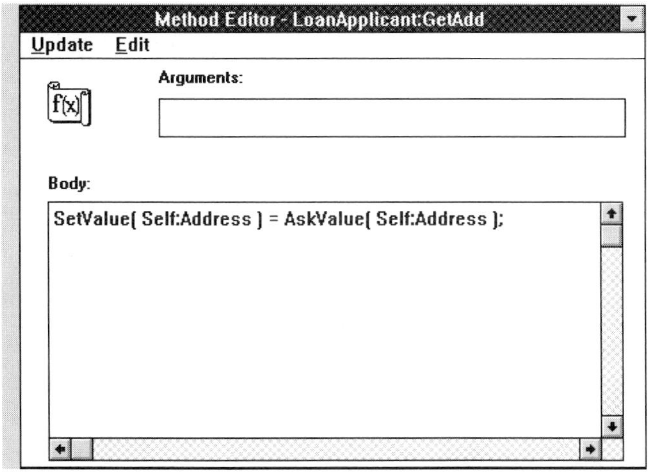

Figure 9.8   The Method Editor for the GetAdd Method

In this example, the KAL function **AskValue** asks the user for the value of the **Address** slot and stores the value in this slot. One continues this process by defining the slots and methods for other classes.

To show the inheritance structure in KAPPA, let us examine the class editor for **IndApplicants**, as shown in Figure 9.9.

When editing a class with a subclass, the slots and methods of the parent class automatically show up in its class editor, with a (*) next to the name of the inherited method and slot. One can remove the (*) by clicking the mouse on the name of the slot or method, and selecting the **Local** option. If one makes the method local, it acts as though the parent has been declared virtual for this class (as described in Chapter 8). This makes the polymorphism possible, because the subclass has the same method name as its parent, but the content of the method differs from that of the parent, hence it would respond differently when it receives an activation message.

For example, if we remove the (*) from the method **AreYouSure**, it responds differently when it receives the message for executing this method. All the children of this class inherit the method in its altered form, unless they, too, change the content of the method by removing the (*) from the method and defining their own content for the **AreYouSure** method.

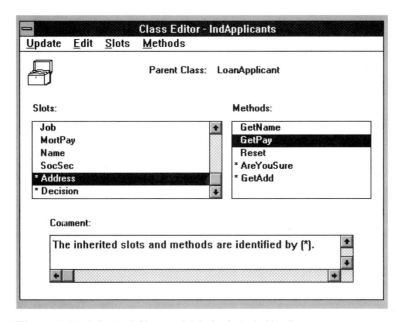

Figure 9.9 Inherited Slots and Methods in **IndApplicants**

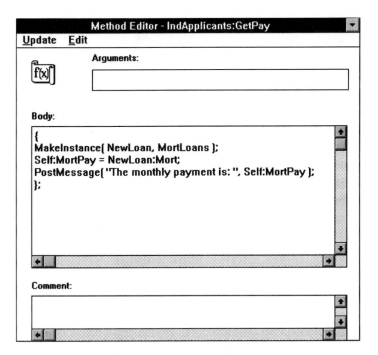

Figure 9.10   An Example of a More Complex Method in KAPPA

Figure 9.10 shows a more complex method, GetPay for the class IndAppli-cants. This method creates an instance of the class Loans by using the KAL function MakeInstance, and calls it NewLoan. Assume that the *Loans* class is designed such that when its instance is created, it automatically gets the loan information from the user, computes the monthly mortgage payment, and stores it in its own slot called Mort. The second operation of this method sets the value of its own slot MortPay by getting the information from the newly created instance. The third KAL function prints the mortgage information for the user into a pop-up window with an explanatory message.

Rule-based Representation in KAPPA (Optional)

Rules have their own editors that could be activated by a mouse click on the Rule icon in the Knowledge Tools window. One can create new rules or modify an existing one. An example of the rule editor is shown in Figure 9.11.

In the rule editor, one can assign priority to a rule, with 0 as the default priority, and $32,767$ and $-32,767$ as the highest and lowest priority, respec-tively. In the case of a conflict, the rule with a higher priority will fire first. In the rule editor, one can specify that a particular rule applies to a class and all its subclasses and their instances. One can accomplish this in the

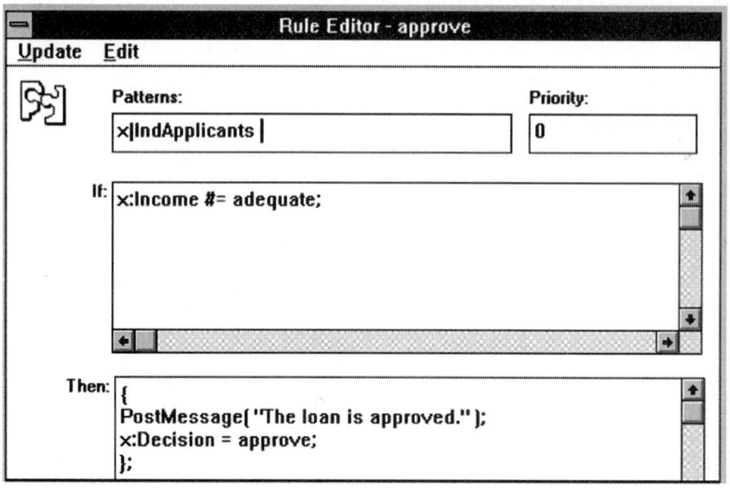

Figure 9.11   An Example of the Rule Editor in KAPPA

Patterns part of the rule editor. In Figure 9.11, we have x | IndApplicants, and have used x as the class name in the body of the rule. It means that this rule applies to the class IndApplicants, its instances and subclasses. This increases the power of reasoning with the rules, because one can specify one rule that applies to a hierarchy of classes.

The body of the rule has two parts: If and Then. The conditions of the rules consist of comparing the slot values of classes, and their antecedents assign values to the slots and take actions. In Figure 9.11, the Income slot of the class x (which is IndApplicants and all its instances and subclasses) is compared to the string adequate. The symbol "#=" represents the equality operator. If the comparison succeeds, the Then part takes the action of informing the user that the loan is approved, and assigns approve to the slot Decision of class x. If we create an instance for the class IndApplicants called smith, it has an inherited slot called Income, and this rule also applies to the instance smith.

The consequent part of the rule in Figure 9.11 has two parts. In one part, the value approve is assigned to the slot Decision in x—the object to which this object is applied. It also has an action part, which sends a message to the screen by the function PostMessage. One can call any one of the KAL functions in the rules, including functions for drawing windows and images, or any user-defined functions.

To show the relations among rules, KAPPA has the Rule Relations window, which can be activated by a click on the icon with the same name

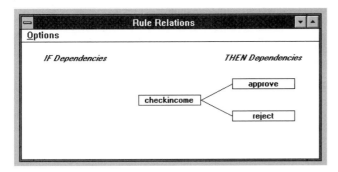

Figure 9.12   An Example of the Rule Relations Window in KAPPA

in the **Knowledge Tools** window. KAPPA automatically creates the decision tree, which shows the interrelations of different rules. When the result of the consequent of a rule is used in the antecedent of another rule, a decision tree is created to show the relations. Since there could be numerous relations, KAPPA asks for the rule that should be the root of the tree.

An example of the rule relation window is shown in Figure 9.12. Here there are three rules called: **checkincome**, **approve**, and **reject**. Before opening this window, KAPPA displays the list of the rules and asks which one should be the root. It then draws the decision tree.

Inference in KAPPA (Optional)

KAPPA offers forward and backward inference mechanisms. The developer has control over the type of inference, the search methods in the inference, and the rules to which the inference applies. The developer defines goals in a different window, activated by clicking the last icon in the **Knowledge Tools** window (shown in Figure 9.4). One can choose to create a new goal, which opens the **Goal Editor**, shown in Figure 9.13.

A goal reasons about class instances. For example, we create an instance of the class **IndApplicants**, called by the generic name **smith**. The goal in Figure 9.13 is asking whether the slot value of **smith:Decision** has the value **approve**. The operator "$\#=$" tests the equality of two single values. The developer can create many such goals, and use them in the inference process as needed.

KAPPA allows the developer to select the inference mechanism by the KAL functions: **ForwardChain** and **BackwardChain**. One can use the **KAL Interpreter** window to interactively call KAL functions, and get answers. Figure 9.14 shows an example of using the **KAL Interpreter** in performing the backward chaining using the created rules, and their related objects.

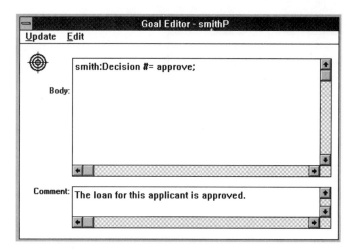

Figure 9.13   An Example of Goal Editor

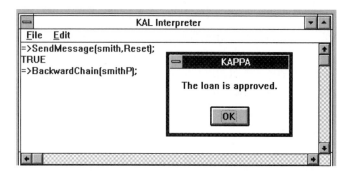

Figure 9.14   The Use of KAL Interpreter for Inference

The first line in this window is to reset the slot values of the instance smith. The reason for the necessity of reset is that once the reasoning is finished, the user's answers to questions are stored in the relevant objects, in this case, smith. There is a method in the IndApplicants class called Reset, which resets its slot value (Figure 9.9). As an instance of this class, smith inherits the Reset method.

The first line of the interpreter is sending a message to this object to reset its own slot values. The success of the operation is shown by the TRUE response of the interpreter.

The third line in the KAL interpreter in Figure 9.14 shows the function for backward chaining, in which the goal to pursue is called smithP, created as shown in Figure 9.13. The inference engine starts from the goal, asks the user for the values of the slots it needs by opening a series of windows and prompting the user to respond. The conclusion is in the last window. The example of the final window is the smaller window in Figure 9.14. Once the inference ends, the interpreter returns TRUE, FALSE, or NULL, depending on whether the goal has succeeded or failed or the user has selected UNKNOWN as a response, resulting the goal status to be UNKNOWN.

In the BackwardChain function call, one can specify the subset of rules (stored as a multi-valued slot in the Global class), which the inference engine must use. For example, we can store the three rules as the values of a slot called RuleSet1, and use it in the function call as:

```
BackwardChain(smithP, Global:RuleSet1);
```

which will cause the inference engine to use only the rules in RuleSet1 in the inference process. All such function calls are performed in the KAL interpreter, as shown in Figure 9.14.

KAPPA has the forward chaining function. One has the option of including a goal and the subset of rules it must use. In forward chaining, KAPPA has an agenda, on which the asserted or established facts are stored. The inference engine matches these facts with the antecedents of rules to assert other facts. The developer can access the agenda by including new facts in it as well as modifying its content.

For example, take the following functions calls in the KAL interpreter:

```
SetForwardChainMode(BREADTHFIRST);
smith:Income = adequate;
Assert (smith, Income);
ForwardChain(NULL, Global:RuleSet1);
```

These functions tell the inference engine to:

- Use the breadth first search method in forward chaining

- Enter the fact that the slot value of smith:Income is adequate

- Tell the inference engine to add the fact to its agenda by the Assert function

- Use forward chaining in inference, without using any goal (NULL), and only using the subset of rules, as specified in the slot RuleSet1 of the Global class

In this case, the inference engine applies the fact to the antecedents of all rules in the set, and draws all possible conclusions from the consequents of the rules that have fired. It stops when no new conclusion could be reached. Replacing NULL by the name of a goal limits the search to achieving that goal. For debugging purposes, the developer can step through the inference process one step at a time, while viewing the agenda and the rules that have fired and modified the slots.

User Interface in KAPPA (Optional)

KAPPA provides the developer with a number of facilities for custom-designing the user interface. It has about 27 image functions by which one can import, store, and display images at the appropriate time. Examples of such functions are: DrawImage and SetImageLink, which draws an image on the screen and sets a graphical image link to a slot. It also has numerous functions for manipulating windows and communicating with the user.

From the Session icon (Figure 9.4), one can access the layout mode for designing graphical displays, using the facilities within the systems. An example of the graphical facilities of KAPPA is shown in Figure 9.15. Note that the image of the party items is imported to the system from a Window's bitmap file.

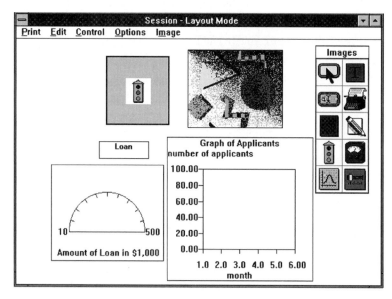

Figure 9.15   Some Graphical Tools in KAPPA

The KAL functions could be stored in an ASCII file, and called from the KAL interpreter. All the system specification in KAPPA is in the form of KAL functions. The designed system is stored either in KAL or in binary form. Thus, the developer has access to all aspects of the design in the form of KAL functions within the stored file, and can alter it by any editor that has an ASCII output file.

Outside Hooks in KAPPA (Optional)

KAPPA can import graphical and CAD files. The most advanced hook in KAPPA is to the C function libraries. It can import texts in ASCII files and images in bitmap. KAPPA has functions that can open, retrieve values from, and close dBASE and Lotus 1-2-3 files. It can also update a record within the dBASE with data from an instance. Thus, its interaction with the dBASE is active because it can change the content of the database.

Case: Expert System for Buying Decisions

Touche Ross of Seattle, Wash., developed a knowledge-based expert system for Associated Grossers. The Buyer's Workbench, built in Neuron Data's Nexpert Object, supports buyers in making investment-buying decisions.

Buyer decisions are based on inventory and price information, point of sale, and speculation about supply and demand. Associated Grocers wanted to capture the experience, judgment, and quantitative-analysis abilities of senior buyers in a knowledge base with access to inventory and product information for based goods. Touche Ross chose an AI approach because although decision models for the task were fairly simple, they required deep experience and could number in the thousands. Nexpert Object was selected for its mainframe-integration capabilities.

The buyer uses a Windows interface to call up a list of potential investment buys, evaluates them using the knowledge base, and may issue purchase orders. (The interface and knowledge base are separate applications in Buyer's Workbench that communicate as client and server.) Expert knowledge of seasonality, consumer performances, vendor characteristics, and other factors is structured as objects and classes in the knowledge base.

A Buyer's Workbench prototype is under evaluation, and has already been useful for detecting good investment-buying decisions. Associated Grocers plans to deploy versions of the system for various food items.

By Justin Kestelyn, "Application Watch," *AI Expert*, March 1990, p. 72, reprinted with permission from *AI Expert*.

9.3.3   Other Hybrid Products

Many of the recent and advanced expert system software products combine rule-based and object-oriented knowledge representation methods, and have the capability of calling functions written in the conventional mode of programming. KAPPA is one example of such products. In this section, we briefly review a few additional products in this category.

G2

G2 (by Gensym, Cambridge, Mass.) is a powerful hybrid expert system that combines rule-based and object-oriented knowledge representation methods. It, too, has the capability of adding user-defined mathematical functions to the knowledge base. G2 provides a foreign function interface by which the developer can call up C and FORTRAN functions.

One of G2's strong features is its simulator. It can simulate the working of the system, and has the capability of modeling discrete and continuous event systems. The simulator can run in parallel, when G2 is used to control a real system.

Another strong feature of G2 is its graphic representation of the structure of a system. For example, one can model the structure of a factory and model its objects and their relations in a graphical mode. Clicking on any object within the schematic diagram of the system shows all information about that object. Its simulator capability gives the developer the opportunity to design and test the expert system on simulated data before running it on a real system. The simulator also can feed data to the system if any of the flows from the real system are temporarily disrupted. G2 is used for real time control of manufacturing processes.

NEXPERT Object

NEXPERT Object (by Neuron Data, Palo Alto, Calif.) is another hybrid expert system product. It has classes and objects, and rules by which one can reason about the objects. It has the capability of forward and backward reasoning. It runs on Microsoft Windows, thus giving the developer windowing and editor capabilities.

One of the interesting features of NEXPERT Object is its open architecture, which allows the developer to embed the product as an intelligent component of other systems. As discussed later, the ability of a product to have open and active interactions with other systems is an increasingly important feature.

NEXPERT Object can import the knowledge base from NEXTRA. The Neuron Data's brochure calls NEXTRA a knowledge acquisition tool for interviewing experts and comparing their opinions. The developer can use it for acquiring knowledge by identifying relevant factors and rating their importance. At the completion of the knowledge acquisition process, NEXTRA automatically generates rules and objects to NEXPERT Object.

KEE

KEE, the Knowledge Engineering Environment (by IntelliCorp, Mountain View, Calif.), is a large hybrid expert system product that requires at least the power of workstation computers for hardware.

KEE has rule-based and object-oriented representations, and has image processing and windowing capabilities. It, too, has a number of functions that allow the developer to control the inference process. For example, backward chaining is activated by the function: QUERY, and forward chaining by functions: FORWARD.CHAIN and ASSERT. The developer must program methods in Lisp or call Lisp functions.

The KEEworlds facility allows the developer to partition facts into different worlds. The basic knowledge does not change from one world to another. Only facts differ from one world to another. Thus, the system could include a number of hypothetical worlds, which could be in conflict with each other, yet each would contain consistent facts. This facility allows the user to apply the truth maintenance mechanism, discussed briefly in Chapter 11.

Worlds could have a hierarchical relation, in that one can create one world from another. KEE has functions for creating, deleting, changing, and merging worlds. Each world should have consistent facts.

The developer can import and present various types of images and create a number of graphical presentations in designing the user interface.

Case: Expert System in Bakery

When most of us think of baked goods, we rarely consider what it takes for a major bakery to get its products made, baked, and packaged. The methodology for producing bakery items is as complex as any other industrial process—in some cases, it is more stringent because of FDA and health regulations that accompany the production of foodstuffs.

Mrs. Baird's Bakery, the largest independent bakery in the United States, has just completed a state-of-the-art bakery in Fort Worth, Texas, that uses Gensym's G2 real-time expert system to schedule and monitor all aspects of production. The company's aim is to keep the production process completely balanced in real-time, so that it can keep a delivery schedule that ships baked items to customers as quickly as possible. After all, stale muffins don't exactly make for repeated customers.

So G2 schedules tasks during production, from ingredient loading and mixing to specific oven operations. Once it has set the schedule, G2 monitors the process to ensure that all is running as planned. Since bakeries are highly automated (and have been for the last few decades), the use of G2 to oversee the integration of specialized machines makes more sense than having each machine supervised by an individual (human or computer) that is responsible only for that machine's performance. Thus, quality control (avoiding those stale muffins) is coordinated at every point along the production line.

From the article by Harvey P. Newquist III, "Where You Least Expect AI," *AI Expert*, September 1991, pp. 59–60, reprinted with permission from *AI Expert*.

9.4 Future Hybrid Designs

Each technology and method of knowledge representation has its strong points and disadvantages. One approach is to combine them, and use each technology where it can best serve the goal of the system. There are a number of other approaches being tested at labs that hold great promise. The following are two samples of what may be ahead.

9.4.1 Knowledge-based Integrated Information Systems

The idea of the *knowledge-based integrated information systems* (KBIIS) is to provide *interoperability* among various heterogeneous information systems within an organization. This takes system compatibility and system interconnectivity a few steps forward [Manola 1990].

The proliferation of various types of software within an organization has created numerous autonomous islands of information systems within an organization. The idea of *system compatibility* is that the output of one information system (say, in KAPPA) is available to another system (say, dBASE IV, a DBMS product), and vice versa. System compatibility is passive, in that the two systems do not interact with each other, and do not send messages, or ask for an output.

Interconnectivity means that the computer communication systems make it possible for a user to access various systems located in different locations, call on each system to get the answer that system could provide, and integrate the answers into a usable form. This takes advantage of the compatibility among the systems and gives it an active nature.

The interconnectivity puts the burden of connection on the developer, who should know how to call on each one of the systems. The concept of *system interoperability* takes the system integration further by designing a system that uses a number of heterogeneous information systems (including expert systems) to solve a given problem, or to answer a given question.

For example, assume that the mortgage loan expert system (written in KAPPA and located in Boston) may need input for the credit history of the applicant smith. The needed data is on the database management system of an organization in Los Angeles, and is stored in dBASE IV. The system interoperability means that the developer has a tool to design the system in such a way that it can send a message from Boston to Los Angeles asking for smith's credit history. The database sends back the data, the expert system uses it to process smith's loan application, and stores the data in, say, an RBase database file in New York. In doing so, the developer does not need to know or program the interfaces among these products.

The concept of knowledge-based integrated information systems (KBIIS) is based on the idea that one can create an overall umbrella that allows interoperability among various heterogeneous information systems. One way to operationalize the KBIIS idea is to view each information system as a class of objects. The overall umbrella should be a *distributed object manager*, which embodies each one of the heterogeneous information systems as a class of objects and has an interface with each class. Passing the message in the distributed object manager is a call to one of the information systems to produce an output. The GTE Laboratories have produced a couple of prototypes for such a system.

Case: Smart Toxicology Assistant

There's more to marketing a new brand of toothpaste than ensuring it tastes good. Every chemical must be cleared for safety and adherence to federal, corporate, and plain common sense rules. A company like Colgate-Palmolive has hundreds of such products—soaps, salves, flavorings, and powders—so you can imagine the scope of its safety-clearance mission.

The company's toxicology staff in Piscataway, N.J., monitors the chemicals in new Colgate-Palmolive formulas to ensure they comply with a huge set of complex rules. To make matters worse, these rules are in constant flux. (For example, a certain coloring that had been used in the past may not be acceptable.) The three-member staff handled anywhere from 12–20 chemical formulas per day, an average of about 3,000 annually, and paperwork really piled up. Colgate-Palmolive decided to help its toxicologists out and implement an intelligent "information/knowledge access system" under the leadership of Senior Research Associate William Gregory.

The Safety Clearance Request Automated Processing System (SCRAPS), which is implemented in IntelliCorp's Knowledge Engineering Environment (KEE), greatly enhances the speed, accuracy, and consistency of toxicology review. Developed on T1 Explorer in about four person-years and originally delivered on a DEC VAX, SCRAPS helps toxicologists "get in touch" with old formulas closely related to the one under scrutiny and gather the information necessary for proper analysis. (This research of old formulas was perhaps the most time-consuming task performed by the staff.) And because SCRAPS captures all relevant rules, it provides the toxicologists with, according to Gregory, a "rule language they can use to change the rules that apply to a given case... and they catch every single rule, every time."

The system works like this: A user enters a case and queries the staff's Ingress database. (Users typically need five hours of training to use the system.) SCRAPS, running in batch mode overnight, combs the database for similar cases and all relevant safety regulations and rules. The system then makes a toxicology assessment and returns a "go" or "no go" decision to the user. All told, the system has reduced data-input time from 30 minutes to five. But more importantly, SCRAPS lets toxicologists spend less time on routine paperwork and more on difficult formula assessment and has improved consistency, quality, and efficiency.

Gregory is quick to add that IntelliCorp's Apprenticeship Program, in which KEE customers are walked though development of their system, was a major reason for his project's success. "(IntelliCorp's Program) was a marvelous experience in Lisp coding.... It really worked," Gregory said.

Development of SCRAPS is continuing, and Colgate-Palmolive hopes to expand its knowledge base to cover federal labeling regulations and European health codes. Gregory is also attempting to reduce SCRAPS training time.

By Justin Kestelyn, "Application Watch," *AI Expert*, February 1991, p. 71, reprinted with permission from *AI Expert*.

9.4.2   Object-Oriented Neural Expert Systems

One can combine the power of logic-based reasoning with the modularization ability of the object-oriented approach and the learning capability of the neural networks to create *object-oriented neural expert systems*. The topic of neural networks is discussed in Chapters 13 and 14. Here, we briefly review one of the ways to combine the three technologies, without discussing how the neural network component accomplishes its function.

One way to combine object-oriented knowledge representation, logic-based reasoning, and neural networks is in the following form [Knaus 1990]. The domain objects and concepts are represented in the form of classes of objects, as in the object-oriented programming approach. The logic-based rules or predicates reason about the attributes of the objects, and send messages to objects as a part of the consequence of a rule, or function call. A group of neurons could also be categorized as a class of objects, which are used for a particular problem. In some cases, the expert system may require some analysis of the input provided by the end-user before it can use it in its antecedents. In this case, the rule may send a message to the class of object embodying the neurons to perform the analysis, and return the result. The rule uses this result to carry out its reasoning process.

Let us demonstrate this approach with the mortgage loan system. In this system, all real objects are modeled in the classes of objects within the system. Thus, we have classes such as **LoanApplicants**, **MortgageLoans**, **IndividualApplicants** and so forth. The credit rating is delegated to a neural network that is represented by a class called **NeuralRating**. When an instance of **NeuralRating** is created, its methods take in input data regarding the credit history of the applicant. One of its methods called **GetRate** returns the credit rating as a number such as 1, 2, ..., 5, where 5 represents the best rating. Now, we can have a rule, such as

```
IF NeuralRating:GetRate > 4
THEN the applicant has adequate credit worthiness
```

Note that in this example, the data and procedures, including the neural network methods, are encapsulated into classes of objects. The logic-based representation reasons about the objects by using the object's attributes or passing messages to their methods.

Conclusion

In Chapters 3, 4, and 8, we discussed two major categories of knowledge representation methods: logic-based and object-oriented. Each method has its particular strengths in representing knowledge. Thus, combining the two approaches holds the promise of using the strengths of both methods. There are now a number of methods and areas that utilize both approaches. Hybrid methods include opportunistic reasoning, production systems, and blackboard systems, which combine logic-based method with object-oriented approach in designing complex problems.

A number of expert system tools have been developed to combine the two approaches in representing knowledge and in making inferences. These tools include intelligent database management systems, in which an intelligent component is added to the conventional database systems. In the object-oriented database systems, the object-oriented approach is the data modeling method for the database.

In this chapter, we reviewed methods and software tools that take a hybrid approach to knowledge representation and reasoning in expert systems. KAPPA was reviewed in detail, and other hybrid expert system tools were discussed briefly. We predicted that the future hybrid designs would include information systems with knowledge base as their integral part, as well as expert systems in which the object-oriented approach and a neural network are embedded within the system.

References

Engelmore, R. S. and Morgan, T. (Eds.) 1988. *Blackboard Systems*, Addison-Wesley Publishing Co., Reading, MA.

Engelmore, R. S.; Morgan, A. J.; and Nii, H. P. 1988. "Introduction [to Blackboard Systems]," in Engelmore, R. S. and Morgan, T. (Eds.) 1988. *Blackboard Systems*, Addison-Wesley Publishing Co., Reading, MA, pp. 1–22.

Engelmore, R. S. and Morgan, A. J. 1988. "Conclusion [about Blackboard Systems]," in Engelmore, R. S. and Morgan, T. (Eds.) 1988. *Blackboard Systems*, Addison-Wesley Publishing Co., Reading, MA, pp. 1–22.

Erman, L. D.; Hayes-Roth, F.; Lesser, V. R.; and Reddy, D. R. 1988. "The Hearsay-II Speech-Understanding System: Integrating Knowledge to Resolve Uncertainty," in Engelmore, R. S. and Morgan, T. (Eds.) 1988. *Blackboard Systems*, Addison-Wesley Publishing Co., Reading, MA, pp. 31–86.

Feiner, S. K. and McKeown, K. R. 1990. "Coordinating Text and Graphics in Explanation Generation," *Proceedings of the Eighth National Conference on Artificial Intelligence–AAAI–90*, AAAI Press/The MIT Press, Menlo Park, CA, pp. 443–449.

KAPPA *Reference Manual, Version 1.0* 1990. IntelliCorp, Inc. Mountain View, CA.

Kerschberg, Larry. 1986. *Expert Database Systems; Proceedings from the First International Workshop*, Benjamin Cummings, Menlo Park, CA.

Knaus, Rodfer. 1990. "Object-Oriented Shells," *AI Expert*, Vol. 5, No. 9, September, pp. 19–25.

Larner, Daniel L. 1990. "Factories, Objects, and Blackboards," *AI Expert*, April, Vol. 5, No. 4, pp. 38–45.

Loomis, Mary E. S. 1990. "OODBMS, the Basics," and "OODBMS vs. Relational," *Object-Oriented Programming*, Vol. 3, No. 1, pp. 77–81, No. 2, pp. 79–82.

Manola, Frank. 1989. "Applications of Object-Oriented Database Technology in Knowledge-Based Integrated Information Systems," in A. Gupta (Ed.) *Integration of Information Systems: Bridging Heterogeneous Databases*, IEEE Press, New York, NY.

Manola, Frank. 1990. "Object-Oriented Knowledge Bases, Parts I and II" *AI Expert*, March, pp. 26–36, April, pp. 46–57.

Moore, J. D. and Swartout, W. R. 1990. "Pointing: A Way Toward Explanation Dialogue," *Proceedings of the Eighth National Conference on Artificial Intelligence—AAAI-90*, AAAI Press/The MIT Press, Menlo Park, CA, pp. 457–465.

Newell, Allen and Simon, Herbert. A. 1972. *Human Problem Solving*, Prentice Hall, Englewood Cliffs, NJ.

Nii, H. P. and Aiello, N. 1979. "Attempt to Generalize: A Knowledge-Based Program for Building Knowledge-Based Programs," *Proceedings of IJCAI-79*, Morgan Kaufmann, San Mateo, CA, pp. 645–655.

Nii, H. P. 1986. "Blackboard Systems—Part I," and "Blackboard Systems—Part II," *AI Magazine*, Vol. 7, No. 2, pp. 38–53, and No. 3, pp. 82–106.

Parsaye, K.; Chignell, M.; Khoshafian, S.; and Wong, H. 1989. *Intelligent Databases: Object-Oriented, Deductive, Hypermedia Technologies*, John Wiley and Sons, Inc., New York, NY.

Parsaye, K.; Chignell, M.; Khoshafian, S.; and Wong, H. 1990. "Intelligent Databases," *AI Expert*, Vol. 5, No. 3, March, pp. 38–47.

Rowan, D. 1989. "On-Line Expert Systems in Process Industry," *AI Expert*, August, pp. 30–37.

Schur, S. "Intelligent Databases," *AI Expert,* January, Vol. 3, No. 1, pp. 26–34.

Tello, Ernest R. 1989. *Object-Oriented Programming for Artificial Intelligence: A Guide to Tools and System Design,* Addison-Wesley Publishing Co., Reading, MA.

Questions

9.1   What is the difference between production systems and blackboards?

9.2   Why are blackboard systems called a hybrid method?

9.3   What is an intelligent database management system? What are its advantages and disadvantages?

9.4   What are the important features of OODBMS?

9.5   As a business user, what are the circumstances in which you would prefer to use OODBMS?

9.6   As a business user, what are the circumstances in which you would prefer to use a relational DBMS?

9.7   Compare OODBMS and relational DBMS. What are the advantages and disadvantages of each?

9.8   Compare the capabilities of KAPPA with LEVEL5 and 1st-CLASS discussed in Chapters 5 and 6. What are the advantages a hybrid tool offers?

9.9   Discuss the complexities a hybrid approach introduces to an expert system tool.

9.10   What hybrid systems do you envision for the future?

9.11   Review the literature on the new developments in hybrid systems since the publication of this book. If you were to expand this chapter, what sections would you add? Why?

9.12   Search the literature to identify other hybrid tools, such as GoldWorks II, ART, and LOOPS. Compare their capabilities and features with those discussed in this chapter.

Case: Expert System Applications in Corporate Control

A business needs to control its investment in inventory to avoid both overstocking and stockouts. In multi-location businesses, the location of inventory and the movement of inventory from location to location are critical to meeting customer demands. Also, in many industries, special merchandise offers or special price offers frequently are available.

The success of a business with a high volume of inventory often hinges on its availability to take advantage of these opportunities when they arise. Buyers with substantial experience have developed skills over time for deciding which special offers to accept and which ones to ignore based on their customers' demands. The wholesale and retail grocery industries, for example, have many of these special merchandise and price offers. As the grocery industry operates on very small profit margins, the acceptance or rejection of their offers can have a major impact on overall profitability.

1. *Associated Grocers' Buyer's Workbench.* Associated Grocers, located in the Pacific Northwest, is a large wholesale and retail chain with more than 400 member stores. Since no commercial expert systems for purchasing inventory were available, the company hired Deloitte & Touche, to help develop the application using the expert knowledge of Associated Grocers' buyers.

The long-run goal of the project is to provide an integrated Merchandiser's Workbench that will assist with buying, pricing, promotion planning, assortment selection, and retail space allocation. The first stage implemented was the Buyer's Workbench, which captures the company's buying expertise in a knowledge base. The key issues in the knowledge base include consumer preference trends, price trends, vendor distinctions, seasonality, mix change indicators or triggers, product movement volatility, and distribution factors.

Deloitte & Touche recommended the use of NEXPERT Object, because it permits the categorization of items into hierarchies. While the Buyer's Workbench operates with a limited number of rules, the large number of different inventory items in Associated Grocers' stores makes the class hierarchies a vital requirement. A prototype has been completed and evaluated with satisfactory results.

2. *Arthur D. Little's Expert System.* The analysis of variances for cost control, budgeting, and future planning is vital to the success and profitability of manufacturing operations. The analysis becomes more critical as profit margins narrow, competition increases, technology advances, or market demand changes. Arthur D. Little has developed an expert system to perform variance analysis for a high technology company with $75 million in sales.

This expert system, in use since 1987, analyzes the variance for budget line items as well as budget line groups. Based on its internal model of the company, the system determines the variances that are significant and provides an explanation for the variance without additional user input. The system is integrated at the menu level with a budgeting system developed in Lotus 1-2-3. The expert system also is integrated with the accounting system through the use of file transfers that bring the accounting information into the spreadsheet. Thus, the system has two types of integration: tight coupling with a commonly used spreadsheet and loose coupling with accounting records.

3. *Digital Equipment's Expert Systems.* Digital Equipment Corp. (DEC) is one of the leaders in the use of expert systems, with more than 140 expert systems in use. DEC's most well-known expert system, XCON, assists in the configuration

of its computer lines, VAX. DEC estimates XCON saves $20 million per year in manufacturing costs and that its entire set of expert systems saves the company more than $100 million per year. Among DEC's other expert systems is a division evaluation program, Business Control Knowledge System (BUCKS).

BUCKS, in operation since 1986 in Europe, is designed to assist controllers and managers in analyzing the performance of division projects and consulting activities by region. The expert system considers the environmental and resource differences between regions within a country as well as the long-run consequences of short-run performance changes.

The system evaluates net operating revenue compared to budget, business contribution margin compared to budget, and business contribution margin in relation to net operating revenue. The manager can set the parameters of BUCKS, thus customizing it for a particular situation. BUCKS is integrated with other DEC systems that provide accounting information used by the expert system.

Users of the system can send comments regarding the expert system directly to the experts in charge of maintenance of the system. DEC has found that the system discovers trends and underlying factors often overlooked by managers, saves managers time, and improves the quality of managers' decisions.

Excerpts from "Expert Systems for Management Accountants," by Carol Brown and Mary Ellen Phillips, *Management Accounting*, January 1990, pp. 18–23, reprinted with permission from *Management Accounting*.

Case Questions

1. Discuss the nature of the applications in this case that make them good candidates for a hybrid approach.

2. Suggest other areas of corporate control in which the deployment of an expert system may improve the quality of decisions.

3. Pick an application in the case. If you were to design this application, what type of software product would you choose? What should be the special features of this software product? Justify your answer.

4. In the application of Question 3, do you attempt to integrate the expert system with other components of the information system? Which components? How?

5. Discuss the advantages of object-oriented databases in communicating their data to a hybrid-based expert system.

CHAPTER 10

LEVEL5 OBJECT: A Hybrid Tool

Intelligence ... is the faculty of making artificial objects, especially tools to make tools.

Henri Bergson, *Creative Evolution*

Chapter Objectives

The objectives of this chapter are:

- To review the structure of LEVEL5 OBJECT, a hybrid software product for expert systems

- To demonstrate how the object-oriented approach is implemented in modeling knowledge in expert systems

- To show how LEVEL5 OBJECT combines the rule-based and object-oriented approaches to modeling knowledge

- To demonstrate the window-based user interface in an expert system software

- To discuss the working of LEVEL5 OBJECT in some detail

KEY WORDS: Object-oriented knowledge representation, classes, attributes, methods, hierarchies, rules, demons, goals, hypertext, confidence factor, system parameters, user interface, multiple knowledge bases

---

This chapter could be used with the demonstration diskettes attached to this book for hands-on experiments with the tool. Those who prefer to have a general understanding of the tool without practicing with the diskettes can read the chapter and refer to the figures, which demonstrate the working of the software.

Introduction

This chapter reviews a hybrid tool in detail and gives you a chance to get hands-on experience with it. We have chosen LEVEL5 OBJECT for this purpose because you have already been exposed to the rule-based version of the product in Chapter 5. The syntax of LEVEL5 for creating rules applies here as well. However, LEVEL5 OBJECT goes much further. It structures the knowledge base with an object-oriented approach, and the software itself has an object-oriented design. It has classes, hierarchies, inheritance (no polymorphism, though), methods (as demons), and many functions. Objects are used within the rules for reasoning. It runs under Microsoft Windows, and has great graphics and hypertext capabilities.

In this chapter, we learn how to create classes, attributes, and methods in LEVEL5 OBJECT, and use them within the rule-based reasoning method. We also review how to create a user interface and its graphical displays, and discuss the treatment of uncertainty in LEVEL5 OBJECT.

This chapter continues the mortgage loan case, and the examples in the text draw upon this case. A demo diskette for the software is attached to the book. This demo diskette is the full version of the software, but you cannot store a knowledge base on it. You can, therefore, practice with the demo diskette to understand how the software works, but you will not be able to store your knowledge base for later access.

10.1 General Features of LEVEL5 OBJECT

LEVEL5 OBJECT brings together a number of facilities, which makes it a truly hybrid tool. These facilities include:

- Object-oriented knowledge representation

- Rule-based knowledge representation

- The treatment of uncertainty

- Windows and graphics

- Database

- Hypertext

LEVEL5 OBJECT for the PC runs under Microsoft Windows, using Microsoft's windowing facilities and standards. In this chapter, we assume that the reader is familiar with opening, closing, and resizing windows.

The structure of LEVEL5 OBJECT is based on object-oriented representation, in that every part of the knowledge is represented as a class of objects. Rules, too, are considered a class of objects. However, one does not have to always reason with attributes of objects. LEVEL5 OBJECT allows the developer to represent knowledge purely in the rule-based form, without the use of objects.

The treatment of uncertainty in LEVEL5 OBJECT is similar to that in LEVEL5, in that it uses simple certainty factors associated with rules, as well as the attributes of objects. However, in LEVEL5 OBJECT, the display of confidence factors for the final results requires additional effort.

LEVEL5 OBJECT interacts with dBASEIII files. It considers a database file as a class of objects, and each record within the file as an instance of that class. In this respect, it uses an object-oriented database management system (OODBMS) approach in its interaction with database files. (The concept of OODBMS is covered in Chapter 9.)

LEVEL5 OBJECT gives the developer the ability to create various types of displays and attach imported images to these displays. The process is interactive, in that the developer, in creating the displays, does not need to program. The creation process is window-driven.

Another interesting feature of LEVEL5 OBJECT is its hypertext capability, which the developer can use to allow the user to explore different facets of the system. Combined with displays, the hypertext feature allows the user to click into various displays to explore the system, get information, and enter data in various forms.

The inference engine in LEVEL5 OBJECT has both forward and backward chaining capabilities. One can also use a mix of forward and backward chaining. The inference engine could also work from procedures written in PRL, or purely from the object-oriented message passing.

LEVEL5 OBJECT offers the developer a number of debugging facilities. The developer can actually observe the reasoning process as the inference engine goes through its reasoning process, or trace and record the process in a history file for a later analysis.

10.2 Object-Oriented Knowledge Representation

The basis of LEVEL5 OBJECT is *object-oriented*, in that all pieces of knowledge are grouped into classes of objects. The developer can create a hierarchy of classes, where the child class can inherit all attributes of the parent classes.

The product has two types of classes: system-defined and user-defined. The software components are all structured in a series of system-defined classes. One of the system-defined classes is domain. If the user creates any rules or variables that do not belong to any class, the system automatically makes them the attributes of the domain class.

LEVEL5 OBJECT classes have attributes and methods. The attributes can take a variety of types, including multiple values, pictures, colors, and arrays. In addition to type, an attribute has a confidence factor representing the degree of certainty with respect to its value.

Methods in LEVEL5 OBJECT are attached to attributes, and are limited to WHEN CHANGED and WHEN NEEDED methods. (These types of methods are discussed in Chapter 9.) In this respect, the product has a more limited capability than the standard object-oriented programming software.

A class can inherit from more than one parent. In this sense, LEVEL5 OBJECT has the multiple inheritance capability (discussed in Chapter 8). However, one can not modify the class attributes inherited from its parents. Thus, LEVEL5 OBJECT does not have the polymorphism capability, as defined in Chapter 8. The plan for the future enhancement of the product includes the addition of the polymorphism capability and a security mechanism to control its use.

LEVEL5 OBJECT provides a number of powerful facilities to the developer, within a relatively simple and easy-to-use framework. All developmental features of the product are window-driven, which relieves the developer from the need to learn a programming language for coding the knowledge base into the system.

Let us see how the software works in action by creating the mortgage loan system, the example we have developed in the previous chapters. LEVEL5 OBJECT has a main window, as shown in Figure 10.1. (In the demo version, the software may open into the Knowledge Tree window. Close this window by double clicking in the top left corner box to see the main window appear.)

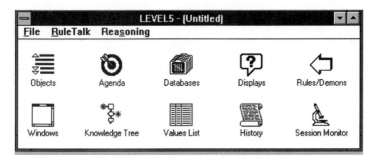

Figure 10.1   Main Window in LEVEL5 OBJECT

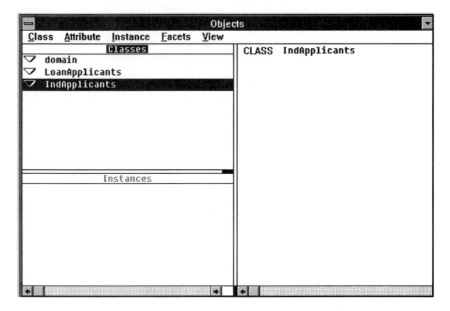

Figure 10.2   Objects Window in LEVEL5 OBJECT

The main window has a number of icons, representing the categories of the software functions. The object-oriented features of the software are grouped under the **Objects** icon.

- To start developing a new system, one must open a new file by selecting the **FILE** menu and choosing the **New** option. (Failing to do this in the full version of the product leads to a fatal error when creating a new class.)

- Double click on the **Objects** icon to open the window shown in Figure 10.2.

10.2.1 Creating Classes

The **Objects** window consists of three sub-windows, and a number of pull-down menu options. The left side has two windows showing the classes and instances. The right window is the editor for the class under consideration.

- To create a new class, click on the **Class** menu, and select the **New** option. It creates a class with a default name. Change its name to **LoanApplicants**, and do not forget to hit the return key for the name to take effect.

- Repeat the process to create a class called **IndApplicants**.

To create a parent-child hierarchical relation between two classes, one must have the child class in the class editor (in the right window in Figure 10.3) by clicking twice on the class name. The parent class must be highlighted in the class window (the top left window in Figure 10.3). Then, one must select the option of **Inherit** from the **Class** menu, the top left menu option in Figure 10.3. Note that in Figure 10.3, the class attributes are already created; we will see in the next section how to create attributes for a class. Furthermore, if we compare the attributes of **IndApplicants** in the left window of Figure 10.3 with those in the right window, we see that the left window has two more attributes. These are the attributes that IndAppli-

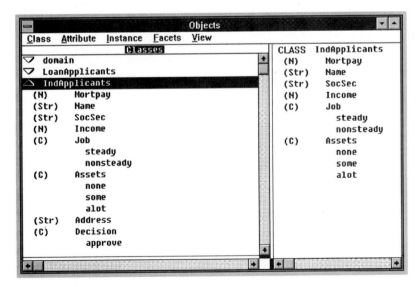

Figure 10.3   Attributes of IndApplicants Class in the Mortgage Loan System

cants has inherited from its parent LoanApplicants, as discussed in the next section.

- Make the IndApplicants class inherit from LoanApplicants class by following the above procedure.

One can check the inheritance relations by selecting the Show Inheritance option from the Class menu.

10.2.2 Creating Attributes

One can add attributes to the class in the class editor window by choosing the Add option of the Attribute menu. This automatically opens a sub-window for selecting the attribute type, as shown in Figure 10.4.

The simple type attribute takes true or false values. The compound type attribute takes one value of a given list of values. The multicompound attribute type can simultaneously take more than one value from a group of values. The picture attribute type takes a bitmap graphic image as its value. The time type represents date and time together, as 3/30/91 14:59:45.320, which represents the date, hour, minutes, seconds, and milliseconds. The interval type represents the time interval. For example, taking the difference

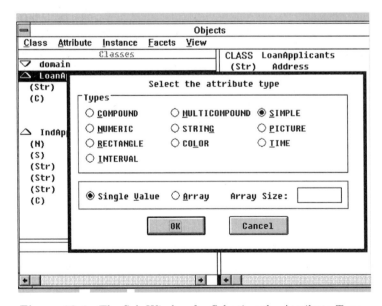

Figure 10.4 The Sub-Window for Selecting the Attribute Type

of two time-typed attributes results in a time interval, showing number of days, hours, minutes, seconds, and milliseconds as 4 17:54:59.130.

The color type attribute represents colors red, green, or blue. In assigning value to such an attribute when the instance of the object is created, a color editor pops up to let the developer choose the desired color combinations. The rectangle attribute type represents four coordinates, left, top, right, and bottom, which can be used to identify the location of a display or window.

After choosing the attribute type, one gets a default name for the attribute, with an editing prompt that can be used to give a more meaningful name to the attribute. When the attribute type is compound or multicompound, one should highlight the attribute and choose the Add Compound Item option from the Attribute menu to create (one at a time) the values the compound or multicompound attribute can take.

- Create attributes Address (string type) and Decision (compound with values approve and reject) for the class LoanApplicants.

- Use the class editor (right window) to create the attributes for the IndApplicants class, including the allowable compound values for Job and Assets attributes, as shown in Figure 10.3.

- Create a class called Loans, with three numeric attributes: Duration, Rate, and Amount.

Clicking on the triangle next to a class name in the Class window shows the attributes of the class. The inherited attributes are shown in blue, and do not show up in the class editor (the right window). That is why the attributes Address and Decision (with compound values approve and reject) are part of the attributes of IndApplicants in the left window in Figure 10.3, while they do not show up in the class editor (right window). They are the inherited attributes of the parent class: LoanApplicants. In other words, the inherited attributes of a class cannot be changed, hence polymorphism is not allowed.

10.2.3   Creating Methods

In LEVEL5 OBJECT, one can attach two types of methods to attributes of a class: WHEN CHANGED and WHEN NEEDED. The Attribute menu contains the option for creating a method for an attribute, as shown in Figure 10.5.

- Highlight the Mortpay attribute in IndApplicants class. Click on the Attribute menu, and choose the WHEN NEEDED method, as shown in Figure 10.5.

In writing methods, LEVEL5 OBJECT uses a procedural language similar to the PRL in LEVEL5. In LEVEL5 OBJECT, the language has 49 functions, 49 symbols, and 9 commands, which could be used in encoding methods. They are accessible by clicking on one of the two arrows of the left side sub-window in the Objects window.

Figure 10.6 shows the code for the computation of the monthly mortgage payment of a loan, using the Duration, Rate, and Amount attributes of the Loans class. The intermediate variables created in this method, such as n, r and x, do not belong to any class. Therefore, they become the attributes of the system class domain.

BEGIN and END delimit the chunks of codes, including the entire code for a method, and the FOR loop. The latter performs a fixed number of iterations of the statements within BEGIN and END, located immediately after FOR. One can use any of the functions, symbols, and commands in coding a method.

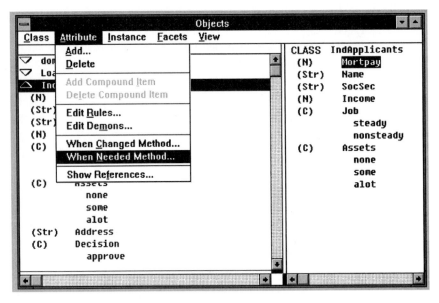

Figure 10.5 Creating a Method for an Attribute

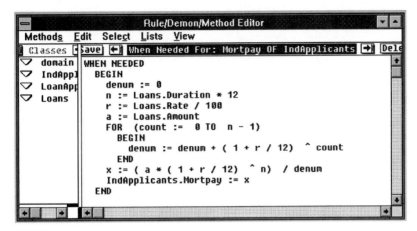

Figure 10.6   Method for Computing the Monthly Mortgage Payment

10.2.4   Facets

The Facets menu provides a number of additional features for an attribute, as shown in Figure 10.7. The first three options of this menu make it possible to initialize and reinitialize an attribute or assign a default value to it. to the attribute when using the system. The Unknown Prompting option makes it possible to assign UNKNOWN as an acceptable value to an attribute.

LEVEL5 OBJECT has default query displays for obtaining attribute values from the user. However, if the developer wishes to design customized displays, texts, or explanations for an attribute, the Query from, Text, and Expand options allow the developer to accomplish such designs.

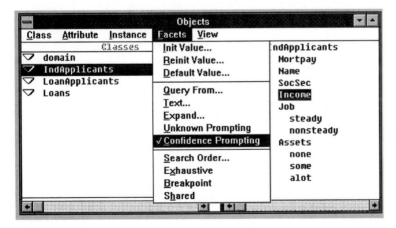

Figure 10.7   Facets Options that Could Be Attached to an Attribute

The last four facets allow the developer to:

- Change the default search order that the inference engine uses to find the value of the attribute (**Search Order**). This gives the developer control over the way the inference engine performs its search.

- Check all rules in which an attribute is used (**Exhaustive**). This forces the inference engine to test all rules containing the attribute and select the one with the highest confidence factor. One can consider this option hypothetical reasoning, because the inference engine tests all hypotheses regarding the attribute.

- Create a breakpoint in the reasoning process when the inference engine evaluates an attribute (**Breakpoint**). As we will see later, this is a debugging tool for testing the system.

- Declare an attribute as shared with other knowledge bases (**Shared**). This is used in processing multiple knowledge bases, discussed in Section 10.5.

10.3 Rule-based Knowledge Representation

The rule-based knowledge representation of LEVEL5 OBJECT has two main components: rules and goals. Rules and goals in LEVEL5 OBJECT are similar to those in LEVEL5, discussed in Chapter 5, with the additional feature that here the rules and goals could include attributes of both the user-defined as well as system-defined classes.

10.3.1   Creating Rules and Demons

Rules and *demons* have the same structure and syntax in LEVEL5 OBJECT. The only difference is that rules are used in backward chaining, while demons are used in forward chaining, as discussed in Section 10.5.

One can create rules in LEVEL5 OBJECT from the **Objects** window by selecting the **Rule** option in the **Attributes** menu. Another way to reach the rule editor is to double click on the **Rules/Demons** icon in the main window. This opens the **Rule/Demon/Method** window as shown in Figure 10.8. In both cases, the system automatically groups rules based on the attributes used in them. Obviously, a rule may belong to more than one group.

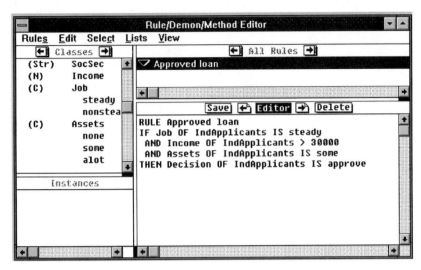

Figure 10.8   The Rule/Demon/Method Window

This window has four sub-windows and five menus. The right window is the rule editor, which consists of two sub-windows. The top sub-window lists the names of the existing rules, and the bottom sub-window is the editor where one can enter the text of the rule. On the left, there are class and instance windows, similar to those in the Objects window.

By selecting the New option from the Rules menu, the software activates the editor, by which one can enter rules. If a rule contains attributes of a class, by highlighting that attribute in the class window on the left and double clicking on it, the attribute and its class appear on the rule with the correct syntax, at the cursor position. This reduces coding and avoids possible typographical errors. (This facility is available for coding functions and commands, as well.) In this aspect, the software is developer-friendly.

As shown in Figure 10.8, an attribute of a class is identified as attribute name OF class name. Another way to refer to an attribute is class.attribute. The rule syntax of LEVEL5 OBJECT is an expanded version of the PRL in LEVEL5, covered in Chapter 5, with the exception that one can use the class attributes within the rules. Figure 10.9 shows another rule for the mortgage loan system.

- Use the rule window to create the rules shown in Figures 10.8 and 10.9.

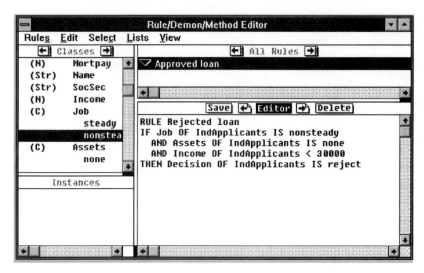

Figure 10.9 Another Rule for the Mortgage Loan Example

As in LEVEL5, the developer can assign a *confidence factor* to a rule, by adding, say, CF=80 to the consequent of the rule. The default value of confidence factors is 100.

When some information is needed from the user, one can ask for it by using the **ASK** command. For example, in the mortgage loan system, to get the applicant's IDs, such as name, social security number, and address, one can ask the user by the **ASK** command. One can enter this command before the antecedent of a rule, as shown in Figure 10.10. When the inference engine checks this rule for the purpose of backward chaining, it executes the **ASK** command, regardless of the truth value of the rule's antecedent.

In Figure 10.10, the antecedent **Mortpay OF IndApplicants**> 0 requires knowledge of the **Mortpay** value. This triggers the **WHEN NEEDED** method attached to **Mortpay**, shown in Figure 10.6. Since the execution of this method requires the knowledge of the **Duration**, **Rate**, and **Amount** of the loan, the software automatically prompts the user to enter the values of these attributes, which are used to compute the value of **Mortpay**.

This demonstrates that the developer does not need to program the entry of all needed attribute values. In backward chaining, when the inference engine needs a value that is unavailable within the system context, it prompts the user to enter it.

The inference engine searches for the value of an attribute in the following order: the context already established, **WHEN NEEDED** method, components of rules, query from the user, and the default value of the at-

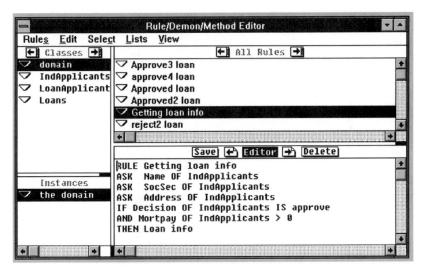

Figure 10.10   Using the ASK Command in a Rule

tribute. One can change this search order by selecting the **Search Order** option of the **Facets** menu, shown in Figure 10.7. This selection opens a window that allows the developer to change the search order for a given attribute.

10.3.2   Creating Goals

Goals in LEVEL5 OBJECT are defined as a numbered list, similar to what we have seen in LEVEL5. The goals could be organized in a hierarchy. The inference engine attempts to establish the truth of a subgoal, when the truth of its parent is established. A goal could be an attribute of an already defined class of objects, or a proposition that is not part of any class. In the latter case, the proposition would be automatically assigned as an attribute of the **domain** class.

To encode goals, one should double click on the **Agenda** icon in the main window (shown in Figure 10.1). This opens the **Agenda** window, which consists of three sub-windows: the goals editor on the right, and class and instance windows on the left. The left windows are the same as those in the **Objects** window. It also has two menus: **Goals** and **View**, as shown in Figure 10.11.

One can enter a goal in two ways. One way is by selecting the **New** option of the **Goals** menu. This prompts the user to enter the code for the goal. The

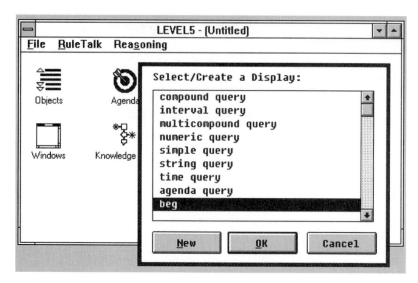

Figure 10.11 Agenda Window

second way to enter a goal is to click on the triangle of the class whose attribute is to be a goal, in the class window. This brings out the attributes of the class. A double click on the class attribute that should be the goal creates the goal in the goal editor. The second method saves the developer from entering the code, and reduces the typographical errors associated with entering codes.

To make a subgoal, one should first create it as a goal, then highlight it and click on the Move In option of the Goals menu. This makes the highlighted goal the subgoal of the goal above it.

- Highlight the class IndApplicants, and click on its triangle to bring out its attributes. Highlight the approve value of the Decision attribute, and double click on it. This creates the goal number 1, as shown in Figure 10.11.

- Enter the second goal, and use the Move In option of the Goals menu to make it a subgoal.

- Enter the last goal shown in Figure 10.11 by double clicking on the reject value of the Decision attribute of the IndApplicants class in the class window.

10.4 Creating the User Interface in LEVEL5 OBJECT

After creating classes, rules, and goals, the knowledge base is ready for backward chaining inference. If we run the system, it prompts the user for all needed information using the default displays. However, it does not display final results. This is because LEVEL5 OBJECT does not have a default conclusion display; the developer must create it. This could be easily accomplished via the Displays window. Moreover, the *hypertext* facility makes it possible for the developer to create with ease elaborate displays for system users. In display creation too, the software is developer-friendly.

10.4.1 The User Interface

One can access the display window by clicking on the Displays icon in the main window. It brings out a window that already contains a number of display names, as shown in Figure 10.12. These are the default displays for querying the user for different types of attribute values. The last name beg in Figure 10.12 is the name of a display created for this application.

Selecting the New option opens a window that gives the developer the option to designate the new display as the Title or Conclusion display. Every application has one title and one conclusion display. Once used, these options become disabled. The Title display is the display the user sees at the beginning, and the Conclusion display shows the user the final outcomes of

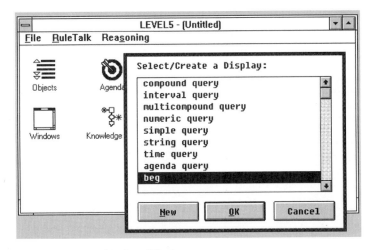

Figure 10.12 Displays Window

running the system. One can create any number of displays that are neither title nor conclusion. Such displays are normally linked to other displays, attached to the **Expand** option in the **Facets** menu (Figure 10.7), or displayed to the user by the **ASK** command,

- Open the display editor and choose the **New** option. Name the new display **beg**, and select it as the **Title** display. You should get the display editor shown in Figure 10.13.

The **Tools** menu (and the toolbox icons) allow the developer to create displays with ease.

- Select the Textbox option. The arrow turns into crosshairs.

- Position the crosshairs at a desired location and hold down the mouse button to open a text box in the display. When the box is of the desired size, release the mouse button. This prompts a window where you can enter the text for the box.

- Enter the text for the title display, as shown in Figure 10.14. (This window is what you see first when you run the system, as discussed later.)

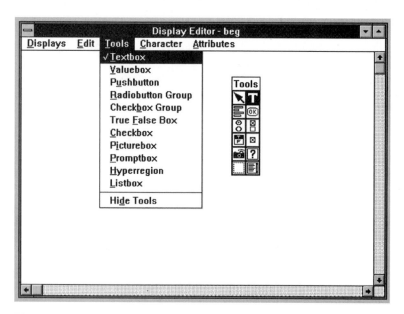

Figure 10.13   Display Editor and its Tools Menu

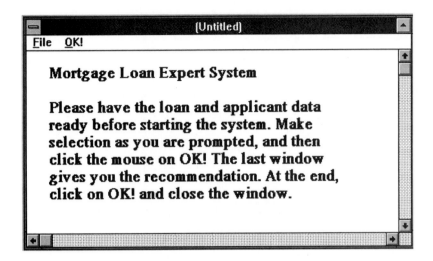

Figure 10.14   The Title Display when Running the Mortgage Loan System

The Textbox can be dragged to a new location. Its fonts and other features could be adjusted via the Character menu. Closing the display editor automatically saves the display.

In the conclusion display, we would like to display the final results to the user. This can be accomplished by using the Valuebox tool. Selecting the Valuebox turns the arrow into the crosshairs, which makes it possible to open a box. It then prompts for the selection of the attribute whose value should be attached to the Valuebox. This way one can display the value of the attribute in the Valuebox.

- Create a new display called end. Select the conclusion option, making it the Conclusion display.

- Create a Textbox, and enter name: as the text.

- Create a Valuebox next to it, and attach the attribute Name in the class IndApplicants to it. The box will have the word UNDETERMINED, because the value of this attribute is undetermined at this stage.

- Continue creating other textboxes and valueboxes in Figure 10.15, except the last box with the broken line.

The last box in Figure 10.15 is an application of the hypertext concept, discussed in the next section. Other tools in the display editor allow the

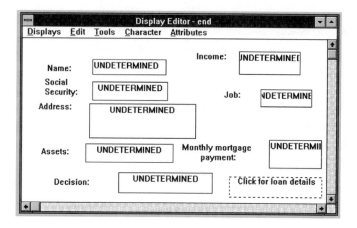

Figure 10.15 Design of Conclusion Display for the Mortgage Loan Example

developer to create a number of other types of boxes. We will discuss the Pushbutton and Hyperregion in the next section.

The Picturebox allows the developer to show a bitmap file in a *Picturebox*. The bitmap file must be in the LEVEL5 OBJECT bitmap format. One way to import a foreign bitmap file to the system is to capture it in the clipboard. The selection of the Picturebox option allows the developer to capture the image from the clipboard. Once captured, one can save the image in the LEVEL5 OBJECT format. One can also create an attribute that takes an image as its value type. Then, one can attach the picture attribute to a Valuebox. Once an instance of the class is created, and the picture attribute is assigned the bitmap file, the image from the bitmap file appears in the valueboxes to which the picture attribute is attached. Furthermore, by combining rules and picture attributes, the developer can create animated displays for the user.

Another interface development feature of the product is the Windows window, accessible from the starting window, shown in Figure 10.1. In this window, one can change the characteristics of windows within the system. Thus, the developer can custom design the windows for an application.

10.4.2 Hypertext Applications

The hypertext capability of LEVEL5 OBJECT allows the developer to create and link displays. This lets the user navigate through the displays to get more information. The developer could use this capability to create elaborate help displays as well.

The hypertext capability of the software is in the combination of the Hyperregion and Pushbutton tools in the display editor.

To demonstrate the process, assume that we want to link the end display to another display, which contains the information on the amount, rate, and duration of the loan. This display is called details. We can accomplish the creation of the link by the following steps:

- Create the details display, which contains the loan amount, rate, and duration, using the Textbox and Valuebox tools. Close the display.

- Open the conclusion display end. In this display, create a Textbox with the text Click for loan details.

- Choose the Hyperregion tool, and use the crosshairs to create a box over text. The software prompts for the choice of a display. Select the details display. Close the end display. Now the display end is linked to details.

- To make it possible for the user to return to the original display, we should create a pushbutton in the details display. Open the details display.

- Select the Pushbutton option, and create a box. When prompted for attaching an attribute, choose cancel, because we do not wish to attach an attribute in this case.

- In the Attributes menu of the display editor, choose the Label option, and give the box the label: Go back.

- From the Attributes menu, choose the Attach Display option. The list of displays appears. Choose the end display. Now the user can go back to the end display by clicking on the pushbutton.

Thus, the Hyperregion tool allows the developer to create forward links to other displays, and the Pushbutton tool makes it possible to create a backward link to the calling display.

10.4.3 Running the Expert System

One can save and run the system from the main window, Figure 10.1. Selecting the Save option of the File menu saves the knowledge base, and the choice of the Run option from the same menu initiates the processing of the knowledge base.

Figure 10.14 shows the title display for the mortgage loan example when processing the system begins. Each display will remain on the screen until the user clicks on the OK! option in the display. Figure 10.16 shows the Query display for the compound attribute Job. The user makes the selection and clicks on OK! to enter the answer.

In the query of the attributes for which the confidence prompting option in the Facets menu is selected (Figure 10.7), the user is given the Confidence option, which opens the confidence editor window, and allows the user to change the default confidence factor, as shown in Figure 10.17. In the last section of this chapter, we discuss how one can display the confidence factor of an attribute in the conclusion display.

The Conclusion display of the run is shown in Figure 10.18. We saw the design of this display in Figure 10.15. Now the attributes have values, which are displayed in the value boxes attached to them.

Figure 10.16   Query Display for a Compound Attribute

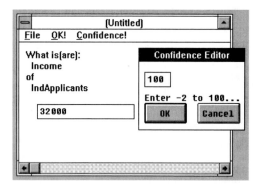

Figure 10.17   Query Display with the Confidence Factor

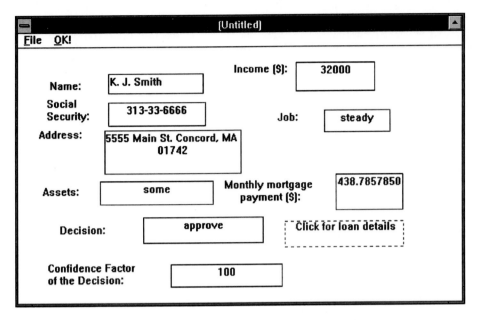

Figure 10.18   The Conclusion Display of the Mortgage Loan Example

If the user clicks on the hyperregion area, the display links to the Details display, which contains the details of the loan, as shown in Figure 10.19. Clicking on the Go Back pushbutton takes the user back to the conclusion display.

The Conclusion display allows the user to restart the session or end it by selecting the appropriate option from the File menu.

10.5   Other Features of LEVEL5 OBJECT

In this section, we review some of the remaining important features of LEVEL5 OBJECT. Although the following discussion does not show the full capabilities of these features, it provides an overview of the working of the product.

10.5.1   System Parameters

LEVEL5 OBJECT has a number of system classes, which may be viewed by selecting System Objects from the View menu in the Objects window. One of the important system classes is applications. This class can have only

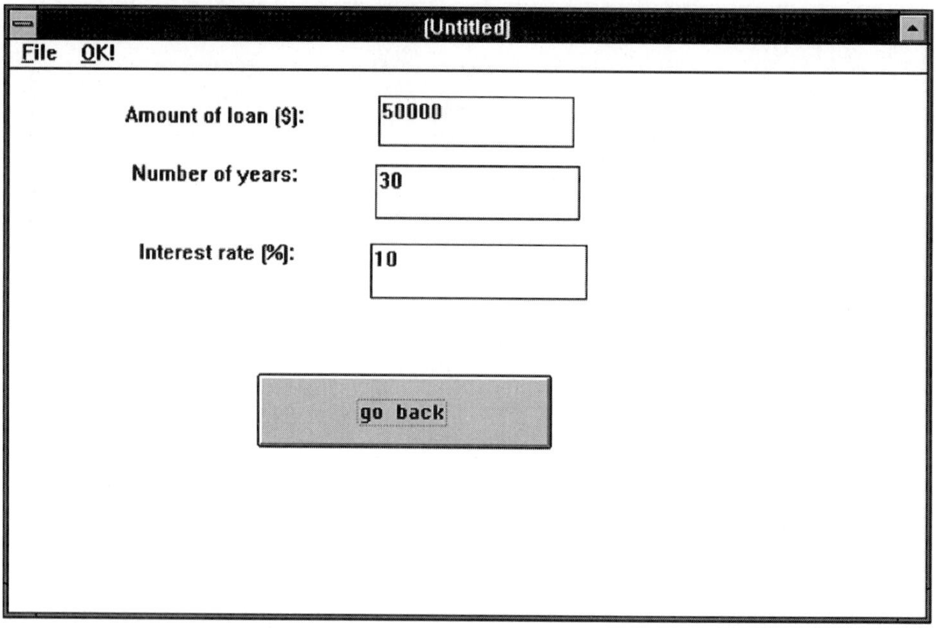

Figure 10.19 The Linked Display for the Details of the Loan

one instance, called the application. The *system parameters* are stored as the attribute values of the application instance.

The developer can change the values of system parameters by highlighting an attribute of the instance in the Objects window and using the edit option of the Instance menu to edit it. To see the values assigned to the attributes of the application instance, the lower left window should be widened. This can be done by dragging the window when the mouse arrow becomes a double-headed arrow on the window border. This is a standard window operation. Figure 10.20 shows a partial list of the attributes of the application instance.

- In the Objects window, edit the goal select attribute of the application and assign a true value to it. This allows the user to select the goal on which the inference engine must concentrate in the backward chaining inference process.

The values of the application instance could be altered in the Objects window, and they also could be accessed and changed in rules and methods in the form of attribute name OF application, or application.attribute name.

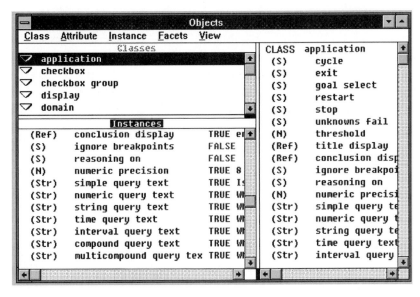

Figure 10.20 The System Parameters in the Application Instance

For example, the consequent of a rule may contain the following:

```
IF a given attribute is true
THEN cycle OF the application := TRUE
ELSE exit OF the application := TRUE
```

In a forward-chaining inference, when the antecedent of the rule becomes true, the system starts to cycle, which restarts processing the knowledge base while preserving the facts obtained in the previous session. When exit OF the application is true, the system stops.

Another system parameter is the threshold attribute of the application. When the confidence factor of an attribute reaches below the threshold, that attribute is considered to be undetermined. The default value of this attribute is set at 50, but the developer can alter it by editing this attribute.

Another interesting system parameter is the save context attribute of the application instance. It allows the developer to capture the context of a session, store it in the file specified by the context filename attribute, and restore it with the restore context attribute. This too could take place within the consequent of a rule, such as

```
IF an attribute is true
THEN context file OF the application := "c:\L5\filename"
AND save context OF the application := TRUE
```

As Figure 10.20 shows, every element of LEVEL5 OBJECT is in the form of classes of objects and their attributes. We have seen that system parameters are attributes of the class application. The display and other components of the system are also in the form of classes of objects. Any object or item that can not be classified within the system- or user-defined classes will automatically become an attribute of the class domain.

10.5.2   Inference Mechanisms

The inference mechanism in LEVEL5 OBJECT takes the following forms:

- Backward chaining

- Forward chaining

- A combination of both forward and backward chaining

The inference engine uses the backward chaining strategy when the system contains goals and rules methods. The inference engine applies the forward chaining strategy when the system contains demons, WHEN NEEDED, or WHEN CHANGED methods.

Demons have the same syntax as rules, but are entered in the system as demons. These are rules specifically used in forward-chaining inference. For a demon to fire, its antecedent must be true. The antecedents of the demons may contain display information, such as a click on a pushbutton within the display. For example, assume that the title display has a pushbutton labeled compute, and the system has a demon in the following form:

```
IF compute button
THEN net := income - cost
```

When the user clicks on the pushbutton, the antecedent of the demon becomes true, and it executes the consequent part, assuming that the user has already provided the values of income and cost. In demons, the developer can access and change many aspects of the user interface, hence allowing the user to start, stop, exit, and control the forward-chaining inference process.

When the knowledge base contains a combination of rules, demons, and WHEN NEEDED and WHEN CHANGED methods, the inference engine uses both forward and backward chaining in the following fashion. The inference engine starts backward chaining, using the rules in the knowledge base.

When an antecedent of a demon becomes true, or a WHEN CHANGED or WHEN NEEDED method is activated, the inference engine reverts to forward chaining and continues the process until no more forward chaining is possible. At this stage, the inference engine continues with the backward chaining.

10.5.3 Database Interface

In LEVEL5 OBJECT, the developer can get data from a dBASEIII file, change the data, and write it back to the database file. In this sense, LEVEL5 OBJECT has an active interaction with dBASEIII. Furthermore, the software treats the imported record from the database file as an instance of a class of objects. In this sense, it has an OODBMS approach, as discussed in Chapter 9.

In the Objects window, one can declare the source of the class as External in the class menu. The data must be in the dBASEIII file with the extension ".DBF". One does not need to have the database software present for this interaction to work, the access to the data file suffices.

One can also access the Databases window from the main window. The software prompts for the choice of a database. In the present version, there is only one choice—dBASEIII. It then prompts for the selection of one of the dBASEIII files in the directory. Choosing a file automatically creates a class with the name of the database file. The attributes of this class are the field names of the file records. That is, a relation in dBASEIII becomes a class in LEVEL5 OBJECT. The fields of this relation become the attributes of the class. The data types of these fields become the types of attribute values. Figure 10.21 shows the dB3 employee class, which is automatically created from the Databases window.

As the left window in Figure 10.21 shows, the class created by the Databases window inherits the attributes of the dB3 system class within LEVEL5 OBJECT. These attributes are the commands that allow the developer to access and take action on the database file. The possible values of the attribute access allow the developer to read from and write into the database file. The compound values of the action attribute allow the developer to advance, append, insert, delete, and recall records within the file, as well as open and close it. These are the common access and modification commands for a relational database management system software.

One can attach any of these attribute values to a pushbutton in an interface display, such that when the user clicks on the pushbutton, the system takes the action attached to the button, such as read or append.

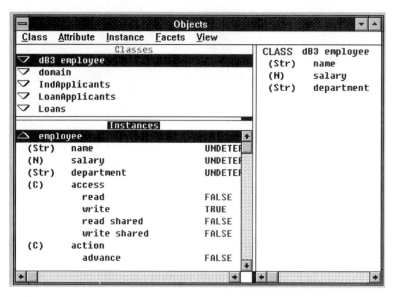

Figure 10.21   An Example of a Class Created from the Databases Window

Furthermore, one can use FIND and MAKE system commands in conjunction with the database class to make a query and retrieve a desired record (FIND), and store the result as an instance of the class (MAKE) within a rule or demon. Take the following example:

```
FIND dB3 employee
WHERE salary OF dB3 employee > 30000
AND department OF employee = "Systems Design"
WHENFOUND
MAKE qualified employee
WITH name := name OF dB3 employee
WITH salary := salary OF dB3 employee
FIND END
THEN found qualified employee
```

In this rule, the system searches the database file and attempts to find the record that matches a given list of attribute values. Once such a record is found, the MAKE command makes an instance called qualified employee, and then the THEN part makes the proposition found qualified employee true.

In sum, LEVEL5 OBJECT allows the developer to actively interact with the dBASEIII file. The construct of the Databases window is such that adding other types of database files could be easily accommodated. One expects to see more variety of database and spreadsheet files in the future versions of the software.

10.5.4 Debugging Tools

LEVEL5 OBJECT has a number of development aids and debugging tools. The Knowledge Tree window is a development aid that shows the structure of the knowledge base. This window is the opening display for the software. It shows a summary of goals, rules, methods, and displays in the system. The view menu of this window allows the developer to exhibit the structure of the knowledge base from the forward- or backward-chaining points of view. Figure 10.22 shows the backward-chaining view of the mortgage loan knowledge base.

As Figure 10.22 shows, the Knowledge Tree window shows the name of the title and conclusion displays at the beginning and end of this window. If these displays are not defined yet, the color of the box will be red on the screen. By highlighting a rule and touching the space bar, one can turn on and off the details of each rule. One can enter windows for rules, methods,

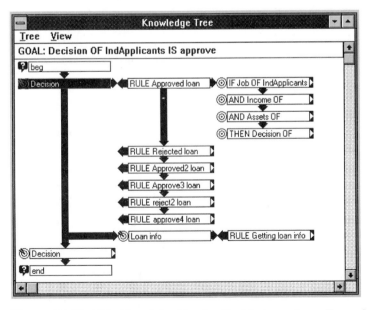

Figure 10.22   The Knowledge Tree for the Mortgage Loan Example

goals, and displays from the Knowledge Tree window. One can display the Knowledge Tree on a corner window at the run time. This display window changes in real-time and shows the branches of the Knowledge Tree being used by the inference engine.

Another development aid is the References option in the Attribute option of the Objects window. By choosing this option, one can see the rules, demons, methods, and displays in which the attribute has been used.

Among the debugging tools is the Breakpoint option in the Facets menu of the Objects window, shown in Figure 10.7. By choosing this option, the inference engine stops when the attribute to which the breakpoint is attached is evaluated.

Another development aid is the Value List window, which one can enter by clicking on its icon from the main window. The Value List window shows the values of various attributes within the system. By checking this window, the developer can ensure that the system does not contain erroneous attribute values. For a large knowledge base in which values are assigned to attributes at various points, this window is quite helpful.

Yet another development aid is the system's ability to capture and store the context of a session, or restore the facts of a session from a file. Section 10.5.1 describes how to accomplish this task. This development aid is helpful in the validation and verification process of the system, discussed in Chapter 7.

An important debugging feature of LEVEL5 OBJECT is the History window, which can be selected by clicking on the history icon in the main window. In the History window, one can choose the option in the Start menu, which turns the tracing process of the system on, and stores the trace in a file with the extension ".HST". After turning the tracing on, one should close the window and run the system. This window captures every step of processing the knowledge base. An example of the history of processing the mortgage loan example is shown in Figure 10.23.

As this figure shows, the tracing is an all-encompassing process. For even a moderate-size knowledge base, tracing could be quite long, and would slow down the processing of the knowledge base. For example, the history of the mortgage loan example captures and records every operation within the FOR loop in the WHEN NEEDED method shown in Figure 10.6. If the loan duration is 30 years, the method goes through 360 iterations, and the trace captures and records every operation in these 360 iterations. This makes the tracing file quite lengthy, and slows down the processing of the knowledge to a great extent.

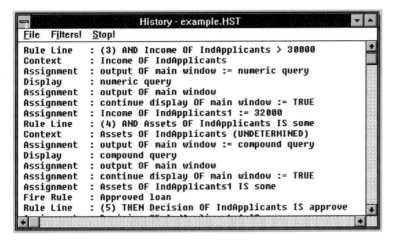

Figure 10.23 A Partial List of the Traced Processing History of the Mortgage Loan Example

For this reason, the developer can select to capture only a given set of operations. This can be done through the **Filters** menu in this window, as shown in Figure 10.24.

As Figure 10.24 shows, the default filter contains all inference engine actions. By removing the × sign from the box next to the action in this window, one can disable the tracing of that action, hence reducing the tracing load.

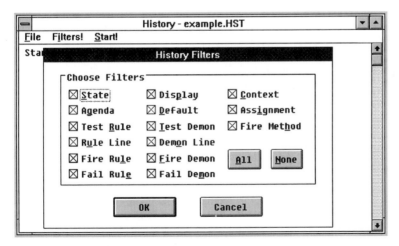

Figure 10.24 The History Filters for Selecting the Operations the Tracing Should Capture

Finally, another debugging tool of LEVEL5 OBJECT is the **Session Monitor** window. This window allows the developer to observe the firing of rules and processing of methods as the inference engine works.

LEVEL5 OBJECT stores the knowledge base in an ASCII file in the PRL language. The developer has the option of editing this file with any word processor that outputs an ASCII file. Thus, the developer has the option of programming or debugging the system off-line.

10.5.5 Multiple Knowledge Bases

In LEVEL5 OBJECT, the developer can break down the knowledge base into a number of independent modules, thus creating *multiple knowledge bases*. The CHAIN command allows the developer to connect to another knowledge base and use its contents. The **Shared** option of the **Facets** menu in the **Objects** window makes an attribute shared among chained knowledge bases. That is, only the shared attributes will be communicated among the chained knowledge bases.

10.6 Treatment of Uncertainty in LEVEL5 OBJECT

In LEVEL5 OBJECT, all attributes have a confidence factor. The default value of the confidence factor is 100. However, the developer can change this value in a number of ways.

10.6.1 Assigning Confidence Factors

The confidence factor takes values 0 to 100, -1 representing an undetermined value (for which the system has no information), and -2 representing an unknown value (which is declared as unknown by the user). To assign a confidence factor to an attribute, the **CONFIDENCE PROMPTING** option of the **Facets** menu should be turned on, which causes the inquiry display to contain the **Confidence** option when the system is run by the user, as shown in Figure 10.17.

The system instance **the Application** has an attribute called **Threshold**, which is set to 50. This means that when the confidence factor of an attribute falls below 50, the value of that attribute will be assumed to be false. One can change the threshold value in the **Objects** window or within a demon by incorporating the following:

```
threshold OF the Application := 80
```

One can assign, change, and access the confidence factor of an attribute within a rule or demon, using CF and CONF functions, as shown in the following example:

```
IF income OF IndApplicants > 30000
AND CONF(credit rating OF IndApplicants IS good) > 90
AND assets OF IndApplicants IS some
THEN Decision OF IndApplicants IS approve  CF 95
```

In this example, the CONF(attribute) function returns the confidence factor of the attribute. The CF function assigns a confidence factor to the consequent of the rule.

10.6.2   *Displaying Confidence Factors*

So far, we have discussed how one can assign and access confidence factors within the system. The next question is how to display confidence factors to the user. In the present version of the software, this uncharacteristically requires some effort in the following form. Assume that we want to display the confidence factor of the decision in the mortgage loan example to the user.

- Define a class attribute in which the confidence factor should be stored. Define a numeric attribute for the IndApplicants class, and call it Con.

- Add the following statement to the THEN part of the rules that has the loan approval as their consequents:

```
Con OF IndApplicants := CONF(Decision OF IndApplicants IS
    approve)
```

- Repeat the same process for the loan rejection with the exception that the value of the Decision attribute is reject.

- In the conclusion display, create a Textbox that reads: The confidence factor of the decision is.

- In the conclusion display, create a Valuebox to which Con attribute of the IndApplicants is attached.

10.6.3 The Computation of Confidence Factors

LEVEL5 OBJECT uses a combination of fuzzy set and probability (Chapter 11) in the internal computation of confidence factors. When the system uses connectors AND and OR, the inference engine usesfuzzy set. That is, when two propositions are combined with AND, the minimum of the confidence factors of the two propositions would be the confidence factor of the resultant proposition. When two propositions have OR as their connectors, the maximum of their confidence factors is the confidence factor of the result. When the proposition contains a computation or comparison such as $A = B + C$, the confidence factor of the result is the minimum of confidence factors of the three attributes A, B, and C.

For example, assume the system context has the following facts and rule:

```
confidence factor of attribute1 is 90
confidence factor of attribute2 is 80
confidence factor of attribute3 is 70

IF attribute1
AND attribute2
OR attribute3
THEN achieved goal   CF 95
```

Since in PRL, OR has priority over AND, the connection of **attribute2** and **attribute3** results in a confidence factor of 80, the maximum of the two confidence factors. Since this is above the threshold, it is connected with **attribute1**, which results in the confidence factor 80 for the antecedent.

To combine the confidence factor of the antecedent and consequent, LEVEL5 OBJECT uses the probability computation of two independent propositions (discussed in Chapter 11), and multiplies the two confidence factors and the antecedent and consequent, and normalizes the result by dividing it by 100.

In the above example, the proposition **achieved goal** gets the confidence factor: $80 * 95/100 = 76$.

As discussed in Chapter 11, this type of confidence factor computation is ad hoc, and common in products that address uncertainty in the knowledge base. When scholars within the field reach a consensus on a theoretical framework for dealing with uncertainty, software developers will pay more attention to the treatment of uncertainty on a more theoretical foundation.

Conclusion

In this chapter, we reviewed in some detail the working of a hybrid tool called LEVEL5 OBJECT. This software is the extension of LEVEL5 (covered in Chapter 5), and uses a PRL-like language. However, LEVEL5 OBJECT has a structure completely different from LEVEL5, in that it combines rule-based and object-oriented knowledge-representation methods, and includes advanced facilities for user-interface development.

The object-oriented approach in LEVEL5 OBJECT allows for the creation of classes, attributes, methods, facets. One can use objects within rules, demons, and goals, thus combining the object-oriented approach with the rule-based methods of knowledge representation and reasoning.

In LEVEL5 OBJECT, one can create a sophisticated user-interface that has graphical and hypertext features. The inference mechanism in LEVEL5 OBJECT includes backward chaining, forward chaining, or a combination of the two. It has interface with databases, and tools for debugging. One can create multiple knowledge bases in LEVEL5 OBJECT and connect them together to work as a single system. LEVEL5 OBJECT also allows for uncertainty in rules and facts.

In facilities and structure, LEVEL5 OBJECT represents the type of tool that will become commonplace in expert systems software products.

References

Information Builders, Inc. *LEVEL5 OBJECT: Object-Oriented Expert System for Microsoft Windows User's Guide*, 1990, Information Builders Inc., New York, NY.

Information Builders, Inc. *LEVEL5 OBJECT: Object-Oriented Expert System for Microsoft Windows Reference Manual*, 1990, Information Builders Inc., New York, NY.

Questions

10.1 Discuss the hybrid features of LEVEL5 OBJECT. Using the discussions in Chapter 9, identify the areas of possible enhancement in the software.

10.2 Compare LEVEL5 in Chapter 5 and LEVEL5 OBJECT. What are the advantages and disadvantages of the two products? Identify the application areas where each product has a comparative advantage.

10.3   Compare object-oriented features of LEVEL5 OBJECT with those of the object-oriented programming languages discussed in Chapter 8. Is LEVEL5 OBJECT a complete OOP tool? Why?

10.4   Discuss the similarities and differences between WHEN NEEDED and WHEN CHANGED methods in LEVEL5 OBJECT.

10.5   What is the role of hypertext in LEVEL5 OBJECT? Where are other areas in which hypertext could be of use?

10.6   Discuss the OODBMS feature of LEVEL5 OBJECT. Suggest possible enhancements in this area.

10.7   Discuss the development tools in LEVEL5 OBJECT. Test them extensively by using the mortgage loan example in the text.

10.8   What is the difference between demons and rules in LEVEL5 OBJECT?

10.9   Discuss the treatment of uncertainty in LEVEL5 OBJECT.

10.10   If you were to enhance the treatment of uncertainty in LEVEL5 OBJECT, which one of the methods discussed in Chapter 11 would you suggest? Why?

10.11   As a developer, which system parameters in LEVEL5 OBJECT are you likely to change? How do you change them?

10.12   Identify the tools available in LEVEL5 OBJECT for developing the user interface. Identify the type of applications where each type of tool could be of great importance.

10.13   As a developer, what additional user interface development tools would you like to have in LEVEL5 OBJECT?

Problems

10.1   Give an example of a forward-chaining application using LEVEL5 OBJECT.

10.2   Enhance the mortgage loan example to include rules and methods for establishing the credit rating and level of assets for an applicant.

10.3   In the mortgage loan example, make it possible for the user to assign confidence factors to attributes that take numerical or categorical values, and display their confidence factors in a display attached to the conclusion display.

10.4   In the mortgage loan example, create a picture in Windows 3.0 paintbrush, import to LEVEL5 OBJECT, assign it to a picture type attribute, and display it in the conclusion display.

10.5   In the mortgage loan example, design a display that shows the user how the monthly mortgage is computed, and link it to the conclusion display by the Hyperregion tool.

10.6   Assuming that you intend to use LEVEL5 OBJECT as the software, create a physical design for a job application expert system that recommends the suitability of an applicant for various job categories.

Case: Hybrid System for Product Configuration

Anderson Consulting developed an integrated product configuration system for Microsoft Corp. that incorporates a Nexpert Object (from Neuron Data of Palo Alto, Calif.) rule base, accessed via Nexpert Forms. The Bill of Material Workbench (BOM), which runs under Microsoft Windows v. 3.0 on a PC, helps project managers configure products that conform to corporate guidelines.

During the manual configuration process, planning engineers would spend a lot of time assuring marketing managers that a product would be in accordance with specified guidelines (density and number of diskettes, type of packaging, price ceiling, and so on). Microsoft wanted a system that could provide uniform visibility into configuration guidelines, provide cost-modeling capabilities, and access CAD files and bills of material.

BOM's architecture integrates client-server functions, Windows, Excel, Nexpert Object, AutoManagers, and DynaComm. The program guides users through domains such as "documentation," "packaging," and "distribution," allowing them to enter product information. The Nexpert component loads default production-guideline constraints and fires rules incrementally at each domain, advising users if a guideline is violated (BOM allows guideline violations with user justification). An end-processing base applies guidelines to all domain inputs and advises users if they don't conform: product information can then be modified. BOM allows access to CAD designs, cost data, and current bills of material from remote systems, and maintains an on-line record of rule violations and justifications.

Microsoft claims speeded accurate design, a more consistent application of guidelines, and benefits from a central source of guidelines and cost of goods sold. BOM is currently in use with 30 project managers; BOM v. 2.0, which will add internationalized guidelines and SQL Server support, will be implemented for about 100 managers soon.

From "Application Watch: Smart Product Configuration," by Justin Kestelyn, *AI Expert*, July 1990, p. 72, reprinted with permission from *AI Expert*.

Case Questions

1. Discuss the nature of this expert system and the degree of its integration with other components of information systems.

2. Which the features of this application necessitate the use of an object-oriented approach and a hybrid tool?

3. Take a product you are familiar with. Try to identify classes of objects and their attributes that are essential for putting the product together.

4. Write the rules that should guide the design of the product in Question 3. Use the syntax of LEVEL5 Object.

5. Describe the ideal user interface you envision for your product-design system.

6. If you were to implement your expert system, what components of the firm's information system would you like to integrate with or connect to your expert system? Why?

7. What are managerial implications of deploying the expert system for product configuration?

PART V

ADVANCED TOPICS IN EXPERT SYSTEMS

The objective of Part V is to introduce the reader to advanced topics in expert systems. This part consists of Chapters 11 and 12.

Chapter 11 discusses uncertainty in expert systems (when the knowledge is uncertain, error-laden, or vague) and methods for dealing with such uncertainty. The introductory sections of this chapter are essential for decision makers and managers in understanding the sources of uncertainty and the shortcomings of expert systems in dealing with uncertainty. Chapter 12 contains methods for evaluating expert system products.

In business expert system courses with minimal quantitative requirements, covering the first few sections of Chapter 11 that do not have "optional" in their titles will be sufficient. The rest of Chapters 11 and 12 can be used in more advanced graduate courses in expert systems or as reference materials.

Uncertainty in Expert Systems

What men really want is not knowledge but certainty.

Bertrand Russell

As far as the laws of mathematics refer to reality, they are not certain, and as far as they are certain, they do not refer to reality.

Albert Einstein

Chapter Objectives

The objectives of this chapter are:

- To discuss the sources that cause uncertainty in expert systems

- To review the issues involved in reasoning in expert systems when there is uncertainty in the knowledge base and facts

- To review the methods for dealing with uncertainty, including the Bayesian approach, the Dempster-Shafer theory of evidence, fuzzy sets theory, and mixed approaches

- To discuss the importance of having the proper structure for uncertainty in an expert system application

---

KEY WORDS: Sources of uncertainty, reasoning with uncertainty, Bayesian approach, Bayesian-based method, belief net, theory of evidence, fuzzy set theory, fuzzy logic, possibility theory, certainty factor, mixed approaches, uncertainty structure

---

Introduction

This chapter is the first of a two-chapter part discussing the advanced topics in expert systems. The focus of this chapter is the treatment of uncertainty in expert systems.

We have seen in Chapters 3 and 4 that the mathematical logic assumes error-free logic. That is, we assume that our experts are certain and 100 percent correct in their knowledge and that no vagueness exists in the domain.

We also assume that the user has error-free, certain, and crisp (as opposed to vague) data for the case under analysis. Similar assumptions hold for the object-oriented approach. However, the real world does not work according to these assumptions. Knowledge could be vague, experts could be uncertain or even wrong, and the user may not have the ideal data for the case. How can we formalize these features in expert systems? This is the question this chapter deals with.

Section 11.1 discusses the sources of uncertainty and vagueness. The following five sections discuss alternative methods of dealing with uncertainty: the probability approach, theory of evidence, fuzzy sets and fuzzy logic, the possibility theory, and mixed approaches. These sections are relatively theoretical and, to a practical reader, rather dry. That is why they are optional readings for the most part. However, uncertain knowledge is a fact of life, and no matter how much you may like to avoid a theoretical discussion, you need to be aware of the methods of dealing with it. Moreover, what is theoretical and dry today will become commonplace and practicable tomorrow, so scan through the optional readings to be ready for what is in store for you in the future.

11.1 Uncertainty in the Real World

Mathematical logic, which is the foundation of logic-based methods in expert systems, is inherently deterministic. That is, it allows truth values of 1 or 0—a statement form is either true or false with certainty. Therefore, reasoning in logic-based expert systems is theoretically exact and deterministic.

In reality, human knowledge is for the most part inexact and uncertain. People make decisions in an environment where facts and rules contain various shades of vagueness, imprecision, and errors. An expert system as a decision-making tool must have the ability to accommodate the inexact nature of human knowledge processing. This need was recognized early in the development of expert systems, and a number of methods have been proposed to superimpose uncertainty over the logical structure of expert systems. On the other hand, there are theories, mainly in the field of fuzzy sets and fuzzy logic, which have vagueness as their fundamental premise.

To understand the need for dealing with uncertainty, one must identify the sources of uncertainty and how the uncertainty accumulates within the expert system. The next two sections address these topics.

11.1.1 Sources of Uncertainty

There are a number of *sources of uncertainty*:

- Uncertainty within the knowledge domain

- Uncertainty related to the expert, knowledge engineer, and data

- Uncertainty related to the user

The knowledge domain may contain uncertainty in the following forms (Figure 11.1):

- The existing state of knowledge in a domain may be imperfect and incomplete

- The knowledge may be vague by nature

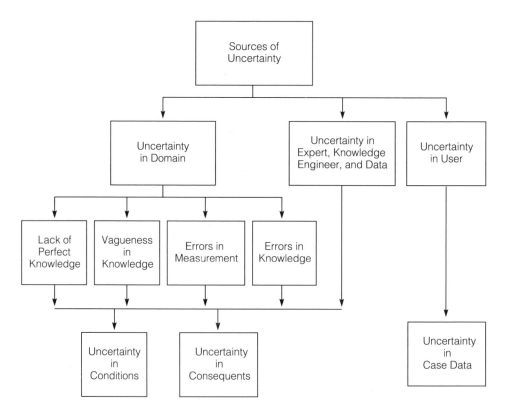

Figure 11.1 Sources of Uncertainty in the Knowledge Base

- The measurements in the domain knowledge may contain errors

- The domain may contain conflicting and erroneous information

There is hardly any domain with complete and perfect knowledge; the imperfection of the domain knowledge is a matter of degree. In some cases, the developer has to incorporate the inadequacy of knowledge in the knowledge base to make it more representative of the real system. For example, in the mortgage loan system, one does not know with certainty the profile of an applicant who will be delinquent in the course of loan payment. The expert expresses this uncertainty by the statement that loan applicants with a given profile (job history, credit ratings, and monthly income and expenses) normally have loan delinquency in 95 percent of cases. For the system to be realistic, the developer must incorporate this uncertainty in the knowledge base.

The knowledge domain may contain vagueness. For example, the best available knowledge in the domain indicates that **an applicant with a steady job is more likely to pay back the loan than an applicant without a steady job.** The words **steady** and **more likely** are vague concepts within the domain, and do not lend themselves to exact quantification.

Measurement error is another way the knowledge domain may be uncertain. For example, the method of evaluating the loan applicant's assets may be flawed, such as using the wrong source for evaluating the market value of the applicant's assets.

The conflicting information within a knowledge domain is quite common. For example, an expert believes that the applicant's assets should be evaluated based on the income that the applicant can earn from the ownership of the asset. Another expert believes that the assets must be evaluated at their present market value. The two methods do not coincide in cases where there is no active or efficient market for the assets. This causes an uncertainty regarding the value of the applicant's assets.

The second major source of uncertainty is the expert whose knowledge is the basis of the expert system, and the knowledge engineer who acquires the knowledge from experts. In such cases, the expert may not be 100 percent sure of a particular rule. For example, in the mortgage loan application example in Chapter 4, we had

```
IF the applicant has a job
   AND the applicant has been more than 2 years at the
      present job
THEN the applicant has a steady job.
```

The expert loan officer may be unsure of the rule, and assign the reliability of 90 percent to it. Or, the knowledge engineer may be in doubt about the quality of the expert's judgment in this regard, and assign a reliability of 90 percent to the rule. Although the knowledge engineer may increase the certainty of the knowledge base by additional field research, he or she may decide to limit the knowledge base to the expertise of the expert, and enter the rule with a parameter that reflects the lack of full confidence about it.

If the system uses the inductive inference method (discussed in Chapters 4 and 6), the data used to derive a decision tree and rules may contain inconsistencies. Contradictory observations in the data set indicate the presence of error or lack of consistent rules in the practice. For example, in two identical applications, the bank may have granted the loan to one and rejected the other. The developer needs a mechanism to incorporate this type of uncertainty in the knowledge base.

Another source of uncertainty could be in the input data that the user provides to the system for solving a particular problem. The user may not be sure of the correctness or accuracy of the evidence or data for a case. For example, in the mortgage loan system, we had the following rule:

```
IF  the applicant has properties with a value greater than
       10 times the loan
   OR  the applicant has liquid assets greater than 5 times
       the loan
THEN the applicant has adequate assets
```

The value of the applicant's property may change from one day to another; therefore, the user may not be sure that the first condition of the antecedent holds with certainty.

The uncertainties related to the domain, expert, data, or user are reflected in the knowledge base in the condition of rules, in the consequent of rules, or in the input data provided for solving a given case. Figure 11.1 summarizes this discussion.

The uncertainty in rules creates problems in the single and multiple inference process. The reasoning in such cases becomes inexact, and the conclusions lack complete certainty.

11.1.2 Reasoning with Uncertainty

The inference engine, in processing knowledge, propagates the uncertainty of a single piece of knowledge throughout the system. For example, assume that there is only uncertainty in one rule in the knowledge base. This rule has the consequent that the applicant's job is steady. Because of this uncertainty, the conclusion arrived from the rule is uncertain. When the steadiness of the applicant's job is used as a condition in a second rule for making the loan decision, the conclusion of the second rule will also become uncertain. Thus, the uncertainty in one rule propagates throughout the system as the conclusion reached from firing the uncertain rule is used in other rules.

Therefore, there are two parts to *reasoning with uncertainty* within an expert system. The first part entails issues regarding the uncertainty within a rule, or single inference with uncertainty. The second part is the process by which the uncertainty within a rule is propagated throughout the system. The issues related to this part are termed multiple inference with uncertainty.

Single Inference with Uncertainty

When a rule has uncertain conditions and consequent, and its conditions are matched with facts that themselves are uncertain, the question becomes: What is the degree of uncertainty attached to the conclusion of the rule when it fires?

The general label *certainty parameter* indicates a measure for the degree of certainty. In the theoretical discussions of this chapter, we see that this parameter takes different names in different uncertainty methods.

To see the issues involved in single inference with uncertainty, take the following example:

```
IF   the applicant has properties with a value greater than
       10 times the loan
   OR the applicant has liquid assets greater than 5 times
       the loan
THEN   the applicant has adequate assets C=0.95
```

where C denotes the certainty parameter or *degree of belief* about the consequent.

Assume that for the applicant smith, the user believes with the certainty parameter of 0.90 that the applicant has property with a value greater than 10 times the loan. Furthermore, the user believes with the certainty parameter 0.85 that smith has liquid assets greater than 5 times the loan. In this case, what is the value of the certainty parameter in inferring that smith has adequate assets?

To answer this question, one must know how to combine a rule's certainty parameters in the following circumstances:

- How to match the first condition of the rule **the applicant has properties with a value greater than 10** with that of the input data for **smith** with the certainty parameter $C = .90$, and what is the certainty parameter of the matched condition?

- Similarly, how to combine the second condition with that of the uncertain input data for **smith** with $C = .85$.

- Since the data for **smith** satisfies the two conditions of the rule, the question is how to combine the certainty parameters of the two satisfied conditions in order to determine the certainty parameter of the antecedent that the applicant (**smith**) has met the conditions of the rule. This is important because the certainty parameter of the antecedent impacts the certainty parameter of the consequent.

- Since the consequent of the rule itself has a certainty parameter $C = 0.95$, then the question is how to combine the certainty parameter of the antecedent's satisfied conditions with that of the consequent. In other words, how certain is the conclusion that **smith** has adequate assets?

These are the types of questions raised within a single rule, or the *intra-rule* treatment of uncertainty. In mathematical logic, there is no theory for guiding the combination of certainty parameters. Therefore, in dealing with uncertainty, we have to superimpose a theory or a method of uncertain or approximate reasoning over the existing structure of knowledge representation.

In summary, single inference with uncertainty poses a number of questions for which the inference engine should have answers before it can make any inference using a single rule. The intra-rule questions are:

- When the conditions in the antecedent are uncertain, how does this uncertainty affect the conclusions?

- When both the condition and the rule itself are uncertain, how should these two types of uncertainty be combined? One can summarize questions 1 and 2 as: how do we combine the certainty parameters for the $\rightarrow$ (or THEN) operator?

- How do we combine uncertainties of the antecedent's conditions, separated by the operators AND, OR, and NOT? In other words, how do we combine the certainty parameters for the $\wedge$, $\vee$, and $\neg$ operators?

- When the fact of a case is uncertain, how should its uncertainty be combined with the uncertainty within various parts of a rule in the computation of the uncertainty of the result? In other words, how do we combine uncertainty in the matching operation?

- If a condition or a consequent is the result of a mathematical computation that has uncertain components, how should the system compute the certainty parameter of the computed result? In other words, how do we combine the certainty parameters for the mathematical operations?

- Should the case in which the same input data (such as a bank credit report) determine the certainty parameter of more than one part of a rule be treated differently than the case where the source of the certainty parameters are independent from one another? This question raises the issue of *conditional dependency*, which is discussed in the next section.

- Should the system accept a consequent as true even if the certainty parameter of the consequent is very low? If not, what is the *threshold* of the certainty below which the uncertain consequent could not be considered true? In other words, what is the threshold at which the knowledge could be considered as "known"?

The list of questions shows that designing a model for incorporating various facets of uncertainty is not an easy task. In this chapter, we will discuss a number of methods that address these questions to a varying degree. In selecting a method for modeling uncertainty, one should strike a balance between the complexity of the method and the extent of the answers it provides to the above questions.

Multiple Inference with Uncertainty

When the knowledge is uncertain, multiple inference loses its clarity. For example, two different rules result in the conclusion that the applicant has a good credit rating, one with the certainty parameter of .90, and the other with the certainty parameter of .80. What is the certainty parameter for this conclusion? Should arriving at the same conclusion via two different rules be considered a strengthening factor and further confirmation that the conclusion is true?

Consider another case in which one rule has fired with the consequent that the applicant has a good credit rating with the certainty parameter .80, and another has concluded that the applicant has a bad credit rating with the certainty parameter of .82. What should the conclusion be? What is the certainty parameter of the conclusion?

The common questions regarding the combination of certainty parameters across rules, or the *inter-rule* combination of certainty parameters, could be summarized as follows:

- If two different conclusions are reached, each with a different certainty parameter, what inference engine strategy should be used in chaining with the other rules?

- When the same conclusion is formed from two rules, each with its own certainty parameter, what is the certainty parameter of the conclusion?

- How should the system resolve two contradictory conclusions, and what is the certainty parameter of the outcome? If two conclusions are contradictory, will the certainty parameter be lower for both?

- Should it make any difference if the same uncertain input is used to arrive at more than one conclusion? Does this make the conclusions statistically dependent, in that if one conclusion is true, the other one also has a higher probaility to be true? Should the treatment of dependent conclusions be different than that of independent conclusions?

In the following sections, we review the methods that provide answers to such questions.

11.2 Probability Methods

Probability theory has long been used to deal with the concept of uncertainty. Therefore, it is the first candidate for the treatment of uncertainty in expert systems.

Probability theory is based on three axioms or accepted assumptions that:

- The probability $p(h)$ is nonnegative and less than or equal to 1

- The probabilities of all possible simple events sum to 1

- The probability that any one of the k simple events will happen is the sum of their probabilities.

In other words:

$$0 \leq p(h) \leq 1$$

$$\sum_{\forall i} p(h_i) = 1$$

$$p(h_1 \vee h_2 \vee \ldots \vee h_k) = \sum_{i=1}^{k} p(h_i)$$

where in the last two axioms, the h_i's are the simple events that are *mutually exclusive* and *exhaustive*. That is, only one of the h_i's could happen or be true at any one time, and together they represent all possible simple events. Another important aspect of probability theory of particular interest to expert system researchers is that the probability of an event (or a hypothesis) and its *complement* should sum to 1. That is,

$$p(h) + p(\neg h) = 1$$

where $p(\neg h)$ is the probability that the hypothesis is false or the event does not happen.

There are two interpretations of probability:

- The frequentist or objective interpretation

- The Bayesian or subjective interpretation

In the *objective* or *frequentist* interpretation of probability, $p(h)$ represents the actual or theoretical frequency of a hypothesis being true. In this approach, probability values should be measured by observing the events, or by theoretically deriving them from the underlying model of the system.

The underlying assumption in the frequentist approach is that h is an event or hypothesis that occurs repeatedly, and we can measure its frequency by observing the number of times it has been true (n) in N observations. We use the relative frequency $f = \frac{n}{N}$ to represent the estimate of the true probability of h. The larger the value of N, the closer f would be to the true probability of h. In other words, in the frequentist approach to probability, we assume a true probability exists out there, and we can get an estimate of it by using the frequency approach.

In the *subjective* or *Bayesian approach*, h may not be a hypothesis that could repeatedly be true. For example, in the case of a particular applicant smith, the hypothesis of a good credit rating could be true only once for this particular applicant, because the applicant is not normally in the habit of repeatedly asking for the same loan over and over again.

With a history dating back to Thomas Bayes's work in 1763, the subjective approach to probability treats $p(h)$ as the degree of belief that h may be true. This belief is expressed by the decision maker, in this case, the expert. The expert may use the frequency data to update his or her opinion. However, the updated opinion is still the revised *belief* of the expert. In the subjective approach, one does not assume that a true value for $p(h)$ necessarily exists. Rather, the expert revises his or her belief to represent a better understanding of the domain knowledge.

While the basic formulas of probability are the same in the frequentist and subjective schools of thought, the collection of data, the application of the formulas, and the interpretation of the results differ in the two approaches. The Bayesian approach has been the predominant method for decision making, and naturally, by extension, for expert systems.

11.2.1   *Bayesian Approach (Optional)*

When the system has uncertainty, it is common to refer to the antecedent as *evidence*, and the consequent is called the *hypothesis*. That is, in place of

$$< antecedent > \ \rightarrow \ < consequent >$$

we have

$$< evidence > \ \rightarrow \ < hypothesis > .$$

The naming has no impact on the rule content. It only reminds us that when a rule contains uncertainty, the consequent is in the form of a hypothesis, which receives its support from the fact or evidence in its conditions.

Consider the condition of a rule as the evidence and the consequent as the hypothesis, in form:

$$IF < evidence > \ THEN \ < the \ hypothesis \ i >$$

or

$$IF < e > \ THEN \ < h_i > .$$

The probability of concluding the hypothesis (h_i), given the evidence (e), has the form of a conditional probability:

$$p(h_i|e).$$

defined by the ratio

$$p(h_i|e) = \frac{p(h_i \wedge e)}{p(e)}. \tag{1}$$

We have the following equalities for the conditional probabilities:

$$p(h_i \wedge e) = p(h_i|e)p(e) = p(e|h_i)p(h_i). \qquad (2)$$

where $p(h_i \wedge e)$ is the probability that h_i and e occur together.

From this, we get the Bayes formula:

$$p(h_i|e) = \frac{p(e|h_i)p(h_i)}{p(e)}. \qquad (3)$$

Assume that the system has a number of rules that have e in their antecedent, with different consequents $h_1, h_2, \ldots h_n$. Then, the probability of the event e is the sum of the intersections of e with all the possible hypotheses, as:

$$\begin{aligned} p(e) &= \sum_{j=1}^{n} p(e \wedge h_j) \\ &= \sum_{j=1}^{n} p(e|h_j)p(h_j). \end{aligned} \qquad (4)$$

We replace the denominator of (3) with either of the two equalities in (4).

In Bayesian probability, $p(h_i)$ is called the *prior probability*, and $p(h_i|e)$ is called the *posterior probability*. The prior is the expert's belief in the truth of the hypothesis. The posterior is the revised belief of the expert, after observing the evidence of e as a fact in a case.

Normally, the application of the Bayesian approach is better understood by depicting the rules or the inference process in graphical form, such as *inference network* or a *belief net*. A belief net is similar to the decision tree discussed in Chapter 4, except that in a belief net, a node represents the probability of an evidence or a hypothesis (in the form of an event), and can have more than one parent.

Let us demonstrate this by an example. Assume that there are two hypotheses: $h_1 =$ to approve the loan is financially prudent and $h_2 =$ to approve the loan is not financially prudent. Note that this example emphasizes the appropriateness of the decision, because the probability of the prudence of the decision helps the decision maker select a course of action. The evidence that can be used in both of the above hypotheses is $e =$ the applicant has a steady job. The belief net for this example is given in Figure 11.2. The expert should specify the prior probabilities as:

$$p(h_1) = .70$$

$$p(h_2) = .30$$

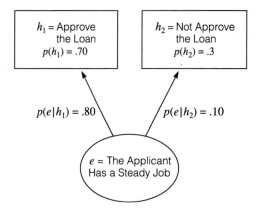

Figure 11.2   Example of the Belief Net in the Bayesian Approach

and the conditional probabilities of:

$$p(e|h_1) = .80$$

$$p(e|h_2) = .10$$

The prior $p(h_1)$ represents the expert's belief that, without any evidence, the probability that a loan application is approved is .70. The conditional probability $p(e|h_1)$ is the answer to the question: of those applicants whose loans were financially prudent to be approved, what percentage had a steady job? These probabilities are expressed by the expert as a belief, or derived from bank or industry data. The expert system contains these probabilities. The user gives the evidence that e is true, that is, the applicant has a steady job. Applying the Bayes formula in (3), the system generates the posterior probabilities as:

$$p(h_1|e) = \frac{p(e|h_1)p(h_1)}{p(e|h_1)p(h_1) + p(e|h_2)p(h_2)}$$

$$= \frac{(.80)(.70)}{(.80)(.70) + (.10)(.30)}$$

$$= \frac{.56}{.56 + .03}$$

$$= .95$$

$$p(h_2|e) = \frac{.03}{.56 + .03}$$

$$= .05$$

Note that the evidence of a steady job has increased the probability of h_1 from the prior value of .70 to the posterior value of .95, and decreased that of h_2 from .30 to .05. Thus, the evidence has increased the belief that the loan will be approved.

The problem becomes more involved when there is more than one e in the rule. In that case, we have

$$p(h_i|e_1 \land e_2 \land \ldots \land e_k) = \frac{p(e_1 \land e_2 \land \ldots e_k|h_i)}{\sum_{j=1}^{n} p(e_1 \land e_2 \land \ldots \land e_k|h_j)\, p(h_j)}. \qquad (5)$$

To compute (5), we need the following:

$$p(e_1 \land e_2 \land \ldots \land e_k|h_i) = p(e_1|e_2 \land \ldots \land e_k \land h_i)\, p(e_2|e_3 \land \ldots \land e_k \land h_i) \ldots p(e_k|h_i),$$

where $p(e_1|e_2 \land \ldots \land e_k \land h_i)$ means the probability that the evidence e_1 is true, given that other pieces of evidence $e_2 \ldots e_k$ and the hypothesis h_i are true.

It is clear that this formula requires a number of complex conditional probabilities. Furthermore, the formula is dependent on the context and structure of the knowledge base, because the expert must know of the interdependencies of the pieces of evidence and the hypotheses, as well as their probabilities. While the formula allows the knowledge engineer to incorporate the special structure of the domain knowledge into the system, the complexity and the sheer number of required conditional probabilities could make such a design prohibitive in most real-world applications.

One way to curb the complexity is to assume that the pieces of evidence are *conditionally independent*. This assumption implies that once we know h_i, the fact that we have observed e_1 does not have any consequence on observing e_2. For example, given we know it is financially prudent to approve a loan application, the fact that the applicant has a steady job does not impact the probability that the applicant has a good credit rating.

In this case, we can use the following in equation (5):

$$p(e_1 \land e_2 \land \ldots \land e_k|h_i) = p(e_1|h_i)\, p(e_2|h_i) \ldots p(e_k|h_i). \qquad (6)$$

This resolves the problem of the complexity of the conditional probabilities. But the number of required conditional probabilities increases as more pieces of evidence are used in the system. For example, if we add just one more piece of evidence to the example in Figure 11.2, the number of the required conditional probabilities increases from 2 to 4, as shown in Figure 11.3. Applying (6) and (5) to this belief net, given that the applicant

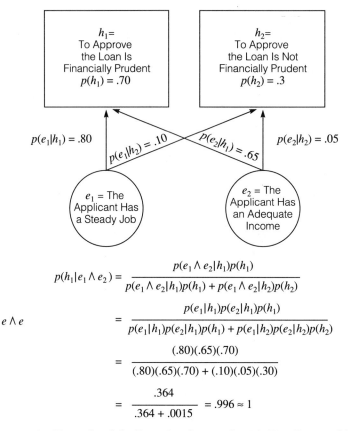

Figure 11.3   Example of the Bayesian Approach with Two Pieces of Evidence

has a steady job and an adequate income, the probability of getting the loan is about 1. The details of this computation are given in Figure 11.3.

With the assumption of conditional independence, when the antecedent has conditions e_1 and e_2 separated by an OR operator, the probability of the antecedent is computed as:

$$p(e_1 \lor e_2|h_i) = p(e_1|h_i) + p(e_2|h_i) - p(e_1|h_i)p(e_2|h_i). \qquad (7)$$

The case of the AND operator is covered in (6), and the negation is the probability of the complement of the hypothesis: $p(\neg h) = 1 - p(h)$.

In the Bayesian approach, when the evidence is uncertain, the computational complexity increases. The probability of the hypothesis with the uncertain evidence ($\tilde{e}$) is

$$p(h_i|\tilde{e}) = p(h_i|e)p(e|\tilde{e}) + p(h_i|\neg e)p(\neg e|\tilde{e}), \tag{8}$$

where $\neg e$ means that the evidence e is not true. When the conclusion itself is uncertain, the value of $p(h_i|e)$ would be multiplied by the probability of the conclusion, again assuming conditional independence.

The Bayesian approach has encountered a number of objections:

- That in many expert systems, the objective estimation of the conditional probabilities is impossible or prohibitive. This objection is not valid, because the conditional probabilities could be the subjective belief of the expert, and could be elicited in the process of knowledge engineering.

- That the assumption of conditional independence of the conditional probabilities is not always valid. For example, having an adequate income could depend, in a probability sense, on having a steady job. As Judea Pearl [1988] points out, this is the price to pay for the simplification the assumption provides. This assumption allows reasoning in a *modular* form in that the expert does not need to know the full content of the knowledge base for expressing the conditional probabilities.

- That the multiplication of probabilities makes the probability of the outcome unrealistically low.

- That many experts are not comfortable with the underlying implication of the Bayesian approach when we have, say, $p(h_i|e) = .7$, then $p(h_i|\neg e) = 1 - .7 = .3$. In other words, a piece of evidence may support a hypothesis, but the lack of the evidence may not have any impact on the hypothesis. This was the experience of the developers of MYCIN, who encountered the physician experts' objection that the lack of a positive test result does not impact the hypothesis. Two relatively new methods of the Dempster and Shafer theory of evidence and the Bayesian-based method by Pearl deal with this objection.

- That the probability approach does not distinguish between ambiguity inherent within the domain knowledge, and the uncertainty due to errors and lack of complete knowledge. Zadeh's fuzzy set theory and fuzzy logic deal with this problem.

- That, for a real world expert system with many rules, the Bayesian approach requires too many probabilities. Pearl's approach addresses this concern.

11.2.2   *Pearl's Bayesian-based Method (Optional)*

In 1986, Pearl noticed that in many domains, the hypotheses of interest can be organized in a tree hierarchy. In this hierarchy, every node in the tree represents a subset S of singleton hypotheses, h_i's. The evidence e impacts the singleton hypotheses within the set S. The expert should only assess the impact of the evidence on the most directly affected set S, not on its singleton hypotheses. Therefore, the expert must provide the prior probabilities $p(h_i)$, and the likelihood ratios:

$$\lambda_s = \frac{p(e|S)}{p(e|\neg S)}, \tag{9}$$

where $p(e|S)$ means the probability of the evidence e being true given that the hypotheses in set S are true, and $p(e|\neg S)$ is the probability that the same evidence is true given that the hypotheses outside set S are true. Note that S and $\neg S$ are mutually exclusive. Within each set, too, only one hypothesis could become true.

The likelihood ratio calculates the odds of observing the evidence e when one of the hypotheses in S is true, as opposed to when one of the hypotheses of $\neg S$ is true. Experience has shown that experts are more comfortable expressing the impact of evidence in the form of such ratios, rather than absolute probabilities. When the odds are favorable to S, λ_s is greater than 1, otherwise it is less than 1. Each hypothesis in S gets a weight $w_i = \lambda_s$, and those outside S get 1 as their weight.

In running the system, if the user inputs the presence of evidence e, the system assesses its impact on the hypotheses of S and computes the posterior probabilities as:

$$p(h_i|e) = \alpha_s w_i p(h_i), \qquad i = 1, 2, \ldots, n \tag{10}$$

where n is the number of hypotheses in the system, and α_s is used to normalize the probabilities such that the sum of the probabilities of all possible hypotheses would add to 1. This is one of the axioms of the probability: The the sum of the probabilities of all the simple mutually exclusive events must add to 1. Therefore, α_s has the form

$$\alpha_s = [\sum_{j=1}^{n} w_j p(h_j)]^{-1}. \tag{11}$$

Pearl's *Bayesian-based method* simplifies to a great extent the computational requirements of the system and demands a careful analysis of the structure of the hypotheses by the knowledge engineer. Although the structural analysis of hypotheses in Pearl's method is an additional burden, such analysis gives the knowledge engineer a valuable insight and a general overview of the knowledge base. It gives the developer the opportunity to discover errors and contradictions in the knowledge base that otherwise are hard to identify.

11.3 The Dempster-Shafer Theory of Evidence (Optional)

Dempster in 1967 and later Shafer in 1976 developed a theory in which the probabilities are expressed in the form of an interval and the probabilities $p(h)$ and $p(\neg h)$ do not have to add to 1, as is required as an axiom in probability theory.

In the Dempster-Shafer (D-S) *theory of evidence*, the *environment* is defined as a set θ, which consists of all mutually exclusive hypotheses. As in probability theory, in mutually exclusive hypotheses no two hypotheses can be true at the same time. For example, the θ for the credit rating of a loan applicant could be

$$\theta = \{x, \ v, \ g, \ f, \ b\},$$

where x, v, g, f, and b stand for **excellent**, **very good**, **good**, **fair**, and **bad**. These elements are mutually exclusive in that an applicant can get only one of them as a credit rating. In this case, θ is also called a *frame of discernment*.

The set θ could have subsets, such as

$$\theta_1 = \{x, \ v\}$$
$$\theta_2 = \{g, \ f, \ b\}$$
$$\theta_3 = \{x\}$$
$$\theta_4 = \emptyset = \{\}$$
$$\theta_5 = \theta = \{x, \ v, \ g, \ f, \ b\}$$

Assuming that θ has n elements, then one can form 2^n subsets of n, including the empty set $\emptyset$ and θ itself. The set that contains all such subsets is called the *power set* of θ. For the simplicity of presentation, denote the power set as Θ. Note that Θ has all subsets of θ, including $\theta_1, \ldots, \theta_5$, and others. A piece of evidence could impact or have relevance to some subsets in Θ. Such subsets are called the *focal element*.

The *basic probability assignment* (b.p.a) m in D-S theory is a function that maps Θ to the interval $[0,1]$, such that

$$m(\emptyset) = 0$$

$$\sum_{S_i \subset \Theta} m(S_i) = 1.$$

In other words, the m value for the empty set is zero, and the sum of the m values for all possible subsets in Θ should always sum to 1. One intuitive interpretation of the m value is the weight of evidence for the subset. The empty set does not receive any weight from the evidence. The summation to 1 ensures that all the possible subsets are included in Θ.

The *belief* for the focal element S is defined as

$$Bel(S) = \sum_{s \subset S} m(s). \tag{12}$$

For example, assume that $S = \{x,\ v\}$ is a focal element because the evidence from the field is relevant to it. The $Bel(S)$ is the sum of the m values of $\{x\}$, $\{v\}$, and $\{x,\ v\}$. The belief in θ is always 1. That is, $Bel(\theta) = 1$. This means that the environment set contains all possible hypotheses.

The belief in the D-S theory defines an *evidential interval* for the focal element. Once a piece of evidence becomes known, it generates the evidence interval for S. The lower end of this interval is $Bel(S)$, and the upper end of this interval is the *plausibility* of S, which is defined as:

$$Pls(S) = 1 - Bel(\neg S), \tag{13}$$

where $\neg S$ is the compliment set of S. *Pls* represents the extent of belief in the consistency of the evidence with S.

The m values generated from different pieces of evidence could be combined. For example, assume that one piece of evidence has arrived in the form of a credit report from a credit card company, and the following m values are formed by the expert:

$$m_1(\{x,\ v\}) = .70$$

$$m_1(\{g,\ f,\ b\}) = .10$$

$$m_1(\{\theta\}) = .20$$

where $m_1(\{\theta\})$ is the part for which no belief is formed. In other words, in the D-S theory, the decision maker, based on the evidence, assigns weights in the form of m values to the focal elements. The remaining weight (which makes the m's add up to 1) is assigned to the environment, as the weight of evidence for the subsets of θ that are not considered yet. The second report produces the following b.p.a.'s or m values:

$$m_2(\{x\}) = .80$$

$$m_2(\{\theta\}) = .20$$

The combination of the two sets is computed in the following form:

	$m_2(\{x\}) = .80$	$m_2(\{\theta\}) = .20$
$m_1(\{x, v\}) = .70$ $m_1(\{g, f, b\}) = .10$ $m_1(\{\theta\}) = .20$	$\{x\}^* \; .56$ $\{\emptyset\} \;\; .08$ $\{x\} \;\; .16$	$\{x, v\} \;\; .14$ $\{g, f, b\} \;\; .02$ $\{\theta\} \;\; .04$

* (the resulting intersection set)

In other words, the intersection of the m values is the multiplication of the values. However, the set that owns the result of the multiplication is the one that is the intersection subset of the two. For example, $\{x\}$ is the intersection subset of the second column and first row sets. When the two sets do not have an intersection, the empty set gets the value, as shown in the cell on the second row and second column. The intersection of any set with θ is the set, and the intersection of θ with itself is θ.

From the table, we can compute the combined belief values as

$$m_3(\{x\}) = m_1 \oplus m_2(\{x\}) = .56 + .16 = .72$$

$$m_3(\{x, \; v\}) = m_1 \oplus m_2(\{x, \; v\}) = .14$$

$$m_3(\{g, \; f, \; b\}) = m_1 \oplus m_2(\{g, \; f, \; b\}) = .02$$

$$m_3(\{\theta\}) = m_1 \oplus m_2(\{\theta\}) = .04$$

$$m_3(\{\emptyset\}) = m_1 \oplus m_2(\{\emptyset\}) = .08$$

where $\oplus$ represents the operation of combining the belief values.

The problem with the above result is that the empty set has a nonzero m value. D-S theory requires that the m value of the empty set be zero, because it is not a focal element, and the m values of the focal elements should add up to 1. To achieve this, all m values of the focal elements should be normalized by dividing them by the normalization factor $1 - m(\emptyset)$, and making the m value of the empty set equal to zero. If there is more than one m value for the empty set $\emptyset$, the normalization factor is one minus the sum of the m values of the empty set.

In doing so, we get

$$m_3(\{x\}) = .72(\frac{1}{1 - .08}) = .783$$

$$m_3(\{x, \ v\}) = .14(\frac{1}{1 - .08}) = .152$$

$$m_3(\{g, \ f, \ b\}) = .02(\frac{1}{1 - .08}) = .022$$

$$m_3(\{\theta\}) = .04(\frac{1}{1 - .08}) = .043$$

Now, we can compute the belief value of the credit rating set $\{x, \ v\}$ as:

$$Bel(\{x, \ v\}) = .783 + .152 = .935,$$

because the belief in $\{x, \ v\}$ consists of the sum of the m values of all of its subsets, here $\{x\}$ plus that of the set itself. The plausibility of the set is

$$Pls(\{x, \ v\}) = 1 - Bel(\neg\{x, \ v\}) = 1 - .022 = .978$$

In the computation of the plausibility, the m value of θ is not considered as part of the belief in the complement of the set, because θ in this context represents the unknown. Thus, the evidential interval of the set $\{x, \ v\}$ is the interval $[.935, .978]$. A wide interval such as $[0, 1]$ does not have any informational value.

The D-S theory addresses a number of concerns regarding the use of probability theory:

- The number of m values is limited, because we group the hypotheses into focal elements or relevant sets on which the evidence could have some impact. Grouping of hypotheses is similar to the sets in the Pearl approach.

- Since we allow for ignorance in the form of $m(\theta)$, then the m value of a focal element when the evidence is lacking is not necessarily one minus that when the evidence is present. The likelihood ratio in Pearl's method has a similar property.

- The D-S theory is not based on probability theory, and could produce results that conflict with people's intuitive notion about how to measure belief. The Pearl approach has probability theory as its foundation.

- The D-S theory assumes that the n hypotheses that form the environment are mutually exclusive. Pearl makes a similar assumption.

- The most problematic aspect of the D-S theory is the arbitrary nature of the normalization of the m values, which could lead to counterintuitive results. To show this, let us assume that we have:

$$m_1(\{x\}) = .90$$
$$m_1(\{b\}) = .10$$
$$m_2(\{v\}) = .90$$
$$m_2(\{b\}) = .10$$

When we form the table of the intersection, compute $m_1 \oplus m_2$ values, and normalize the result, we get

$$m_3(\{b\}) = m_1 \oplus m_2(\{b\}) = 1.$$

This is because the intersection of the sets with high m belief values are the empty set, and normalization leads to an extremely high value for the set, which before the normalization had only .01 as its m_3 value (0.1×0.1). This is quite a counterintuitive result. This demonstrates that grouping the hypotheses into sets is of crucial importance to the D-S theory. Avoiding such erroneous conclusions requires a very careful design of the hypothesis sets.

- Neither the D-S theory nor Pearl's method distinguishes between the ambiguity and perceived inconsistency inherent in the domain as opposed to the errors caused by the incomplete or erroneous knowledge of the expert or the user. Fuzzy logic is designed to make this distinction.

11.4 Fuzzy Sets and Fuzzy Logic

Mathematical logic is based on Aristotelian logic, which considers propositions to be either true or false. In other words, it is a *bivalent* or *two-value* logic, which considers propositions as either true or false. In reality, a proposition could be partially true or partially false. For example, the categories of credit risk are vague. Assume we have numerical values of 0 to 1 for rating, and have decided that those with the rating .71-.80 are considered **good** credit risks. Does this mean that an applicant with a rating of .70 could not be considered a good risk? Or, say the bank requires an annual income of $40,000. Does it mean that an applicant with $39,990 in yearly income would be rejected?

In two-value logic, the answer is "yes" to both questions. In reality, the expert may answer "no" to both. The two-value logic does not have the flexibility to accommodate such cases, where the human expert constantly deals with such ambiguities.

Lukasiewicz in the 1920s proposed the n-value logic. Zadeh in his pioneering work in 1965 proposed the theory of fuzzy sets, and created a new field for dealing with the vagueness of the human environment. Fuzzy logic extends fuzzy sets theory into reasoning with fuzzy propositions and fuzzy rules.

Case: Applications of Fuzzy Systems

Fuzzy systems have been around since the 1920s, when they were first proposed by Lukasiewicz (also the inventor of reverse Polish notation). The intellectual appeal of fuzzy systems is clear when faced with the restraints of Aristotelian logic, which says a thing is either something or isn't something.

We contradict that kind of logic every day in the real world. For example, we look at someone and say they are somewhat tall. Does that mean they're of average height? Does it mean they're short? In fact, someone's height is a subjective judgment based on our own height and perception of social norms. But why is a person's height important?

Certainly, height is important when you buy clothes, but is it important in bottom-line dollars? The answer is yes. You might not be aware of this, but for people taller than average, a negative correlation exists between life expectancy and height if all other factors are equal: in general the taller you are, the shorter your life expectancy. But how much is "above average," and what is the "shorter life expectancy"?

Many life insurance companies use what are called "box car" classification schemes. For a given weight and sex, a height of 5'9"–5'11" might be average. Therefore, someone who is 5'11$\frac{1}{2}$" tall is above average, where above average might be classed from 5'11"–6'1". Consequently, this person will pay the same premium as someone who is 6'1" and is clearly more at risk. Why? Because as we all know, most conventional programming methods, and even expert systems, force us to use a box-car classification scheme for computational simplicity and because of our own unfamiliarity with fuzzy systems.

1. *Process Control.* In 1965, Lotfi Zadeh codified and expanded on Lukasiewicz's work and gave the world enough mathematical theory to work with the concept of fuzzy sets. A fuzzy set suggests an item can have partial membership in two seemingly contradictory sets. A man who is 5'11$\frac{1}{2}$" is mostly a member of the set of average height men, but also holds some membership function in the set of above average height men. It was Zadeh's math that allowed the commercial fuzzy system to be deployed in an industrial control setting.

In most manufacturing processes, the production of cement is "fuzzy." In 1980, F. L. Smidth & Co. of Copenhagen, in conjunction with a research team from Queen Mary College from Denmark, decided to attack this problem. To present the scale of the control problem, let's look at the Canada Cement Lafarge Plant in Ontario, Canada. The kiln is 19' in diameter, 655' long, and can produce 1,000,000 tons of cement annually.

Interestingly, while humans can learn to operate such a kiln quite efficiently, the pursuit of a mathematically representative control function has been elusive. Most of the easily constructed functions can't do the job as well as humans, whereas exact mathematical specification of the process has to be too comprehensive and complex to build.

The factors in the kiln managed by the fuzzy controller include the rate of fuel introduction, kiln rotation speed, product feed, and kiln draft (amount of air introduced). The computer program was developed by F. L. Smidth & Co. because at that time no expert system tools that could implement fuzzy logic were commercially available. The entire fuzzy system is incorporated into F. L. Smidth's process-monitoring system known as FLS Supervision, Dialog and Reporting System (SDR). SDR is implemented on a Hewlett-Packard Micro 26 A600 in only 256K of memory with no floppy or hard drives. A color display, keyboard, and printer are used to inform the operator and create logs of conditions and actions taken. Before the SDR, Lafarge was controlled by human operators using a Foxboro I computer. Lafarge reports substantial savings in coal consumption and significantly longer brick life in the kiln, which means less down time and greater productivity for the plant. Lafarge is only one of the more than 30 sites using the SDR.

This commercial application of fuzzy systems illustrates several important points. First, in some cases, fuzzy systems can be added to existing control systems with substantial savings on very modest computers. Second, conflicting rules can be fired and rationally resolved. Third, energy is saved, a consistent theme in almost every fuzzy system process control application I've seen. Fourth, very complex control functions can be generated using a few simple rules.

2. *Fuzzy Expert System Tool.* One of the leading companies pursuing the commercialization of fuzzy systems is Togai InfraLogic Inc. (TIL) of Irvine, Calif. In addition to producing TILSHELL, a development tool for fuzzy-based expert systems, the company also manufactures a coprocessing chip for fuzzy interfacing. The following TIL applications are good examples of what can be done with fuzzy reasoning.

3. *Focusing Camcorders.* Anyone who uses a camera or camcorder realizes that it uses some form of autofocusing system. TIL's application sounds like an oxymoron—a fuzzy-focusing system for camcorders. Almost all camcorders use one of two types of focusing systems, the inferred system (IR) or through-the-lens (TTL).

The IR system is very accurate but has two problems: your finger should not cover the system and it is useless for shooting through a glass window. TTL is not very accurate and focuses correctly only 20–30 percent of the time. This degree of accuracy is not acceptable to Canon, a major manufacturer of 8mm camcorder. Enter fuzzy systems.

The fuzzy system uses seven inputs as variables and produces one output, the camcorder focus. The prototype fuzzy system was developed in less than one calendar week; the real work was spent in tuning the class of membership functions for the input variables. This task was done by three domain experts using a trial-and-error method. The output of the fuzzy system was "defuzzyfied" using a centroid method.

The fuzzy system has only 20 rules, some using as many as five predicates. The performance of the fuzzy system is equal to the IR system and three times better than the TTL system; and does not have the drawbacks of either. Canon began shipping the camcorder in June 1990 and expects to sell more than 200,000 units.

4. *Climate Control.* The recent events of Earth Day raised our awareness of conservation, and conservation of energy is a high priority with Mitsubishi Heavy Industries Inc. (MHII). In April 1988, MHII engineers approached Togai with the problem of building-environment control.

Most large office buildings have an environmental control system for heating and cooling. The systems going into new buildings in Japan are generally quite sophisticated in their ability to control building environments. Typically, these systems have sensors in every chamber for room and wall temperature. In addition, the systems can control the rate of heat exchange, fan speed, and the direction of louvers in each room. However, MHII thought that a fuzzy system might do better than their conventional proportional integral differential (PID) method of control.

The TIL system uses 25 rules for heating and 25 rules for cooling. The inputs to the system include items such as room and wall temperature and rate of change in those temperatures. The initial rules were written in just three days, and the domain experts provided the initial class membership functions in one calendar month. The final system needed three more months of tuning to optimize performance. The results were dramatic.

The fuzzy system reduced heating and cooling times by a factor of five, and temperature stability improved by a factor of two; when doors are opened and closed the perceived disturbance in the room environment is reduced. The fuzzy system also requires fewer sensors and, most importantly, reduces the energy consumption of the heating and cooling system by 24 percent.

5. *Other Applications.* Hundreds of fuzzy-system applications are deployed in Japan. For example, the Sendai subway system is a great success. Sanyo is already using a fuzzy-system focusing mechanism in their single-lens reflex camera. Fuzzy systems are also used in a financial application at Yamaichi Securities, which uses a 800-rule fuzzy system to trade stocks on the Nikkei Stock Exchange. (This system is out-performing the exchange by more than 20 percent.) One Japanese manufacturer is using a fuzzy system in conjunction with a video camera and sensory foot pad to help match its golf clubs with the customer's swing to minimize the strokes it takes to get around the golf course.

Fuzzy systems are also finding many consumer applications. Panasonic is using a fuzzy system in a shower-head controller to regulate the water temperature, to prevent scalding as the water temperature and pressure change. The Japanese automotive industry is very active in developing fuzzy systems—almost all of the manufacturers are developing fuzzy automatic breaking systems (ABSs) to prevent skidding during panic stopping and dangerous weather conditions. Two Japanese firms are shipping home-laundry machines with fuzzy controllers. The fuzzy system monitors the temperature, wash-cycle time, detergent concentration, and washing quality. One of the machines uses the murkiness of the wash water as an input to the controller.

6. *Fuzzy Systems in U.S.* The acceptance of fuzziness in the United States lags behind not only the Japanese but the European as well. To date, few users of fuzzy systems are around. One is NASA, at both the Ames Research Center and Johnson Space Center. Engineers at Johnson have used a fuzzy controller in a shuttle-station minding (keeping the shuttle in one place in space) simulation. In the simulation, the fuzzy system reduced shuttle fuel consumption by a factor of three.

Rod Taber, of the Center for Applied Optics at the University of Alabama in Huntsville, is one enthusiastic user of fuzzy systems and neural networks. Taber integrates neural networks and fuzzy systems. His systems, designed with data from Hubbs Marine Research Institute of San Diego, Calif., helps marine biologists identify the dialect of killer whales by using intelligent hydrophones that combine these technologies.

The Future of Fuzzy Systems. I believe that fuzzy logic will become a valuable component in the next generation of computer systems. In such systems, each of the central technology building blocks can be used in series or in parallel.

For example, the neural networks could be used to identify classes of membership for the fuzzy system. Neural networks could be used for rule discovery in large databases with the rules fed into the conventional expert system. The output of the "defuzzyfied" fuzzy system could be used as an input to an expert system, and the output in a decision-making process such as speech recognition.

All of these components exist, and very difficult problems use some if not all of them. The components don't compete, they complement. As you approach real-world problems, remember that if the only tool you have is a hammer, all your problems look like nails.

Condensed from "Fuzzy Systems in the Real World," by Tom J. Schwartz, *AI Expert*, August 1990, pp. 29–36, reprinted with permission from *AI Expert*.

11.4.1   Fuzzy Set Theory

In set theory, which is called *crisp* as opposed to fuzzy, an element either belongs to a set or not. In *fuzzy set theory*, the membership of elements in a set is not in the form of yes or no. The elements have membership values that show the strength of their membership in a set. Take the set representing **adequate income**. An applicant with an income of $40,000 ($40K$) and above belongs to this set with the membership of 1. However, an applicant with $35K$ income belongs to this set with the membership value of .75. An element of a set is denoted by a pair of $<$ *its membership value/its value* $>$, as:

$$adequate\ income = \{0/10K, .125/20K, .50/30K, .75/35K, 1/40K\}.$$

The membership could be shown as the list of values, or in the form of a function. For example, if we plot the values of income against the membership values, we get an S-shape function, shown in Figure 11.4a. The membership value of x is denoted by μ_x, and Γ denotes the membership function.

a. S–shaped membership function (Π)

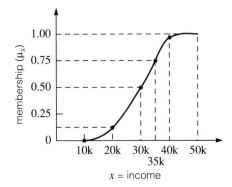

b. Bell–shaped membership function (Π)

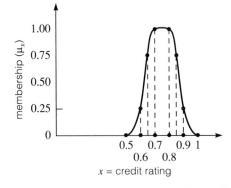

Figure 11.4 Membership Functions in Fuzzy Set Theory

The membership function could have a bell-shaped curve. For example, assume that credit ratings are categorized as .91–1 as excellent, .81–.90 as very good, and .71–.80 as good. The set good could have the following elements:

$$good = \{0/.50, .125/.60, .75/.65, 1/.71, 1/.80, .75/.85, .125/.90, 0/1\}.$$

Figure 11.4b is the plot of the membership function for this set.

Fuzzy set theory utilizes the logical operators ¬ (NOT), ∧ (AND), and ∨ (OR). The complement of a set has $1 - \mu_x$ as the membership value of the element x in the set. For example, the ¬ or the complement of the adequate income set is

$$\neg adequate\ income = \{1/10K, .875/20K, .50/30K, .25/35K, 0/40K\}.$$

Note that any element, such as an income of $35K$, could be a member of both an adequate income and not adequate income sets, because it has nonzero membership value in both sets. Since its membership value in the first set is .75, as opposed to .25 in the second set, then $35K$ is more of an adequate income than not. Thus, the fuzzy set theory codifies the way we normally address vague concepts, such as adequacy.

The AND operator (the conjunction or the intersection) chooses the minimum membership values for the common elements in the two sets. For example, assume we have the set low income as

$$low\ income = \{1/0K, .95/10K, .90/20K, .30/30K, .10/40K\}.$$

The intersection of the two sets ¬adequate income and low income is

$$low\ income \wedge \neg adequate\ income =$$
$$\{1/0K, .95/10K, .875/20K, .30/30K, 0/40K\}.$$

The OR (union or disjunction) of the two sets has the combined elements of the two sets, each with a membership value equal to the maximum of two membership values. That is

$$\mu_{x\varepsilon set1 \vee set2} = \max[\mu_{x\varepsilon set1}, \mu_{x\varepsilon set2}].$$

For example,

$$low\ income \vee \neg adequate\ income =$$
$$\{1/0K, 1/10K, .90/20K, .50/30K, .25/35K, .10/40K\},$$

where, again, the elements with zero memberships are omitted from the set.

In fuzzy set theory, there are a number of operators that do not exist in the classical (or crisp) set theory. For example, one can *concentrate* or *dilate* the set to represent modifiers such as very or quite for concentration and somewhat or approximately for dilation. To represent concentration of a set, it is enough to raise the membership values to the power 2, and for dilation, to the power 0.5. For example, a set of very adequate income is

$$CON(\textit{adequate income}) = \{.016/20K, .25/30K, .56/35K, 1/40K, 1/50K\},$$

where the membership values of the set adequate income are raised to the second power. The set representing somewhat adequate income is the following dilation:

$$DIL(\textit{adequate income}) = \{.35/20K, .71/30K, .87/35K, 1/40K, 1/50K\},$$

which consists of the elements of the set adequate income with the membership values raised to power 0.5. There are many more set operations in the fuzzy set theory than covered here. (For additional linguistic modifiers, see, for example, Zimmermann 1987, Chapter 7, or Giarratano and Riley 1989, Chapter 5.)

11.4.2 Fuzzy Logic (Optional)

Fuzzy logic is a method for approximate reasoning, when the propositions are inexact and vague. In fuzzy logic, the truth value of a proposition falls in the interval between 0 and 1. The propositions are specified in terms of their membership to the sets called true and false. For example, the proposition that the applicant has adequate income could have the membership value or the *truth value* of .80 in the true set, and a membership value of .20 in the false set. We can have a set called somewhat true, whose membership values are the dilation of the set true. In this case, the membership value of the above proposition is .89 in the set somewhat true.

The Operators in Fuzzy Logic

From the set operators, we can easily establish that for propositions A and B with the truth values $\mu(A)$ and $\mu(B)$, the following holds:

$$\mu(\neg A) = 1 - \mu(A)$$

$$\mu(A \wedge B) = \min[\mu(A), \mu(B)]$$

$$\mu(A \vee B) = \max[\mu(A), \mu(B)]$$

$$\mu(A \rightarrow B) = \mu(\neg A \vee B) = \max[(1 - \mu(A)), \mu(B)]$$

where the $A \rightarrow B = \neg A \vee B$ has the same meaning as that in the mathematical logic discussed in Chapter 3. Note that fuzzy logic contains an inherent structure to deal with the ambiguity in the intra-rule structure.

For example, consider the rule

```
IF  the applicant has adequate income
   AND the applicant has a steady job
THEN approve the loan
```

Assume that the user gives the "truth" membership values of .90 and .80 to the two conditions of the antecedent. Because of the AND operator, the antecedent has the membership value of min[.90, .80] = .80. Hence, the hypothesis or the consequent of **approve the loan** has the truth value of .80.

If more than one hypothesis is formed, the one with the maximum value for the truth value would be chosen, based on the interpretation that the disjunction or the union of these hypotheses is of interest. This is the consequence of the compositional rule of inference, which will be discussed in the next subsection.

The consequent may have a truth value other than 1, due to the expert's doubt in the applicability of the rule. Assuming that the consequent has the truth value of .95, then the conclusion of **approve the loan** has a truth value equal to min[.80, .95] = .80. The argument for this conclusion is that the truth value of the conclusion could not be stronger than the evidence leading to the conclusion. Note that this is not the direct consequence of the theory. A more structured method of dealing with the ambiguity in the rule itself is discussed in the next subsection.

One of the direct and useful consequences of the theory is the truth value of the rule itself. In the above example, the rule itself has a truth value of max[1 − .80, .95] = .95. This is the direct result of applying the fourth operation above. The membership value of the rule could be used as a criterion for rule selection by the inference engine.

Reasoning in Fuzzy Logic

In two-value logic, we had two quantifiers: "for all" or $\forall$ and "there exists one or more" or $\exists$. Fuzzy logic deals with many *inexact quantifiers* such as **approximately, more or less, little, a lot, many** and so forth. In the two-value logic, when we have the predicate **adequate income(x)**, the result is either true or false. In fuzzy logic, the fuzzy predicate (called *relation* or *fuzzy restriction*) has an accompanying membership function, such as

$$adequate\ income(x) = \{.125/20K, .50/30K, .75/35K, 1/40K\}.$$

The predicate could have two parameters, such as approximately equal income(x,y). In this case, the truth value of the predicate is expressed in the form of a matrix or a table as:

$$approximately\ equal\ income = \begin{array}{c} \\ 20K \\ 30K \\ 35K \\ 40K \end{array} \begin{array}{cccc} 20K & 30K & 35K & 40K \\ \begin{pmatrix} 1 & .50 & 0 & 0 \\ .50 & 1 & .70 & .10 \\ 0 & .70 & 1 & .80 \\ 0 & .10 & .80 & 1 \end{pmatrix} \end{array}$$

Now, we can combine the predicates with inexact quantifiers into a new predicate as:

$$approximately\ adequate\ income(y) =$$

$$adequate\ income(x)\ o\ approximately\ equal\ income(x, y)$$

where o denotes the compositional operator. The truth values of the predicate approximately adequate income(y) is computed in the following manner.

- Set up the truth values of the two predicates in the form of a matrix multiplication:

$$(.125 \quad .50 \quad .75 \quad 1) \begin{pmatrix} 1 & .50 & 0 & 0 \\ .50 & 1 & .70 & .10 \\ 0 & .70 & 1 & .80 \\ 0 & .10 & .80 & 1 \end{pmatrix}$$

- Take the row vector (the one-row table) and match pairwise with one column of the matrix (the two-dimensional table). This match for the row and first column is

$$\{(.125, 1), (.50, .50), (.75, 0), (1, 0) \}.$$

- Choose the minimum of each pair. For the above example, this results in

$$\{.125, .50, 0, 0\}.$$

- Choose the maximum of the numbers. For this example, the maximum is .50. This is the truth value of $20K$ for the predicate approximately adequate income.

- Repeat steps 1–4 using the second column to get $.70/30K$. Repeat 1–4 using the third column to get $.80/35K$. Repeat 1–4 using the last column to get $1/40K$.

Thus, the *max-min-composition* results in the truth values for the combined predicate as

$$approximately\ adequate\ income(y) = \{.50/20K, .70/30K, .80/35K, 1/40K\}.$$

Now we can express a rule with the fuzzy quantifier as:

```
IF   x is an adequate income
   AND  y is an approximately equal income as x
THEN  y is approximately adequate income
```

or

$$adequate\ income(x) \wedge approximately\ equal\ income(x, y)$$

$$\rightarrow approximately\ adequate\ income(y)$$

Assume that the user enters \$35,000 as the applicant's income. This rule concludes that the applicant's income is approximately adequate with the truth value of .80. One can even dilate this result by taking the square root of .80, and conclude that the applicant's income is **somewhat** approximately adequate income with the truth value of .89. Alternatively, we can concentrate this conclusion by taking the second power of the truth value, and conclude that the applicant's income is an approximately **close** to adequate income, with the truth value of .64. Here, **somewhat** and **close** are called the *linguistic modifiers*.

Multiple Inference in Fuzzy Logic

As discussed in Chapter 4, multiple inference is the process of combining more than one rule to arrive at a conclusion. The rules of inference, such as modus ponens, syllogism, and modus tollens have fuzzy logic counterparts. The question is how the truth values move from one rule to another. In the case of forward or backward chaining, the truth value of a proposition travels with it through the multiple inference.

If a hypothesis is formed using different rules with different truth values, what should be the truth value of the hypothesis? Or, could there be a number of hypotheses that form the final hypothesis of the system? In such cases, the max-min-compositional inference dictates that the maximum of the truth values should be chosen. This is called the *maximum* criterion.

Combining inexact quantifiers in multiple inference could become complicated. For example, assume we have **many** in the antecedent of one rule, and **some** in the antecedent of another rule. What is the resulting quantifier when the two rules are chained? This is one of the many advanced features of fuzzy logic that are beyond the scope of this introductory discussion. (See Zadeh [1983, 1985] for a thorough coverage of the advanced topics.)

11.5 Possibility Theory (Optional)

In *possibility theory*, the possibility of a hypothesis is the degree to which the decision maker considers the hypothesis to be feasible, or simply possible. Possibility is quite different from probability, in that the probability shows the frequency of a hypothesis or the strength of belief in its occurrence. *Possibility*, on the other hand, is the extent of feasibility of the hypothesis, even though it has not yet occurred in reality. Possibility values vary between 0 and 1.

The *necessity* of a hypothesis is defined as one minus the possibility of its negation. For example, assume that the possibility of **a good credit rating** is .95, and the possibility of **not a good credit rating** is .3. The necessity of **a good credit rating** is $1 - .3 = .7$. A tautology (as defined in Chapter 3) has the possibility of 1 and the necessity of 1. A contradiction has the possibility of 0, and the necessity of 0.

The possibility measure does not require that the possibility values for a given universe add up to 1. The only requirement is that the possibility value must be between 0 and 1.

Possibility theory covers a vast area and has counterparts in many methods of approximate reasoning. For example, the possibility has an interpretation similar to the theory of evidence. We can have the evidential interval for possibility, with the necessity measure at its lower end and possibility at its upper limit. To make this point simple, assume that we denote necessity as Bel and possibility as Pls, then the evidential interval is $[Bel(h), Pls(h)]$ for the hypothesis h. Now, assume we have h_1 and h_2 with the intervals $[Bel(h_1), Pls(h_1)]$ and $[Bel(h_2), Pls(h_2)]$. Then we have

$$Bel(h_1 \wedge h_2) = \min[Bel(h_1), Bel(h_2)]$$

$$Pls(h_1 \vee h_2) = \max[Pls(h_1), Bel(h_2)],$$

which provides a method for combining belief values. (For further details of the connection between the possibility measure and other methods, see Klir and Folger [1988, Chapter 4].)

In possibility theory, one can specify a *possibility distribution* for uncertain values. It has the look of a membership function, but is interpreted as the possibility of an uncertain event or hypothesis, rather than the grade of membership to a set.

A rule in fuzzy logic has the general form or *canonical form* as:

IF e is F with $Poss(e)$
THEN h is G with $Poss(h)$,

where $Poss(e)$ is the possibility distribution that e takes the values in F. Similarly, $Poss(h)$ is the possibility distribution that the h takes the values in G.

The following is an example of the above general form:

```
IF    credit reports are mostly positive with Poss(e)
THEN  the credit rating is G with Poss(h)
```

where e=credit reports, F=mostly positive, h=the credit rating, and G={bad, fair, good, very good, excellent}. The possibility distributions are:

$$Poss(e) = \{.5/3, .9/4, 1/5, 1/6\}$$

and

$$Poss(h) = \{.1/bad, .4/fair, .90/good, 1/very\ good, 1/excellent\}.$$

In the case of e, credit reports, the possibility distribution reflects the possibility of considering 3, 4, 5, and 6 positive reports as mostly positive.

The conditional possibility is defined as:

$$Poss(h = u | e = v) = 1 \wedge (1 - \mu_F(u) + \mu_G(v)),$$

for all values of u in the set F and v in the set G. For example,

$$Poss(h = bad | e = 3) = 1 \wedge (1 - .5 + .1) = \min(1, 1.5) = 1.$$

Thus, the conditional possibility for the above rule is:

	bad	fair	good	very good	excellent
3	1∧(1+.1-.5)	1∧(1+.4-.5)	1∧(1+.9-.5)	1∧(1+1-.5)	1∧(1+1-.5)
4	1∧(1+.1-.9)	1∧(1+.4-.9)	1∧(1+.9-.9)	1∧(1+1-.9)	1∧(1+1-.9)
5	1∧(1+.1-1)	1∧(1+.4-1)	1∧(1+.9-1)	1∧(1+1-1)	1∧(1+1-1)
6	1∧(1+.1-1)	1∧(1+.4-1)	1∧(1+.9-1)	1∧(1+1-1)	1∧(1+1-1)

The final table for the combination of the fuzzy quantifier and the possibility values is in the form of:

	bad	fair	good	very good	excellent
3	.6	.9	1	1	1
4	.2	.5	1	1	1
5	.1	.4	.9	1	1
6	.1	.4	.9	1	1

Depending on how many reports are positive, the system decides the possibility of the outcome from this table. For example, if the applicant has four positive reports, there is a possibility of 1 that the credit rating is **good** or better.

The number of positive reports for the case of an applicant, say, **smith** could be uncertain, because of the vagueness of the reports. Therefore, an uncertain or fuzzy fact may have a possibility distribution or a membership function. This could be combined with the conditional possibility distribution, using the max-min-composition, described in the previous section. In sum, the possibility distributions within the fuzzy rule are combined to get the conditional possibilities. Then, the conditional possibilities are combined with the possibility distribution of the observed fact (using the max-min-composition method) to make an inference based on the fuzzy rule and the imprecise fact. Thus, one can model both uncertainty and ambiguity by combining fuzzy logic with the theory of possibility.

11.6 Mixed Approaches

Some expert systems have used a mix of theories to manage the uncertainty in the expert system. Such approaches could produce unpredictable and unrealistic outcomes. It would be much safer to choose one method and use it consistently, because there is more information about the advantages and disadvantages of each theory than the ad hoc combination of theories. Here, we briefly review the well-known methods of mixed approaches.

11.6.1   Certainty Factors (Optional)

In developing MYCIN, Shortliffe and Buchanan developed the concept of *certainty factors* [1975]. They observed the necessity of updating beliefs with partial evidence and criticized the extensive requirements of the frequentist approach to probability theory and the requirement that the hypothesis could be revised even when evidence is lacking, in the form of

$$p(h|\neg e) = 1 - p(h|e).$$

They developed the certainty factors method for MYCIN. In this approach, the system has measures for belief and disbelief. A new piece of evidence changes the measure of belief and the measure of disbelief, according to the following formula:

$$MB(h|e) = \begin{cases} 1 & \text{if } p(h) = 1 \\ \frac{\max[p(h|e),p(h)]-p(h)}{\max[1,0]-p(h)} & \text{otherwise} \end{cases}$$

$$MD(h|e) = \begin{cases} 1 & \text{if } p(h) = 0 \\ \frac{\min[p(h|e),p(h)]-p(h)}{\min[1,0]-p(h)} & \text{otherwise,} \end{cases}$$

and the certainty factor is computed as

$$CF(h|e) = MB(h|e) - MD(h|e).$$

The certainty factor ranges from -1 to 1. A negative certainty factor means that the evidence does not support the hypothesis.

For example, the expert believes that 70 percent of those who apply for a loan have good credit ratings, $p(h) = .70$. After receiving positive reports from an applicant's banks, this ratio increases to, say, .95. Then,

$$MB(h|e) = \frac{\max[.95, .70] - .70}{1 - .70} = .83$$

$$MD(h|e) = \frac{\min[.95, .70] - .70}{0 - .70} = 0$$

$$CF(h|e) = .83 - 0 = .83,$$

where $MB(h|e)$ measures the increase in the expert's belief after observing the evidence of positive bank reports for an applicant, and $MD(h|e)$ measures the decrease in the expert's belief given the bank reports.

For combining rules and evidence, Shortliffe and Buchanan suggest the following:

- When two hypotheses are in the form of a conjunction (AND or ∧), one should choose the minimum values for the two MB. The MD value of the joint hypotheses would be the minimum of the two MD values, as well. That is,

$$MB(h_1 \wedge h_2|e) = \min[MB(h_1|e), MB(h_2|e)]$$

$$MD(h_1 \wedge h_2|e) = \min[MD(h_1|e), MD(h_2|e)].$$

- When the two hypotheses are in the form of the disjunction (OR or ∨), the min in the above formula is changed to max.

- When the evidence itself is uncertain, the certainty factor of the uncertain evidence ($\tilde{e}$) and the measure of the belief and disbelief in the rule (when the evidence is certain) are multiplied in the following form:

$$MB(h|\tilde{e}) = MB(h|e) \; . \; \max[0, CF(\tilde{e})]$$

$$MD(h|\tilde{e}) = MD(h|e) \; . \; \max[0, CF(\tilde{e})].$$

When the evidence for the same hypothesis is incrementally acquired, the measures are updated according to the following:

$$MB(h|e_1 \wedge e_2) = \begin{cases} 0 & if \; MD(h|e_1 \wedge e_2) = 1 \\ MB((h|e_1) + MB(h|e_2)(1 - MB(h|e_1)) & otherwise \end{cases}$$

$$MD(h|e_1 \wedge e_2) = \begin{cases} 0 & if \; MB(h|e_1 \wedge e_2) = 1 \\ MD((h|e_1) + MD(h|e_2)(1 - MD(h|e_1)) & otherwise. \end{cases}$$

The combination rules of the certainty factor are mostly ad hoc, and have little theoretical underpinnings. The disjunction and conjunction of hypotheses by using max and min is similar to the operations in fuzzy sets and fuzzy logic.

The certainty factors are successfully used in MYCIN, and are simple to compute. The problem with this approach is that it is an ad hoc approach, which may result in unexpected or unacceptable conclusions. For example, assume that we have the following belief values from the expert:

$$p(h_1) = .90 \quad p(h_1|e) = .95$$

$$p(h_2) = .10 \quad p(h_2|e) = .70.$$

Using the formula for the measures of belief and disbelief, the certainty factors for the first and second hypotheses are

$$CF(h_1|e) = .50$$

$$CF(h_2|e) = .86,$$

which is an unexpected result, because the certainty factor of h_1 is far below h_2, while the probabilities of h_1 are far higher than those of h_2 before and after observing the evidence e.

11.6.2   *Mixed Applications of Uncertainty Methods (Optional)*

As was mentioned in the previous subsection, MYCIN is among the early, successful applications in which mixed uncertainty theories were applied. Another successful application is PROSPECTOR. This system uses the Bayesian approach for updating probabilities, and represents its rules in the form of a belief network. For an inter-rule probability update, this system uses the min and max operators of fuzzy set theory. In this system, too, the treatment of uncertainty is an ad hoc mix of uncertainty methods. PROSPECTOR has a successful track record in geological decision-making. However, its ad hoc nature of treatment of uncertainty may produce unacceptable outcomes in other applications.

One of the reasons for mixing the probability approach with the fuzzy set operators is that the multiplication of probabilities drastically reduces the probability of the outcome. Taking the minimum of the two probabilities yields a higher probability value for the outcome. On the other hand, combining probabilities using the union operation gives a higher result than taking the maximum of the two probabilities. Some have suggested using the average of the two operations. The Bonczek-Eagan method [Holsapple and Whinston 1987, Chapter 10] also produces outcomes similar to taking the average of the two methods. In the Bonczek-Eagan method, the conjunction (intersection) is computed as

$$\frac{x.y}{100}(2 - \frac{\max[x, y]}{100}),$$

and the disjunction (union) is computed as

$$\max[x, y] + \frac{x.y}{100}(1 - \frac{\max[x, y]}{100}),$$

where x and y represent $p(h_1)$ and $p(h_2)$, respectively, expressed in the 0 to 100 interval.

This *mixed approach* is one of the methods available for modeling uncertainty in Guru, an expert system software product.

The danger here is that the use of methods without a theoretical structure may produce unexpected or erroneous outcomes, and damage the integrity of the knowledge base in a hidden and unpredictable manner.

11.7 Uncertainty Structure as the Critical Factor

This chapter introduced only some of the best-known approaches to address uncertainty in expert systems. There are other methods for modeling uncertainty. One such method is *multi-valued crisp logic*, where the logic is crisp, but there are multiple truth values. Another approach is the *truth maintenance system*, in which the reasoning is *non-monotonic*. In monotonic reasoning, the system moves from one rule to another; once the truth of a rule is established, it remains unchanged in the process of reasoning. In truth maintenance systems, the system chooses the best assumption with uncertain knowledge, and proceeds through reasoning until it encounters contradictory or impossible results or changes in facts. In such cases, the system withdraws the assumption and the results obtained from it, and selects another assumption to follow [deKleer 1986].

From the wealth and diversity of the methods for managing uncertainty in expert systems, it is clear that no consensus exists about various methods, and no one method addresses all issues in the management of uncertainty in expert systems. Indeed, this area is under active research at present, dealing with unanswered questions, such as:

- How can we reconcile the deterministic nature of rule-based systems with the methods of managing uncertainty?

- What are the criteria for judging the suitability of a method for various types of expert system applications or domains?

- What are the salient features of each method?

- What is the best representation method for each method?

- How should we treat uncertainty in expert systems software in order to give the developers and users the most flexibility in design, without forgoing the integrity of the reasoning and outcomes?

One emerging concept is the serious attention to structure as opposed to numbers in modeling uncertainty in expert systems. Shafer and Pearl [1990, Chapter 1] point out that in addressing the uncertainty aspect of an expert system, two factors are of critical importance. The design of *uncertainty structure* (such as the belief network) and understanding of the interrelations of the structure's components prior to selecting a method could both contribute greatly in preserving the integrity of the system. The knowledge engineering and knowledge modeling methods for the design of the uncertainty structure have yet to be developed.

Conclusion

In the theoretical development of knowledge representation and reasoning, we assumed complete certainty in every step. This means that the domain knowledge is certain and clear, the expert applies his or her expertise with full certainty, the knowledge engineer can elicit and formalize knowledge with no error, and the user can express the facts regarding a particular case with certainty. Such assumptions do not hold in reality.

In this chapter, we reviewed the sources of uncertainty in expert systems, and identified the areas and impacts of uncertainty in the single- and multiple-inference processes of expert systems.

Since mathematical logic lacks an uncertainty component, to make the system a more representative model of the real world, the uncertainty within the domain should be molded into the knowledge base using other formalisms or theories. We reviewed a number of these theories, including probability-based methods, Dempster-Shafer theory of evidence, fuzzy logic, possibility theory, and mixed approaches. Although each method has its proponents, no clear consensus exists in the choice of the best method, and no method provides answers to all issues in the management of uncertainty in expert systems.

Since the incorporation of uncertainty in expert systems is an unresolved issue, there are expert system software products that either do not have an uncertainty component, or offer the developer complete control over how to deal with uncertainty within the system. This results in a systems design that either lacks the important uncertainty component or deals with uncertainty in an ad hoc and haphazard manner. Both of these alternatives damage the integrity of the knowledge base and produce unexpected and erroneous results. Therefore, an understanding of uncertainty models with a theoretical underpinning is of great importance in designing real-world expert systems. We reviewed a number of uncertainty models in this chapter.

References

deKleer, J. 1986. "An Assumption-based Truth Maintenance System," *Artificial Intelligence*, Vol. 28, pp. 127–162.

Dempster, A. P. 1967. "Upper and Lower Probabilities Induced by Multivalued Mappings," *Annals of Mathematical Statistics*, Vol. 38, pp. 325–329.

Giarratano, Joseph and Riley, Gary. 1989. *Expert Systems: Principles and Programming*, PWS-KENT Publishing Co., Boston, MA.

Holsapple, C. W. and Whinston, A. B. 1987. *Business Expert Systems*, Richard D. Irwin, Inc. Homewood, IL.

Klir, George J. and Folger, Tina A. 1988. *Fuzzy Sets, Uncertainty, and Information*, Prentice Hall, Englewood Cliffs, NJ.

Pearl, Judea. 1986. "On Evidential Reasoning in a Hierarchy of Hypotheses," *Artificial Intelligence*, Vol. 28, pp. 9–15.

Pearl, Judea. 1988. *Probabilistic Reasoning in Intelligent Systems*, Morgan Kaufmann, Los Altos, CA.

Shafer, Glenn. 1976. *A Mathematical Theory of Evidence*, Princeton University Press, Princeton, NJ.

Shafer, Glenn and Pearl, Judea. 1990. *Readings in Uncertain Reasoning*, Morgan Kaufmann Publishers, San Mateo, CA.

Shortliffe, E. H. and Buchanan, B. G. 1975. "A Method of Inexact Reasoning," *Mathematical Biosciences*, Vol. 23, pp. 351–379, reprinted in edited form in *Readings in Uncertain Reasoning*, G. Shafer and J. Pearl (eds.), 1990, Morgan Kaufmann Publishers, San Mateo, CA, pp. 255–273.

Zadeh, L. A. 1965. "Fuzzy Sets," *Information and Control*, Vol. 8, pp. 338–353.

Zadeh, L. A. 1975. "Fuzzy Logic and Approximate Reasoning," *Synthese*, Vol. 30, pp. 407–428.

Zadeh, L. A. 1983. "The Role of Fuzzy Logic in the Management of Uncertainty in Expert Systems," *Fuzzy Sets and Systems*, Vol. 11, pp. 199–227.

Zadeh, L. A. 1985. "Syllogistic Reasoning in Fuzzy Logic and its Application to Usuality and Reasoning with Dispositions," *IEEE Transactions on Systems, Man, and Cybernetics*, Vol. 15, pp. 149–194.

Zimmermann, Hans J. 1987. *Fuzzy Sets, Decision Making, and Expert Systems*, Kluwer Academic Publishers, Boston, MA.

Questions

11.1 What are the sources of uncertainty?

11.2 What is the difference between single inference with uncertainty and multiple inference with uncertainty?

11.3 What are the differences between the frequentist and subjective interpretation of probability? What is the significance of such differences in expert systems?

11.4 What is conditional independence? What is its relevance to expert systems?

11.5 What is the difference between the prior and posterior probabilities? Give an example of a case in an expert system where both are used.

11.6 What are the evidence and hypothesis components in a rule? What is the justification for using such terms in reasoning with uncertainty?

11.7 What is the difference between Pearl's method and the Bayesian approach? What are their advantages and disadvantages?

11.8 What is modularity in reasoning with uncertainty? Is modularity a desirable aspect of an uncertainty method? Why?

11.9 What are the differences and similarities of the probability methods and the Dempster–Shafer theory of evidence?

11.10 What is an evidential interval, and what is its use in expert systems?

11.11 What is the difference between fuzzy and crisp sets?

11.12 What are the operations in fuzzy set theory? Give an example for each. Which of the operators are unique to fuzzy set theory?

11.13 Describe the max-min-composition operation.

11.14 What is possibility theory, and what is its difference from probability theory?

11.15 Discuss how one uses possibility theory and fuzzy logic to model the error and ambiguity aspects of uncertainty in expert systems.

11.16 Discuss the issues in mixing uncertainty methods to reason with uncertainty.

11.17 What is the significance of uncertainty structure in expert systems? Discuss its importance in the knowledge acquisition and design of the system.

Problems

11.1 Give an example for each source of uncertainty.

11.2 Give an example of a rule with uncertain components.

11.3 Give an example of a belief net, and identify the input probabilities that are needed for the belief net.

11.4 In Figure 11.3, change the prior probability values to $p(h_1) = .50$ and $p(h_2) = .50$, and recompute the probability of h_1 given the pieces of evidence e_1 and e_2. What is the direction of change? Is the posterior probability of h_1 sensitive to the evidence?

11.5 Give an intuitive interpretation for the plausibility measure.

11.6 In the example of Section 11.3, assume that

$$m_2(\{x\}) = .60$$

$$m_2(\{v, g\}) = .20$$

$$m_2(\{\theta\}) = .20$$

and recompute the evidential intervals for the sets that are the focal element.

11.7 What is the difference between fuzzy logic and two-value logic? Why is fuzzy logic important in expert systems? Give an example that illustrates the difference.

11.8 Give an example of reasoning in fuzzy logic.

11.9 Change the membership function of **adequate income** in Section 11.4.1. to the following

$$\{.05/20K, .20/30K, .60/35K, 1/40K\}$$

and recompute the membership function for **approximately adequate income**. Discuss the impact of this change in the computed membership function.

Case Questions

The following questions refer to the case box: "Applications of Fuzzy Systems."

1. Review the applications of fuzzy systems and characterize the type of applications reported in this case.

2. Discuss possible applications of fuzzy systems in management decision making.

3. Discuss the advantages and disadvantages of using fuzzy systems for decision making.

4. Discuss possible reasons why the U.S. companies lag behind the Japanese and Europeans in the applications of fuzzy systems.

5. If a part of your expert system has a fuzzy nature, how would you integrate a fuzzy system with an expert system?

6. Describe the features of an ideal expert system in which the uncertainty and fuzziness of the domain knowledge and experts are formally accounted for.

CHAPTER 12

Software Evaluation in Expert Systems

"Your face is the same as everybody has—the two eyes, so ... nose in the middle, mouth under. It's always the same. Now, if you had two eyes on the same side of the nose, for instance—or the mouth at the top—that would be some help."

Lewis Carroll

Chapter Objectives

The objectives of this chapter are:

- To discuss the issues involved in selecting the software product for creating an expert system application

- To present a structured approach for decomposing various aspects of the expert system software products

- To show the method of rating various parts of expert system software

- To demonstrate how to rank various expert system software products

- To discuss the liability involved in selling and using expert systems

---

KEY WORDS: Software selection, attribute hierarchy, software aspects, functional aspects, components, facilities, primitives, relative importance, simple rating, pairwise comparison, analytical hierarchy process, ranking expert system tools, liability issues

---

Introduction

If we had only one method to create an expert system and only one software tool to use, most sections of this chapter would be unnecessary. That not being the case, we need a structured method to evaluate our priorities for what we expect from an expert system and to rate the many available software products. When an expert system project is small and the system needs are commonplace, we may be able to evaluate our available options informally. However, for large projects with complex requirements, a formal analysis could save the project from many pitfalls down the road.

Section 12.1 justifies why a formal structure is needed to evaluate expert system products, and the following two sections construct a hierarchy for the various features of an expert system tool. Sections 12.4 and 12.5 develop a numerical approach (analytic hierarchy process) for ranking the software products. The final outcome of the process is a numerical rank for each software tool that reflects its ability to satisfy the requirements of the expert system project.

The last section of this chapter discusses the liability issues as related to expert systems. As expert systems are deployed in various fields and functions of business, the legal repercussions of their improper development and deployment will become more consequential. The awareness and sensitivity to these issues may save the developer, expert, distributor, and user of an expert system a great deal of legal expenses and headaches.

12.1 Software Evaluation Issues in Expert Systems

As we have seen in Chapters 3, 4, 8, and 11, there are a number of methods for knowledge representation, inference, and the treatment of uncertainty in expert systems. In addition to the theoretical diversity of methods, there are a number of practical facets that increase the complexity of expert system tools.

With expert system technology maturing as a cost-effective tool for decision making, the complexity and variety of applications increase. This growth creates demands for more flexible features that allow a developer to custom-design the expert system to fit the requirements of a particular decision problem. However, the technical flexibility and variety must not translate to technical complexity, because a product that requires a lengthy learning period would make the project too costly to develop. Moreover, with microcomputers as the most common hardware in business offices, any widespread use of expert systems must work on microcomputers. The widespread use of expert systems requires that the system development be affordable, and work in conjunction with other information systems within the organization. Thus, on the demand side of expert system tools, developers need powerful, flexible, easy-to-program, easy-to-use, affordable products that run on small machines and communicate with other business systems.

On the supply side of expert system tools, the producers of such tools jockey for technical leadership in a market that has begun to stabilize. In a state-of-the-art technology such as expert system tools, technical leadership translates to high market share and standard-setting for the industry. This phenomenon has occurred in almost all areas of computer-related fields, from the dominance of IBM in mainframes in the early days of the computer industry, to Lotus 1-2-3 and dBASE leadership in spreadsheets and database management systems for micro computers, and the de facto standard of SQL for database query language. It is only natural for expert system tool producers to try hard to achieve an early technical leadership in the market.

That is why the producers of expert system tools actively modify and enhance their products to incorporate the technical and financial requirements of the developers. The increasing power of microcomputers has eliminated the major hardware constraints on increasing the capability of expert system tools.

The trend in expert system tools is toward more powerful knowledge management, which includes a greater flexibility and ease in creating custom-designed user interfaces with unique features. The producers also offer flexibility for the choice of knowledge representation and inference. A number of tools have an embedded programming language of their own. Such a language gives a developer the freedom of programming functions common to conventional programs, and includes them in the expert system. The recent versions of these tools offer a greater capability for outside connections to other systems and languages. The micro tools increasingly have features that used to be available exclusively in expensive products running on large machines.

With this growth in the technical capability of expert system tools, the selection of the appropriate tool for an application is not limited to an investigation of a small number of software features. Many applications do not need all the features of a tool. At the same time, some features could be crucial to the success of an application. In sum, the selection of the expert system tool appropriate for an application is not a simple choice. It is a decision problem of its own.

12.1.1   *The Selection Problem*

Evaluating expert system products is a complex decision problem for the following reasons:

- The recency of products, and the lack of standards

- The evolving nature of products

- The variety of products

The expert system concepts and the related product lines are relatively new. As we have seen in Chapter 9, the functionality of expert system software is still evolving. Hence, although there are some common features among the products, there is no standard—not even a well-accepted list of functions that an expert system software product should contain. Thus, there is no *typical* product or market leader whose product would be considered the de facto standard. In selecting the software for a project, the developer may have to compare dissimilar products. This makes the *software selection* difficult.

Furthermore, new conceptual components are still being introduced, and components that are in place are continuously being modified and enhanced. Therefore, the components or functions that are considered optional, esoteric, or experimental could become essential in a relatively short time.

The variety and number of products on the market have grown with impressive speed. There are now numerous products on the market, with prices ranging from less than $100 to $100,000. An expensive product does not necessarily mean a better product. For the same price, a newer product or version may have more capabilities than the old one.

12.1.2   *The Common Approach to Choice*

Obviously, expert system software products have multiple attributes, and any comparison of these products must be based on all of these attributes. The problem is that the expert system products have many functions, which make the comparison difficult, though not impossible.

The common practice in a comparative reporting of expert system products is to select a few seemingly important or complicated functions within the products, and compare the products based on them. This approach has several shortcomings:

- It is evaluator-specific and unreliable

- No product could be judged by only a few attributes

- It excludes the relevant issues in a particular application

- It lacks an evaluation measure, reflecting the strength of a product or its rating compared with its competitors

There is no consensus on what attributes of products form the salient features of expert system products. Hence, in evaluating and reporting the comparative analysis of such products, the selection of attributes depends on the background and preferences of the evaluator. If the evaluator does not consider an attribute important, or lacks information or knowledge about it, that attribute would be excluded from the analysis. Thus, the review reports of products are insufficient for the software selection.

Furthermore, as the complexity and sophistication of expert systems products increase, it becomes impossible to summarize their capabilities into just a few attributes. A careful software selection requires considering all attributes and capabilities of these products.

Even when the evaluator is well-known in the field and takes into account numerous attributes of software products, the analysis does not include the importance or relevance of attributes for particular applications. For example, in the mortgage loan expert system, it may be important for the project to use a software product that can take voice-activated input, while in many other projects, this attribute may be irrelevant. Thus, in the real-world applications of expert systems, the logical design of the system should decide which attributes of tools are important. The published technical reviews could hardly take into account all project-specific needs of customers.

It is obvious that an ad hoc and unstructured approach to software selection does not produce the best choice for a given project.

12.1.3   A Structured Approach

From the discussion in the previous section, one can establish a number of requirements for a software evaluation method. Such a method must:

- Contain all of the important features of expert system products

- Make it possible to compare different types of products

- Accommodate the special needs and requirements of the expert system project

- Summarize the results of evaluation into a quantitative or qualitative measure of fitness for each product

The first requirement necessitates a model with a structured approach, which includes all attributes of the products. Since the attributes vary in their degree of generality and detail, one needs to organize them in an *attribute hierarchy.*

The second requirement means that the attribute hierarchy must accommodate various types of systems within the same framework.

The third requirement includes the developer of the expert system as the decision maker whose preferences (based on his or her knowledge of the task at hand) decide the relative importance of various attributes within the model.

Finally, the last requirement calls for a decision analysis method, which takes into account the preference of the decision maker (the system developer, in this case), and produces a measure or a rating for each product. This measure reflects the relative fitness of each product in satisfying the requirements of an application project.

Therefore, the structured software evaluation method consists of four steps:

- The identification of the software structure, resulting in the construction of the attribute hierarchy

- The quantification of the relative importance of attributes of expert system tools

- The comparison of the candidate tools based on the attribute hierarchy

- The aggregation of the comparisons into a single measure for each tool, reflecting the relative ratings of candidate tools

12.2 Attribute Hierarchy of Expert System Tools

In setting up the attribute hierarchy of expert systems, we can use a concept similar to the class structure used in object-oriented design (discussed in Chapters 7 and 8). We categorize attributes of products into general groups. Within each group, we identify groups of more specialized subclasses, and

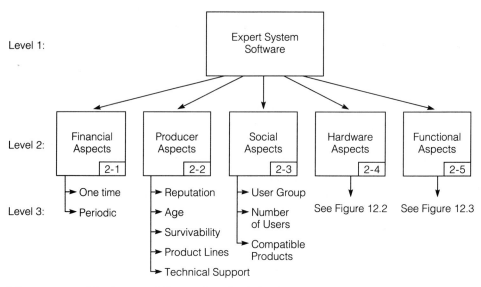

Figure 12.1   The First and Second Levels of the Attribute Hierarchy

continue down the hierarchy. This provides a structured framework for comparing different attributes at different levels of abstraction.*

In expert systems, as in any other type of software, one can identify five groups of attributes, called *software aspects* (Figure 12.1):

- Financial aspects
- Producer aspects
- Social aspects
- Hardware aspects
- Functional aspects

The functional aspects are the most important ones. However, the other aspects may play an important role in some applications as well.

12.2.1   Financial Aspects

As the name indicates, the financial aspects of a product involve any monetary payments to obtain the right of using the product. The financial aspects

---

*Parts of this and the following sections are based on the paper "A Method for Quantitative Evaluation of Expert Systems," by Fatemeh Zahedi, *European Journal of Operational Research*, Vol. 48, No. 1, 1990, pp. 136–147, with permission from the Elsevier Science Publication.

of a software product consist of two subclasses:

- One-time costs

- Periodic costs

The one-time costs include the initial cost of buying the product. The periodic costs involve any costs that occur over an interval of time, such as licensing costs, education costs, and maintenance costs. For products with complex financial deals, this hierarchy could be expanded to accommodate the complexity.

12.2.2   Producer Aspects

The producer aspects of a product are those attributes of the producer that are relevant to the evaluation of the product. Among them are:

- The producer's reputation

- The producer's age

- The producer's probability of survival

- The producer's line of products

- The producer's technical support

The producer's reputation and length of time in business are indicators of the product's quality. When all attributes are the same, a buyer prefers a product with a reputation for quality over its unknown rivals. The survival of the producer is important for maintenance, future expansion, and continuation of the technical support for the product. Using the product of a defunct producer leaves the buyer on its own in dealing with the product's errors and shortcomings.

The producer's line of products is important for those expert system projects that have a great number of outside hooks. When all other things are the same, most organizations prefer to stay with the producer whose products are already in place in the organization, especially when product compatibility is of importance to the firm.

The producer's technical support for the product is one of the most important attributes of the producers of expert system software. When the expert system project is large and the software product is complex, technical support becomes a critical factor in the success of the project.

The producer may provide the technical support in a variety of forms, including: training workshops, in-place advising, telephone support, technical consulting, and active participation in the development process.

12.2.3 Social Aspects

The social aspects of a software product relate to the social standing of the product. They include:

- The number of product users

- The product's user group

- The number of compatible products in the market

The social aspects of a product indicate its acceptability within the user community and the industry. The number of users is an indicator of the dependability and quality of the product. Furthermore, when the number of users is high, the developer will have an easier time recruiting professionals to install the product, produce the physical design for the application, and encode the physical design into the system. The product's user group, if it has one, provides the users with shared information regarding the technical aspects of the product, hence adding to the degree of technical support for the product.

The number of compatible products shows the technical leadership of a product. This is an indicator that the producer will continue to enhance the tool, as the application system enhances in the future and requires more advanced features.

12.2.4 Hardware Aspects

Hardware aspects have the following subclasses (Figure 12.2):

- Platform

- Input/output devices

- Resource requirements

- Efficiency

The subclasses of the platform node are:

- The operating system

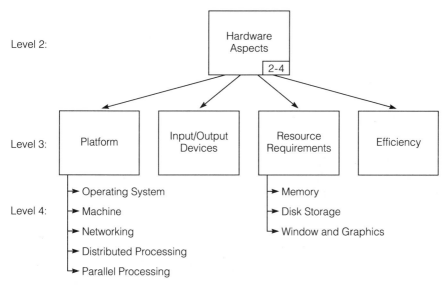

Figure 12.2 The Attribute Hierarchy for Hardware Aspects

- The machine

- The networking capability

- The distributed processing capability

- The parallel processing capability

The platform is the combination of the machine and the operating system on which the product resides. The platform is relevant in the evaluation of products, because the existing platform within an organization imposes a constraint. A product that runs on an organization's platform is preferred, because it saves the cost of buying the hardware and training its users.

The networking capability becomes an issue when the system is designed to be used over a network of computers. Distributed processing is important for expert systems with knowledge bases distributed over a network of computers. This aspect of expert systems is yet to be developed. The parallel processing capability in expert systems is another attribute still in its infancy. However, with the availability of Prolog running on multiple processors, the technology has already entered the market.

Input/output devices are crucial when the system is designed for use in special circumstances, such as voice-activated input or input from analog devices such as medical instruments.

The resource requirements consist of the following subclasses:

- Memory

- Disk storage

- Windows and graphics

The computer resource requirements are the suggested needed memory and disk storage for installing the product. With the inclusion of object-oriented representation, the additional requirements of windows and graphics capability are added to the required resources.

For large applications, the efficiency of the system becomes important. In such systems, the long response time could discourage the system use. On the other hand, when the application requires a real-time response, the efficiency attribute becomes one of the most significant features of the product.

12.3 Functional Aspects

Functional aspects are the most important attributes of expert system tools, and have the most involved attribute hierarchy. The functional aspects of a product are those attributes that are related to the way the product performs its intended tasks, and are directly related to the program code of the product, as opposed to the platform it runs on, or other aspects. We can identify three levels below the functional aspects. Because of the complexity of the hierarchy, we name these levels:

- Level 2: functional aspects (and other aspects)

- Level 3: components

- Level 4: facilities

- Level 5: primitives

The *components* are the abstract classes that exist within the functional aspects, and are generally distinguishable from one another both on the basis of the visibility to the user and on theoretical grounds. The *primitives* are the classes of software functions that are concretely identifiable within a product. A primitive performs one well-defined task. The *facilities* are the grouping of primitives into more manageable classes. Although the definitions of components, facilities, and primitives are inexact, when applied to a given type of software, they fall into place.

12.3.1   *Components*

One can identify four components for expert system products (Figure 12.3):

- Knowledge representation component

- Inference engine component

- Knowledge management component

- Outside hooks component

The components level is the most abstract type of class within the hierarchy. At the lower levels of the hierarchy, the level of abstraction decreases. On the theoretical basis, these four components are relatively distinct. Furthermore, the inference engine is the least visible component of a product, while the outside hooks are visible to the developer, not to the user. The knowledge representation and knowledge management components are visible to both the developer and the user.

Although one may compare candidate products based on their components, this type of class is too general for a meaningful comparison. Thus, we look into facilities that are the subclasses of components.

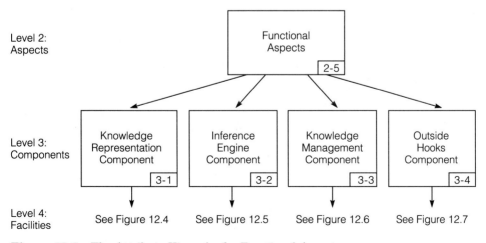

Figure 12.3   The Attribute Hierarchy for Functional Aspects

12.3.2   *Facilities and Primitives*

Facilities are subclasses of components, and embody a set of primitives. Primitives are the well-defined and relatively independent functions within the product. The following discussion on the facilities and primitives of each component makes the point more clear.

Facilities and Primitives of Knowledge Representation

The facilities or the subclasses of the knowledge representation component are (Figure 12.4):

- Logic-based representation

- Object-based representation

- Uncertainty representation

- Meta-knowledge representation

- Mathematical representation

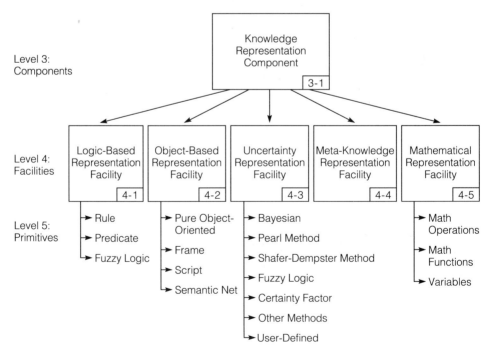

Figure 12.4   The Attribute Hierarchy for Knowledge Representation Component

Chapters 3, 4, 8, and 11 have discussed the first four facilities of knowledge representation. The mathematical representation is the facility to create functions and perform procedural computations independently. This facility represents a conventional programming capability within the knowledge representation component.

Figure 12.4 shows the primitives of facilities of the knowledge representation component. Primitives perform well-defined functions. For example, the primitive **rule** is the collection of codes within the product that the developer uses to represent knowledge as a set of rules. The primitives of Figure 12.4 are those we have covered in other chapters or are self-explanatory.

The only facility without a set of primitives is the meta-knowledge representation facility. The reason is that the methodologies of meta-knowledge representation are lacking in this area, and few products have the facility.

Facilities and Primitives of the Inference Engine

As shown in Figure 12.5, the inference engine component has the following facilities:

- Chaining

- Induction

- Object-oriented

- Blackboard

- Truth maintenance

- Conflict resolution

The chaining facility has the primitives of backward chaining, forward chaining, or mixed forward-backward chaining. (See the discussion on chaining in Chapter 4.)

The induction facility also has a number of well-defined methods, such as decision tree and ID3 (which are covered in Chapters 4 and 6, and Appendix A).

Object-oriented reasoning is discussed in Chapter 8, which includes a review of the nature of inheritance and concurrency in the object-oriented approach. Blackboard systems are discussed in Chapter 9, and Chapter 11 has a brief description of the truth maintenance mechanism in Section 11.7. The primitives of the conflict resolution facility are discussed in Chapter 9.

476

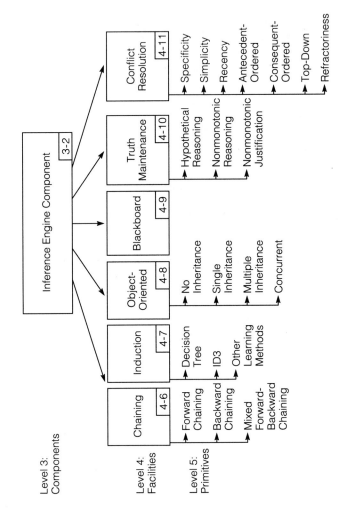

Figure 12.5 The Attribute Hierarchy for the Inference Engine Component

Facilities and Primitives of Knowledge Management

The knowledge-base management component consists of all attributes of a tool that allow the developer to code the system design into the system, and allow the user to access and interact with the system. This component is the most visible one to both developers and users, thus playing an important role in the evaluation of a product.

One can divide the facilities of this component into the following classes, as shown in Figure 12.6:

- User interface
- User-interface creation
- Debugging tools
- Knowledge maintenance
- System security
- Integrated tools
- Developer-user assistance

The *user interface* facility consists of all the interface attributes that are available to the user as the system default. The developer does not need to program these capabilities into the system. The primitives of this facility are listed in Figure 12.6. We have seen a number of these primitives in Chapters 5, 6, and 10. There are two primitives we have not seen before: what-if and initial pruning. The *what-if* primitive allows the user to give a number of assumptions, and ask the expert systems to produce the results of these assumptions. The *initial pruning* primitive allows the user to exclude some of the goals from the start, saving the searching time for the system. A product with a higher number of primitives in this facility would require less programming, and would be easier to use.

The *user-interface creation* facility allows the developer to custom-design some parts of the user interface. A product with a higher number of primitives in this facility gives the developer more flexibility in the user interface design. The primitives of this facility are listed in Figure 12.6, and enumerate what the developer can create for the user interface.

The *debugging tools* facility is what is available to the developer in checking and debugging the system once the physical design is coded. A longer list of primitives for this facility means more help for the developer in identifying possible errors and testing the system. Within this facility, the

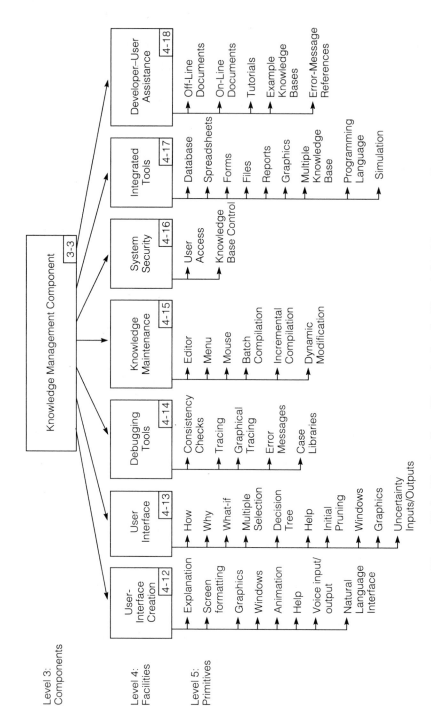

Figure 12.6 The Attribute Hierarchy for the Knowledge Management Component

478

consistency checks primitive identifies various types of inconsistencies within the knowledge base. *Tracing* traces the execution process of the system step by step. One type of tracing is to list the line of reasoning for making sure that the correct answer is reached for the correct reason—the reason intended by the expert. An incorrect reasoning process indicates errors in the knowledge base. The *case libraries* primitive lets the developer run the system with the inputs from the case libraries. This is helpful in the validation and verification stages of system development.

The *knowledge maintenance* facility of this component contains the primitives allowing the developer to enter the coded knowledge into the system, compile it, and modify it. Figure 12.6 shows the primitives of this facility. The *incremental compilation* primitive of this facility makes it possible for the developer to compile the knowledge base in an incremental fashion. In large knowledge bases, this is a helpful primitive for locating errors and observing how the reasoning advances as additional pieces are added to the system. The *dynamic modification* primitive makes the developer and user able to modify the content of the knowledge base while the system is running. This, too, could be helpful in observing the behavior of the system and its sensitivity to a particular piece of knowledge or the uncertainty method.

The *system security* facility of the knowledge base component gives the developer the ability to restrict access to the system by user type, by knowledge type, or both. Different types of users may have different access privileges to various components of the system. For example, a user may not be allowed to change the content of the knowledge base or see the codes for the access to databases. The knowledge base, also, could be partitioned into different levels of access privileges. Some portions of the knowledge base, containing sensitive information, may be off-limits to all or some users.

The *integrated tools* facility contains the attributes of the product that make the product hybrid in content (as discussed in Chapter 9), thus containing other types of information in addition to the knowledge base. Examples of additional contents are: databases, spreadsheets, forms, files, reports, graphics, and multiple knowledge bases, listed as the primitives of this facility in Figure 12.6. The programming languages and simulation primitives are not additional contents, but give the developer the capability to create additional contents to the system, other than the knowledge base.

Finally, the *developer-user assistance* facility consists of all attributes of the product that help the developer and user in understanding, coding, and using the system. It includes the on-line and off-line documents and other sources, listed as primitives for this facility in Figure 12.6.

Facilities of the Outside Hooks

The outside hooks component is the class of attributes that allows the developer to connect the product to the other systems within the organization, or lets other systems access the expert system. The facilities of this component are shown in Figure 12.7 as:

- Data access

- Text access

- Graphics access

- Knowledge-base access

- Language access

- Rehostability

The difference between facilities of this component and the integrated tools facility of the knowledge management component is that the integrated tools exist within the product, while the facilities of this component are the interface hooks and connections to the systems outside the product.

The *data access* facility of this component allows the system to have access to the data on the other systems, including the data in databases, spreadsheets, and files. The primitives of this facility are listed in Figure 12.7.

The *text access* facility plays a similar role, with the exception that it creates access to texts, such as reports, forms, and wordprocessing files. The *graphics access* permits the system to access and import graphics files and hard copy images.

The *knowledge-base* facility aids system interaction with other expert systems. The type of interaction could be multiple knowledge base, concurrent access, or distributed access to other systems. This facility is not common in most of the existing products.

The *language access* facility is those attributes of the product that create interaction between the expert system and programs written in various programming languages.

The *rehostability* facility is the capability of the product to export its knowledge base to other platforms or even to other expert systems, and to import knowledge bases from other platforms and expert systems. It also includes the capability of the product to create a standard file of its content, such as translating its contents to an ASCII file.

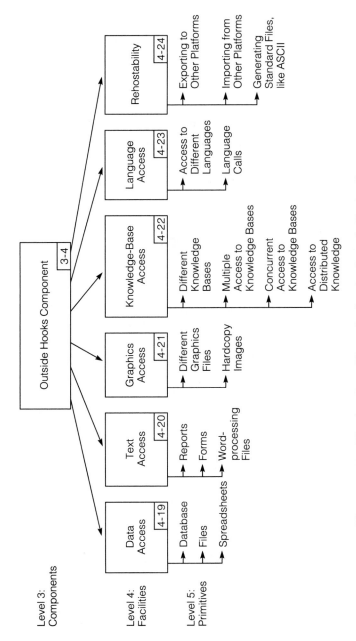

Figure 12.7 The Attribute Hierarchy for the Outside Hooks Component

12.3.3 Attribute Hierarchy in One Glance

Figures 12.1 through 12.7 depict the attribute hierarchy as abstract models of the expert system software. As the content of these figures shows, the attribute hierarchy is not a simple model, and any attempt to compare expert system products on the basis of only a portion of these attributes would be incomplete and hence inaccurate.

On the other hand, a nonsystematic comparison of products based on all attributes would be humanly impossible. Therefore, one needs to use a systematic approach to compare the candidate products using the attribute hierarchy. This is a case for using a decision analysis method to accomplish this systematic evaluation.

12.4 Computing the Relative Importance of Attributes (Optional)

After setting up the hierarchy for the structure of expert system tools, one must quantify the *relative importance* of attributes, because the attributes within the hierarchy do not have the same importance in an application. In this section, we discuss the methods for quantifying the relative importance of attributes.

One of the simple decision-analysis tools in evaluating various choices within a hierarchy of attributes is the analytic hierarchy process (AHP) [Saaty 1977; Zahedi 1986]. AHP requires that attributes of the decision problem be structured into a decision hierarchy, as we have done in the previous section for the decision problem of selecting and evaluating expert system tools. To quantify the relative importance of attributes within the hierarchy, one can adopt two methods: *simple rating* and *pairwise comparison*.

12.4.1 Simple Rating of Attributes Within the Hierarchy (Optional)

The first step in computing of the relative importance of attributes within the hierarchy is to assign relative weights to each set. However, the relative weight should be in connection with the role of the children attributes in serving the purpose of their common parent or superclass.

Let us show this by a number of examples that focus on the functional aspects of tools. Consider Figure 12.3, where there are four components:

knowledge representation, inference engine, knowledge management, and out-side hooks. For the mortgage loan example, assume that knowledge management is twice as important as the other three. The other three components are considered equally important. In this case, we assign the following relative weights to the four components accomplishing the functional aspects:

$$wc_{1,5} = .20$$

$$wc_{2,5} = .20$$

$$wc_{3,5} = .40$$

$$wc_{4,5} = .20$$

where wc is the estimate of the relative weights of each component in accomplishing the goal of the functional aspects, the fifth aspect type shown in Figure 12.1. The subscripts of wc show the component number (1, 2, 3, or 4) and the aspects type that is the parent of the components, 5 in this case.

One can continue to assign relative weights to attributes at the lower levels of the hierarchy. For example, consider Figure 12.4, the knowledge representation component. This component has five facilities: *logic-based, object-oriented, uncertainty, meta knowledge,* and *mathematical* representations. Assume that the first three facilities are equally important for the mortgage loan example, and are twice as important as the other two.

Since we have quite a number of relative weights throughout the hierarchy, we must name them more systematically so that the values do not get confused. Looking at Figures 12.3 through 12.7, we see that there are four components. These components together have 24 facilities, as the numbered boxes at the fourth level of the hierarchy indicate. We show the relative weights of the facilities at the fourth level of the hierarchy with wf, and use two subscripts for it. The first subscript denotes the facility number, and the second subscript shows the component number the facility serves. Thus, for the facilities of the first component, we have:

$$wf_{1,1} = .250$$

$$wf_{2,1} = .250$$

$$wf_{3,1} = .250$$

$$wf_{4,1} = .125$$

$$wf_{5,1} = .125$$

Thus we rate the elements of the hierarchy in their roles for accomplishing the goal of their immediate parent at one level higher on the hierarchy. Assume that for the mortgage loan system, the developer has produced the following relative ratings for the facilities at level 4 of the hierarchy:

Table 12.1.   The Relative Weights of Facilities

Weights of Facilities Serving			
Component 1	Component 2	Component 3	Component 4
$wf_{1,1} = .250$	$wf_{6,2} = .20$	$wf_{12,3} = .125$	$wf_{19,4} = .30$
$wf_{2,1} = .250$	$wf_{7,2} = .20$	$wf_{13,3} = .125$	$wf_{20,4} = .10$
$wf_{3,1} = .250$	$wf_{8,2} = .20$	$wf_{14,3} = .125$	$wf_{21,4} = .10$
$wf_{4,1} = .125$	$wf_{9,2} = .10$	$wf_{15,3} = .125$	$wf_{22,4} = .10$
$wf_{5,1} = .125$	$wf_{10,2} = .10$	$wf_{16,3} = .250$	$wf_{23,4} = .10$
	$wf_{11,2} = .20$	$wf_{17,3} = .125$	$wf_{24,4} = .30$
		$wf_{18,3} = .125$	

Note that the relative weights of facilities serving each component add to one, because we are measuring the role of the facilities in serving the functionality of each component. If a facility happens to serve, say, two components, it will be rated twice, once for its role for serving the first component, and once for serving the second component. For example, if the facility uncertainty representation, facility 3, serves both component 1 and 2, then we will have $wf_{3,1}$ for its role in serving the first component. This relative weight would be part of the weights of the facilities serving the first component. Furthermore, we will have $wf_{3,2}$ for the role of facility 3 in serving component 2. This weight would be part of the relative weights of the second component. In other words, we allow multiple parents for each child within the attribute hierarchy.

Now that we have all the relative weights for the attributes within the hierarchy, we should be able to combine them to find the global weights for the facilities.

12.4.2   Computing Global Weights of Attributes (Optional)

The relative weights assigned so far are called *local relative weights* because they represent the role of an element of the hierarchy in accomplishing the goal of its immediate parent within the hierarchy. In this section, we compute the *global relative weights*, which represent the role of each attribute within the hierarchy in accomplishing the goal of its ancestor at the top of the hierarchy.

To show this computation process, let us assume that we want to see the role of each component and facility attribute in accomplishing the goal of the functional aspects. Since components are one level below the functional aspects, their local weights are also global weights. However, facilities are two levels below the functional aspects. Therefore, we have to compute the global weights of facilities, which show the relative importance of facilities in accomplishing what is expected from the functional aspects. To compute the global weights of facilities, we should multiply their local weights by the weights of their immediate parents.

For example, take component 1: knowledge representation. It has a relative weight of $wc_{1,5} = .20$. To get the global weight of the facilities serving this component, the local weights of the children of this component should be multiplied by .20. Similarly, local relative weight of the facilities serving components 2, 3, and 4 in Table 12.1 should be multiplied by $wc_{2,5} = .20$, $wc_{3,5} = .40$, and $wc_{4,5} = .20$, respectively. The results would be the global weights of the facilities serving the goal of functional aspects (their grandparent). The following table shows the global weights of facilities with respect to the functional aspects.

Table 12.2.   The Global Weights of Facilities

Global Weights of Facilities with Respect to the Functional Aspects			
$gwf_1 = .050$	$gwf_6 = .040$	$gwf_{12} = .050$	$gwf_{19} = .060$
$gwf_2 = .050$	$gwf_7 = .040$	$gwf_{13} = .050$	$gwf_{20} = .020$
$gwf_3 = .050$	$gwf_8 = .040$	$gwf_{14} = .050$	$gwf_{21} = .020$
$gwf_4 = .025$	$gwf_9 = .020$	$gwf_{15} = .050$	$gwf_{22} = .020$
$gwf_5 = .025$	$gwf_{10} = .020$	$gwf_{16} = .100$	$gwf_{23} = .020$
	$gwf_{11} = .040$	$gwf_{17} = .050$	$gwf_{24} = .060$
		$gwf_{18} = .050$	

In Table 12.2, the global weights of facilities are denoted by *gwf*, and subscripted by the facility number. Note that the subscript for the component the facility serves locally has disappeared, because the global relative weights show the role of the facilities with respect to their grandparent class: functional aspects. To be accurate, one should add the subscript of the grandparent to the global relative weights. In this case, we omit this subscript to keep the presentation simple, with the understanding that all global relative weights are computed with the functional aspects serving as the ultimate ancestor.

One can go one level higher and compute the global weight of the facilities with respect to their great grandparent by multiplying the attained global weight by the weight of the functional aspects. In this case, the global weights of the children of other aspects, such as those of financial aspects, producer aspects, social aspects, and hardware aspects should also be computed for the global weights to add to 1.

Going back to the global relative weights of facilities with respect to the functional aspects, notice that the global weights of facilities under each component add up to the global weight of that component. For example, the global weights of facilities serving component 1 add up to .20, which is the global weight of component 1. Thus, the hierarchy takes the global weight of a parent and distributes it among its children according to their importance to the parent.

Thus, the global relative weights of children reflect the relative importance of their immediate parents as well as their own role in serving their topmost ancestor. As one moves down the hierarchy, this feature recursively propagates into global relative weights of attributes at the lower levels. Therefore, the global relative weights of children at the lowest level of the attribute hierarchy embody the relative importance of all their ancestors or superclasses in serving the goal of the topmost ancestor.

One can continue the process of identifying the local relative weights, and aggregating to find the global relative weights downward in the attribute hierarchy to the primitive level (level 5). This leads to the computation of about 100 global relative weights of primitives with respect to the functional aspects. Thus, we are able to identify the relative importance of each piece of the tool with respect to its overall functionality in a particular expert system application, in a systematic and structured manner.

For example, in an application where the outside hook or access to a database is important, the developer can give a higher rating locally to these facilities, and observe its result in the global relative weights. As the rating moves down the hierarchy, the evaluation becomes more exact and less subjective, but the process takes more time and requires more detailed information about the candidate tools. The developer decides how far down to go in the hierarchy, based on the size and importance of the project. The developer of a large and important project in which a significant investment is made has to apply extra caution in the choice of the expert system tool.

12.4.3   Pairwise Comparison of Attributes (Optional)

In many cases, assigning weights to various attributes is not an easy task. The analytic hierarchy process (AHP) offers the method of pairwise comparison for solving this problem. In this method, the attributes are compared pairwise. Take the four components in Figure 12.3. The developer may not be able to rate these four components with ease. One can ask the developer to compare them pairwise, asking a typical question: "Is component 1: knowledge representation, equally important as component 2: inference engine?" If not, is it twice as important, half as important? The answers to the pairwise comparisons form a table (or matrix) as shown in (1).

In the matrix of pairwise comparisons, the elements in the main diagonal of the matrix are always 1, because an attribute is equally important when it is compared with itself.

$$
\begin{array}{c}
\begin{array}{cccc} comp-1 & comp-2 & comp-3 & comp-4 \end{array} \\
\begin{array}{c} comp-1 \\ comp-2 \\ comp-3 \\ comp-4 \end{array}
\left(
\begin{array}{cccc}
1 & 1 & 0.5 & 2 \\
1 & 1 & 0.5 & 3 \\
2 & 2 & 1 & 4 \\
0.5 & \frac{1}{3} & \frac{1}{4} & 1
\end{array}
\right)
\end{array}
\tag{1}
$$

The elements on the lower diagonal are always the inverse of those symmetrically located from the main diagonal. For example, the last element in column 1 is the inverse of the last element in row 1. So we do not need to get the pairwise comparison for the elements of the main diagonal. In the *eigenvalue* method of Saaty [1977], one does not need the elements of the lower triangle of the matrix, either.

The eigenvalue method takes the above matrix and computes the local relative weight from the following formula:

$$
A = W.\lambda_{max}
\tag{2}
$$

where A is the matrix of pairwise comparisons, W is the vector (or the list) of estimated local relative weights, and λ_{max} is the greatest eigenvalue of the matrix. There are algorithms that compute W and λ_{max} for any given A.

Note that the user can be inconsistent in expressing pairwise values. For example, in the input matrix, the first and second components are judged to be equally important. However, the first row shows that component 1 is twice as important as component 4, while the second row shows that component 2 is three times as important as component 4. When a pairwise matrix is fully consistent, the computation yields λ_{max} equal to the size of the matrix. In the case of matrix (1), the size is 4. The inconsistency of an input matrix could be computed as

$$inconsistency \; measure = \frac{\lambda_{max} - n}{n - 1} \qquad (3)$$

where n is the size of the matrix (or the number of elements being compared), and λ_{max} is computed from (2).

There is a software product in the market called Expert Choice (Decision Support Software, Pittsburgh, Penn.) that takes in the pairwise comparisons from the user and produces local and global relative weights for the hierarchy.

Using Expert Choice for the input matrix (1), we get

$$W = (\; .22, \quad .24, \quad .44, \quad .10 \;),$$

and the measure of inconsistency is .008. It is recommended that if this measure goes above .1, the user should try to check the input matrix to reduce the inconsistency. The pairwise comparison helps in identifying the relative weights when the evaluator has difficulty rating the attributes.

In the next section, we see how we can use the global relative weights of attributes for ranking software tools.

12.5 Computing the Rank of Expert System Tools (Optional)

When the global relative importance or weights of various attributes are established, we can use them for *ranking expert system tools*. We compare the candidate tools attribute by attribute. These attributes are the lowest level of the hierarchy, and their global relative weights reflect all their ancestors' importance in accomplishing the goal of the topmost element.

For example, we can compare candidate tools facility by facility. Assume that the system developer is interested in comparing KAPPA, LEVEL5 OBJECT, and 1st-CLASS on a facility basis for the mortgage loan system. In this case, the three products must be compared 24 times, once for each facility.

Take the first facility in Figure 12.4, the logic-based representation. The developer (or an evaluator who helps the developer and knows the products' capabilities) may feel that for the purpose of the mortgage loan system, these three tools have equal capability. Therefore, we have:

$$WT_1 = (\, wt_{1,1}, wt_{2,1}, wt_{3,1} \,)$$

$$\begin{array}{cccc} & KAPPA & LEVEL5OBJECT & 1st\text{-}CLASS \\ = \Big(& .33 & .33 & .33 \quad \Big) \end{array}$$

where $wt_{2,1}$ is the local relative weight of tool number 2 (LEVEL5 OBJECT) in facility 1. To get the global weight of each tool in facility 1, these local weights must be multiplied by the global relative weight of facility 1. That is, each of the above rates must be multiplied by .05, the global weight of facility 1, shown in Table 12.2.

For the second facility **object-based representation**, KAPPA and LEVEL5 OBJECT have equal capability, while 1st-CLASS lacks the capability, thus a rating of, say, .49, .49, .02. These local weights also should be multiplied with the global relative weight of the second facility (.05).

Columns 2–4 of Table 12.3 show a hypothetical rating of the three products for the 24 facilities. When we multiply the ratings of the three products for each facility by the global weight of that facility, we get columns 5–7 of Table 12.3. Columns 5–7 show the global weights of the three products for each one of their facilities.

To get the single score as the relative rating of a tool, it is enough to sum its global weights. For example, in Table 12.3, the final scores of KAPPA, LEVEL5 OBJECT, and 1st-CLASS are .343, .377, and .287, respectively. Thus, in this example, the developer chooses LEVEL5 OBJECT if the functional aspects were the only criteria of choice. Note that these scores are relative to the selection set and sum to 1. If we add other candidates, the scores would change.

While a product may be far stronger than its competitors in one facility, if the global relative weight of that facility is not high for a particular case, this strength would not contribute much to the final score of the tool. On the other hand, when a facility is very important for an application, a slight edge in a tool's rating for that facility may contribute significantly to its final score. Thus, this method of software evaluation allows the developer to combine the requirements of a particular application with the features available in various expert system tools.

In a real-world evaluation of tools, the developer may decide to evaluate the tools primitive by primitive. In this case, one must find the global weights of primitives, and evaluate the tools based on each primitive. This

**Table 12.3.   Relative and Global Weights of
the Three Tools for the Mortgage Loan Example**

Facility No.	Global Weights of Facilities	Local Weights(*)			Global Weights(*)		
		K	L	F	K	L	F
1	.050	.333	.333	.333	.017	.017	.017
2	.050	.490	.490	.020	.025	.025	.001
3	.050	.010	.700	.290	.001	.035	.015
4	.025	.333	.333	.333	.008	.008	.008
5	.025	.400	.400	.200	.010	.010	.005
6	.040	.400	.400	.200	.016	.016	.008
7	.040	.010	.010	.980	.000	.000	.039
8	.040	.490	.490	.020	.020	.020	.001
9	.020	.350	.350	.300	.007	.007	.006
10	.020	.333	.333	.333	.007	.007	.007
11	.040	.333	.333	.333	.013	.013	.013
12	.050	.400	.400	.200	.020	.020	.010
13	.050	.400	.400	.200	.020	.020	.010
14	.050	.333	.333	.333	.017	.017	.017
15	.050	.350	.350	.300	.018	.018	.015
16	.100	.400	.400	.200	.040	.040	.020
17	.050	.333	.333	.333	.017	.017	.017
18	.050	.333	.333	.333	.017	.017	.017
19	.060	.333	.333	.333	.020	.020	.020
20	.020	.333	.333	.333	.007	.007	.007
21	.020	.400	.400	.200	.008	.008	.004
22	.020	.350	.350	.300	.007	.007	.006
23	.020	.400	.400	.200	.008	.008	.004
24	.060	.333	.333	.333	.020	.020	.020
Total	1.00	-	-	-	.343	.377	.287

(*) K=KAPPA, L=LEVEL5 OBJECT, F=1st-CLASS.

would require the computation of about 100 primitive weights, and the comparison of tools based on 100 primitives. The tedium of computation could be reduced considerably by the use of Expert Choice.

In this section we computed an example of the rankings of tools based on their functional aspects. However, no evaluation is complete without the inclusion of other aspects. The evaluation process for other aspects has the same procedure. At the end, the scores for various aspects should be multiplied by the relative weights of each aspect, and then summed. This will give an overall score for each tool.

The evaluation method presented in this chapter is simplified to a great extent. The *qualitative programming* method extends this evaluation approach for cases where the developer imposes constraints and assigns extra penalties on tools for their lack of important attributes.

12.6 Potential Liabilities Associated with Expert Systems

As the popularity of expert systems increases and the use of expert systems becomes commonplace, users and developers have to deal with the legal ramifications of selling and using expert systems. For example, if a doctor uses the advice of a defective or incomplete expert system, and the decision leads to the death of a patient, is the doctor liable? Can the doctor be considered negligent for following the advice of the system? Is the company that developed the system liable? Can there be a completely fault-free expert system? If not, then how can a company market an expert system, such as a tax advisor?

Although legal precedents with regards to expert systems have not been established, there are potential liabilities for any system used for making consequential decisions, the type of decisions that justifies the use of an expert system.

A number of individuals and organizations are involved in the development and use of an expert system, and each could become the target of litigation. They can be grouped into:

- Users

- Domain experts

- Knowledge engineers

- Seller organizations

The novelty of expert systems precludes any legal discussions on the basis of past cases and precedents. The intention of this section is to raise liability issues that could be potentially damaging in the application of expert systems, and to increase awareness for the necessity of their careful evaluation and testing before being sold to customers and used for making decisions.

Case: Computer-related Legal Cases

In their article ["Legal Perspectives on Expert Systems"], Peter and Kathleen Mykytyn discuss specific legal issues in development and deployment of expert systems. They specifically discuss the fact that the expertise of domain experts is often clouded with some degree of uncertainty. The second issue is related to the liabilities resulting from the use or nonuse of expert systems. The following eight legal cases are reported by the above authors and reprinted below.

- *Triangle Underwriters v. Honeywell, Inc (1979)*: Triangle Underwriters purchased a complete computer system from Honeywell that never functioned properly in spite of efforts by Honeywell to correct the defects. Because the statute of limitations from the time of purchase under the Uniform Commercial Code (UCC) has ran out, Triangle argues that Honeywell's continuing efforts to correct the difficulties were analogous to the concept of "continuing treatment," which is applied to medical malpractice actions. The court rejected this argument, noting that this case lacked the professional relationship existing under the "continuing treatment" doctrine.

- *Chatlos Systems v. National Cash Register Corp. (1979)*: The plaintiff asked the court to consider computer malpractice, which the court rejected. The court reasoned that the requisite degree of trust and professional relationship required for malpractice was lacking in the relationship between the software provider and the consumer.

- *Diversified Graphics v. Groves Ltd. (1989)*: Professional standards of care were applied to information-systems consultants. They were held liable for professional malpractice for not meeting the standards of the Management Advisory Services Practice Standards for the American Institute of Certified Public Accountants in their procurement of a turn-key system for Diversified Graphics.

- *Data Processing Services Inc. v. L.H. Smith Oil Corp. (1986)*: This case is on appeal. The Indiana Court of Appeals upheld a lower court's verdict that the firm that performed the computer programming, Data Processing Services, Inc., was liable for professional malpractice.

- *Invacare Corp. v. Sperry Corp.*: Invacare alleged that Sperry negligently recommended the purchase of its own computer system. The court held that such actions were a valid claim for fraud if the alleged facts were proven. The court also held that, since all the contractual agreements were not independent of one another, no statute of limitations existed until all portions of the contract had been completed.

- *United States Welding v. Burroughs Corp. (1984)*: U.S. Welding sued Burroughs because they were dissatisfied with the performance of a leased computer system, including the software. The court held that a claim for monetary losses caused by misrepresentation was allowed if parties had sufficient privity (a private relationship upon which the person you relied is a person on whom you are entitled to rely). In this case, the court noted that pure economic harms may be recoverable in a strict products liability claim.

- *Black, Jackson, and Simmons Ins. Brokerage v. IBM Corp. (1982)*: IBM was sued because a computer system and software they provided did not function as represented. The court did not permit an action based on negligence for purely economic harms, but did allow a claim based on warranty.
- *Quad County Distributing Company v. Burroughs Corp. (1979)*: this case involved a dispute over the contract. The case is particularly significant because the court held that a computer program is covered by the UCC provisions concerning the sale of products. If the courts have established that computer programs are products, the legal doctrine of strict liability will apply. Strict liability makes it much easier for the plaintiff to recover, because the injured party does not have to prove negligence on the part of the manufacturer.

Excerpt from "Legal Perspectives on Expert Systems," by Peter P. Mykytyn, Jr. and Kathleen Mykytyn, *AI Expert*, December 1991, pp. 41–45, reprinted with permission from *AI Expert*.

12.6.1 Liability of Expert System Users

Who is responsible if a decision maker uses a defective expert system to make a decision that leads to personal or financial damage? Although legal precedents have not yet been established for expert systems, there are cases that indicate the user could be held responsible even though he or she has been unaware of the fault, and has used the system with the best of intentions. For example, when a software error caused a machine to dispense a lethal dose of radiation to a patient, the doctor was sued alongside the manufacturer of the machine and the institution where the machine was being used.

On the other hand, there could be legal consequences for NOT using an available expert system. Take the case of a nurse who does not have access to a doctor, and chooses not to use an expert system that could potentially help save a patient's life. Is the nurse liable for negligence?

When an expert system could provide advice that has potentially high financial or personal consequences, the user organization of the system must make sure that the system is evaluated and its reliability is tested thoroughly. Furthermore, a clear procedure for the use of the system should be established, and adherence to the procedure should be monitored regularly. The organization should also provide liability insurance coverage for those who use the system.

12.6.2   Liability of Domain Experts

When the expert system is created based on the expertise of one or more domain experts, the erroneous, incomplete, or conflicting opinions of experts could lead to the development of a faulty system. When the faulty system causes damage, the domain experts might be potentially held liable. Here, the importance of careful knowledge engineering could not be overemphasized. Experts who do not have adequate expertise to stand the test of a court challenge should altogether avoid getting involved in the development of the system. The system developer must perform a careful evaluation of domain experts before engaging them in the knowledge acquisition process. The differences among experts should be carefully resolved or managed in the system, as discussed in Chapter 7. Again, the reliability testing of the system plays an important role in ensuring the integrity of the system.

12.6.3   Liability of Knowledge Engineers

Of all those involved in developing an expert system, the knowledge engineer can influence the content of the knowledge base the most. The knowledge engineer could damage the integrity of the knowledge base by his or her personal biases, negligence, and lack of understanding of the knowledge domain.

The documentation process and paper trail of the knowledge engineering process (discussed in Chapter 7) would be of critical importance in auditing and checking the quality of knowledge engineering.

12.6.4   Liability of Seller Organizations

An organization may develop an expert system to sell to the public, such as a tax advisor expert system helping individual taxpayers prepare income tax forms. If the system is defective and gives wrong tax advice that leads to financial losses, is the company liable?

Almost all software companies have limited warranties, and disclaim any damage caused by their software products. In their article, Mykytyn, Mykytyn, and Slinkman [1990] discuss that, as long as a software system is considered a *product*, such warranties would protect the seller organization. However, when the system is considered to be providing a *service* to customers, then such disclaimers could not prevent litigations. That is why many software companies announce that what they sell is a *product*.

However, the best policy for a company selling a popular expert system is to have a tight quality control and regular reliability testing and updating.

Furthermore, the company must make sure that the customers are aware of the limitations and inflexibility inherent to the expert system.

At present, the legal consequences of producing and using expert systems are not adequately explored. There will be more discussions on this topic as the use of expert systems in the work place expands.

Conclusion

In the 1980s, expert system software products grew from research projects and esoteric and expensive products into decision-support tools for business. One of the principal contributors to the popularity of expert systems is the availability of various types of software products in the commercial market. As the number of choices for software tools and their complexity have increased, the choice of an appropriate product has become an evaluation decision problem of its own.

The selection of the expert system software, especially for large and complex systems, requires a formal structure. This chapter discussed a hierarchy of expert system attributes that includes financial, producer, social, hardware, and functional aspects of expert systems. The functional aspects were the focus of discussion and were broken down into lower levels: components, facilities, and primitives. This chapter discussed two methods (simple rating and analytic hierarchy process) for evaluating the functional aspects of expert systems.

Finally, this chapter introduced the liability issues involved in the use and development of expert systems. The legal precedents related to expert systems have not yet been established, but there must be organizational awareness of potential liabilities that require careful planning in evaluating, testing, and use of such systems.

References

Citrenbaum, Ronald; Geissman, James; and Schultz, Roger. 1987. "Selecting a Shell," *AI Expert*, Vol. 2, No. 9, September, pp. 30–39.

Expert Choice Manual. 1988. Decision Support Software Co. Pittsburgh, PA.

Freedman, Roy. 1987. "27-Product Wrap-up: Evaluating Shells," *AI Expert*, Vol. 2, No. 9, September, pp. 69–74.

Gevarter, William B. 1987. "The Nature and Evaluation of Commercial Expert System Building Tools," *IEEE Computer*. Vol. 20, No. 5, May, pp. 24–41.

Gilmore, John F.; Pulaski, Kirt; and Howard, Chuck. 1986. "A Comprehensive Evaluation of Expert System Tools," *SPIE Applications of Artificial Intelligence III*, Bellingham, Wash. Vol. 635, pp. 2–16.

Karna, Animesh and Karna, Amitabt. 1985. "Evaluating the Existing Tools for Developing Expert Systems in PC Environment," *Proc. Expert Systems in Government*, K. N. Karna, Ed. October 24–25, Computer Society Press, Los Alamitos, CA, 295–300.

Mykytyn, K.; Mykytyn, P. P. Jr.; and Slinkman, C. W. 1990. "Expert Systems: A Question of Liability," *MIS Quarterly*, March 1990, pp. 27–38.

Richer, M. H. 1986. "An Evaluation of Expert System Development Tools," *Expert Systems*, Vol. 3, No. 3, July, pp. 166–183.

Saaty, T. L. 1977. "A Scaling Method for Priorities in Hierarchical Structures," *Journal of Mathematical Psychology*, Vol. 15, No. 2, pp. 234–281.

Tuthill, G. Steven. 1991. "Legal Liabilities and Expert Systems," *AI Expert*, March 1991, pp. 44–51.

Zahedi, F. 1985. "Database Management Systems Evaluation and Selection Decisions," *Decision Sciences*, Vol. 16, No. 1, pp. 91–116.

Zahedi, F. 1986. "The Analytic Hierarchy Process—A Survey of the Method and its Applications," *Interfaces*, Vol. 16, No. 4, pp. 96–108.

Zahedi, F. 1987. "Qualitative Programming for Selection Decisions," *Computers and Operations Research*, Vol. 14, No. 5, pp. 395–407.

Zahedi, F. 1990. "A Method for Quantitative Evaluation of Expert Systems," forthcoming in *European Journal of Operational Research*.

Questions

12.1 Discuss the importance of software evaluation in expert system applications. What factors have contributed to the necessity of a formal evaluation?

12.2 Why do we need to organize the attributes of expert system tools in a hierarchy?

12.3 What factors contribute to the inequality in the importance of the attributes within the attribute hierarchy?

12.4   What is the difference between the local and global relative weights?

12.5   Do you think we need another level of attributes below the primitive level? If so, what type of attributes should be included in that level?

12.6   What is the pairwise comparison method? What is its use in rating attributes or candidate tools?

12.7   Who may be sued in case an expert system does not function as it supposed to?

12.8   If an expert system is available for use but a negligent employee does not use it for a customer and this leads to damage, who may be legally held responsible?

Problems

12.1   In Figures 12.1 through 12.7, identify areas where future software developments may change or expand.

12.2   Go through the evaluation process of the components and facilities. Consider the job application system. Rate the components and facilities for the purpose of this system, and compute the global relative weights for the 24 facilities within the functional aspects.

12.3   Compare your answers to Problem 12.2 with the entries in Tables 1 and 2. Which facilities have you rated differently? Why?

12.4   Complete the chapter example by a hypothetical evaluation of the three software products for all software aspects, and produce a score for each tool that reflects all five types of aspects.

12.5   Add LEVEL5 to the three candidate tools, and repeat the evaluation process. Analyze the impact of adding the additional candidate to the selection set.

Case Questions

The following questions refer to the case box "Computer-related Legal Cases," in this chapter.

1. Review each of the eight cases, and identify how each may apply to a legal action related to an expert system.

2. What additional groups of people get involved in an expert system related legal action?

3. What differences between expert systems and ordinary information systems may lead to get more individuals involved in an expert system related legal action?

4. Take the case of *Black, Jackson, and Simmons Ins. Brokerage v. IBM Corp.* Assume that the software was an expert system, advising the user about investment opportunities. If the lawsuit was brought by an individual who had lost all his fortune because of a flaw in the software, do you think the case would have the same outcome?

5. Answer Question 4 assuming that the expert system was for diagnosing cancer and a patient loses his life because of an error in the system.

6. What precautions should a developer of an investment-advisor expert system take to avoid legal actions similar to that in Question 4?

7. Do you think that the trend in legal actions might hamper the development and mass marketing of ready-to-use expert systems?

8. As a user of a ready-to-use expert system, how would you evaluate the system before relying on it for important decisions?

9. Can we use the evaluation method discussed in this chapter to compare and evaluate future ready-to-use expert systems? If yes, how?

10. Assume that there are five different ready-to-use expert systems for individual income-tax preparation. Draw the decision hierarchy for evaluating these systems.

NEURAL
NETWORKS

The objective of Part VI is to introduce the reader to the new field of neural networks. It consists of Chapters 13 and 14.

Chapter 13 introduces neural network systems, discusses their structure, and compares expert systems and neural networks. The section on the general building blocks of neural network systems identifies the numerous design parameters that have to be decided by the system developer. Chapter 14 covers well-known architectures and designs of neural network systems, and identifies unique design issues in developing such systems. The section on training a system in neural networks shows the difficulties involved in developing a neural network system.

In undergraduate courses and for readers interested in acquiring a general understanding of neural networks, a review of Chapter 13 (with no emphasis on the formulas) and the last section of Chapter 14 will suffice to give students a general understanding of the field. Advanced graduate courses and readers interested in inner workings of neural network systems can cover both chapters in detail.

Components of Neural Networks and a Comparison with Expert Systems

It is because I am not an Expert. Experts invent themselves. Whereas I was born with my mind made up.

        J. L. Carr, *How Steeple Sinderby Wanderers Won the FA Cup*

Is there intelligent life on earth?
Yes, but I'm only visiting.

        Graffiti

Chapter Objectives

The objectives of this chapter are:

- To give the reader a historical perspective of the development of the neural networks field

- To provide the reader with an understanding of the major building blocks and design parameters of neural network systems

- To highlight the advantages and disadvantages of expert systems and neural network systems by comparing and contrasting the two types of systems

KEY WORDS: Brain model, neurons, dendrites, synaptic connection, excitation, inhibition, firing, layers, transfer functions, learning, similarities of expert systems and neural networks, differences between expert systems and neural networks

Introduction

In this chapter, you are introduced to the components of the brain on which neural networks are loosely modeled. The brain is the least understood organ, and what we know about the brain is relatively recent. A brief review of the landmark discoveries about the brain discusses the origin of attempts to model brain functions, which eventually led to what we call today the field of neural networks.

Section 13.2 discusses the building blocks of neural networks. These components are common in all neural net structures, and a general understanding of the interactions among these components gives you the necessary background for understanding the architecture of various neural net designs. One of the important features of neural networks is the learning method. Although the learning equations are optional in this chapter, a general familiarity with the learning methods is crucial for designing a neural net system.

Sections 13.3 and 13.4 compare and contrast different features of expert systems and neural networks. This comparison shows that the two fields have common goals, but have a different approach in achieving them. Their differences show that each field has its own strengths and weaknesses.

There are a number of cases reporting the applications of neural networks in this chapter. They demonstrate the diversity and range of fields in which neural networks are applied as well as the nature of such applications. A couple of cases in this chapter highlight the integration of expert systems and neural networks, a trend that will become more pronounced in the future.

13.1 The Brain as the Underlying Model

The basic components of neural networks are modeled after the structure of the brain. Not all neural network structures adhere closely to the *brain model.* If a neural network of a particular type has proven to work in practice, the fact that it does not have a biological counterpart in the brain has not prevented its use. However, neural network systems have a strong similarity to the biological brain, and a great deal of the terminology in the field is borrowed from neuroscience, which embodies the fields studying the brain and mind. Thus, a brief review of the basic components of the brain could facilitate the understanding of the neural network building blocks.

13.1.1   Components of the Brain

The brain consists of *neurons*, which are small processing units, capable of simple processing. A neuron receives input either from the outside environment or from the other neurons. The neurons are connected in a large and complex network, as shown in Figure 13.1. The network consists of *dendrites*, which transmit messages across various paths in the network. One can imagine dendrites as roads and highways connecting various towns (neurons).

The interconnection of this network with a particular neuron is called a *synapse* or *synaptic connection*. In our road terminology, a synapse is the interconnection where a highway enters a town. When many roads lead to a town, there would be many interconnections in that town. This indeed is the case with neurons and synapses. There are numerous paths of dendrites leading to a neuron, and therefore, a neuron has numerous synapses. Or, one may consider a synapse as the connecting hook where a neuron latches to the network to capture the messages passing at that dendrite. Neurons have many such latch-points to the network. A neuron could have up to 10,000 synapses.

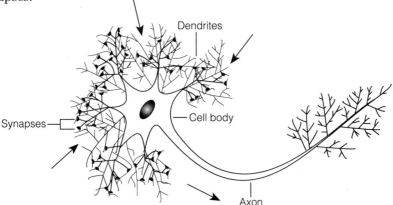

Figure 13.1   The Network of Neurons in the Brain

A neuron has activity in the form of a chemical or electrical impulse. The synapses bring the input to a neuron in the form of either a chemical or electrical impulse. Each input brought in from a synapse could *excite* or *inhibit* the neuron's activity, or, more accurately, the neuron's action potential. The inhibitory charge reduces the action potential of the neuron, and the excitatory charge increases its action potential. At any given time, when the net effect of the *excitation* and *inhibition* from the inputs of all synapses increases the action potential of the neuron beyond a threshold level, the neuron is activated and begins to fire by emitting output in the form of a chemical or electrical impulse. The strength of the neuron's activity (or *firing*) is determined by the frequency per second of the neuron's firing.

The synapses of a neuron are unidirectional. That is, they bring in input signals to the neuron, but they do not take out the output from the neuron. A neuron has a single *axon* that transmits the output signal from the neuron to the dendrite network, as shown in Figure 13.1. An axon is thicker than dendrites. It stems from a neuron, connects to the network of dendrites, and carries the neuron's output to the network.

The brain is massively parallel. There are an estimated 10^{12} neurons in a human brain. They are structured in layers or sheets of neurons. Each layer consists of a network of interconnected neurons. The layers are also interconnected.

13.1.2   A Brief History of Brain Research

This brief review is based on Shepherd's book on neurobiology [1988], which provides an account of the major breakthroughs and discoveries about the brain. This book is an excellent source for those who wish to learn more on the anatomy of the brain.

Case: Neural Net for Financial Market Analysis

Want to apply neural network technology to financial-market analysis? Karl Bergerson of Seattle's Neural Trading Co. found a way. His Neural$ trading system features a neural net trained with California Scientific Software's (Grass Valley, Calif.) BrainMaker and a C-based expert system that applies money-management rules. Says Bergerson, "I always look for the best trading tools, and I consider neural nets to be where the intelligence is going in the AI world."

Bergerson used nine years of "ultra-hand-picked" financial data to train the network and ran it against a theoretical $10,000 investment. After two years, the fictional account had grown to $76,034—a 660% appreciation. When tested on new data, Neural$ was 89% accurate. Bergerson attributes this phenomenal success rate to proper training data: "Neural nets are the best tools for pattern recognition, but you can't just dump data into one and expect to get wonderful results. The most important factor is your training data. You have to have your whole act together: training, design, and the right tools."

To train networks for Neural$, Bergerson inputs financial data like price, volume, and advance/decline into BrainMaker and calls the trained network from the system. The network predicts market fluctuation and the expert system component flags appropriate buying or selling opportunities.

Bergerson used Neural$ in the fourth quarter of the 1990 U.S. Investing Championship, which turned out to be his best quarter in business.

By Justin Kestelyn, "Application Watch," *AI Expert*, May 1991, p. 72, reprinted with permission from *AI Expert*.

Shepherd points out that the discussion of the separation of mind and brain goes back to 600 B.C., when the Greek philosophers raised the issue of thinking and its dependence on the brain, and speculated that the brain emanates spirits, which flow through nerves to muscles. However, it was Vesalius who in 1543 gave a description of the brain anatomy, and Descartes in 1637 who described the brain as a machine, which works independent of the soul. In 1791, Luigi Galvani from Bologna stimulated a frog's muscles with electricity; this led to the discovery that the brain has electrical activity.

As late as 100 years ago, scientists did not know that the brain and nervous system have cellular structure. They were unable to observe neurons because of the complexity and compactness of the brain cells. Gocli, in 1837, happened to stain a selected number of brain cells, which made it possible to observe the structure of neurons with its axons and connections to dendrites. At the time, the significance of this breakthrough went mostly unnoticed, until Santiago Cajal used the method to prove in 1888–1891 that the nervous system consists of neuron cells, which have axons connected to the network of dendrites. Later, the synaptic interconnection was suggested by Sherrington in 1897.

In the 1920s, it was discovered that neurons communicate via chemical impulses, called *neurotransmitters*. In the 1930s, research began on the chemical processes that produced the electrical impulses. This led to Hodgkin and

Huxley's Nobel Prize–winning work in the 1950s on developing the model and recording the electrical signals of the brain at the cellular level.

In the 1970s, the neuromodulator substances were discovered, leading to the belief that the interactions among neurons are of greater complexity than previously believed. As we can see, accurate and detailed knowledge of the physical mechanism of the brain is relatively new.

Although progress in the physical mechanism at the brain cell level has been substantial, there are still many unanswered questions about the collected mechanism of neurons in processing information. This is where the computer comes into the picture.

In the 1970s, computerized techniques were developed that made it possible to have visualization of the brain's activities, and the observation of groups of neurons in the act of information processing. This introduced computers as an effective tool for neurobiological research. The natural next step for the neuroscientists was to attempt to simulate brain activities on the computer, and neural networks offered the models neuroscientists could use in their research. In the 1980s, the connection between neurobiology and neural networks became stronger, and the two fields began to have an effective communication in their research efforts.

13.1.3   Neurobiology and Neural Networks

The field of neural networks began as an approach to imitating human intelligence for the purpose of creating intelligent machines. In the 1980s, neurobiologists began to accept neural network models as a method for testing various hypotheses about the structure and functional aspects of the brain.

The following are some of the facets of brain functions, to which neural networks have been applied as a tool for research [Grossberg 1988].

- One of the activities of the brain is various visual and audio perceptions like three-dimensional forms, color distinction, and dealing with various levels of brightness or sound.

- A second type of brain activity is the functioning of the memory, including long-term memory, short-term memory, recalling, and forgetting.

- A third aspect of brain function is the relationship between our cognition and emotion, which may lead to irrational behavior and abnormal emotions. One can easily observe that this aspect involves a wealth of knowledge on psychology and psychotherapy.

- The fourth aspect of brain function is its control mechanism of muscular movements, such as the way we use our arms and hands to achieve a particular goal, like writing or grabbing an object.

The use of neural networks in testing hypotheses about brain functions has created a close bond between neurobiology and neural networks. At the same time, this bond has given rise to a dual role for neural networks:

- First, as technological systems for complex information processing and machine intelligence

- Second, as simplified biological models for testing various hypotheses about the neuronal information processing in the brain

This dual role of neural networks has also created a dichotomy within the field. There are now two schools of thought on evaluating new theories and designs in the field. One group believes that the validity of a new theory or design depends on its direct or indirect confirmation by what we know about the neural activities of the brain. This group believes that the neural network designs should be able to explain the data collected and observations made about the various activities of the brain. Those designs that do not pass such a test are not true neural networks. This group emphasizes the neurobiological aspects of neural networks.

The second group treats neural networks as technological inventions that borrow ideas from neurobiology but do not have to be necessarily confirmed by the data on brain functions. This group emphasizes the engineering and *neurocomputing* aspects of neural networks. For this group, if a neural network structure works in practice, then it is a good system.

The dual role of neural networks will continue to give rise to lively discussions in years to come, and will color the writing of researchers. Some will promote theories and designs on the basis that they can explain the data on brain functions, others will advance their methods on the basis of practical tests, such as recognizing a tank from a piece of rock based on fuzzy and distorted pictures. The criteria for the comparisons of neural networks theories and designs have yet to be established.

Case: Neural Networks in Sales Support

Veratex Corp., a Detroit, Mich.-based distributor of medical and dental products, is a good example of a company that's not afraid to use the best that AI technology has to offer. Among other applications it employs, Veratex has deployed neural network and expert system based sales-support systems running on the heralded but underutilized IBMAS/400. Both projects were developed by Churchill Systems Inc. of Troy, Mich. Here we look at the neural network system.

Veratex has a unique approach to marketing its products. The company mails unsolicited catalogs to physicians and dentists. When a customer makes a buy from the catalog, his or her name is added to a customer database. Veratex's team of 40 telemarketers then calls the names in that database for reorders.

The company's problem was that before long, huge numbers of "dormants"— customers who had not made reorders for significant length of time—would accumulate without a telephone call. Veratex's small telemarketing force is not trained to prospect for new sales, and the portion of the telemarketers' time allotted to calling dormants is typically limited to 20%. Given that Veratex's database contains 44,000 customer names, that adds up to a lot of lost and relatively accessible business. In addition, the credibility of older data as a whole was called into question more and more as time went on.

The company had to verify its older data and then decide to which members of the dormant pool it should assign the limited telemarketing time. In a stroke of imagination, Veratex contracted with Churchill Systems to build a backpropagation neural network that would help identify the dormants with the highest probability of being the "best" customers—the ones most likely to place reorders. Similarly, the network would be trained to weed out the customers less likely to reorder from the "good" ones. The telemarketers would take it from there, making the most of their available time to contact the best customers thus identified by the network.

Built with IBM's NNU400 neural network utility and running on an AS/400, the neural network inputs comprised various statistical and demographic data called from Dun & Bradstreet and other sources. The network was then applied against Veratex's accounts to get a numerical output—a "rating"—for each customer. These ratings were then plugged directly into the customer records, which were sorted down to the best accounts. The result for each account is a rating relative to the "best" Veratex customer.

According to Harvey Light, president of Churchill Systems, following the network's installation two years ago, "More Veratex accounts were reopened in five months than similar periods (that didn't have the benefit of the network)." In addition, he said, the patterns and interrelationships uncovered by the neural network proved to be an extremely valuable resource for Veratex marketing analysts.

Light claims that apart from its effectiveness, the Veratex project has other important lessons for neural network developers: "A lot of people think you can avoid knowledge engineering (for neural networks). Forget it—you can't do it. You really have to get down to the business problem before you can do anything else." In fact, Light claims that a large part of the neural network's development time entailed gathering, cleaning up, and organizing the appropriate data.

Condensed from "Application Watch," by Justin Kestelyn, *AI Expert*, January 1992, pp. 63–64, reprinted with permission from *AI Expert*.

13.2 General Building Blocks of Neural Networks

Section 13.1 described the relevant parts of the brain on which the building blocks of neural networks are modeled. In this section, we see how these components are translated into the structure of neural networks.

To set the record straight, it must be mentioned that there is no consensus as to what degree neural networks are based on the structure of the brain. The field goes by numerous names, such as *connectionism, parallel distributed processing, neurocomputing, naturally intelligent systems*, and *artificial neural networks*. One can observe even from these names that there is a tension between engineering a new technology for information processing, and developing the biological model of the brain. Here, we acknowledge the existence of this dual nature of neural networks, and cover the field from the perspective of the practical utility of the topics for application purposes.

In this section, we first look at the neurons as a closed box, and review how they are grouped together into layers. Later, we open the box, and investigate how neurons process their inputs, and send out their outputs. This sets the stage for a general presentation of the learning process, which will be expanded in the next chapter. (The original papers of some of the pioneering work referenced in this chapter are reprinted in the comprehensive book edited by Anderson and Rosenfeld [1988].)

13.2.1   Neurons and Their Interconnections

A neural network structure consists of nodes modeled after a neuron, hence the word *neural*. Some use the word *processing element*, or just *element*, or *neurode* in place of neurons. In this book, we will use neurons and processing elements interchangeably.

Neurons are connected via a network of paths carrying the output of one neuron as input to another neuron. These paths are normally unidirectional. This, however, does not prevent a two-way connection between two neurons,

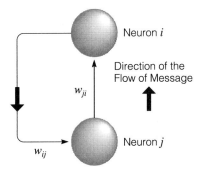

Figure 13.2   Two Connected Neurons in Neural Networks and Their Connection Weights

because one can just add another path in reverse direction to make the communication two-way.

One of the most important elements in the design of a neural network system is the strength of connection between two neurons, which is denoted by the weight value of the connection. For example, if neuron j is connected to neuron i such that the output of neuron j is the input to neuron i, then the strength of connection between j and i is stored in w_{ji}, as shown in Figure 13.2. If there is a reverse connection from i to j, the weight of this connection is stored as w_{ij}. Normally, the two weights do not have the same value. The direction of the arrow in Figure 13.2 shows the direction of the flow of impulses from one neuron to another.

A neuron receives input from many neurons, but produces a single output impulse each time, which is communicated to other neurons. For example, neuron i in Figure 13.3 is connected to neurons called 1, 2, 3, through n. The strength of connection of these neurons to neuron i are stored in the weights w_{1i}, w_{2i}, through w_{ni}. We will see later that the domain knowledge is stored as the values of these weights, and the system learns new knowledge by adjusting the connection weights.

There are two types of connections between two neurons:

- Excitatory

- Inhibitory

In the *excitatory* connection, the output of a neuron increases the action potential of the neuron to which it is connected. When the connection type of two neurons is *inhibitory*, then the output of the neuron sending a message would reduce the activity or action potential of the receiving neuron. In many

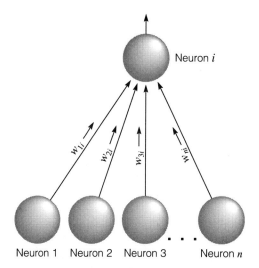

Figure 13.3   A Group of Neurons Connected to Neuron i

neural network designs, all the connections are excitatory. That is why when the type is not specified, the connection is assumed to be excitatory. The inhibitory connections are used in more complex designs, especially in the intra-layer connections discussed later.

Case: Application of Neural Networks in Bankruptcy Prediction

One can't pick up a newspaper or tune into a news broadcast without being painfully aware of the rising number of bankruptcies. Within the realm of finance, the FDIC reported that 1,000 banks closed over the last five years. The disaster within the savings and loan industry is now a national issue.

Financial institutions are not alone in suffering. Commercial and individual bankruptcies are also steadily rising. In 1990 there were about 725,000 filings for chapter 7 or chapter 11 bankruptcies. As a natural result, debt associated with bankruptcies is at its largest point in our history.

While bankruptcies pose grave problems for credit institutions, they are also a nightmare for accounting firms. Aside from losing the income from a paying client, accounting firms can share the liability for bankruptcies. Liability was one of the major reasons for the Laventhal liquidation. The state of California sought to have Ernst & Young's accounting license suspended for their role in the collapse of the Lincoln Savings and Loan Association.

It's clear that the ability to accurately predict if an institution, company, or individual will become bankrupt is of paramount importance. NeuralWare's Application Development Services and Support (ADSS) group has been involved with a number of successful bankruptcy prediction applications. These applications were built using the NeuralWorks Professional neural network development system. One of the highlights of the NeuralWorks development system is that, after development, NeuralWare Designer Pack can be used to port the network to an ANSI standard "C" module for deployment in a customer's computing system.

Both applications I'm about to describe used standard backpropagation networks, with the addition of a proprietary error function created by the ADSS staff. The first application was developed for Peat Marwick, and was used to predict banks that were certain to fail within a year. The predicted certainty of failure was then given to bank examiners dealing with the bank in question.

The backpropagation network the ADSS developed has 11 inputs, each of which was a ratio developed by Peat Marwick. The inputs were connected to a single hidden layer, which in turn was connected to a single node in the output layer. The network output was a single value denoting whether the bank would or would not fail within that calender year. The network employed the normalized cumulative delta learning rule and the hyperbolic-tangent transfer function, both standard choices within the development system. In fact, with the exception of applying the custom error function, the entire network could be constructed within a single dialog box in the NeuralWorks Professional II/Plus development system.

The network was trained on a set of about 1,000 examples, 900 of which were viable banks and 100 of which were banks that had actually gone bankrupt. Training consisted of about 50,000 iterations of the training set.

Peat Marwick has published that the model can predict 50 percent of the population of banks that are viable, and predict failed banks with an accuracy of 99 percent (with an accepted error of 1 percent). If the accepted error is increased to 10 percent, the network can predict both viable and bankrupt banking institutions with an accuracy of 90 percent.

NeuralWare's ADSS has also developed a bankruptcy prediction application for one of the nation's leading credit card institutions. This prediction application is currently used in identifying those credit card holders which have a 100 percent probability of going bankrupt, allowing the institution to take action before this occurs.

NeuralWare isn't the only group that has had success in applying neural computing to bankruptcy prediction. Odom and Sharda, at the Oklahoma State University, have compared the prediction capabilities of a backpropagation neural network with a discriminant analysis technique. Using a training set divided into 10 percent bankrupt firms and 90 percent non-bankrupt firms, the neural network was able to predict bankruptcy with an accuracy of 77.78 percent. This was opposed to an accuracy of 59.26 percent produced by discriminant analysis. By changing the ratio of the bankrupt to non-bankrupt firms in the training set to 50 percent each, bankruptcy predicting accuracy of the neural network improved 81.48 percent. Through techniques developed by the ADSS group, NeuralWare has further improved accuracy over that reported by Odom and Sharda.

What Lies Ahead? The next step is a system that integrates a neural network and an expert system. This hybrid application feeds data from conventional programs (data entry screens, links to external databases, etc.) to both the database and neural network. The neural network then produces a single output value which is actually a probability of whether or not the company, institution, or individual will declare bankruptcy. Using the Explain Net function, a unique feature in the NeuralWorks Professional II/Plus development system, the neural network can also inform the knowledge base about which of the input parameters has the most effect on its prediction.

The expert system can then apply its rule-based decision making capabilities and recommend remedial actions to improve the financial condition of the company, institution or individual. It can also recommend a course of action to be taken by its owner, i.e., a credit institution or accounting firm. This is a vital capability, as the system is not only able to pinpoint potential problems, it can also suggest ways to avoid problems or at least minimize losses.

A fascinating feature of this system is its ability to play "what-if" games to determine the efficacy of remedial action. Because the knowledge base also has access to the conventional programs supplying data to the neural network, it can then vary the parameters that were originally fed to the neural network. By experimenting with changes to the most significant parameters, and then checking the resultant probability of bankruptcy, the system can actually establish what suggested actions are likely to have the most effect.

Finally, the probability of bankruptcy and the suggested actions are added to the database. The result is a self-contained system that both predicts bankruptcy and advises the credit institution or accounting firm on what to do.

Condensed from "Neural Networks for Bankruptcy Prediction: The Power to Solve Financial Problems," by Kevin G. Coleman, Timothy J. Graettinger, and William F. Lawrence, *AI Review.* Summer 1991, pp. 48–50, reprinted with permission from NeuralWare Inc.

13.2.2   *Processing Knowledge in Neural Networks*

In a neural network, neurons are grouped into *layers* or *slabs*. There are different types of layers. For example, an *input layer* consists of neurons that receive input from the external environment. One can consider the input layer as the input unit of the neural network system. The *output layer* consists of neurons that communicate the output of the system to the user or external environment.

The input to the input layer consists of the facts about a given decision problem, such as the facts about a loan application. Once the external input enters the network, the neurons of the input layer become excited and produce output to the neurons on the other layers of the system. The knowledge processing of a neural network system consists of the interactions among layers of neurons in the system. This processing continues until a certain condition is satisfied, or the neurons of the output layer get excited and fire their output to the external environment.

Thus, designing the interactions among neurons is equivalent to programming a system to process an input and produce the desired output. Designing a neural network consists of:

- Arranging neurons in various layers

- Deciding the type of connections among neurons of different layers, as well as among the neurons within a layer

- Deciding the way a neuron receives input and produces output

- Determining the strength of connections within the network by allowing the network to learn the appropriate values of connection weights by using a training data set

The design controls the interactions among the neurons, and hence the output that the system produces. In this section, we discuss the main components of neural network design.

13.2.3   Inter-Layer Connections of Neurons

In a neural network system, there are many interconnected neurons. Normally neurons are grouped into *layers* or *slabs*. The neurons in each layer are of the same type.

In this and the next section, we discuss different types of connections among groups of neurons, and introduce some of the well-known neural networks from a purely structural design perspective. The introduction is brief, and is intended to impress upon the reader the variety and importance of the structural designs in neural networks. In the next chapter, we return to some of the well-known neural networks, and examine more details of their design.

The neurons in a slab may communicate with each other, or they may not have any connections. Normally, in many of the simpler designs, the neurons on a layer do not have interconnections. We discuss the case of intercommunicating neurons within a layer in Section 13.2.4.

The neurons of one layer always are connected to the neurons of at least another layer, as shown in Figure 13.4. There are different types of layer-to-layer or inter-layer connections:

- Fully connected

- Partially connected

- Feed-forward

- Bi-directional

- Hierarchical

- Resonance

In the *fully connected* connection, each neuron on the first layer is connected to every neuron on the second layer. In the *partially connected* layers, a neuron of the first layer does not have to be connected to all neurons on the second layer. It may be connected to only one or more (but not all) neurons on the second layer.

In the *feed-forward* connection, the neurons on the first layer send their output to the neurons of the second layer, but they do not receive any input back from the neurons on the second layer. In the *bi-directional* connection, on the other hand, in addition to a set of connections going from neurons of the first layer to those on the second layer, there is another set of connections carrying the outputs of the neurons of the second layer into the neurons of the first layer. Feed-forward and bi-directional connections could be fully connected or partially connected. Bi-directional connection is also called *association fascicles* in some designs.

The design of a network may not be limited to two layers; it may have many layers. In a *hierarchical* connection, the neurons of the lower layer communicate only with the neurons on the next level. Figure 13.5 shows an example of a hierarchical connection. If a design is not hierarchical, the neurons of one layer may communicate not only with those on the next immediate layer, they may send their output to other layers.

In the *resonance* type of inter-layer connection, the two layers have bi-directional connection, with the added complexity that they continue sending messages across the connections a number of times until a certain condition is achieved. One can imagine the resonance interconnection as two groups sending messages back and forth until they arrive at a consensus.

a.

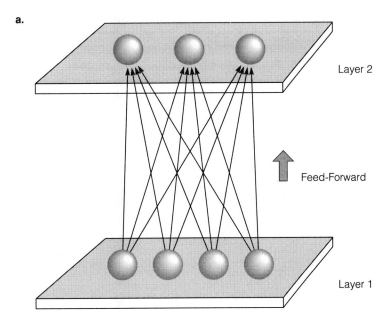

Layer 2

Feed-Forward

Layer 1

b.

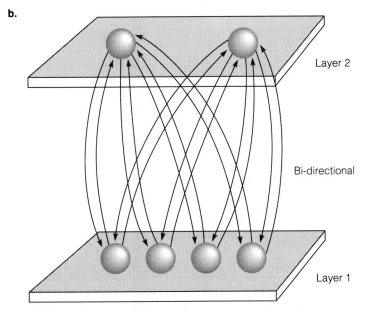

Layer 2

Bi-directional

Layer 1

Figure 13.4 Two Layers or Slabs of Neurons

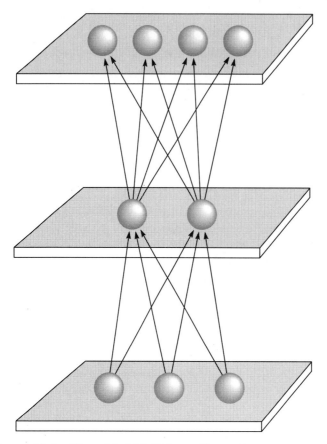

Figure 13.5 Hierarchical Multi-Layer Connection

The above categories of inter-layer connections are used in different well-known neural network designs. (The details of some of these designs are discussed in the next chapter.) The simplest structure is grouping neurons into two layers or slabs: input layer and output layer. The input layer receives input from the environment and passes it to the output layer. The two layers are fully connected. This was the structure of the first neural network: *Perceptron* (developed in 1957 by Frank Rosenblatt), and a later network called *ADALINE* (developed in 1962 by Bernard Widrow and Marcian E. Hoff).

Another neural network called *backpropagation* (developed first by Paul Werbos in 1974, and extended and popularized by Rumelhart, Hinton, and Williams in 1986) has a three-layer, feed-forward, hierarchical structure. In this network, the first layer is the input layer and the third layer is the output layer. The middle layer is called the *hidden* layer, because it is the only layer that does not communicate with the external environment either by taking in the external input or sending out the system output. The backpropagation could have more than one hidden layer, but the hidden layers have a hierarchal structure—a lower level communicates only to its immediate upper level.

The resonance inter-layer connection was used in *Adaptive Resonance Theory (ART)*, developed by Stephen Grossberg in 1976, and later was used in *ART 1*, *ART 2*, and *ART 3* neural networks (developed by Stephen Grossberg and Gail Carpenter in 1987 and 1989). The ART series of neural networks have a more complex structure. They have three layers: the input layer is fully connected to the next layer in a hierarchical manner; the other two layers have a resonance connection.

Another neural network with a relatively complex structure is the *feedforward counterpropagation* neural network (developed by Robert Hecht-Nielsen in 1987). It has a structure similar to that of the backpropagation network, but it is nonhierarchical in that the input layer connects to the output layer as well as the middle layers. In the *full counterpropagation* neural network, the structure is not only non-hierarchical, it is also bidirectional. Another difference is that in the backpropagation neural network, the neurons of one layer do not communicate with one another, while in the middle layer of the counterpropagation network, there are intra-layer connections. More complex neural networks usually have neurons that communicate within one layer. We discuss the intra-layer connections in the next section.

13.2.4   *Intra-Layer Connections of Neurons*

In simple structures, the neurons of one layer only communicate with those on the other layers. In more complex structures, the neurons of a layer are also connected. In the intra-layer connections, the neurons communicate among themselves within a layer. The intra-layer connection may not be present in all layers of a network. For example, the input layer rarely has intra-layer connection.

There are two types of intra-layer connections:

- Recurrent

- On-center/off-surround

In the *recurrent* intra-layer connection, the neurons within a layer are fully or partially connected to one another. When these neurons receive input from another layer, they communicate their outputs with one another a number of times before they are allowed to send their outputs to another layer. Normally, a stable condition among the neurons of the layer should be achieved before they are allowed to communicate their outputs to another layer.

The *Hopfield* network (developed in 1982 by John Hopfield), is a two-layer, fully connected network. The output layer neurons have recurrent intra-layer connections. The recurrent intra-layer connection could also be found in the *recurrent backpropagation* network (developed first in 1986 by David Rumelhart, Geoffrey Hinton, and Ronald Williams). The structure of this network consists of a single layer, part of which receives input from outside, and the rest is fully connected with the recurrent intra-layer connection type.

The *on-center/off-surround* type of intra-layer connection has a more complex design. In this type of connection, a neuron within a layer has excitatory connections to itself and its immediate neighbors, and has inhibitory connections to other neurons. One can imagine this type of connection as a competitive gang of neurons. Each gang excites itself and its gang members (who live close by), and inhibits all members of other gangs.

The idea behind this type of connection is that after a few rounds of signal interchange (or gang fights), the neuron with an active output value will win, and is allowed to update its weight (and possibly also its gang member weights). Since updating weight is equivalent to learning new knowledge, the neuron and its gang win the learning competition.

The on-center/off-surround is a powerful design. It was first developed by Grossberg in a variety of forms in the late 1960s. It has been used in the resonating layers of *ART1, ART2,* and *ART3*.

Teuvo Kohonen has used and popularized this type of intra-layer connection in his *self-organizing* network, developed in 1982. The intra-layer connection in the *counterpropagation* neural network also uses the on-center/off-surround intra-layer connection. We will see later that this type of connection is closely associated with a category of learning called *competitive learning*, and in many publications, the on-center/off-surround is referred to as the competitive learning structure.

13.2.5   Input to Neurons

So far, we have treated information processing within a neuron as a closed box. It is time to open the box, and see how a neuron processes the input messages it receives.

Take node i that receives impulses from n other neurons to which it is connected. We do not distinguish whether the messages are from the neurons on the same layer or on another layer. The impulse a neuron sends to neuron i is modified by the strength of connection between that neuron and neuron i. For example, if neuron 1 sends its output $output_1$ to neuron i, the input to neuron i is equal to $w_{1i} \cdot output_1$. That is, the output of neuron 1 is weighted by the interconnection weight between the two. Since neuron i receives many input impulses, its net input is:

$$input_i = \sum_{all\ j\ neurons\ connected\ to\ i} w_{ji}\ output_j. \tag{1}$$

In equation (1), $input_i$ is the net value of all weighted impulses coming to the neuron. There could be two more terms added to the net input. One term is $extinput_i$, which represents any input the neuron receives from the external environment. Another term is $bias_i$, which represents a bias value used in some networks to control the activation of the neuron.

In some networks, the absolute values of the interconnection weights are limited to the interval 0 to 1. This normalization prevents the input to a neuron from exploding to large values. This is of crucial importance in some networks such as Kohonen's *self-organizing* design. In some networks, the external inputs are also normalized to be in the range 0 and 1. The input data types are discussed in Chapter 14.

Equation (1) has a universal appeal, and it is used both in biological modeling of the brain and in neurocomputing. It also represents the simple computational capability that a neuron is supposed to have. The net input to the neuron creates an action potential. Once this potential reaches a given level, the neuron fires and sends out output messages or impulses to others.

13.2.6 Output from Neurons

For the neuron to send out output, the action potential or the net input should go through a filter or transformation. One of the design issues in neural networks is the type and nature of the *transfer function* used in generating the output in a neuron. There are a number of alternatives for this function. Among the popular transfer functions are:

- Step function
- Signum function
- Sigmoid function

- Hyperbolic tangent function

- Linear function

- Threshold-linear function

In the *step function*, the neuron remains inactive until its net input reaches a *threshold* value T. Once this threshold is reached, it fires and sends out a discrete value, such as 1. This transfer function could be summarized in the following form:

$$output_i = \begin{cases} 0 & \text{if } input_i \leq T \\ 1 & \text{if } input_i > T. \end{cases} \tag{2}$$

When the threshold is 0 in (2), the step function is called *signum*. Another form of *signum* transfer function is

$$output_i = \begin{cases} 1 & \text{if } input_i > 0 \\ 0 & \text{if } input_i = 0 \\ -1 & \text{if } input_i < 0. \end{cases} \tag{3}$$

Among the networks utilizing a *signum* transfer function are *Perceptron* and *bi-directional associative memory* networks. Figure 13.6a shows both the step and signum functions.

The *sigmoid* transfer function produces a continuous value in the 0 to 1 range. It has the following form:

$$output_i = \frac{1}{1 + e^{gain \cdot input_i}}. \tag{4}$$

In this transfer function, no matter what the value of $input_i$ is, the output would be limited to the $[0, 1]$ range. The parameter *gain* is to be determined by the system designer. In some cases, it is defined as $gain = \frac{1}{T}$, where T is defined before as the threshold. The value of *gain* affects the slope of the transfer function around zero. Figure 13.6b shows the shape of this function. The sigmoid transfer function is used in many networks, including the *backpropagation* and *Hopfield* networks.

Another version of the sigmoid transfer function is *hyperbolic tangent* transfer function. It has the following form:

$$output_i = \frac{e^u - e^{-u}}{e^u + e^{-u}}, \tag{5}$$

where $u = gain \cdot input_i$. This function has a form similar to the sigmoid function, with the difference that the value of $output_i$ ranges between -1 to 1 in this transfer function. When $u = 0$ in this transfer function, the value

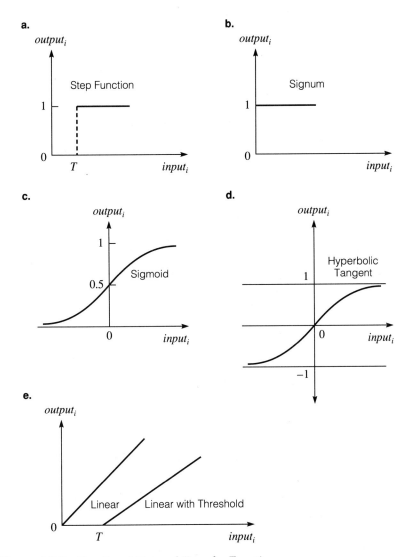

Figure 13.6 Functional Form of Transfer Functions

of output is also zero. Figure 13.6b shows both the sigmoid and hyperbolic tangent functions.

The *linear* transfer function has the simple form of

$$output_i = gain \cdot input_i. \tag{6}$$

Again, *gain* is a system parameter, and in some designs its value is equal to 1. This transfer function is used in *brain-state-in-a-box* neural network.

Threshold-linear transfer function is another form of the linear function:

$$output_i \begin{cases} 0 & \text{if } input_i \leq T \\ input_i - T & \text{if } input_i > T. \end{cases} \tag{7}$$

This function allows the neuron to fire only after it has reached the threshold value, and its output value is the value of input minus the threshold. Figure 13.6c shows both types of linear transfer functions.

An inspection of the transfer functions in Figure 13.6 reveals that the output of a neuron could be binary (0 and 1), or it could be continuous and constrained in the $[0, 1]$ interval or $[-1, 1]$ range. The output could also take continuous values, not limited to the $[0, 1]$ interval. The choice of the transfer function normally goes with the network design chosen for the system. In some networks, the developer has the flexibility of selecting the transfer function for the network. In this case, the selection of the transfer function becomes a design issue for the system developer.

Even when the system developer decides to use a neural network design in which the form of transfer function is already specified, the system developer still has to determine the parameter of the transfer function, such as threshold (T) in equations (2) and (7), and *gain* in equations (4) and (6). The determination of the transfer function and its parameter are design issues that the system developer should resolve through experimentation with the system.

13.2.7   General Types of Learning in Neural Networks

In equation (1), we can easily observe that the connection weights decide what is the net input to a neuron. Furthermore, the net input of the neuron determines its output value. Thus, the connection weights are the single most important factor in the input and output processes of a neuron. Since a neural network consists of a collection of interacting neurons, the values of weights determine the outcome of the network.

In almost all neural network systems, it is the system itself that computes the interconnection weights among the neurons. The process by which the system arrives at the values of connecting weights is called *learning*. For the system to learn, it should be given a learning method to change the weights to the ideal values and a domain data set that represents the domain knowledge.

Learning method is the most important distinguishing factor in various neural networks. We will discuss the details of these networks and their learning methods in the next chapter. Here, we discuss the learning methods from a more general perspective.

There are two distinct types of learning:

- Supervised

- Unsupervised

In *supervised* learning, the system developer tells the system what the correct answer is, and the system determines weights in such a way that once given the input, it would produce the desired output. Of course, it is understood that the input could be noisy and incomplete. When in operation, the system may receive input data that is not exactly the same as what the system has used to determine the weights.

The main idea in supervised learning is that the system is repeatedly given facts about various cases, along with the expected outputs. The system uses the learning method to adjust the weights in order to produce outputs close to what are expected. Supervised learning has the analogy of a child learning new lessons with the help of a teacher.

In *unsupervised* learning, the system receives only the input, and no information on the expected output. In this type of learning, the system learns to produce the pattern of what it has been exposed to. This type of learning conjures up the image of an infant who learns by repeated exposure to its environment. The *self-organizing* neural network (developed by Kohonen) is the network that created this category of learning.

Most of the neural networks employ the supervised learning method, because this type is of more immediate use for problem solving. On the other hand, unsupervised learning has the potential for creating intelligent systems more powerful than what other methods could accomplish.

One can categorize the learning methods into yet another group:

- Off-line

- On-line

The system could be in one of two states: *training mode* and *operation mode*. When the system uses input data to change its weights to learn the domain knowledge, the system is in the *training* or *learning* mode. When the system is being used as a decision aid to make recommendations, it is in the *operation* mode. In the *off-line* learning methods, once the system enters into the operation mode, its weights are fixed and do not change any more. Most of the network designs are of the off-line learning type.

In *on-line* or *real-time* learning, when the system is in the operation mode, it continues to learn while being used as a decision tool. When the system encounters a new input data that is different from what it has seen before, it decides that the input data represents new knowledge, and changes its weights to reflect the new knowledge. This type of learning has a more complex design structure. The Grossberg–Carpenter ART networks series utilizes the real-time learning.

13.2.8   *Types of Learning Equations (Optional)*

Neural network systems are in one of two states: training mode or operation mode. When a system is in training mode, and the input data is presented to the system, it is allowed to modify its weights. This is the mode in which the system learns new knowledge by modifying its weights.

In most of the learning methods, when the system is in the training mode, weights are changed gradually in an iterative process. The system is repeatedly presented with case data from a training data set, and is allowed to change its weights after one (or a predetermined number of) iteration(s).

One of the important building blocks in training a system is the learning equation. (We will see the other issues involved in training a system in Chapter 14.) This is the formula the system uses to alter its weights. Although there are numerous learning methods, the equations used in most of these methods could be considered variations of four basic rules:

- Hebb rule

- Delta rule

- Generalized delta rule

- Kohonen rule

Hebb Rule

The *Hebb rule* has a biological basis, and is the oldest learning equation. The Hebb rule was inspired by an observation by the well-known Canadian psychologist Donald Hebb, who stated in 1949 that

> "When an axon of cell A is near enough to excite a cell B and repeatedly or persistently takes place in firing it, some growth process or metabolic

change takes place in one or both cells such that A's efficiency, as one of the cells firing B, is increased." (Hebb [1949], quoted by Carpenter [1989].)

The Hebbian rule has a number of interpretations. The simplest formulation of Hebb's idea is:

$$w_{ji}^{new} - w_{ji}^{old} = \alpha \ . \ output_j \ . \ output_i. \tag{8}$$

The weight w_{ji} is the weight of the connection from neuron j to neuron i. This equation shows that when neuron j sends the output ($output_j$) to neuron i, and neuron i is excited at the same time and produces ($output_i$), the interconnection weight from neuron j to neuron i increases by the product of the two outputs. In this learning equation, α is called the *learning parameter* or *learning coefficient*, and represents the speed of learning.

Another interpretation of the Hebb rule is to use $input_i$ in place of $output_i$, as

$$w_{ji}^{new} - w_{ji}^{old} = \alpha \ . \ output_j \ . \ input_i. \tag{9}$$

(Grossberg and Carpenter use this interpretation of the Hebb rule.)

A more common formulation of Hebb's idea is to use the "desired" output of neuron i (we call it $desoutput_i$) in place of $output_i$ in equation (8).

$$w_{ji}^{new} - w_{ji}^{old} = \alpha \ . \ output_j \ . \ desoutput_i. \tag{10}$$

The desired output is what is expected from neuron i to produce, and this value is known if the neuron sends its output to the external environment. This interpretation is used in many neurocomputing engineering applications of the Hebb rule. In this interpretation, it is mathematically shown that for the Hebbian learning rule to learn the domain knowledge correctly, the data for the cases in the training data set should be *orthogonal*. This means that the data for the cases should not have any correlation. Otherwise, the system output would contain an error, which is proportional to the correlation among the data in the training data set.

The learning parameter α varies in the $[0, 1]$ range. The higher the value of this parameter, the faster the system learns. However, when the value of the learning parameter is high, the system will have a lower capability to generalize. The generalization capability is important in neural network systems, because it enables the system to make the correct decisions from noisy and incomplete input data. In some implementations of this learning equation, the value of the learning parameter is changed as the training progresses.

Delta Rule

The *delta rule* was first developed by Widrow and Hoff, and it has an engineering, rather than biological, basis. This rule is also known as the *Widrow/Hoff rule, least mean square rule*, and *LMS rule*. The delta rule is the prominent example of optimizing an objective function in determining the weight values. In the case of the delta rule, the objective is to minimize the sum of the squared errors, where an error is defined as the distance between an actual output of the system from the desired (or the correct) output, for a given input data.

The rule has the following equation:

$$w_{ji}^{new} - w_{ji}^{old} = \alpha \ . \ output_j \ . \ error_i, \tag{11}$$

where $output_j$ is the message that neuron j has sent to neuron i over the connection $j \rightarrow i$. In (11),

$$error_i = output_i^{old} - desoutput_i, \tag{12}$$

is the distance between the actual output of neuron i in the previous iteration ($output_i^{old}$) and the desired output of neuron i ($desoutput_i$). α is the learning parameter, similar to that in the Hebb rule.

Generalized Delta Rule

The generalized delta rule is similar to the delta rule, with the exception that the derivative of the transfer function is added to the equation as:

$$w_{ji}^{new} - w_{ji}^{old} = \alpha \ . \ output_j \ . \ error_i \ . \ f'(input_i), \tag{13}$$

where $f'(input_i)$ is the derivative of the transfer function evaluated at $input_i$. This rule is used when the transfer function is nonlinear, such as sigmoid (4) or hyperbolic tangent transfer function (5). Otherwise, the transfer function either does not have a derivative (such as the case of step function), or its derivative is constant, such as the linear transfer function.

Kohonen Rule

In the neurocomputing interpretation of the Hebbian rule and in the delta rule, the system is given the "desired" output (*desoutput*) for each of the neurons in the output layer. This means that the "correct" answer is known.

The learning equations (11) and (13) are used in the supervised methods of learning. The *Kohonen rule* does not require the desired output. Therefore, it is implemented in the unsupervised methods of learning.

The Kohonen rule has the following equation:

$$w_{ji}^{new} - w_{ji}^{old} = \alpha(extinput_i - w_{ji}^{old}), \tag{14}$$

where $extinput_i$ is the input the neuron i receives from the external environment. Kohonen has used this rule combined with the on-center/off-surround intra-layer connection (discussed before) to create the *self-organizing* neural network, which has an unsupervised learning method.

In the next chapter, we see how these learning equations are combined with inter-layer and intra-layer connections and interactions to create various types of neural networks.

Case: Using Neural Networks for Identifying Horse Pedigree

The University of California School of Veterinary Medicine at Davis is preoccupied with horse pedigrees. Thoroughbred breeders cannot race a horse without proof of its parentage, and that means running 142 separate reaction tests on a sample of the horse's blood, something that the veterinary school does under contract to horse registries. This adds up to a monumental volume of reaction tests, as many as 72,000 a day. How to automate the business? The lab's scientists trained a computer to peer through a microscope and judge, like a human technician, whether a blood reaction is positive or negative.

The significance of this accomplishment is that it involves a developing technology called neural network computing. Neural networking is much theorized about these days but rarely capable of commercially practical results. If neural nets do all that is expected of them, they will someday be able to solve all kinds of problems for which conventional computers have proven inadequate—such as the recognition of handwriting, speech or battlefield targets.

In essence, neural networking amounts to teaching computers to think and learn more like human beings. From a practical standpoint, though, the question arises whether imitating nature is an intelligent way to design a thinking machine. Isn't that rather like designing an airplane with wings that flap, or a car that gallops? The success of the blood-testing computer, which has been in development since April 1987 and in pilot testing for the last year, should help allay such concerns.

To some degree neural networks resemble, in the abstract, the wiring style of the human brain. The network is structured as a layered series of nodes. Nodes of the input layer receive signals of varying strength coming into the network.

These signals are in turn passed on to the next layer of nodes. After processing within this layer, these nodes transfer an answer out of the system—in this case, a simple yes or no. Is this blood sample reaction a positive one? The process of learning in neural networks is one of gradually and systematically adjusting the signal strengths in the network until a given set of input data gives rise to the correct output.

Most neural nets in use or in experimental work today, including Davis' lab system, are software simulations that run on ordinary IBM and IBM clone personal computers or Apple Macintoshes. You can display a network diagrammatically on a monitor screen and actually watch it learn. The wiring scheme looks rather like a plan for a train yard.

One of the most level-headed and successful practitioners of neural network technology is Wasyl Malyj, 43, chief development engineer with the Serology Laboratory at the veterinary school in Davis. A lot is at stake for the lab. The accuracy of its results must be unquestioned. Horse breeders and owners depend on these tests to assure the value of their animals.

To confirm the genetic heritage of a racehorse, the lab does blood typing tests similar to those done in hospitals. (If you are type AB, for example, then genetic logic states that both of your parents must have had A or B antigens, neither of them could have been completely genetically type O.) The same sort of genetic reasoning holds true for a horse. Most such logic rules out, rather than rules in, a family relationship. This reasoning by exclusion is why many different blood groups must be tested to confirm a thoroughbred's parentage.

Computers are, of course, vital to keeping track of all the horses and all their potential relatives. At the Serology lab, an array of hard-disk drives store 2 gigabytes (2 billion characters) of genetic archives on 456,000 horses tested to date. But this is conventional computing, not tougher than keeping 456,000 checking account records on a bank's mainframe.

Malyj's neural net tackles an altogether different and, at least to a computer, more difficult assignment: deciding whether the cells in a tiny droplet of blood have agglutinated, that is, clumped together. A technician can make this judgment instantly, but no technician is eager to do 72,000 of these a day.

Malyj's system sees with a video camera that divides its field of view into 262,144 pixels of photographic information. In principle it should be possible to use this array of data as input to a neural network. In order to learn the concept of clumpiness, the computer would be trained with perhaps tens of thousands of reaction images that could be considered clumpy. But this is just too much raw data for a neural net to handle. Malyj estimates the time required to train his particular network to learn the concept of clumpiness this way at something like 28 million years.

To make the network function here and now, Malyj had to find a shortcut. He found it in a scientific paper published in 1970 by George Lendaris, who pioneered in scanning aerial surveillance photographs by computer. Lendaris, who was then at General Motors' military research laboratory in Santa Barbara, Calif., was asking his computer to simulate human eye and ferret out orderly man-made features on the ground—orchards, road intersections, buildings and the like.

This is a bit of a tangent but stay with us. Lendaris' contribution involves a ubiquitous mathematical object called the Fourier transform, named after an early

19th-century French physicist and mathematician. The transform takes in a blizzard of data and, using mathematical operations, converts them into oscillating waves of energy. Musical sound, for example, has components that repeat at different frequencies corresponding to different pitches. A Fourier transform of a bit of symphonic music would tell you how much sound is being heard at middle C, how much at D and so on. The transform can also highlight sharp gradations, such as at the edge of a building—or the edge of a clump of blood.

Aided by the Fourier transform, Malyj found that he could condense the 262,144 pixels from a blood sample to a mere 48 data points. The neural net computer can quickly learn to read from the 48 features whether a clump is present. The neural net doesn't have to memorize every possible angle, dimension, and position in which a clump has turned up in blood test images.

As Davis' Malyj puts it, "Similar features have really similar transforms." What was impossible for conventional computing logic became possible and commercially feasible using neural networking.

Malyj uses a neural network system supplied by Science Application International Corp., a San Diego, Calif., firm that does a lot of military and other government-funded research. The $25,000 SAIC product, Delta II, consists of both the network simulation software and a powerful accelerator board. These neural net add-ons greatly enhance an ordinary $5,000 desktop computer of the sort using the Intel 386 chip. In developing the system, Malyj also used a product on his Macintosh called MacBrain, from Neurix of Cambridge, Mass.

The implications of Malyj's success in applying neural nets to the analysis of horse bloodlines is evident. Human diagnostic work may follow. In Seattle a neural net is already being applied in reading the results of pap smear tests. These machines cannot distinguish fine structure, but they can readily recognize simple patterns like agglutination.

Despite his own success, Malyj believes that commercial development of neural nets is problematical. "The difficulty is, what will you sell? A neural net is just an algorithm—a method of calculation like a [statistical] regression or multiplication. It is hard to protect a product like that—hard to get a commercial handle on it." What will succeed, he believes, is a variety of hardware systems in which the neural net learning method is to some degree automated and embedded in the computer system, so that the user won't have to understand it to the same degree today's pioneers do.

Among many companies developing chips, boards, software of whole computers specially configured to support neural nets besides Scientific Applications, Intel and Apple: MasPar Computer Corp., a Sunnyvale, Calif., firm working on parallel-processing computers, Ariel Corp. of Highland Park, N.J., a firm specializing in array processors, and Applied Intelligent Systems, an Ann Arbor firm working on machine vision. But the field is still largely one of theoretical triumphs. At the level of practical applications, where progress in neural nets has been slow, meager and difficult, it appears that Wasyl Malyj is the man on horseback.

Condensed from "The Eye is a Computer," by Michael Giantureo, *Forbes*, November 12, 1990, pp. 326–330, reprinted with permission from *Forbes*.

13.3 Similarities of Expert Systems and Neural Networks

In this section, we review the *similarities of expert systems and neural network systems.** We can categorize the similarities of the two fields into:

- Common origin and common goal

- Imitating human intelligence

- The mix of quantitative and qualitative information processing

- Nonautomatic nature of design

- Multi-disciplinary domain and applications

13.3.1 Common Origin and Common Goal

Expert systems and neural networks have a common origin and a common goal. The dream of creating objects with human intelligence is as old as recorded history. In Homer's *Iliad*, Hephaestus's golden robots are "in appearance like living women./ There is intelligence in their hearts, and there is speech in them / and strength and from the immortal gods they have learned how to do things" (as quoted in McCorduck [1979]). Old Chinese, Jewish, and Arab tales, among many, allude to mythical robots with artificial intelligence. In modern times, intelligent robots in science-fiction stories have created an expectation that someday, such machines will become a reality. This could partly explain why any news about artificial intelligence or thinking machines can grasp the attention of an audience much larger than those who have a direct stake in the topic.

Although the history of mankind is a testament to the continuous fascination with intelligent machines, by many accounts, the beginning of the

---

*Parts of this section are based on the paper "An Introduction to Neural Networks and a Comparison with Artificial Intelligence," by Fatemeh Zahedi, *Interfaces*, Vol. 21, No. 2, March–April 1991, pp. 25–38, with permission from the Operations Society of America and the Institute of Management Sciences.

modern scientific research in artificial intelligence goes back to 1943, when McCulloch and Pitts developed a simple neural network that could produce outputs of logical and mathematical functions. Their interest was using neural networks to perform logical reasoning.

When Hebb in 1949 provided an explanation for conditional learning in animals, the idea became one of the fundamental methods for making intelligent systems learn. Animal conditioning goes back to Pavlov's famous experiment, in which a bell was rung before food was given to a dog. After a while, without being offered any food, the dog salivated whenever the bell was rung. Hebb suggested that animal conditioning is due to the strengthening of interconnection among individual neurons, where the memory of food and the memory of bell ringing are stored.

In 1951, Marvin Minsky created *Snark*, the first of what we call neurocomputers today. By the time the well-known Dartmouth conference was convened in 1956, declaring the goal of artificial intelligence as simulating all aspects of human intelligence, both artificial intelligence and neural networks had laid some groundwork for methods of achieving this common goal.

Thus, neural networks have the same goal as artificial intelligence and expert systems. They both strive to create intelligent computer systems.

13.3.2 *Imitating Human Intelligence*

In 1956 and 1957, Rosenblatt developed the first successful neurocomputer, *Mark I Perceptron*, and developed the first neural network system, called *Perceptron*. By this time, two distinct approaches to the simulation of human intelligence were developed: one was what today we call artificial intelligence, and the other was neural networks.

In the 1960s, the two fields competed to prove the superiority of their approach in giving computers intelligence similar to what we observe in humans. Artificial intelligence advocated the imitation of human logical reasoning, while neural networks prescribed designs roughly similar to the structure of neurons in the brain. Artificial intelligence made bigger advances in the 1960s, and when Minsky and Papert published their book *Perceptrons*, criticizing the shortcomings of one popular design for neural networks, artificial intelligence emerged as the winner. The research in neural networks subsided in the 1970s, except for the continuous efforts of a handful of researchers.

In the 1980s, interest in neural networks was revived for a number of reasons. A well-known physicist, John Hopfield, showed that a neural network design corresponds to a similar structure in a physical phenomenon, called spin glass. Robert Hecht-Nielsen proved that the criticism of Minsky and Papert does not hold for the more general type of neural networks. Furthermore, although the successes of artificial intelligence and expert systems became well-known in the 1980s, so did the limitations of artificial intelligence in pattern recognition and learning. Moreover, advances in computer hardware have made the time ripe for the revival of neural networks. Thus, researchers started to look to neural networks for dealing with aspects of human intelligence for which the existing technology of artificial intelligence lacked a clear answer.

13.3.3   The Mix of Quantitative and Qualitative Information Processing

As we have seen in expert systems, the knowledge base mostly contains qualitative information and knowledge. The strength of an expert system is its ability to store, formalize, and process qualitative information. However, as shown in the discussion on logic-based knowledge representation in Chapters 3 and 4, and object-oriented knowledge representation in Chapters 8, 9, and 10, one can include quantitative computations in the form of functions and methods.

In neural networks, too, one can combine qualitative and quantitative processing of information. In neural networks, one can have system input and output of a qualitative nature, such as colors or patterns, as well as quantitative input or output, such as the amount of a loan. The qualitative or quantitative nature of input and output data, in principle, does not alter the structure of the neural networks, because neural networks are trained from raw data. However, we will see later that one must code the data, and choose the method for training the system that is more appropriate for the domain data. Therefore, despite the ability of neural networks to deal with a mix of qualitative and quantitative data, the design process for such systems is far from automatic and predetermined.

13.3.4   Nonautomatic Nature of Design

One of the features of human intelligence is that its learning, at least in the early stages of life, is automatic, in that an infant does not have to be coaxed to learn to recognize its mother, or to take food. A robot that automatically learns a new type of knowledge from its environment has been the dream of many innovators, and the goal of many scientific research projects.

Artificial intelligence is far from approaching this dream. The discussion of knowledge engineering in Chapter 7 demonstrates that creating the knowledge base for expert systems is not an automatic process. It requires careful planning and extensive participation of a variety of groups, such as experts, systems designers, knowledge engineers, and users.

The early attraction of neural network systems was their potential for learning automatically from raw input data, and creating their own internal knowledge base. However, neural networks, too, are still far away from this goal. Although a neural network system does not have the knowledge engineering problems common in expert systems, it requires extensive and careful structural design, which is dependent on the domain and the nature of the decision problem. For the foreseeable future, systems designers will have a secure job in creating expert systems and neural network systems.

13.3.5 *Multi-disciplinary Domain and Applications*

Intelligence is a multi-faceted concept that encompasses many functions, such as language, speech, memory, recognition, reasoning, learning important new knowledge, and gradually forgetting what has become unimportant or irrelevant. Hence, the study of intelligence and its simulation would interest a heterogeneous group of researchers in disciplines that investigate one or more aspects of intelligence. This group includes psychologists, cognitive scientists, linguists, philosophers, engineers, and computer scientists. Since artificial intelligence uses mathematical logic as its basis, mathematicians and logicians have interest in this field. In neural networks, because of its focus on the brain structure, and its similarity with some physical phenomena, neurosientists, biologists, and physicists should be added to the above list. Thus, both expert systems and neural networks, by the nature of their goals, have a multi-disciplinary theoretical domain.

The applications of intelligent systems are also multi-disciplinary. Humans apply their intelligence in solving problems and making decisions in all walks of life. An intelligent system will be of interest to almost all fields of human endeavor. The application of intelligent systems in business is of great interest because of the capability of mixing qualitative and quantitative knowledge processing. However, the scope of the application of intelligent systems is virtually limitless, ranging from decision systems in medicine, geology, and fishery, to arts and entertainment. We are just beginning to discover the innovative applications of expert systems in divergent fields, and the applications of neural networks will have even more diversity and variety.

13.4 Differences Between Expert Systems and Neural Networks

Although artificial intelligence (including expert systems) and neural networks have common goals, they use very different means to achieve them.*
We can categorize the *differences between expert systems and neural networks* into:

- Foundation
- Scope
- Processing techniques
- Learning
- Reasoning method
- Underlying theory
- Solution algorithm
- Knowledge representation
- Knowledge engineering
- Design issues
- Reliability issues
- User interface
- State of recognition and maturity
- Applications

13.4.1   Foundation: Logic vs. Brain

Artificial intelligence and neural networks have different foundations: one is founded on *logic*, and the other on the *brain*.

To accomplish the mission of endowing computers with intelligence, researchers pursued two fundamental approaches. The artificial intelligence group chose to concentrate on simulating and formalizing human reasoning

---

*Parts of this section are based on the paper "An Introduction to Neural Networks and a Comparison with Artificial Intelligence," by Fatemeh Zahedi, *Interfaces*, Vol. 21, No. 2, March–April 1991, pp. 25–38, with permission from the Operations Society of America and the Institute of Management Sciences.

and logical processes. Simon and Newell were the pioneers of this approach. This school of thought advocated a symbolic system representing human logic and reasoning. This became the foundation of artificial intelligence, which focuses on how a person logically justifies actions and decisions, and attempts to give the machine a similar logical and reasoning capability. On the other hand, when issues such as uncertainty or other types of presentation have gained relevance in expert systems, the researchers have not hesitated to stray from absolute adherence to the principles of logic to include them in their systems.

In neural networks, researchers opted for simulating intelligence functions of the brain. Rosenblatt in 1958 stated that the perceptron (the neural network design that he developed) was a model of a biological brain and "seems to come closer to meeting the requirements of a functional explanation of the nervous system than any system previously proposed." Thus, the foundation of neural networks was the modeling of the brain. However, as we will see in the following chapter, researchers of neural networks have not adhered to the exact modeling of the biological brain, and have developed systems for which we have yet to find a parallel in the biological brain.

Hence, while human logic and reasoning are the foundation of artificial intelligence, and the structure and functioning of the brain is the ideal model of neural networks, neither logic nor the brain have constrained the development of useful approaches that may not conform to the basic foundation.

13.4.2   Scope: Macro vs. Micro

Artificial intelligence has a *macro* scope, while neural networks have a *micro* scope. Artificial intelligence treats the brain as a black box. Its structure is closer to models of human decision making. In decision science and cognitive science, researchers focus on actions, underlying motives, and the formal process that links the actions to motives. The axiomatic foundation of these sciences is logic, its consistency, and its completeness. Artificial intelligence has a similar focus.

The neural network approach, on the other hand, opens the brain and looks at its known structure and functions. The focus here is to create a system that functions like the brain because it has a structure similar to some areas of the brain, and has functionalities observed in the operations of the brain. For example, the structure of a neural network consists of connected nodes. Each neuron or processing element in neural networks is fashioned after one neuron (or a group of neurons with similar functions) in the brain. The connections among neural network nodes is a model of the connectivity of neurons in the brain. The modeling of human intelligence in neural networks is obviously at the micro level of the physical and functional structure of the brain.

Obviously, the limitations of our knowledge of how the brain works, and the fact that none of the existing hardware could even begin to approach the number and connectivity of neurons in the brain, make any claim of modeling the biological brain quite superficial. But neural network researchers use the brain both as the source of inspiration and ideas on design and functionality, and as the major criterion for the verification of the validity of theoretical developments.

13.4.3   Processing Techniques: Sequential vs. Parallel

The processing method in artificial intelligence is inherently *sequential*. Take the rule-based processing in expert systems. The knowledge is coded in the form of IF-THEN rules. The backward chaining takes the known THEN part of a rule and matches it with the IF part of other rules. Such a matching process takes one rule at a time, hence the processing method is inherently sequential. The developments of artificial intelligence parallel systems and parallel Prolog are attempts to overcome the sequential nature of artificial intelligence.

The processing method in neural networks is inherently *parallel*. Each of the neurons in a neural network system functions in parallel with the other nodes. The neurons in a neural network system could be considered simple CPUs, operating simultaneously. Since most of the existing hardware systems are sequential machines, neural network software has been developed to simulate the parallel nature of neural networks in the present serial machines. There are add-on chips in the market that give some virtual parallelism to the hardware. However, the full power of neural networks will become evident when the parallel processing computers enter the mass market.

13.4.4   Learning: Static and External vs. Dynamic and Internal

In artificial intelligence and expert systems, learning usually takes place outside the system. The knowledge is obtained outside the system, and then coded into the knowledge base. In more complex expert systems, it may be possible to include meta-rules in the knowledge base to make the system more adaptive to the environment. But even in such cases, the learning would take place according to a static set of rules. Thus, in artificial intelligence and expert systems, learning is *static* and *external* to the system. (In recent years, numerous attempts have been made to make the AI systems capable of learning automatically. Together, this body of research has been called *machine learning*. Machine learning in AI at this stage lacks a biological or theoretical underpinning.)

In neural networks, learning is an integral part of the system, and plays an important role in the design of the system. In neural networks, knowledge is stored as the strength of connections among the nodes or neurons. It is the neural network's job to learn by determining these weights from a set of training data. Hence, in neural networks, learning is *internal* to the system, and could be made *dynamic*.

In Chapter 14, we see that the selection of the method by which a neural network system learns is one of the most important design issues in neural networks. The variety and diversity of learning methods in neural networks is one of the interesting, and at the same time, confusing aspects of creating neural network systems.

13.4.5   *Reasoning Method: Deductive vs. Inductive*

The traditional methods in artificial intelligence and expert systems are *deductive* in nature, in that the generalized domain knowledge is developed outside the systems and is coded into it. The use of the system involves a deductive reasoning process, applying the generalized knowledge to a given case, as we have seen in Chapters 4, 5, 8, and 10. More recent expert systems do have a mechanism for developing rules from data, hence formalizing the knowledge engineering process. An example of such a system is 1st-CLASS (covered in Chapter 6), which uses ID3 to develop a decision tree for the knowledge base by induction. However, induction is not the common approach in artificial intelligence and expert systems.

The reasoning method in neural networks is decidedly *inductive*. Neural networks construct an internal knowledge base from the raw training data. In other words, the system generalizes from the data, such that when it is presented with a new set of data that it had not seen before, it can make a decision based on the generalized internal knowledge.

This difference also underlines the fact that the two systems have different data requirements. Artificial intelligence and expert systems require knowledge coded in advance. The source of the coded knowledge is of little importance to the system. The knowledge could be engineered from experts, it may be based on data, it may come from books or other sources such as application reports. Neural networks, on the other hand, require data in raw form, and in most designs, a massive amount of data is needed. In areas where little data exists, neural networks would find few applications.

13.4.6   Underlying Theory: Mathematical Logic, Object-Oriented, and Deterministic vs. Statistics and Stochastic

As we have seen in Chapters 3, 4, and 8, the underlying theory of artificial intelligence is *mathematical logic* and *object-oriented* approach. By nature, this theory is *deterministic*. As we have seen in Chapter 11, the treatment of uncertainty in expert systems is an add-on to the system, which is necessitated by a practical reality, rather than a theoretical imperative. Thus, even in deriving knowledge rules or decision trees from raw data by inductive methods in expert systems, the data set is to be complete and error-free.

In neural networks, on the other hand, the underlying assumption is that data is noisy and error-ridden. The learning methods attempt to come up with the best representation of knowledge based on stochastic and ambiguous data. Thus, the underlying theory of neural networks is *statistical* and *stochastic* in nature.

The statistical and probabilistic nature of neural networks puts it in direct competition with statistical techniques for processing data and making inference from it. As a matter of fact, Halbert White, a well-known econometrician, has been doing research on the interface of statistics and neural networks (see, for example, his 1989 article in *AI Expert*). Statistical and econometrics methods mostly deal with quantitative data and require functional specifications among the variables or attributes. Neural networks have the advantage of dealing with both qualitative and quantitative data and do not require a mathematical function for specifying the relationships among the decision attributes. However, as we will see in Chapter 14, neural networks require careful design specifications, the details of which are yet to be developed.

13.4.7   Solution Algorithm: Exact Matching vs. Approximate Matching

Many algorithms of artificial intelligence and expert systems are based on variable bindings of predicate calculus. When the production rule is the method of knowledge representation, the system uses either backward chaining or forward chaining in traversing through the knowledge base. Thus the solution algorithms in most of artificial intelligence and expert systems are based on *binding* and *chaining*. Both require the *precise matching* of components.

Neural networks use *approximate matching* or *nearest matching* to recall what the system has learned before. This gives a neural network system the ability to recognize a pattern or recommend a decision from incomplete, altered, noisy, and uncertain data about a case. This aspect of neural networks brings the system closer to the human method of recognition and decision process. However, it also adds the complexity that the system may over-generalize, or attribute a new case to a wrong category and pattern. The generalization ability of the system is one of the design issues of neural network systems.

13.4.8 Knowledge Representation: Explicit vs. Implicit

Artificial intelligence and expert systems represent knowledge in an *explicit* form. Production rules, predicate calculus, frames, and object-oriented representations contain knowledge in a form recognizable by a human. One can inspect and alter a rule within an expert system, or identify an object and change its attributes.

In neural networks, the knowledge is stored in the form of the interconnection strengths among the neurons. Nowhere in the system can one pick a piece of computer code or a numerical value as a discernible piece of knowledge. The knowledge representation in neural networks is *implicit*. This aspect of neural networks may be considered the most dramatic departure from conventional information processing. At the same time, it causes a number of problems, among which are the difficulty in inspecting the content of the knowledge base and in creating a user-friendly interface.

13.4.9 Knowledge Engineering: People-oriented vs. Data Driven

In artificial intelligence and expert systems, knowledge engineering is mostly *external* to the system. As we have seen in Chapter 8, the definition of domain and the acquisition of knowledge from experts must take place prior to any coding. The knowledge engineer does not need to be an expert in expert system software in order to compile the domain knowledge relevant to the decision problem at hand. The knowledge engineering in expert systems is *people-oriented*.

Knowledge engineering in neural networks is mostly *internal* to the system, in that, once the problem is defined and relevant raw data is identified, the design and experimentation with the system could immediately commence. However, the developer must work longer with the system to make sure that its performance is satisfactory. Thus, neural networks do not have the lengthy knowledge engineering process, but the developer must be familiar with the field of neural networks and design the system with a great deal of care. The knowledge engineering in neural networks is *data driven*.

In sum, while knowledge engineering may be considered the bottleneck of developing an expert system, design could be considered the bottleneck in developing a neural network system.

13.4.10 Design Issues: Simple vs. Complex

The domain knowledge dictates most of the design issues in expert systems. Once the content of the knowledge base is determined, there are not many design alternatives. The developer must choose between a couple of approaches for knowledge representation, and select the appropriate software for coding the knowledge base. The technical side of expert system development is relatively *simple*, and does not involve difficult design choices.

In neural network systems, the developer embarks on design at the early stage of the project, and has to make a number of difficult decisions on the structure of the system. As we will see in Chapter 14, the developer must make a number of decisions for which well-defined rules are not available. For example, the developer must determine the number of layers, type of connectivity, method of learning, and the learning parameters of the system. Since neural network systems are still at their infancy, the guidelines for the design parameters are yet to be fully developed. Thus, the developer must go through a period of trial and error in the design decisions before coming up with a satisfactory design. The design issues in neural networks are *complex* and will remain the major concern of system developers in years to come.

13.4.11 Reliability Issues: Expert-based vs. Data-based

The reliability of expert systems has a definite criterion, which is the performance of a human counterpart in similar cases. The knowledge base of an expert system does not contain the vehicle for validation and verification except for consistency cases. The expert system is tested against the performance of a selected expert. Thus, the emphasis in testing the reliability of an expert system is its performance against the *expert*.

The emphasis of reliability tests of neural networks is on *data*. The developed system must be tested against new data. The source of new data could be experts, machines, or any other data-producing process, such as the stock market. One can also divide the original data set into two parts, using one part to develop the system and the second part to test its reliability. Because of the noisy nature of the raw data in neural networks, the neural network systems require extensive reliability checks.

13.4.12   User Interface: White-box vs. Black-box

One of the attractive features of expert systems is the user interface, especially the explanatory features, such as why and how. The user can ask the system why a particular decision was recommended, and receive a user-friendly account of the rules or logic used in arriving at a conclusion, or why the system asked for a particular piece of information. The user interface in expert systems opens the process of reasoning to the user, creating a confidence and an understanding of the underlying process. The expert systems' user interface is one of the unique features that the other decision models lack. The user interface in expert systems is an inherent part of these systems, and makes the system a *white box* to the user, in that the user can see and understand the piece of knowledge applied by the system.

Neural network systems lack such an inherent user interface, because the knowledge representation in these systems is internal to the structure, and a user or even the developer is usually unable to understand or interpret the internal knowledge. Thus, the knowledge base in such systems is a *black box* to the user.

The development of user interface in neural networks is at its infancy, and the developer has to make an extra effort to design an interface that makes the system's recommendation understandable to the user. The internal structure of the knowledge base in such systems is of no help to the developer in this effort.

13.4.13   State of Recognition and Maturity: In-place and Now vs. New and Future

Artificial intelligence and expert systems emerged from research labs almost a decade ahead of neural networks. They formed a relatively well-established field, with a clear demarcation of its potential and limitations. The operating words in the state of expert systems are *in-place* and *now*.

The operating words for neural networks, on the other hand, are *new*, *potential*, and *future*. As compared to expert systems, neural network systems are newcomers. Some major work on neural network theories and their application issues are still taking place in labs. The hardware and software products that make the neural networks easier to apply and faster to work are in the developmental stage. Neural networks require parallel processing. Thus, the future developments in the hardware in this area will promote the application of neural networks. The software products utilizing the parallel processors and with user friendly interface make neural networks accessible to less technically trained developers.

Furthermore, neural networks have an affiliation with the research in neurobiology and studies of the brain. New advances in brain research could potentially be a new source of ideas and designs for neural networks. On the other hand, some of the neural network structures have been used to study and simulate brain functions. The outcomes of such studies could help in reducing the large number of learning methods now available in neural networks. One can categorize the state of neural networks as *future-oriented*.

13.4.14 Applications: Advanced vs. Starting

The applications of expert systems have long passed from research projects into real-world prototypes and large applications. Although many new approaches of artificial intelligence and expert systems are still being tested at the research labs, one can categorize the state of the applications of expert systems as *advanced*.

Although there are a number of successful real-world applications of neural networks, because they are so recent, the wealth of application reports in this area comes from research labs and research projects, at present. These applications are in the problem areas for which easy and affordable solutions have not been available before, and have a surprisingly diverse range. The application of neural networks is just *starting*.

Case: Combining Expert Systems and Neural Networks for Intelligent Flexible Manufacturing Systems

Flexible manufacturing systems (FMS) are automated manufacturing systems consisting of numerical control machine tools, material handling devices, automated inspection stations, storage areas, and a computational (hardware-software/processing-communications) scheme to provide databases handling, supervisory and monitoring functions. FMS are characterized by high flexibility and complexity. Consequently, it is difficult to schedule jobs, machines and other resources in FMS to achieve the production goals while taking into consideration their decision making time frame.

The ISS/FMS (intelligent scheduling system for FMS) is designed to utilize AI technologies so that expected performance levels can be accomplished. Neural networks and expert systems can be integrated to strengthen the best features of each. The following is a list of possible ways to integrate the two technologies.

- Development of innovative knowledge acquisition strategies using neural networks to extract and synthesize the knowledge. The expert systems would provide justification and explanation support.

- Expert systems could be utilized to generate a first cut solution. Neural networks would utilize its learning and generalization properties to refine the strategy and perform the task with a higher efficiency.

- Expert systems could monitor the performance of neural networks and automate the learning of neural network units. Expert systems could generate procedures to modify and update the training files, and retrain neural networks.

- Neural networks would perform the tasks for which expert systems have performance degradations such as pattern recognition and hypertext retrievals.

- Integrating expert systems and neural networks enhances the learning and inference mechanisms. The neural network modularity enhances the knowledge representation and the manipulation of uncertainty. On the other hand, the symbolic part improves the complexity dimension of the inference strategy.

Such an integrated approach is used to develop ISS/FMS, which has been designed based on the principles of modularity and distributed knowledge bases. ISS/FMS consists of the following units: Expert Scheduler, Heuristics Programs, Artificial Neural System for Heuristics, Expert Look-Ahead Scheduler, Artificial Neural System for Coefficients, Learning Unit, Decision Support Unit, and databases.

Expert Scheduler is the knowledge controller of ISS/FMS. It has three knowledge base modules. The first knowledge base is the Interpretation and Feasibility module which receives requests (from databases and commands) and scheduling objectives. Based on the existing resources and the current status, it interprets the requests. If the information is incomplete, it will ask for more information.

It decides to call Artificial Neural System for Heuristics to solve the scheduling problem. The second knowledge base is the Controller module, which takes the output from the neural network, and calls the Look-Ahead Scheduler based on the time frame of the problem. The third knowledge base is the Discriminator module, which receives the answers to the scheduling problem and selects the best among them. If the final schedule does not meet some of the high priority constraints, it checks the time frame of the problem, changes the time constraint, makes changes in the job database and restarts the scheduling process.

The Heuristics Programs module contains different scheduling heuristics. The Artificial Neural System for Heuristics gets its parameters from the Interpretation and Feasibility module which determines which network to use. This system has several networks based on the number of machines, number of jobs, and desired performance measure. The networks are three-layer, feedforward networks trained using the backpropagation method.

The Look Ahead Scheduler implements another round of feedback for generating optimal schedules and calls on the Artificial Neural System for Coefficients, which is designed to accelerate the performance of the feedback heuristic. This network also uses the backpropagation method.

The system was trained on 1600 data samples. It was tested with 200 job databases. It was found that the system chose the best rule in 92% of cases, and the rest were the second best choices.

Condensed from "Synergy of Artificial Neural Networks and Knowledge-Based Expert Systems for Intelligent FMS Scheduling," by Luis Carlos Rabelo, Sema Alptekin, and Ali S. Kiran, *Proceedings of International Joint Conference of Neural Networks*, San Diego, June 1990, Volume I, pp. I.359–I.366, reprinted with permission from The Institute of Electrical and Electronics Engineers (IEEE). ©1990 IEEE.

Conclusion

This chapter introduced the fundamental components of neural network systems, without plunging into the mathematical details of their learning methods. It painted a general picture of neural networks, and discussed some of the major issues that become important in the systems analysis and design phases of system development. This approach alerts the reader to the design parameters the learning methods in neural networks entail.

Here, we first discussed the basic components of the brain on which the structure of neural networks is based. This set the background for a review of the building blocks of neural network systems, such as nodes, connections, and layers, as well as the neurons' input and output processes. The learning method is one of the most important components of a neural network system. A general overview of learning methods and parameters was presented in this chapter. The details of different types of learning methods are postponed to the next chapter.

This chapter also compared and contrasted neural networks with expert systems. This comparison allows us to demonstrate that both fields attempt to give intelligence to computer systems. In doing so, both incorporate aspects of decision making that have received little attention in most of the existing quantitative decision models and information systems. Both expert systems and neural network systems deal with hard decision problems that involve qualitative and unstructured information.

Expert systems and neural networks, however, approach decision problem-solving from two drastically different points of view. Expert systems imitate human reasoning process while neural networks model the structure of the brain. Although neither expert systems nor neural networks remain faithful to what they imitate, this difference in the primary philosophy has produced two distinct and interesting approaches to solving difficult decision problems.

References

Anderson, James A. and Rosenfeld, E. (Eds.) 1988. *Neurocomputing: Foundations of Research*, MIT Press, Cambridge MA.

Carpenter, Gail A. 1989. "Neural Network Models for Pattern Recognition and Associative Memory," *Neural Networks*, Vol. 2, No. 4, pp. 243–257.

Caudill, Maureen and Butler, Charles. 1990. *Naturally Intelligent Systems*, MIT Press, Cambridge, MA.

Caudill, Maureen. 1991. "Neural Networks Training Tips and Techniques," *AI Expert*, Vol. 5, No. 1, January, pp. 56–61.

Grossberg, Stephen (Ed.). 1988. *Neural Networks and Natural Intelligence*, MIT Press, Cambridge, MA.

Hebb, Donald O. 1949. *The Organization of Behavior*, Wiley, New York, NY.

Hecht-Nielsen, Robert. 1990. *Neurocomputing*, Addison-Wesley Publishing Company, Reading, MA.

McCorduck, Pamela. 1979. *Machines Who Think*, W. H. Freeman, San Francisco, CA.

McCorduck, Pamela. 1988. "Artificial Intelligence: An Aperçu," *The Artificial Intelligence Debate—False Starts and Real Foundations*, S. Graubard (Ed.), MIT Press, Cambridge, MA, pp. 65–83.

McCulloch, W. S. and Pitts, W. 1943. "A Logical Calculus of the Ideas Immanent in Nervous Activity," *Bulletin of Mathematical Biophysics*, Vol. 9, pp. 127–147.

Minsky, M. and Papert, S. 1969. *Perceptrons*, MIT Press, Cambridge, MA.

Newell, Allen and Simon, Herbert. 1981. "Computer Science as Empirical Inquiry: Symbols and Search," *Mind Design*, John Haugeland (Ed.), MIT Press, Cambridge, MA, p. 41.

Rosenblatt, Frank. 1958a. "The Perceptrons: A Probabilistic Model for Information and Organization in the Brain," *Psychological Review*, Vol. 56, pp. 386–408.

Rosenblatt, F. 1958b. "Mechanism of Thought Processes," *Proceedings of a Symposium at the National Physical Laboratory*, Her Majesty's Stationary Office, London, Vol. 1, p. 449.

Rumelhart, David E.; Hinton, Geoffrey E.; and Williams, Ronald J. 1986. "Learning Representation by Backpropagation Errors," *Nature*, Vol. 323, pp. 533–536.

Shepherd, Gordon M. 1988. *Neurobiology*, Second Edition, Oxford University Press, New York, NY.

Simpson, Patrick. 1990. *Artificial Neural Systems*, Pergamon Press, Oxford, England.

White, Halbert. 1989. "Neural Network Learning and Statistics," *AI Expert*, December, Vol. 4, No. 12, pp. 48–52.

Zahedi, Fatemeh. 1991. "An Introduction to Neural Networks and a Comparison with Artificial Intelligence and Expert Systems," *Interfaces*, Vol. 21, No. 2, pp. 25–28.

Questions

13.1   What are the main components of the brain that are used in modeling neural networks?

13.2   There are two schools of thought about the relationships between modeling the brain and neural networks. Discuss these two schools of thought. What is the implication of each in developing neural network systems?

13.3   What are the general building blocks of neural networks? What are their similarities and differences to the components of the brain?

13.4   What are the main functions of a neuron in a neural network?

13.5   What is the difference between the inter-layer and intra-layer connections?

13.6   What is the difference between the feed-forward and bi-directional inter-layer connections?

13.7   What is the difference between the bi-directional and resonance connections?

13.8   Why is a transfer function needed in generating an output of a neuron?

13.9   What are the main types of transfer functions? How do they determine the type of a neuron's output?

13.10   How is knowledge stored in neural networks?

13.11   What features of knowledge storage and processing in neural networks make such systems a parallel type?

13.12   What is the relation between the connection weights and learning in neural networks?

13.13   What are the main types of learning?

13.14   What is the significance of the learning equation in neural networks?

13.15   Describe the major types of learning equations.

13.16   What is the difference between the Hebb rule and the delta rule?

13.17   What is the major difference between the Kohonen rule and the other three types of learning equations?

13.18   Describe the similarities of expert systems and neural networks.

13.19   Describe the differences between expert systems and neural networks.

13.20   Identify the areas where expert systems are superior to neural networks.

13.21   Identify the areas where neural networks are superior to expert systems.

13.22   If you could come up with a system that had the capabilities of expert systems and neural networks, which aspects of expert systems and neural networks would you include in it?

Case: Neural Networks Research in Japan

In engineering labs across Japan, scientists are turning increasingly to chemistry and biology to create new designs of neural networks computer systems. It is believed that the neural networks can be particularly effective for computer functions based on sensory experiences, such as recognizing handwriting and spoken words. In a report released last year [1988] by Japan's Ministry of International Trade and Industry, neural computing was one of several key areas the agency is targeting for original research.

In its research, NEC (a Japanese company) has been studying *caeorhabditis elegance*, a type of microscopic worm, in order to understand how humans process information. These organisms are useful to study in the lab because of their sheer simplicity. They have only 955 neurons—302 for what could be defined as brain functions and 635 to control motor functions; their growth period, from birth to adulthood, takes only three days.

By focusing laser beams on particular cells or neurons and the eggs that these organisms generate, NEC researchers hope to learn about the process of inherited characteristics, according to Kazumoto Iinuma, general manager of NEC's Computer and Communications Information Technology Research Laboratories.

In March [1989], NEC announced success in developing a personal computer-based "neural net music sound arranging system." Researchers feed a melody into the system that, in turn, automatically generates harmonic accompaniment for the music, depending on the style of music required—jazz, pop, or children's songs.

NEC has also sold some 200 PCs to date, equipped with "neuro-engine" boards and neural network software. In summer, NEC also announced its development of a neural net character recognition system that can recognize up to 12,840 Japanese characters with 100% accuracy.

Fujitsu Ltd. scientists, in adapting the learning process to information processing applications, have tried to model their neural networks after the actual learning experiences of students in school. They found that if they feed selected patterns into the network in a progressively more difficult manner—inputting the easier problems first and saving the more serious problems for later—the networks were able to absorb the information faster. As a result, Kazuo Asakawa, section manager for Fujitsu's artificial intelligence laboratory, predicts that "the speed of learning in our products will be far quicker than those of other manufacturers."

Fujitsu, in fact, already has several PC-based neural network products on the market and expects to ship 2000 "neuro boards" and associated software over the next three years.

Fujitsu demonstrated its research with a comical minirobot demonstration at its 50th anniversary celebration, entitled, "Sherlock Holmes' Arresting Drama." A minirobot named Sherlock Holmes—equipped with two motors, two tires, 12 sensors and 50 to 60 neurons—was programmed to pursue a "criminal" into a corner. The Holmes robot was able to do the task quicker than two other less developed "detective" minirobots because the processor for Holmes robot was based on a type of neural network known as "backpropagation." If Holmes made a mistake during the case, turning one way instead of another, the signal, indicating an error, was fed back to it for relearning.

Not to be outdone, Hitachi Ltd. also is feverishly at work, doing neural network-related research in five of its nine basic and applied research labs. Hitoshi Matsushima, a senior researcher, says Hitachi is doing research in several areas, including neural network wafer scale integration chips for very high fault tolerance applications. The company has also introduced an all-digital "neuro chip," jointly developed with Yuzo Hirai of Tsukuba University for neural network applications.

In addition, Hitachi says it has invented a neural network simulator to assist in voice recognition. Part of the research involves developing a computer model of starfish to see how and why they right themselves after they've been turned upside down. It is hoped that the research will give Hitachi some understanding of instinct. The "theme" of the research, says Akira Ichikawa, head of Hitachi's speech research unit, is "how we deal with the left [lobe of the] brain, which controls the logical world, and the right [side of the] brain, which controls the analog world, and how we integrate both."

Mitsubishi Electronic Corp. is working with sea slugs to see how their neurons respond to stimulation. Researchers hope that basic research in this area will help the company develop better computer models for how the process of learning and remembering works. The research also involves developing actual hardware– including optical and large-scale integration components.

Kazuo Kyuma, manager of the Photonics Group at Mitsubishi's Central Research Laboratory, heads up a 10-researcher team that has created a prototype of an "associative optical neurocomputer" capable of recognizing several characters in the English alphabet. His team has also created an optical neuron chip incorporating 32 neurons. "The greater the number of neurons, the more difficult becomes the interconnection in the case of hand writing," Kyuma says.

Condensed from "Expanding Neural Marketplace Challenges Japanese Engineers," by Shohei Kurita, *Electronic Business*, September 18, 1989, pp. 79-80, reprinted with permission from *Electronic Business*.

Case Questions

1. Discuss and characterize the nature of the neural networks R & D projects in Japanese companies.

2. For each company in the case, discuss the potential commercial applications of its R & D projects.

3. In addition to software and new designs, some Japanese companies are developing the hardware for neural networks applications. Discuss the potential competitive advantage for a company that succeeds in developing new designs, software and hardware for neural networks applications.

Case: Neural Networks + Expert Systems = Manufacturing Solutions

Many problems involve a variety of issues, and call upon information in a variety of formats. Combinations of technologies are often appropriate for particular problems and environments. For this reason, neural nets are often embedded within expert systems, and vice versa. The expert systems handle rule-based data and may also provide the user interfaces. The neural net receives input through the expert system interface, and performs estimation and correlation. Rule-based decision making may overlay net output fed to the expert system. In other cases, an expert system is embedded within a neural net. A neural net analyzes data, and a rule-based system then selects among several discrete responses. This accommodates many situations in which only discrete actions are possible or rules serve to quanitize estimated values. In both cases, we call upon the best features of each technology, as summarized in the following table.

There are many applications in industry that exemplify the functionality and power of combining expert systems and neural nets in manufacturing environments. In each case, neural nets automatically learn correlations to model situations and provide decision support beyond traditional computer capabilities.

Table of Features

Neural Nets	Expert Systems
Example based	Rule based
Domain free	Domain specific
Finds rules	Needs rules
Little programming	Much programming
Easy to maintain	Difficult to maintain
Fault tolerant	Not fault tolerant
Needs a database	Needs a human expert
Fuzzy logic	Rigid logic
Adaptive systems	Requires reprogramming

1. Quality Control. A manufacturer uses infrared spectroscopy to verify product quality. Samples are taken at regular intervals and are tested to verify that product components are in the proper ratios and contaminants are below target levels. Since each product component has characteristic emission spectra, seen on the instrument output plot as distinct peaks at specific wavelengths, analysis of single components is straightforward. Analysis of multicomponent compound is not the sum of the plots of individual components. The components of the compound interact chemically, and the resulting spectrometer output exhibits the interaction. These plots often provide only subtle indication of the quality problem. Only experts understand these chemical interactions sufficiently to interpret compound plots reflecting this interaction.

Interpretation expertise is not widely available. The quality control challenge is to provide this scarce expertise to support a three-shift operation. Neural nets provided a sophisticated but easy to use solution. A neural net analyzes infrared spectrometer output to verify product quality. Technicians load a material test sample into the infrared spectrometer and initiate the test. The neural net-based system interprets the instrument output to provide quality validation or an indication that a contaminant has entered the process.

The system is trained by providing examples of known compositions paired with the associated spectroscope output. This data is available in existing records.

The neural net uncovers correlations in the data that effectively provide an understanding of the relationship between product formula and the spectroscope plot.

The trained system then estimates compositions falling anywhere within the ranges taught. The neural net analyzes spectroscope data from a sample of unknown composition, and provides percentages of contaminants and desired components as output. This validates the production sample, or directs plant personnel to correct or shut down the process.

2. Machine Diagnosis. Machine condition impacts product quality and production rate. A machine failure requires expensive and disruptive unscheduled maintenance. Thus, the maintenance staff must balance the needs to maintain the quality and rate of production, while minimizing time and expense for preventive maintenance. Catastrophic failures must be predicted to prevent unanticipated shut downs.

A neural net imbedded in an expert system analyzes sensor data to determine machine condition. This determination schedules and specifies machine rebuilds for a manufacturer of parts for extremely tight dimensional and surface finish tolerances. Grinders used to manufacture these parts were rebuilt extensively and frequently to maintain product quality. A project was initiated to reduce machine rebuild costs with no compromise in product quality. Smarter machine rebuilding has been implemented in two steps. In the first step, an expert system determined machine condition. Inputs from machine adjusters and accelerometers located near vital machine components such as bearings were fed to an expert system. The system scheduled machine downtime for maintenance and rebuild based on identified need rather than on a time basis.

In the second step, the system was upgraded to embed a neural net into the existing expert system. The neural net was presented data from accelerometer as well as product quality data.

From this data, the neural net learned the correlation between machine condition and product quality. The understanding of correlations between specific aspects of machine condition, as captured in specific sensor readings, and quantified measures of product quality allowed determination of aspects of machine rebuild crucial or immaterial to product quality. This understanding significantly decreased rebuild and down time expense with no compromise in product quality. Subsequent implementation of this system on other grinders were less expensive since the neural net also determined that many of the original sensors were redundant, and could be eliminated without degrading system performance.

3. Process Control. Process designers desire stable, robust control with response time, overshoot, and other parameters held within acceptable limits. In a continuous process control application, liquid level in a tank is maintained at a target level as unmeasured output flow is varied. An input valve, driven by the neural net controller, maintains or changes the input flow to achieve the target level. The challenge is to provide smooth level changes as the level passes through the different tank cross-sections and transition points.

The neural net controller was trained through cause and effect examples. "Cause" was incremental opening of the inlet valve, and "effect" was the rate of change of liquid level. The neural net "learned" to control the tank with no further user input. The neural net controller accommodates the system changes over time and provides robust supervisory control.

Condensed from "Solving Manufacturing Problems with Neural Nets: Neural Nets + Expert Systems = Manufacturing Solutions," by William VerDuin, *Automation*, July 1990, pp. 54–58, reprinted with permission from *Automation*.

Case Questions

1. Discuss the table comparing the features of neural networks and expert systems. Do you agree with the author's point of view? Why?

2. Discuss and characterize the nature of the neural network applications as reported in this case.

3. Identify a potential integration of expert systems and neural networks in managing manufacturing functions.

CHAPTER 14

Neural Network
Architectures

The great end of learning is nothing else but to seek for the lost mind.

Mencius, *The Chinese Classics*

We know the human brain is a device to keep the ears from grating on one another.

Peter De Vries, *Comfort Me with Apples*

Chapter Objectives

The objectives of this chapter are:

- To provide a uniform framework for reviewing and understanding various well-known network architectures that already exist in the field

- To discuss the advantages and shortcomings of each neural network architecture

- To discuss unique training issues in developing neural network systems

---

KEY WORDS: Neural network architecture, auto-associative networks, hetero-associative networks, two-layer networks, multi-layer networks, deterministic networks, stochastic networks, cross-bar networks, hierarchically partitioned networks, static networks, dynamic networks, perceptron, ADALINE, MADALINE, Kohonen's self-organizing network, Hopfield network, brain-state-in-a-box network, instar and outstar networks, backpropagation network, counter propagation network, recurrent backpropagation network, ART1, ART2, ART3, training

---

If the equations look ominous to you, read the content of this chapter without worrying about the details of the equations, because in most cases they are either the same or minor variations of the basic equations covered in Chapter 13.

Introduction

This last chapter takes you further into the structure of various designs and architectures used in applying neural networks. The first section introduces the types of neural network architectures. Sections 14.2 through 14.4 review three groups of neural net designs: two-layer networks, multiple-layer networks, and the ART networks. We have tried to use the same format for reporting the structure of each design. Therefore, once you overcome the hurdle of reading the first design, the next design should be easier to follow. As before, you can scan over the equations and still be able to grasp the structure of the network.

Although the details of neural net architectures are optional in this chapter, it is important for you to be aware that there are various designs with varying complexity. Furthermore, they are applied in various fields and there are reports on their performance and special characteristics. Therefore, in many cases, we do not have to invent the design of a new neural net from scratch. Instead, we can try various architectures, and eventually select the one that is most appropriate for our problem. Some of the cases reported in this and previous chapters demonstrate this fact.

For the practically minded reader, Section 14.5 is of great importance. It shows that creating a neural net is anything but automatic. Not only does one have to select the design and determine the parameters of the design, but also training and testing the neural net system is quite a big task by itself. The same iterative process in system development that we see in other system types is present in designing and training a neural net application.

14.1 Types of Neural Network Architectures

The field of neural networks has an impressive number of designs and architectures, which could overwhelm the novice and the experienced alike. Categorizing the existing neural networks facilitates the discussion of various *neural network architectures.* However, the structural complexity of neural networks means that they can be grouped based on a number of different criteria, including:

- Nature of learning methods

- Correspondence of input and output data

- Number of layers

- Certainty of firing

- Type of connectivity

- Temporal feature

- Timing of learning

14.1.1   Nature of Learning Methods

We have already seen in Chapter 13 that the learning methods in neural networks could be divided into *supervised* and *unsupervised* learning.

In supervised learning, the "correct" answer is given to the network. In unsupervised learning, the objective of the network is to produce an output that is close to the correct output for each case. The supervised networks have, implicitly or explicitly, an underlying error function which they strive to minimize. Most of the existing networks fall in the supervised category.

The unsupervised networks are also called *self-organizing* networks. This type of network is given only the input data, without any hint of what the correct outputs are. These networks learn the patterns of the input data, and are able to produce their stored pattern, once a similar pattern is presented to them. The self-organizing networks hold the promise of simulating the automatic learning ability of the brain.

14.1.2   Correspondence of Input and Output Data

One of the important features of the brain is its associative memory. We remember by association. For example, a bank officer sees a customer, remembers that he had applied for a loan two weeks ago, then discusses the loan with the supervisor.

The early (two-layered) neural networks were designed to have an associative memory nature, by producing an associative output for any given input. For example, for a given set of attributes of a loan application, the network is expected to output the decision about the loan. This type of network is called *associative*.

However, almost all existing neural networks are either associative by nature or have components that perform the function of an associative memory.

The associative networks are divided into

- Auto-associative networks

- Hetero-associative networks

In an *auto-associative network*, the input vector is the same as the output vector. This type of network is useful for recognizing patterns from incomplete and erroneous data, such as identifying a person from an old or faded picture, recognizing handwritten letters, or finding a customer from fragmented information. In such cases, the input and output are of the same type; the only difference is that the output is a completed and recognizable version of the input.

In a *hetero-associative network*, the input and output vectors are not of the same type. For example, in a mortgage loan system, the input could be the applicant's profile and the loan data, and the output of the system could be the decision to grant or deny the loan.

By nature, self-organizing networks are auto-associative, because there is no teacher to tell the network to produce an output that is not the same as the input. On the other hand, the networks with supervised learning can have hetero-associative input and output.

14.1.3   Number of Layers

The networks could be grouped by the number of their layers as:

- Two-Layer

- Multi-Layer

The earlier networks had two layers, in that only the interconnections of two layers are allowed to change and accomplish learning. We will see that simple *two-layer networks* are unable to accommodate all types of patterns. This limitation is overcome by *multi-layer networks*, in which the interconnections of more than one pair of layers are allowed to change. In the next section, we study the networks grouped into two-layer and multiple-layer types.

14.1.4   *Certainty of Firing*

One can group neural networks based on the certainty of the firing of their neurons as:

- Deterministic

- Stochastic

Most networks are deterministic. In *deterministic networks*, once a neuron reaches a certain level of activation dictated by the transfer function, it fires and sends out impulses to other neurons. Thus, the firing of the neurons takes place with certainty. This is not the case in the *stochastic networks*, in which firing of a neuron is not certain, but takes place according to a probability distribution. Among the well-known stochastic networks is the Boltzman machine (which is based on an optimization method called *simulated annealing*). The Boltzman machine network design is not covered in this book. (For a good exposition of the design see Hecht-Nielsen [1990].)

14.1.5   *Type of Connectivity*

In Chapter 13, we discussed the inter-layer connection types used singly or in combination in neural networks. There are, however, some neural networks that are distinguished by the special type of their inter-layer connections. Among them are:

- Cross-bar networks

- Hierarchically partitioned networks

Cross-bar connections are the connectivity among two layers of a network, with feedback, as shown in Figure 14.1. The feedback allows for the iterative change of interconnection weights among the two layers of the network. Many pioneering two-layer networks used this type of connectivity, and have come to be called *cross-bar networks*.

The *hierarchically partitioned networks* are of recent vintage. We have added the word *partitioned* to avoid the confusion with the general hierarchical structure of multiple-layer networks. In the hierarchically partitioned network, each layer is designed to deal with a particular feature or attribute of the input pattern. Normally in this type of network, the lower layers of the hierarchy deal with the simple features of the pattern. The higher layers of the hierarchy combine the simple features to deal with more aggregate and

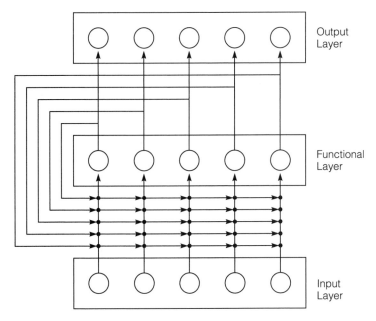

Figure 14.1   Cross-Bar Connectivity

complex aspects of the input pattern. The design issues of the hierarchically partitioned networks are complex, and are yet to be formalized.

Among the well-known hierarchically partitioned network are Neocognitron and Combinotorial Hypercompression. These designs are not covered here. (For a simple exposition of these designs see Hecht-Nielsen [1990].)

14.1.6   Temporal Feature

Neural networks could be grouped by their temporal nature into:

- Static

- Dynamic

In *static networks*, there is no element of time; that is, it accepts inputs one at a time, and produces outputs without any connection to the next input. For example, a network that takes the loan application and produces a decision is a static network.

A *dynamic network* processes a series of inputs through time, and generates output accordingly. This type of network is also called a *spatio-temporal network*. A network that receives a series of patterns and recognizes that they represent, say, an aircraft in motion is an idealized example of a spatio-temporal network.

Case: Neural Network for Diagnosing and Treating Hypertension

Computer-based medical systems are playing an increasingly relevant role in assisting both diagnosis and treatment. When designing such tools, certain objectives must be considered. First of all, physicians should be able to use low-cost, user-friendly instruments—for example, programs running on personal computers. Nevertheless, to satisfy physicians' requirements, processing time should be short.

Since any failure of such tools could prove harmful to patients, fault tolerance and reliability are the most crucial characteristics. At the same time, end users must be provided with as much information as possible about how the processing is carried out.

In the effort to reach these objectives, developers of computer aids for physicians face a variety of problems deriving from the complex nature of biological data. Such data is characterized by an intrinsic variability that can occur as the result of spontaneous internal mechanism or as a reaction to occasional external stimuli. Furthermore, most biological events result from the interaction of many systems whose different effects are almost indistinguishable.

Clinicians are accustomed to such problems, but their skills cannot easily be incorporated into computer programs. Most clinical decisions are based on experience as well as complex inferences and extensive pathophysiological knowledge. Such experience cannot be condensed into a small set of relations, and this limits the performance of algorithmic approaches to many clinical tasks. The breadth of clinical knowledge is an obstacle to the creation of symbolic knowledge bases comprehensive enough to cope with the diverse exceptions that occur in practice.

Experience-based learning, fault tolerance, graceful degradation, and signal enhancement are properties of artificial neural networks that make them effective in solving the above problems. This points to a way for implementing reliable computer-based medical systems that can closely emulate a physician's experience.

Here we describe Hypernet (Hypertension Neural Expert Therapist), a neural network expert system for diagnosing and treating hypertension. Hypernet has been developed through the cooperative efforts of the Department of Electronic Engineering of the University of Florence, the Interuniversity Center of Clinical Chronobiology, and the CNR Institute of Physiology.

The inputs to the Hypernet are the subjects' health-related data and the 24-hour diastolic and systolic blood pressure time series. The system output includes four 24-item arrays, whose values specify the hourly dosage to be administered to the patient for each of the most common antihypertensive drugs. The presence and degree of hypertension (diagnosis) can be inferred from the drug dosage: No treatment is required for normal subjects.

To simulate a physician's reasoning, the system is divided into three main modules: the reference generating module (RGM), the drug compatibility module

(DCM), and the therapy-selecting module (TSM). Each module consists of one or two feed-forward neural networks trained by the backpropagation algorithm.

This kind of architecture increases the user's confidence in the system, providing a set of internal testing points that give explicit information about the processing. (Internal representations of neural networks are often too complex to be meaningful to the end user.).

The RGM comprises of two identical three-layer networks, each consisting of two input, four hidden, and 24 output units. These networks compare a patient's 24-hour blood-pressure time series with the time series typical for normal subjects of the same sex and age. The purpose of this module is to call on medical knowledge regarding the concept of normality for blood-pressure recordings.

The DCM is a simple two-layer neural network with 17 input and four output units. Its function is to analyze the most important entries of the patient's clinical report (inputs) and determine the patient's degree of compatibility with each drug (outputs). To do this, it must discover and apply the set of rules a physician usually employs for discarding unsuitable drugs.

The TSM is a six-layer neural net whose inputs are (1) the degrees of compatibility, (2) the differences between the systolic and diastolic reference blood pressures and those derived from the patient's monitoring, and (3) five health-related data that can influence the diagnosis. The activation of 96 output units (24 hours times 4 drugs) of this module represents the final results of the system, indicating the dosage of the drug to be prescribed at a given hour of the day.

Hypernet has a user interface which translates the input data from a simple symbolic description into a suitable data structure for the system. Although neural network technology does not require users to be capable of programming, preparing the examples for training can be complex. Hypernet has some example-generating programs for converting the raw blood pressure data and the clinical data into language statements.

For instance, to generate the example for the TSM, an example-generating program helps the physician integrate blood pressure and health-related data with drug compatibility for selection of the therapy. All crucial data about the patient is summarized on the graphics screen: the physician selects the timing and dosage of each drug simply by moving a cursor. A similar screen displays the final results. The user can quickly verify the consistency of the system's operation by checking the consistency of its output with the drug compatibility, the health-related information, and the blood pressure data.

The network was trained and tested using 300 clinically healthy and 85 suspect hypertensive subjects. The trained network produced output which followed eight general criteria used by physicians in treating hypertensive patients. The system performance was evaluated on the basis of its accuracy in both diagnoses and prescriptions. The test set included 35 subjects, 10 normal and 25 suspect hypertensive. A diagnosis was judged correct if the system and the specialist agreed on treating or not treating. Hypernet correctly diagnosed 33 out of 35 (94 percent). The specialist evaluated the recommended treatment by the system and judged 82 percent to be correct or acceptable. The system developers continue to collect more data and to enhance the system.

Condensed from "A Neural Network Expert System for Diagnosing and Treating Hypertension," by Riccardo Poli, Stefano Cagnoni, Riccardo Livi, Giuseppe Coppini, and Guido Valli, *Computer*, March 1991, pp. 64–71, reprinted with permission from The Institute of Electrical and Electronics Engineers (IEEE). ©1991 IEEE.

14.1.7   Timing of Learning

We have already seen in Chapter 13 that one can group neural networks based on the timing of their learning as:

- Batch learning

- On-line learning

In batch or off-line learning, the network is trained in the training phase by changing the interconnection weights. Once the training is over, the interconnection weights are fixed, and the network is used in the operational phase. Most neural networks learn in batch mode.

In on-line learning, although the network is trained in the training phase, it continues to learn in the operational phase. This type of network is closer to the way the brain learns new concepts, and alters existing ones.

14.2 Two-Layer Neural Networks (Optional)

Almost all of the early ground-breaking networks were two-layer networks. We defined a two-layer network as a network in which the interconnection between only two layers of the network changes in the learning process. In other words, the network may have more than two layers, but only one set of inter-layer connections can be trained. In many of the networks discussed in this section, we show the network with more than two layers, mostly because we have added an input layer that acts as a buffer, storing the external input data and passing it on to the next layer. In other cases, an output layer is added that passes the outcome to the external environment. However, in all cases, the definition of the two-layer network remains operational.

In this section, we review some of the two-layer networks that created the foundation of the field. These networks have been developed in an interval of about two decades and are still acceptable architectures, used either as a stand-alone network or as a part of a more complex network system.

The networks reviewed in this section are:

- Perceptron

- ADALINE and MADALINE

- Kohonen's Self-organizing Network

- Hopfield

- Brain-state-in-a-box

- Instar and outstar

14.2.1 Perceptron Network (Optional)

Perceptron, the first neural network, was developed by Frank Rosenblatt in 1957. A psychologist by training, Rosenblatt developed perceptron to reflect the psychological aspects of the brain. The focus of the model was to show that the network could simulate the associative memory feature of the brain, with its random connections among layers of neurons that are capable of learning even when the external input is noisy and inaccurate.

However, the perceptron's potential for learning complex patterns made it an attractive model for engineers and physicists. In 1958, Rosenblatt and Charles Wightman developed one of the first computer applications of the design, called Mark I Perceptron. Its function was to distinguish patterns, such as characters, well before character recognition became an important business problem in computerized information systems.

The original perceptron used many ideas that are still in use, including an inhibitory feedback from one layer to another, which is an elementary version of the winner-takes-all concept. In what follows, we present one type of the perceptron architecture.

Layer Structure

The perceptron has a three-layer, hierarchical, feed-forward structure, with no intra-layer connections. The first layer is the input layer, which gets the external data, as shown in Figure 14.2. It has a fan-out nature. That is, the neurons on the input layer send their output to either all neurons or a randomly selected number of neurons on the next layer. The connection weights between the first and second layer are fixed, and are equal to 1. Therefore, the first layer works as an input buffer that receives the external stimuli, and passes them to all or some of the neurons on the second layer, without any alteration due to the connection weights. Since the connection weights are fixed from the first to the second layer, no learning takes place on these weights.

The neurons on the second layer are designed to detect special attributes or features of a case or pattern. The third layer is the output or the perceptron layer, where each neuron represents the presence or absence of an

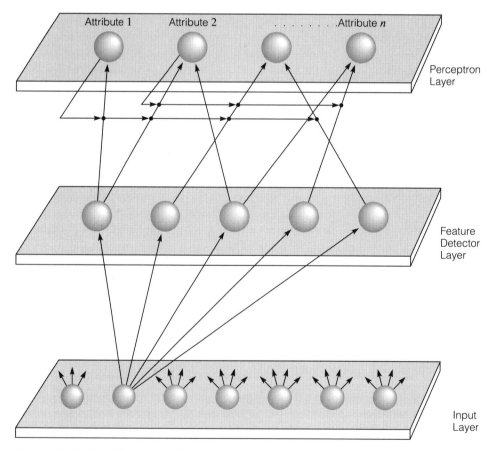

Figure 14.2 The Structure of a Simple Perceptron

attribute or feature. The third layer feeds back to the second layer. The original perceptron did not have full connectivity between the second and third layers. These connections had to be created at random at the start of the training session.

Input and Output of Neurons

The neurons on the second and third layers compute their input according to the input equation (1) in Chapter 13, with a bias factor for the neurons of the third layer:

$$input_i = \sum_{j=1}^{n} w_{ji} \cdot output_j + w_{0i} \cdot output_0, \tag{1}$$

where $output_j$s are the outputs from the neurons of the previous layer. The neurons on the third layer have a bias factor $output_0$ with a value fixed at 1. The weight of the bias factor (w_{0i}) changes in the learning process. In this context, one can imagine the bias factor $output_0$ as the output of an imaginary neuron on the second layer with an output always equal to 1.

The neurons of the second and third layers utilize the signum transfer function of (2) discussed in Chapter 13, in the form of:

$$output_i = \begin{cases} 1 & \text{if } input_i > 0 \\ 0 & \text{if } input_i \leq 0. \end{cases} \tag{2}$$

From equation (2) one can observe that the input and output data types in perceptron are discrete and binary. That is, the input and output values are either 0 or 1.

Learning Equation

The learning of connection weights between the second and third layers takes place according to the following equation:

$$w_{ji}^{new} = w_{ji}^{old} + \alpha(desoutput_i - output_i), \tag{3}$$

where, as defined in Chapter 13, w_{ji} is the connection weight of neuron j on the second layer with neuron i on the third layer, $desoutput_i$ is the "desired" or correct output of neuron i on the third layer, and $output_i$ is the actual output of neuron i.

The learning equation in perceptron has a simple interpretation. If neuron i sends out the correct impulse to the external environment, then its weights to the neurons on the second layer do not change. However, if neuron i sends out 1, when the correct impulse is 0, then its connection weights with the neurons of the second layer are reduced by an amount equal to α. If, on the other hand, neuron i sends out 0, when the correct impulse is 1, then its connection weights to the neurons on the second layer are increased by an amount equal to α. The value of α could be set to a positive value less than or equal to 1.

It is possible to vary the change of weights depending on the amount of error. In this case, the error is computed as the difference between the desired output and the actual input to neuron i, before the transfer function is applied. To accomplish this, we should substitute $input_i$ for $output_i$ in the perceptron learning equation (3).

Limitations

The perceptron network works well for the *linearly separable* cases. However, when the condition of linear separability is not satisfied, the network does not function properly. In linearly separable cases, one can separate categories of output by a line.

To demonstrate the linear separability concept in a two-dimensional case, consider the simple form of the mortgage example. Assume there are only two attributes in each application: job status (employed=1 and unemployed=0) denoted by x_1, and credit rating (good=1 and bad=0) denoted by x_2. The possible paired input values of x_1 and x_2 are $(0,0)$, $(1,0)$, $(0,1)$, and $(1,1)$. These four points are shown in Figure 14.3 as a, b, c, and d.

Now, let us put this simple example in the perceptron network, shown in Figure 14.4. In this example, we have a direct connection from the input layer to the second layer with the interconnection weights fixed to 1. The

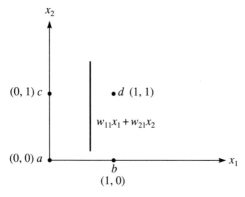

Figure 14.3   The Graphical Presentation of the Perceptron Example

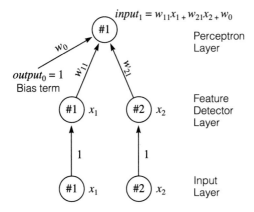

Figure 14.4   The Structure of the Perceptron Example

second layer has two neurons. Each takes the input from the input layer, and passes its output to the output layer. The output layer has one neuron, which represents approving (1) or denying (0) the loan. The connection weights from the second to the third layer are denoted as w_{11} and w_{21} for connections of neurons 1 and 2 in the second layer to neuron 1 on the third layer. The input to the neuron in the third layer (or the output layer) is

$$input_1 = w_0 + w_{11}x_1 + w_{21}x_2. \tag{4}$$

Note that equation (4) is the equation for a line, with known values for x's and unknown values for the weights (ws).

Assume that the desired output is that the loan should be granted when the applicant is employed ($x_1 = 1$) and the applicant's credit rating is either good ($x_2 = 1$) or bad ($x_2 = 0$). The training of the network determines the weight values in equation (4) such that the points $(1,1)$ and $(1,0)$ fall on one side of the line and the other points fall on the other side of the line, as shown in Figure 14.3.

The weights would be determined such that the points b and d would produce an output from the network with a value equal to 1, and the other points would produce 0 impulse from the network. Thus, the equation (4) belongs to a line that separates loans into "approve" and "deny" categories. In this example, the cases are "linearly separable," in that a line can separate them into two groups.

If we were to solve equation (4) manually with data free of noise, we would have the following equations to solve in order to determine the interconnection weights:

$$w_0 + w_{11}.1 + w_{21}.1 = 1$$
$$w_0 + w_{11}.0 + w_{21}.1 = 0$$
$$w_0 + w_{11}.1 + w_{21}.0 = 1 \tag{5}$$
$$w_0 + w_{11}.0 + w_{21}.0 = 0$$

When the number of attributes increases to three, the line in Figure 14.2 becomes a three-dimensional plane. When the number of attributes is more than three, the line becomes what is called a *hyperplane*, which is a plane in an n dimension. But the idea remains the same. For the perceptron to work, the knowledge domain cases should be such that the possible responses could be categorized into n sides of the hyperplane in the n dimensional geometry.

Although one can perceive many decision problems with a linearly separable nature, this requirement limits the applicability of the network. For example, assume that we had a case where the bank would grant loans to applicants with $(1, 1)$ and $(0, 0)$ qualifications in the above example, (a bank with a special program for the poor). In that case, points a and d in Figure 14.2 should produce an output impulse of 1, and 0 for the other points. There is no line that could separate points a and d into one side, and b and c into the other.

The above example is the XOR problem, which Minsky and Papert used in their book *Perceptrons*, to conclude that the perceptron network is inadequate to solve even a simple problem. Later, Hecht-Nielsen used a theorem proved by the well-known Russian mathematician Kolmogorov in a context unrelated to neural networks to prove that if we add a layer between the second and third layers in the perceptron network, the linear separability requirement vanishes. This proof helped the field of neural networks return to a sound theoretical footing in solving complex problems.

The discussion in this subsection also demonstrates one of the interesting features of neural networks—that neural networks are capable of representing complex relationships between the input and output data, without the need to specify this relationship in the form of a complex mathematical formula. Thus, although in some networks one can find the correspondence between a complex mathematical function relating the input to the output and the neural network that produces the same outcome, in designing the neural network, the developer does not need to worry about the mathematical specification of the relationship between the input and output data. Instead, the developer must design the structure of the network and train the system to accomplish the task. Therefore, in neural networks, finding and computing the mathematical function(s) relating the input data to the output data (as is the case in statistics) is replaced by the requirement of finding the appropriate structural design and parameters for the system. This underlies the crucial role that the structure and training process of a network plays in its reliable and successful operation.

14.2.2   ADALINE and MADALINE Networks (Optional)

ADALINE stands for ADAptive LINear Element, and MADALINE stands for Multiple ADALINE, developed by Bernard Widrow and Marcian E. Hoff in 1960. *ADALINE* describes the input and output of one neuron or processing element, and *MADALINE* combines many ADALINEs into one network.

Widrow and Hoff assumed the existence of a teacher (they called it a "boss") who knows what the correct answer is for each input. They introduced the concept of *error signal*, which is the distance between the "correct" output and the actual output of the system, and developed the delta learning rule (discussed in Chapter 13) such that the square values of error signals would be minimized. This network was one of the important designs in neural networks that was implemented in a number of systems. Later, it was generalized in the backpropagation network, one of the most popular networks at present.

Layer Structure

MADALINE has an input layer, which fans out to the second layer. The connection weights of the first and second layers are variable and must be trained. The second layer consists of a set of ADALINEs (or adaptive neurons). The third layer or the output layer has a single neuron, called MADALINE. The connection weights between the second and third layers are fixed at 1, and are not trainable. The structure is hierarchical and forward, with no intra-layer connections.

Input and Output of Neurons

The neurons on the input layer send their input values directly to the second layer. The neuron on the second layer is called ADALINE. The system's data type is binary, with $+1$ and -1 values. The input computation for an ADALINE is the same as that of the perceptron, equation (1). The transfer function of the ADALINE is also similar to that in perceptron. It uses the signum transfer function, producing $+1$ if the input reaches above 0, and -1 otherwise. The connection weights take negative to positive values.

The single neuron in the third layer (MADALINE) receives $+1$ and -1 values from the neurons of the second layer, and takes a majority vote. It sends out a $+1$ impulse if the majority is with $+1$, and a -1, otherwise.

Learning Equation of ADALINE

The learning equation in ADALINE is the delta rule, discussed in Chapter 13. This rule minimizes the mean square distance of the actual output from the desired output. To show this mathematically, when the network is trained, it determines the connection weights such that

$$\frac{1}{n}\sum_{i=1}^{n}(desoutput_i - output_i)^2 \tag{6}$$

is at minimum. The starting values of the connection weights should be determined at random, and then the training should begin to let the system alter its weights according to the delta rule. In doing so, it minimizes the mean square error, as shown in (6). The system developer may vary the learning coefficient α between 0.1 to 10, starting with 0.1, and gradually increasing the coefficient as the system learns.

Thus, the network has a supervised and off-line learning type.

Limitations

In training the network, the system may get stuck in what is called a *local minimum* point. That is, in minimizing (6), the system is walking from one point to the next (always in a downward direction), trying to find the set of connection weights that yield the lowest value for (6). This is like trying to find the bottom of the deepest valley in a terrain by moving only in the direction that goes down.

The problem is that the system may get into the bottom of a ditch, and conclude that it has found the bottom of the deepest valley, because it cannot find any better neighboring point farther down, even though the best point (the lowest value or the bottom of the deepest valley) lies some distance away.

If (6) has only one valley, by going from one point to the next in a downward direction, the system finds it with no problem. If (6) has many ditches and valleys, and the system starts on a road that leads to the deepest valley, with no ditches in between, it will find the set of weights that represent the best point. However, if there is more than one valley, the system may get to the bottom of the one that is not the deepest.

To check whether the best set of weights has been found, the developer should start the system with another random set of starting values for the connection weights, and see whether it produces the same solution. Although this is not a fool-proof solution, repeating this process a number of times increases the developer's confidence that the system has indeed found the best set of weights.

Another limitation of ADALINE and MADALINE is that the decision problem should be linearly separable, as is the case for the perceptron network. We will see that in backpropagation, this limitation is removed by adding another layer to the network.

14.2.3   Kohonen's Self-organizing Network (Optional)

Kohonen's self-organizing network is another ground-breaking network, in that it popularized a new type of learning: unsupervised learning. Although the idea of unsupervised learning and clustering has been around before, Teuvo Kohonen from Helsinki Technical University in Finland was the first to formalize the concept within the neural network paradigm by developing his self-organizing network in 1982.

The idea behind the network is elegant and simple. At the start, the neurons respond randomly to the input impulse. As on-center/off-surround impulse interchanges take place among the neurons with competitive learning, the interconnection weights of the winners increase at the expense of interconnection weights of the losers (the weights are required to be normalized to sum to a fixed value), and the neurons of the network end up mimicking the topology of the input data.

Layer Structure

Kohonen's self-organizing network has two layers: one input layer that works as an input buffer, and a second layer, called the Kohonen layer. The connection weights between the two layers are variable and trainable. The second layer has intra-layer connections of the on-center/off-surround type. The intra-layer connections at the second layer have weight values fixed at 1.

The second layer also sends out impulses to the external environment, after the on-center/off-surround interchanges are completed. The winning neuron sends out the impulse 1, and the output of the remaining neurons remains at 0.

Input and Output of Neurons

There is more than one type of input computation in Kohonen network, but all have the objective of computing the distance between the external input and the connection weights. One common method of distance computation in this network is:

$$input_i = [|w_{1i} - extinput_1|, |w_{2i} - extinput_2|, \ldots, |w_{ni} - extinput_n|], \quad (7)$$

where n is the number of neurons at the input layer, and $extinput_k$ is the external input to the kth neuron in the input layer, where $k = 1, 2, \ldots, n$. The symbol $|\ |$ represents the absolute value of the distance. Thus, the input to the neuron at the Kohonen layer has a column of numbers (or a vector) as its value. The neuron with the *lowest* input value wins the competition.

The transfer function at the Kohonen layer is in the form of "winner-takes-all," in that a single winner neuron (the one with the lowest input value) sends out 1 as the output to the external environment, and the rest have 0 as the output value.

Let us examine equation (7) and the concept of winners within the context of recalling what happens when the training is over and the network is in operation. Assume that the network is given a case input. We can perceive the attributes of the case as a column of numbers (or a one-dimensional array of numbers or a vector). The external input impulse goes through the system, and equation (7) is used to compute the net input impulses to each neuron. The final winner neuron is the one with the smallest difference between its weight vector (or the column) and the vector of the input data, which means that the neuron with the weight vector closest to the input vector wins the competition.

Let us show this with the mortgage loan example. Assume the system is trained on the application profiles representing the knowledge domain. The objective of the system is to produce a loan application profile stored in the system that is closest to the case under investigation. Now, according to the profile of smith, the applicant is age 34, and has a good credit rating, non-steady job, and some assets. We would like to match this profile (coded appropriately for the system) with what we have in the system. smith's profile forms the external input to the system.

The input impulses lead to the computation of equation (7) for all the neurons. Assume neuron 5, which has the lowest $input_i$, wins. This means that the weight vector of neuron 5 has been closest to smith's profile. The firing of neuron 5 produces an output that represents the pattern of profile closest to smith's profile. The example shows that the Kohonen network is of the auto-associative type.

Learning Method

The Kohonen network uses the Kohonen learning rule, which was discussed in Chapter 13 and is reproduced here:

$$w_{ji}^{new} - w_{ji}^{old} = \alpha(extinput_j - w_{ji}^{old}). \tag{8}$$

One must notice that the only interconnection weights that are trainable are those between the first and second layers. From the learning method, one can see that the network tries to gradually move the connection weights to the input values, by a fraction equal to α. It is recommended to start with a large value for the learning coefficient α, such as 0.8, and gradually reduce it to 0.1 or less [Hecht-Nielsen 1990].

No desired output exists in this learning equation. The network is the unsupervised, off-line type. The weights should be normalized to sum to a fixed value, such as 1, and the starting value of the weights should be assigned in a random fashion.

Limitations

Since no desired or correct answer exists for the network, one may ask: What does the network accomplish? The network stores the pattern of case data used for its training. In other words, once the training is completed, the network has the probability distribution (or the topology) of the data, and the number of positive connection weights is higher in areas where the data has been more common or dense.

When the training data set has many cases of various types with rare frequency of occurrences, the network does not learn their pattern as well as the cases with high frequency [Hecht-Nielsen 1990].

For example, assume that in the mortgage loan network, the majority of applicants are employed, their ages are between 25 to 45, and they have some assets. The majority of weights vectors would be trained to represent these common cases. In the training process, the system has one rare case— adam—who is retired, age 76, with a great deal of assets. Next case in the training is a retired applicant called jones, age 60, with some assets. Since this profile is closest to the first rare case, the winner is the neuron with the weight vector closest to **adam**'s profile. This weight vector gets revised to represent both cases. Now, a third case is an unemployed applicant, age 58, with a great deal of assets. Again, this case is closest to that of **adam** and **jones**. Again, the same neuron wins, and its weights get revised to represent all three *dissimilar* rare cases.

In other words, the rare cases do not get the appropriate weight representation. The network requires cases with density or distribution that is spread relatively evenly across different attributes.

One way to get around this limitation is to add what is called a *conscience* to the network, suggested by Duane Desieno in 1988. Conscience is a control mechanism that keeps count of how many times a neuron has won in a training process. If a neuron wins more than a given limit (such as $\frac{1}{N}$ where N is the number of cases), that neuron is removed from competition for a while. This allows the other neurons to win in order to achieve a better representation of the input patterns. This is a practical fix, which has reportedly produced good results.

14.2.4 Hopfield Network (Optional)

John Hopfield, a well-known physicist, was one of the researchers who helped to revive interest in neural networks by his network design in 1982. He renewed enthusiasm in neural networks by comparing the neural networks process with that of the "spin glass" in physics, and coupling his network design with physical features, such as the energy function, and the minimization of this function in achieving a stable state.

The idea behind the *Hopfield network* is that the network system (with recurrent cross-bar connectivity) arrives at an answer by minimizing a function that he called the *energy function*. He observed that the energy function has a direct counterpart in physical systems.

Layer Structure

This network has three layers: input layer, the middle layer called the Hopfield layer, and the output layer. Both input and output layers are used as buffers, receiving the input from the external environment and sending the output to the environment. The main layer in this network is the Hopfield layer. The number of neurons in the input and output buffers are the same as those in the Hopfield layer, and the connection is one-to-one from the input layer to the Hopfield layer with fixed connection weights of 1, and one-to-one from the Hopfield layer to the output, with fixed connection weights of 1.

The Hopfield layer neurons have a cross-bar connectivity, with the exception that no neuron is connected to itself. The connection type is recurrent. The neurons at the Hopfield layer keep on interchanging impulses, until a certain criterion is achieved. The connection weights of the Hopfield layer are symmetric. That is, the weight value from neuron i to neuron j is the same as the weight value from neuron j to neuron i. In other words, $w_{ji} = w_{ij}$.

Input and Output of Neurons

The input to the neurons of this network is the same simple summation as that of equation (1), with no bias term. The input at the Hopfield layer has the same form, with the additional term t, which denotes the iteration number of the impulse interchange among the neurons:

$$input_i^t = \sum_{j=1}^{n} w_{ji} \; output_j^{t-1}, \tag{9}$$

where n represents the number of neurons at the Hopfield layer.

The output of the neurons follows the signum function. That is,

$$output_i^t = \begin{cases} 1 & \text{if } input_i^t > 0, \\ 0 & \text{if } input_i^t \leq 0. \end{cases} \tag{10}$$

Some variations of the Hopfield network use the signum transfer function, with output values of -1, 0, and $+1$ and the threshold T_i (instead of 0).

Minimum Energy Function

The additional question in the Hopfield network is: When should the impulse interchange among the neurons of the Hopfield layer end, and the output be transmitted to the output layer?

The interesting aspect of the Hopfield network is that the impulse iterations among the neurons reduce what is termed the energy function, or the objective function of the system:

$$E = -\frac{1}{2} \sum_{j \neq i}^{n} \sum_{i=1}^{n} w_{ji} \; output_j \; output_i. \tag{11}$$

Learning Equation

Originally, the Hopfield network did not have a learning equation. The weights were assumed to be fixed and determined outside the system. In the present application of the network, one can use either the Hebb rule or the delta rule (discussed in Chapter 13) as the learning equation.

Limitations

The limitation of the Hopfield network is that it requires input patterns to be linearly separable. Furthermore, the minimum of the energy function could be a local one. These are the same limitations present in MADALINE, or any two-layer network that has an objective function to minimize its learning process. (The Boltzman machine network, an advanced architecture not covered in this book, attempts to overcome these limitations.)

Case: Neural Networks in Forecasting, Control, Scheduling, and Diagnosis

If you believe some of the press neural networktechnology has attracted recently, you probably aren't holding your breath for widespread applications in the "real-world." According to some experts in the field, neural nets are a long way off from practical implementation in areas such as scheduling, process control, and diagnosis—the traditional domain of expert systems. Well, don't believe everything you read.

The following applications illustrate that neural network technology isn't as esoteric as you might think. Neural networks, in one form or another, have been employed for system monitoring, scheduling, manufacturing diagnosis, and process control, as well as for more exotic pursuits. By some accounts, revenues from this technology may total as much as five billion dollars by the end of the decade. *Neurocomputers*, an industry newsletter, claims that every major company will have a neural network department by then. Although no one expects the technology to replace conventional computing, it has only begun to realize its potential.

1. *Bond-rating Prediction.* G. R. Pugh & Co. of Cranford, N.J., has employed a neural network built with California Scientific Software's (Grass Valley, Calif.) BrainMaker. The network forecasts the next year's corporate-bond ratings of 115 companies.

Pugh advises public-utility industry clients on the selection of corporate bonds that would be good investments for their customers. (Corporate bonds are rated by industry-standard indexes such as *Standard & Poor's* and *Moody's*.) He uses discriminate analysis methods to classify bond ratings into broad categories and subcategories and make forecasts, but these methods are usually only 85% accurate within a category.

The BrainMaker application takes 23 financial-analysis factors (such as debt load, income, and five-year sales growth) and the previous year's index ratings as inputs; each factor is assigned its own neuron. The network produces a ratings forecast for the next year as output.

The network was trained on a PC XT in about four hours. Pugh claims that the network is 100% accurate in categorizing ratings among categories, and 95% accurate among subcategories. It has also detected hidden trends in the data quite capably.

2. *Refinery Process Control.* Engineers at Texaco's Puget Sound Refinery, which processes 120,000 barrels of oil daily, has integrated neural network models into the plant's process-control strategies. The models were built on a PC with NeuroShell from Ward Systems Group of Frederick, Md. and ported to Data General MV10000s for implementation.

One of the neural network models has been applied to control a debutanizer, which separates and condenses hydrocarbons according to their molecular weights. This process requires careful monitoring of temperature, pressures, and flows, and a 17-hour batch cycle subjects the process to a constant instability. Refinery engineers used NeuroShell to build and train a neural network that would help ensure product quality during flux.

1,440 data sets, each comprising seven inputs (for control and disturbance variables) and two outputs (for manipulated variables such as "steam to an exchanger for heating") were entered into the network for learning. The model will usually correct errors in the control parameters before they appear; a feedback mechanism helps eliminate unexpected errors that do occur. Analysis has shown that the neural network model is in control about 80% of the time, and even more often during unstable processing.

3. *Hubble Telescope Scheduling.* Scientists at the Space Telescope Science Institute, which will manage planning and scheduling operations for NASA's Hubble Space Telescope, have implemented a Hopfield network-based system to assist the extremely complex business of space-telescope scheduling.

This task must account for about 30,000 exposures of 3,000 celestial sites annually and is constrained by mission precedence, orbital viewing occultations, propulsion, and communication limitations. In addition, schedules must be flexible enough to accommodate spacecraft problems and astronomical events such as supernovas. The Institute has developed several scheduling tools (collectively called SPIKE) for the task, one of which is the Hopfield Network.

Think of the network as a matrix of time segments (columns) and scheduling clusters (rows), the lowest-level schedule entities (such as branching sequences or multistate missions). Each network neuron represents the possible commitment of a cluster to a segment; a solution is reached when that commitment occurs. Segment neurons are interconnected to signify time constraints and cluster neurons are similarly connected, an arrangement that prevents a cluster from committing to more than one segment. The network's architecture is designed to find many "good" solutions rather than a single ideal one—multiple partial or complete schedules can be generated.

4. *Loudspeaker Diagnosis.* CTS Electronics of Brownsville, Texas, has also implemented a NeuroShell network for the classification of loudspeaker defects on its Metamoros, Mexico, assembly line. (The facility produces several million speakers annually.) Audible defects in the speakers has been detected by human operators, which introduced a great deal of subjectivity to the testing and made its accuracy liable to worker fatigue.

CTS implemented a PC-based audio-test system in conjunction with statistical pass/fail limits that detected defects well enough, but wasn't "smart" enough to classify them—an essential for process control.

The company has solved the problem by training a neural network to classify speakers into four output classes. Ten input nodes represent distortion at 10 discrete frequency points; four output nodes denote the speaker-defect classes. After a 40-minute training period, network parameters are incorporated into the audio-test software.

The trained network correctly classified loudspeakers under laboratory conditions within a week; a test sweep and evaluation takes only a second. The efficiency of the NeuroShell network has exceeded CTS's original specifications.

CTS is planning a production pilot run that will help define procedures for workers to train and maintain the network.

By Justin Kestelyn, "Application Watch," *AI Expert*, June 1990, pp. 71–72, reprinted with permission from *AI Expert*.

14.2.5   Brain-State-in-a-Box Network (Optional)

The *brain-state-in-a-box network* was developed by James A. Anderson and his colleagues in 1977. Anderson, a neurophysiologist by training, developed this network for recognizing patterns by their "distinctive features."

The main process in the network is that no matter where one starts in the network, the recurrent process within the network leads the network to one corner of a hypercube (a cube in n dimensions). The corner represents a pattern identified by its distinctive features. The network, therefore, acts like a brain in a box, which settles at one of its corners after its internal impulse processing is ended.

Layer Structure

This network has one functional layer. The input and output layers are buffer layers. The neurons on the input and output layers have a one-to-one connection to the neurons on the functional layer. The interconnection weights between functional layer and others are fixed at 1. The functional layer of this network has cross-bar connectivity, and its connections are recurrent. The interconnection weights are not symmetric.

Input and Output of Neurons

The input to a neuron of the functional layer is the simple summation as in equation (1), with a bias term.

The output of a neuron at the functional layer to the output layer is binary, with values -1 and $+1$. However, prior to sending any message to the output layer, the neurons of the functional layer interchange messages among themselves a number of times. The input of a neuron is similar to that of the Hopfield network, equation (9).

Each time, the output of a neuron to the others in the functional layer is computed as:

$$output_i^t = LIMIT(\alpha \ \ input_i^t + \beta \ \ output_i^{t-1}), \tag{12}$$

where $LIMIT$ means that if the computed value goes above the upper limit 1 (or below the lower limit -1), the computed value is set equal to 1 (or -1). (In the implementation of this design, the limit values are altered and set to values such as 1.5 and -1.5.)

The message interchange among the neurons at the functional layer continues until the outputs of the neurons do not change from one iteration to another. At that point, the system is said to have approached a *stable state*. At this state, if the system is in the learning mode, the values of the weights are updated according to the learning equation. When the weight update is over, or if the system is in the operation mode, the neurons of the functional layer send their output to the output layer.

To understand how the system reaches the stable point, imagine a hypercube (a cube with n dimensions) that has corners with values either -1 or $+1$ in each dimension. The system starts at a point somewhere within the cube. The iterative message interchange among the neurons according to equation (12) moves the point to one of the corners of the hypercube, where it remains. Thus, one can imagine that the brain is a box (in an n-dimension space) and each one of its corners represents a pattern in its memory. When a pattern is presented to the brain, it bounces the pattern around, until it ends up at one of its corners which is the closest to the pattern. This corner is the stable state reached by applying (12). The stable corner sends out the answer.

The network is used for both auto-associative and hetero-associative designs. When the system is auto-associative, equation (12) has as additional term: $\gamma \, input_{i}^{0}$, which represents the initial input received from the input layer. This additional term forces the network to produce a pattern closest to the input pattern, thus completing and correcting an input pattern that is incomplete or inaccurate.

As in other designs, the parameters α, β, and γ should be determined by the developer.

Learning Equation

When the network reaches the stable state, then the weights could be updated. The learning equation in the brain-state-in-a-box could be either the Hebb rule or the delta rule. The Hebb rule implemented in this network could be either equation (8) or (10) from Chapter 13. The output of each neuron is the output at the stable state. It is shown that this network minimizes an energy function.

Limitations

This network is similar to the Hopfield network, and has the same limitations.

14.2.6   Instar–Outstar Networks (Optional)

The concepts of *instar and outstar networks* were proposed by Stephen Grossberg in 1969. In 1972, he combined the two into instar–outstar design, and in 1976 added competitive learning at the middle level. This network, as in all networks developed by Grossberg and his colleagues, is intended to model the brain, and to be used as a tool for explaining the brain's existing data and abnormalities. For this reason, the computation of the input to a neuron is a more complicated version of the simple weighted sum shown in equation (1).

Although this network is not commonly used as a stand-alone network, its main features are used in other networks, including the ART series of networks, which are among the most promising designs for modeling the on-line learning nature of the biological brain.

Layer Structure

The instar–outstar design has three layers: an input layer with connections to a competitive middle layer, and an output layer. The connections are hierarchical and feed-forward. The neurons at the middle layer have on-center/off-surround type of connections.

Input and Output of Neurons

The computation of input to a neuron in the networks developed by Grossberg has a more complex structure, and is designed to model the biological process.

The input to a neuron is computed as the change in the activation of a neuron, denoted by $\frac{d\ input_i}{dt}$, indicating the change in the activation potential of a neuron ($d\ input_i$) in a short time interval dt:

$$\frac{d\ input_i}{dt} = -input_i + (A - input_i) \sum_{\forall excitatory\ j} w_{ji}\ output_j - \tag{13}$$

$$(B + input_i) \sum_{\forall inhibitory\ j} w_{ji}\ output_j,$$

where $input_i$ denotes the initial activation of the neuron i.

In this input equation, the impulses received from the output of other neurons ($output_j$) are divided into two sets: excitatory and inhibitory. The weighted sum of the excitatory impulses are multiplied by a factor ($A - input_i$) to ensure that the activation does not go above the upper limit of A. As the strength of excitatory activation increases, this term reduces its effect on the neuron.

Similarly, the weighted sum of the inhibitory impulses are multiplied by a factor ($B + input_i$) to ensure that the activation of a neuron does not fall below ($-B$). Thus, as the strength of the inhibitory impulses increases, their effect on the neuron is offset by this term.

This formulation is a generalization of the simple summation, and is called the *shunting* model. The shunting model is designed to model a biological phenomenon—when the level of external stimula increases, the sensitivity of the biological system decreases in order to protect and adapt the system to extreme external stimuli. For example, if the amount of light in our environment is increased, the sensitivity of our vision to the light decreases to allow us to see objects around us. Otherwise, the extreme flow of light could flood the neurons receiving visual inputs, thus stopping us from distinguishing other objects within the environment. Similar analogies exist in sudden changes in other sensational or emotional stimuli.

The output of the network uses the threshold-linear transfer function, given in equation (7), Chapter 13.

Learning Equation

The learning equation for the connections between the input and middle layers is called the *instar* learning equation. This learning equation is an interpretation of the Hebb rule as:

$$w_{ji}^{new} - w_{ji}^{old} = \alpha(output_j - w_{ji}^{old})\ input_i, \qquad (14)$$

where neuron i is located in the middle layer, and neuron j is in the input layer, as shown in Figure 14.5.

The idea of instar learning is that when a strong output impulse at the input layer corresponds with a strong impulse at the middle layer, the connection weight of the two neurons emitting the strong simultaneous impulses should increase. One simplified interpretation of this learning equa-

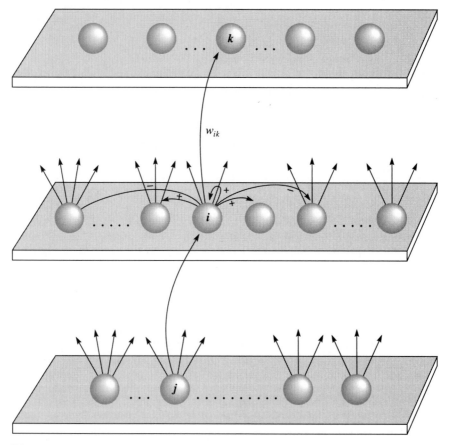

Figure 14.5   The Instar–Outstar Networks

tion is that it allows an input pattern (say, $j = 1, 2, \ldots, n$ neurons) to be condensed in a neuron i in the middle layer.

The learning equation for the connection weights between the middle layer and the output layer is called the *outstar* learning equation. Its form is similar but slightly different from the instar equation:

$$w_{ik}^{new} - w_{ik}^{old} = \alpha(input_k - w_{ik}^{old}) \, output_i, \qquad (15)$$

where neuron i is located at the middle layer, and neuron k is on the output layer. The term $input_k$ at the output layer could be replaced by the desired output from neuron k: $desoutput_k$.

The idea of outstar learning is that once *one* outstar neuron (i) is strongly activated, its impulse to the output layer would activate a set of neurons that represent the desired output pattern. Thus, each one of the neurons at the middle layer could represent a given pattern, or the average of a set of patterns related to a given input pattern. Since the neurons at the middle level compete, one can imagine this as a competition among rival patterns. When the winner succeeds in sending its output to the output layer, it causes the pattern it can activate at the output layer to become the output of the system.

Case: Neural Network Projects at Lockheed

Beginning in 1981, Lockheed has started developing what it calls a probabilistic neural network (PNN) and applied it successfully to the control of active or "rubber" mirrors. Active mirrors are segmented, and each segment can be moved by an actuator to alter the image reflected from the mirror. They are used to counteract the distortion induced in telescope images by Earth's atmosphere. The scientists at Lockheed Missiles & Space are finding practical applications now for the technology that someday duplicate functions of the human brain.

Lockheed recently has won three contracts to apply neural network computing to specific problems from the Defense Advanced Research Projects Agency:

• Automatic target recognition. Lockheed's Digital Image Processing Laboratory will be the prime contractor for studies to apply neural networks automatic target recognition.

• Seismic signature classification. This work will attempt to differentiate between seismic events and underground nuclear tests. Lockheed's Applied Physics Laboratory will be the prime contractor.

• Continuous speech recognition. Lockheed will be a subcontractor to Stanford Research Institute to explore the use of neural networks in continuous speech recognition equipment.

Other Lockheed neural network projects include:

    • Electronic intelligence. A neural network could recognize a complex signature inside a complex signal.

    • Resource allocation. The pilot of a modern fighter could use a neural network to help decide what weapons and defensive measures to use and when to use them.

    • Autonomous vehicles. These would include air or ground vehicles that need to make decisions on the information they gather with their sensors.

Condensed from "Neural Network Computers Finding Practical Applications at Lockheed," by Breck W. Henderson, *Aviation Week & Space Technology*, January 15, 1990, pp. 53–55, reprinted with permission from *Aviation Week & Space Technology*.

14.3 Multiple-Layer Networks (Optional)

Most of the networks discussed in Section 14.2 were presented in three layers. However, these networks could be considered as one- or two-layer networks, because in all of these networks, the weight connections among at most two layers are trainable. For this reason, all have the limitation of the linear separability requirement, and suffer from the same problem as the perceptron.

The backpropagation network and its variants, counterpropagation and recurrent propagation, overcome the linear separability requirement by adding another layer to the network, with trainable connection weights. In this section, we cover this category of multiple-layer networks, all of which have the supervised learning type.

14.3.1 Backpropagation Network (Optional)

The *backpropagation network* was first introduced by Paul Werbos in 1974, and was popularized by David Rumelhart and his colleagues in 1986. This network is one of the most widely applied designs at present.

The basic idea behind backpropagation is that the neurons of lower layers send up their impulses to the next higher layer until they reach the output layer. At this layer, there is a "teacher" that determines the amount of error in each neuron. The connection weights of the output layer and its previous layer get updated based on the amount of error at the output layer (by the generalized delta rule). The error of the output layer propagates back to the hidden layer via the backward connections. Then, the connection weights between the input and hidden layer get updated based on the generalized delta rule. If there is more than one hidden layer, the same backpropagation and weight update is repeated for the additional layers. In summary, there is a forward flow of impulses, and a backward update of the weights based on the errors at the output layer.

While the network can easily compute the errors at the output layer by comparing its output to the "desired output," there is no direct way to compute the errors at the hidden layer(s), because there is no "desirable" or "correct" answer for the neurons of this type of layer. The contribution of the backpropagation network is its ingenious and simple method of propagating the output-layer errors back to the hidden layer(s).

It is proven that the backpropagation network minimizes the sum of the square of output-layer errors. Thus, it has the same type of objective function as MADALINE.

Layer Structure

This network has three or more layers: the input layer, one or more hidden layers, and the output layer. It has a hierarchical, feed-forward structure. There is no intra-layer connection among the neurons within a layer. There is full connectivity in the inter-layer connections of the input and hidden layers, as well as between the hidden and output layers.

There is a backward connection from the output layer to the hidden layer, from the hidden layer to the next lower hidden layer if there is any, and from the hidden layer to the input layer. The backward connections between each pair of layers have the same weight values as those of the forward connection, and are updated together with the forward connections.

For example, as shown in Figure 14.6, the forward connection between the neuron j on the first layer and neuron i on the second layer is w_{ji}. The backward connection between the two neurons has the same weight value, and is updated as soon as the forward connection is changed.

Input and Output of Neurons

The input to each neuron is computed as the simple summation, as in equation (1) with no bias term. The output of a neuron is computed according to the sigmoid transfer function, equation (4) in Chapter 13. The neurons of each layer send their outputs forward to the neurons on the next higher layer.

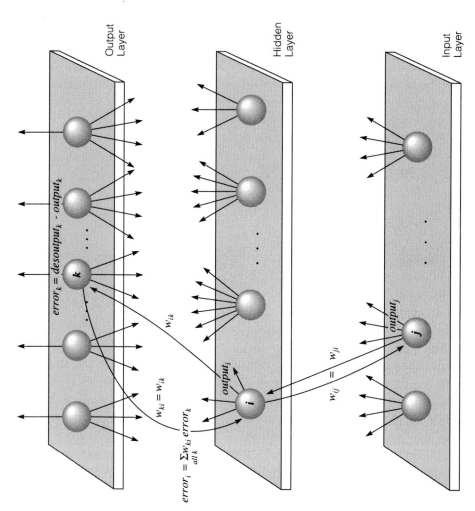

$error_k = desoutput_k - output_k$

$error_i = \sum_{all\ k} w_{ki}\ error_k$

$w'_{ki} = w_{ik}$

w_{ik}

$output_i$

$w_{ij} = w_{ji}$

$output_j$

Output Layer

Hidden Layer

Input Layer

Figure 14.6 The Backpropagation Network

Learning Equation

In the following discussion, we assume that there is only one hidden layer in the network. Later, we see that one can easily extend the process to more than one hidden layer structure.

The learning equation in the backpropagation network is the delta rule, equation (11) in Chapter 13, reproduced here:

$$w_{ik}^{new} - w_{ik}^{old} = \alpha \; output_i \; error_k, \tag{16}$$

where neuron i is located on the hidden layer, and neuron k is located on the output layer, as shown in Figure 14.6. The term $error_k$ represents the deviation of the actual output of neuron k from its desired output: $desoutput_k - output_k$.

To update the connection weights between the output and hidden layers, one can also use the generalized delta rule equation (13) in Chapter 13, reproduced here:

$$w_{ik}^{new} - w_{ik}^{old} = \alpha \; output_i \; input_k \; (1 - input_k) \; error_k, \tag{17}$$

where the additional terms $input_k \; (1 - input_k)$ is the derivative of the sigmoid transfer function used to generate the output of the neurons in the backpropagation network.

To update the connection weights between the hidden and input layers, one has to modify the learning equation. The reason is that, at the hidden layer, the values of the error terms are not known, because we do not know the desired output of the neurons at the hidden layer.

Once the connection weights between the output and hidden layers are updated, we move backward to update the connection weights between the hidden and input layer. At the hidden layer, we define the error term as:

$$error_i = \sum_{\forall k \; in \; output \; connected \; i} w_{ik} \; error_k. \tag{18}$$

Here we assume that the error term $error_i$ of the hidden layer's neuron i is a weighted sum of all the neurons it is connected to on the output layer. Notice that in this process, we are moving backward from the output layer to the hidden layer, as shown in Figure 14.6.

Once the error term for the hidden layer is determined, we can use it in the generalized delta rule (17) to determine the learning equation for the hidden layer. Note that the terms of equation (17) change to follow our notation for the hidden layer as shown in Figure 14.6:

$$w_{ji}^{new} - w_{ji}^{old} = \alpha \ output_j \ input_i \ (1 - input_i) \ error_i, \qquad (19)$$

where $error_i$ is computed according to equation (18). If the system has more than one hidden layer, one can apply (18) and (19) repeatedly to update the interconnection weights of the hidden layers in the backward propagation of errors to the first layer.

Limitations

It has been shown that the backpropagation method minimizes the sum of the square error of the system. Like all networks that optimize an objective function, this method may lead to a local minimum (as in the Hopfield and MADALINE networks). That is, it may find a set of weights that are not necessarily the best answer. The solution to this problem is the same as in other cases: one must train the system with different starting values for the interconnection weights.

14.3.2 Counterpropagation Network (Optional)

The *counterpropagation network* was developed by Robert Hecht-Nielsen in 1987. This network is designed to overcome the shortcoming of the backpropagation network, which lacks the guarantee of producing the best weights (or the globally-minimum-error weights).

Layer Structure

There are a number of counterpropagation-network architectures, with a varying degree of complexity. The *full* version of this network has five layers, and receives external input data from both top and bottom ends of the network. The impulses move in both directions, and the final output of the network is the pattern that matches a combination of the two inputs to the system at both ends.

Here, we focus on the *feed-forward-only* variant of the counterpropagation network, which has a simpler structure. This network consists of three layers, an input layer, a Kohonen layer in the middle, and Grossberg's outstar layer as the third layer. The output layer also receives the desired output.

The inter-layer connections are fully-connected, feed-forward, and hierarchical. The first and third layers do not have any intra-layer connections.

However, the middle layer (the Kohonen layer) has recurrent, cross-bar connectivity, as seen in the Kohonen network.

Input and Output of Neurons

The computation of the input to neurons is the simple weighted sum as in equation (1), with no bias term. The transfer function of the first layer is the linear transfer function. The input to the middle layer should be normalized to be between 0 and 1. The output of the middle layer is a Kohonen network output. That is, only one neuron wins the competition, and sends out an output value equal to 1, while the rest have 0 as their output. The output at the third layer is computed according to a linear transfer function.

Learning Equation

The inter-layer connection weights between the first and second layers are updated the same way as those in the Kohonen network. The inter-layer connection weights between the second and third layer are updated according to the outstar learning equation, in which the desired output ($desoutput_k$) is used in place of $input_k$ in equation (16).

The single winning neuron at the middle layer sends an impulse to the output layer, causing the system to generate the pattern that is the average of patterns represented by that single middle-layer neuron. The advantage of counterpropagation over backpropagation is that it generates near-optimal (or best) weights when the input and output patterns are related by a mathematical function.

14.3.3 Recurrent Backpropagation Network (Optional)

The *recurrent backpropagation network* was first developed by David Rumelhart, Geoffrey Hinton, and Ronald Williams in 1986. This network generalizes backpropagation to include the element of time into the system. As such, this network could be considered the spatio-temporal extension of the backpropagation network.

The main idea in this network is that it receives a series of input patterns in an interval of time, and produces the corresponding series of output patterns in the same interval.

For example, the network receives the payment pattern of a person holding a mortgage loan for six months, and recognizes that it matches the payment pattern of an individual who is going to default on his loan. One can easily extend the example to the case of defaulting credit card holders and patterns of financially troubled firms and so forth. The addition of the time element to the network substantially increases the usefulness of the network.

Layer Structure

The recurrent backpropagation network has two layers: the input layer and the functional layer. The input layer has two types of neurons: one set of neurons (say, n of them) receives the external input from the environment. One can imagine these neurons representing a column of inputs with n elements. Denote this column of external input as $EXINPUT$. The second set of neurons (say N of them) does not have any external input, but receives impulses from the neurons at the functional layer. There are N neurons at the functional layer, which send their impulses both to the input layer and to the external environment, as shown in Figure 14.7.

There is full connectivity between the neurons on the input layer and those on the functional layer. There is also full connectivity from the neurons on the functional layers back to the N (nonexternal) neurons in the input layer.

The exchange of impulses among the neurons on the two layers takes place in discrete time, represented by $t = 1, 2, \ldots, stoptime$, where $stoptime$ is the end of one training epoch. (The training epoch is defined in Section 14.5.)

The external input $EXINPUT$ column changes from one time to another. Thus, in the impulse exchange at time $t = 0$, the external input is $EXINPUT^0$, the external input in the next exchange of impulses is $EXINPUT^1$, and so forth. Thus the system receives a series of temporal (or time-related) input impulses from the external environment, in the form of columns of numbers represented by $EXINPUT^0$, $EXINPUT^1$, $EXINPUT^2, \ldots, EXINPUT^{stoptime}$.

The functional layer has N outputs at time t, shown as $OUTPUT^t$ in Figure 14.7. Of these, the first m output goes to the external environment as the output of the system at time t. These m outputs are summarized in a column of numbers called $EXOUTPUT^t$ at any time t. Thus, the network sends out output in columns of numbers as $EXOUTPUT^1$, $EXOUTPUT^2$, $EXOUTPUT^3$, to $EXOUTPUT^{stoptime}$ at time $1, 2, 3, \ldots, stoptime$. The external output at time 0 should be provided to the system as input.

Thus, at time 0, the network receives $EXINPUT^0$ and $EXOUTPUT^0$, and it produces $OUTPUT^1$, part of which is $EXOUTPUT^1$. It sends out $EXOUTPUT^1$ to the environment. At time 1, the network feeds back

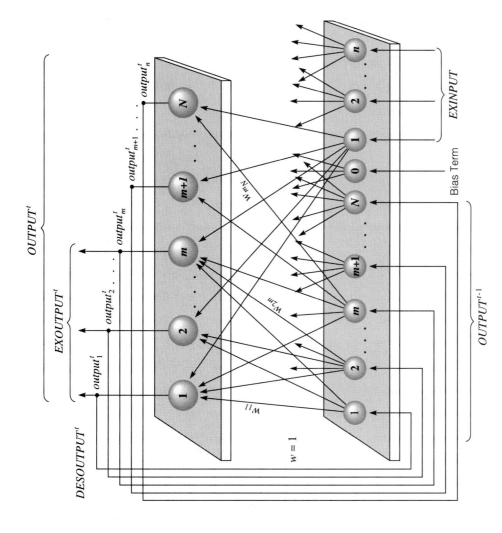

Figure 14.7 The Recurrent Backpropagation Network

$OUTPUT^1$ to the input layer and receives external input $EXINPUT^1$, and produces $OUTPUT^2$, of which $EXOUTPUT^2$ is sent out, and the process continues.

The system requires desired values for the output for learning purposes. Thus, the m desired output of the system at time t is denoted in a column of numbers of $DESOUTPUT^t$. The network does not need to see the desired output for every time unit, but it must have correct outputs for some of the time units.

This structure allows the developer to enter a series of time-sensitive input values, and produce output values that are also time-dependent.

Input and Output of Neurons

The input layer is a buffer layer and its neurons receive only one input, which they send out directly to the functional layer. The input function of the neurons on the functional layer is the simple weighted summation (1), including the bias factor in the form of:

$$output_i^t = \sum_{j=1}^{N} w_{ji} \ output_j^{t-1} + \sum_{k=1}^{n} w_{ki} \ exinput_k^{t-1} + w_{0i} \ output_0. \quad (20)$$

The transfer function for the output is a nonlinear transfer function, such as sigmoid or hyperbolic tangent discussed in Chapter 13, equations (4) and (5).

Learning Equation

The learning equation in the recurrent backpropagation network is relatively complex. The reason is that the network allows for both the single update or cumulative update (discussed in Chapter 13). When the correct or desired output is not known for every single time, one must update cumulatively. Here we give only a simplified version of the learning equation for the single update with one desired output in each time unit, and the sigmoid transfer function:

$$w_{ji}^{new} - w_{ji}^{old} = 2 \ (\ desoutput_i^t - output_i^t \ ) \ r_{ji}^t, \quad (21)$$

where r_{ji}^t is defined as:

$$r_{ji}^t = f'(input_i^t) \ (\ output_j^{t-1} + \sum_{k=1}^{N} w_{ki}^{old} \ ) \ r_{ki}^{t-1}, \quad (22)$$

where r_{ji}^0 is set equal to 0.

Since we use the sigmoid transfer function, then f' in (22) is:

$$f'(input_i^t) = input_i^t(1 - input_i^t).$$

The learning equation for this network could be more involved when there is more than one desired output in some units of time, and no desired answer in others (see Hecht-Nielsen [1990], Chapter 6 for a more detailed treatment of the subject).

Limitations

The network requires a large number of runs for training. If there is a small number of the desired outputs available, training and evaluating the system could pose a great challenge to the developer. Furthermore, the temporal nature and the interdependency of the input and output of the system may cause problems in training the system. Temporal generalization of networks is in its infancy, and the issues related to the temporal aspects of neural networks have yet to be spelled out.

14.4 ART Networks (Optional)

The adaptive resonance theory (ART) was developed by Stephen Grossberg in 1976. Later, Gale Carpenter and Stephen Grossberg developed *ART1* and *ART2* in 1987, and ART3 in 1990. The ART series of neural networks is developed with a closer link to the biological models of the brain than other networks discussed in this chapter. The prominent feature of this network type is its on-line learning capability, and its correspondence with some of the observations on brain functions.

The ART1 network has the simplest structure of the ART series. The network has binary (0, 1) inputs and outputs. The ART2 network has gray scale input and output, in that the interval $[-1, +1]$ is divided into finer intervals. The ART3 network is recently proposed, and is reported to have a hierarchically partitioned structure. In this section, we review the ART1, and briefly discuss ART2 and ART3.

14.4.1   ART1 Network (Optional)

The structure of ART1 is more complex than what we have seen in other networks. In addition to the layered structure, ART1 has two control features (*gain unit* and *vigilance unit*) that make the network operate more in line with the functioning of the brain.

Layer Structure

ART1 has two functional layers: F1 and F2, as shown in Figure 14.8. The inter-layer connections are bi-directional; that is, F1 neurons are fully connected to F2 neurons in the feed-forward, bottom-up manner. The neurons of F2 layer send back their impulses to F1 neurons, in a top-down flow, again with full connectivity.

The intra-layer connection at the F2 layer is the on-center/off-surround type. The competition among neurons leads to one winner. (Although the method theoretically allows for more than one winner, the F2 layer has only one winner in most ART1 networks created so far.)

At the F2 layer, neurons are grouped into what Grossberg calls *dipoles*, or groups of similar neurons. Therefore, at the F2 layer, when we mention one neuron, it means one group of neurons. The competition lets one group of neurons win.

In ART1, the F1 layer may be considered the short-term memory layer, which creates different hypotheses regarding the nature of the external input. The F2 layer is the storage or the long-term memory of the network, in which different patterns are stored. It is against these stored patterns that the F1 layer tests its hypotheses regarding the external input.

Two-Thirds Rule for Activation

In ART1, a neuron is activated when it receives two sets of excitatory inputs. We can see in Figure 14.8 that the neurons of F1 and F2 layers receive three excitatory inputs. For example, a neuron at the F1 layer may receive excitatory impulses from the external input, from F2 layer, and from what we have called the *gain* control unit on the left side of the figure. For the neuron to be activated, it should receive two excitatory impulses out of the three sources. We will see below that this rule provides the network with a sophisticated structure.

Matching Criterion: Vigilance Parameter

The F1 layer receives input from the external sources (we call it *external* pattern), and passes it to the F2 layer across the interconnections. The neurons of F2 compete, and a group of neurons (a dipole) wins. This group represents a pattern (in the form of an outstar structure). We call this pattern the

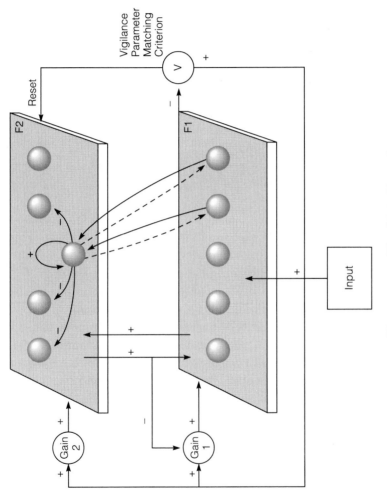

Figure 14.8 The ART1 Network

expectation pattern. The F2 layer sends the expectation pattern top-down to the F1 layer. The neurons of the F1 layer are now activated by both the expectation pattern and the external pattern, producing a combined result called the *trial* pattern.

If the expectation pattern is highly similar to the external pattern, each activated neuron at the F1 layer is now reinforced (by the two-thirds rule), the neurons of the F1 layer with the trial pattern will have a high level of activation, and the expectation pattern becomes the suitable network output to the external environment.

However, if the expectation pattern is not similar to the external pattern, the trial pattern at F1 becomes defused, and the level of activation of the neurons decreases at this layer. This decrease is caused by the fact that each neuron that receives the expectation pattern from F2 is not equally reinforced by the external input pattern (by the two-thirds rule). Thus, the activation level of the neurons representing the trial pattern decreases with the degree of dissimilarity between the top-down (expectation) pattern and the external pattern.

When the two patterns do not match, we need a mechanism to erase the expectation pattern from F2, and let another group of neurons win. This is the function of a neuron called the *vigilance* neuron with what is called a vigilance parameter V, shown on the right-hand side of Figure 14.8.

When activated, the neurons of F1 layer always send inhibitory impulses to the vigilance neuron. The external input always sends excitatory impulses to the vigilance neuron. When the trial pattern at F1 is defused and has low activation potential, the inhibitory impulses to the vigilance neuron would be less than the excitatory impulses from the external input, thus increasing the vigilance neuron's activation potential. Once activated beyond the threshold V (the vigilance parameter), the vigilance neuron sends its output impulse to F2. This has the effect of inhibiting the active group of neurons on F2 for some time, without affecting any of the neurons that are inactive at that moment.

The inhibitory impulse from the vigilance neuron in effect resets the neurons at the F2 layer, and gives another group of neurons an opportunity to win, in response to the bottom-up impulses received from F1. Thus, the next time around, when F2 receives the input from F1, the group of neurons that won the last time around will remain inhibited, and another group will have a chance to win.

The above process of resonance continues until a pattern that sufficiently matches the external input pattern is found. If no pattern stored in F2 neurons matches the external input, then the network learns the external pattern as a new pattern, and stores it in a group of neurons at F2 layer.

The vigilance parameter V determines the extent of dissimilarity allowed between the input and stored patterns. When the vigilance is high, a small amount of dissimilarity will trigger a rest impulse from the vigilance neuron. A low value for the vigilance parameter permits a more coarse categorization of patterns, and tolerates more dissimilarity between the input and stored patterns.

Gain Control

On the right side of Figure 14.8, we have the *gain* control units. These units are necessary to control the activation of the neurons at F1 and F2 layers, by the two-thirds rule.

In ART1, as in the brain, the flow of impulses takes place regularly. Therefore, it is possible that the neurons of F2 become activated by some random noise without any input from F1. This is similar to hallucination in humans. The gain units are designed to control the activation of neurons at F1 and F2 according to the two-thirds rule.

The gain unit is a neuron, which receives excitatory impulses from the external input, and inhibitory impulses from the top-down impulses of the F2 layer. When the external input sends impulses to F1 layer, the **gain 1** and **gain 2** control units receive excitatory impulses. **Gain 1** sends an excitatory impulse to F1, which together with the external input satisfies the two-thirds rule; thus activating the appropriate neurons at F1.

Then F1 sends impulses to F2 layer, so does **gain 2**, which is activated by the external input. The neurons of F2 receive two excitatory impulses, one from F1, and one from **gain 2**. Then, the winner group of neurons at F2 sends its impulses back to F1. The top-down impulses also inhibit **gain 1**, thus offsetting any excitatory impulse from the external input. Now, F1 neurons get activated by F2 top-down impulses only when there are impulses coming from the external input as well. Otherwise, receiving impulses only from F2 would not activate F1 neurons (because the two-thirds rule is not satisfied). This process prevents any activation of F1 neurons when the external input is absent.

Input and Output of Neurons

The input and output of neurons are binary (0 and 1). The input to neurons are computed according to the extended summation formula (14). The weights are normalized to remain between 0 and 1. The output of F1 neurons have a linear transfer function.

Plasticity and Stability Dilemma

If one wants to design a real-time neural network, which learns at the same time it is in operation (like the brain), the developer encounters the dilemma of plasticity versus stability of the network. The developer would like the network to have *plasticity*, which means that the network should be able to learn new patterns and knowledge. It also should have stability in that a single outlier pattern should not be allowed to distort those patterns already stored in the network, or the recent new pattern should not be allowed to quickly replace the old pattern. The ART1 network comes closest to solving the plasticity–stability dilemma, by allowing the network to search for closest matches, before learning it as a new pattern. Furthermore, as we see below, the search process slightly changes the interconnection weights in each iteration, thus providing the network the ability of learning gradually.

Learning

Every time one layer sends impulses to the other layer, the interconnection weights are slightly altered. If a match is found quickly, these alterations have very little effect. Otherwise, a new set of interconnection weights would be established as the network learns a new pattern. The learning formulas for bottom-up interconnections are not the same as those for the top-down. The learning equations for ART1 are reported in the Carpenter paper [1987].

Limitations

The ART1 network demonstrates the complexity of creating systems that have the same real-time nature as the brain. Its binary input and output capability limits the ability of the network to represent complex patterns. Furthermore, the fact that each group of neurons at F2 represents only one pattern limits the storage capacity of neurons at F2 level. For example, if there are $n = 10$ groups of neurons at F2 layer, the network can store only $n = 10$ patterns. A combinatorial representation, as discussed in the combinatorial hypercompression network, could considerably increase this storage capacity.

14.4.2   ART2 and ART3 Networks (Optional)

Complete and detailed information on ART2 and ART3 networks is limited, partly because of the network developers' patent application. From what is available in the literature, we can gather that there have been a number of versions for ART2. The principle feature of ART2 is that it allows for gray scale input and output.

The gray scale is different from real or analog input and output. In the gray scale, the interval is divided into distinct subintervals, while in the real or analog type, there are theoretically infinite possible real numbers between −1 and +1.

The introduction of gray scale increases the complexity of the network to a great extent, because there is no longer a crisp distinction between a neuron being active (1) and inactive (0). Thus, the difference between a noise and the increment to the next gray level becomes fuzzy. To deal with this complexity, some of the ART2 systems have as many as five input layers, each with its own gain control unit.

The limitation of both ART1 and ART2 is that they do not process different attributes of a pattern separately, as is possible in the hierarchically partitioned networks already discussed. This limits the ability of the network for complex pattern recognition, such as picking up a relevant object from a background of irrelevant objects. It seems that the newly developed ART3 was designed to address this issue.

14.5 Training the System in Neural Networks

When a neural network system is designed, it should be trained with a *training* data set. To train a system, the developer repeatedly presents it with data from the training data set, and allows the system to change its weights. This process continues until a given criterion is satisfied. Training is not an automatic process. Here is where the experience and art of the developer make a difference.

Since neural networks have recently entered the market, publications on issues surrounding the practical application of neural networks are not abundant. However, the reported experiences of those who have applied the system show that in the real-world application of the method, the developer must commit as much time to designing the training process as to designing the network itself. In many instances, the lack of success in training the system returns the developer to the drawing board for the redesign of the system. Thus, the developer goes through designing the system, training it, and evaluating its performance in an iterative fashion. The developer normally goes through a number of design-train-evaluate cycles before arriving at a system design with a satisfactory performance.

The issues of training could be grouped into the following categories:

- Training data set

- Training strategies

Case: Neural Network Application in Stock Market Prediction

Fujitsu and Nikko Securities of Japan have designed a modular neural network to predict the timing of buying and selling stocks for the TOPIX (Tokyo Stock Exchange Prices Indexes). TOPIX is a weighted average of market prices of all stocks listed on the First Section of the Tokyo Stock Exchange. It is weighted by the number of stocks issued for each company, and is similar to the Dow-Jones averages.

Neural networks are being applied to a widely expanding range of applications in addition to the traditional areas such as pattern recognition and control. Its non-linear learning and smooth interpolation capabilities give the neural network an edge over standard computer programs and expert systems for solving certain problems.

The input to the network consists of several technical and economic indexes. In this system, several modular neural networks learn the relationships between the past technical and economic indexes and the timing for when to buy or sell. The system predicts the best time to buy or sell for one month ahead.

The neural network has a number of modules, each module consists of a three-layer network, consisting of the input, hidden, and output layers. The three layers are completely connected to form a feed-forward hierarchical network.

Each node in the network receives input from the lower level units and perform weighted addition to determine the output. A standard sigmoid function is used as the output function. The output is analog in the [0,1] range. The learning method is the backpropagation, and is modified to increase the speed of learning for the large volume of data involved in this system.

Two-thirds of data is used for training the system and the rest is used for testing the system. To prevent overlearning, a special learning control was developed for the system.

To verify the effectiveness of the prediction system, a simulation of buying and selling of stock was done. Buying and selling according to the prediction of the system made a greater profit than buying stocks and holding them. The TOPIX index of January 1987 was considered as 1.00. By the end of September 1989, the buy-and-hold policy would have an index value of 1.67, and buying and selling according to the prediction of the neural network system would have an index value of 1.98, which indicates an excellent profit.

Condensed from "Stock Market Prediction System with Modular Neural Networks," by Takashi Kimoto, Kazuo Asakawa, Morio Yoda, and Masakazu Takeoka, *Proceedings of the International Joint Conference on Neural Networks*, San Diego, June 1990, Volume I, pp. I.1–I.6, reprinted with permission from the Institute of Electrical and Electronics Engineers (IEEE). ©1990 IEEE.

14.5.1   Training Data Set

One can categorize the issues in the training data set as follows:

- size
- noise
- knowledge domain representation
- training set and test set
- insufficient data
- coding the input data

Size

In neural networks, the domain knowledge is summarized into a set of data used for training the system. Although the required size of the training data is not well-established, and depends on the type of neural network and its design, the size of the data set must be relatively large. When the problem domain lacks adequate data, the use of neural networks is not recommended.

Noise

The training data set could be noisy and may contain errors. In some cases, such as the backpropagation neural network, it is reported that the training is more successful when the data contains errors [Caudill 1991].

Knowledge Domain Representation

The training data set should include a good representation of the cases of the problem domain. On the other hand, when the number of distinct cases increases in some neural networks, the developer may need to change the number of neurons in some layers of the system, and redesign their connections. Many questions are yet to be answered about the number of neurons and size of the training cases for different types of neural networks.

Training Set and Test Set

The accessible data on the domain knowledge should be divided into two parts: training set and test set [Hecht-Nielsen 1990, Chapter 5]. The reason is that any neural network performs better in cases it has seen in its training process. Therefore, it is not enough to measure the performance of the system based on the data used for its training. There must be an exogenous data set for testing the system. (The issues related to the reliability of the system are covered in Hecht-Nielsen, Chapter 17.)

This requirement means that the developer needs a large data set, and must decide on the proportion of training and test sets. Obviously, the more data that is allocated to training the system, the more accurately the data would represent the domain knowledge. However, a small set of test data may damage the validity of the performance test.

Insufficient Data

When the data is scarce, the allocation of data for training and testing becomes critical. One may resort to one of the following options when the data set is limited and the opportunity for collecting more data does not exist:

- Rotation scheme
- Creating made-up data
- Expert-made data

Rotation scheme. Hecht-Nielsen [1990, Chapter 5] suggests that when the domain data is not sufficiently large to be divided into two sets for training and testing, the developer may use the rotation scheme. In this scheme, if the data set has N points in it, the developer sets aside only one data point for testing, and trains the system with $N - 1$ data points. Then, another data point is set aside, and the system is trained on $N - 1$ points. This process continues N times. That is, the system is trained N times, each time with $N - 1$ points, with a different excluded data point from the training set.

Creating made-up data.   Another scheme to increase the size of the data set is to create *made-up* data by looking at the existing data, and interpolating the possible data if new circumstances are present. For example, in a loan application system, the data set may not include applicants with some particular profile, such as the applicant of age 75 with sufficient assets and a small retirement income. If the existing data set has an applicant with age 73 and a similar financial profile, one may use the decision of the 73-year-old applicant for the 75-year-old applicant, and add this made-up data to the data set.

The danger of creating made-up data is that it may distort the actual distribution of profiles. For example, if the developer adds numerous data points on applicants over age 70, the data set will have a larger proportion of older applicants than the real data set. To remedy this situation, one may use the idea of *bootstrapping* in statistics. In bootstrapping, the distribution of made-up data should follow the distribution of the real data. In this way, the proportion of real data does not change. For example, if in the real data set, the proportion of applicants above age 70 with the given financial profile is 3 percent, then only 3 percent of the made-up data should belong to applicants aged over 70 with a similar financial profile. This requires a careful categorization of real data in the creation of made-up data.

Expert-made data.   Another method for creating new data, when the size of the real data set is not adequate, is to ask a panel of experts to review the data set, and create data for the missing circumstances. For example, in the loan application case, the developer may create a forum of all senior loan officers of the bank with the mission of reviewing the real data set, and creating *expert-made* data for missing profiles in the data set.

In creating the expert-made data, the decision must be made as to whether the distribution of the real data should be preserved. The forum of experts could help the developer in this decision. If the forum decides the original data set correctly reflects the knowledge domain, then the bootstrapping scheme of the previous subsection must be applied. Otherwise, the forum of experts could add data in the categories that they believe are insufficiently represented in the real data set.

Coding the Input Data

Although neural networks use raw data for input, and produce output used for making a decision (or taking an action), the input and output data must be coded for the system. For example, assume in a given design, each neuron in the input layer of the network takes 0 or 1 as the input impulse. In the case of a loan application network, the input record may contain the applicant's job (employed or not employed), the level of the applicant's assets (none, some, high), the credit rating of the applicant (bad, good, very good, excellent), and the amount of the loan (up to $500,000). The outcome of the network is either to grant or deny the loan.

To code the input, the input layer needs one neuron for the job status ("1" for employed and "0" for not employed), two neurons for coding the level of asset ("00" for none, "01" for some, and "11" for high), two neurons for credit rating ("00" for bad, "01" for good, "10" for very good, and "11" for excellent). To code 500 in binary value, one needs 9 neurons because each neuron can code 2 values, and $2^9 = 512$, a little more than what is needed. The output requires one neuron, with the output 1 representing grant the loan, and 0 denoting the denial of the loan. Thus, the network needs 14 neurons in the input layer to receive the external input, and one neuron in the output layer to send the result to the external environment.

Now, if the type of network is such that it could take real values of any size, we could use one input neuron for every real value. In this case, we could use one neuron to take the input for one data item, such as one for the job status, one for the asset status, one for the credit rating, one for the amount of loan, and one for the output. Thus, this design requires four input neurons and one output neuron.

Thus, in designing a network, one must pay attention to the neurons type of input and output. The combination of the knowledge domain data and the type of neurons determine the number of neurons needed. Furthermore, the raw data must be coded to accommodate the network design.

14.5.2 Training Strategies

Training a network depends on the characteristics of its design. Many networks require iterative training, in that data is presented to the system many times and the system gradually changes its connection weights. For training a system, the developer faces a number of training issues, such as:

- Proportional training

- Over-training and under-training

- Generalization

- Updating

- Scheduling

Proportional Training

In training a system, the developer presents data to the system repeatedly. As many as half a million iterations is not uncommon.

In training the network system, a data record may be input to the system many times. The question is how many times a given case should be presented to the system. A simple answer is to present all cases equally. For example, assume that the training data set has 500 cases in it. (In the loan application example, each case represents the data for one loan application and its loan decision.) Furthermore, assume that it takes the system $500,000$ iterations to be trained. The simple answer to the above question is that each case must be input to the system $1,000$ times.

The simple proportional training is appropriate if each case represents a unique set of data. Now, assume that the set of 500 observations could be categorized into 100 categories of unique cases. That is, the data set has cases with identical data items, such as applicants with exactly the same profiles. Then, each unique case should be presented to the system in proportion to its occurrence in the real data set. For example, if a case is repeated 5 times in the data set, then it must be presented $5,000$ times to the system (instead of $1,000$ times in the simple case above). This proportional presentation gives an appropriate share of each unique case in training the system. A case with a larger number of occurrences in the training data set has a more important share in determining the weights within the system.

Over-training and Under-training

In the iterative training of a system, a higher number of interactions does not always mean a better training outcome. In other words, one may *over-train* or *under-train* a system. Too many iterations or too few iterations in training a system may lead to inferior system performance. The reason for over-training is not completely clear, and requires further research. However, the reported experience shows that in some networks, training beyond a certain point may lower the performance of the system. The developer must determine when this point is reached. This is accomplished through trial and error.

Generalization

The performance of a system is normally measured with the *endogenous* data (data used in training the system) and *exogenous* data (test data, not used in training the system and representing cases not seen by the system). In practice, when the learning coefficient of a network is high, the number of training iterations is smaller, and the system learns faster. In such systems, the performance of the system with the exogenous data is normally poor. That is, when the system is presented with a case that it has not seen before, its outcome has a high degree of error. In this case, the system is not capable of *generalization*. That is, it cannot extrapolate from what it has been trained on to the cases it has not seen before.

To increase the system's generalization ability, the developer must use a lower value for the learning coefficient and a higher number of iterations in the training. In some designs, the learning coefficient may be changed in the training process. The developer may start the training with a high value of the learning coefficient, and gradually reduce it as the training progresses. Again, the choice of the learning coefficient and decision of a fixed or variable learning coefficient are design issues that should be resolved by the system developer.

Updating

Another training issue is determining when the weights should be updated. There are two main updating strategies:

- Single update

- Epoch or cumulative update

In the *single update* strategy, when the system is in the learning mode, it may change its connection weights every time that it is presented with a new case data. Thus, the system updates its weights every single time it is presented with an input.

In the *epoch* or *cumulative update* strategy, the system may change its weights after it is presented the whole training data set. In this case, the changes in the weights are accumulated from one input to another, but the weights are actually altered after the presentation of the entire data set, which is called an *epoch*.

Some neural network designs come with a recommended updating strategy. In others, the system developer must choose the updating strategy. This strategy is another aspect of the system with which the developer could experiment to fine-tune the system's performance.

Scheduling

Another training issue is the priority and sequence by which the connection weights are changed within the system. In some networks, all the weights are changed *simultaneously*. That is, the system determines the values by which all the connection weights are to be changed, and then changes the weights all at the same time.

In another type of network, the connection weights are changed *sequentially*. That is, a given set of neurons may change their connection weights before another. The network type determines which neurons have the priority to change their connection weights.

In some networks, one may have both sequential and simultaneous types of weight change. For example, the connection within one layer (intra-layer connections) may change simultaneously, while connections among layers (inter-layer connections) are changed sequentially.

In another type of network, one layer must be completely trained before another layer is allowed to change its weights. In this case, the high-priority layer is allowed to change its intra-layer connection weights, while other layers keep theirs fixed (or *clamped*). Once the higher-priority layer is trained, its weights are fixed (or clamped), and the next-priority layer starts training. This process continues until the entire system is trained.

Almost all well-known network designs recommend their own scheduling. However, this is an important design aspect, which has a major impact on the training efficiency of the system, and on which the system developer must keep a watchful eye.

Conclusion

This chapter discussed some of the well-known neural networks, and brought the reader up to date with the basic categories of architectures in the field. More importantly, it alerted the reader to the limitations that exist in each design type.

The first section of this chapter showed that one can group the existing neural networks by various criteria, such as their learning methods, input and output data, number of layers, certainty of firing, type of connectivity, temporal feature, and timing of learning.

Most of the earlier networks were two-layer networks. Section 14.2 reviewed some of the most influential two-layer networks, such as perceptrons, ADALINE and MADALINE, Kohonen's self-organizing, Hopfield, brain-state-in-the-box, and instar–outstar. The review contained a discussion of the layer structure, input–output, learning equations, and limitations of each network.

Although ground breaking, most of these networks have been superseded by the more recent multiple-layer networks. Sections 14.3 and 14.4 reviewed some the well-known multi-layer networks, including backpropagation, counterpropagation, recurrent backpropagation, and ART series.

For a system to learn, one must train it. The issues involved in training do not have a great deal of theoretical implications. However, in the application of neural networks, training is an important factor. Section 14.5 discussed issues involved in implementing networks, such as the training data set and training strategies.

References

Ackley, D. H.; Hinton, G. E.; and Sejnowski, T. J. 1985. "A Learning Algorithm for Boltzman Machines," *Cognitive Science*, Vol. 9, pp. 147–169.

Anderson, James A.; Silverstein, Jack W.; Ritz, Stephen A.; and Jones, Randall S. 1977. "Distinctive Features, Categorical Perception, and Probability Learning: Some Applications of a Neural Model," *Psychological Review*, Vol. 84, pp. 413–451.

Carpenter, Gail A. and Grossberg, Stephen. 1987. "A Massively Parallel Architecture for a Self-Organizing Neural Pattern Recognition Machine," *Computer Vision, Graphics, and Image Processing*, Vol. 37, pp. 54–115.

Carpenter, Gail A. and Grossberg, Stephen. 1987. "ART 2: Self-Organization of Stable Category of Recognition Codes for Analog Input Patterns," *Applied Optics*, Vol. 26, pp. 4919–4930.

Carpenter, Gail A. 1989. "Neural Network Models for Pattern Recognition and Associative Memory," *Neural Networks*, Vol. 2, No. 4, pp. 243–257.

Carpenter, Gail A. and Grossberg, Stephen. 1990. "ART 3 Hierarchical Search: Chemical Transmitters in Self-Organizing Pattern Recognition Architectures," *The Proceedings of the International Joint Conference on Neural Networks*, January 1990, Washington DC, Lawrence Erlbaum Associates, Hillsdale, NJ, Vol. II, pp. 30–33.

Caudill, Maureen. 1991. "Neural Network Training Tips and Techniques," *AI Expert*, Vol. 6, No. 1, pp. 56–61.

Desieno, Duane. 1988. "Adding a Conscience to Competitive Learning," *Proceedings of International Conference on Neural Networks*, Vol. I, IEEE Press, New York, July 1988, pp. 117–124.

Hecht-Nielsen, Robert. 1987. "Counter-Propagation Networks," *Proceedings of the International Conference on Neural Networks*, Vol. II, IEEE Press, New York, pp. 19–32.

Hecht-Nielsen, Robert. 1990. *Neurocomputing*, Addison-Wesley Publishing Co., Reading, MA.

Hertz, John; Krough, Anders; and Palmer, Richard G. 1991. *Introduction to the Theory of Neural Computation*, Addison-Wesley Publishing Co., Reading, MA.

Hopfield, John J. 1982. "Neural Networks, and Physical Systems with Emergent Collective Computational Abilities," *Proceedings of the National Academy of Science*, Vol. 79, pp. 2554–2558.

Kohonen, Teuvo. 1982. "Self-Organizing Formation of Topologically Correct Feature Maps," *Biological Cybernetics*, Vol. 43, pp. 59–69.

Rosenblatt, Frank. 1958. *The Perceptron: The Computer and the Brain*, Yale University Press, New Haven, CT, pp. 66–82.

Rumelhart, D. E. and McClelland, J. L. 1986. *Parallel Distributed Processing: Explorations in the Microstructure of Cognition*, Vols. I and II, MIT Press, Cambridge, MA.

Questions

14.1   Discuss distinctive features of a network structure that could be used to categorize the existing architectures.

14.2   Why should the developer of a neural network be aware of the existing architectures?

14.3   Compare and contrast the two-layer networks.

14.4   What are the advantages and disadvantages of the multiple-layer networks over the two-layer networks?

14.5   Which networks generalize the backpropagation network? What is the price of these generalizations?

14.6   What is the main idea behind the hierarchically-partitioned networks?

14.7   What are the advantages of the ART series of networks? What are their disadvantages?

14.8   Assume that you want to design a network to find the loan application profile best matching an existing application. What network will you choose for your system? Justify your answer.

14.9   As a developer, what criteria would you use in selecting a network architecture for (a) a large and complex system, (b) a small prototype system, (c) a system with a time factor, such as the spending profile of a loan applicant through time?

14.10 What are the issues related to the capacity of a network in storing many patterns? What type of structure could help increase the storage capacity of the network?

14.11 What is the significance of associative memory in the design of networks? Identify the networks in this chapter that have the associative memory capability.

14.12 Which of the networks discussed in this chapter are of the self-organizing type? How are they different from other types of networks?

14.13 What is the significance of self-organizing networks? Give examples for possible applications of the self-organizing networks in business.

14.14 Why is a real-time network important in business applications of neural networks? Give examples of the possible use of real-time networks in business.

14.15 What are the issues of plasticity and stability? What is their significance in the applications of neural networks in business?

14.16 What does training a neural network system mean?

14.17 What are the major issues related to the data sets used for training a neural network?

14.18 If the training data set is not large, what schemes could the developer use in order to increase the size of the data set?

14.19 What is proportional training? Why is it important in training a neural network system?

14.20 What is the "generalization" capability of a system? What are the factors affecting the generalization capability of a system?

14.21 What are the two major types of updating in training?

14.22 What is "scheduling"? Does the developer have any control over it?

14.23 In reviewing the design and training aspects of developing a neural network, list and discuss the factors over which a system developer has control. How should the developer make decisions regarding these control factors?

Case: Neural Networks Application for Monitoring the Environment

Images transmitted by satellites help scientists monitor our environment. Neural networks are used to analyze these images.

In addition to their commercial value as telecommunications devices, orbiting earth satellites have proven their worth in scientific research. Satellites take pictures of our planet and send these pictures back in a digital format. When scientists receive these digitized pictures of earth, they have to make sense of them. Specifically, the earth's surface features have to be detected, identified, and classified. *Satellite remote sensing* encompasses a set of techniques for doing just that.

Among its many successful applications, satellite remote sensing has been used extensively to

- explore mineral and petroleum resources

- monitor the rate of deforestation in the world's tropical rain forests

- assess environmental impacts from major disasters such as the Valdez oil spill

- predict annual crop yields

- monitor the Kuwaiti oil field fires

- map urban sprawl

Of all civilian satellites, the Landsat series, initiated in 1972, has been depended on the most for earth resource issues and problems.

Designed primarily for earth resources observation, these satellites carry sensors which record reflected and emitted radiation in several wavelength bands of the electromagnetic spectrum. These sensors scan the earth's surface recording radiance for discrete elements (called picture elements, or pixels).

The radiance data often reveal the unique spectral reflectance properties of various earth surface cover types. Vegetation reflects light in one particular way, soil in another, and water still another. These reflectance differences enable scientists to detect and map the features of the earth's surface.

One way to make sense of a Landsat picture is to try and classify each pixel. Does a particular pixel indicate vegetation? Water? Soil?

Traditionally, scientists have used statistical techniques for the classification of pixels. Analysts have begun to use neural networks to classify satellite image data. The Landsat TM (Thematic Mapper) reflective data have been used for an area in Coventry, Connecticut. The classification categories included: urban areas, agriculture, deciduous forests (trees that shed their leaves), coniferous forests (trees, like evergreens, that bear cones), water, wetland, barren land. The NeuralWorks Explorer was used to construct backpropagation neural networks of one input layer, either one or two hidden layers, and a one-element output layer. In each network, all processing elements in the network were fully connected. A weighted sum algorithm combined inputs from contributing processing elements. A sigmoid function was used to transfer a processing element's value along the output path.

In the one-hidden-layer network, fifteen processing elements were in the hidden layer. In the two-hidden-layer network, six processing elements were in one hidden layer and fifteen processing elements were in the other.

For all networks, six processing elements were in the input layer—one for each of the TM reflective bands. The mean vectors of the land cover classes were the training data for network learning. Network training, accomplished via the *delta learning rule*, was iterated for 10,000 to as many as 250,000 times with root mean square error (RMS) calculated every 25,000 iterations. RMS, a commonly used statistical measure, gets smaller as classification accuracy increases.

For neural network classification, the TM image was segmented into regions of homogeneous spectral properties. This was accomplished by a statistical cluster technique. The mean spectral response per TM reflective band was calculated for each region and supplied to the neural network during classification.

The neural networks were tested and their overall classification accuracies were 66.7% (for the one hidden layer network) and 64% (for the two hidden layer network). (The statistical technique of maximum likelihood has 91.5% accuracy.)

Much of the inaccuracies resulted from miscalculations of coniferous forest land, barren land, and to some extent, wetlands. In the remaining categories, the neural networks performed about as well as the statistical technique.

Apparently, the chosen architecture does not yield sufficient accuracy, and the research group is developing and testing alternative neural network architectures. Output layers are being structured with as many neurons as land cover classes. Preliminary results show improvement in the accuracy of results and shorter training time. Multiple output neuron approach lends itself to the concept of *fuzzy class membership*.

Condensed from "AI and the Environment: Neural Networks Analyzes Satellite Images," by Daniel Civco, *PC AI*, January/February 1992, pp. 43–45, reprinted with permission from *PC AI*.

Case Questions

1. Discuss the type of neural net architecture used in this case. Suggest alternative design(s) for this application. Support your proposal based on the special features of the proposed architecture.

2. Refer to Chapter 11 and the fuzzy logic. How does fuzzy class membership apply to the outcome of a neural net system?

3. Find the article by Casimir Klimasauskas: "Applying Neural Networks—Part VI: Special Topics," in *PC AI*, November/December 1991, pp. 46–49. Discuss how one can assign probability to the output of a neural net system.

4. Compare and contrast the application of the neural net in environment here with that of the expert system in Chapter 7. Discuss possible avenues for integrating neural networks and expert systems in addressing the environmental issues.

5. Are the organizational roadblocks in deploying neural networks different from those in using expert systems?

The Computational Method in ID3

In Chapters 4 and 6, we discussed ID3 as one of the methods for inductive reasoning in expert systems. In this appendix, we discuss the computational method of ID3 in more detail. To do this, we use the example in Chapter 4 and repeat it here:

steady job	*adequate assets*	*adequate income*	*approve loan*
yes	yes	yes	yes
yes	no	yes	yes
no	yes	yes	yes
no	no	yes	no
yes	yes	no	no
yes	no	no	no
no	yes	no	no
no	no	no	no

We want to find the first node that has the highest discriminatory power of the decision action: approve loan. To do this, ID3 goes through the following steps:

1. Choose one attribute; call it attribute #1 on node #1.
2. Categorize the data according attribute #1, setting up a branch for each value of attribute #1.
3. For the branch i of attribute #1, compute

$$B_i = -p^+ log_2 p^+ - p^- log_2 p^-$$

where p^+ is the fraction of *yes* decisions under branch number i and p^- is the fraction of *no* decisions under the same branch i.
4. Compute for the node 1

$$M_1 = \sum_{i=1}^{n} r_i \, B_i$$

where the decision tree so far has branches leading to n leaves, and r_i is the proportion of the observations under leaf i with respect to the total number of observations that the decision tree is to classify.
5. Repeat steps 1–4 for other decision attributes to get $M_2, M_3, \ldots$.
6. Choose the attribute with the smallest M. This is the chosen node on the decision tree.
7. Continue steps 1–6 for the selection of the node at the next level of the decision tree.
8. Stop when all observations under each leaf have the same decision type. M values become zero at this stage.

Let us apply this algorithm to the example:

Step 1. We choose the attribute *steady job* as node #1.

Step 2. Node #1 has two branches, *yes* and *no*. We categorize eight observations according to this attribute and each branch gets four observations (see Figure A.1a).

Step 3. For the first branch of node #1, we compute

$$B_1 = -p^+ \log_2 p^+ - p^- \log_2 p^-$$

$$= -\frac{2}{4} \log_2 \frac{2}{4} - \frac{2}{4} \log_2 \frac{2}{4}$$

$$= -.50 \frac{\log .50}{\log 2} - .50 \frac{\log .50}{\log 2}$$

$$= 2[-.50 \frac{-0.3010}{0.3010}] = 1$$

Repeating the computation for the second branch, we get

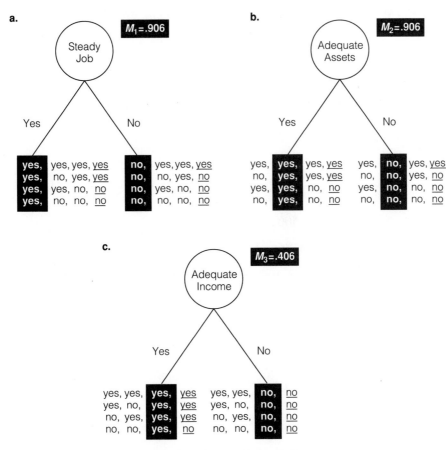

Figure A.1 The First Step of ID3 for the Example Data

$$B_2 = -\frac{1}{4} \log_2 \frac{1}{4} - \frac{3}{4} \log_2 \frac{3}{4}$$

$$= -.25 \frac{\log .25}{\log 2} - .75 \frac{\log .75}{\log 2}$$

$$= -.25 \frac{-.6021}{.3010} - .75 \frac{-.1249}{.3010}$$

$$= .811$$

Step 4. We compute M for the node #1 representing the *steady job* attribute as:

$$M_1 = \frac{4}{8}(1) + \frac{4}{8}(.8113) = .906$$

Step 5. When we repeat steps 1–4 for *adequate assets*, we get (Figure A.1b):

$$M_2 = .906$$

because the number of observations and the decision types of each branch are similar to those on node #1. Repeating Steps 1–4 for *adequate income*, we get (Figure A.1c):

$$M_3 = \frac{4}{8}[\ -\frac{3}{4}\log_2\frac{3}{4} - \frac{1}{4}\log_2\frac{1}{4}\ ]+$$
$$\frac{4}{8}[\ -\frac{4}{4}\log_2\frac{4}{4} - \frac{0}{4}\log_2\frac{0}{4}\ ]$$
$$= .406 + 0$$
$$= .406$$

Step 6. We choose *adequate income* as the node at level #1 of the decision tree.

Step 7. Now that we have decided on the first node, we must decide which of the two other attributes should be used as the next node at level #2. An inspection of Figure A.2 shows that both nodes have the same M value at level #2. In Figure A.2a, we have

$$M_4 = \frac{4}{8}\ \{\frac{2}{4}[\ 0\ ] + \frac{2}{4}[\ -\frac{1}{2}\log_2\frac{1}{2} - \frac{1}{2}\log_2\frac{1}{2}\ ]\ \}$$
$$+ \frac{4}{8}(0)$$
$$= .25$$

M_5 has the same number of observations under each branch as those in M_4, and the decision types of data under each branch are the same as those in M_6. Therefore, $M_6 = .25$. Thus, we can continue the decision tree using either *steady job* or *adequate assets*. In doing so, we get to the last level (level #3) in each decision tree, as shown in Figure A.2.

At level #3, both M_6 and M_7 are zero because when a branch has data with decisions of the same type, the value of its B is equal to zero. This is true for branches of *adequate assets* and *steady job* in the last level of the two decision trees in Figure A.2. Therefore the problem has two answers, as shown in Figure A.3.

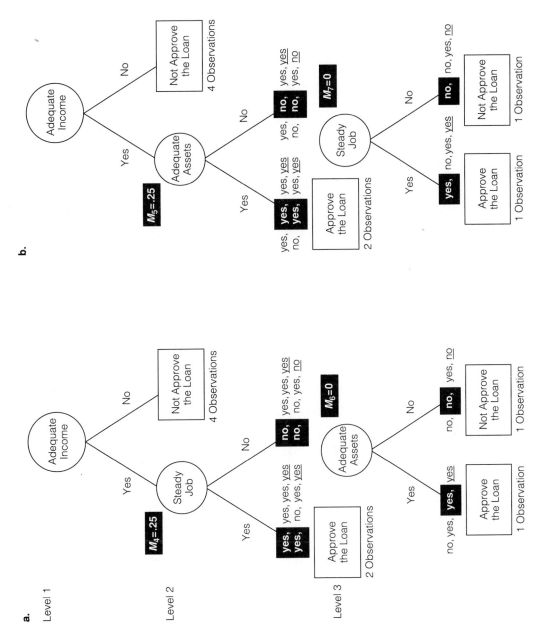

Figure A.2 The Choice of the Second and Third Nodes for the Decision Tree

621

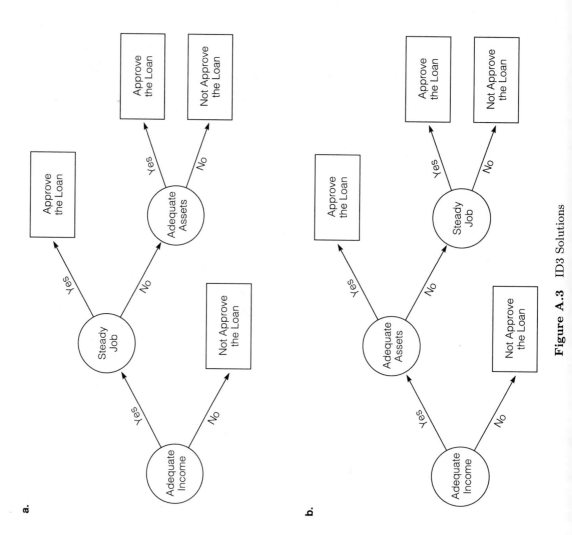

Figure A.3 ID3 Solutions

Sources for Expert Systems

This appendix lists sources for expert system software products as of 1991. Be aware that the only constant features in expert system markets are: frequent introductions of new products, enhancements of existing ones, and changes and mergers of software companies. Therefore, this list may be out of date by the time it reaches you. Use it as an indication of what is available in the market, rather than an exhaustive and up-to-date list of companies and products.

This appendix is an abbreviated version of a survey by Patty Enrado ["Expert-System Resource Guide," *AI Expert*, May 1991, pp. 52–59], and was reprinted with permission from *AI Expert*. The survey is based on the information provided by those vendors who responded to the survey and does not constitute a review of products. Not all companies in the original article are included in this appendix.

In the following list, the name of the software company appears first and is followed by the name of the expert system products the company offers. For more detailed information on addresses and list prices, consult the original article.

1. ABTECH CORP., Charlottesville, Va.

AIM Problem Solver is a numeric knowledge acquisition tool. It does not generate rules, but its functional models can be used to manage uncertainty, handle numeric knowledge, or manage automatic knowledge acquisition. It works with DOS and Macintosh platforms.

2. AICORP, Waltham, Mass.

1st-CLASS is an inductive tool that is discussed in Chapter 6. It works with DOS, VAX VMS, OS/2 platforms.

KBMS (Knowledge-Base Management System) is an integrated, multiplatform, hybrid knowledge-base system. It applies backward- and forward-chaining, hypothetical reasoning, and object-oriented programming. The natural-language facility speeds development by writing rules in English. The graphical developer and user interface simplify and enhance the delivery of knowledge-base applications. It works with MVS, VM, OS/2, and DOS platforms.

3. AI SQUARED, Chelmsford, Mass.

Idea is an expert system tool that incorporates high-resolution graphics, hypertext, and integration with information systems. It works with DOS platform.

4. AION CORP., Palo Alto, Calif.

The Aion Development System (ADS) is a logic-based system that is designed for traditional IBM environments, and is interoperable with existing applications, databases, languages, and hardware platforms. It works with IBM System/370 under MVS, VM, CICS, IMS, ISO, CMS, and DOS platforms.

5. ALBATHION SOFTWARE, San Francisco, Calif.

Entrypaq Professional is a hybrid development tool and combines rule-based and object-oriented methods. It works with DOS and Macintosh platforms.

6. ARITY CORP., Concord, Mass.

The Arity/Expert Development Package is a hybrid tool that combines frames and rule-based methods. It supports multiple inheritance and allows for negative result, concluding that something is not true. The package works with DOS and OS/2 platforms.

7. ARTIFICIAL INTELLIGENCE TECHNOLOGIES, Hawthorne, N.Y.

Mercury KBE is an object-oriented programming tool for building intelligent applications. It features an SQL-compliant interface to relational databases, an interactive development environment, high-performance rule-based programming, and a comprehensive presentation-management facility that includes automatic generation of a user interface. Mercury works with VME and UNIX platforms.

8. ATTAR SOFTWARE, Lancaster, England

Xper Rule is a powerful expert system development tool that has inductive and deductive methods. It can generate entire applications as source code in high-level languages, including COBOL, Pascal, C, RPG/400, DataFlex, and Mantis. Xper Rule works with DOS platform.

9. BELL ATLANTIC SOFTWARE SYSTEMS, Princeton, N.J.

Laser is a hybrid tool that has a C environment with several subsystems, including object-oriented, rule-based inference, and simulation. It works with DEC and Sun workstations platforms.

10. CARNEGIE GROUP, Pittsburgh, Penn.

TestBench is a knowledge-management shell for developing and delivering troubleshooting systems. It uses Sun workstations for development and DOS for delivery of systems.

Knowledge Craft is a toolkit for developing large knowledge-based systems. It is particularly suitable for applications such as scheduling, design, and configuration, which require a solution to account for complex information brought to bear in a consistent, straightforward manner. It works with VAXstation, DECstation, and Sun workstation platforms.

Text Categorization Shell is a problem-specific shell for automatic content-based categorization of on-line text. It works with MicroVAX platform.

IMKA Technology is a knowledge-representation technology that provides organizations with power and flexibility to build knowledge-based systems that are easily integrated and embedded into existing computing environments. It works with DECstation, VAXstation, SparcStations, and OS/2 platforms.

11. COGENT SOFTWARE, Framingham, Mass.

Personal HyperBase and HyperBase Developer combine hypertext, graphics, and rule-based links with an expert system shell in a hypertext environment. They work with DOS platform.

12. COMPUTER-AIDED KE SYSTEMS, Pearl River, N.Y.

Knowledge Analysis Tool and Knowledge Quest are graphic knowledge acquisition tools. One is based on the principles of influence diagrams and flowcharts, and the other is based on decision trees. They produce knowledge-base reports and support code generation for popular expert system shells. These tools work with DOS and Macintosh platforms.

13. COMPUTER ASSOCIATES, Garden City, N.Y.

CA-DB: Expert/VAX is a rule-based expert system that lets users integrate knowledge-base systems with their existing commercial production applications and database processing. It extends the functionality of existing 3GL and 4GL applications by enhancing them with knowledge-base components, and works with VAX VMS platform.

CA-DB: Expert/Voice provides simple voice access and response for virtually any application, turning telephones into interactive, easy-to-use terminals. It works with VAX VMS platform.

14. EMERALD INTELLIGENCE, Ann Arbor, Mich.

Diagnostic Advisor helps diagnose problems with products, machinery, and equipment on the plant floor. It works with Windows 3.0 and Macintosh platforms.

Mahogany HelpDesk helps automate help-desk, customer support, and technical-support centers. It works with Windows 3.0 and Macintosh platforms.

Mahogany Professional is a hybrid expert system tool, and works with DOS and Macintosh platforms.

15. EXSYS, Albuquerque, N.M.

Exsys EL is an introductory tool that provides a full environment for the development of rule-based systems. It works with DOS platform.

Exsys Professional is a hybrid development tool that provides the developer with a procedural-command language, interface with LP modeling tools, extensive validation capabilities, frames, tables, common-data blackboard, speech and graphics interface, and hypertext. It works with DOS, OS/2, VAX VMS, and UNIX platforms.

16. FIRSTMARK TECHNOLOGIES, Ottawa, Canada

Knowledge Seeker is designed for use as a database-analysis package for use on record-oriented data. It scans an existing database or report for significant relationships among all fields and any indicator field, developing a decision model that is useful for understanding and directing decisions affecting business, research, and so on. Knowledge Seeker displays the multi-dimensional models in a graphic decision tree format or as a set of expert system rules. It works with DOS platform.

17. GENSYM CORP., Cambridge, Mass.

G2 is a hybrid tool that is discussed in Chapter 9. It works on UNIX workstations.

18. GINSYS CORP., Greenville, S.C.

K-Base Corporate is an expert system development shell with advanced natural-language capabilities and user-defined multiple windows. All products listed for this company work with DOS platform.

K-Base Builder has all K-Base Corporate features plus a complete implementation of uncertainty representations.

K-Base Educator is an educational version of K-Base Builder.

K-Induction combines neural networks and rule-based expert systems. Its inputs consist of data tables. It generates subjective rules based on the input data.

ES-Assessor is an expert system that predicts the likelihood of success of any proposed rule-based expert system development and suggests, when applicable, how to increase that likelihood of success.

19. GOLD HILL INC., Cambridge, Mass.

GoldWorks II is a hybrid expert system tool for developing and delivering advanced applications. It supports frames, rules, and object-oriented programming, and works with DOS, OS/2, Macintosh, and Sun workstation platforms.

20. THE HALEY ENTERPRISE, Sewickley, Penn.

Eclipse DOS Developer's Edition is a rule-based, data-driven expert system tool. It maintains a set of user-defined rules in real time as facts are asserted into or retracted from a database, and checks the rules. It works with the protected mode of Windows and DOS platforms.

Eclipse Toolkits enhances the basic Eclipse Developer by adding features such as rule sets, agenda, opportunistic backward chaining, and binary saving. It works with DOS, Windows, OS/2, and SparcStations platforms.

21. IBM, Palo Alto, Calif.

The Integrated Reasoning Shell (TIRS) is a powerful hybrid knowledge-base development and application tool, which combines rule-based and object-oriented methods. It works with OS/2, CMS, TSO, VAX VMS, CICS platforms.

22. INFERENCE CORP., El Segundo, Calif.

Xi Plus is a rule-based expert system tool. It works with DOS platform.

CBR (Case-Based Reasoning) Express is an expert system tool that uses the case-based reasoning approach. It works with Windows 3.0 platform.

ART, the Automated Reasoning Tools, provides an integrated Lisp-based development environment for developing symbolic-processing applications, and includes incremental knowledge-base acquisition, incremental rule compilation, and graphical presentation of the knowledge base. It works with UNIX, Symbolics, TI Explorer, and VMS platforms.

ART-IM is a hybrid development tool that contains procedural programming, object-oriented programming, rule-based reasoning, hypothetical reasoning, and case-based reasoning. It works with DOS, OS/2, Windows, VMS, UNIX, and MVS platforms.

23. INFERENCE ENGINE TECHNOLOGIES, Cambridge, Mass.

Sienna OPS5 is a complete OPS5 development and delivery system. It works with DOS and OS/2 platforms.

24. INFORMATION BUILDERS, New York, N.Y.

LEVEL5 is a rule-based system discussed in Chapter 5. It works with MVS, TSO, VM/CMS, VAX VMS, DOS, and Macintosh platforms.

LEVEL5 for FOCUS is a complete application development environment that combines fourth-generation language tools and database management with a rule-based inference system. It works with the same platforms as in LEVEL5.

LEVEL5 OBJECT is a hybrid tool discussed in Chapter 10. It works with Windows 3.0 platform.

25. INTEGRATED SYSTEMS, Santa Clara, Calif.

RT/Expert is a complete development environment for knowledge-based real-time systems. Simulation and code generation are provided for accelerating the development and implementation of real-time software that incorporates rule-based logic. It works with VAX, Sun-3, Sun-4, SparStations, and Appolo platforms.

26. INTELLICORP, Mountain View, Calif.

Knowledge Engineering Environment (KEE) is a hybrid tool discussed in Chapter 9. It works with Sun-4, HP 9000/300 and 9000/400 platforms.

ProKAPPA and KAPPA-PC are hybrid tools that are discussed in Chapter 9. ProKAPPA works with Sun-3, Sun-4, SparcStations, and HP 9000/300 and 9000/400 platforms. KAPPA-PC works with Windows 3.0 platform.

27. KDS CORP., Wilmette, Ill.

KDS3.8 can automatically produce as many as 24,000 rules from 4,096 cases. It uses frame-based architecture with object-oriented blackboard and extensive math capability. Development is in plain English. It works with DOS platform.

KDS/VOX3.8 has all capabilities of KDS3.8 plus the ability to speak with users over a regular telephone. The user can respond by using the buttons on a touch-tone telephone. It works with DOS platform.

28. KNOWLEDGE GARDEN, Nassau, N.Y.

KnowledgePro lets experts, authors, and writers create tutorials and explain complex procedures or regulations using a unique combination of object-oriented programming, expert systems, and hypertext techniques. Underlying this environment is a symbolic language and a new programming paradigm, "topics." Topics are "chunks of knowledge" containing rules, calculations, commands, hypertext, or graphics. It works with DOS platform.

KnowledgePro (Windows) is a tool for rapid application development under Windows 3.0. It has an object-oriented environment.

29. MICRO DATA BASE SYSTEMS, Lafayette, Ind.

Guru is an expert system/4GL programming environment. It is rule-based, but is integrated with business graphics, text processing, report generation, communications, natural-language interface, and more. It works with DOS, OS/2, and VAX VMS platforms.

Guru Solveur is an application generator for diagnostic expert systems. This software is designed for the direct use by an expert, without the help from the knowledge engineer. It works with DOS platform.

30. M.I.S. INTERNATIONAL, Cincinnati, Ohio
Consult-I 2.0 is an expert system in which each category has subcategories providing subsystems within each subsystem. It works with DOS platform.

31. NEURON DATA, Palo Alto, Calif.
NEXPERT Object is a hybrid tool discussed in Chapter 9. It works with DOS, Macintosh, VAX, and UNIX platforms.

32. NORRAD, Nashua, N.H.
NetLink+ is a series of related bridge products to NEXPERT from NeuralWare's NeuralWorks Professional II/Plus, AbTech's AIM, Togai Infralogic's TILShell, and Mind's Eye's genetic algorithms package. It works with DOS, Macintosh, and SparcStations platforms.

33. OXKO, Annapolis, Md.
INDUCPRL is an inductive tool that uses the ID3 method and produces rules in the production-rule language of the LEVEL5 or LEVEL5 OBJECT expert system development tools. It works with DOS and Windows 3.0 platforms.

INDUCEXS performs the same function as INDUCPRL, and produces Exsys Professional source code as its output. It works on DOS platform.

MAINGEN is a knowledge acquisition system for maintenance problems. It asks questions about a maintenance problem area that a user has and then generates production-rule language code from the automated interview. MAINGEN works with DOS platform.

PRLREF is a cross-reference tool that cross-references facts with rules in the production-rule language. It works with DOS platform.

Expert System Database Developer's Toolkit is a compendium of tools to help expert system developers utilize dBASE database and index files within an expert system. Any expert system tool that allows the execution of external programs can utilize this toolkit. It works with DOS platform.

34. PAPERBACK SOFTWARE, Berkeley, Calif.

VP-Expert is a rule-based development tool that contains certainty factors, dynamic graphic objects, hypertext, and links to dBASE and Lotus 1-2-3. It works with DOS platform.

35. PERCEPTICS, Knoxville, Tenn.

Knowledge Shaper is an expert system design and development tool that automatically generates portable C and Ada source code that could be embedded in decision-making systems. It works with VAX VMS.

36. PRODUCTION SYSTEMS TECHNOLOGY, Pittsburgh, Penn.

OPS83 is a rule-based language for expert system applications. It supports rules and ordinary Pascal-like procedures. It works with DOS platform.

RAL is an extended dialect of C that adds rules and objects to C. RAL code is compatible with existing C tools. It works with DOS platform.

37. ROSH INTELLIGENT SYSTEMS, Needham Heights, Mass.

Computer-Aided Intelligent Service (CAIS) is an expert system-based network for service and maintenance functions in high-tech industries. CAIS lets service and maintenance organizations computerize their troubleshooting expertise. It works with UNIX platform.

Knowledge-CAIS is a knowledge-acquisition workstation that lets product specialists computerize their diagnostic knowledge programming or rules. A graphical user interface enables rapid description of a product's physical structure, functional relationships, available tests and repair procedures, and symptoms of malfunction and their significance. It works with UNIX platform.

Brief-CAIS is a delivery vehicle for troubleshooting knowledge, which is carried by a service engineer or installed at customer site. It offers step-by-step troubleshooting guidance with a graphical interface. It also offers electronic logging and reporting, automatic test injection, an electronic service manual, and an interface to service-management systems. It works with DOS platform.

Hyper-CAIS supplements the Brief-CAIS user interface with hypermedia capabilities. It works with DOS platform.

Show-CAIS is a comprehensive maintenance, troubleshooting, training, and operations management environment for supporting high-tech equipments. It works with DOS platform.

Central-CAIS is a communication and control center for CAIS system, providing managers and technical specialists with a centralized workstation for managing remote operations. It enables real-time monitoring of field operations and the generation of a range of logistical and diagnostic reports based on a service-call history database. It works with UNIX platform.

38. SOFTWARE A & E, Arlington, Va.

Knowledge Engineering System (KES) is a robust hybrid expert system tool that supports rapid development of prototypes and production of expert systems. It supports production-rule reasoning, hypothesis-and-test inference, and object-oriented and truth-maintenance methods. It works with DOS, UNIX, mini, and mainframe platforms.

39. SOFTWARE ARTISTRY, Indianapolis, Ind.

PC Expert Professional is a simple rule-based expert system development tools. It works with DOS platform.

Knowledge Engine is a complete hypermedia development environment with support for graphics, animation, full-motion video, and scripting languages. It works with DOS platform.

Application Software Expert is a platform independent 4GL with an embedded expert system inference engine. It has animation and graphics, and works on DOS, OS/400, and OS/4680 platforms.

40. SOFTWARE PLUS, Crofton, Md.

Cxpert integrates expert systems and hypertext technology into C. Knowledge bases translated by Cxpert into C code are compiled and linked to produce executable applications that require no royalties or run-time interpreters. It works with many platforms, including DOS.

41. SYMBOLOGIC CORP., Redmond, Wash.

Symbologic Adept is a procedure-based expert system technology and graphical user interface that can convert all types of procedures into expert system applications. It works with 386-based PCs and Windows 3.0 platforms.

42. WANG LABORATORIES, Lowell, Mass.

CommonKnowledge is a knowledge-based development tool for creating decision-support or problem-solving applications. It uses a patented "definitional" model of knowledge representation and conversational method of knowledge acquisition, which lets users with little experience create complex applications. Applications can be integrated with DOS files, images, and word-processing documents. It works with DOS platform.

APPENDIX C

Sources for Neural Networks

This appendix lists sources for neural network products as of 1991. As with expert systems, be aware that the only constant features in neural network markets are: frequent introductions of new products, enhancements of existing ones, and changes and mergers of software companies. Therefore, this list may be out of date by the time it reaches you. Use it as an indication of what is available in the market, rather than an exhaustive and up-to-date list of companies and products.

This appendix is an abbreviated version of a survey by Patty Enrado ["Neural-Net Resource Guide," *AI Expert*, July 1991, pp. 60–70], and was reprinted with permission from *AI Expert*. The survey is based on the information provided by those vendors who responded to the survey, and does not constitute a review of products. Not all companies in the original article are included in this appendix.

In the following list, the name of the software company appears first and is followed by the name of neural net products the company offers. For information on addresses and list prices, consult the original article.

1. ADAPTIVE SOLUTIONS, Beaverton, Ore.

CNAPS Server is a stand-alone neurocomputer that runs more than five billion connections per second (CPS). It has an array of 256 processors, and is designed to run large neural network algorithms. The Server also executes feature extraction routines without additional hardware. It includes 8MB to 64MB of data-storage memory and built-in Ethernet LAN support.

CNAPS CodeNet is an integrated set of software-development tools designed to facilitate the development, modification, and execution of neural network programs for CNAPS architecture. The architectures supported by CodeNet include backpropagation, LVQ2, self-organizing map, and frequency-sensitive learning methods. The development toolset includes a host-based neurocomputer simulator, assembler, symbolic debugger, and CNAPS Server control software. CodeNet provides a graphical and command-line interface.

CNAPS-C is a C compiler for the CNAPS architecture.

2. AI WARE, Cleveland, Ohio

N-NET EX, N-NET 500, and the N-NET 600 Neural Net Development System are neural net development tools that support supervised and unsupervised learning methods. They work with DOS, Microsoft C, Sun-4, SparcStations, Sun OS 4.0, Sun C, VMS, and VAX platforms.

CAD/Chem Custom Formulation System can determine an optimized formulation of desired product properties. Given a set of ingredients and processing attributes, CAD/Chem can determine the product's properties. It is a "what-if" design tool, providing answers to questions on the effects of varying ingredients and process conditions. CAD/Chem supports supervised and unsupervised learning methods, and works with Sun OS 4.0, DEC under Windows, and IBM under VMS platforms.

3. AND CORP., Hamilton, Ontario, Canada

HNET is a neural-based development system. It uses a proprietary holography network technology. It works with Borland C or Microsoft C compilers.

4. CALIFORNIA SCIENTIFIC SOFTWARE, Grass Valley, Calif.

BrainMaker and BrainMaker Professional are neural net tools. They import data from Lotus 1-2-3, Excel, dBASE, binary, or ASCII files. BrainMaker has pull-down menus, dialog boxes, color graphics, and a mouse. BrainMaker Professional accepts larger datasets than BrainMaker, provides more flexible modeling and graphics, and includes run-time license. The package includes NetMaker which automatically constructs networks from Lotus 1-2-3, dBASE, ASCII, and binary files. They work with DOS and Macintosh platforms.

5. COGNITION TECHNOLOGY CORP., Cambridge, Mass.

NeuroSmarts is a hybrid neural network and expert system tool that integrates pattern recognition and explicit rules. It permits use in real-time environments, and has manager-level, rather than an engineer-level, user interface, and insulates operators from network details. NeuroSmarts imports data from various spreadsheet/database files, has single proprietary algorithm (four-layer, single-pass training gives Bayesian optimal classification), and works with DOS and OS/2 platforms.

6. NHC, San Diego, Calif.

ExploreNet is an icon-based neural network development system. **KnowledgeNet** is a supplemental capability to ExploreNet, and its patented technique is used within ExploreNet to show the rationale used by the network to make a decision or choice. These two products import data from almost any file, including Windows 3.0. They support Balboa 860, ANZA Plus, and 19 neural network architectures. They work with Windows 3.0 platform.

NeuroSoft is a library of C functions used by programmers to embed neural networks in their applications. It supports Balboa 860, ANZA Plus DP, ANZA Plus, ANZA, and multilayer backpropagation. It works with Sun-3, Sun-4, and DOS platforms.

Balboa 860 is an i860-based neural network coprocessor available for AT-bus or VME configurations. It provides up to 25 interconnections per second for neural network computation. Optional memory configurations provide from 8MB to 64MB of memory for neural network applications. It supports all NHC software products and neural networks.

7. HYPERLOGIC CORP., Escondido, Calif.

OWL Neural Network Library provides a set of neural networks simulation in the form of a programming library for C-language development. The portable source code has run without change on many platforms. A graphical user-interface library is included with the IBM AT product. It supports more than 20 neural net architectures, and works with DOS and Macintosh platforms.

8. INTEGRATED INTERFACE MACHINES, Anaheim, Calif.

Neural-Inference-System (N-I-S) combines Nestor Inc.'s neural net algorithms with rule-based and fuzzy-logic technologies in a Common Lisp environment. It provides the AI developer the freedom to select the technology to fit the requirements of the application to the technology, and works with Windows 3.0 platform.

9. INTEL CORP., Santa Clara, Calif.

Intel Neural Network Training System (iNNTS) provides complete development support for Intel's 80170NX high-speed neural network chip. The iNNTS contains two Intel 80170NX ETANN chips, two new learning-simulation software programs, diagnostic software, and a programmer interface and adapter that can run on any PC. It supports backpropagation, MADALINE III, recurrent backpropagation, or user-written learning methods, and works with DOS platform.

10. LORAL SPACE INFORMATION SYSTEMS, Houston, Texas

Neural Emulation Tool (NET) is a programmable processing system, and includes two accelerator-board types, processor and memory boards, firmware, system software, user interface, and a host computer. It is designed for efficient large-networks simulation, and supports backpropagation, feature-map classifier, ART2, ARP, and shared weights. NET works with DOS platform.

11. LUCID, Menlo Park, Calif.

Plexi is an interactive, graphical environment for the development of sophisticated neural networks on general-purpose workstations. Its flexibility and extensibility promote experimentation and the generation of unique network designs. Plexi can import data from ASCII files and can have live connections to Lisp and C programs. It supports backpropagation, backpropagation with momentum, competition, and self-organizing map. It works with Sun-3, Sun-4, and SparcStations platforms.

12. MARTINGALE RESEARCH CORP., Allen, Texas

Tocof is a neural network that can predict the long-term buy/sell positions in a commodity-futures market. Tocof uses backpropagation and proprietary methods. It imports data from ASCII files and works with DOS platform.

Syspro implements a simulation protocol for hierarchically defined neural networks and systems. It will survive the migration from uniprocessor to multiprocessor to parallel asynchronous processor hosts. Syspro supports backpropagation, Klopf drive reinforcement, Grossberg avalanche, and Hopfield net. It imports data from ASCII files and works with DOS platform.

13. NESTOR, Providence, R.I.

Nestor Development Systems (NDS1000) is a software development environment that utilizes the patented Nestor Learning System (NLS) multiple neural network technology for pattern recognition applications. It can achieve high levels of accuracy and process large volumes of data. NDS1000 can import data from Lotus 1-2-3, dBASE, and ASCII files, and works with Sun workstations and DOS platforms.

14. NEURAL SYSTEMS, Vancouver, Canada

Genesis is a neural network development environment. In Genesis, network configuration is menu-driven with a context sensitive help system. Options for network size, data scaling, weight constraint, connection updating, measure of performance, and type of transfer function are available. It works on DOS platform.

15. NEURALWARE, Pittsburgh, Penn.

NeuralWorks Professional II/Plus provides a complete, flexible, neural network development and deployment tool. It supports more than 20 neural net architectures. Diagnostic capabilities let you monitor weights, errors, and activations. Data is read from ASCII files, the keyboard, spreadsheets, and databases. User-written C programs can be executed to gather and process data. It works with DOS, Macintosh, Sun, and VAX platforms.

NeuralWorks Explorer is an introductory learning tool that is a fully functional multiparadigm development package with many of the same features found in the NeuralWorks Profession II/Plus. It supports eight architectures, and works with DOS and Macintosh platforms.

NeuralWorks Designer Pack is a deployment package that converts neural networks designed with NeuralWorks Professional II/Plus in C source code. This source code can then be embedded into user applications running on different computing platforms. It works with DOS, Macintosh, RS/6000, Sun, or VAX platforms.

NeuralWorks User-Defined Neuro-Dynamics (UDND) is an advanced optional extension of NeuralWorks Professional II/Plus that lets you write your own summation, transfer, output, error functions, and learning rules in C. UDND's user-defined routines can be compiled and linked with NeuralWorks libraries to create a new customized NeuralWorks Professional II/Plus. It supports backpropagation, the Boltzman Machine, and the probabilistic neural network architectures, and works with DOS, Macintosh, RS/6000, Sun, and VAX platforms.

16. NEURIX, Boston, Mass.

MacBrain is a neural network software package for Macintosh. It is a fully interactive program with an intuitive graphic interface. It imports data from ASCII files, and provides many built-in functions and learning methods. MacBrain is fully modifiable and includes HyperBrain, a toolkit that runs simulations from within Hypercard or SuperCard.

17. NEURODYNAMX, Boulder, Colo.

DynaMind is a neural network software that reads data from many types of spreadsheets. It is menu driven and supports backpropagation and MADALINE III architectures, and works with DOS platform.

18. NEUROSYM CORP., Houston, Texas

NeuroSym Neurocomputing Library is a collection of functions written in ANSI C that lets neural networks be added to an application. It supports 12 neural network architectures, Microsoft C, Turbo C, Turbo C++, and Zortech C++.

19. NORRAD, Nashua, N.H.

Net-Link+ is a bridge between NEXPERT Object and other advanced technologies, including neural nets, abductive reasoning, generic algorithms, and fuzzy logic. It provides the C functions to embed and link these technologies. It imports data from many databases and spreadsheets, and requires NEXPERT Object and NeuralWorks Professional II, AIM, or the TILShell. Net-Link+ works with DOS, Macintosh, and Sun platforms.

20. PEAK SOFTWARE, Denver, Colo.

Autonet automatically constructs neural networks determining the most appropriate architecture, weights, nodes, and layers for solving a problem. The access facility lets application programs access constructed networks. It has a proprietary algorithm, and works with DOS platform.

21. PROMISED LAND TECHNOLOGIES, New Haven, Conn.

Braincel is a C-based program that embeds seamlessly into Excel for Windows 3.0. It supports backpropagation and backpercolation architectures, and works with Windows 3.0 platform.

22. RACECOM, Ormand Beach, Fla.

Magic! is a group of 12 neural network architectures running under Windows 3.0 for Microsoft's Excel. It works with Windows 3.0 platform.

23. SCIENCE APPLICATIONS INTERNATIONAL CORP., San Diego, Calif.

ANSpec is an object-oriented neural systems language that lets users specify novel and complex network architectures. It works with DOS, Macintosh, and UNIX platforms.

24. VISION HARVEST, Hatch, N.M.

NeuroVision is designed for developing and deploying applications in image analysis, signal processing, and neural networks. The package supports graphical menu systems and library-call interfaces. It includes backpropagation, functional link nets, adaptive vector quanitization, image filtering and segmentation, morphological operations, region analysis, and feature extraction. It works with 386 and 486 PC platforms.

Direct Digital NeuroComputer (DDNC) is a PC coprocessor board for high-speed, feed-forward neurocomputing. DDNC can process 20 million connections per second. It supports all common neural network models, and works with 32-bit DOS-based PCs.

NeuroSimulator is a high-speed PC coprocessor board on the Intel i860 RISC processor, which facilitates neural net training and recall and pattern-recognition operations. It can perform 20 million connections per second in feedforward mode and 9 million CPS in learning mode. It works with 32-bit DOS-based PCs.

25. WARD SYSTEMS GROUP, Frederick, Md.

NeuroShell is a ready-to-use software shell for neural network applications. It imports data from ASCII, Lotus 1-2-3, and dBASE III files, and works with DOS platform.

NeuroBoard is a neural network accelerator board that runs NeuroShell approximately 100 times faster then a 20MHz 80386 processor with math coprocessor. It works with DOS platform.

APPENDIX **D**

NeuralWorks
Professional II/Plus

In this appendix, we give a brief review of NeuralWorks Professional II/Plus, which is developed by NeuralWare, Inc., and is one of the comprehensive neural net development tools. The demo diskette attached to this book could be used in conjunction with this appendix.

Introduction

NeuralWorks Professional II/Plus (called NWPII/+ for short here) gives the developer quick access to numerous architectures. It also provides the flexibility of developing a network from scratch. In this respect, the software accommodates all types of developers. A novice can build networks based on the well-known backpropagation method. The experienced and advanced developer can choose from an extensive menu of architectures, including more complex and less known structures. Furthermore, the developer can design and program his or her own architecture and add it to the system.

NWPII/+ offers flexibility in external hooks and user interface. The developer can import C programming instructions into the system, and export the trained network as a C program to be incorporated into other programs and software products.

NWPII/+ has a user interface that allows one to explore the dynamics of an already-trained net or change its structure and retrain it. The developer has the option of creating a new interface using the available system commands. In rare cases where the developer wishes to create user interfaces not available in NWPII/+, the developer can import an interface written in the C language.

Creating a Network

NWPII/+ allows the developer to create a network in four different ways:

- BackProp Builder
- InstaNet
- From scratch by graphical pallets
- User-defined neuro-dynamics

The demo diskette attached to the book demonstrates the methods of creating a net. Here, we briefly review each one in order to provide a background for the use of the demo disk.

BackProp Builder. This option allows the developer to define a back-propagation network in one menu. The developer is presented with a menu in which all information needed for creating a backprop net is listed. The developer provides information such as the training data file, the test data file, the number of layers, and number of neurons or processing elements (or PEs). Once the needed information is entered in the menu, the system builds the backprop net and is ready for the developer to examine, test, change, and use it. This is a simple and powerful way to get started in building a net.

InstaNet. To the developer who wishes to build a net other than a backprop type, NWPII/+ offers the InstaNet option. In this option, the developer can select from a list of 22 network architectures, some of which were discussed in Chapter 14. Again, once the developer selects the model, the software prompts the developer for the needed information and creates the network. The demo diskette goes through the steps for creating a net via InstaNet.

Thus, the prerequisite for developing a net is the familiarity with various known architectures, and their strengths and limitations. That is why in Chapter 14 we cover some well-known models in a comparative fashion. To provide the developer with the necessary background, NWPII/+ comes with a book called *Neural Computing*, which discusses the history of neural computing and reviews the 22 architectures available in the software. The demo diskette gives a brief overview of some of these models.

From Scratch by Graphical Pallets. NWPII/+ allows the developer to modify an existing architecture or design his or her own net from scratch. In the design of a customized net, if the developer can use the functions available in the software, then he or she can use the graphical pallets for identifying processing elements (neurons or PEs), their connections, learning methods, and other needed functions. The developer can design his or her net and add it to the system's list of options via the InstaNet script. The demo diskette shows how one such net is created.

User-Defined Neuro-Dynamics. In rare cases when the developer is experimenting with a completely new design and wishes to define a new summation, transfer, or error function that is unknown to the software, then the developer can write these functions in the C language, and link it to NWPII/+. Since the software provides an extensive menu of functions, it is unlikely that many developers would need to write their own functions. The developer also has the option of using IDL (the proprietary language of NeuralWare) to design a new architecture. Again, given the variety of and the knowledge about existing architectures, the developer should first try to utilize the known models before embarking on designing a new neural net architecture.

External Hooks

NWPII/+ allows the developer to identify two data files: one for training and one for recall and testing. The files could be in ASCII or binary. The file selection menu has a User IO or UIO option. This file contains procedures defined by the developer who wants to import instructions to the system and use them in the design.

The developer can export the trained net by FlashCode, and create an ANSI standard C code of the backprop net. This way the trained net could be incorporated in other systems, such as an expert system.

Interface Instruments

NWPII/+ exhibits the network's PEs and connections. One way to learn about the inner working of a network is to monitor the computed values within the network. For example, the developer can exhibit information about one or a group of PEs and one or a group of weight connections. This is done via the **probes/instruments** combination. **Instruments** are the windows that appear in the network view screen. A **probe** is the computed value in the network, or the contact point of an **instrument** with the network.

For example, on the view screen of the network, we can have a side window that contains the graph of the actual output values as opposed to the network-generated outputs. Or, the connection weights may be shown on a bar graph. Alternatively, the mean square errors (or delta rule) of the backprop model (discussed in Chapter 14) can be graphed for a particular epoch.

There are three ways the developer can design **probe/instruments** windows in NWPII/+:

- EasyProbe

- InstaProbe

- Probe Add Tools

The **EasyProbe** facility has a menu from which the developer can choose standard probe instruments. The menu allows the developer to select the variable to be graphed (such as the output value or mean square error), the probe type (such as the entire network, output layer, or selected PE), and the graph type (such as bar or histogram).

The **InstaProbe** option loads a set of "pre-fabricated" probes. These are in addition to those available in the **EasyProbe** facility.

Finally, NWPII/+ lets the developer create new combinations by using the graph and probe add tools. These are customized probe/instrument combinations, however, that rarely are needed since **EasyProbe** and **InstaProbe** cover most known types of information needed about a network.

Explanation

As discussed in Chapter 13, one of the advantages of expert systems compared to neural nets is that expert systems have the explanation component that shows the user the reasoning behind a particular recommendation.

NWPII/+ has a unique facility called **Explain** that displays the input factors with the greatest effect on the output. The **Explain** command changes the input values by a percentage and computes how much the output has been changed as a percentage of the input change. It then ranks the input factors on their impact on the output.

Control Strategies

NWPII/+ defines the architecture of a network to consist of:

- Topology (the PEs, layers, and their connections)

- Layer parameters (the summation function, transfer function, output, error-correction, and the learning rule)

- Control strategy

The topology and layer parameters are created using one of the four ways of creating a network. The control strategy is the sequence of activities within a layer and the transfer of information from one layer to another.

Every network architecture has a corresponding control strategy. The control strategy of backprop is resident in memory in NWPII/+. If the developer uses InstaNet to create a network, then the control strategy of that architecture is loaded to the system and will be saved with the network.

The developer has the option of choosing a different control strategy. This can be accomplished by using the Control Strategy menu.

Pruning, Changing, and Editing

NWPII/+ has a relatively extensive set of facilities that permits the developer to prune, change, and edit the network and set up check points for observing the network. It also has an extensive help facility.

Documentation

NWPII/+ has four volumes of documentation:

- *Neural Computing*

- *Reference Guide*

- *Using NWorks*

- *System Guide*

The *Neural Computing* volume provides a historical background on the field and discusses the theoretical aspects of the architecture available in NWPII/+. The *Reference Guide* volume gives a description of the features in NWPII/+. The *Using NWorks* volume is a short one and starts the developer on a tutorial for creating a net. The *System Guide* shows how to install the software and contains special information for various platforms on which the software could be installed.

Reduced Version

Explorer is a reduced version of NWPII/+. It has the **BackProp Builder** facility. Its **InstaNet** supports seven architectures other than backprop. The control strategies in **Explorer** are fixed, resident in the memory, and accessible from the **Network Parameter** menu. It contains the **EasyProbe** facility and the graphical user interface, and allows the developer to define and use C procedures (**User IO**). Explorer runs on PC and Macintosh.

Index